Modern Spanish

A Project of the Modern Language Association

Advisory Staff

CONSULTANTS

Daniel N. Cárdenas *University of Chicago*
Rodger A. Farley *U. S. Naval Academy*
S. N. Treviño *Foreign Service Institute*

ADVISORY COMMITTEE

Frederick B. Agard *Cornell University*
Richard Armitage *Ohio State University*
Ralph S. Boggs *University of Miami*
D. Lincoln Canfield *University of Rochester*
John A. Crow *University of California, Los Angeles*
Rodger A. Farley *U. S. Naval Academy*
Lewis U. Hanke *University of Texas*
Francis Hayes *University of Florida*
Hayward Keniston *University of Michigan (Emeritus)*
Robert Lado *University of Michigan*
J. Kenneth Leslie *Northwestern University*
George E. McSpadden *George Washington University*
Robert G. Mead, Jr. *University of Connecticut*
Sarah M. Pereira *West Virginia State College*
Ruth Richardson *Adelphi College*
Hilario S. Sáenz *University of Nebraska*
Sol Saporta *Indiana University*
William H. Shoemaker *University of Illinois*
Robert K. Spaulding *University of California, Berkeley*
Charles N. Staubach *University of Michigan*
Robert P. Stockwell *University of California, Los Angeles*
S. N. Treviño *School of Languages, Foreign Service Institute*
Laurel H. Turk *DePauw University*
Donald D. Walsh *The Choate School*

Administrative Staff

DIRECTORS OF
THE FOREIGN LANGUAGE PROGRAM, MLA

Theodore Andersson, 1956–57

Kenneth W. Mildenberger, 1957–59

Archibald T. MacAllister, 1959

Donald D. Walsh, 1959–

PUBLISHING COMMITTEE

Albert H. Marckwardt *University of Michigan*

Kenneth W. Mildenberger *Chief, Language Development
    Section, U. S. Office of Education*

William R. Parker *Indiana University, formerly Executive Secretary
    of the MLA and Director of the Foreign Language Program*

George Winchester Stone, Jr. *Executive Secretary, MLA*

HARCOURT, BRACE & WORLD

New York and Burlingame

Modern Spanish

A Project of the Modern Language Association

Editorial Staff

WORKING COMMITTEE

Dwight L. Bolinger *Coordinator, University of Southern California*

J. Donald Bowen *University of California, Los Angeles*

Agnes M. Brady *University of Kansas*

Ernest F. Haden *University of Texas*

Lawrence Poston, Jr. *University of Oklahoma*

Norman P. Sacks *Oberlin College*

AUTHORS OF DIALOGS
AND ORIGINAL READINGS

Domingo Ricart (SPAIN) *University of Kansas (readings)*

Guillermo Segreda (COSTA RICA) *Foreign Service Institute (dialogs)*

Ismael Silva-Fuenzalida (CHILE) *Foreign Service Institute (dialogs)*

PRINTED IN THE UNITED STATES OF AMERICA

[d · 7 · 61]

LIBRARY OF CONGRESS CATALOG CARD NUMBER: 60-10695

Thanks go to the University of Missouri Press (and Ralph E. Parker and
Mildred Johnson) for permission to quote the translation of "Puentes"
by Pablo Neruda; to the Librería y Editorial Nascimento, Santiago, Chile,
for permission to quote "Puentes" by Pablo Neruda; to the late Alfonso
Reyes for permission to quote from his book *Ultima Tule;* to Francisco
L. Urquizo for permission to quote from his book *Ahora Charlemos;* to Félix
Coluccio for permission to quote from his "Artes populares en México" in
Folklore de las Américas; and to Vicente T. Mendoza for permission to
quote from his book *Vida y Costumbres de la Universidad de México.*

DRAWINGS BY MICHAEL TRAIN

Contents

Introduction   xi

1   **Pronunciation**   1

2   **La familia de Cecilia**   24

    1   The subject pronouns   *27*
    2   Present tense of *ser,* to be   *28*
    3   Present tense of *–ar* verbs   *29*
    4   The articles; gender of nouns   *32*
    5   Number: the plural   *33*
    6   Adjectives: agreement of nouns and adjectives   *35*
    7   The numerals, 1–10   *38*

3   **Una conversación por teléfono**   40

    8   Interrogative words   *44*
    9   Word order in questions   *46*
    10   Placement of *no*   *48*
    11   Intonation   *48*
    12   Tag questions   *52*
    13   Present tense of *estar,* to be   *54*
    14   *Ser* versus *estar*   *55*

    READING: Morenas y rubias   *57*

4   **El día del santo**   58

    15   Present tense of *–er* and *–ir* verbs   *62*
    16   Verbs with changes in the stem: $o \rightarrow ue, e \rightarrow ie, e \rightarrow i$ *63*
    17   Present with future meaning   *65*
    18   The with-verb pronouns   *66*
    19   Possessive adjectives   *69*
    20   Possession with *de*   *71*

    READING: El teléfono   *72*

5   **Problemas de una dueña de casa**   73

    21   Present tense of irregular verbs   *77*
    22   Direct commands: the *usted, ustedes* forms   *79*
    23   Direct commands: the *tú* form   *82*

24   With-verb pronouns in commands *84*

25   The personal *a* *86*

READING: Conversación en un restorán *88*

6   **Lío de tráfico**   **89**

26   Preterit of regular verbs and *dar* *93*

27   The demonstratives *96*

28   The conjunctions *e* in place of *y* and *u* in place of *o* *97*

29   The contraction of *a* plus *el* to *al* *98*

30   The article with classifying nouns *99*

31   The article with things possessed *100*

32   *Conocer* and *saber* *100*

READING: "The Policeman's Lot" *102*

7   **Tema del día**   **103**

33   The infinitive after another verb *107*

34   *Ir a* plus infinitive *109*

35   *Al* plus infinitive *111*

36   The verb *haber,* there to be *112*

37   Reflexives with nonpersonal subjects *113*

READING: Paquito y la relatividad *117*

8   **Hombre respetable**   **118**

38   The infinitive after prepositions *121*

39   The infinitive with verb-plus-relator *123*

40   The *–ndo* form *125*

41   The present progressive *126*

42   The position of the with-verb pronouns in verb constructions *128*

43   The cardinal numerals above ten *130*

READING: Juanito en la barbería *133*

9   **En un café**   **134**

44   Irregular preterits *137*

45   The preterit and *–ndo* form of *–ir* stem-changing verbs *140*

46   Limiting adjectives *141*

47   The ordinal numerals *143*

48   Days, months, years *144*

49   The plural of nouns with singular ending in [s] *145*

50   Shortened adjectives *145*

READING: Lección de aritmética *148*

10 **El campo y la ciudad**   **149**

51   The imperfect   *153*
52   Imperfect versus preterit   *155*
53   The past progressive   *159*
54   The with-preposition pronouns   *160*
55   With-preposition pronouns as objects with *a*   161
56   With-verb pronouns that repeat noun objects   *162*

READINGS: La familia Alvarez va a la feria   *166*
              Las lenguas de América   *167*

11 **En la tintorería**   **169**

57   Two with-verb pronoun objects   *171*
58   Meaning of the indirect object   *175*
59   Nominalization   *177*
60   Possessives that do not precede nouns   *180*
61   Nominalized possessives   *182*
62   Telling time   *183*
63   Anticipation of number and person   *185*

READINGS: Fragmento de una conferencia sobre la etimología hispánica   *187*
              Dos triángulos americanos   *187*

12 **Una visita al médico**   **190**

64   Descriptive adjectives   *192*
65   The reflexive with-verb pronouns   *195*
66   Reflexive constructions, direct object   *196*
67   Reflexive constructions, indirect object   *198*
68   The reflexive for unplanned occurrences   *201*

READINGS: Una visita al médico   *203*
              España y la formación de la lengua española   *203*

13 **La universidad y la política**   **206**

69   The position of negative words other than *no*   *209*
70   Negative words (other than *no*) and their affirmative counterparts   *210*
71   Negatives other than *no* both before and after the verb   *211*
72   The position of *no* in contradictions and reservations   *212*
73   The personal *a* with indefinites   *213*
74   The indefinites in affirmative questions   *214*
75   The definite article for "definite wholes"   *215*
76   The definite article with days and places   *217*

READINGS: Dos puntos de vista   *219*
              Entrevista de dos periodistas   *220*

14   Problemas de un turista   223

77   Nominalization with the neuter article *lo*   226
78   Comparatives   228
79   The comparison of inequality   230
80   *Lo* with compared adverbs   233
81   The comparison of equality   233
82   The comparison of identity   234
83   Certain uses of the indefinite article: identification and individualization   235

READINGS: Problema de pronunciación   239
En la sala de matrícula en una universidad de los Estados Unidos   239

15   Temprano en la oficina   243

84   Nominalization of indefinites   245
85   The *each-other* construction   248
86   The equivalents of *that, which, who,* and *whom*   249
87   Word order   251
88   The position of adjectives with *qué*   252
89   Singular for "one each"   254
90   Idioms with *tener* and *dar*   254
91   *Hacer* in expressions of time   257

READINGS: Orden de las palabras   259
Los estudiantes hispanos y sus actividades políticas   260

16   Problemas del crecer   263

92   The *–do* form as an adjective   265
93   The *–do* form with *estar* and *ser*   267
94   The present perfect   268
95   Forms of the present subjunctive; subjunctive or indicative with *tal vez*   270
96   The equivalents of *–ly*   274

READINGS: A la mesa   276
Las riquezas de la América hispánica   277

17   La política en la casa   279

97   Indicative and subjunctive in noun clauses   282
98   Indirect commands   287
99   Present subjunctive for *let's*   289
100   Colors   290
101   Nouns and *todos* with first- and second-person verbs   291

READINGS: Escojamos una carrera   293
De compras   294

18 Un hombre de negocios **297**

    102 Indicative and subjunctive in adverb clauses *299*
    103 Indicative and subjunctive in adjective clauses *304*
    104 Mass nouns and countables *307*

       READINGS: ¿Quiere usted empleo? *308*
                Las comidas en Hispanoamérica *309*

19 El nuevo gerente **311**

    105 The imperfect subjunctive *313*
    106 The present and present perfect subjunctive after a verb in the present *319*
    107 The equivalents of *I wish* and *as if* *320*
    108 The diminutive suffix *–ito* *322*
    109 Singular and plural with collective nouns *323*

       READINGS: La puntualidad *325*
                La familia *326*

20 La lotería **328**

    110 The future tense *329*
    111 The conditional *332*
    112 Additional progressives *334*
    113 Additional perfects *335*
    114 The future of probability; *deber,* must, ought *337*
    115 Clauses with *si,* if *338*
    116 Softened requests and criticisms *342*

       READINGS: Sinfonía: Conjugación del verbo "amar"—by Alarcón *344*
                La rúbrica en la modalidad hispana *345*

21 De duelo **348**

    117 Indicative or subjunctive in exclamations *349*
    118 Infinitive and subjunctive with verbs of suasion *351*
    119 Perceived actions *353*
    120 *El* and *un* with feminine nouns *354*
    121 *De* and *por* for *by,* after a *–do* form *355*
    122 *De* as equivalent of *with* and *in* *357*
    123 *En* and *a* for *at* *358*

       READINGS: Muere un destacado miembro del foro *361*
                La religión *362*

22 El robo **365**

    124 Probability in past time *367*
    125 The meanings of *por* *369*
    126 The meanings of *de* *372*

127 The *–do* form for postures *375*

128 *Tener, haber,* and *estar* without complements *376*

READINGS: Noticia del día *378*

El conquistador español del siglo XVI *379*

23 **Celebrando la Independencia** **381**

129 The meanings of *para* *383*

130 *Para* versus *por* *385*

131 The equivalents of English nouns modifying nouns *387*

132 Infinitive phrases and noun clauses as modifiers *389*

133 The masculine referring to both sexes *392*

READINGS: Un poquito sobre la derivación *394*

Las literaturas hispánicas *395*

24 **La OEA** **399**

134 Derivation *402*

135 Compounding *405*

136 Compound prepositions *406*

137 Forms of pronouns after relator words *408*

138 *¿Cuál?* and *¿qué?* for *what?* *410*

139 *¿De quién, –es?* for *whose?* *411*

READINGS: La composición *414*

La Organización de los Estados Americanos (OEA) *415*

25 **Una tertulia: Cervantes** **418**

Una charla: Deportes **421**

26 **La corrida de toros** **425**

El gaucho y el cowboy **428**

27 **Una velada musical** **432**

La música hispánica **433**

28 **El arte hispánico** **437**

Las artes populares en México **439**

29 **Emigrantes** **442**

La llegada de un emigrante del siglo XX **444**

30 **Charlas sobre el folklore** **446**

El folklore español **450**

Appendix *451*

Vocabulary *458*

Index *487*

Introduction

One of the most rewarding events in my term of office as President of the Modern Language Association of America was the development of the College Language Manual. It is now my privilege to introduce this long-awaited text to you. This is an exciting book, whose publication will mark a number of "firsts" in the history of foreign language study in the United States. The MLA, now seventy-six years old, has never before endorsed a textbook but is proud to sponsor this one, for reasons I want to explain.

"There are always new textbooks; what we need is a new *kind* of textbook." For years I have heard language teachers say this. What kind was rarely spelled out by the speaker, but the remark usually implied that foreign language study has become more important to all of us since World War II, that students now expect more of their language teachers (and can be expected, in turn, to do more than used to be asked of them), that a lot of important things have been learned in recent years about making language learning more efficient, and that these things should be more fully exploited in textbooks than has hitherto been the case. What the profession seemed to want was a beginning text that was bold, experimental, keyed throughout to the new spirit in language study. Here it is.

In a sense this is the profession's own book. I say this not because of its conference origin and multiple authorship, not even because it is sponsored by a professional society, but rather because its basic principles, once agreed upon (in May 1956), were widely publicized and talked about long before the book got written, and every Spanish teacher in the United States was invited to agree or disagree and to contribute of his own knowledge and experience. Many did. The reader should know also that the six authors of this book (and twenty-four members of an Advisory Committee) will receive no royalties. All royalties will go into an MLA fund to make possible the writing of other books, as teachers of other languages come forward in a similarly unselfish and cooperative spirit, desiring to achieve another "ideal" text.

Planning and writing a book in the way that this one was planned and written is an expensive, time-consuming matter. Anyone who has watched a committee struggle to compose a single paragraph may doubt that any committee should be entrusted with the writing of a whole book. However, thanks to a grant of $40,500 from the Rockefeller Foundation, and thanks also to the generosity and hospitality of the University of Texas, this committee was able to live and work together long enough to do the seemingly impossible. The adventure was undertaken only because a conference of seventeen veteran teachers of Spanish had agreed unanimously that the best text-book could be produced through *cooperative endeavor*. Since among these conferees were the authors of many of the successful textbooks already available, the argument was as convincing as it was surprising and inspiring.

Equally surprising was the agreement of these seventeen college and university teachers of Spanish (chosen to represent a variety of points of view) on criteria for a truly modern textbook. In arriving at these criteria they assumed these conditions: qualified instructors, students of college age with the usual spread in ability and motivation, a class of manageable size, and a course with a minimum of 300 hours spent in class, laboratory, and outside study. The general approach was then outlined to include the following points:

1. The course should concentrate at the beginning on the learner's *hearing* and *speaking* of Spanish, *whatever his objective*. (The Working Committee therefore developed a teaching tool that adequately presents and drills pronunciation—not the usual brief treatment of pronunciation in an introduction. Pronunciation exercises continue through the first eleven units, or weeks, with emphasis on contrasts within Spanish or comparison of Spanish sounds with English sounds.)

2. The text should make extensive use of *realistic dialogs,* which should also be *recorded*—in an acceptable standard for the Americas. (The Working Committee went further, trying to give the dialogs—and the readings too—*mature content,* interesting to learners of college age. It was decided that the student should *memorize all of these dialogs,* to make them immediately useful for conversational practice. Memorization has always been an indispensable part of language learning; but this book, instead of requiring the student to memorize vocabulary lists or verb paradigms or grammar rules, asks him to memorize full utterances in contextual relationships with each other—sentences one might actually want to speak someday outside the classroom.)

3. Grammar should be presented *inductively,* with summary statements given *after drill.* (The Working Committee therefore produced explanations of grammar that are both accurate and unambiguous, written in a style understandable to the student. It also produced grammar drills that give enough practice in the basic patterns of Spanish to enable the student to learn to use and respond to these patterns *automatically.* All exercise and drill materials are based on comparison of the structures of English and Spanish.)

4. Translation should be used sparingly as a device in teaching reading, since the goal is *direct reading,* without conscious item-by-item decoding. Consequently, although reading of previously heard and memorized material may begin early in the course, reading of previously unheard material should not begin until the student has reasonable control of the pronunciation and principal structural patterns involved in the material.

5. Visual and audio-visual aids should be used as auxiliaries to the text when possible.

6. In order to liberate the student from his single-culture limitations, Spanish and Spanish-American cultural values and patterns of behavior should form a significant part of the content of the linguistic material from the beginning—and at every stage.

This is the basic philosophy; the selection and organization of actual details came from a wealth of experience, cooperatively checked and double checked. The text is divided into thirty units of work, corresponding roughly to the weeks in an academic year. After the first unit, which emphasizes pronunciation and useful classroom phrases, each of the next twenty-three units consists of a *dialog (from which everything else in the unit is drawn),* a section of drills and grammar, and a section of readings. The last six units in the book are exclusively reading units, presenting few new points of grammar.

The drills are ingeniously designed to give the student the "feel" of Spanish as quickly as possible; having memorized a "frame sentence" from the basic dialog, he expands this through whatever range of vocabulary he controls, and soon has a considerable store of *complete utterances* he can use as occasion requires or suggests. The drills are of three main kinds: substitution drills, response drills, and translation drills (mostly structurally oriented). Following each is a discussion of the pattern that has been drilled—not a set of rules to learn and follow, but a clear statement of how the pattern operates. Students should gain confidence rapidly through this *pattern assimilation* (each sentence having elements of novelty), but, if I may say so, they may need to be very patient with their teachers, for whom such *thorough* covering of familiar ground can become dull and tiring. (Drills are, however, for learners, not for teachers.) Teachers accustomed to traditional texts may even find the drills in this book deceptively easy. The variety of drill types has been intentionally limited: there are no paradigm recitations, no fill-the-blanks, no multiple choice, no conjugate-the-infinitives, no matching.

The readings are meant to be *read,* not translated. They are of two different kinds, with different functions. Units Three through Nine contain "reworked readings" (reintroducing situations, topics, vocabulary, and language patterns in somewhat different contexts and arrangements), whereas units Ten through Thirty contain "original readings" (nearly all produced for this text), the last six consisting of longer, more advanced readings. Questionnaires to check student comprehension follow all the original readings, which are designed to enlarge on the *cultural content* of the dialogs and hence to give the Spanish class the range of a liberal arts course on Hispanic society.

One of the most valuable lessons I learned when Director of the MLA's Foreign Language Program (1952–1956) was the potentiality of cooperative solutions to all sorts of problems vexing the profession. I can give many examples of how such solutions were found, but none so heart-warming, none involving the active participation of so many able people, as this book *Modern Spanish.* Since I was present at its inspiring beginning—having called the conference that recommended cooperative production of the book—it is most gratifying to be allowed now to commend the results to you.

Let me say finally that such wonderful cooperation should not end with publication. Having produced this unprecedented textbook, the profession will, I trust, see to it that it is later improved with each revision.

February, 1960

WILLIAM RILEY PARKER
Distinguished Service Professor of English
Indiana University

Acknowledgments

For a venture to which so many people have contributed, it is virtually impossible to make a complete list of acknowledgments. We wish to thank first, in the name of the MLA, the many Spanish teachers throughout the country who volunteered advice and constructive criticism. Our thanks go too to the Rockefeller Foundation and to the cooperating institutions:

> University of Texas (host to writers working in residence)
> Foreign Service Institute
> University of Kansas
> University of Oklahoma
> University of Southern California

We owe a special debt of gratitude to the six members of the Working Committee, the twenty-four members of the Advisory Committee, the editors of *Hispania,* Kenneth W. Mildenberger (now with the U. S. Office of Education, but chiefly responsible for MLA liaison in the critical months of the project), and to all those whose names are listed below.

SPECIAL SERVICES   Richard Beym *Foreign Service Institute*
D. Lincoln Canfield *University of Rochester*
Odette Scott (CHILE) *University of Kansas*
Jack L. Ulsh *Foreign Service Institute*
Howard Walker *University of Kansas*

Modern Spanish

A Project of the Modern Language Association

Of all the animals on earth, man alone has developed *language,* an oral means of communication extending his effectiveness beyond the here and now. Unlike other animals, man is able to recall past events and to speculate about the future and the imaginary.

Nothing definite is known about the origins of speech. But indirect evidence suggests that a hundred thousand years ago man already possessed a highly organized system of oral communication. Compared with this, the period during which man has expressed himself in writing has been insignificantly short. The earliest evidence of a system of writing dates back only about six thousand years. Even today there are scores of languages with no written form. These are every bit as complex and systematically organized as the languages that have been written for centuries and that have been the vehicle for the great literatures of the world. The spoken language, then, is primary, both in the history of the race and in the experience of the individual speaker. For this reason, it is important to distinguish a language from the system of writing which represents it.

Among the oldest writing systems known are the Chinese, the Greek, and the Latin. The writing system of Latin, or at least the Latin alphabet, has been adapted increasingly over the centuries to the writing of the languages of Europe and recently even of Chinese,

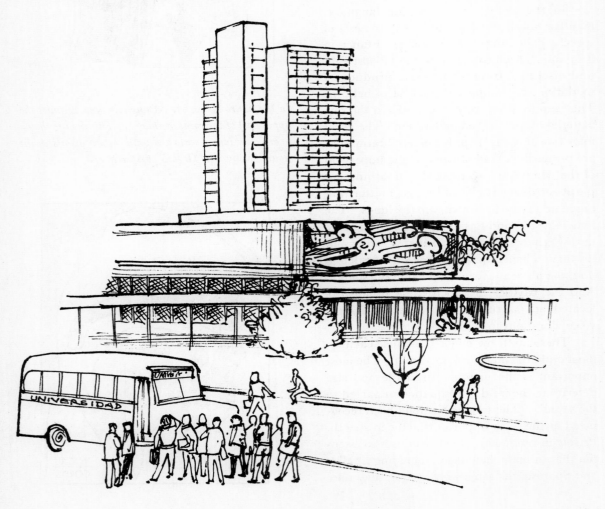

while spoken Latin has continued, with modifications, in the various forms of the Romance languages, including Spanish.

In this text we will be primarily concerned with spoken rather than written Spanish. Hence it is appropriate that we begin with a discussion of pronunciation. In order to produce the sounds of another language satisfactorily, the student must become aware of the mechanism with which he produces his own language and must gain conscious control of it. As an aid to doing so, some details are given about the organs of speech and how they perform. Then follows a discussion of the articulation of the sounds of Spanish and the accompanying phenomena of stress and pitch. With these explanations, the student will be able to hear and imitate more accurately what he hears in the recorded models.

The Organs of Speech

In the process of developing language, man has adapted various organs to the uses of speech. The lungs, whose biological function is to absorb fresh oxygen into the bloodstream and discharge from it the waste products of oxidation, act in speech as a sort of bellows. They supply what may be considered the raw material of speech: compressed air. The vocal folds (vocal cords) supply voice vibration but are primarily a kind of valve at the upper end of the windpipe to protect the breathing apparatus from particles of foreign matter that might otherwise be drawn into the lungs. The tongue, teeth, and lips are basically organs for tasting, chewing, sucking, drinking, and swallowing. Their function in speech is articulation: the process of forming meaningful sounds. And the cavities in which these organs are located act as resonators which modify the voice vibrations from the vocal folds.

There are three major resonance cavities: the mouth, the nose, and the throat. The most important is the mouth. Its shape and size determine the kind of resonance imparted to the sound. (The tongue has long been recognized as the most important factor in speech. Its role in producing speech sounds is so essential that in many languages, including English and Spanish, the same word, *tongue,* may refer

to both the organ and the language.) In modifying the shape and size of the mouth cavity, the tongue and lips have an important function.

The roof of the mouth is formed by the hard palate and the soft palate. The hard palate is divided, in phonetic descriptions, into teeth, alveolar region (gum ridge), and palate proper. The soft palate is often called the velum.

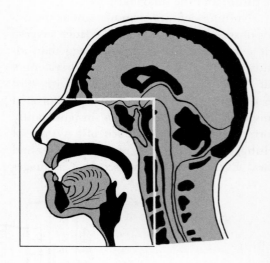

In the figure above, the rectangular area delimits the upper part of the vocal mechanism. This area is shown again on a larger scale and with certain details in the figure below: The Organs of Speech.

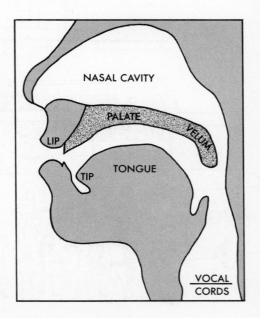

Articulation of Vowels

To produce a vowel sound, the tongue is arched higher or lower in the mouth: high, mid, low. This arching is either toward the front of the palate or toward the back (near the velum), and these two positions for vowel sounds are called front and back. Combining high, mid, and low with front and back, we obtain a set of descriptions for the five Spanish vowels: *high front* is [i], *mid front* is [e], *low central* is [a], *mid back* is [o], and *high back* is [u]. (Symbols between brackets are phonetic symbols rather than letters of the alphabet. The five symbols used above should not be pronounced as the English letters— "eye," "ee," "ay," "oh," "you"—but by shaping the mouth as indicated to approximate the Spanish vowel sounds.)

Two positions of the lips are also important: *spread* and *rounded*. These terms are also used to describe the vowel sounds. Thus we have a high-front spread vowel, a high-back rounded vowel, and so forth.

The characteristic of vowels is that air, set in motion by the vibration of the vocal folds (this is called voice vibration or voicing), resonates in the mouth cavity which has been shaped by the position of the tongue and lips. For each separate vowel sound, the shape and size of the resonance cavity is different.

Voice vibration also accompanies some of the consonants, which are therefore known as *voiced* consonants. Consonants articulated without this voice vibration are said to be *voiceless*. One way of telling whether a sound is voiced, say a sound like *ah* or *mm*, is to see whether it can be sung to a musical note. Voiceless sounds like *f* or *s* cannot be sung.

Speech sounds are thus described scientifically in three ways: (1) how the speech organs are placed (place of articulation); (2) how they perform in producing the sound (manner of articulation); and (3) whether or not the vocal folds vibrate (voiced-voiceless).

The next step is to describe how the voiced and voiceless consonants are articulated, and to do this we must state the *place* where the lips or tongue make contact or near-contact, and the *manner* in which they perform.

Articulation of Consonants

PLACES OF ARTICULATION

In the figure below the places of articulation are indicated by numbered arrows:

1. The arrow joins the upper and lower lips and is labeled *bilabial,* meaning "two lips." A bilabial articulation is one involving both lips, which are either pressed together or brought close together.

2. *Labiodental* involves contact with little pressure between the lower lip and the upper teeth.

3. *Dental* involves contact between the tongue tip and the upper teeth.

4. *Alveolar* involves the tongue, either the tip or the blade, touching or approaching the alveolar ridge, just back of the upper front teeth.

5. *Palatal* indicates either complete or partial contact between the tongue and the hard palate.

6. *Velar* involves contact or narrowing of the passage between the tongue and soft palate or velum.

7. *Nasal* requires the opening of the nasal cavity, by lowering the velum.

MANNER OF ARTICULATION

The following terms describe the kinds of articulation found in Spanish:

1. *Stop* refers to consonants characterized by a complete closure of the air passage, stopping the flow of air.

2. *Nasal* refers to consonants which involve closure of the air passage somewhere in the mouth, but with voiced air admitted from the

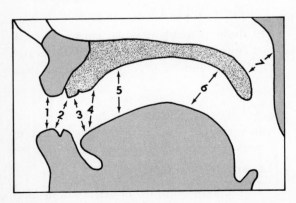

1. *Bilabial* 2. *Labiodental* 3. *Dental* 4. *Alveolar* 5. *Palatal* 6. *Velar* 7. *Nasal*

throat into the nasal cavity, resonating there and passing out through the nose.

3. *Fricative* refers to consonants made by narrowing the mouth passage at some point so that the air, voiced or voiceless, is forced out with an audible sound of hissing or friction.

4. *Affricate* refers to consonants involving momentary closure of the mouth passage at a given point, followed by a rather slow movement of release, during which a friction noise is produced (cf. *fricative,* 3 above).

5. *Lateral* refers to the kind of consonant made when the tongue touches only the median line of the palate, so that air escapes around one or both sides of the tongue.

6. *Tap* refers to the kind of consonant in which there is a single rapid contact made with the tip of the tongue against the alveolar ridge.

7. *Vibrant* refers to the kind of consonant in which the tip of the tongue vibrates against the alveolar ridge.

Just as in writing we line up letters from left to right to spell words, so in speaking we combine sounds in time sequences to form utterances. While words are separated by blank spaces in the written form of the language, words in speech are not always separated from each other. The "spaces" in the flow of speech are called pauses, short periods of silence. The individual utterances which fill the time lapses between pauses are called phrases.

Within each phrase utterance, i.e., an uninterrupted period of speech activity, there are other phenomena which occur simultaneously with the articulations. These are the phenomena of *stress* and *pitch.*

Stress

Stress is the term applied to the relative prominence of certain syllables as compared with the neighboring syllables in the same phrase. We distinguish two degrees of stress: strong stress and weak stress. Every phrase has at least one strong stress. In a phrase with more than one strongly stressed syllable, the one nearest the end is usually reinforced, i.e., a little stronger than the other strong syllables.

All the strong stresses are marked in the phonetic transcriptions in this book with the accent [']. The accent mark ' which follows regular rules in Spanish spelling (appearing only over small letters, not over capital letters) almost always indicates a strong stress.

The term *weak stress* is used here for the lower degree of prominence which characterizes all syllables that are not strongly stressed. Such weakly stressed syllables are left unmarked both in the spelling and in the phonetic transcriptions.

Spanish words of two or more syllables are strongly stressed (1) on the last syllable, (2) on the next-to-last, and (3) on the third-from-last (or earlier in the case of certain compounds).

Spanish spelling, unlike English, shows clearly what syllable is stressed:

1. Words having the *last syllable* stressed can be arranged in two classes, according to the spelling devices used:

   a. those spelled without an accent mark: **estoy, verdad, español, reloj, estar, feliz.** (NOTE: These end in consonant letters other than **n** or **s.**)

   b. those spelled with an accent mark on the last syllable: **está, perdón, después.** (NOTE: These end in a vowel or **n** or **s.**)

2. The majority of Spanish words have strong stress on the *next-to-last syllable.* Again the spelling clearly shows the place of the stress by two means:

   a. those spelled without an accent mark: **clase, puerta, llegan, alumnos.** (NOTE: These end in a vowel or **n** or **s.**)

   b. those spelled with an accent mark: **fácil, cónsul, azúcar, césped, Martínez.** (NOTE: These end in a consonant other than **n** or **s.**)

3. Words having the stress on the *third-from-last,* or earlier, are all spelled with an accent mark, regardless of their endings:

   a. **ángeles, lástima, teléfono;**

   b. compounds formed of verb (strong) plus pronoun forms (weak), written together: **siéntense, dándomelo, vendiéndosela;**

c. compounds combining two stressed forms, i.e., verb plus noun, adjective plus –**mente,** etc., of which the first would have the written accent if it appeared alone: **fácil + mente = fácilmente, rápida + mente = rápidamente.**

These compounds then have two strong stresses, the one nearer the end being a little stronger. The same is true of other compounds, such as **tocadiscos (toca + discos)** and **exactamente (exacta + mente),** which do not have a written accent.

Pitch

Pitch refers to a musical tone, i.e., to the frequency of the voice vibration. All the voiced sounds of speech have pitch.

It is sufficient to recognize three levels of pitch in Spanish. By this we mean not that Spanish speakers use only three pitches, but that the variety of pitches they do use can be grouped into three heights. We use the term *levels* rather than *notes* because the intervals between them are not fixed as are the intervals between notes in a musical scale. Furthermore, the levels vary with individual speakers, and are not at specific frequencies as are the notes of our musical scale, like F or B flat. We refer to the three pitch levels as *low, middle,* and *high,* or by numbers 1, 2, and 3 respectively:

high   3
middle   2
low   1

In the intonation of Spanish, shifts from one level to another, whether up or down, either coincide with the stress or immediately follow the stress. They are, in fact, one of the ways by which the stressed syllable is made to stand out.

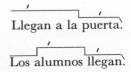

Llegan a la puerta.

Los alumnos llegan.

In the second example, the two syllables with weak stress which precede the first strong are on level 1 (low). The last two syllables, the strong and the weak one following, are

also on level 1. The downward slant at the end indicates that during the final syllable a slight but quick drop in pitch occurs.

The following example includes a larger number of syllables, but with essentially the same intonation pattern:

Los alumnos llegan a la puerta de la clase.

All the syllables from the first strong to the next-to-last strong of the phrase are on level 2, with the last strong on level 1. The variation of actual pitch between strongs and weaks within level 2 is very slight. The drop in pitch to level 1 on the last strong in this sentence is a typical Spanish intonation and requires practice, because in English one is apt to rise on the last strong.

The preceding patterns all had a drop in pitch at the end, on the last strong. The following example shows a rise in pitch at the end of the first phrase:

Cuando los alumnos llegan, el profesor los

invita a entrar.

There is a slight pause after **llegan.**

Three frequent intonation patterns which characterize questions are:

1) ¿Llegan a la puerta?

The upward slant at the end indicates that the pitch rises very quickly within the final syllable. Not infrequently a slight drop in pitch occurs on the strong syllable just preceding this rise, or on the weak syllable before that.

2) ¿Está la puerta abierta?

This type of question intonation indicates that the speaker assumes a confirmation, rather than really asking for information.

3) ¿Quién llega a la puerta?

Such an intonation pattern is typical of questions beginning with interrogative words, like *who, which, when, where,* etc.

In answer to this last question we might well have:

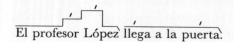

El profesor López llega a la puerta.

The rise to level 3 on the strong syllable Ló– is a device for giving prominence to the name, which is the specific information called for.

Specific comparisons of English and Spanish intonation are given in Unit 3.

On the following pages are drawings that show the position of the vocal organs for successive articulations in the order of their first occurrence in the drill sentences (pp. 11–14, 21–22). The drill sentences are built up, one sound at a time, to form syllables, then phrases. These are set apart from the descriptive material with an appropriate intonation marking in each case.

LETTER	SYMBOL	SYLLABLE
l	[l]	

Voiced alveolar lateral. The vocal folds vibrate; the tip of the tongue touches the alveolar ridge, while the sides of the tongue, being lowered, allow the air to escape laterally, on one or both sides of the central obstruction. The surface of the tongue, being somewhat arched toward the palate, imparts the quality of [i] (see below, p. 15, **invita**).

a	[a]	

Low-central spread vowel. The vocal folds vibrate. The mouth cavity is wide open, with the tongue rather flat in the mouth and the corners of the mouth pulled back slightly. Keep the vowel short.

	[la]	Weak

p	[p]	

Voiceless bilabial stop. The vocal folds do not vibrate. The lips, pressed together for a brief time, are then separated without the strong puff of air which occurs in English in such a word as *pool*. We say therefore that Spanish [p] is unaspirated.

u	[w]	

Voiced labiovelar semiconsonant. The vocal folds vibrate. The lips are pushed forward in a pouting position, while the back of the tongue is arched toward the velum. The term *semiconsonant* refers to something in between a consonant and a vowel.

e   [e]

Mid-front spread vowel. As with the vowel [a] above, and all other vowels, the vocal folds vibrate. The tongue is arched forward in the mouth to a level between low and high.

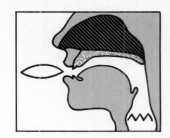

r   [R]

Voiced alveolar tongue trill. The vocal folds vibrate. The tip of the tongue taps repeatedly against the alveolar ridge. By making several taps you will more readily separate this articulation from the next one in the word.

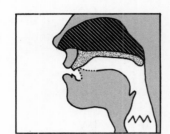

[pwér–]   Strong

It is permissible to replace [R] in this position (before another consonant) with the single-tap [r] described below, for in this position there is no significant contrast betwen [R] and [r].

t   [t]

Voiceless dental stop. The vocal folds do not vibrate. When the closure is released, there is no strong escape of air as in English *top*. Like [p] above, this consonant is unaspirated.

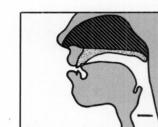

a   [a]

[–ta]   Weak

In the sequence of three syllables [la pwérta], the second has a strong stress with higher pitch. We symbolize the greater stress by putting an accent mark over the vowel of the strong syllable [la pwérta]. We show the relative levels of pitch by means of a diagram:

la–pweR–ta. The situations here are typical: low pitch for the first (weak) syllable, a rise to the next higher level coinciding with the greater stress and a drop to low pitch again on the last (also weak) syllable. Where, as happens here, the word is at the end of the phrase, i.e., comes just before a pause point, the pitch normally describes an additional downward or upward movement (here downward) accompanied by a slowing down and weakening of articulation. This feature is the one that appears in the diagrams in the form of an upward or downward slant line. It is called "terminal juncture." (Sometimes there is a break without the additional rise or fall in pitch and without a slowing down; this form of juncture is shown simply by a gap in the line of pitch. See the diagrams at the end of this unit.)

a   [a]   [a]   a–la–pweR–ta

In this utterance, as in the preceding one, there is only one strong syllable. Note that two weak ones precede it and one weak one follows it.

ll   [y]   *Voiced palatal semiconsonant.* The vocal folds vibrate. The tongue is arched high in the fore part of the mouth and touches the hard palate except for a rather narrow channel down the middle (or median) line.

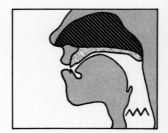

[λ]   A variant pronunciation, which is used by many speakers in various parts of the Spanish-speaking world, is a *voiced palatal lateral affricate.* The vocal folds vibrate. The tip of the tongue touches the lower teeth while the blade makes contact with the hard palate. Upon releasing this contact, the median line of the tongue pulls away first and a fricative sound occurs as a result of voiced air escaping through this narrow channel. In some speakers the fricative sound is particularly noticeable.

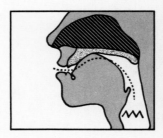

e   [e]

[yé–]   Strong

g   [g̶]   *Voiced velar fricative.* The vocal folds vibrate. The tongue, high in the rear of the mouth, does not quite touch the soft palate as for the velar stop (cf. English *go*). The narrow space left unobstructed between the surface of the tongue and the soft palate allows the voiced air to keep on escaping—a characteristic of the fricative articulation.

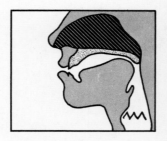

a   [a]

[–ga–]   Weak

LETTER	SYMBOL	SYLLABLE

n   [n]

Voiced alveolar nasal. The vocal folds vibrate. The tongue, pressed against the alveolar ridge and the sides of the palate, obstructs the mouth as in English [n]. The velum is lowered, thus opening the nasal passage. The voiced (vibrating) air escapes then through the nose where it resonates, giving the acoustic effect that is called nasality.

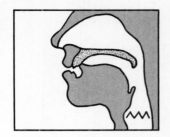

[–na]   Weak

ye–g̶a–na–la–pweʀ–ta

Note that the syllable division shown by [–] in the transcription indicates that [n] attaches to the following vowel [a], thus linking the two words and bridging the gap that appears in the written or printed form.

In this utterance there are two strong syllables (marked with [′]). The first strong syllable of the series determines the pitch as being on level 2. The second strong syllable is characteristically on level 1, followed by the final weak, which again is marked by the falling terminal juncture [⌐]. The weak syllables between the two strongs are, as indicated in the diagram, on level 2, although their pitch may be slightly lower than the syllable [yé].

l   [l]

o   [o]

Mid-back rounded vowel. The tongue is arched somewhat toward the rear of the palate, and the lips are rounded, forming a rather elongated mouth opening.

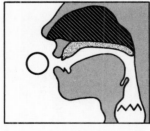

[lo–]   Weak

s   [s]

Voiceless alveolar fricative. The vocal folds do not vibrate. The tongue forms a narrowed channel in the area of the alveolar ridge, and voiceless air escapes through it to produce the fricative sound.

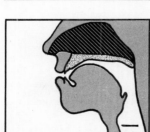

a   [a]

[–sa–]   Weak

Note again that the syllable constitutes a sequence of consonant-plus-vowel across the word boundary, as happened in **llegan a** [yé–g̶a–na], above.

LETTER	SYMBOL	SYLLABLE
l	[l]	
u	[u]	

High-back rounded vowel. The tongue is arched high in the rear of the mouth, and the lips are energetically pushed forward to form a small, round opening.

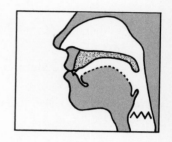

Speakers of English often imitate this sound inaccurately by giving it too much duration and ending it with an offglide like *w,* or will make it too open if they keep it short. In some parts of the U. S., speakers tend to arch the tongue too far forward while failing to round the lips enough. It is best to push the lips far forward. But keep the vowel short.

| m | [m] | |

Voiced bilabial nasal. As in English [m], the mouth is closed at the lips while the lowered velum allows the voiced air to escape through the nose where it resonates (nasality).

[–lúm–] Strong

[–nos] Weak

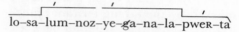

lo–sa–lum–noz–ye–ga–na–la–pweʀ–ta

Note the first and second strong syllables on level 2 and the last strong on level 1, followed by a weak with falling terminal juncture. At normal conversational tempo, the whole utterance (ten syllables of which three are strong) would be said without interruption. However, the diagram is broken after **alumnos** to indicate that if a break is made it will be at this point rather than any other.

At normal conversational tempo, the [s] of –**nos** (defined as voiceless) would be immediately followed by the voiced semiconsonant [y]. In this situation, typically, there occurs *assimilation.* This means that one speech sound comes to resemble another in some respect. What happens here is that the [s] acquires the voicing of its neighbor [y], and in place of voiceless [s] we have voiced [z].

Note in the recorded model that the articulation of this [s] plus voice is very lax, i.e., lacking in tenseness. If a break is made at this point (after [nos]), the [s] automatically reverts to the voiceless quality which is characteristic of it.

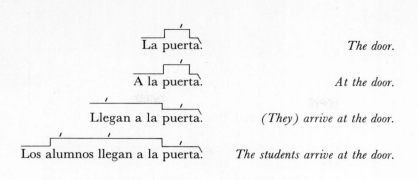

La puerta.	The door.
A la puerta.	At the door.
Llegan a la puerta.	(They) arrive at the door.
Los alumnos llegan a la puerta.	The students arrive at the door.

● RESPONSE DRILL WITH LONG ANSWERS

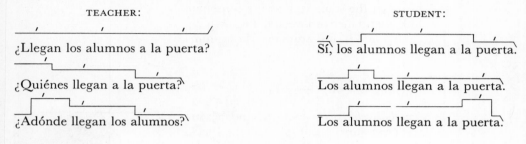

TEACHER:

¿Llegan los alumnos a la puerta?

¿Quiénes llegan a la puerta?

¿Adónde llegan los alumnos?

STUDENT:

Sí, los alumnos llegan a la puerta.

Los alumnos llegan a la puerta.

Los alumnos llegan a la puerta.

● RESPONSE DRILL WITH SHORT ANSWERS

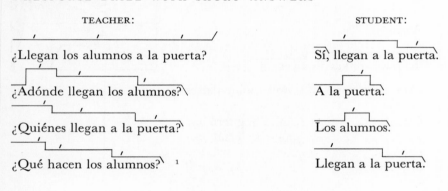

TEACHER:

¿Llegan los alumnos a la puerta?

¿Adónde llegan los alumnos?

¿Quiénes llegan a la puerta?

¿Qué hacen los alumnos? [1]

STUDENT:

Sí, llegan a la puerta.

A la puerta.

Los alumnos.

Llegan a la puerta.

LETTER	SYMBOL	SYLLABLE	
		[a–]	Weak

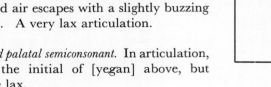

b	[ƀ]	*Voiced bilabial fricative.* The upper and lower lips, instead of being pressed together, are merely brought close, leaving a space between them through which voiced air escapes with a slightly buzzing noise. A very lax articulation.	
i	[y]	*Voiced palatal semiconsonant.* In articulation, like the initial of [yeǥan] above, but more lax.	
		[–ƀyér–]	Strong
		[–ta]	Weak

---

[1] In these three questions a rising terminal is also possible, and makes them more wheedling.

a–ƀyeʀ–ta

es–ta–ƀyeʀ–ta

At normal speed the vowel [a] of the weak syllable is absorbed into the [á] of the strong syllable immediately preceding. Such fusion of contiguous similar vowels is common in Spanish. It bridges the division between words in a phrase in much the same way as the consonant link mentioned above (cf. **llegan a** . . . [yé–ga–na–]; **los alumnos** [lo–sa–lúm–nos]).

la–pweʀ–ta–es–ta–ƀyeʀ–ta

qu   [k]   *Voiceless velar stop.* Like [p] and [t], this voiceless stop is unaspirated, i.e., lacks the strong air puff that occurs in English *cat*.

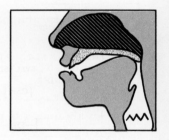

[ke]   Weak

la–pweʀ–ta kes–ta–ƀyeʀ–ta

Note two cases of vowel fusion [ke–es–tá–a].

ye–ga–na–la–pweʀ–ta kes–ta–ƀyeʀ–ta

Abierta   *Open.*

Está abierta.   *(It) is open.*

La puerta está abierta.   *The door is open.*

La puerta que está abierta.   *The door which is open.*

Llegan a la puerta que está abierta.   *They arrive at the door which is open.*

● RESPONSE DRILL WITH LONG ANSWERS

TEACHER: STUDENT:

¿Está abierta la puerta?   Sí, la puerta está abierta.

¿Está la puerta abierta?   Sí, la puerta está abierta.

TEACHER:

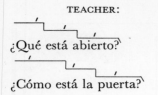

¿Qué está abierto?

¿Cómo está la puerta?

STUDENT:

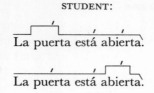

La puerta está abierta.

La puerta está abierta.

(Repeat question, leaving pauses for long responses.)

● RESPONSE DRILL WITH SHORT ANSWERS

TEACHER:

¿Está la puerta abierta?

¿Está abierta la puerta?

¿Qué está abierto?

¿Cómo está la puerta?

STUDENT:

Sí.

Sí.

La puerta.

Abierta.

LETTER	SYMBOL	SYLLABLE		
		[es–]	Weak	
		[–pa–]	Weak	

ñ [ñ] *Voiced palatal nasal.* There are two steps: (1) The back of the tongue is pressed against the hard palate to close off the mouth cavity (the tongue tip touches the lower teeth), while the voiced air escapes through the nose, producing nasality. (2) The closure is released by first moving the median portion of the tongue forward and downward, and following this by the sides of the tongue. The narrow channel momentarily opened to the escaping air gives rise to a brief sound like [y] (palatal fricative).

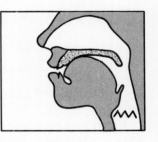

[–ñól] Strong. Make it short. Remember the [i]–like quality of [l], here as well as in the earlier occurrences.

es–pa–ñol

	[la]	Weak
	[klá–]	Strong
	[–se]	Weak

LETTER   SYMBOL   SYLLABLE

d   [đ]

Voiced dental fricative. The tip of the tongue lightly touches the upper incisors. Very lax and short articulation.

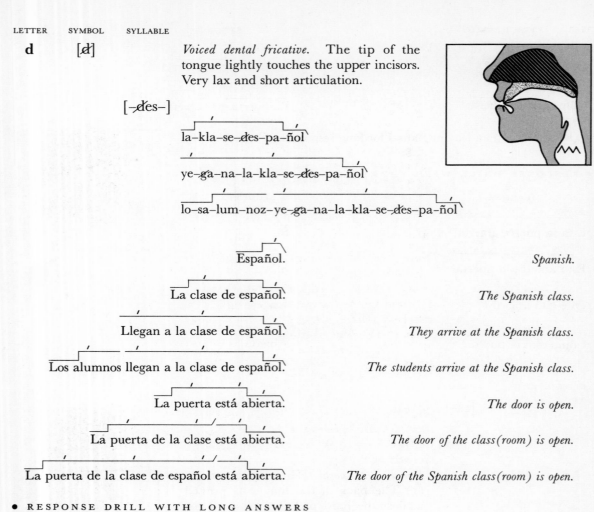

[–đes–]

la–kla–se–đes–pa–ñol

ye–ga–na–la–kla–se–đes–pa–ñol

lo–sa–lum–noz–ye–ga–na–la–kla–se–đes–pa–ñol

Español.	*Spanish.*
La clase de español.	*The Spanish class.*
Llegan a la clase de español.	*They arrive at the Spanish class.*
Los alumnos llegan a la clase de español.	*The students arrive at the Spanish class.*
La puerta está abierta.	*The door is open.*
La puerta de la clase está abierta.	*The door of the class (room) is open.*
La puerta de la clase de español está abierta.	*The door of the Spanish class (room) is open.*

● RESPONSE DRILL WITH LONG ANSWERS

INSTRUCTIONS: Give long answers to the following questions.

¿Está abierta la puerta?

¿Está la puerta abierta?

¿Cómo está la puerta?

¿Está abierta la puerta de la clase?

¿Cómo está la puerta de la clase?

¿Qué puerta está abierta?

¿Está abierta la puerta de la clase de español?

¿Cómo está la puerta de la clase de español?

¿Qué puerta está abierta?

¿Llegan los alumnos a la puerta abierta?

¿A qué puerta llegan los alumnos?

¿Quiénes llegan a la puerta abierta?

¿Llegan los alumnos a la puerta de la clase?

¿A qué puerta llegan los alumnos?

¿Quiénes llegan a la puerta de la clase?

● RESPONSE DRILL WITH SHORT ANSWERS

INSTRUCTIONS: Give short answers to the above questions.

[en–] Weak

The [n] of this syllable assimilates to the dental [t] of the following syllable, becoming itself dental.

r [r] *Voiced alveolar single tap.* The tip of the tongue makes a single brief tap against the alveolar ridge. It is important to complete the [t] before beginning the [r].

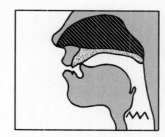

[–trár] [en–trár]

[a̗en–trár]

Note that the coming together of two vowels is characterized by the first one being very weak and short, so that the two together constitute one syllable. The ‿ mark under the vowel symbol indicates such a weak, short variant.

[lo–] Weak

s [s]

i [i] *High-front spread vowel.* The tongue is arched quite high in the mouth, toward the fore part of the palate; the lips are spread wide.

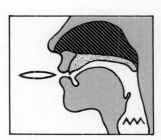

n [m] *Voiced bilabial nasal.* Exactly like [m] previously described in [–lum–] of the word **alumnos,** although spelled differently.

[–sim–] Weak

v [b] *Voiced bilabial stop.* [m] and [b] form a related sequence (the same is true of [m] and [p]). Among nasal consonants only [m] immediately precedes a [b] or [p]. And the [b] here is invariably the [b] stop, never the fricative [b̶] of **abierta** (see p. 11). The letters **v** and **b** represent the same two sounds, [b̶] and [b]. The latter occurs under limited conditions.

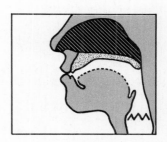

[–bí–] Strong

[–ta] Weak

lo–sim–bi–ta̗en–trar

	[el]	Weak

Remember the [i]–like quality of [l], here as well as in the earlier occurrences.

	[pro–]	Weak

f   [f]

Voiceless labiodental fricative. The lower lip lightly touches the edge of the upper incisors, and breath escapes with a slight friction noise.

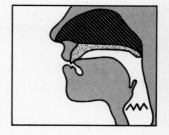

	[–fe–]	Weak
	[–sór]	Strong

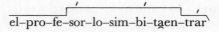

el–pro–fe–sor–lo–sim–bi–tạen–trar

c   [k]   [kwán–]   Strong

In [n] before dental [d] the tongue tip makes contact against the inner face of the upper incisors, as in **entrar.**

d   [d]

Voiced dental stop. Preceded by [n], the voiced dental is a stop [d], never the fricative variant [đ] as in [la–klá–se–đes–pa–ñól].

As in the [mb] sequence described above, the nasal consonant which immediately precedes a dental stop [t, d] is also dental.

	[–do]	Weak

kwan–do–lo–sa–lum–noz–ye–g̃a–na–la–pwer–ta

el–pro–fe–sor–lo–sim–bi–tạen–trar

	[el]	Weak
	[pro–]	Weak
	[–fe–]	Weak
	[–sór]	Strong
	[đí–]	Strong

c   [s]

Voiceless alveolar fricative. The letter **c** in spelling represents this sound when followed by the letter **e** or **i** (cf. **gracias** [grasyas] below).

[−se]   Weak

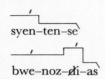

el–pro–fe–sor–di–se̜a–lo–sa–lum–nos

pa–se–nus–te–des

[syén–]   Strong

[−ten–]   Weak

[−se]   Weak

syen–ten–se

bwe–noz–di–as

In **buenos** there is a voiced bilabial stop, since it occurs right after *pause*. This is the same stop encountered after [m], above. Spelling, whether with **b** or **v**, makes no difference.

[se–]   Weak

[−ñó–]   Strong

r   [r]   *Voiced alveolar single tap.* In this position, between vowels, no more than a single tap is permissible.

[−res]   Weak

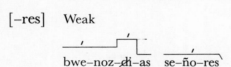

bwe–noz–di–as   se–ño–res

[se–]   Weak

[−ñór]   Strong

bwe–noz–di–as   se–ñor

[mar–]   Weak

t   [t]

i   [i]   [−tí–]   Strong

z   [s]   *Voiceless alveolar fricative.* The letter **z** represents the same sound as **s.**

[−nes]   Weak

c   [s]   [syé–]   Strong

rr   [R]

Voiced alveolar vibrant multiple trill. The tip of the tongue vibrates, making two or more rapid taps, against the alveolar ridge. In this position, between vowels, it contrasts with the single tap [r]. Many pairs of words are distinguished by this contrast: **perro** *dog,* **pero** *but.*

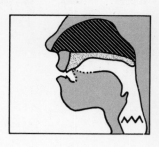

[–Re]   Weak

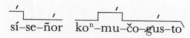

se–ñor–mar–ti–nes   sye-Re-la-pwer-ta   por–fa–bor

[sí]   Strong

[se–]   Weak

[–ñór]   Strong

[kon]   Weak

[mú–]   Strong

ch   [č]

Voiceless palatal affricate. There are two steps: (1) The tongue blade is pressed rather energetically against the fore part of the palate, the tip touching the lower incisors. (2) The pressure is then released a little more slowly than for a stop consonant, so that the escaping air causes a momentary fricative sound before the following vowel begins.

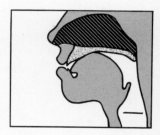

[–čo]   Weak

[gús–]   Strong

[–to]   Weak

sí–se–ñor   koⁿ–mu–čo–gus–to

The small superscript [n] signifies that the articulation is very weak, a case of partial assimilation.

g   [g]

Voiced velar stop. Identical with [k] in place and manner of articulation, but with voicing. Note that this is preceded by silence, hence it is in absolute initial position, and is therefore a stop.

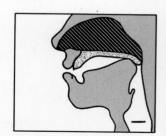

[grá–]   Strong

[–syas]   Weak. In this syllable note the spelling of [s] with **c** followed by **i**.

gra–syas

d	[d]	*Voiced dental stop.* The articulation is the same as in the sequence [–nd–] in the word [kwándo]. Here it is preceded by silence.
	[de]	Weak
	[ná–]	Strong
	[– đa]	Weak
	[se–]	Weak
	[–ñór]	Strong

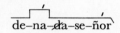

de–na–đa–se–ñor

b	[b]	*Voiced bilabial stop,* since it is preceded by silence (cf. [grásyas], [de náđa]).
	[bwé–]	Strong
	[–no]	Weak

bwe–no

	[a–]	Weak
h		In Spanish the letter **h** does not represent a sound. Its occurrences in spelling will be dealt with in a later section (Unit 15).
	[–ó–]	Strong
	[–ra]	Remember the single tap. The word **ahorra** [aóɾa] *he saves (money)* with a multiple trill has a different meaning from that of **ahora** *now.*
v	[ƀ]	[ƀóy] Strong. Be sure to end this syllable with a high tongue position, for this is a fricative semiconsonant.
	[a]	Weak
	[pa–]	Weak
	[–sáɾ]	Strong
	[lís–]	Strong
	[–ta]	Weak

a–o–ra–ƀoy–a–pa–saʀ–lis–ta

Notes: (1) The semiconsonant [y] may attach itself to either a preceding or a following vowel (cf. [yé–ǥan]). (2) In the syllable [–sáʀ] the trill is very common preceding [l], but the single tap [r] is also appropriate here. (3) The falling terminal juncture is normal at this place where in the written form we find the colon (:).

[se–]	Weak
[–ño–]	Weak
[–rí–]	Strong
[–ta]	Weak
[fló–]	Strong
[–res]	Weak

se–ño–ri–ta–flo–res

The strong syllable [–rí–] stays on level 1. The rise on the strong syllable of the proper name is normal.

[pre–]	Weak
[–sén–]	Strong. Dental point of contact for [n], in anticipation of the articulation of [t] (cf. assimilation). Beware of any voicing of [s].
[–te]	Weak

pre–sen–te

[se–]	Weak
[–ñó–]	Strong
[–rar–]	Weak

j   [x]   *Voiceless velar fricative.* The rear part of the tongue is arched toward the velum so that only a narrow passage remains open between it and the soft palate (velum); the noise produced by the air escaping is the characteristic of a fricative.

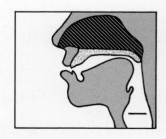

[–xó–]	Strong

LETTER	SYMBOL	SYLLABLE		
		[–na]	Weak

se–ño–rar–xo–na

		[se–]	Weak
		[–ñó–]	Strong
		[–ra–]	Weak
		[đe]	Weak
		[lo–]	Weak

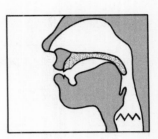

n [ŋ] *Voiced velar nasal.* The tongue touches the velum and voiced air escapes through the nose. The nasal consonant that precedes a velar consonant [x, k, g] (and sometimes [w]) is velar.

| | | [–sáŋ–] | Strong |

g [x] This sound is spelled in two ways: with **j** as in **Arjona** and with **g** followed by **e** or **i**.

| | | [–xe–] | Weak |
| | | [–les] | Weak |

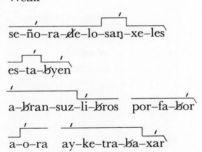

se–ño–ra–đe–lo–saŋ–xe–les

es–ta–ƀyen

a–ƀran–suz–li–ƀros   por–fa–ƀor

a–o–ra   ay–ke–tra–ƀa–xar

INSTRUCTIONS: Repeat the following phrases:

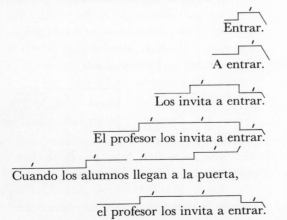

Entrar. — *To come in.*

A entrar. — *To come in.*

Los invita a entrar. — *(He) invites them (to come) in.*

El profesor los invita a entrar. — *The professor invites them in.*

Cuando los alumnos llegan a la puerta, — *When the students arrive at the door,*

el profesor los invita a entrar. — *the professor invites them in.*

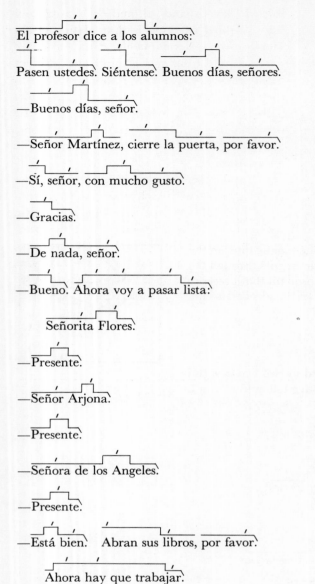

El profesor dice a los alumnos: — The professor says to the students:

Pasen ustedes. Siéntense. Buenos días, señores. — "Come in. Sit down. Good morning."

—Buenos días, señor. — "Good morning."

—Señor Martínez, cierre la puerta, por favor. — "Mr. Martínez, shut the door, please."

—Sí, señor, con mucho gusto. — "Yes, sir, be glad to."

—Gracias. — "Thanks."

—De nada, señor. — "You're welcome."

—Bueno. Ahora voy a pasar lista: — "All right. Now I'm going to call the roll:

Señorita Flores. — Miss Flores."

—Presente. — "Here."

—Señor Arjona. — "Mr. Arjona."

—Presente. — "Here."

—Señora de los Angeles. — "Mrs. los Angeles."

—Presente. — "Here."

—Está bien. Abran sus libros, por favor. — "All right. Open your books, please.

Ahora hay que trabajar. — It's time to get to work."

Some of the distinctions among the sounds which have been described on the preceding pages are necessary for communication; others are not but are important for the sake of natural-sounding Spanish. How do we distinguish these two kinds of difference?

In the following Spanish words, only the vowel of each first syllable is changed, but the meanings are completely different:

piso	*I trample*
peso	*weight*
paso	*step*
poso	*I lodge*
puso	*he put*

Since the meaning changes, the distinctions among these vowels are significant. We say that each one *contrasts* with all the others. Such a contrastive element in the sound system is called a *phoneme*. We have already pointed out a few of the many similar contrasts among the consonants, for example:

pero *but* versus **perro** *dog*
ahora *now* versus **ahorra** *he saves (money)*

We therefore have two phonemes, /r/ and /ʀ/. Similarly, **peso** and **beso** *kiss* show that /p/ and /b/ are different phonemes.

Among the distinctions that make no difference in meaning are the two varieties of /s/

that occur in different environments. In [lo–sa–lum–nos] we have [s], but in [loz–li–bros], as a result of assimilation to the following [l], we have [z]. These two submembers, [s] and [z], are called *allophones* of the phoneme /s/. (In English, /s/ and /z/ are independent phonemes, because they signal differences in meaning, e.g., between *fuss* and *fuzz*.) Another example is that of the consonants /b/, /d/, and /g/. Besides the fricative allophones, each of these has a stop allophone that occurs under limited conditions (e.g., when preceded by a nasal consonant or a pause):

[a–byér–ta]	but	[im–bí–ta]	
[ná–da]	but	[kwán–do]	
[yé–gan]	but	[án–gu–lo]	*angle*

The phoneme /b/ has the allophones [b] and [b]; /d/ has [d] and [d]; and /g/ has [g] and [g]. A third example is that of the nasals. Here, in the series **cama** *bed,* **cana** *gray-haired (woman),* and **caña** *cane,* we find three distinct nasal phonemes: /m/, /n/, and /ñ/. But in the words **entrar** with its dental [n], **Angeles** with its velar [ŋ], and **bueno** with its more common alveolar [n], we have three allophones of /n/, the dental and velar ones being due to assimilation.

It sometimes happens that two phonemes do not contrast with each other in certain positions. This is to say that either one may occur, with no difference in meaning. In the word **puerta,** we find either [pwérta] or [pwéRta]. The phonemes /r/ and /R/, which always contrast with each other between vowels, do not contrast before consonants.

Summary of the Sounds of Spanish

PHONEMES AND ALLOPHONES

	Bilabial VE.[1]	Bilabial VD.[2]	Labiodental VE.	Labiodental VD.	Dental VE.	Dental VD.	Alveolar VE.	Alveolar VD.	Palatal VE.	Palatal VD.	Velar VE.	Velar VD.
Stops	p	b			t	d					k	g
Affricate									č			
Fricatives		b	f			d	s	z			x	g
Nasals		m				n		n		ñ		ŋ
Lateral								l				
Trill								R				
Tap								r				
Semiconsonants									y		w	
Vowels: *High*									i		u	
Mid									e		o	
Low										a		

[1] Voiceless [2] Voiced

2

Cecilia's Family

P. *Pablo*   M. *Julio's mother*   J. *Julio, Pablo's friend*
B. *Betty*   C. *Cecilia, Julio's sister*   S. *Susana*

P. Good afternoon, Doña Mercedes. Is Julio in?

M. Yes, he must be in the kitchen or the patio. Julio, Pablo's here!

J. Come on in, Pablo! Here I am, in my room.

La familia de Cecilia

P. *Pablo*   M. *madre de Julio*   J. *Julio, amigo de Pablo*
B. *Betty*   C. *Cecilia, hermana de Julio*   S. *Susana*

P. Buenas tardes, doña (1) Mercedes. ¿Está Julio?

M. Sí, debe estar en la cocina o en el patio. ¡Julio, aquí está Pablo!

J. ¡Entra, Pablo! Estoy aquí, en mi cuarto.

24

P. Excuse me, ma'am.

M. Of course.

* * *

P. Who are the two girls [who are] in the living room?

J. A couple of my sister's schoolmates [companions of school of my sister]. Why? Do you like them [they please you]?

P. Yes, they're really [how] pretty! You [are] a friend of theirs [them]?

J. Yes, the blonde's name is [calls herself] Betty, and the brunette's Susana. They're cousins.

P. Where are they from?

J. From the United States. Betty's father is the new American consul.

P. Too bad I don't speak English.

J. You don't need to know any English; they speak [know] Spanish perfectly.

P. Then, what are we waiting for? Let's go talk to [with] them. We'll study later.

* * *

B. Your house is so nice, Cecilia.

C. Thanks, you're very kind.

S. And so big, too.

P. Con permiso, señora.

M. Cómo no.

* * *

P. ¿Quiénes son las dos chicas que están en la sala?

J. Compañeras de escuela de mi hermana. ¿Por qué? ¿Te gustan?

P. Sí, ¡qué bonitas! ¿Tú eres amigo de ellas?

J. Sí, la rubia se llama Betty y la morena Susana. Son primas.

P. ¿De dónde son?

J. De los Estados Unidos. El padre de Betty es el nuevo cónsul americano.

P. Lástima que yo no hablo inglés.

J. No necesitas saber inglés; ellas saben español perfectamente.

P. Entonces, ¿qué esperamos? Vamos a hablar con ellas. Después estudiamos.

* * *

B. ¡Qué bonita es tu casa, Cecilia!

C. Gracias, eres muy amable.

S. Y qué grande, también.

c. It's because we're a big family [many]: dad, mom, ten children, my grandmother, and an aunt.

c. Es que somos muchos: papá, mamá, diez hijos, mi abuela y una tía.

B. Fourteen altogether! That many! You have nine brothers and sisters?

B. ¡Catorce en total! ¡Tantos! ¿Tú tienes nueve hermanos?

c. Yes, five brothers and four sisters. I'm the youngest.

c. Sí, cinco hermanos y cuatro hermanas. Yo soy la menor.

s. My gosh! What a family!

s. ¡Dios mío! (2) ¡Qué familia!

Cultural Notes

(1) **Doña,** from Latin *domina* "mistress," is a title of respect used with the given name of a woman, generally one who is married, older, or distinguished. As a form of address, **doña** with the given name is a common substitute for **señora** (*Mrs.*) with the family name; e.g., Mrs. Mercedes López might be addressed as doña Mercedes or as señora López. This title, once reserved for the upper strata of society, has come to be used in some regions of Spain and America to address any woman of a certain age and social position, while elsewhere it may be used for women of all classes.

(2) The use of sacred words in exclamations, such as **Dios, Jesús,** and **María,** is common even among women and does not imply profanity, as the English equivalents might.

Introductory Note to the Student

The drills in this book are designed for oral recitation in class with books closed. You can best prepare yourself for recitation by doing the drills in the language laboratory, without referring to the text. Tape recordings have been made for this purpose. If no laboratory is available, then use the written directions in the text; but when you do this, cover any answers that may be there.

A few simple direction words will be used to cue the drill procedures. Some of these are:

ADDRESSING ONE STUDENT	ADDRESSING MORE THAN ONE STUDENT	
repita	**repitan**	*repeat*
conteste	**contesten**	*answer*
traduzca	**traduzcan**	*translate*
cambie	**cambien**	*change*
escuche	**escuchen**	*listen*

In addition, some references to grammatical categories will be needed: **singular** *singular,* **plural** *plural.* As other terms are needed, they will be introduced.

The drills will move fast. Answers should be given without hesitation, and preparation is not complete until this can be done. If the basic dialogs have been properly memorized, the drills should be done very easily.

● PRONUNCIATION EXERCISE

Minimal vowel contrasts under weak stress. INSTRUCTIONS: The teacher will read the following pairs of words. The student will repeat them just as he hears them.

/a/	/e/	/a/	/i/	/a/	/o/	/a/	/u/
mesas	meses	pañal	piñal	cara	caro	lagar	lugar
sobras	sobres	matad	mitad	habla	hablo	pajar	pujar
marcado	mercado	pasar	pisar	derecha	derecho	cañada	cuñada
preguntas	preguntes	charlar	chirlar	esposas	esposos	sabido	subido
españolas	españoles	paquete	piquete	hermanas	hermanos	palidez	pulidez

/e/	/i/	/e/	/o/	/e/	/u/
pecar	picar	deje	dejo	lechar	luchar
pesar	pisar	vine	vino	legar	lugar
remar	rimar	hable	hablo	temor	tumor
rezar	rizar	leche	lecho	pechero	puchero
pesada	pisada	quiere	quiero	retina	rutina

/i/	/o/	/i/	/u/	/o/	/u/
mirar	morar	ligar	lugar	bocal	bucal
timó	tomó	mirar	murar	morar	murar
imito	omito	birlar	burlar	plomero	plumero
mirada	morada	pintar	puntar	motilar	mutilar
pisada	posada	pidiendo	pudiendo	acosar	acusar

All the above pairs involve minimal vowel contrasts under weak stress. You have noticed that two words may be differentiated in Spanish merely by a weak-stressed vowel. Since this feature is not characteristic of English, it is important that you develop the habit of saying the Spanish vowels clearly. Slurring the vowels or reducing them to an "uh" sound may distort the meaning.

1 The subject pronouns

EXAMPLES
1. **Yo** soy la menor.
2. ¿**Tú** eres amigo de ellas?
3. ¿**Usted** es amigo de ellas?
4. Pasen **ustedes.**
5. **Ellas** saben español perfectamente.

SINGULAR		PLURAL	
I	yo	we	**nosotros** (**nosotras**, *feminine*)
you	**tú**	you	**ustedes**
you	**usted**		
he	**él**	they	**ellos** (**ellas**, *feminine*)
she	**ella**		

● DISCUSSION

In the singular there are two equivalents of *you,* **usted** and **tú,** which call for different forms of the verb (see the conjugations of **ser** and **hablar,** below). **Tú** is used when the speaker is on an intimate footing with his hearer (approximately at the point where in English we begin to address a person by his first name): *You, John, sit here* **Tú, Juan, siéntate aquí.** **Usted** is used when the speaker is on a "Mr., Mrs., or Miss" footing: *You, Mr. Gómez, sit here* **Usted, señor Gómez, siéntese aquí.** In the plural, however, no distinction is made, and **ustedes** serves for both.[1]

---

[1] English at one time had this same distinction between intimate *thou* and formal *you.* In Spain the distinction persists in the plural, with **vosotros, -as** opposed to **ustedes.** In many parts of Spanish America **tú** is replaced by **vos,** with a different set of verb and other forms, but this usage is not generally regarded as standard.

Gender is distinguished in **él** and **ella, ellos** and **ellas,** and **nosotros** and **nosotras. Ellos** and **nosotros** refer either to male beings alone or to a mixed group. Many nouns behave similarly: **alumnos,** either *men students* or *men-and-women students;* **hermanos,** either *brothers* or *brother(s) and sister(s).*

2 Present tense[1] of *ser*, to be

EXAMPLES
1. Yo **soy** la menor.
2. **Eres** muy amable.
3. El padre de Betty **es** el cónsul.
4. **Somos** muchos.
5. ¿Quiénes **son** las dos chicas?

ser *to be*			
yo	soy	nosotros, –as	somos
tú	eres		
usted		ustedes	
él	es	ellos, –as	son
ella		Betty y Susana	
Cecilia			

The present tense of **ser** is irregular. Each form must be learned separately. The subject pronouns are not required for the meaning,

● PERSON-NUMBER SUBSTITUTION DRILL

INSTRUCTIONS: The teacher says the model sentence and asks a student to repeat it. Then the teacher gives a word to be substituted for a word in that sentence. If the student has any difficulty in making the new sentence, the teacher should prompt, using a stage whisper. The students' books are closed during class recitation.

	TEACHER:	STUDENT:
A. 1.	¿De dónde son *ellos? Repita.*	**¿De dónde son ellos?**
2.	_____ él?	¿De dónde es él?
3.	_____ ustedes?	¿De dónde son ustedes?
4.	_____ usted?	¿De dónde es usted?
5.	_____ ellas?	¿De dónde son ellas?
6.	_____ tú?	¿De dónde eres tú?
7.	_____ Pablo?	¿De dónde es Pablo?
8.	_____ Pablo y Julio?	¿De dónde son Pablo y Julio?
9.	_____ la señora de Arjona?	¿De dónde es la señora de Arjona?
10.	_____ nosotros?	¿De dónde somos nosotros?

	TEACHER:	STUDENT:
B. 1.	*Ellos* son de los Estados Unidos. *Repita.*	**Ellos son de los Estados Unidos.**
2.	El _____	El es de los Estados Unidos.
3.	Yo _____	Yo soy de los Estados Unidos.
4.	Ustedes _____	Ustedes son de los Estados Unidos.
5.	Susana y yo _____	Susana y yo somos de los Estados Unidos.
6.	Tú _____	Tú eres de los Estados Unidos.
7.	El señor Martínez _____	El señor Martínez es de los Estados Unidos.
8.	Ellas _____	Ellas son de los Estados Unidos.
9.	El profesor _____	El profesor es de los Estados Unidos.

_____

[1] The term *tense* as used here covers all those changes in the verb that relate to time and aspect (how the action is viewed), and includes the constructions that are usually referred to as compound tenses. Examples of various tenses in English are: *he works* (present), *he worked* (past), *he **will** work* (future), *he **has** worked* (present perfect).

INSTRUCTIONS: The teacher asks the question and prompts the answer.

TEACHER:	STUDENT:
A. 1. ¿De dónde es el padre de Betty? *Conteste.*	**Es de los Estados Unidos.**
2. ¿De dónde son Betty y Susana?	Son de los Estados Unidos.
3. ¿De dónde es el profesor?	Es de los Estados Unidos.
4. ¿De dónde son las compañeras de escuela?	Son de los Estados Unidos.
5. ¿De dónde es usted?	Soy de . . . (*home town or state*)
6. ¿De dónde es usted?	Soy de . . .
7. ¿De dónde es usted?	Soy de . . .
8. ¿De dónde son ustedes?	Somos de . . .
B. 1. ¡Tú no eres amigo de ellas!	**Sí soy.**
2. ¡Julio no es amigo de ellas!	Sí es.
3. ¡Ustedes no son amigos de ellas!	Sí somos.
4. ¡Doña Mercedes no es amiga de ellas!	Sí es.
5. ¡El señor Flores no es amigo de ellas!	Sí es.
6. ¡El profesor no es amigo de ellas!	Sí es.
7. ¡Usted y Pablo no son amigos de ellas!	Sí somos.
8. ¡La alumna no es amiga de ellas!	Sí es.
9. ¡Usted no es amigo de ellas!	Sí soy.

● DISCUSSION

Verb endings in Spanish carry more information than those of English. Thus, in **Nosotros hablamos** we can omit the **nosotros** and still know that *we* is understood as the subject; whereas, if *we* is omitted in *We speak,* all reference to *we* is lost.

Because of this, where English has to include the pronouns for meaning and emphasis, Spanish omits them except for emphasis: **Somos muchos** *We are many;* **Nosotros somos muchos** *We are many.* English almost never stresses the subject *it:* Spanish almost never uses it: **Es grande** *It's big.*

If the subject is a noun, normally the verb is the same as for *he, she, it,* or *they: Betty (= she) is nice* **Betty es amable;** *Betty and Susana (= they) are schoolmates* **Betty y Susana son compañeras de escuela.** On the other hand, *Betty and I = we,* and *Betty and you = you* (plural): *Betty and I study Spanish* **Betty y yo estudiamos español;** *Betty and you are from the United States* **Betty y usted son de los Estados Unidos.**

3 **Present tense of -ar verbs**

EXAMPLES
1. No **hablo** inglés (from **hablar** *to speak*).
2. No **necesitas** saber inglés (from **necesitar** *to need*).
3. El profesor los **invita** a entrar (from **invitar** *to invite*).
4. ¿Qué **esperamos?** (from **esperar** *to wait for*)
5. Los alumnos **llegan** a la puerta (from **llegar** *to arrive*).

hablar *to speak*			
habl–		habl–	
yo	–o	nosotros, –as	–amos
tú	–as		
usted él } ella	–a	ustedes ellos, –as }	–an

The present tense of –**ar** verbs is formed by replacing –**ar** with the above endings. The subject pronouns are not required for the meaning.

TEACHER:		STUDENT:

A. 1. *Yo* no hablo inglés.   *Repita.*   **Yo no hablo inglés.**
   2. Nosotros _____ Nosotros no hablamos inglés.
   3. El _____ El no habla inglés.
   4. Ellas _____ Ellas no hablan inglés.
   5. Usted _____ Usted no habla inglés.
   6. Usted y yo _____ Usted y yo no hablamos inglés.
   7. La señorita Flores _____ La señorita Flores no habla inglés.
   8. Ustedes _____ Ustedes no hablan inglés.
   9. Tú _____ Tú no hablas inglés.
  10. Mi abuela _____ Mi abuela no habla inglés.
  11. Pablo y Julio _____ Pablo y Julio no hablan inglés.
  12. Ella _____ Ella no habla inglés.

B. 1. No necesitas saber inglés.   **No necesitas saber inglés.**
   2. (usted) _____ No necesita saber inglés.
   3. (nosotros) _____ No necesitamos saber inglés.
   4. (él) _____ No necesita saber inglés.
   5. (ellos) _____ No necesitan saber inglés.
   6. (el profesor) _____ No necesita saber inglés.
   7. (yo) _____ No necesito saber inglés.
   8. (ella) _____ No necesita saber inglés.
   9. (nosotras) _____ No necesitamos saber inglés.
  10. (ellas) _____ No necesitan saber inglés.

C. 1. *El profesor* los invita a entrar.   *Repita.*   **El profesor los invita a entrar.**
   2. Doña Mercedes _____ Doña Mercedes los invita a entrar.
   3. Ellos _____ Ellos los invitan a entrar.
   4. Nosotros _____ Nosotros los invitamos a entrar.
   5. Yo _____ Yo los invito a entrar.
   6. El _____ El los invita a entrar.
   7. Pablo y Julio _____ Pablo y Julio los invitan a entrar.

D. 1. *Pablo* llega a la clase.   *Repita.*   **Pablo llega a la clase.**
   2. Yo _____ Yo llego a la clase.
   3. Tú _____ Tú llegas a la clase.
   4. Nosotros _____ Nosotros llegamos a la clase.
   5. Ellas _____ Ellas llegan a la clase.
   6. Usted _____ Usted llega a la clase.
   7. Pablo y yo _____ Pablo y yo llegamos a la clase.
   8. Ellos _____ Ellos llegan a la clase.
   9. El padre de Betty _____ El padre de Betty llega a la clase.

E. 1. *Nosotros* entramos con las chicas.   *Repita.*   **Nosotros entramos con las chicas.**
   2. Usted _____ Usted entra con las chicas.
   3. Yo _____ Yo entro con las chicas.
   4. Ellos _____ Ellos entran con las chicas.
   5. Tú _____ Tú entras con las chicas.
   6. Ustedes _____ Ustedes entran con las chicas.
   7. El profesor _____ El profesor entra con las chicas.

F. 1. *Yo* trabajo mucho aquí.   *Repita.*   **Yo trabajo mucho aquí.**
   2. El _____ El trabaja mucho aquí.
   3. Nosotros _____ Nosotros trabajamos mucho aquí.
   4. Pablo _____ Pablo trabaja mucho aquí.
   5. Tú _____ Tú trabajas mucho aquí.
   6. El y yo _____ El y yo trabajamos mucho aquí.
   7. Ellos _____ Ellos trabajan mucho aquí.
   8. Nosotras _____ Nosotras trabajamos mucho aquí.
   9. El cónsul _____ El cónsul trabaja mucho aquí.

G. 1. ¿Qué esperamos?   *Repita.*   **¿Qué esperamos?**
2. (usted) _____   ¿Qué espera?
3. (yo) _____   ¿Qué espero?
4. (ellas) _____   ¿Qué esperan?
5. (usted y él) _____   ¿Qué esperan?
6. (ella) _____   ¿Qué espera?
7. (ustedes) _____   ¿Qué esperan?
8. (nosotras) _____   ¿Qué esperamos?
9. (él) _____   ¿Qué espera?

H. 1. Después estudiamos.   *Repita.*   **Después estudiamos.**
2. (yo) _____   Después estudio.
3. (usted) _____   Después estudia.
4. (ustedes) _____   Después estudian.
5. (él) _____   Después estudia.
6. (nosotros) _____   Después estudiamos.
7. (tú) _____   Después estudias.
8. (ellos) _____   Después estudian.

● PATTERNED RESPONSE DRILL

INSTRUCTIONS: In the first part of the drill, the teacher asks the questions and the students give the answers. In the second part, the teacher cues one student who asks the question. Then the teacher selects a second student to answer.

TEACHER:	STUDENT:
A. 1. ¿Qué espera Juan? *Conteste.*	**Espera la clase de español.**
2. ¿Qué esperan los alumnos?	Esperan la clase de español.
3. ¿Qué esperamos Susana y yo?	Esperan la clase de español.
4. ¿Qué esperamos usted y yo?	Esperamos la clase de español.
5. ¿Qué espera usted?	Espero la clase de español.
6. ¿Qué esperan ustedes?	Esperamos la clase de español.

TEACHER:	STUDENT 1:	STUDENT 2:
B. 1. (Juan)	**¿Qué espera Juan?**	**Espera la clase de español.**
2. (los alumnos)	¿Qué esperan los alumnos?	Esperan la clase de español.
3. (Julio)	¿Qué espera Julio?	Espera la clase de español.
4. (él)	¿Qué espera él?	Espera la clase de español.
5. (usted)	¿Qué espera usted?	Espero la clase de español.
6. (yo)	¿Qué espero yo?	Espera la clase de español.
7. (usted y yo)	¿Qué esperamos usted y yo?	Esperamos la clase de español.

TEACHER:	STUDENT:
C. 1. ¿Adónde llega el profesor? *Conteste.*	**Llega a la puerta.**
2. ¿Adónde llegan los alumnos?	Llegan a la puerta.
3. ¿Adónde llega la chica?	Llega a la puerta.
4. ¿Adónde llegan los compañeros de escuela?	Llegan a la puerta.
5. ¿Adónde llega usted?	Llego a la puerta.
6. ¿Adónde llegas tú?	Llego a la puerta.
7. ¿Adónde llegamos usted y yo?	Llegamos a la puerta.
8. ¿Adónde llegamos él y yo?	Llegan a la puerta.

TEACHER:	STUDENT 1:	STUDENT 2:
D. 1. (el profesor)	**¿Adónde llega el profesor?**	**Llega a la puerta.**
2. (los alumnos)	¿Adónde llegan los alumnos?	Llegan a la puerta.
3. (la chica)	¿Adónde llega la chica?	Llega a la puerta.
4. (los compañeros de escuela)	¿Adónde llegan los compañeros de escuela?	Llegan a la puerta.
5. (usted)	¿Adónde llega usted?	Llego a la puerta.
6. (yo)	¿Adónde llego yo?	Llega a la puerta.
7. (usted y yo)	¿Adónde llegamos usted y yo?	Llegamos a la puerta.

4 The articles; gender of nouns

MASCULINE	FEMININE
el *the* ⟶ el patio el padre el cónsul un *a, an (one)* → un patio	la familia la cocina ← la *the* la sala una tía ⟵ una *a, an (one)*

The masculine article goes with masculine nouns, the feminine with feminine.

MASCULINE FOR MALE	FEMININE FOR FEMALE
abuelo	abuela
alumno	alumna
amigo	amiga
compañero	compañera
chico	chica
hermano	hermana
hijo	hija
primo	prima
tío	tía
profesor	profesora
señor	señora

These are the nouns that have appeared in the dialogs in either masculine or feminine. Given one, the other may be inferred: **abuela** *grandmother*, **abuelo** *grandfather*.

● ITEM SUBSTITUTION DRILL

	TEACHER:		STUDENT:
A.	1. Estamos con el *cónsul.*	*Repita.*	**Estamos con el cónsul.**
	2. _____hermano		Estamos con el hermano.
	3. _____papá		Estamos con el papá.
	4. _____tía		Estamos con la tía.
	5. _____abuela		Estamos con la abuela.
	6. _____mamá		Estamos con la mamá.
	7. _____compañera		Estamos con la compañera.
	8. _____padre		Estamos con el padre.
	9. _____hermana		Estamos con la hermana.
	10. _____chica		Estamos con la chica.
	11. _____señor		Estamos con el señor.
	12. _____profesor		Estamos con el profesor.
	13. _____señorita		Estamos con la señorita.
	14. _____amigo		Estamos con el amigo.
	15. _____señora		Estamos con la señora.
	16. _____prima		Estamos con la prima.
	17. _____hermano		Estamos con el hermano.
	18. _____abuelo		Estamos con el abuelo.
	19. _____profesora		Estamos con la profesora.
	20. _____amiga		Estamos con la amiga.
	21. _____tío		Estamos con el tío.
	22. _____alumna		Estamos con la alumna.
B.	1. ¿Tú tienes un *hermano?*	*Repita.*	**¿Tú tienes un hermano?**
	2. _____abuela		¿Tú tienes una abuela?
	3. _____hermana		¿Tú tienes una hermana?
	4. _____primo		¿Tú tienes un primo?

5. _____hijo	¿Tú tienes un hijo?	
6. _____hija	¿Tú tienes una hija?	
7. _____amiga	¿Tú tienes una amiga?	
8. _____abuelo	¿Tú tienes un abuelo?	
9. _____alumna	¿Tú tienes una alumna?	
10. _____profesor	¿Tú tienes un profesor?	
11. _____profesora	¿Tú tienes una profesora?	
12. _____clase	¿Tú tienes una clase?	
13. _____libro	¿Tú tienes un libro?	
14. _____cuarto	¿Tú tienes un cuarto?	
15. _____casa	¿Tú tienes una casa?	
16. _____patio	¿Tú tienes un patio?	

C.
1. La *chica* está en la *sala*.   *Repita.*   **La chica está en la sala.**
2. _____ clase   La chica está en la clase.
3. — chico _____   El chico está en la clase.
4. _____ cuarto   El chico está en el cuarto.
5. — chica _____   La chica está en el cuarto.
6. _____ patio   La chica está en el patio.
7. — chico _____   El chico está en el patio.
8. _____ cocina   El chico está en la cocina.
9. — chica _____   La chica está en la cocina.
10. _____ escuela   La chica está en la escuela.
11. — chico _____   El chico está en la escuela.
12. _____ casa   El chico está en la casa.
13. — chica _____   La chica está en la casa.

● DISCUSSION

Every noun in Spanish falls into one of two classes traditionally called "masculine" and "feminine." The relatively few nouns that have a sex connotation usually assign masculine gender to male beings and feminine gender to female. Among these nouns with sex connotation are most of the familiar names of relatives and the like; given a masculine word such as **hijo** (*son*), it is usually safe to infer a feminine **hija** (*daughter*), and vice versa (**tía** *aunt,* **tío** *uncle*).

A large proportion of nouns have endings that indicate their gender. Nouns ending in –o and –or are almost all masculine, and nouns ending in –a are usually feminine. With other nouns it is helpful to learn the article as a reminder of the gender (for example, **la clase** *the class,* **el total** *the total*).

The definite article (equivalent to *the*) is **el** with masculine nouns and **la** with feminine nouns. The indefinite article (equivalent to *a, an*) is **un** with masculine nouns and **una** with feminine nouns. In Spanish, the indefinite article is the same as the adjective meaning *one* (just as in English *an* and *one* used to be the same word); accordingly, it is stressed as much as *one* is stressed in English not weak-stressed like *a, an*.

5 Number: the plural

Masculine				Feminine			
SINGULAR		PLURAL		SINGULAR		PLURAL	
el	estado padre cónsul	los	estados padres cónsules	la	chica clase pared[1]	las	chicas clases paredes

When *the* accompanies a plural noun, it is **los** with masculine nouns and **las** with feminine nouns.

---

[1] **pared** *wall*

● NUMBER SUBSTITUTION DRILL

	TEACHER:		STUDENT:
1.	¿Tú tienes el *libro?*	*Repita.*	**¿Tú tienes el libro?**
		Plural.	**¿Tú tienes los libros?**
2.	¿Tú tienes la *casa?*	*Repita.*	¿Tú tienes la casa?
		Plural.	¿Tú tienes las casas?
3.	¿Tú tienes el *cuarto?*	*Repita.*	¿Tú tienes el cuarto?
		Plural.	¿Tú tienes los cuartos?
4.	¿Tú tienes la *clase?*	*Repita.*	¿Tú tienes la clase?
		Plural.	¿Tú tienes las clases?
5.	¿Tú tienes la *puerta?*	*Repita.*	¿Tú tienes la puerta?
		Plural.	¿Tú tienes las puertas?
6.	¿Tú tienes la *lista?*	*Repita.*	¿Tú tienes la lista?
		Plural.	¿Tú tienes las listas?

● ITEM SUBSTITUTION DRILL

		TEACHER:		STUDENT:
A.	1.	¿Quiénes son las dos *chicas?*	*Repita.*	**¿Quiénes son las dos chicas?**
	2.	_____señoras		¿Quiénes son las dos señoras?
	3.	_____alumnos		¿Quiénes son los dos alumnos?
	4.	_____americanos		¿Quiénes son los dos americanos?
	5.	_____profesoras		¿Quiénes son las dos profesoras?
	6.	_____cónsules		¿Quiénes son los dos cónsules?
	7.	_____señoritas		¿Quiénes son las dos señoritas?
	8.	_____señores		¿Quiénes son los dos señores?
	9.	_____primas		¿Quiénes son las dos primas?
	10.	_____chicos		¿Quiénes son los dos chicos?
	11.	_____compañeras de escuela		¿Quiénes son las dos compañeras de escuela?

		TEACHER:		STUDENT:
B.	1.	El *padre* de Betty es de aquí.	*Repita.*	**El padre de Betty es de aquí.**
	2.	___ abuela _____		La abuela de Betty es de aquí.
	3.	___ amigo _____		El amigo de Betty es de aquí.
	4.	___ compañera _____		La compañera de Betty es de aquí.
	5.	___ abuelos _____		Los abuelos de Betty son de aquí.
	6.	___ padres _____		Los padres de Betty son de aquí.
	7.	___ hermanas _____		Las hermanas de Betty son de aquí.
	8.	___ alumnos _____		Los alumnos de Betty son de aquí.
	9.	___ amigas _____		Las amigas de Betty son de aquí.
	10.	___ primos _____		Los primos de Betty son de aquí.
	11.	___ compañeros_____		Los compañeros de Betty son de aquí.
	12.	___ hijos _____		Los hijos de Betty son de aquí.
	13.	___ tías_____		Las tías de Betty son de aquí.
	14.	___ profesores _____		Los profesores de Betty son de aquí.

● DISCUSSION

The meanings of singular and plural are the same in Spanish as in English: singular = "one" and plural = "two or more."

If the singular of the noun ends in a vowel (**estado, chica, clase**), the plural is formed by adding –s (**estados, chicas, clases**). If the singular ends in a consonant (**cónsul, pared**), –es is added to form the plural (**cónsules, paredes**).

Adjectives: agreement of nouns and adjectives

EXAMPLES   1. El **nuevo** cónsul americano.   3. ¡Qué **bonita** es tu casa!
              2. Los Estados **Unidos.**   4. **Buenas** tardes.

SINGULAR	PLURAL
(M) el cuarto bonito (*ending* –**o**) (F) la cocina bonita (*ending* –**a**)	(M) los cuartos bonitos (*ending* –**os**) (F) las cocinas bonitas (*ending* –**as**)

Adjectives agree in number and gender with the nouns they modify. The majority of adjectives show agreement by the four endings listed above.

● TRANSLATION DRILL

INSTRUCTIONS: The teacher says the English sentence. Then he selects a student to give the Spanish equivalent.

TEACHER:	STUDENT:
1. The house? It's really pretty! *Traduzca.*	**¿La casa? ¡Qué bonita!**
2. The room? It's really pretty!	¿El cuarto? ¡Qué bonito!
3. The living room? It's really pretty!	¿La sala? ¡Qué bonita!
4. The youngest? She's really pretty!	¿La menor? ¡Qué bonita!
5. The cousins? They're really pretty!	¿Las primas? ¡Qué bonitas!
6. The brunettes? They're really pretty!	¿Las morenas? ¡Qué bonitas!
7. The children? They're really pretty!	¿Los chicos? ¡Qué bonitos!
8. The blondes? They're really pretty!	¿Las rubias? ¡Qué bonitas!
9. The school? It's really good!	¿La escuela? ¡Qué buena!
10. The professor? He's really good!	¿El profesor? ¡Qué bueno!
11. The class? It's really good!	¿La clase? ¡Qué buena!
12. The children? They're really good!	¿Los chicos? ¡Qué buenos!
13. The consul? He's really new!	¿El cónsul? ¡Qué nuevo!
14. The house? It's really new!	¿La casa? ¡Qué nueva!
15. The book? It's really new!	¿El libro? ¡Qué nuevo!
16. The kitchen? It's really new!	¿La cocina? ¡Qué nueva!

● SUBSTITUTION DRILL

TEACHER:		STUDENT:
A. 1. Es *el cónsul* americano.	*Repita.*	**Es el cónsul americano.**
2. — la prima _____		Es la prima americana.
3. — el amigo _____		Es el amigo americano.
4. — la escuela _____		Es la escuela americana.
5. — los tíos _____		Son los tíos americanos.
6. — las chicas_____		Son las chicas americanas.
7. — los alumnos _____		Son los alumnos americanos.
8. — los profesores _____		Son los profesores americanos.
9. — las señoras _____		Son las señoras americanas.
10. — los primos _____		Son los primos americanos.
11. — las profesoras _____		Son las profesoras americanas.

TEACHER:		STUDENT:
B. 1. *El patio* es muy bonito.	*Repita.*	**El patio es muy bonito.**
2. La sala _____		La sala es muy bonita.
3. Los hijos _____		Los hijos son muy bonitos.
4. Las primas _____		Las primas son muy bonitas.
5. La profesora _____		La profesora es muy bonita.
6. Las rubias _____		Las rubias son muy bonitas.
7. La española _____		La española es muy bonita.

EXAMPLES 1. La chica **inglesa.** *The English girl.*
           2. **Mis** amigos **españoles.** *My Spanish friends.*
           3. Las hermanas **menores.** *The younger sisters.*

Singular		*Plural*	
MASCULINE	FEMININE	MASCULINE	FEMININE
bonito	bonita	bonitos	bonitas
mi		mis	
menor		menores	
grande		grandes	
amable		amables	
inglés	inglesa	ingleses	inglesas
español	española	españoles	españolas

Adjectives whose masculine singular does not end in –**o** are the same in masculine and feminine, except that adjectives of nationality whose masculine ends in a consonant add –**a** for the feminine. Adjectives form their plurals like nouns.

● TRANSLATION DRILL

TEACHER:

1. The house? It really is big! *Traduzca.*
2. The professor? He really is big!
3. The class? It really is big!
4. The family? It really is big!
5. The room? It really is big!
6. The school? It really is big!
7. The roll? It really is big!
8. The patio? It really is big!
9. The living room? It really is big!
10. The rooms? They really are big!
11. The doors? They really are big!
12. The books? They really are big!
13. The children? They really are big!
14. The consuls? They really are big!
15. The ladies? They really are big!
16. The blonde? She really is nice!
17. The blond? He really is nice!
18. The brunette? She really is nice!
19. The dark-haired boy? He really is nice!
20. The cousin? She really is nice!
21. The cousin? He really is nice!
22. The teachers? They really are nice!
23. The students? They really are nice!
24. The aunt and uncle? They really are nice!
25. The brothers and sisters? They really are nice!
26. The girls? They really are nice!

STUDENT:

¿La casa? ¡Qué grande!
¿El profesor? ¡Qué grande!
¿La clase? ¡Qué grande!
¿La familia? ¡Qué grande!
¿El cuarto? ¡Qué grande!
¿La escuela? ¡Qué grande!
¿La lista? ¡Qué grande!
¿El patio? ¡Qué grande!
¿La sala? ¡Qué grande!
¿Los cuartos? ¡Qué grandes!
¿Las puertas? ¡Qué grandes!
¿Los libros? ¡Qué grandes!
¿Los hijos? ¡Qué grandes!
¿Los cónsules? ¡Qué grandes!
¿Las señoras? ¡Qué grandes!
¿La rubia? ¡Qué amable!
¿El rubio? ¡Qué amable!
¿La morena? ¡Qué amable!
¿El moreno? ¡Qué amable!
¿La prima? ¡Qué amable!
¿El primo? ¡Qué amable!
¿Los profesores? ¡Qué amables!
¿Los alumnos? ¡Qué amables!
¿Los tíos? ¡Qué amables!
¿Los hermanos? ¡Qué amables!
¿Las chicas? ¡Qué amables!

● GENDER-NUMBER SUBSTITUTION DRILL

TEACHER:

A. 1. *El señor Martínez* está presente.   *Repita.*
   2. La señora de los Angeles _____
   3. El señor Arjona _____
   4. La señorita Flores _____
   5. Los alumnos _____
   6. Las alumnas _____
   7. El profesor _____

STUDENT:

El señor Martínez está presente.
La señora de los Angeles está presente.
El señor Arjona está presente.
La señorita Flores está presente.
Los alumnos están presentes.
Las alumnas están presentes.
El profesor está presente.

TEACHER:		STUDENT:
B. 1. Es *la familia* española.	*Repita.*	**Es la familia española.**
2. — la señora ————		Es la señora española.
3. — el cónsul ————		Es el cónsul español.
4. — la escuela ————		Es la escuela española.
5. — el amigo ————		Es el amigo español.
6. — la casa ————		Es la casa española.
7. — la puerta ————		Es la puerta española.
8. — la morena ————		Es la morena española.
9. — las amigas ————		Son las amigas españolas.
10. — los alumnos ————		Son los alumnos españoles.
11. — las señoritas ————		Son las señoritas españolas.
12. — los chicos ————		Son los chicos españoles.

TEACHER:		STUDENT:
C. 1. Es *el profesor* inglés.	*Repita.*	**Es el profesor inglés.**
2. — la casa ————		Es la casa inglesa.
3. — el señor ————		Es el señor inglés.
4. — la familia ————		Es la familia inglesa.
5. — los alumnos —		Son los alumnos ingleses.
6. — las primas ————		Son las primas inglesas.
7. — las compañeras —		Son las compañeras inglesas.
8. — los amigos ————		Son los amigos ingleses.
9. — las chicas ————		Son las chicas inglesas.

TEACHER:		STUDENT:
D. 1. Es que somos *muchos hijos* ahora.	*Repita.*	**Es que somos muchos hijos ahora.**
2. ———————— tantos ————————		Es que somos tantos hijos ahora.
3. ———————— hijas ————		Es que somos tantas hijas ahora.
4. ———————— muchas ————————		Es que somos muchas hijas ahora.
5. ———————— alumnos —		Es que somos muchos alumnos ahora.
6. ———————— tantos ————————		Es que somos tantos alumnos ahora.
7. ———————— alumnas —		Es que somos tantas alumnas ahora.
8. ———————— muchas ————————		Es que somos muchas alumnas ahora.
9. ———————— compañeros —		Es que somos muchos compañeros ahora.
10. ———————— tantos ————————		Es que somos tantos compañeros ahora.
11. ———————— compañeras —		Es que somos tantas compañeras ahora.
12. ———————— muchas ————————		Es que somos muchas compañeras ahora.

TEACHER:		STUDENT:
E. 1. ¡Qué *bonita* es tu *casa!*	*Repita.*	**¡Qué bonita es tu casa!**
2. ———————— cuarto		¡Qué bonito es tu cuarto!
3. — grande ————		¡Qué grande es tu cuarto!
4. ———————— clase		¡Qué grande es tu clase!
5. — buena ————		¡Qué buena es tu clase!
6. ———————— profesor		¡Qué bueno es tu profesor!
7. — amable ————		¡Qué amable es tu profesor!
8. ———————— mamá		¡Qué amable es tu mamá!
9. — bonita ————		¡Qué bonita es tu mamá!
10. ———————— prima		¡Qué bonita es tu prima!
11. — buena ————		¡Qué buena es tu prima!
12. ———————— libro		¡Qué bueno es tu libro!

7 The numerals, 1–10

EXAMPLES
1. **Una** o **dos** chicas.   *One or two girls.*
2. **Cinco** hermanos y **cuatro** hermanas.
3. ¿Tú tienes **nueve** hermanos?
4. **Diez** hijos.

SINGULAR 1	(M) **un chico**	(F) **una chica**
PLURAL 2	dos	
3	tres	
4	cuatro	
5	cinco	
6	seis	chicos
7	siete	chicas
8	ocho	
9	nueve	
10	diez	

The numeral *one* has separate forms for masculine and feminine.   The other numerals have only one form.   (*Zero* is **cero**.)

uno AND un	
I need one book.	**Necesito un libro.**
I need one.	**Necesito uno.**
One boy.	**Un chico.**
One or two boys.	**Uno o dos chicos.**

The numeral *one*, masculine, is **un** directly before a noun but **uno** elsewhere.

● COUNTING DRILL

1. Cuente[1] de uno a cinco.   Uno, dos, tres, cuatro, cinco.
2. Cuente de seis a diez.   Seis, siete, ocho, nueve, diez.
3. Cuente de uno a diez.   Uno, dos, tres, cuatro, cinco, seis, siete, ocho, nueve, diez.

● ITEM SUBSTITUTION DRILL

TEACHER:		STUDENT:
1. ¿Tú tienes *nueve* hermanos?	*Repita.*	**¿Tú tienes nueve hermanos?**
2. _____ cinco _____		¿Tú tienes cinco hermanos?
3. _____ cuatro _____		¿Tú tienes cuatro hermanos?
4. _____ ocho _____		¿Tú tienes ocho hermanos?
5. _____ tres _____		¿Tú tienes tres hermanos?
6. _____ seis _____		¿Tú tienes seis hermanos?
7. _____ diez _____		¿Tú tienes diez hermanos?
8. _____ siete _____		¿Tú tienes siete hermanos?
9. _____ dos _____		¿Tú tienes dos hermanos?
10. _____ un _____		¿Tú tienes un hermano?

---

[1] **Cuente(n)** *count*

INSTRUCTIONS: These drills are like substitution drills except that the items replacing those in the model sentence are put in different slots. The teacher says the model sentence and asks a student to repeat it. Then the teacher gives a word to replace some word in the model. The student determines where the replacement item fits and makes the substitution, also making any changes that are correlated with the new form. This modified sentence becomes a model sentence for the insertion of the next replacement item. Thus each modification is made on the sentence just preceding. If the student hesitates in making the new sentence, the teacher should prompt, using a stage whisper. The students' books are closed during class recitation.

	TEACHER:		STUDENT:
A. 1.	Ella es la hermana menor.	*Repita.*	**Ella es la hermana menor.**
2.	_____ bonita		Ella es la hermana bonita.
3.	_____ son _____		Ellas son las hermanas bonitas.
4.	_____ amable		Ella es la hermana amable.
5.	_____ hermanos _____		Ellos son los hermanos amables.
6.	Tú _____		Tú eres el hermano amable.
7.	_____ grande		Tú eres el hermano grande.
8.	_____ la _____		Tú eres la hermana grande.
9.	Ellos _____		Ellos son los hermanos grandes.
10.	_____ tío _____		El es el tío grande.
11.	_____ español		El es el tío español.
12.	_____ son _____		Ellos son los tíos españoles.
13.	_____ cónsul _____		El es el cónsul español.
14.	Usted _____		Usted es el cónsul español.
15.	_____ profesora _____		Usted es la profesora española.
16.	El _____		El es el profesor español.
17.	_____ americano		El es el profesor americano.
18.	_____ abuelo _____		El es el abuelo americano.
19.	_____ son _____		Ellos son los abuelos americanos.
20.	_____ americana		Ella es la abuela americana.

B. 1.	Los alumnos estudian en la clase.	*Repita.*	**Los alumnos estudian en la clase.**
2.	_____ patio		Los alumnos estudian en el patio.
3.	El _____		El alumno estudia en el patio.
4.	_____ espera _____		El alumno espera en el patio.
5.	_____ sala		El alumno espera en la sala.
6.	_____ alumna _____		La alumna espera en la sala.
7.	_____ hablan _____		Las alumnas hablan en la sala.
8.	_____ cocina		Las alumnas hablan en la cocina.
9.	_____ trabajan _____		Las alumnas trabajan en la cocina.
10.	_____ mamá _____		La mamá trabaja en la cocina.
11.	_____ casa		La mamá trabaja en la casa.
12.	_____ entra _____		La mamá entra en la casa.
13.	_____ chica _____		La chica entra en la casa.
14.	_____ escuela		La chica entra en la escuela.
15.	Las _____		Las chicas entran en la escuela.
16.	_____ profesor _____		El profesor entra en la escuela.
17.	_____ trabajan _____		Los profesores trabajan en la escuela.
18.	_____ cuartos		Los profesores trabajan en los cuartos.

3

A Telephone Conversation

o. *Olga*   j. *José María*
m. *María Elena*   a. *María Elena's aunt*

o. Fine thing! [What a pity!] The record player's broken.

j. Why don't we call María Elena? She has a portable [one].

o. Good idea. Do you know her number?

j. I think it's 17-26-58, if I'm not mistaken. Can I use your telephone?

Una conversación por teléfono

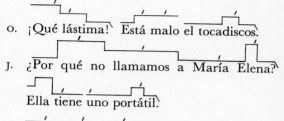

o. *Olga*   j. *José María*
m. *María Elena*   t. *tía de María Elena*

o. ¡Qué lástima! Está malo el tocadiscos.

j. ¿Por qué no llamamos a María Elena?

Ella tiene uno portátil.

o. Buena idea. ¿Sabes el número?

j. Creo que es el diecisiete, veintiséis, cincuenta

y ocho, si no estoy equivocado. ¿Puedo usar

el teléfono?

O. Yes, sure. It's over there, by the dining-room door [doorway, entrance].

O. Sí, claro. Está ahí, a la entrada del comedor.

* * *

J. Hello. Is this Dr. Fernández' house?

J. ¿Aló? (1) ¿Hablo con la casa del Dr. Fernández?

A. Yes. Who do you want to speak to?

T. Sí, señor. ¿Con quién desea hablar?

J. María Elena, please. Are you her mother, may I ask?

J. Con María Elena, por favor. Perdón (2), ¿es usted la mamá?

A. No, this is her aunt. María Elena just left [finishes leaving], but she'll be back [returns] in [inside of] ten minutes. Would you like [do you wish] to leave a [some] message?

T. No, habla con la tía. María Elena acaba de salir pero regresa dentro de diez minutos. ¿Desea usted dejar algún recado?

J. No, thanks. I'll call later [more late].

J. No, gracias, señora. Yo llamo más tarde.

A. Who may I say is calling [on behalf of whom, in-order-to tell her]?

T. ¿De parte de quién, para decirle?

J. José María Romero, thank you [if you do me the favor].

J. De José María Romero (3), si me hace el favor.

* * *

M. Hi, Pepe. Where are you? What's all that noise I hear [that I hear so much noise]?

M. ¿Qué tal, Pepe? (4) ¿Dónde estás que oigo tanto ruido?

J. At Olga's. She's got some new records, some Venezuelan *joropos*. We're all here. Why don't you come over?

J. En casa de Olga, que tiene unos discos nuevos, unos joropos (5) venezolanos. Aquí estamos todos. ¿Por qué no vienes?

M. Oh, I'd love to [what desires of going]. But you know mom ...

M. Ay qué ganas de ir. Pero tú conoces a mamá ...

J. Yes, but your dad . . .

M. No, not him; her, —mom. She says I have to stay with my aunt. How dull. But [however; still], maybe I can come. What time is it?

J. It's three-thirty [half]. If you come, can you bring your record player? We'll come by for you.

M. Don't you have one there?

J. Yes, but it isn't working [is broken].

M. Oh, so that's how come [because-of that] the invitation, huh?

J. No, girl. What crazy ideas you have!

J. Sí, pero tu papá . . .

M. No, él no; ella, mi mamá. Dice que tengo que estar con mi tía. ¡Qué aburrido! Sin embargo, tal vez puedo ir. ¿Qué hora es?

J. Son las tres y media. Si vienes, ¿puedes traer tu tocadiscos? Nosotros pasamos por ti.

M. ¿No tienen ustedes uno allá? (6)

J. Sí, pero está descompuesto.

M. Ah, por eso la invitación, ¿eh?

J. No, chica, ¡qué ideas tienes!

Cultural Notes

(1) The Spanish equivalents of the English telephone greeting, *Hello,* are several: in Spain, **Diga** or **Dígame;** in Mexico, **Bueno;** in Cuba, **Oigo** or **¿Qué hay?;** in Colombia, **A ver;** in Argentina, **Holá;** and in most other Spanish-speaking countries, **Aló.**

(2) One-for-one semantic equivalents, like the Spanish equivalents of *Hello* explained above, are rare between any two languages (see footnote 1, p. 56). The use of **Perdón** in this dialog, and that of **Con permiso** in the previous one, both translated as *Excuse me,* illustrate the fact that one word or phrase in English often covers a semantic range requiring more than one verbal equivalent in Spanish. (The reverse is also true.) Thus, in excusing oneself from people with whom one is speaking, in passing in front of someone at a theater, or in making one's way through a crowded elevator or public conveyance, **Con permiso** is normally used; but in interrupting a conversation to inquire about something, **Perdón** is one of the commonly used expressions.

(3) The name **María** is not uncommon as the second element of a male double name, e.g., José María Morelos, the Mexican patriot, and Carlos María Ocampos, the Argentine novelist.

(4) **Pepe** is a nickname for **José,** in Old Spanish **Josep.** The form **Pepe** is just a reduplicated syllable (cf. English *tom-tom, choo-choo, chitchat*) and is paralleled by the Italian *Beppo,* "Joe," a nickname of *Giuseppe.*

(5) The **joropo** is the most typical Venezuelan folk song and rustic dance. In tempo—usually 6/8 or 3/4—and in liveliness, the **joropo** resembles the jig.

(6) There are three Spanish adverbs corresponding to English *there:* **ahí, allí,** and **allá.** In general, **allá** indicates greater remoteness from the speaker, and often

a less precise location than do the other adverbs.   In Spanish America, **ahí** has tended to crowd out **allí** so that the former distinction (**ahí** referring to something nearer the person addressed, and **allí** to something distant from either speaker in a conversation) has to some extent been lost, though still preserved in Spain.

● PRONUNCIATION EXERCISE

A. The variants [b] and [ƀ].   INSTRUCTIONS: Repeat the following pairs of words just as you hear them.

[b]	[ƀ]	[b]	[ƀ]
vez	la vez	un bus	este bus
voz	la voz	un baile	este baile
vaca	la vaca	un banco	este banco
boca	la boca	un vaso	este vaso
vista	la vista	un velo	este velo
banca	la banca	un balcón	este balcón
banda	la banda	un verano	este verano
bocina	la bocina	un billete	este billete

In the above pairs the first column has the stop [b], which occurs at the beginning of an utterance (i.e., when preceded by silence) or after [m].   The second column has the fricative [ƀ], which is found everywhere else.   Note that the letters **b** and **v** represent the same sound.

B. The variants [d] and [đ].

[d]	[đ]	[d]	[đ]	[d]	[đ]
día	ese día	un día	este día	el dios	la diosa
disco	ese disco	un disco	este disco	el danés	la danesa
deporte	ese deporte	un dólar	este dólar	el dicho	la dicha
desfile	ese desfile	un deporte	este deporte	el ducho	la ducha
dinero	ese dinero	un desfile	este desfile	el diestro	la diestra
discurso	ese discurso	un discurso	este discurso	el dichoso	la dichosa
despacho	ese despacho	un despacho	este despacho	el discreto	la discreta
director	ese director	un director	este director	el director	la directora

In the above pairs the first column has the stop [d], which occurs at the beginning of an utterance (i.e., when preceded by silence) or after [n] and [l].   The second column has the fricative [đ], which is found everywhere else.

C. The variants [g] and [g̵].

[g]	[g̵]	[g]	[g̵]
gato	este gato	un galgo	mi galgo
gaucho	este gaucho	un ganso	mi ganso
globo	este globo	un gasto	mi gasto
golpe	este golpe	un gato	mi gato
gordo	este gordo	un globo	mi globo
grito	este grito	un grupo	mi grupo
grupo	este grupo	un gusto	mi gusto
gusto	este gusto	un galón	mi galón

In the above pairs, the first column has the stop [g], which occurs at the beginning of an utterance (i.e., when preceded by silence) or after [ŋ].   The second column has the fricative [g̵], which is found everywhere else.

8 Interrogative words

EXAMPLES 1. **¿Por qué** no llamamos a María Elena?
2. ¿Con **quién** desea hablar?
3. **¿Quiénes** llegan a la puerta?
4. **¿Cómo** está el profesor?   *How's the teacher?*

when?	**¿cuándo?**
how? [1]	**¿cómo?**
why?	**¿por qué?**
who, whom?	**¿quién?** (*plural,* **¿quiénes?**)
which, which one?	**¿cuál?** (*plural,* **¿cuáles?**)
how much?	**¿cuánto?** –a?
how many?	**¿cuántos?** –as?

These English words regularly have only the equivalents shown.

● **TRANSLATION DRILL** [2]

A. 1. When is the lady arriving?
   2. How is the lady arriving?
   3. Why is the lady arriving?
   4. With whom is the lady arriving?

B. 1. Who is arriving?
   2. Who all [3] are arriving?
   3. Which one is arriving?
   4. Which ones are arriving?
   5. Which family is arriving?

6. Which families are arriving?
7. How much is arriving?
8. How many are arriving?

C. 1. Who is he?
   2. Who are they?
   3. Which is it?
   4. Which are they?
   5. How much is it?
   6. How many are they?

● **CONSTRUCTION SUBSTITUTION DRILL**

TEACHER:

1. Pregúntele [4] al señor cómo se llama.
2. Pregúntele al señor cuándo viene.
3. Pregúntele al señor cómo viene.
4. Pregúntele al señor por qué viene.
5. Pregúntele al señor con quién viene.
6. Pregúntele al señor con quiénes viene.
7. Pregúntele al señor cuál viene.
8. Pregúntele al señor cuáles vienen.
9. Pregúntele al señor quién viene.
10. Pregúntele al señor quiénes vienen.
11. Pregúntele al señor cuántos vienen.

STUDENT:

¿Cómo se llama, señor?
¿Cuándo viene, señor?
¿Cómo viene, señor?
¿Por qué viene, señor?
¿Con quién viene, señor?
¿Con quiénes viene, señor?
¿Cuál viene, señor?
¿Cuáles vienen, señor?
¿Quién viene, señor?
¿Quiénes vienen, señor?
¿Cuántos vienen, señor?

● **PATTERNED RESPONSE DRILL**

1. TEACHER: ¿Cómo se llama?
   STUDENT: **Pablo Arjona.**
   TEACHER: ¿Cómo?
   STUDENT: **Pablo Arjona.**

2. ¿Cómo se llama usted?---
   ¿Cómo?---
3. Etc. con otros alumnos de la clase.

---

[1] To ask for the repetition of what someone has just said, Spanish uses the equivalent of *how?* **¿cómo?** Compare English *How? How was that? What did you say?* etc.
[2] In order to present more drills in the space available, instructions and answers will appear in this and in subsequent units only when needed; e.g., when a new type of drill is introduced.
[3] English expressions with *all* will be used in the drills to cue a plural where the English form does not show plurality: *who all, you all.* If the teacher prefers, he can give this cue with a gesture that indicates he is talking to more than one person.
[4] **Pregunte(n)** *ask*

EXAMPLES   1. **¿A qué** puerta llegan los alumnos?
2. **¿Qué** hora es?
3. **¿Qué** hacen los alumnos?

What? BEFORE NOUN	*What?* BEFORE VERB
¿qué { **puerta?** **hora?** **libro?**	**¿qué** { **hacen?** **esperamos?** **dice?**

English *what?* followed directly by a noun is **¿qué?**   The same is usually true of English *what?* followed by a verb.

● TRANSLATION DRILL

A. 1. What time is it?
   2. What day is it?
   3. What number is it?
   4. What book is it?
   5. What record is it?
   6. What part is it?
   7. What room is it?
   8. What class is it?
   9. What door is it?
  10. What entrance is it?
  11. What school is it?
  12. What house is it?

B. 1. What is he saying?
   2. What is he leaving?
   3. What is he studying?
   4. What is he waiting for?
   5. What is he doing?
   6. What is he using?

C. 1. What does he say?
   2. What does he need?
   3. What does he leave?
   4. What does he study?
   5. What does he have?
   6. What does he want?

EXAMPLES   1. **¿Adónde** llegan los alumnos?
2. **¿De dónde** son?
3. **¿Dónde** está Julio?

where? where from? for where? etc.	**¿dónde?** **¿de dónde?** **¿para dónde?** etc.		where? where to?	**¿adónde?**

Where? in the sense *where to?* is **¿adónde?**   In other senses, *where?* is **¿dónde?**

● CONSTRUCTION SUBSTITUTION DRILL

A. 1. TEACHER: Pregúntele adónde llega.
     STUDENT: **¿Adónde llega usted?**
   2. Pregúntele adónde tiene que ir.
   3. Pregúntele adónde tiene que salir.

B. 1. Pregúntele dónde está.
   2. Pregúntele dónde trabaja.

   3. Pregúntele dónde estudia.
   4. Pregúntele dónde habla.

C. 1. Pregúntele de dónde es.
   2. Pregúntele de dónde viene.
   3. Pregúntele de dónde regresa.

● DISCUSSION

Most English interrogative words have just one equivalent in Spanish.   *Where?*, however, has two possibilities: when it means *where to?*, it is translated by **¿adónde?** (meaning, literally, *to where?*), but the rest of the time it is translated by **¿dónde?**   ***Where*** *are you going?* therefore calls for **¿adónde?**, ***Where*** *are you?* for **¿dónde?**, and ***Where*** *are you* ***from?*** for **¿de dónde?**

9 Word order in questions

	INTERROGATIVE WORD	VERB	SUBJECT (IF ANY)
QUESTIONS WITH INTERROGATIVE WORDS	¿Adónde ¿Quiénes ¿Qué ¿De dónde ¿Con quién	llegan son esperamos? son? desea hablar?	los alumnos? las chicas?

In this pattern, the subject, if any, follows the verb, and any preposition understood with the interrogative word precedes it.

● TRANSLATION DRILL

A. 1. Where is Julio from?
   2. Who is she?
   3. Which ones are they?
   4. How much is it?
   5. When is it?
   6. What is it?
   7. Which is it?

B. 1. Where are you working?
   2. When are you coming?
   3. Why are you studying?
   4. What are you waiting for?
   5. What is he saying?

C. 1. Why does he study?
   2. What does he have?
   3. When does he arrive?
   4. When do you go in (enter)?
   5. What do you want?
   6. Which one do you need?

	SUBJECT	VERB	REMAINDER (IF ANY)
SUBJECT BEFORE VERB	¿Tú ¿Tú ¿Julio	eres tienes está?	amigo de ellas? nueve hermanos?

	VERB	SUBJECT	REMAINDER (IF ANY)
SUBJECT AFTER VERB	¿Es ¿Llegan ¿No tienen ¿Está	usted los alumnos ustedes Julio?	la mamá? a la puerta? uno allá?

In these two patterns, verb and subject interchange positions, as in English *Julio is here?* and *Is Julio here?*

● CONSTRUCTION SUBSTITUTION DRILL

INSTRUCTIONS: Repeat the question as you hear it. Then change the order of the subject and verb.

A. 1. TEACHER: ¿Tú eres amigo de ellas?
      STUDENT: **¿Eres tú amigo de ellas?**
   2. ¿Tú tienes nueve hermanos?
   3. ¿Usted es el señor Arjona?
   4. ¿Usted estudia español?
   5. ¿Pablo está en la clase?
   6. ¿La morena tiene un hijo?
   7. ¿Ustedes son catorce en total?

B. 1. ¿Es usted la mamá?
   2. ¿Tiene usted algún joropo?
   3. ¿Tienen ustedes uno allá?
   4. ¿Llegan los alumnos a la puerta?
   5. ¿Tiene la casa un patio grande?
   6. ¿Vamos todos a casa de Olga?
   7. ¿Son ellos compañeros de escuela?

	VERB	REMAINDER
NO SUBJECT EXPRESSED	¿Sabes ¿Puedes	el número de su casa? traer tu tocadiscos?

Questions, like other sentences, do not need an expressed subject to make them complete.

● CONSTRUCTION SUBSTITUTION DRILL

INSTRUCTIONS: Repeat the question as you hear it. Then repeat again omitting the subject.

A. 1. TEACHER: ¿Tú eres amiga de las dos chicas?
     STUDENT: **¿Eres amiga de las dos chicas?**
  2. ¿Ellas son compañeras de escuela?
  3. ¿Ella tiene un tocadiscos?
  4. ¿Usted desea hablar con Olga?
  5. ¿El dice de parte de quién?
  6. ¿Es que nosotros somos muchos?
  7. ¿Es que yo soy la menor?

B. 1. ¿Llegan los alumnos a la clase?
  2. ¿Voy yo a pasar lista?
  3. ¿Está Julio en la cocina?
  4. ¿Son ellos primos?
  5. ¿Puedo yo usar el teléfono?
  6. ¿Regresa Olga dentro de diez minutos?
  7. ¿Es que no oigo yo bien?

	VERB	REMAINDER	SUBJECT
SUBJECT AFTER REMAINDER	¿Está ¿Llegan	abierta a la puerta	la puerta? los alumnos?

	VERB	SUBJECT	REMAINDER
SUBJECT AFTER VERB	¿Está ¿Llegan	la puerta los alumnos	abierta? a la puerta?

Emphasis can be placed on subject or on remainder by shifting it to the end. **¿Está abierta la puerta?** means *Is the **door** open?*; **¿Está la puerta abierta?** means *Is the door **open?***

● TRANSLATION DRILL

INSTRUCTIONS: Translate the following paired sentences, emphasizing the italicized items by placing them last in your Spanish sentence.

1. Is *the record player* broken?
   Is the record player *broken?*
2. Is *everybody* here? (Are all here?)
   Is everybody *here?*
3. Does *Cecilia* have lots of friends?
   Does Cecilia have *lots of friends?*
4. Don't *you* have one?
   Don't you have *one?*
5. Are *the students* arriving at the class?
   Are the students arriving *at the class?*
6. Is the *professor* present?
   Is the professor *present?*
7. Do *you* have a sister?
   Do you have *a sister?*

● DISCUSSION

In questions with interrogative words, the subject normally comes after the verb. In other questions, it may precede or follow the verb, with effects similar to those in English: **¿Es usted la mamá?** *Are you her mother?*; **¿Usted es la mamá?** *You are her mother?* (The words *do* and *did,* as markers of interrogation and negation, have no parallel in Spanish: the question *Do you have the invitation?* appears in the same order as *Have you the invitation?* **¿Tiene usted la invitación?**)

Where Spanish omits the subject, there is no problem of word order.   Whether **¿Puedes traer tu tocadiscos?** means *You can bring . . . ?* or *Can you bring . . . ?* depends on context and intonation.

English emphasizes a word by stressing it.   Spanish emphasizes a word both by stressing it and, more often than is possible in English, by shifting it to the end of the sentence.

10 Placement of *no*

EXAMPLES   1. **No** necesitas saber inglés.   3. ¿Por qué **no** vienes?
             2. Si **no** estoy equivocado.   4. **¿No** puedes traer tu tocadiscos?

no	+	verb

When **no** accompanies a verb, it is placed directly before the verb.

● CONSTRUCTION SUBSTITUTION DRILL

INSTRUCTIONS: Repeat the following sentences.   Then say them again making the verbs negative.

A. 1. TEACHER: Los alumnos llegan a la puerta.
     STUDENT: **Los alumnos no llegan a la puerta.**

2. La puerta está abierta.
3. Ahora voy a pasar lista.
4. Ahora hay que trabajar.
5. Debe estar en la cocina.
6. Son primas.
7. El padre de Betty es el nuevo cónsul americano.
8. Ellas saben español perfectamente.
9. Después estudiamos.
10. Eres muy amable.
11. Yo soy la menor.
12. Está malo el tocadiscos.
13. Ella tiene uno portátil.
14. No, habla con la tía.
15. Yo llamo más tarde.
16. Pero tú conoces a mamá.
17. Sin embargo, tengo que estar con mi tía.
18. Son las tres y media.
19. Pero está descompuesto.

B. 1. ¿Está Julio?
2. ¿Tú eres amigo de ellas?
3. ¿Sabes el número de su casa?
4. ¿Puedo usar el teléfono?
5. ¿Desea hablar con María Elena?
6. ¿Es usted la mamá?
7. ¿Tienen ustedes uno allá?
8. ¿Desea dejar algún recado?
9. ¿Es aburrida la clase?
10. ¿Por qué vienes?

11 Intonation[1]

EXAMPLES

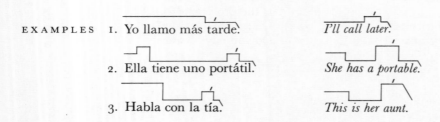

1. Yo llamo más tarde.   *I'll call later.*
2. Ella tiene uno portátil.   *She has a portable.*
3. Habla con la tía.   *This is her aunt.*

---

[1] The examples, with contrasting English and Spanish intonation patterns, are on a recording.   You will understand the explanations better if you listen to the recording as you read the examples and diagrams.

The pitch of the main stress in nonquestions

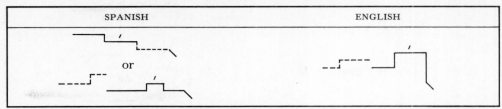

SPANISH	ENGLISH

Where American English tends to rise higher at the main stress than anywhere else and then drop steeply, Spanish normally drops to the main stress or rises less than English.

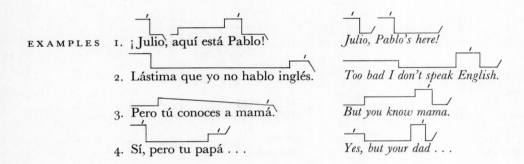

EXAMPLES
1. ¡Julio, aquí está Pablo! *Julio, Pablo's here!*

2. Lástima que yo no hablo inglés. *Too bad I don't speak English.*

3. Pero tú conoces a mamá. *But you know mama.*

4. Sí, pero tu papá . . . *Yes, but your dad . . .*

Emphasis plus inconclusiveness

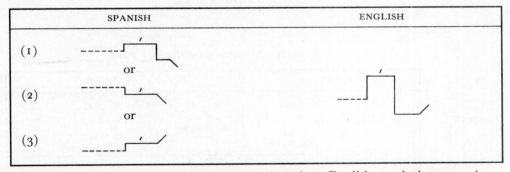

SPANISH	ENGLISH

To show emphasis plus inconclusiveness, American English regularly uses a rising-falling-rising pitch curve starting at the main stress. Spanish treats most such utterances as if they were conclusive (1 and 2 in the box), but for extreme inconclusiveness it may make a simple rise at the main stress without any following fall-rise (3 in the box).

EXAMPLES

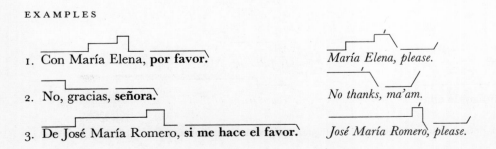

1. Con María Elena, **por favor.** *María Elena, please.*

2. No, gracias, **señora.** *No thanks, ma'am.*

3. De José María Romero, **si me hace el favor.** *José María Romero, please.*

Statement tags

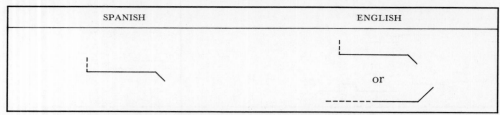

SPANISH	ENGLISH

The low-pitched statement tags which in English may either rise or fall at the end, in Spanish regularly have only the fall.

EXAMPLES

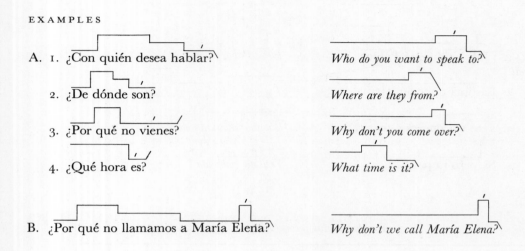

A. 1. ¿Con quién desea hablar?   Who do you want to speak to?

2. ¿De dónde son?   Where are they from?

3. ¿Por qué no vienes?   Why don't you come over?

4. ¿Qué hora es?   What time is it?

B. ¿Por qué no llamamos a María Elena?   Why don't we call María Elena?

Questions introduced by interrogative words[1]

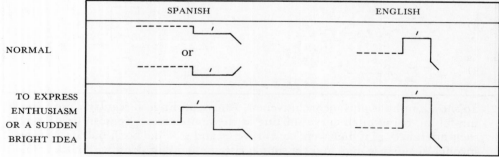

	SPANISH	ENGLISH
NORMAL	or	
TO EXPRESS ENTHUSIASM OR A SUDDEN BRIGHT IDEA		

In these questions, American English normally goes up at the main stress, while Spanish normally goes down except when expressing enthusiasm, inspiration, or other strong emotion (here, American English tends to go still higher at the main stress).

EXAMPLES

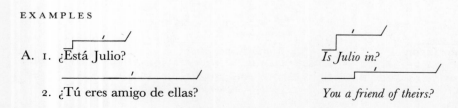

A. 1. ¿Está Julio?   Is Julio in?

2. ¿Tú eres amigo de ellas?   You a friend of theirs?

---

[1] These same intonations, with similar differences between English and Spanish, are often encountered in yes-no questions.

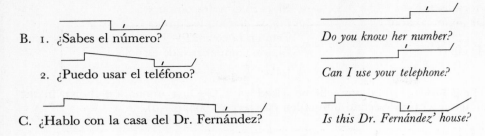

B. 1. ¿Sabes el número?

    Do you know her number?

   2. ¿Puedo usar el teléfono?

    Can I use your telephone?

C. ¿Hablo con la casa del Dr. Fernández?

    Is this Dr. Fernández' house?

Yes-no questions

SPANISH		ENGLISH
Informal	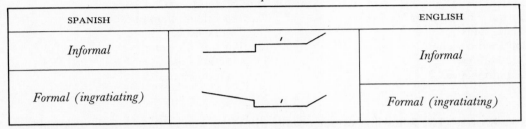	*Informal*
Formal (ingratiating)		*Formal (ingratiating)*

English and Spanish use essentially the same curves: a rise (without fall) at the main stress in informal questions (Examples *A*) and a drop to the main stress and rise afterward in formal questions (Example *C*); but Spanish often uses the formal type where American English favors the informal (Examples *B*).

● INTONATION DRILL

A. INSTRUCTIONS: The following questions will be asked and answered with the intonations shown (see second box p. 50 and box p. 51 for the questions, and first box, p. 49, for the answers).

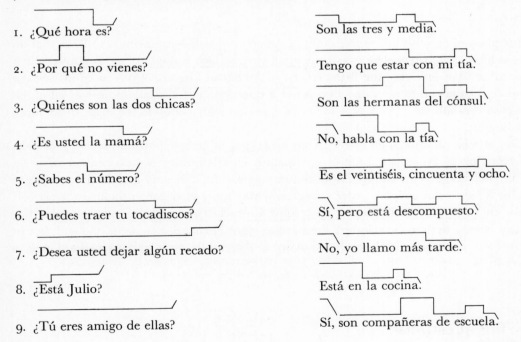

1. ¿Qué hora es?

   Son las tres y media.

2. ¿Por qué no vienes?

   Tengo que estar con mi tía.

3. ¿Quiénes son las dos chicas?

   Son las hermanas del cónsul.

4. ¿Es usted la mamá?

   No, habla con la tía.

5. ¿Sabes el número?

   Es el veintiséis, cincuenta y ocho.

6. ¿Puedes traer tu tocadiscos?

   Sí, pero está descompuesto.

7. ¿Desea usted dejar algún recado?

   No, yo llamo más tarde.

8. ¿Está Julio?

   Está en la cocina.

9. ¿Tú eres amigo de ellas?

   Sí, son compañeras de escuela.

B. INSTRUCTIONS: Questions 4–9 of the preceding set will be asked again, using the intonation shown in the example (see second box, p. 50 and footnote), and answered in the same way as before.

4. ¿Es usted la mamá?

No, habla con la tía.

5. ¿Sabes el número?

Es el veintiséis, cincuenta y ocho.

6. ¿Puedes traer tu tocadiscos?   Sí, pero está descompuesto.
7. ¿Desea usted dejar algún recado?   No, yo llamo más tarde.
8. ¿Está Julio?   Está en la cocina.
9. ¿Tú eres amigo de ellas?   Sí, son compañeros de escuela.

C. INSTRUCTIONS: The following questions will be asked with the first intonation shown in the example, then asked again with the second intonation (see second box, p. 50).

1. ¿Qué esperamos?	¿Qué esperamos?
2. ¿De dónde son?	¿De dónde son?
3. ¿Por qué no llamamos?	¿Por qué no llamamos?
4. ¿Dónde estás?	¿Dónde estás?
5. ¿Por qué no vienes?	¿Por qué no vienes?
6. ¿Qué hora es?	¿Qué hora es?
7. ¿Cuándo vienes?	¿Cuándo vienes?

D. INSTRUCTIONS: The following statement tags will be spoken as shown in the example (see first box, p. 50).

1. Entra, Pablo.
2. Buenas tardes, doña Mercedes.
3. Con permiso, señora.
4. ¿De parte de quién, por favor?
5. De parte de José María, gracias.
6. Deseo dejar un recado, si me hace el favor.

● DISCUSSION

The intonation of Spanish differs from that of American English in having: (1) Rises that do not go quite as high. (2) A tendency to put the main stress, which is the last one, at a lower pitch than some or all of what precedes; this is the reverse of American English. (3) A more sparing use of upward glides at the end in anything that is not a question, and virtually no use at all of the common English rise-fall-rise. (4) A type of yes-no question with a drop to the main stress, more as in British English.

The effect of Spanish intonation to American ears is one of greater restraint, sobriety, or even gruffness, while that of American English on Spanish ears is one of overexcitement or over-emphasis. English also gives a gliding impression as against the crisp and angular impression of Spanish. This is partly due to word order. English syntax more often forces the main stress well back from the end, with the result that the upward or downward glides at the end are drawn out. In **¿Hablo con la casa del Dr. Fernández?** the stressed word **Fernández** comes at the end; but in *Is this Dr. Fernández' house?* English has to make room at the end for *house,* and the upward glide is extended over it.

12   Tag questions

EXAMPLES

1. Por eso la invitación, **¿eh?**
2. Tiene uno portátil, **¿no?** (**¿verdad?**).   *She has a portable one, hasn't (doesn't) she?*
3. No regresa, **¿verdad?**   *She isn't coming back, is she?*

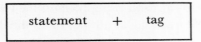

EXAMPLES

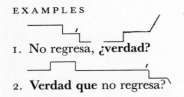

1. No regresa, **¿verdad?**

2. **Verdad que** no regresa?

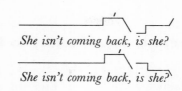

She isn't coming back, is she?

She isn't coming back, is she?

Intonation of tag questions

SPANISH	ENGLISH
¿verdad? ¿no?	*English tag with rise at end* is she? etc.
¿Verdad que . . . . ?	*English tag with fall at end* is she? etc.

Both English and Spanish have tags that rise at the end; but where English has a tag with a fall at the end (this occurs in questions that do not really ask), Spanish puts **verdad que** at the beginning and a fall in pitch at the end.

● CONSTRUCTION SUBSTITUTION DRILL

A. INSTRUCTIONS: Repeat the following statements. Then repeat them again and make them tag questions by adding **¿no?** or **¿verdad?**

1. Los alumnos llegan a la puerta.
2. La puerta está abierta.
3. Ahora hay que trabajar.
4. Debe estar en la cocina.
5. Ay, qué ganas de ir.
6. ¡Qué lástima que está descompuesto!
7. Ustedes son catorce en total.
8. Son primas.
9. El padre de Betty es el nuevo cónsul.
10. Después estudiamos.
11. Ella tiene uno portátil.
12. Pero tú conoces a mamá.
13. Son las tres y media.
14. Pero está malo.

B. INSTRUCTIONS: Repeat the following negative statements. Then make them tag questions by adding **¿verdad?**

1. No está Julio.
2. Tú no sabes el número.
3. No oigo tanto ruido.
4. No es aburrida la clase .
5. Ella no es la menor.
6. Las chicas no saben español.
7. No tienes que estar en casa.
8. No está el Dr. Fernández.

● DISCUSSION

¿Eh? is equivalent to English *eh?, huh?, hm?* and the like, as a tag or as an independent question.

¿No? or **¿no es verdad?** (after an affirmative) and **¿verdad?** (after either an affirmative or a negative) correspond to the English tags in *You don't like it, do you? You like it, don't you? He won't eat* *it, will he? He'll eat it, won't he?* etc., all with rising pitch at the end. Where English puts a falling pitch at the end, Spanish does not use a tag at all, but starts the utterance with **¿Verdad que?** and ends it with a falling pitch.

13 Present tense of *estar*, to be

EXAMPLES
1. **Estoy** aquí.
2. ¿Dónde **estás?**
3. **Está** ahí, a la entrada del comedor.
4. Aquí **estamos** todos.

I am	estoy	we are	estamos
you are	estás		
you are he, she, it is }	está	you are they are }	están

● PERSON-NUMBER SUBSTITUTION DRILL

1. *Las chicas* están en la sala.
   (mi hermano, nosotros, Julio, tú y yo, ellos, usted, ustedes, él, yo)[1]
2. ¿Dónde está *el profesor?*
   (los alumnos, papá, los tíos, el recado, la invitación, los cónsules, tú)

3. *¿Yo?* Estoy aquí en la cocina.
   (Pablo, Betty y Susana, nosotros, ellos, Cecilia, todos, Julio y yo, los chicos)

● PATTERNED RESPONSE DRILL

TEACHER:	STUDENT:
A. 1. ¿Cómo está doña Mercedes? *Conteste.*	**Está bien.**
2. ¿Cómo están los señores Fernández?	Están bien.
3. ¿Cómo está María Elena?	Está bien.
4. ¿Cómo está usted?	Estoy bien, gracias.
5. ¿Cómo están ustedes?	Estamos bien, gracias.
6. ¿Dónde están las chicas?	Están en la sala.
7. ¿Dónde está Julio?	Está en la sala.
8. ¿Dónde están Pepe y Susana?	etc.
9. ¿Dónde está el teléfono?	
10. ¿Dónde está usted?	
11. ¿Dónde están ustedes?	

TEACHER:	STUDENT 1:	STUDENT 2:
B. (*mamá*)	**¿Dónde está mamá?**	**Está en la sala.**
(la profesora, mi abuela, la familia, los discos, Olga, usted, ustedes)		etc.

---

[1] In order to present more drill material in the space available, the substitution items are listed in parentheses following the sentence. These items replace the words in italics in the model. The drill is conducted in the same way as similar drills in Unit 2.

14 *Ser* versus *estar*

ser	estar
A. 1. El padre de Betty **es** el nuevo cónsul. 2. **Son** primas. 3. ¿Tú **eres** amigo de ellas? 4. ¿Quiénes **son** las dos chicas? 5. ¿**Es** usted la mamá? 6. **Somos** muchos. 7. Yo **soy** la menor.	
B. 1. ¡Qué bonita **es** tu casa! 2. **Eres** muy amable. 3. Pero mi tocadiscos no **es** portátil. *But my record player isn't portable.*	E. 1. La puerta **está** abierta. 2. Si no **estoy** equivocado. 3. **Está** descompuesto.
C. 1. ¿De dónde **son?** 2. ¿De quién **es** la casa? *Whose house is it?* 3. **Es** de Cecilia. *It's Cecilia's.*	F. 1. ¿**Está** Julio? 2. Debe **estar** en la cocina. 3. **Estoy** aquí, en mi cuarto.
D. 1. ¿Qué hora **es?** 2. **Son** las tres y media.	

The two verbs **ser** and **estar** cover most of the meanings of *to be*.

● PERSON-NUMBER SUBSTITUTION DRILL

Pablo es de Chile, pero está en los Estados Unidos.
   (yo, mi tía, ellos, nosotros, Cecilia, tú, Susana y yo, mis padres, él)

● TRANSLATION DRILL

1. The record player? It's portable, but it's broken.
2. The door? It's big, but it's open.
3. The professor? He's nice, but he's wrong.
4. The telephone? It's new, but it's bad (not working).
5. The hour? It's late, but it's okay.
6. My cousin? She's pretty, but she's not here.
7. The school? It's big, but it's not open.
8. The record? It's pretty, but it's not clear.
9. Pepe? He's American, but he's not here.
10. Gloria? She's brunette, but she's not present.

● PATTERNED RESPONSE DRILL

TEACHER:	STUDENT:
1. ¿Está mi primo? Es Pedro González.	**¿Quién es su primo?** **No, no está aquí.**
2. ¿Está mi prima? Es Elena Fernández.	¿Quién es su prima? No, no está aquí.
3. ¿Está mi tío? Es Julio Arjona.	¿Quién es su tío? No, no está aquí.

4. ¿Está mi tía?   ¿Quién es su tía?
    Es Mercedes Flores.   No, no está aquí.
5. ¿Está mi profesor?   ¿Quién es su profesor?
    Es José María Martínez.   No, no está aquí.
6. ¿Está mi profesora?   ¿Quién es su profesora?
    Es María Romero.   No, no está aquí.

● DISCUSSION

The verb *to be* ties something to the subject of the sentence: *John is sick, John is a lawyer, John is here*—*is* ties *sick, lawyer,* and *here* to *John.*

With **estar,** the things tied are thought of as not really "belonging to" the subject. The speaker already has an impression of the subject, and **estar** adds something from outside. So **estar** is used to tell *where* the subject is (examples *F* above) or the *way* the subject is (examples *E* above).

Ser tells *what* the subject is. So it is used for tying the subject to the following kinds of things: (1) nouns or pronouns (examples *A* above), (2) adjectives when they are thought of as belonging to the subject and not added to it (examples *B* above), and (3) expressions of origin and possession (examples *C* above). Time of day is a special case (examples *D* above).

The "what" and the "way" are hard for the English-speaker to distinguish, especially with adjectives. *How pretty your house is!* might be translated with **está** as well as with **es.** With **es** the spreaker tells *what kind of* house it is: a pretty house, one of that class of houses. With **está** he implies a comparison with some idea already held: perhaps he has got an impression from the neighboring houses and wants to suggest "How your house stands out from the rest!"; or perhaps he remembers the house before it was redecorated, and wants to suggest "What an improvement over the way it was!"; or perhaps he wants to be highly complimentary, and to suggest "This really surpasses any possible expectation!"

By the same token, **estar** implies "change" and "becoming." *He's old* is **Es viejo** to tell *what* he is (an old man) but **Está viejo** to tell the *way* he is (old-looking, old when I expected him to be young).[1]

● COMBINED PATTERN REPLACEMENT DRILL

A.
1. **Tengo que estar con mi tía.**
2. _____ hablar _____
3. Tiene _____
4. _____ papá
5. _____ salir _____
6. Acaba de _____
7. _____ compañero
8. _____ regresar _____
9. Voy a _____
10. _____ el profesor
11. _____ estudiar _____
12. Hay que _____
13. _____ trabajar _____
14. _____ clase

B.
1. **¿Cuándo viene la prima bonita?**
2. _____ profesora _____
3. _____ nueva
4. De dónde _____
5. _____ es _____
6. Cuál _____
7. _____ española
8. _____el _____
9. Dónde _____
10. _____ están _____
11. Cómo _____
12. _____ americano
13. Con quién _____
14. _____ señora _____
15. _____las _____
16. Dónde _____
17. _____ señor _____
18. _____ trabaja _____
19. Por qué _____
20. _____ grande

---

[1] Note: A foreign language often forces you to make distinctions that seem irrelevant or unnecessary in your own language. **Ser** and **estar** compel you to see "being" from two points of view and to decide between them. English compels similar "unnecessary" distinctions from the point of view of Spanish-speakers: for example, in place of one word **hacer,** English requires a choice between *make* and *do.*

Morenas y rubias

(Pablo y Julio son dos amigos, compañeros de escuela. Están en la casa de Julio, donde estudian. ¿De qué hablan dos amigos cuando estudian?)

P. *Pablo*   J. *Julio*   O. *Olga, prima de Julio*

P. ¡Julio! ¿Quién es la rubia que acaba de llegar?

J. Es mi prima. ¿Por qué?

P. ¿Cómo? ¿Tu prima? ¡No es posible, es muy[1] bonita!

J. ¡Gracias, eres muy amable!

P. ¿De dónde es?

J. Es de Venezuela, de Caracas.

P. ¿Está aquí su[2] familia?

J. Sí. Su padre es el nuevo cónsul venezolano.

P. ¿Y tiene mucha familia?

J. No tanta: su papá, su mamá, tres hermanos, una hermana . . .

P. Hmm . . . ¿Es rubia la hermana?

J. No, es morena.

P. ¿Y cómo se llama la rubia?

J. Olga. ¿Deseas conocerla[3]?

P. Sí, claro.

J. Olga, quiero[4] presentarte a[5] mi buen amigo Pablo Fernández.

O. & P. Tanto gusto.

J. ¿Qué haces, Olga?

O. Espero a[5] Pepe.

P. ¿Su hermano, señorita?

O. No, mi marido.[6]

P. ¡¡¡!!!. . . Julio.

J. ¿Eh?

P. ¿Tiene marido la morena?

---

[1] *so (very)*   [2] *her*   [3] **la** *her (pron.)*   [4] *I want*   [5] *Omit in translation.*   [6] *husband*

4

The Saint's Day

F. *Francisco*   R. *Don Rafael, friend of Francisco*

F. I'm hungry [have hunger]; I'm going to go eat something. Won't you come with me, Don Rafael?

R. I can't right now, thanks. However, since you're going, can you send me up a cup of coffee?

F. Be glad to. With or without milk?

El día del santo

F. *Francisco*   R. *Don Rafael, amigo de Francisco*

F. Tengo hambre; voy a ir a comer algo. ¿No quiere venir conmigo, don (1) Rafael?

R. Ahora no puedo, gracias. Sin embargo, ya que va, ¿puede mandarme una taza de café?

F. Con mucho gusto. ¿Con o sin leche?

58

R. Black, with very little sugar, please.

R. Negro, con muy poquito azúcar, por favor.

* * *

* * *

F. (*a short time later*) Here's your coffee, Don Rafael. Careful, [because] it's hot.

F. (*un rato después*) Aquí está su café, don Rafael. Cuidado que está muy caliente.

R. You shouldn't have gone to so much trouble. Why are you bringing it instead of sending it up with the girl in the restaurant?

R. Mi amigo, tanta molestia; pero ¿por qué lo trae usted en vez de mandarlo con la muchacha del restorán?

F. Because she's not there; they say she's sick. Besides, it's no trouble.

F. Porque no está; dicen que está enferma. Además, no es ninguna molestia.

R. Well, thanks a lot. By the way, Francisco, what day is today, Thursday or Friday?

R. Pues, muchas gracias, entonces. A propósito, Francisco, ¿qué día es hoy, jueves o viernes?

F. Friday, all day. Are you writing to someone, Don Rafael?

F. Viernes, todo el día. ¿Le escribe a alguien, don Rafael?

R. Yes, to my niece who lives in Mexico. I'm writing to congratulate her on her birthday this month.

R. Sí, a mi sobrina que vive en México. Le escribo para felicitarla por su cumpleaños este mes.

F. What a thoughtful [so good] uncle you are! I've got lots of relatives abroad, but I never write to them.

F. ¡Qué tío tan bueno es usted! Yo tengo muchos parientes en el extranjero pero nunca les escribo.

R. I don't either, except to this niece. You see I'm her *padrino* [godfather].

R. Yo tampoco, excepto a esta sobrina. ¿No ve que soy su padrino? (2)

F. Oh well, that's different [another thing]. Now I understand. How old is [what age has] she?

F. Ah, bueno; eso es otra cosa. Ahora entiendo. ¿Qué edad tiene ella?

R. She must be around twenty-one [have some twenty-one years]. She's been living there about four years. She's married to a Mexican.

* * *

F. Speaking of dates, October 4 is a holiday, St. Francis' Day, remember?

R. Yes, and it's your saint's day, too. Do you expect to celebrate like last year?

F. No, this time we're planning to have [make] a dinner. How about you and your wife—can you come?

R. Sure we can; delighted. But it's still two weeks off [are lacking]. What day is it [does it fall]?

F. I think Tuesday—let me see: Sunday is the first, Monday the second; no, it's on Wednesday. You know where we live?

R. I know that you live near Central Park, but I don't remember the exact address.

F. Very easy; it's not far. You go [follow; continue] straight up North Avenue till you come to Twentieth Street, and then . . .

R. Now I remember: then I turn right and go three more blocks, the last house on the left, right?

R. Debe tener unos veintiún años. Hace como cuatro años que vive allá; está casada con un mexicano.

* * *

F. Hablando de fechas, el 4 de octubre es día feriado, día de San Francisco, ¿recuerda?

R. Sí, y es el día de su santo (3), también. ¿Piensa celebrarlo como el año pasado?

F. No, esta vez pensamos hacer una comida. Usted y su señora (4), ¿pueden venir?

R. Claro que podemos; encantados. Pero todavía faltan dos semanas. ¿Qué día cae?

F. Creo que martes; déjeme ver: el domingo es primero, lunes dos . . . No, cae miércoles. ¿Usted sabe dónde vivimos?

R. Yo sé que viven cerca del Parque Central pero no recuerdo la dirección exacta.

F. Muy fácil; no está lejos. Usted sigue derecho por la Avenida Norte hasta llegar a la Calle Veinte, y luego . . .

R. Ya recuerdo: ahí doblo a la derecha y sigo tres cuadras más; la última casa a la izquierda, ¿verdad?

F. That's it, a small green house on the corner.

F.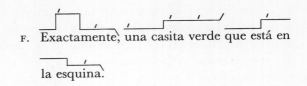
Exactamente, una casita verde que está en la esquina.

Cultural Notes

(1) **Don** is a title of respect used with the given name of a man. As a form of address, its use parallels that of the feminine **doña** (see Unit 2, Cultural Note 1).

(2) The **padrino,** sponsor for a child at baptism, is a regular feature of Hispanic life. The relationship of the **padrino** to his godchild (**ahijado** or **ahijada**) may vary from the merely nominal to the actual assumption of certain responsibilities toward the child. A set of specific family relationships with the child's parents may also be implied.

(3) The Catholic calendar is full of saints' days, and people who are named for saints ordinarily celebrate their saint's day. In practice, this means that all men bearing the given name Francisco, for example, will celebrate **el día de San Francisco** (St. Francis' day), October 4. Certain saints' days are recognized as national holidays in some countries.

(4) The equivalents for *wife* are **señora, esposa,** and **mujer.** In referring to his own wife, a gentleman often uses **esposa,** and sometimes **mujer.** In referring to someone else's wife, he is likely to use the more formal **señora.**

● PRONUNCIATION EXERCISE

A. /d/ and /r/ between vowels. INSTRUCTIONS: Repeat the following pairs of words just as you hear them.

[đ]	[r]	[đ]	[r]
cada	cara	pida	pira
codo	coro	seda	sera
lodo	loro	todo	toro
mida	mira	oda	hora
modo	moro	hada	ara
mudo	muro		

The Spanish fricative [đ] is similar to the voiced *th* in English *this,* though pronounced much more laxly. Spanish [r] is similar to English [d] in words like *reader, rider.* A stop [d] rather than a fricative [đ] between vowels in a Spanish word might be interpreted by the Spanish ear as an [r] sound. Thus Spanish **todo** (*all, every*) if incorrectly pronounced with a stop [d] between vowels, might be heard by a native Spanish speaker as **toro** (*bull*). To avoid this kind of misunderstanding, be sure to use the fricative [đ] between vowels in Spanish.

B. /r/ and /ʀ/. INSTRUCTIONS: Repeat the following pairs of words just as you hear them.

[r]	[ʀ]	[r]	[ʀ]
caro	carro	fiero	fierro
cero	cerro	torero	torrero
coro	corro	amara	amarra
foro	forro	serete	se rete
mira	mirra	seraje	se raje
para	parra	seronda	se ronda
pero	perro	serosa	se rosa
vara	barra		

The Spanish voiced alveolar tap [r] is spelled **r** between vowels, while the voiced alveolar multiple trill [ʀ] is spelled **rr,** as in the preceding list of words. When initial in a word, or when following [n], [l], or [z] (i.e., the variant of /s/ before the voiced consonant), only the multiple trill [ʀ] is found, and in these positions, it is spelled **r.**

At the end of a syllable, either [r] or [ʀ] may be heard, both of which are spelled **r.** (You may sometimes hear a fricative type of alveolar sound [ɹ] at the beginning or at the end of a word. The multiple trill [ʀ] can always be substituted for the fricative sound.)

15 Present tense of –*er* and –*ir* verbs

EXAMPLES

A. 1. **Creo** que martes (from **creer** *to think, believe*).
   2. Nunca les **escribo** (from **escribir** *to write*).

B. 1. **Debe** estar en la cocina (from **deber** *must, ought*).
   2. ¿Le **escribe** a alguien, don Rafael?
   3. Mi sobrina que **vive** en México (from **vivir** *to live*).

C. 1. **Comemos** en casa (from **comer** *to eat*). *We eat at home.*
   2. ¿Usted sabe dónde **vivimos?**

D. **Viven** cerca del Parque Central.

	comer *to eat* **com–**	**vivir** *to live* **viv–**
I (eat, live)	**–o**	
you	**–es**	
you he, she, it	**–e**	
we	**–emos**	**–imos**
you they	**–en**	

Except in the forms corresponding to *we*, **–er** and **–ir** verbs have the same endings in the present tense.

● PERSON-NUMBER SUBSTITUTION DRILL

1. *Rafael* nunca come en el restorán de la esquina.
   (ellos, nosotros, usted, tú, él, Pepe, mi señora y yo, Cecilia)
2. *Yo* creo que es la última vez.
   (Olga, mis abuelos, nosotros, ustedes, Susana, tú, ellos)
3. Debo estar equivocado esta vez.
   (él, tú, Julio, Susana, nosotros, ellos, nosotras, ellas, alguien)

4. *Ella* vive muy cerca del Parque Central.
   (Francisco y su señora, yo, mis padres, mi padrino, tú, ella, mi señora y yo, la profesora)
5. Le escribo a un pariente en el norte.
   (él, nosotros, mi papá, Francisco, ellos, mi compañero de escuela)
6. *Mi tía* nunca abre esta puerta.
   (yo, mi mamá, ellos, nosotros, tú, usted, doña Mercedes, ellas)

INSTRUCTIONS: Answer the following questions by selecting one of the alternatives proposed in each question.

1. TEACHER: ¿Usted come en el restorán o en casa?
   STUDENT: **Como en casa.**

2. ¿Usted cree que son dos cuadras o tres?
3. ¿Usted vive en una calle o en una avenida?
4. ¿Viven ustedes cerca o lejos del parque?
5. ¿Vive su sobrina aquí o en el extranjero?

6. ¿Le escribe usted a su padrino para su cumpleaños o para el día de su santo?
7. ¿Abre usted primero el libro de inglés o el libro de español?

● TRANSLATION DRILL

1. We eat here.
2. We live here.
3. We write here.
4. We open here.

5. He eats here.
6. He lives here.
7. He writes here.
8. He opens here.

16   Verbs with changes in the stem: $o \rightarrow ue$, $e \rightarrow ie$, $e \rightarrow i$

EXAMPLES

A. 1. No **recuerdo** el color exacto. *I don't remember the exact color.*
   2. Tal vez **puedo** ir.

B. 1. ¿**Puedes** traer tu tocadiscos?
   2. ¡Qué ideas **tienes!**
   3. ¿Por qué no **vienes?**

C. 1. Es día de San Francisco, ¿**recuerda?**
   2. ¿**Puede** mandarme una taza de café?
   3. ¿**Piensa** celebrarlo como el año pasado?
   4. ¿No **quiere** venir conmigo, don Rafael?
   5. Ella **tiene** uno portátil.

D. 1. Claro que **podemos.**
   2. Esta vez **pensamos** hacer una comida.

E. 1. Usted y su señora, ¿**pueden** venir?
   2. ¿No **tienen** ustedes uno allá?

recordar *to remember*	pensar *to intend, think about*
recuerdo	pienso
recuerdas	piensas
recuerda	piensa
recordamos	pensamos
recuerdan	piensan

poder *to be able, can*	querer *to wish, want*
puedo	quiero
puedes	quieres
puede	quiere
podemos	queremos
pueden	quieren

Certain verbs, to be learned from observation, change the last vowel of the stem in the forms shown: **o** becomes **ue** and **e** becomes **ie.**

tener *to have*	venir *to come*
tengo	vengo
tienes	vienes
tiene	viene
tenemos	venimos
tienen	vienen

The verbs **tener** and **venir** are like the other verbs with changes in the stem, except that in the first-person singular (the form corresponding to **yo** *I*) they have a different kind of irregularity.

EXAMPLES
1. **Sigo** tres cuadras más.
2. Te **pido** un favor. *I'm asking you a favor.*
3. Usted **sigue**[1] derecho por la Avenida Norte.

pedir *to request, ask for*
pido
pides
pide
pedimos
piden

A few **–ir** verbs change **e** to **i** in the forms shown.

● PERSON-NUMBER SUBSTITUTION DRILL

A. 1. *Nosotros* no recordamos el número exacto.
   (Julio, ellos, yo, mi profesor, ustedes, tú, Gloria)
   2. *Nosotros* podemos celebrarlo con una comida.
   (tú, don Rafael, mis tíos, yo, Pepe y yo, ella, ellas)

B. 1. Pensamos regresar el lunes o el martes.
   (yo, él, tú, Pablo y yo, Pablo y usted, Susana, ellos)
   2. Entendemos algo, pero no todo.
   (el señor, tú, María Elena, yo, Olga y yo, él, ustedes)
   3. Queremos una casita verde con una puerta negra.
   (yo, mi señora, tú, Cecilia, ustedes, usted, mi señora y yo)

4. *Nosotros* nunca cerramos excepto el domingo.
   (el señor Arjona, yo, ustedes, él, tú, mi hermano y yo)

C. 1. Hoy no tengo mucha hambre.
   (tú, ellos, mi hijo, nosotros, usted, ustedes, ella)
   2. Vengo el miércoles o el jueves.
   (él, ellos, doña Mercedes, nosotros, tú, mi hermana casada, ellas)

D. 1. Después de un rato seguimos.
   (yo, ellos, el señor Flores, él y yo, tú, ustedes, él)
   2. Pedimos una taza de café.
   (tú, él, mis padres, yo, ustedes, ella, alguien)

● CHOICE-QUESTION RESPONSE DRILL

A. 1. ¿Puede usted comer en quince minutos o en media hora?
   2. ¿Recuerda usted el número del teléfono o el número de la casa?

3. ¿Recuerdan ustedes la dirección o la fecha?

---

[1] The spelling **gu** before **e** and **i** represents the same sound as the spelling **g** before **a**, **o**, or **u**. In other words, the **u** is "silent," as in the English words *guess, rogue, beguile.*

B. 1. ¿Quiere café o leche?
    2. ¿Quiere poquito azúcar o mucho?
    3. ¿Piensa estar en México una semana o
       un mes?
    4. ¿Entienden ustedes una parte o todo?
    5. ¿Quiere usted ir primero o después?
    6. ¿Piensa doblar a la izquierda o a la
       derecha?
    7. ¿Cierra usted primero o después?
    8. ¿Quieren oir el joropo o un disco nuevo?

C. 1. ¿Tiene que ir a la casa de Olga o puede
       usar el teléfono?
    2. ¿Su hija tiene catorce o quince años?
    3. ¿Viene la muchacha el jueves o el
       viernes?

D. 1. ¿Piden ustedes un libro fácil o un disco
       aburrido?
    2. ¿La muchacha todavía sigue enferma,
       o ya está bien?

● DISCUSSION

In verbs with changes in the stem, the change is associated with stress. In the present tense, the changes o → ue, e → ie, and e → i occur only when that vowel is stressed. For example, we have i in **pido** but e in **pedimos** because in **pido** the i is stressed, while in **pedimos** the e is not stressed because the stress has shifted to the ending.

17 Present with future meaning

EXAMPLES A. 1. ¿**Abro** la puerta? *Shall I open the door?*
              2. ¿Le **mandamos** una taza de café? *Shall we send you up a cup of coffee?*

          B. 1. Después **estudiamos.**
              2. Yo **llamo** más tarde.
              3. Nosotros **pasamos** por ti.
              4. Ellos lo **hacen,** entonces. *They'll do it, then.*

FUTURE	PRESENT
shall I . . . ?	–o
shall we . . . ?	–amos –emos –imos

The present tense of the first person is used where English has the future with *shall* to ask instructions.

FUTURE	PRESENT
we'll study	**estudiamos**
I'll call	**llamo**
we'll come by	**pasamos**
he'll eat	**come**
they'll write	**escriben**
etc.	etc.

The present tense is also used where the speaker offers or agrees to a future action.

● TRANSLATION DRILL

A. 1. TEACHER: Afterwards, we'll study.
       STUDENT: **Después estudiamos.**
    2. Afterwards, we'll work.
    3. Afterwards, we'll celebrate.
    4. Afterwards, we'll talk.
    5. Afterwards, we'll eat.
    6. Afterwards, we'll write.
    7. Afterwards, we'll come by for you.
    8. Afterwards, we'll bring the record player.
    9. Afterwards, we'll send the coffee.

B. 1. I'll call later.
       Yo llamo más tarde.
    2. I'll arrive later.

    3. I'll leave later.
    4. I'll be back later.
    5. I'll come later.
    6. I'll enter later.

C. 1. But she'll be back in ten minutes.
       Pero regresa dentro de diez minutos.
    2. But she'll call in ten minutes.
    3. But she'll arrive in ten minutes.
    4. But she'll open the door in ten minutes.
    5. But she'll send the message in ten
       minutes.
    6. But she'll write the invitation in ten
       minutes.

The present tense in Spanish is used more frequently than the present tense in English to express a future meaning:

1. As regularly as in English for a *planned* future action: *She's returning (she'll be back) in ten minutes* **Regresa dentro de diez minutos;** *I work (plan to work, am working) here tomorrow* **Trabajo aquí mañana.**

2. Regularly, and hence more often than in English, to ask for instructions (examples *A*): *What do I (shall I) ask for now?* **¿Qué pido ahora?** *Shall we (less likely do we) send you up a cup of coffee?* **¿Le mandamos una taza de café?**

3. Regularly, and hence unlike English, for *unplanned* actions that one proposes or offers on the spur of the moment (examples *B*). The English meaning *can* is appropriate here: *I'll call (I can just as well call) later* **Yo llamo más tarde;** *We'll study (we can study) later* **Después estudiamos.**

The present is possible here because the context makes the future meaning clear. Note the frequency of adverbs of time such as **más tarde, después, mañana** *tomorrow,* etc.

18 The with-verb pronouns

EXAMPLES

A. **Déjeme** ver.
B. **Te** felicito. *I congratulate you.*
C. 1. ¿Por qué **lo** trae usted en vez de mandar**lo?**
   2. Le escribo para felicitar**la.**

D. **Nos** conocen. *They know us.*
E. 1. **Los** invita a entrar.
   2. **Las** recuerdo. *I remember them.*

DIRECT OBJECTS					
me	**me**		us		**nos**
you	**te**				
you him it	MASC.	**lo**	you them	MASC.	**los**
you her it	FEM.	**la**	you them	FEM.	**las**

With-verb pronouns are always joined, in speech, to a verb. Normally they precede the verb, but with the infinitive and with affirmative commands they follow.

● CONSTRUCTION SUBSTITUTION DRILL

A. INSTRUCTIONS: Repeat the following sentences just as you hear them. Then say them again, substituting a with-verb pronoun for the appropriate noun.

1. TEACHER: Pablo ve la casa. *Repita.*
  STUDENT: **Pablo ve la casa.**
  TEACHER: *Cambie.*
  STUDENT: **Pablo la ve.**
  Pablo ve el número.
  Pablo lo ve.
  Pablo ve las calles.
  Pablo las ve.
  Pablo ve los colores.
  Pablo los ve.

2. Yo no tengo *el recado.*
  (la invitación, el tocadiscos, la lista, el café, la dirección, las tazas, el azúcar, los discos)

3. Tampoco necesitas *el libro.*
  (la dirección, el café, la leche, las tazas, la clase, los cuartos, la sala, el total)

4. No recuerdo *el número.*
  (la fecha, el mes, la edad, el día, las semanas, los años, la entrada, el comedor, la avenida, las calles, la dirección, el cumpleaños, las horas, el color)

5. ¿Puedes usar *la invitación?*
   (el joropo, la casa, los discos, el teléfono, la hora, el tocadiscos)
6. Quiero ver *el libro.*
   (la esquina, las calles, la avenida, los discos, las invitaciones, la puerta, el patio, las casas, los cuartos)
7. Pensamos traer *la lista.*
   (el disco, la invitación, las cosas, las direcciones)
8. Rafael va a dejar *los libros.*
   (el número, la dirección, los joropos, el recado, las tazas, los discos)

B. INSTRUCTIONS: The teacher will make the following comments to various students, who will respond with the appropriate comment as indicated in the model.

1. TEACHER: Yo no tengo el libro.
   STUDENT: **Tampoco lo tengo yo.**

   (la invitación, los discos, las cosas, el número, los cafés, la leche, las tazas, el recado)

● PATTERNED RESPONSE DRILL

INSTRUCTIONS: Give negative answers to the following questions, using a with-verb pronoun to refer to the noun in the question.

A. 1. TEACHER: ¿Recuerda la dirección?
      STUDENT: **No, no la recuerdo.**
   2. ¿Celebra su cumpleaños?
      No, no lo celebro.
   3. ¿Abre la puerta?
   4. ¿Quiere el teléfono?
   5. ¿Entiende el libro?
   6. ¿Manda los discos?
   7. ¿Pide la comida?
   8. ¿Entiende la idea?

B. 1. ¿Puede traer el tocadiscos?
      No, no puedo traerlo.
   2. ¿Quiere ver la puerta?
      No, no quiero verla.
   3. ¿Piensa estudiar el libro?
   4. ¿Desea dejar la invitación?
   5. ¿Va a celebrar el cumpleaños?
   6. ¿Necesitas saber la dirección?

● TRANSLATION DRILL

A. 1. The book? I haven't got it.
   2. The records? I haven't got them.
   3. The invitation? I haven't got it.
   4. The address? I haven't got it.
   5. The messages? I haven't got them.
   6. The number? I haven't got it.
   7. The lists? I haven't got them.
   8. The milk? I haven't got it.
   9. The coffee? I haven't got it.
   10. The meal? I haven't got it.
   11. The total? I haven't got it.
   12. The record player? I haven't got it.
   13. The dates? I haven't got them.
   14. The *joropos?* I haven't got them.

B. 1. Pablo wants to congratulate her.
   2. Pablo wants to congratulate him.
   3. Pablo wants to congratulate us.
   4. Pablo wants to congratulate me.
   5. Pablo wants to congratulate you.
   6. Pablo wants to congratulate you all.

C. 1. Do you want to wait for me?
   2. Do you want to wait for us?
   3. Do you want to wait for her?
   4. Do you want to wait for him?
   5. Do you want to wait for them?

EXAMPLES   1. Si **me** hace el favor. *(Please = if you do me the favor.)*
   2. No puedo mandar**te** el café. *I can't send you the coffee.*
   3. **Le** escribo para felicitar**la.** *(I'm writing her to congratulate her.)*
   4. No quieren hablar**nos.** *They don't want to talk to us.*
   5. **¿Les** abro la puerta? *Shall I open the door for them?*

INDIRECT OBJECTS			
me	**me**	us	**nos**
you	**te**		
you him her it }	**le**	you them }	**les**

The indirect object expresses a relationship that is usually expressed with *to* or *for* in English.   Indirect-object pronouns combine with the verb in the same way as direct-object pronouns.

● TRANSLATION DRILL

A. 1. I like the book.
   Me gusta el libro.
   2. He likes the book.
   3. We like the book.
   4. They like the book.
   5. You like the book.
   6. You all like the book.

B. 1. I like the books.
   2. He likes the books.
   3. We like the books.
   4. They like the books.
   5. She likes the books.
   6. You all like the books.
   7. You like the books.

C. 1. Who may I tell her is calling?
   2. Who may I tell them is calling?
   3. Who may I tell him is calling?

D. 1. You do me a favor.
   2. You do her a favor.
   3. You do them a favor.
   4. You do him a favor.
   5. You do us a favor.

E. 1. The professor's writing her.
   2. The professor's writing them.
   3. The professor's writing us.
   4. The professor's writing him.
   5. The professor's writing me.
   6. The professor's writing you all.
   7. The professor's writing you.

F. 1. He never opens the door for us.
   2. He never opens the door for her.
   3. He never opens the door for them.
   4. He never opens the door for me.
   5. He never opens the door for you all.
   6. He never opens the door for him.
   7. He never opens the door for you.

G. 1. Pablo can't speak to me.
   2. Pablo can't speak to us.
   3. Pablo can't speak to her.
   4. Pablo can't speak to them.

H. 1. She wants to tell us the truth.
   2. She wants to tell him the truth.
   3. She wants to tell me the truth.
   4. She wants to tell them the truth.
   5. She wants to tell you the truth.

I. 1. Julio is going to send me the records.
   2. Julio is going to send her the records.
   3. Julio is going to send them the records.
   4. Julio is going to send us the records.
   5. Julio is going to send you the records.
   6. Julio is going to send you-all the records.

J. 1. Susana plans to fix him a dinner.
   Susana piensa hacerle una comida.
   2. Susana plans to fix them a dinner.
   3. Susana plans to fix us a dinner.
   4. Susana plans to fix her a dinner.
   5. Susana plans to fix me a dinner.
   6. Susana plans to fix you a dinner.
   7. Susana plans to fix you all a dinner.

DIRECT			INDIRECT	
me	**me**			me
you	**te**			you
you, him, it (MASC.)	**lo**		**le**	you, him, her, it
you, her, it (FEM.)	**la**			
us	**nos**			us
you, them (MASC.)	**los**		**les**	you, them
you, them (FEM.)	**las**			

Direct- and indirect-object pronouns are the same in the **me, te, nos** forms, and different in the **l–** forms.

● TRANSLATION DRILL

1. I write (to) him.
   Le escribo.
   I write (to) her.
   Le escribo.
   I write it.
   Lo (la) escribo.

   I write (to) them.
   Les escribo.
   I write them (things).
   Los (las) escribo.

2. I say to (tell) him.
   I say to her.
   I say it.

   I say to them.
   I say them.

3. I speak to him.
   I speak to her.
   I speak it.

   I speak to them.
   I speak them.

● DISCUSSION

The with-verb ("conjunctive") pronouns are of two kinds, *direct* and *indirect*. English distinguishes direct and indirect objects by *position*. Thus in *Show me them* we know that *me* means "to me" because it precedes *them,* while in *Show them me* we know that *them* means "to them" because it precedes *me*. Spanish distinguishes direct and indirect objects *partially* by form: **me, te,** and **nos** are the same whether direct or indirect, while **le** is the indirect form corresponding to the direct **lo** and **la,** and **les** is the indirect form corresponding to the direct **los** and **las.**

In the third-person pronouns, agreement in gender and number follows a pattern similar to that of adjectives (see Unit 2 §6). The proper gender must be used even if the noun referred to is a thing rather than a person. Thus *I have it* referring to *cup* (**taza**) is **La tengo,** but *I have it* referring to *coffee* (**café**) is **Lo tengo.**

In English we can usually tell when an object is indirect by seeing whether we can add *to* or *for* to it. Thus *I am writing (**to**) **her** to congratulate her* has the first *her* as an indirect object and the second as a direct; and in *If you will do (**for**) **him** the favor* we know that *him* is indirect.

In writing, the with-verb pronouns are attached to the verb when they follow it. When they precede, they are written as separate words.

19 Possessive adjectives

EXAMPLES

A. 1. Estoy aquí, en **mi** cuarto.
   2. Compañeras de escuela de **mi** hermana.

B. 1. Sí, pero **tu** papá . . .
   2. ¡Qué bonita es **tu** casa!

C. 1. Aquí está **su** café.
   2. Soy **su** padrino.
   3. Usted y **su** señora, ¿pueden venir?

D. Abran **sus** libros.

ONE POSSESSOR	ONE THING POSSESSED	MORE THAN ONE THING POSSESSED	MORE THAN ONE POSSESSOR	ONE THING POSSESSED	MORE THAN ONE THING POSSESSED
my	**mi cuarto** **mi casa**	**mis cuartos** **mis casas**	our	**nuestro cuarto** **nuestra casa**	**nuestros cuartos** **nuestras casas**
your	**tu cuarto** **tu casa**	**tus cuartos** **tus casas**			
your his her its }	**su cuarto** **su casa**	**sus cuartos** **sus casas**	your their }	**su cuarto** **su casa**	**sus cuartos** **sus casas**

● ITEM SUBSTITUTION DRILL

1. ¿Dónde tienes tu *libro?*
   (casa, discos, cosas)
2. Aquí está mi *cuarto.*
   (sala, invitaciones, recados)

3. Su *sobrina* está en la casa.
   (hijo, padres, tías)
4. Nuestro *papá* es de los Estados Unidos.
   (abuela, tíos, primas)

● PATTERNED RESPONSE DRILL

INSTRUCTIONS: Answer the following questions after verifying the noun in an echo question.

TEACHER:	STUDENT:
A. 1. Señor, ¿dónde está mi libro?	¿Su libro? Está en el cuarto.
2. Señor, ¿dónde está su libro?	¿Mi libro? Está en el cuarto.
3. Señor, ¿dónde están mis tíos?	¿Sus tíos? Están en el cuarto.
4. Señor, ¿dónde están sus tíos?	¿Mis tíos? Están en el cuarto.
B. 1. Señores, ¿dónde está mi invitación?	¿Su invitación? Está en el cuarto.
2. Señores, ¿dónde está su invitación?	¿Nuestra invitación? Está en el cuarto.
3. Señores, ¿dónde están mis discos?	¿Sus discos? Están en el cuarto.
4. Señores, ¿dónde están sus discos?	¿Nuestros discos? Están en el cuarto
C. 1. Señor, ¿dónde están nuestros padres?	¿Sus padres? Están en el cuarto.
2. Señor, ¿dónde están nuestras hermanas?	¿Sus hermanas? Están en el cuarto.
3. Señor, ¿dónde están nuestros abuelos?	¿Sus abuelos? Están en el cuarto.
4. Señor, ¿dónde están nuestras sobrinas?	¿Sus sobrinas? Están en el cuarto.
D. 1. Señores, ¿dónde está nuestra invitación?	¿Nuestra invitación? Está en el cuarto.
2. Señores, ¿dónde está nuestro cónsul?	¿Nuestro cónsul? Está en el cuarto.
3. Señores, ¿dónde están nuestros compañeros?	¿Nuestros compañeros? Están en el cuarto.
4. Señores, ¿dónde están nuestras amigas?	¿Nuestras amigas? Están en el cuarto.

● TRANSLATION DRILL

A. 1. My house is on the corner.
   2. Their house is on the corner.
   3. Our house is on the corner.
   4. His house is on the corner.
   5. Your house is on the corner.

B. 1. Our parents just left.
   2. His parents just left.
   3. My parents just left.
   4. Your parents just left.
   5. Her parents just left.
   6. Their parents just left.

● DISCUSSION

The common possessive adjectives are those in the above table. Like the adjectives of Unit 2, they have singular and plural endings to agree with the nouns that accompany them: **mi-mis, tu-tus,** and **su-sus** are like **grande-grandes.** But only **nuestro** is like **bonito** in having different endings for masculine and feminine as well as for singular and plural.

20 Possession with *de*

EXAMPLES 1. Compañeras de escuela **de** mi hermana.
2. En casa **de** Olga.   (*At house of Olga.*)
3. ¿Tú eres amigo **de** ellas?
4. ¿De parte **de** quién?

The friend of my niece My niece's friend	**El amigo de mi sobrina**
A friend of my niece A friend of my niece's	**Un amigo de mi sobrina**
It's *her* friend (not his)	**Es el amigo de ella**
A friend of hers	**Un amigo de ella**

With all nouns, possession is shown by **de**. **De**, plus the pronouns **él, ella, usted**, and their plurals, is used for expressions of the type *a friend of hers*, and also to replace the possessive adjectives **su** and **sus** when the possessive in English is stressed.

● TRANSLATION DRILL

A. 1. My uncle's house is near the park.
2. My friend's school is near the park.
3. My brother's house is near the park.
4. My cousin's restaurant is near the park.

B. 1. They're friends of my sister's.
2. They're companions of my son's.
3. They're students of my uncle's.
4. They're daughters of my professor's.

C. 1. We're in Rafael's living room.
2. We're in my cousin's room.
3. We're in my family's restaurant.
4. We're at Olga's house.

D. 1. Is he a friend of theirs?
2. Is he a friend of yours?
3. Is he a friend of hers?
4. Is he a friend of his?

● DISCUSSION

Spanish has no device like the *'s* of English. Its place is taken by a construction with the preposition **de**.

The possessive adjective **su, sus** is rarely stressed in Spanish. When emphasis is desired, **su** and **sus** are replaced by **de** plus one of the forms that may readily be stressed: **él, ella, usted, ellos, ellas**, and **ustedes**.[1]

● COMBINED PATTERN REPLACEMENT DRILL

A. 1. **Olga debe tener mi libro ahora.**
2. Ustedes _____
3. _____ discos _____
4. _____todavía
5. Tú _____
6. _____ puedes _____
7. _____usar _____
8. _____ nuestro _____
9. Elena _____
10. _____primero
11. _____ quiere _____
12. _____tu _____
13. _____ teléfono _____
14. El _____
15. _____ cosas _____
16. _____después

17. _____ ver _____
18. _____ piensa _____
19. _____mis _____
20. _____traer _____
21. _____café _____
22. _____hoy
23. _____ necesita _____
24. _____invitación _
25. _____nuestras _____
26. _____mandar _____
27. Ellas _____
28. _____ desea _____
29. _____entonces
30. _____dejar _____
31. _____recado _____
32. _____algún _____

---

[1] A comparable substitution for **mi** and **tu** is treated in Unit 11 §60.

B. 1. **Por eso, le escribo para felicitarla.**
2. _____ les _____
3. _____ lo
4. _____ invitar ___
5. Además _____
6. _____ les _____
7. _____ hablo _____
8. _____ la
9. _____ conocer ___
10. Entonces _____
11. _____ las

12. _____ traer _____
13. _____ en vez de _____
14. _____ hablan _____
15. Sin embargo _____
16. _____ me _____
17. _____ esperar ___
18. _____ nos
19. A propósito _____
20. _____ llaman _____
21. _____ ver _____

● TRANSLATION REVIEW DRILL

The construction **acabar de** plus infinitive.

A. 1. TEACHER: She just left.
STUDENT: **Acaba de salir.**
2. She just arrived.
3. She just entered.
4. She just spoke.
5. She just passed.
6. She just returned.

B. 1. We just arrived.
2. We just entered.
3. We just passed.
4. We just returned.

C. 1. She just arrived.
2. We just arrived.
3. You just arrived.
4. I just arrived.
5. He just arrived.
6. They just arrived.

D. 1. She just opened the door.
2. She just used the telephone.
3. She just brought the list.
4. She just left the message.
5. She just studied the book.

E. 1. She just ate it.
2. She just remembered it.
3. She just sent it.
4. She just wrote it.
5. She just left it.

READING

El teléfono

J. *Juanito*   P. *Papá*

J. Papá, Pablo dice que el teléfono tiene mucha importancia.

P. Es verdad, hijo.

J. ¿Y por qué es el teléfono de tanta importancia?

P. Porque hay muchas cosas que uno puede hacer y decir por teléfono. Por ejemplo: si estoy malo, puedo llamar al[1] doctor Fernández.

J. ¿Y qué haces si el doctor Fernández no puede venir?

P. Llamo a otro doctor.

J. ¿Y si no puede venir el otro tampoco?

P. Entonces . . . Juanito, ¿no ves que estoy muy ocupado?

J. Perdón, papá. . . . . . . ¿Papá?

P. . . . . . . Sí, Juanito.

J. Cuando dos hombres[2] hablan por teléfono, habla primero uno y después el otro. Uno habla y el otro escucha.[3] Cuando mamá y Tía Julia hablan por teléfono, las dos hablan al mismo tiempo,[4] y ninguna escucha. Pero creo que se entienden[5] perfectamente. ¿Cómo puede ser eso?

P. Es que . . . es que las señoras son . . . son . . . muy inteligentes, hijo.

J. Papá, Pablo dice también que el teléfono es un servicio público. ¿Cómo sabemos eso?

P. Sabemos que eso es verdad porque . . . porque la compañía de teléfonos lo dice.

---

[1] regular contraction of **a el**   [2] *men*   [3] *listens*   [4] *at the same time*   [5] *they understand each other*

5

Problems of a Housewife

B. *Doña Beatriz*   R. *Rosa, Doña Beatriz's maid*
P. *Paquito, Doña Beatriz's son*   J. *Josefina, maid*

B. I can't go to the market today, Rosa. I have to see the new maid to explain her job to her.   You better go alone.

R. All right, ma'am. What shall I get [bring]?

B. Here's the list: beans, meat, bread, butter, vegetables, a dozen eggs, and some fruit.

Problemas de una dueña de casa

B. *Doña Beatriz*   R. *Rosa, criada de doña Beatriz*
P. *Paquito, hijo de doña Beatriz*   J. *Josefina, criada*

B. No puedo ir al mercado hoy, Rosa. Tengo que ver a la nueva criada para explicarle el oficio.   Mejor vaya usted sola.

R. Muy bien, señora.   ¿Qué traigo?

B. Aquí está la lista: frijoles, carne, pan, mantequilla, verduras, una docena de huevos y algunas frutas.

R. We're almost out of [there almost doesn't remain] lard and flour. Shall I put that on the list too?

B. All right, put down two kilos of each. Take the money; look here—this is fifty pesos. Don't lose it.

R. Don't worry, Doña Beatriz.

B. Another thing, don't let them put anything over on you [don't let yourself be given a cat for a hare]. Do the way I do; if you don't, [even with] a *hundred* pesos won't be enough [it won't reach].

R. Don't worry, ma'am; when it comes to bargaining, nobody beats me [wins on-me].

B. All right, don't be long. Get back as soon as [the soonest] you can. Remember we're having company [people] for dinner tonight.

R. Of course, ma'am. What shall we fix for dinner? What do you say to [how seems to you] a salad, roast beef, and ice cream for dessert?

B. Not roast beef; I prefer a more typical dish, since the guests are a foreign couple. Chicken and rice [rice with chicken], maybe.

* * *

P. Mama, come here so I can show you something. Look how I can walk on my hands.

R. Ya casi no queda manteca ni harina. ¿Pongo eso en la lista también?

B. Está bien, ponga dos kilos (1) de cada uno. Tome la plata; vea que son cincuenta pesos. No los pierda.

R. No tenga cuidado, doña Beatriz.

B. Otra cosa, no se deje dar gato por liebre (2). Haga como yo; si no, no alcanza ni con cien pesos.

R. No se preocupe, señora, que para regatear (3), a mí nadie me gana.

B. Bueno, no tarde mucho. Vuelva lo más pronto posible. Recuerde que esta noche viene gente a comer.

R. Cómo no, señora. ¿Qué hacemos de comida? ¿Qué le parece una ensalada, rosbif y helados de postre?

B. Rosbif no; prefiero un plato más típico porque los invitados son una pareja extranjera. Arroz con pollo (4), tal vez.

* * *

P. Mamá, ven acá (5) para enseñarte una cosa. Mira cómo camino con las manos.

B. Oh, Paquito, for goodness' sake, don't do that; you'll get the wall dirty with your feet. Put those toys away [in their place] and go play in the yard.

J. Ma'am, shall I sweep down here in the dining room first?

B. Yes, and then dust all the furniture. Be careful not to break anything.

P. Mama, give me ten centavos for a poor old man that's outside, will you?

B. I don't have any now, I'm busy. Paquito, good heavens, don't come in here with those [so] filthy shoes!

J. And what'll I do with these clothes they just brought? Shall I take them upstairs?

B. What? I can't hear anything. Please, Josefina, don't turn that radio up so loud. Better turn it off; we can't work with such a racket.

P. Maaama! A man wants to know if we have [says whether there are] any old clothes to sell!

B. Paquito, you're driving me crazy! Leave me alone [in peace]! Tell him we haven't any.

B. Ay, Paquito, por Dios, no hagas eso, que ensucias la pared con los pies. Pon esos juguetes en su lugar y ve a jugar al jardín.

J. Señora, ¿barro primero aquí abajo en el comedor?

B. Sí, y luego sacuda todos los muebles. Tenga cuidado de no romper nada.

P. Mamá, dame diez centavos para darle a un pobre que está ahí afuera, ¿quieres?

B. Ahora no tengo, estoy ocupada. ¡Paquito! ¡Caramba! ¡No entres con esos zapatos tan sucios!

J. ¿Y qué hago con esta ropa que acaban de traer? ¿La llevo arriba?

B. ¿Cómo? No oigo nada. ¡Por favor, Josefina, no ponga ese radio tan fuerte! Mejor apáguelo; no podemos trabajar con tal escándalo.

P. ¡Mamaaaaaa! ¡Dice un señor que si hay ropa vieja para vender!

B. ¡Paquito, me vuelves loca, déjame en paz! Dile que no hay.

Cultural Notes

(1) The metric system is employed throughout the Hispanic world. Thus weight is in **kilos** rather than *pounds,* distance is in **metros** or **kilómetros** rather than *yards* or *miles,* and the quantity of a liquid (e.g., milk, gasoline, etc.) is in **litros** rather than *quarts* or *gallons.*

(2) In **no se deje dar gato por liebre** (lit., "don't allow yourself to be given a cat for a hare"), the infinitive **dar,** without a preposition, has passive force. Compare English *too tough to eat* = *too tough to be eaten.* This construction is common after the verb **dejar.**

(3) **Regatear** *to bargain, haggle,* to bring down the price of an article below the figure quoted by a storekeeper. Haggling is a common practice, especially in markets and small stores and among sidewalk vendors where fixed prices are not taken seriously.

(4) Rice dishes are equally popular in Spain and Spanish America. Two such dishes are **arroz con pollo** and **paella,** both of which originated in Valencia, in the region of Spain on the Mediterranean coast, famous for the cultivation of rice.

(5) Two Spanish adverbs correspond to English here: **aquí** and **acá. Aquí,** the one more commonly used, is more definite in its reference; **acá** (**acá** resembles English *over here*) is often found in set phrases with the command forms of **venir.** See Cultural Note 6 in Unit 3.

● PRONUNCIATION EXERCISE

A. English and Spanish vowels. INSTRUCTIONS: Listen for the difference between the English and the Spanish vowels as an English speaker and a Spanish speaker say alternately the English and Spanish words.

English /ey/	Spanish /e/	English /ow/	Spanish /o/
day	de	low	lo
Fay	fe	no	no
Kay	que	so	so
lay	le	dough	do
may	me		
say	sé		

English /iy/	Spanish /i/	English /uw/	Spanish /u/
bee	vi	boo	bu
Dee	di	coo	cu
knee	ni	moo	mu
me	mí	pooh	pu
see	sí	soo	su
tea	ti	too	tu

In some positions, English vowels are automatically followed by a glide or semivowel. The related Spanish vowels are always short, simple, and tense. The preceding pairs illustrate the difference.

B. English and Spanish /l/. INSTRUCTIONS: Listen for the difference between the English and the Spanish [l] as an English speaker and a Spanish speaker say alternately the English and Spanish words.

English /l/	Spanish /l/
feel	fil
el	él
dell	del
hotel	hotel
tall	tal
coal	col
tool	tul

The principal difference between the English and the Spanish /l/ is that in the Spanish /l/ the back of the tongue is high in the mouth, but in the English /l/ it is usually low.

21 Present tense of irregular verbs

EXAMPLES A. 1. ¿**Pongo** eso en la lista?
2. ¿Qué **traigo?**
3. ¿Qué **hago** con esta ropa?
4. Yo **sé** que viven cerca del Parque Central.
5. **Voy** a ir a comer.

B. 1. Tú **conoces** a mamá.
2. ¿**Sabes** el número de su casa?

C. 1. ¿Qué le **parece** una ensalada?
2. **Cae** miércoles.
3. ¿Por qué lo **trae** usted?
4. **Hace** como cuatro años. *(It makes about four years.)*
5. ¿No **ve** que soy su padrino?
6. ¿Usted **sabe** dónde vivimos?
7. Ya que **va,** ¿puede traerme una taza de café?

D. ¿Qué **hacemos** de comida?

E. ¿Qué **hacen** los alumnos?

conocer *to know*	**parecer** *to seem*	**poner** *to put*	**salir** *to leave (depart)*	
conozco	parezco	pongo	salgo	
conoces	pareces	pones	sales	
conoce	parece	pone	sale	
conocemos	parecemos	ponemos	salimos	
conocen	parecen	ponen	salen	
caer *to fall*	**traer** *to bring*	**hacer** *to make, do*	**ver** *to see*	**saber** *to know*
caigo	traigo	hago	veo	sé
caes	traes	haces	ves	sabes
cae	trae	hace	ve	sabe
caemos	traemos	hacemos	vemos	sabemos
caen	traen	hacen	ven	saben

A number of verbs, mostly ending in –er, are regular in all forms of the present tense except the first-person singular.

dar *to give*	**ir** *to go*
doy	voy
das	vas
da	va
damos	vamos
dan	van

Dar is also irregular only in the first-person singular, and **ir** resembles it. Compare **soy** from **ser** and **estoy** from **estar.**

1. Pero *tú* no conoces a nadie en el extranjero.
   (yo, ella, nosotros, usted, ustedes, nadie)
2. ¿*Pablo* parece muy aburrido?
   (él, yo, usted, tú, Paquito)
3. *Mi mamá* nunca pone verduras en la lista.
   (mi tía, usted, nosotros, ella, yo, ustedes, él)
4. *Don Rafael* sale el domingo a las tres y media.
   (mi hermano y yo, mi hermana, tú, yo, Julio, usted, ellos)
5. No trae manteca ni mantequilla del mercado.
   (yo, las señoras, la muchacha, tú, ellas, nosotros, ella)
6. De comida hacemos una ensalada, rosbif y helados de postre.
   (mi mamá, yo, Susana, ellas, tú, Ana y yo, usted)
7. No veo nada en la última cuadra.
   (usted, ellos, nosotros, él, tú, ella, ustedes)
8. *Yo* no sé si está arriba o abajo.
   (Olga, ellas, nosotros, tú, María, las chicas, usted)
9. *Mi mamá* nunca le da café a Paquito.
   (ella, yo, ustedes, mi abuela, nosotros, tú, ellos)
10. *Ellos* van allá para celebrar los días feriados.
    (mi hermano, nosotros, usted, yo, ustedes, tú, él)

A. 1. TEACHER: ¿Sabe usted si está descompuesto?
      STUDENT: **No, no sé nada.**
   2. ¿Ve usted ese radio viejo?
   3. ¿Trae usted plata?
   4. ¿Sabe usted si el cuatro de octubre es feriado?
   5. ¿Hace usted algo por la tarde?
   6. ¿Pone usted muebles en el patio?
   7. ¿Da usted mucha ropa vieja?

B. 1. Pregúntele si usted los conoce.
      ¿Yo los conozco?
   2. Pregúntele si usted parece un loco.
      ¿Yo parezco un loco?
   3. Pregúntele si usted sale mucho.
   4. Pregúntele si usted hace la comida.
   5. Pregúntele si usted la pone ahí.
   6. Pregúntele si usted lo ve todo.
   7. Pregúntele si usted lo sabe.

C. 1. TEACHER: Pregúntele si él los conoce.
      STUDENT 1: **¿Tú los conoces?**
      STUDENT 2: **Claro que los conozco.**
   2. Pregúntele si él parece un loco.
   3. Pregúntele si él sale mucho.
   4. Pregúntele si él hace la comida.
   5. Pregúntele si él lo pone ahí.
   6. Pregúntele si él lo ve todo.
   7. Pregúntele si él lo sabe.

EXAMPLES
1. No **oigo** nada.
2. **Dice** un señor que si hay ropa vieja.
3. **Dicen** que está enferma.
4. ¿**Incluyen** el azúcar? *Do they include the sugar?*

decir *to say, tell*	oir *to hear*
digo	oigo
dices	oyes
dice	oye
decimos	oímos
dicen	oyen

incluir *to include*[1]
incluyo
incluyes
incluye
incluimos
incluyen

A few other verbs have additional irregularities.
Decir, except for **digo,** is like **pedir** (see Unit 4).

[1] Other verbs ending in –**uir** are like **incluir.**

1. *Yo* no digo que es la verdad.
   (él, ellos, nosotros, tú, usted, ustedes, ella)
2. *Yo* no oigo nada con ese escándalo.
   (nosotros, usted, ellos, tú, él, ustedes, ella)

3. *El* dice que si hay ropa vieja para vender.
   (ellos, ella, yo, nosotros, tú, usted, ustedes)
4. Aquí nunca oímos el ruido de la calle.
   (yo, ustedes, tú, usted, ellos, él, ellas)

● PATTERNED RESPONSE DRILL

A. 1. TEACHER: ¿Qué oye usted?
      STUDENT: **¿Yo?   No oigo nada.**
   2. ¿Qué oyes tú?
   3. ¿Qué oyen ustedes?
   4. ¿Qué oye él?
   5. ¿Qué oyen ellos?
   6. ¿Qué oye ella?

B. 1. ¿Qué dicen ustedes?
      Decimos que no.
   2. ¿Qué dicen ellos?
   3. ¿Qué dice Alicia?
   4. ¿Qué dices tú?
   5. ¿Qué dicen ellas?
   6. ¿Qué dice él?

● DISCUSSION

When an irregularity occurs in the present tense, it is most often in the first person singular. The verbs **tener** (with **tengo**) and **venir** (with **vengo**), studied in Unit 4, are members of this group of verbs.

Certain of the irregularities are systematic; for example, practically all verbs ending in –ecer and –ducir have the same irregularity in the first-person singular as **parecer: merecer** *to deserve, win* (with **merezco**), **pertenecer** *to belong* (with **pertenezco**), **producir** *to produce* (with **produzco**), etc. There are also derivatives, identical, except for a prefix, with the verbs studied: **hacer → deshacer** *to undo* (**hago → deshago**), **poner → componer** *to compose, repair* (**pongo → compongo**), etc.

22 Direct commands: the *usted*, *ustedes* forms

EXAMPLES

A. 1. **Tome** la plata.
   2. No se **deje** dar gato por liebre.
   3. No **tarde** mucho.   *(Don't delay much.)*
   4. No se **preocupe.**
   5. **Pasen** ustedes.

B. 1. No **coma** tanto.   *Don't eat so much.*
   2. **Sacuda** todos los muebles.
   3. **Abran** sus libros, por favor.

C. 1. **Recuerde** que esta noche viene gente a comer.
   2. **Cierre** la puerta, por favor.

D. 1. **Vuelva** lo más pronto posible.
   2. No los **pierda.**
   3. No **pida** eso.   *Don't ask for that.*

E. 1. No **tenga** cuidado.   *(Don't have worry.)*
   2. **Ponga** dos kilos de cada una.
   3. **Haga** como yo.
   4. **Vea** que son cincuenta pesos.   *(See that they are fifty pesos.)*

F. 1. No **sea** tan aburrido.   *Don't be so boring.*
   2. Mejor **vaya** usted sola.

	INFINITIVE	FIRST-PERSON SINGULAR PRESENT		SINGULAR COMMAND (usted)	PLURAL COMMAND (ustedes)
Regular –ar	hablar	habl–	–o	–e	–en
Regular –er and –ir	comer vivir	com– viv– }	–o	–a	–an
–ar with stem changes	recordar pensar	recuerd– piens– }	–o	–e	–en
–er, –ir with stem changes	volver perder pedir	vuelv– pierd– pid– }	–o	–a	–an
Verbs irregular in the first-person singular	conocer parecer tener venir poner salir caer traer hacer decir oir ver	conozc– parezc– teng– veng– pong– salg– caig– traig– hag– dig– oig– ve– }	–o	–a	–an

In almost all verbs the **usted** command is based on the first-person singular of the present tense: in –ar verbs the –o is replaced by –e and in –er and –ir verbs the –o is replaced by –a. The plural, or **ustedes,** command adds –n to the singular.

Irregularly formed commands

INFINITIVE	SINGULAR COMMAND	PLURAL COMMAND
dar	dé	den
estar	esté	estén
ser	sea	sean
ir	vaya	vayan
saber	sepa	sepan

● CONSTRUCTION SUBSTITUTION DRILL

INSTRUCTIONS: Repeat each statement as you hear it. Then make a command, following the models given.

A. 1. TEACHER: El señor[1] habla con el cónsul.
   STUDENT: **Señor, hable con el cónsul.**
   2. La señora acaba pronto.
   3. La señorita pasa a la sala.
   4. El señor entra en el comedor.
   5. La señora camina para el mercado.
   6. La señorita alcanza la fruta.
   7. El señor celebra su cumpleaños.

   8. La señora dobla a la izquierda.
   9. La señorita apaga el radio. *turn off*
   10. El señor estudia inglés.
   11. La señora habla muy fuerte.
   12. La señorita pasa por Susana. *come by for*
   13. El señor regresa el domingo.
   14. La señora toma la plata.
   15. La señorita usa el teléfono.

finish

---
[1] For the purpose of drilling commands, **señor, señora, señorita,** etc. will be used to cue the **usted, ustedes** forms.

B. 1. El señor no ensucia la pared.
   Señor, no ensucie la pared.
   2. La señora no llega tarde.
   3. La señorita no regatea tanto.
   4. El señor no tarda mucho.
   5. La señora no trabaja tanto.
   6. La señorita no apaga ese radio.

C. 1. Los señores pasan por los invitados.
   Señores, pasen por los invitados.
   2. Las señoras celebran sus cumpleaños.
   3. Las señoritas regresan dentro de cinco minutos.
   4. Los señores no ensucian la casa.
   5. Las señoras no esperan la comida.
   6. Las señoritas no estudian los domingos.

D. 1. El señor come en el restorán.
   Señor, coma en el restorán.
   2. La señora sacude los muebles.
   3. La señorita barre aquí abajo.
   4. El señor vende la casa.
   5. La señora vive con nosotros.

E. 1. El señor no come tanto.
   Señor, no coma tanto.
   2. La señora no cree eso.
   3. La señorita no rompe nada.
   4. El señor no vende pan.

F. 1. Los señores abren los libros.
   Señores, abran los libros.
   2. Las señoras comen algo.
   3. Las señoritas no sacuden los muebles aquí arriba.
   4. Los señores no escriben tanto.

G. 1. El señor recuerda la fecha.
   Señor, recuerde la fecha.
   2. La señora vuelve más tarde.
   3. La señorita juega en el jardín.
   4. El señor piensa bien.
   5. La señora no pierde la plata.
   6. La señorita no cierra la puerta.
   7. Los señores entienden bien.
   8. Las señoras siguen derecho.
   9. Las señoritas piden una docena de huevos.

H. 1. El señor no pone los pies en los muebles.
   Señor, no ponga los pies en los muebles.
   2. La señora viene acá.
   3. La señorita tiene mucho cuidado.
   4. Los señores traen café caliente.
   5. Las señoras no hacen tal escándalo.
   6. Las señoritas ven la plata.
   7. Los señores saben la verdad.
   8. La señorita no da nada al pobre.
   9. El señor está aquí a las tres.
   10. La señora oye bien.

● CHOICE-QUESTION RESPONSE DRILL

INSTRUCTIONS: Answer each of the following choice questions with a command.

A. 1. TEACHER: ¿Espero hasta el jueves o salgo ahora?
      STUDENT: **Espere hasta el jueves.**
   2. ¿Abro el libro o sigo con la clase?
   3. ¿Barro la cocina o sacudo los muebles?
   4. ¿Traigo café o hago una comida?
   5. ¿Hablo más fuerte o apago el radio?
   6. ¿Camino con las manos o juego en el jardín?
   7. ¿Llego a las cuatro o salgo ahora?
   8. ¿Vengo solo o traigo a mi sobrina casada?
   9. ¿Escribo a mi sobrina o voy al parque?

B. 1. ¿Vamos ahora o esperamos un rato?
   Vayan ahora.
   2. ¿Doblamos a la derecha o seguimos derecho?
   3. ¿Hacemos una comida o vamos a un restorán?
   4. ¿Entramos ahora o volvemos después?
   5. ¿Regateamos un poquito o salimos a la calle?
   6. ¿Estudiamos español o celebramos mi cumpleaños?
   7. ¿Vamos a la escuela o estudiamos en casa?
   8. ¿Usamos el teléfono o vamos allá?

● DISCUSSION

The **usted** command is used in situations that call for **usted** rather than **tú** (see Unit 2).

The subject pronouns **usted** and **ustedes** need not accompany the verb, but do accompany it more frequently than *you* accompanies the command in English. Using them makes the command somewhat less abrupt; example, **Pasen ustedes.** The usual position is after the verb.

23 Direct commands: the *tú* form

EXAMPLES A. 1. Mamá, **ven** acá.
2. **Pon** esos juguetes en su lugar.
3. **Dile** que no hay.
4. **Ve** a jugar al jardín.

B. 1. **Mira** cómo camino.
2. **Dame** diez centavos.
3. **Déjame** en paz.

C. 1. No **entres** con esos zapatos.
2. No **hagas** eso.

Affirmative commands, irregularly formed

INFINITIVE	STEM	COMMAND
tener	ten–	ten
venir	ven–	ven
poner	pon–	pon
salir	sal–	sal
hacer	hac–[1]	haz[1]
decir		di
ser		sé
ir		ve

Most verbs that are irregular in the **tú** command form simply use the stem as it appears in the infinitive. **Decir, ser,** and **ir** are exceptions.

Affirmative commands, regularly formed

THIRD-PERSON SINGULAR PRESENT = COMMAND		
habla	recuerda	conoce
toma	piensa	cae
come	vuelve	trae
cree	pierde	ve (from **ver**)
vive	pide	oye
escribe	sigue	da
		está
		sabe

Except for the verbs in the box preceding this one (**tener, venir,** etc.), the **tú** command form is the same as the third-person singular present. This includes verbs with stem changes and verbs that are in other respects irregular.

Commands with negative

NEGATIVE OR AFFIRMATIVE **usted** COMMAND	NEGATIVE **tú** COMMAND
(no) **pase**	no **pases**
(no) **cierre**	no **cierres**
(no) **abra**	no **abras**
(no) **vuelva**	no **vuelvas**
(no) **haga**	no **hagas**
(no) **sea**	no **seas**
(no) **dé**	no **des**

Without exception, the negative **tú** command is the same as the **usted** command with an added **–s.**

---

[1] Both **hac–** and **haz** represent the same pronunciation [ás]. See Unit 12, Writing Exercise.

INSTRUCTIONS: Repeat each statement as you hear it. Then make a command, following the models given.

A. 1. Ana[1] viene acá.
   Ana, ven acá.
   2. María tiene cuidado.
   3. Julio sale pronto.
   4. Mercedes hace la ensalada.
   5. Paquito pone los juguetes en su lugar.
   6. Cecilia dice la verdad.
   7. María Elena es buena.
   8. Olga va al jardín.

B. 1. Josefina habla fuerte.
   Josefina, habla fuerte.
   2. Beatriz acaba pronto.
   3. Pablo entra por aquí.
   4. Julio pasa a mi cuarto.
   5. Rosa espera un minuto.
   6. Elena lleva el azúcar a la cocina.
   7. Pepe cierra la puerta.
   8. Ana recuerda la dirección.
   9. Paquito juega en el jardín.
   10. María está aquí a las cinco.

C. 1. Pepe come carne.
   Pepe, come carne.
   2. Olga escribe más.
   3. Josefina barre aquí abajo.
   4. Rosa sacude los muebles.
   5. Pablo vive con los abuelos.
   6. Ana ve la avenida.
   7. Mercedes oye bien.

D. 1. Rosa no habla tanto.
   Rosa, no hables tanto.
   2. Susana no apaga el radio.
   3. Cecilia no gana cada vez.
   4. Betty no usa ese color.
   5. Ana no llega tarde.
   6. Paquito no ensucia el comedor.
   7. José no camina al norte.
   8. Olga no celebra los días feriados.
   9. María no falta el viernes.
   10. Paquito no camina con las manos.

E. 1. Ana no barre el lunes.
   Ana, no barras el lunes.
   2. Mercedes no pone el radio.
   3. Susana no escribe en la pared.
   4. Rosa no pierde la plata.
   5. Olga no trae ninguna fruta.
   6. Cecilia no sigue derecho.

F. 1. Josefina no viene este mes.
   Josefina, no vengas este mes.
   2. Rosa no sale hasta el martes.
   3. Olga no hace eso tampoco.
   4. Paquito no dice eso nunca.
   5. Ana no tiene tanto cuidado.
   6. Julio no va tan lejos.
   7. Pablo no pone la ropa en el comedor.

INSTRUCTIONS: Repeat each of the following affirmative commands. Then make them negative.

G. 1. Entra en la sala.
   No entres en la sala.
   2. Lleva la ropa.
   3. Dobla en esa esquina.
   4. Cierra la puerta.
   5. Vuelve a las cinco y media.
   6. Trae a tus parientes.
   7. Vende las frutas.

H. 1. Pon tus juguetes en su lugar.
   No pongas tus juguetes en su lugar.
   2. Haz la comida ahora.
   3. Ten cuidado.
   4. Di la verdad.
   5. Sé típico.
   6. Sal a las seis.
   7. Ve allá ahora.
   8. Ven conmigo.

INSTRUCTIONS: Repeat each of the following negative commands. Then make them affirmative.

I. 1. No camines con las manos.
   Camina con las manos.
   2. No hables con las chicas.
   3. No juegues en el patio.
   4. No llames a María Elena.
   5. No comas ahora.
   6. No abras la puerta.
   7. No vendas ese libro.
   8. No traigas todas estas cosas.

J. 1. No vengas esta noche.
   Ven esta noche.
   2. No pongas los pies ahí.
   3. No digas esas cosas.
   4. No salgas sin tu hermana menor.
   5. No hagas la comida hoy.
   6. No vayas a la escuela.
   7. No seas típico.
   8. No tengas cuidado.

---

[1] For the purpose of drilling commands, given names will be used to cue the **tú** forms.

● DISCUSSION

There are interlockings that furnish a key to most of the **tú** command forms:

1. The affirmative **tú** command form of the verbs **tener, venir, poner, salir,** and **hacer** is the same as the stem of the infinitive.

2. The affirmative **tú** command form of almost all other verbs is the same as the third-person singular of the present tense.

3. The negative **tú** command form for all verbs is the same as the **usted** command form with an added **–s.**

The **tú** commands are required in situations that call for **tú** rather than **usted.** The subject pronoun **tú** itself, however, is not commonly used with the verb unless it is emphasized, as in **Habla tú** *You talk* (***You** do the talking*).

In the plural, only the **ustedes** command form is used.

24 With-verb pronouns in commands

EXAMPLES

A. 1. **Dame**[1] diez centavos.
2. **Siéntense.**
3. Mejor **apáguelo**
4. **Dile** que no hay.

B. 1. No **me des** diez centavos.
   Don't give me ten cents.
2. No **se sienten.** *Don't sit down.*
3. Mejor no **lo apague.** *Better not turn it off.*
4. No **le digas** que no hay.
   Don't tell him there isn't any.
5. No **los pierda.**
6. No **se preocupe.**

AFFIRMATIVE	
verb	pronoun

NEGATIVE		
no	pronoun	verb

The with-verb pronouns follow the verb in affirmative commands and precede the verb in negative commands.

● CONSTRUCTION SUBSTITUTION DRILL

INSTRUCTIONS: Repeat each statement as you hear it. Then make a command, following the models given.

A. 1. El señor me deja ver.
   Señor, déjeme ver.
2. La señora me espera en la esquina.
3. La señorita me enseña español.
4. El señor me lleva a la dirección exacta.
5. La señora me explica el oficio.
6. La señorita me felicita por mi cumpleaños.

7. El señor me manda una taza de café negro.
8. La señora me vende una casa verde.
9. La señorita me escribe pronto.
10. El señor me dice una cosa.
11. La señora me cree.

B. 1. Paquito me deja en paz.
   Paquito, déjame en paz.
2. Ana me lleva al parque.
3. Mamá me da cinco centavos.
4. Elena me llama a las cinco.

5. Cecilia me invita el domingo.
6. José María me escribe todos los días.
7. Olga me quiere mucho.
8. Pablo me dice la verdad.

---

[1] In writing, the with-verb pronouns are attached to the verb when they follow but not when they precede. Also in writing, when the pronoun is attached to a verb whose stress is not on its last syllable, the accent mark is placed over the stressed syllable. This reflects the fact that the stress stays on that syllable.

INSTRUCTIONS: Repeat each of the following affirmative commands. Then make them negative.

C. 1. Déjeme solo.
    No me deje solo.
    2. Piénselo más.
    3. Llévenos a la escuela.
    4. Póngalos en la cocina.
    5. Tráigalo el domingo.
    6. Enséñeles el libro.
    7. Apáguelo, por Dios.
    8. Pídales perdón.
    9. Dígale que no hay.
    10. Véanlo ahí.
    11. Déjenlos aquí.
    12. Tráigalas el viernes.
    13. Celébrenlo como el año pasado.
    14. Denle un peso.

D. 1. Enséñame cómo caminas con las manos.
    No me enseñes cómo caminas con las manos.
    2. Explícanos el oficio ahora.
    3. Tráelos con leche.
    4. Apágalo, por favor.
    5. Dile que no hay nada.
    6. Felicítanos por la invitación.
    7. Véndeme la casa verde.
    8. Hazlo exactamente como la semana pasada.
    9. Ponlo todo en su lugar.
    10. Siéntate aquí.

● CHOICE-QUESTION RESPONSE DRILL

INSTRUCTIONS: Answer each of the following choice questions with first an affirmative command, then a negative command.

A. 1. TEACHER: ¿Traigo la lista o no, señor?
       STUDENT: **Tráigala. No la traiga.**
    2. ¿Llevo los frijoles o no, señor?
    3. ¿Cierro las puertas o no, señor?
    4. ¿Explico el oficio o no, señor?
    5. ¿Pongo el radio o no, señor?
    6. ¿Vendo el tocadiscos o no, señor?
    7. ¿Traemos el café o no, señor?
    8. ¿Rompemos los platos viejos o no, señor?
    9. ¿Sacudimos los muebles o no, señor?
    10. ¿Damos las gracias o no, señor?

B. 1. ¿Traigo los centavos o no, Pablo?
    Tráelos. No los traigas.
    2. ¿Estudio el libro o no, Ana?
    3. ¿Celebro mi cumpleaños o no, Mercedes?
    4. ¿Explico el recado o no, Elena?

C. 1. ¿Te escribo o no, Julio?
    Escríbeme. No me escribas.
    2. ¿Te hablo o no, Olga?
    3. ¿Te dejo o no, María?
    4. ¿Te enseño o no, Josefina?
    5. ¿Te espero o no, Rosa?
    6. ¿Te explico o no, Beatriz?
    7. ¿Te felicito o no, Betty?
    8. ¿Te invito o no, Rafael?
    9. ¿Te llamo o no, Francisco?
    10. ¿Te llevo o no, Pepe?
    11. ¿Te abro o no, Elena?
    12. ¿Te creo o no, José?
    13. ¿Te digo o no, Ana?
    14. ¿Te oigo o no, Pablo?
    15. ¿Te sigo o no, Mercedes?
    16. ¿Te traigo o no, Susana?
    17. ¿Te veo o no, Olga?

● TRANSLATION DRILL

A. 1. Sit down, gentlemen.
    2. Tell me the number, gentlemen.
    3. Send me a cup of coffee, sir.
    4. Bring me a salad, please.

B. 1. Leave me alone, Paquito.
    2. Bring us the book, Ana.
    3. Tell him there isn't any, Olga.
    4. Turn it off, Josefina.

C. 1. Don't lose them, Mr. Martínez.
    2. Don't tell him the truth, Miss Flores.
    3. Don't worry, Professor Arjona.
    4. Don't let them put anything over on you, Mrs. Fernández.

D. 1. Don't bring us your toys, Pepe.
    2. Don't give him the book, Julio.
    3. Don't sell it yet, Olga.
    4. Don't give me anything, Pablo.

● DISCUSSION

In all direct commands, whether of the **usted, ustedes,** or **tú** forms, the object pronoun follows the verb when the command is affirmative and precedes it when the command is negative.

As explained in Unit 3, the word **no,** when it appears with a verb, always immediately precedes the verb. Since object pronouns actually become a part of the verb expression, the word **no** precedes the combination of object pronoun plus verb.

25 The personal *a*

EXAMPLES

A. 1. Tengo que ver **a** la nueva criada.
   2. ¿Por qué no llamamos **a** María Elena?
   3. Tú conoces **a** mamá.

B. 1. Tome la plata.
   2. Ensucias la pared.
   3. Sacuda todos los muebles.

C. ¿Tú tienes nueve hermanos?

D. Dame diez centavos para darle **a** un pobre.

DIRECT OBJECTS
verb + **a** + personal noun
verb + nonpersonal noun
tener + any noun

INDIRECT OBJECTS
verb + **a** + any noun

The preposition **a** is put before a direct-object noun that refers to a definite person or to definite persons. The verb **tener**, however, does not usually require it. It is always put before an indirect-object noun.

● ITEM SUBSTITUTION DRILL

1. TEACHER: Tengo que ver a la nueva *criada. Repita.*
   STUDENT: **Tengo que ver a la nueva criada.**
   TEACHER: . . . *lista.*
   STUDENT: **Tengo que ver la nueva lista.**
   (profesora, escuela, alumna, casa, compañera, clase)

2. ¿Por qué no dejamos a las *chicas* en la casa?
   (radios, profesores, señoritas, doctores, discos, huevos)

3. Tengo ganas de oir ese *joropo.*
   (gente, tocadiscos, profesora, discos, criada, radio, morena)

4. Voy a esperar a mi *prima.*
   (clase, compañero, cumpleaños, hijo, postre, abuelo, ropa, tía)

5. No conozco el *parque.*
   (rubia, restorán, invitados, lugar, pareja, mercado, española)

6. Caramba, no veo a *Paquito.*
   (la casa, la plata, el número, las chicas, la ropa, los muchachos, la carne)

● TRANSLATION DRILL

1. TEACHER: I know the lady.
   STUDENT: **Conozco a la señora.**
   TEACHER: I know the house.
   STUDENT: **Conozco la casa.**

2. I prefer the more typical couple.
   I prefer the more typical dish.

3. I don't want to lose the boys.
   I don't want to lose the toys.

4. Besides, I want to bring the blonde.
   Besides, I want to bring the record player.

5. I'm waiting for the brunette.
   I'm waiting for the money.

6. I can't bring your godparents.
   I can't bring your things.

7. We're leaving the maid.
   We're leaving the book.

8. We're taking[1] the girl.
   We're taking the butter.

9. Who are we waiting for?
   What are we waiting for?

10. Do you take someone?
    Do you take something?

11. I don't see anybody.
    I don't see anything.

---

[1] Use **llevar,** the *take* that means "conduct, transport." **Tomar** is the *take* that means "get together with"—taking a meal, a pill, a train, etc.

The nouns in examples *A* and *B* above are all direct objects of verbs. Those in example *A*, however, refer to definite persons. Spanish marks objects of this kind by putting the preposition **a** before them.

The verb **tener** does not call for this **a**. It does not matter whether the object is personal or nonpersonal.[1]

An indirect-object noun, as in example *D*, always calls for **a**. Here the **a** generally corresponds to a *to* in English, either expressed or implied: **Le escribo *a* mi sobrina** *I write (to) my niece.*

● COMBINED PATTERN REPLACEMENT DRILL

A.	B.
1. **A propósito, Juan, no me traigas más ensalada.**	1. **No estoy enfermo; es que tengo mucha hambre.**
2. _____ mucha _____	2. _____ganas
3. _____ señor _____	3. _____ malo _____
4. _____ manden _____	4. _____años
5. _____ arroz	5. _____ tantos _____
6. _____ Ana _____	6. _____amigos
7. _____nos _____	7. _____ ocupado _____
8. Hablando de otra cosa _____	8. _____ por eso _____
9. _____ carne	9. _____cosas
10. _____ tanta _____	10. _____ casado _____
11. _____ señor _____	11. _____ muchas _____
12. _____ fruta	12. _____plata
13. _____ enseñe _____	13. _____ hago _____
14. _____ tantas _____	14. _____ruido
15. _____me _____	15. _____ solo _____
16. Si me hace el favor _____	16. _____ hay _____
17. _____ señora _____	17. _____ estamos _____
18. _____ carne	18. _____ ya que _____
19. _____ dé _____	19. _____criados
20. _____ verduras	20. _____ están _____
21. Por favor _____	
22. _____ helados	

● TRANSLATION REVIEW DRILL

Noun-adjective agreement.

1. It's a typical meal.
   It's a typical plate.
2. It's a pretty house.
   It's a pretty patio.
3. It's a new entrance.
   It's a new market.
4. It's a dirty kitchen.
   It's a dirty room.

5. It's an old cup.
   It's an old plate.
6. It's a foreign thing.
   It's a foreign book.
7. It's an American school.
   It's an American record.
8. It's a black door.
   It's a black market.

9. It's a crazy week.
   It's a crazy year.
10. It's a married (girl) student.
    It's a married (boy) student.
11. It's a sick (girl) friend.
    It's a sick (boy) friend.

---

[1] The meaning of **tener,** like that of English *have,* often emphasizes "existence" rather than "possession." When the speaker says **Tengo una sobrina** *I have a niece* he calls attention to the existence of this person so related to him: "There is a niece where I am concerned." But if the speaker views the object as someone whose existence is already established, the **a** is called for: **Tengo a mi sobrina conmigo** *I have my niece with me.*

Conversación en un restorán

PAQ. *Paquito*   P. *papá de Paquito*

MO. *Mozo*   M. *mamá de Paquito*

PAQ. Papá, tengo mucha hambre; quiero arroz con pollo, rosbif, frijoles, un huevo . . .

P. ¡Dios mío, Paquito, tú no te vas[1] a comer todo eso!

PAQ. ¿Por qué no, papá?

P. Porque te vas a enfermar.[2] . . . En primer lugar, no debes pedir tanta carne. Quieres ser tan grande como yo, ¿verdad?

PAQ. No, papá.

P. ¿No? ¿Y por qué?

PAQ. Tú estás muy gordo.[3]

M. ¡Paco, no hables así[4] a tu padre!

PAQ. Pero, mamá, tú le dices siempre[5] que . . .

M. Yo a papá, sí, pero tú eres un niño,[6] y . . . ya viene el mozo,[7] gracias a Dios . . .

MO. Buenas tardes, señores.

M. Buenas tardes. El menú, por favor. Pero primero, leche para el niño, que tiene mucha hambre.

MO. Muy bien, señora.

PAQ. . . . Mamá, ¿quién es esa señora bonita?

M. ¿Cuál?

PAQ. La señora que mira a papá.

P. Pues . . . ejem.

M. Hmm . . .

PAQ. Papá, ¿por qué miran los hombres a las señoritas bonitas?

P. (*mirando a mamá*) Bueno . . . como admiran una pintura[8] . . . es cuestión de arte . . . Ah, aquí viene el mozo. Yo también tengo mucha hambre.

---

[1] *aren't going*   [2] *you'll get sick*   [3] *too fat*   [4] *like that*   [5] *always*   [6] *child*   [7] *waiter*   [8] *painting*

Traffic Row

F. *Fernando* R. *Roberto, Fernando's friend* M. *Don Miguel, Traffic Chief* P. *Patricio, Don Miguel's brother-in-law*

F. Why are you looking so glum? Did you get some bad news?

R. I'm not glum, I'm mad. I've just had a big row with the police.

F. Don't tell me! What happened this time?

R. I went the wrong way on a one-way street [put myself . . . against the traffic].

Lío de tráfico

F. *Fernando* R. *Roberto, amigo de Fernando* M. *Don Miguel, Jefe de Tránsito* P. *Patricio, cuñado de don Miguel*

F. ¿Recibiste alguna mala noticia, que te veo con esa cara tan triste?

R. No estoy triste, estoy furioso. Acabo de tener un tremendo lío con la policía (1).

F. No me digas. ¿Qué pasó esta vez?

R. Es que me metí en una calle en contra del tránsito.

F. What! Where?

R. At that darned corner by the National Theater.

F. But man, didn't you see the arrow?

R. What arrow! Afterwards, they showed me one about five meters up on a wall.

F. Calm down, boy. That's nothing serious.

R. Nothing serious? I not only stopped all the traffic, but this dumb policeman came up, who didn't understand me at all, and we had an argument.

F. Hm. Maybe you didn't understand *him*.

R. Anyway [be that as it may], we didn't understand each other. And it was all his fault.

F. Well, but what else happened?

R. They took [from me] all my papers and fined me [required a fine]. What a system!

F. Did you pay it?

R. No, as a big favor they gave me till tomorrow to pay it.

F. Don't worry. I have a friend who's related to the Traffic Chief. I'll call him this afternoon.

F. ¡Cómo! ¿En qué parte?

R. En esa bendita esquina del Teatro Nacional (2).

F. Pero hombre, ¿no viste la flecha?

R. ¡Qué flecha! Después me mostraron una como a cinco metros en una pared (3).

F. ¡Cálmate, chico! Eso no es nada serio.

R. ¿Nada serio? No sólo paré todo el tráfico, sino que llegó este policía medio bruto que no me entendió nada y nos peleamos.

F. Hmm. Tal vez no le entendiste tú.

R. Sea lo que sea, no nos entendimos. Y todo por culpa de él.

F. Bueno, pero ¿qué más sucedió?

R. Que me quitaron mis documentos (4) y me exigieron una multa. ¡Qué sistema!

F. ¿La pagaste?

R. No, como gran cosa me concedieron hasta mañana para pagarla.

F. No te preocupes. Yo tengo un amigo que es pariente del Jefe de Tránsito. Esta tarde lo llamo (5).

* * *   * * *

P. Hello. I'd like to speak to the Traffic Chief, please. This is his brother-in-law speaking.

P. Aló. Con el Jefe de Tránsito, por favor. Habla el cuñado de él.

M. Hello, I'm glad you called. When can I have a talk with you? A friend of mine wants to get a job at the Ministry.

M. Hola, qué bueno que llamaste. ¿Cuándo puedo hablar contigo? Un amigo mío quiere conseguir un empleo en el Ministerio.

P. Okay. Then what do you say we have dinner together tonight? By the way, I'm calling to ask you a favor.

P. Muy bien. Entonces, ¿qué te parece si comemos juntos esta noche? A propósito, te llamo para pedirte un favor.

M. Glad to help you.

M. A tus órdenes.

P. It seems that a boy who is a friend of mine, Roberto Salazar, had his papers taken away from him [from a boy . . . they took away . . .]. And tomorrow he has to pay a fine. He was just thoughtless [it was a piece of foolishness].

P. Es que a un muchacho amigo mío, Roberto Salazar, le quitaron los documentos y mañana tiene que pagar una multa. Fue una tontería.

M. Well, if you say so . . . I'll take care of [arrange] it and you tell him that tomorrow at 4 o'clock he can come by for his papers.

M. Bueno, si tú lo dices . . . Yo voy a arreglar esto, y que mañana a las cuatro puede pasar por sus papeles.

P. Thanks, old man. Give my regards to everybody.

P. Gracias, viejo. Saludos a todos.

M. Same for me. See you tonight then.

M. Igualmente. Hasta esta noche, entonces.

Cultural Notes   (1) When the noun **policía** is feminine, it means *police* (i.e., police force); when it is masculine (**el policía**) it means *policeman*. There are a number of feminine nouns in Spanish, all ending in **–a**, which when used with the article **el** or other masculine determiner (e.g., **un, este,** etc.), refer to a male person. Examples, in addition to **policía,** are: **la guardia** *the guard* (as a corps) vs. **el guardia** *the guard* (guardsman); **la escolta** *the escort* (a group, e.g., of ships or airplanes, accompanying, say, a convoy) vs. **el escolta** *the escort* (i.e., a man who accompanies a woman in public); **la ayuda** *the aid* (i.e., assistance) vs. **el ayuda** *the aide* (i.e., assistant).

(2) In the Hispanic world, it is considered quite normal for the government to subsidize cultural institutions, such as the theater and the orchestra. The **Teatro Nacional** is an example.

(3) Traffic signs, especially those indicating the direction in which traffic may move, are often informal. In many towns they are painted or attached to a wall. Since a painted sign may fade, or a sign attached to a wall may fall off, misunderstandings with the police are not unusual.

(4) In Latin America it is quite usual for a person, especially one planning to go from one country to another, to carry with him a number of documents or papers, as requested by the host country, which in addition to a passport might include birth, health, vaccination, and police certificates, and an identification card. The police certificate, which a person generally carries with him whether he leaves the country or not, serves as proof of good conduct.

(5) Personal contact or influence is often used in order to resolve a problem or achieve a goal. This working through acquaintanceship rather than through impersonal channels is sometimes termed **amiguismo** ("friend-ism"); it becomes in the political sphere what is termed **personalismo** ("personalism"), the extreme of which is government by men rather than by law.

● PRONUNCIATION EXERCISE

A. Minimal stress contrasts. INSTRUCTIONS: The teacher will read the following pairs of words. The student will repeat them just as he hears them.

calle (street)	callé (I was quiet)	libro (book)	libró (he freed)
jugo (juice)	jugó (he played)	pico (peak)	picó (it stung)
hablo (I speak)	habló (he spoke)	abra (open)	habrá (there will be)
ésta (this)	está (is)	ara (altar)	hará (he will do)
peso (monetary unit)	pesó (he weighed)		

In Spanish it is essential that the stresses be correctly placed when you speak. A misplaced stress is apt to give either a radically different meaning or nonsense.

B. Cognate stress patterns. INSTRUCTIONS: Listen for the difference in stress between the English and the Spanish cognates as an English speaker and a Spanish speaker say alternately the English and Spanish words.

1. *English* (́ –)	*Spanish* (– ́)	2. *English* (́ – –)	*Spanish* (– – ́)
action	acción	animal	animal
actual	actual	capital	capital
altar	altar	criminal	criminal
brutal	brutal	cultural	cultural
civil	civil	doctoral	doctoral
color	color	general	general
favor	favor	liberal	liberal
metal	metal	natural	natural

3. *English* (– ́ –)	*Spanish* (– – ́)	4. *English* (– ́ – –)	*Spanish* (– – – ́)
commission	comisión	activity	actividad
conversion	conversión	barbarity	barbaridad
decision	decisión	conformity	conformidad
informal	informal	facility	facilidad
judicial	judicial	particular	particular
official	oficial		
production	producción		
professor	profesor		

5.	*English* (− − ´ −)	*Spanish* (− − − ´)	6.	*English* (− − ´ − −)	*Spanish* (− − − − ´)
	artificial	artificial		opportunity	oportunidad
	universal	universal		possibility	posibilidad
	constitution	constitución		probability	probabilidad
	opposition	oposición		semicircular	semicircular
	revolution	revolución		sensibility	sensibilidad

The English and Spanish cognates given above illustrate a striking difference between the stress patterns of the two languages. Spanish tends to favor the latter part of a word, English the earlier part. Note also that in the Spanish words only one syllable is stressed and the stressed syllable is not lengthened the way it is in English.

26 Preterit of regular verbs and *dar*

EXAMPLES

A. 1. **Paré** todo el tráfico.
2. Qué bueno que **llamaste.**
   ¿La **pagaste?**
3. ¿**Qué pasó** esta vez?
   Llegó este policía.
4. Nos **peleamos.**
5. Después me **mostraron** una.
   Me **quitaron** mis documentos.

B. 1. Me **metí** en una calle en contra del tránsito.
2. ¿No **viste** la flecha?
   Tal vez tú no le **entendiste.**
   ¿**Recibiste** alguna mala noticia?
3. No me **entendió** nada.
   ¿Qué más **sucedió?**
4. No nos **entendimos.**
5. Me **concedieron** hasta mañana para pagarla.
   Me **exigieron** una multa.

C. Me **dieron** diez centavos. *They gave me ten cents.*

	−ar VERBS		**−er** AND **−ir** VERBS			**dar**	
	hablar		**comer**	**vivir**		**dar**	
	habl−		**com−**	**viv−**		**d−**	
	−é	−amos	−í	−imos[1]		−i	−imos
	−aste		−iste[1]			−iste	
	−ó	−aron	−ió[2]	−ieron[2]		−io	−ieron

The preterit of regular verbs and **dar** is formed by attaching the above endings to the stem.

● PERSON-NUMBER SUBSTITUTION DRILL

1. *Los alumnos* llegaron a la clase.
   (nosotros, Cecilia, tú, usted, el profesor, Pablo y yo, ellos)
2. Entré en el cuarto de Julio.
   (José, nosotros, tú, don Rosario, ustedes, Pepe y yo, mis padres)
3. ¿Por qué no llamaron a María Elena?
   (tú, él, nosotros, usted, ellos, ella, yo)
4. *Francisco* les mandó una taza de café.
   (yo, tú, usted, nosotros, la muchacha, ellos, él)
5. Después, *Paquito* le enseñó una cosa.
   (los chicos, el profesor, yo, ellos, nosotros, tú)
6. Entonces caminamos hasta el Parque Central.
   (yo, él, ellos, el jefe, tú, ella, ustedes)

---

[1] In writing, verbs with stem ending in a vowel place the accent mark over the **i** of **−iste** and **−imos,** for example, **creíste, creímos,** from **creer** with stem **cre−.** This indicates that stress is on **i** and not on **e.**

[2] On verbs with stem ending in a vowel, the **−ió** and **−ieron** are spelled **−yó** and **−yeron,** for example, **creyó, creyeron** (from **creer**); **oyó, oyeron** (from **oir**); **incluyó, incluyeron** (from **incluir**). This does not reflect any necessary difference in sound, though some speakers of Spanish do produce a more fricative sound in **creyó,** for example, than in **comió.**

7. La semana pasada *Rosa* llevó las verduras al mercado.

    (nosotros, la muchacha, yo, ellos, tú, él, alguien)

8. *Mi cuñado* le explicó el sistema a la pareja extranjera.

    (nosotros, ellos, yo, tú, Susana y yo, ella, nadie)

9. *Yo* no comí mucho arroz con pollo en los Estados Unidos.

    (los invitados, Paquito, nosotros, usted, Susana y Betty, tú, la gente)

10. *Fernando* perdió todos los documentos y papeles.

    (yo, doña Beatriz, Rosa y Josefina, tú, nosotros, ustedes, un policía)

11. *Pablo* no vendió ni la manteca ni la mantequilla.

    (la muchacha, ellas, nosotros, tú, yo, la criada, usted)

12. Después volvieron al Teatro Nacional.

    (yo, el señor Salazar, tú, nosotros, los señores, Patricio, ustedes)

13. *El jefe* no entendió tal escándalo.

    (mi mamá, nosotros, doña Mercedes, yo, él, ellos, tú)

14. Ya perdí medio kilo de estos benditos frijoles.

    (Paco y yo, ellos, tú, nosotros, Josefina, ustedes, ella)

15. *La chica* rompió todos los platos.

    (las criadas, tú, usted, yo, María, nosotros, alguien)

16. Escribió para pedir un empleo en el ministerio.

    (ellos, Rafael, nosotros, usted, yo, tú, los alumnos)

17. *Un señor* vivió en esa casa.

    (nosotros, ellos, tú, yo, usted, mi señora y yo, unos pobres, un loco)

18. *Mamá* le dio diez centavos.

    (yo, un señor, tú, ellos, nosotros, ella, ustedes)

● TENSE SUBSTITUTION DRILL

INSTRUCTIONS: Repeat the following sentences just as you hear them. Then repeat each again changing the present-tense verb to preterit.

A. 1. TEACHER: No alcanza ni con cien pesos. *Repita*.

    STUDENT: **No alcanza ni con cien pesos.**
    TEACHER: *Cambie*.
    STUDENT: **No alcanzó ni con cien pesos.**

2. Rosa no se *deja* dar gato por liebre.
3. Josefina no *tarda* mucho en volver.
4. Esta tarde lo *llamo*.
5. Las madres *calman* a los chicos.
6. Una tontería, pero lo *arreglo*.
7. Todos *miramos* a las chicas bonitas.

B. 1. La cosa *parece* fácil.
2. Casi me *vuelves* loca.
3. La culpa del tremendo lío *cae* en el ministerio.
4. Las criadas *barren* abajo y afuera.
5. *Entendemos* muy bien al profesor.
6. *Sacudimos* muy bien todos los muebles.
7. Le *doy* dos pesos.

INSTRUCTIONS: Repeat the following sentences just as you hear them. Then repeat each again, changing the preterit forms to present tense.

C. 1. La criada *apagó* el radio.
2. Yo *caminé* solo con zapatos viejos.
3. Le *explicaron* el oficio.
4. Me *quitaron* los documentos.
5. ¿*Pagaste* la multa?
6. ¡Qué bueno que *llamaste*!
7. Los *invitamos* a entrar.

D. 1. Los chicos *comieron* con las manos sucias.
2. El cónsul *vivió* en paz.
3. ¿No *viste* la flecha?
4. Este policía no me *entendió*.
5. Como gran cosa me *concedieron* hasta mañana.
6. Sea lo que sea, no nos *entendimos*.
7. ¿Por qué no *salimos* juntos?
8. Me *dieron* el radio.

● PATTERNED RESPONSE DRILL

INSTRUCTIONS: Answer the following questions imitating the models.

A. 1. ¿Dónde celebraron?
    Celebramos en casa de Olga.
2. ¿Dónde estudiaron?
3. ¿Dónde trabajaron?
4. ¿Dónde jugaron?
5. ¿Dónde comieron?
6. ¿Dónde vivieron?
7. ¿Dónde escribieron?

B. 1. ¿Dónde dejaste el plato?
    Lo dejé en el mercado.

  2. ¿Dónde usaste el plato?
  3. ¿Dónde mostraste el plato?
  4. ¿Dónde perdiste el plato?
  5. ¿Dónde rompiste el plato?
  6. ¿Dónde vendiste el plato?
  7. ¿Dónde viste el plato?

C. 1. ¿Cuándo ensuciaste los zapatos?
    Los ensucié el viernes.

  2. ¿Cuándo llevaste los zapatos?
  3. ¿Cuándo mandaste los zapatos?
  4. ¿Cuándo pagaste los zapatos?
  5. ¿Cuándo rompiste los zapatos?
  6. ¿Cuándo recibiste los zapatos?
  7. ¿Cuándo metiste los zapatos?

● TRANSLATION DRILL

A. 1. Who called?
    ¿Quién llamó?

  2. Who studied?
  3. Who played?
  4. Who paid?
  5. Who ate?
  6. Who went out?
  7. Who wrote?

B. 1. I called at two-thirty.
    Yo llamé a las dos y media.

  2. I entered at two-thirty.
  3. I played at two-thirty.
  4. I paid at two-thirty.
  5. I ate at two-thirty.
  6. I went out at two-thirty.
  7. I wrote at two-thirty.

C. 1. Who (all) called?
    ¿Quiénes llamaron?

  2. Who studied?
  3. Who played?
  4. Who paid?
  5. Who ate?
  6. Who came back?
  7. Who lost?

D. 1. Then we called.
    Luego llamamos.

  2. Then we studied.
  3. Then we played.
  4. Then we paid.
  5. Then we ate.
  6. Then we wrote.
  7. Then we swept.

E. 1. They explained everything.
    Ellos explicaron todo.

  2. They remembered everything.
  3. They paid for everything.
  4. They believed everything.
  5. They lost everything.
  6. They sold everything.
  7. They saw everything.

● DISCUSSION

Following are examples of the English past tense, occurring in affirmative, negative, and interrogative contexts, as compared with the present tense in the same contexts:

	PAST		PRESENT	
AFFIRMATIVE	I went	I ran	I go	I run
	He went	He ran	He goes	He runs
NEGATIVE	I didn't go	I didn't run	I don't go	I don't run
	He didn't go	He didn't run	He doesn't go	He doesn't run
INTERROGATIVE	Did I go?	Did I run?	Do I go?	Do I run?
	Did he go?	Did he run?	Does he go?	Does he run?

Spanish has *two* past tenses, differing in meaning, covering different aspects of the English past above. The preterit is one of them. Until the other past tense is explained (the imperfect, Unit 10), only those past meanings that are translatable by the preterit will appear in the drills and written exercises.

There is no difference in the preterit endings of regular –er and –ir verbs. The irregular –ar verb **dar** takes these same endings.

In the *we* (**nosotros**) form, –ar and –ir verbs are the same in present and preterit. Thus **hablamos** means either *we speak* or *we spoke*. The two meanings are distinguished by context.

27 The demonstratives

EXAMPLES

A. 1. Llegó **este** policía medio bruto.
2. ¿Qué pasó **esta** vez?
3. Hasta **esta** noche. (*Until this night.*)

B. 1. No ponga **ese** radio tan fuerte.
2. Te veo con **esa** cara tan triste. (*I see you with that face so glum.*)
3. Pon **esos** juguetes en su lugar.
4. **Eso** no es nada serio.

	SINGULAR *this*	PLURAL *these*	SINGULAR *that*	PLURAL *those*
MASCULINE	este	estos	ese	esos
FEMININE	esta	estas	esa	esas
NEUTER	esto		eso	

The usual equivalents of English *this, these, that, those* are shown in the table.

● ITEM SUBSTITUTION DRILL

INSTRUCTIONS: Repeat the following sentences just as you hear them.   Then substitute the items listed for the italicized nouns.   When **esto** or **eso** is the item substituted it replaces both the demonstrative and the noun: **este arroz** becomes **esto.**

1. Este *arroz* es muy bueno.
   (carne, helados, frutas, esto)
2. Este *comedor* es muy grande.
   (sala, cuartos, puertas, esto)
3. Ese *plato* es muy típico.
   (ensalada, frijoles, verduras, eso)
4. Ese *lugar* es mejor.
   (escuela, mercados, clases, eso)
5. Dame un poquito de este *pan.*
   (carne, rosbif, ensalada, harina, postre, leche, arroz, café, mantequilla)

6. Tenga cuidado de no romper ese *plato.*
   (taza, huevo, juguete, radio, puerta, disco, mueble, tocadiscos, cosa, teléfono)
7. ¿De quién son estos *frijoles?*
   (verduras, helados, frutas, zapatos, centavos, pesos, listas, huevos, cosas)
8. ¿Dónde están esos *libros?*
   (listas, muebles, documentos, noticias, papeles, amigas, alumnos, extranjeros, invitaciones)

● PATTERNED RESPONSE DRILL

INSTRUCTIONS: Answer the questions below following the pattern of the models given. The teacher should make an appropriate gesture to indicate the position referred to.

A. 1. ¿De quién es este libro?
   ¿Cuál? ¿Ese?
   Sí, éste.
   Es mío.

2. ¿De quién es esta lista?
3. ¿De quién es este papel?
4. ¿De quién es esta plata?
5. ¿De quién es este centavo?

B. 1. ¿De quién son estos libros?
   ¿Cuáles? ¿Esos?
   Sí, éstos.
   Son míos.

2. ¿De quién son estas listas?
3. ¿De quién son estos papeles?
4. ¿De quién son estas cosas?
5. ¿De quién son estos pesos?

C. 1. ¿De quién es ese libro?
   ¿Cuál? ¿Este?
   Sí, ése.
   Es mío.

2. ¿De quién es esa lista?
3. ¿De quién es ese documento?
4. ¿De quién es esa ropa?
5. ¿De quién es ese juguete?

D. 1. ¿De quién son esos libros?
   ¿Cuáles? ¿Estos?
   Sí, ésos.
   Son míos.

2. ¿De quién son esas listas?
3. ¿De quién son esos papeles?
4. ¿De quién son esas cosas?
5. ¿De quién son esos zapatos?

E. 1. ¿De quién es ese libro?
    ¿Cuál? ¿Ese?
    Sí, ése.
    Es de Roberto.
    2. ¿De quién es esa flecha?
    3. ¿De quién es ese café?
    4. ¿De quién es esa taza?
    5. ¿De quién es ese disco?

F. 1. ¿De quién son esos libros?
    ¿Cuáles? ¿Esos?
    Sí, ésos.
    Son de Fernando.
    2. ¿De quién son esas cosas?
    3. ¿De quién son esos documentos?
    4. ¿De quién son esas listas?
    5. ¿De quién son esos zapatos?

● CHOICE-QUESTION RESPONSE DRILL

INSTRUCTIONS: Answer the following questions by selecting one of the alternatives proposed in each question.

A. 1. ¿Quiere ir esta tarde o esta noche?
    Esta noche.
    2. ¿Quiere ir este sábado o este domingo?
    3. ¿Quiere vivir en esta calle o en esa avenida?
    4. ¿Quiere hablar con esta señora o con ese señor?
    5. ¿Quiere esperar en esta casa o en esa esquina?
    6. ¿Quiere comer en este café o en ese restorán?

B. 1. ¿Quiere estos helados o esas frutas?
    2. ¿Quiere ir con estos amigos o con esos estudiantes?
    3. ¿Quiere comer estos frijoles o esas verduras?

● DISCUSSION

The demonstratives are singular or plural, masculine or feminine, to agree with the noun that they modify or to which they refer.

In addition to masculine and feminine, there is a neuter gender which refers to actions, generalities, or unidentified things. For example, to ask *What is that?* the speaker will say **¿Qué es eso?** since the thing is unidentified. For *Don't do that,* he will say **No hagas eso,** since the reference is to an action, not to a noun with its specific gender and number. And to say *Shall I put that (that stuff) on the list too?* he will say **¿Pongo eso en la lista también?,** because the things referred to, though they may have been identified, are thought of vaguely and generally, and hence summarized by a neuter form. The neuter has no plural.

The phrase **esta noche** translates both *this evening* and *tonight.*

28 The conjunctions *e* in place of *y* and *u* in place of *o*

EXAMPLES

A. 1. Hablan de libros **e** ideas. *They're talking about books and ideas.*
    2. Fernández **e** Hijo. *Fernández and Son.*
    3. Es española **e** inglesa. *She's Spanish and English.*
    4. Tengo siete **u** ocho. *I have seven or eight.*
    5. Quieren verlo **u** oirlo. *They want to see it or hear it.*
    6. ¿Son muchachos **u** hombres? *Are they boys or men?*

B. 1. Hablan de nuevos libros y nuevas ideas. *They're talking about new books and new ideas.*
    2. Tengo siete **o** tal vez ocho. *I have seven or maybe eight.*
    3. Quieren oirlo **o** verlo. *They want to hear it or see it.*

*Equivalents of **and***

DIRECTLY BEFORE A WORD BEGINNING WITH [i]	ELSEWHERE
e	y

*Equivalents of **or***

DIRECTLY BEFORE A WORD BEGINNING WITH [o]	ELSEWHERE
u	o

The equivalent of *and* is **e** rather than **y** when it comes directly before a word beginning with [i]. The equivalent of *or* is **u** rather than **o** when it comes directly before a word beginning with [o].

● TRANSLATION DRILL

1. TEACHER: You say left and right?
   STUDENT: **¿Dice izquierda y derecha?**
   TEACHER: You say right and left?
   STUDENT: **¿Dice derecha e izquierda?**

2. You say son and nephew?
   You say nephew and son?

3. You say English and Spanish?
   You say Spanish and English?

4. You say ideas and books?
   You say books and ideas?

5. You say invitation and message?
   You say message and invitation?

6. You say guests and companions?
   You say companions and guests?

7. You say to go and to come?
   You say to come and to go?

8. You say invite them and wait for them?
   You say wait for them and invite them?

9. You say daughter and mother?
   You say mother and daughter?

10. You say men or boys?
    ¿Dice hombres o muchachos?
    You say boys or men?
    ¿Dice muchachos u hombres?

11. You say eight or seven?
    You say seven or eight?

12. You say October or now?
    You say now or October?

13. You say today or tomorrow?
    You say tomorrow or today?

14. You say to hear or to see?
    You say to see or to hear?

15. You say hours or minutes?
    You say minutes or hours?

16. You say hi or hello?
    You say hello or hi?

17. You say busy or mistaken?
    You say mistaken or busy?

18. You say others or these?
    You say these or others?

29 Contraction of *a* plus *el* to *al*

EXAMPLE   Ve a jugar **al** jardín.

a	+	el	→	al

When **a** and the article **el** come together, they fuse to form **al**.[1]

---

[1] In writing, the fusion of **de** plus **el** is also recognized, with the spelling **del**. In speech, the same fusion occurring, for example, in **de este** or in **le escribe**, does not affect the spelling.

1. Voy a la *sala*.
    (patio, cocina, cuarto, entrada)
2. Vemos a la *gente*.
    (cónsul, morena, alumnos, amigas)
3. ¿Le escribe a la *muchacha?*
    (mexicano, venezolana, americanos, españoles)
4. Las chicas llegaron a la *escuela*.
    (parque, casa, Estados Unidos, clases)

30   The article with classifying nouns

EXAMPLES

A. 1. ¿Hablo con la casa **del** Dr. Fernández?
   2. Invitamos **al** padre Roberto. *We're inviting Father Robert.*
   3. ¿Conoces a **los** señores Arjona? *Do you know Mr. and Mrs. Arjona?*
   4. Usted sigue derecho por **la** Avenida Norte hasta llegar a **la** Calle Veinte.
   5. Con don Rosario, por favor. *I'd like to speak to Don Rosario, please.*

B. 1. Señor Martínez, cierre la puerta, por favor.
   2. De nada, profesor Alvarez. *You're welcome, Professor Alvarez.*
   3. No tenga cuidado, doña Beatriz.
   4. ¿No quiere venir conmigo, don Rafael?

*Speaking **about** a person or thing*			
el, la, los, las	+	classifying noun (esp. title)	proper name

*Speaking **to** a person*	
title	proper name

A common noun that classifies an immediately following proper name calls for the definite article. The typical examples are titles with names of persons. The article is not used, however, when the person is addressed directly, nor is it used at any time with the titles **don** and **doña**.

● TRANSLATION DRILL

A. 1. Good morning, Mr. Arjona.
   2. Good morning, Mrs. Arjona.
   3. Good morning, Miss Arjona.
   4. Good morning, Professor Arjona.
   5. Good morning, Dr. Arjona.
   6. Good morning, Father Arjona.

B. 1. Where's Mr. Arjona?
   2. Where's Mrs. Arjona?
   3. Where's Miss Arjona?
   4. Where's Professor Arjona?
   5. Where's Dr. Arjona?
   6. Where's Father Arjona?

C. 1. Good afternoon, Mr. Arjona. How's Mrs. Arjona?
   2. Good afternoon, Mr. Martínez. How's Mrs. Martínez?
   3. Good afternoon, Mr. Flores. How's Mrs. Flores?
   4. Good afternoon, Professor Romero. How's Mrs. Romero?
   5. Good afternoon, Dr. Fernández. How's Mrs. Fernández?

● DISCUSSION

   In combinations of classifying nouns and proper names, English sometimes uses the article (*the Santa Fe Trail, the Atlantic Ocean, the Ozark Mountains, the Messrs. Jones and Reed*), sometimes not (*Santa Fe Street, Lake Mead, Mount Whitney, Mr. Jones*). Spanish uses the article whenever the thing or person is spoken *about*, but not when the person is spoken *to*. The commonest classifying nouns are the personal and professional titles. **Don** and **doña** are exceptions in that they never call for the article (nor do the words **San, Santo,** and **Santa** used as titles equivalent to English *Saint*).

31 The article with things possessed

EXAMPLES

A. 1. Es el día de **su** santo, también.
   2. Sí, pero **tu** papá . . .
   3. Mañana puede pasar por **sus** papeles.
   4. A **tus** órdenes.

B. 1. Le quitaron **los** documentos.
   2. Mira como camino con **las** manos.
   3. No hagas eso, que ensucias la pared con **los** pies.
   4. ¿Es usted **la** mamá?—No, habla con **la** tía.

Possessor not otherwise obvious

possessive adjective	noun

Possessor otherwise obvious

article	noun

When it is obvious who the possessor is, Spanish generally uses the article rather than a possessive adjective.

● TRANSLATION DRILL

A. 1. Your feet are very dirty.
   Tienes los pies muy sucios.
   2. Your hands are very dirty.
   3. Your face is very dirty.
   4. Your shoes are very dirty.
   5. Your clothes are very dirty.
   6. Your things are very dirty.
   7. Your papers are very dirty.
   8. Your book is very dirty.
   9. Your room is very dirty.

B. 1. Look how I walk with my hands.
   2. Look how I walk with my feet.
   3. Look how I walk without my feet.
   4. Look how I walk without my shoes.
   5. Look how I eat without my plate.
   6. Look how I study without my schoolmate.

● DISCUSSION

By comparison with Spanish, English overworks its possessive adjectives. It is not normal in Spanish to insist, as English does, on a routine possessive adjective in a sentence like **Mira como camino con *las* manos,** since the speaker could hardly walk with any hands but his own.[1] If a possessive adjective is used under these circumstances, it is for some special effect (when the speaker in the dialog says **Me quitaron *mis* documentos** he is probably thinking of the trespass on *his* property).

32 *Conocer* and *saber*

EXAMPLES

A. 1. Pero tú **conoces** a mamá . . .
   2. **Conozco** ese sistema. *I know that system* (am aware of its existence and characteristics).
   3. **Conozco** que es verdad. *I know* (am aware, recognize) *that it is true.*

B. 1. No necesitas **saber** inglés.
   2. **Sé** ese sistema. *I know that system* (can perform the operations).
   3. **Sé** trabajar. *I know how to work.*
   4. ¿**Sabes** el número?
   5. ¿Usted **sabe** dónde vivimos?
   6. Yo **sé** que viven cerca del Parque Central.
   7. **Sé** que es verdad. *I know that it is true* (I can report the fact).

---

[1] Clothing and parts of the body are the most typical examples of nouns which in Spanish call for the article rather than the possessive adjective. This discussion is resumed in Unit 12 §67.

The equivalents of **know**

AWARENESS: **conocer**		CONTROL: **saber**	
ACQUAINTANCESHIP	Conoces a mamá Conozco ese sistema	SKILL	Sé inglés Sé ese sistema Sé trabajar
RECOGNITION	Conozco que es verdad	COMMUNICABLE KNOWLEDGE	Sé el número Sé dónde viven Sé que es verdad

Saber represents knowledge that is learned and can be acted out (verbalized or performed).
Conocer represents degrees of awareness, from acquaintanceship to mere recognition.

● TRANSLATION DRILL

1. TEACHER: I don't know the school.
   STUDENT: **No conozco la escuela.**
   TEACHER: I don't know the number.
   STUDENT: **No sé el número.**
2. I know Mexico very well.
   I know the name very well.
3. I don't know Mr. Martínez.
   No conozco al señor Martínez.
   But I know where he lives.

4. We know the National Theater.
   But we don't know where it is.
5. He knows my daughter.
   But he doesn't know where she works.
6. He knows the professor.
   But he doesn't know the lesson.
7. They know that corner.
   And they know the address.
8. She knows that market.
   But she doesn't know how to bargain.

● DISCUSSION

The range of meaning covered by *know* is divided between **conocer** and **saber**. **Conocer** implies that the knower is aware of the thing known. He may be closely acquainted with it, or may merely be conscious of its existence. **Saber** implies control: the knower can put all his knowledge into words, or can act it out; it is knowledge that can be communicated, taught, and learned. Referring to a game of cards one might say: **Conozco ese sistema pero no lo sé** *I know that system* (it is present to my mind) *but I don't know it* (can't play it). **Conozco las calles de Madrid** *I know the streets of Madrid* means that their existence and characteristics are known to me. **Sé las calles de Madrid** *I know the streets of Madrid* means that I can name them.

Two important particular cases are *to know a person,* which calls for **conocer** (*They know John* **Conocen a Juan**), and *to know how to do something,* which calls for **saber** (*They know how to write* **Saben escribir**).

● COMBINED PATTERN REPLACEMENT DRILL

A.

1. **Después, el abuelo les mandó estos muebles.**
2. _____ mandaron _____
3. _____este _____
4. _____ la _____
5. _____ le _____
6. _____ noticias
7. _____ cuñado _____
8. _____ explicó _____
9. Entonces _____
10. _____ policía _____
11. _____ multa
12. _____ exigió _____
13. _____ jefe _____
14. Más tarde _____

15. _____ documentos
16. _____este _____
17. _____ vendió _____
18. _____ me _____
19. _____ mexicano _____
20. _____ lista
21. _____ los _____
22. _____ llevaron _____
23. _____ saludos

B. 1. ¿El libro? Lo llevaron a la escuela.
 2. _____ los llevaron _____
 3. _____ llevé _____
 4. _____ a la clase
 5. La plata _____
 6. _____ al mercado
 7. Las frutas _____
 8. _____ mandaron _____
 9. _____ a la casa
 10. Los muebles _____
 11. _____ mandamos

 12. _____ lo mandamos _____
 13. _____ a los Estados Unidos
 14. El documento _____
 15. _____ los mandamos _____
 16. _____ mandé _____
 17. El azúcar _____
 18. _____ vendí _____
 19. _____ al restorán
 20. _____ vendemos _____
 21. La carne _____

• TRANSLATION REVIEW DRILL

Gender of nouns ending in –e.

A. 1. Which is the coffee?
 2. Which is the toy?
 3. Which is the father?
 4. Which is the park?
 5. Which is the foot?
 6. Which is the dessert?
 7. Which is the man?
 8. Which is the boss?
 9. Which is the piece of furniture?

B. 1. Which is the street?
 2. Which is the meat?
 3. Which is the class?
 4. Which is the people?
 5. Which is the milk?
 6. Which is the mother?
 7. Which is the night?
 8. Which is the part?
 9. Which is the afternoon?

READING

"The Policeman's Lot"

(*El policía acaba de volver a casa. Va a la sala y se sienta en el sofá. Espera la comida que su esposa le prepara en la cocina.*)

P. *Policía* E. *Esposa* V. *Visitante*

P. ¡Ay, caramba! ¡Me matan los pies!
E. ¡Pobre muchacho!
P. Dime, Rafaela, ¿quién fue el poeta que escribió que la vida[1] del policía es muy triste? . . . Debió pensar[2] en mis pies.
E. ¿Pasó algo hoy?
P. Sí, con uno de esos benditos extranjeros que infestan nuestro país, en vez de quedarse[3] en su casa.[4] Cada día que vienen a nuestra . . .
E. Sí, sí; ya sé . . . Pero sigue; dime qué sucedió.
P. Bueno, allá estaba yo, en la esquina del Teatro Nacional, y ese extranjero se metió en la calle en contra del tránsito. Me acerqué a[5] él y le pregunté: "¿No ve usted esa flecha ahí en la pared?" Y el bruto me

dijo que no; que ¿qué flecha? . . . ¿Hay algo más estúpido? ¿Por qué no miró?
E. ¿Paró el tráfico?
P. Claro, ¡cómo no! . . . Luego nos peleamos. Un tremendo lío. Y todo por culpa de él. Le quité los documentos . . . Después le exigieron una multa, pero le concedieron hasta mañana para pagarla.
E. ¿Va a tener que pagarla?
P. ¿Qué crees tú? Te apuesto a que no.[6]
E. ¿Por qué?
P. Porque debe tener amigos que son amigos de la esposa de algún primo del Jefe, que va a arreglarlo todo. Hasta[7] pueden darme una reprimenda. Estoy acostumbrado a eso. Pero lo que me pone[8] más furioso es que estos extranjeros, que hablan muy mal nuestra lengua,[9] y ni llevan[10] nombres españoles . . . (*Llaman a la puerta.*)
E. Ya voy. (*Va a la puerta.*)
V. ¿Es aquí donde vive el señor O'Reilly?
E. Sí, señor, pase usted . . . Terencio, preguntan por ti.

---

[1] *life* [2] *He must have been thinking* [3] *staying* [4] *at home* [5] *I went up to* [6] *I bet you he won't* [7] *even* [8] *makes* [9] *language* [10] *don't even have*

7

Topic for the Day

B. *Barber*   A. *Alonso*

B. Mr. Alonso, you're next. Sit down, please.
Do you want it short in back and on the
sides, as usual [always]?

A. Yes, and you can cut a little off the top too.
It's too long.

B. All right. Well, Mr. Alonso, what are they

Tema del día

B. *Barbero*   A. *Alonso*

B. Sr. Alonso, usted sigue. Siéntese, por favor.
¿Lo quiere corto atrás y a los lados, como
siempre?

A. Sí, y arriba puede cortarme un poco también. Está muy largo.

B. Muy bien. Bueno, Sr. Alonso, ¿y qué se

saying about the coming Pan-American Olympic Games in Peru? They're going to be great, aren't they?

A. Yes, where I work that's all they're talking about. They're already getting up a group to go. I don't know yet if I'll go or not.

B. But isn't this a fine chance [better chance than this] to take a vacation?

A. It's worthwhile all right, but I'm a little short of money. The cost of the trip alone is [the trip alone costs] pretty high [expensive]. Ouch! You pulled my hair!

B. I'm sorry. It's the clippers; I don't know what's the matter with them. I'd better use the scissors.

* * *

B. Who do you think's going to win the games? The Americans?

A. Probably. They have very good athletes and they're going to send quite a large team.

B. We're going to compete in football, basketball, swimming, boxing, the marathon race . . . What else?

A. Nothing else, but unfortunately we're going

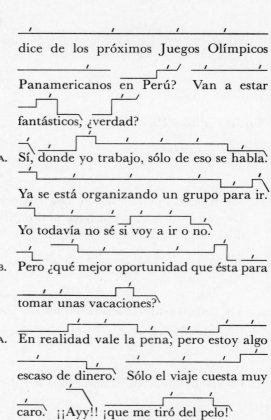

dice de los próximos Juegos Olímpicos Panamericanos en Perú? Van a estar fantásticos, ¿verdad?

A. Sí, donde yo trabajo, sólo de eso se habla. Ya se está organizando un grupo para ir. Yo todavía no sé si voy a ir o no.

B. Pero ¿qué mejor oportunidad que ésta para tomar unas vacaciones?

A. En realidad vale la pena, pero estoy algo escaso de dinero. Sólo el viaje cuesta muy caro. ¡¡Ayy!! ¡que me tiró del pelo!

B. Perdón, es la maquinilla; no sé qué tiene. Mejor uso las tijeras.

* * *

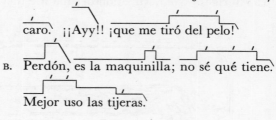

B. ¿Quién cree usted que va a ganar los juegos? ¿Los americanos?

A. Probablemente. Ellos tienen muy buenos

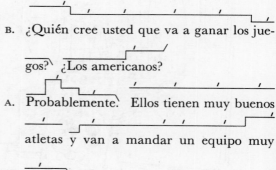

atletas y van a mandar un equipo muy grande.

B. Nosotros vamos a participar en fútbol (1), básquetbol, natación, boxeo, en la carrera de maratón . . . ¿en qué más?

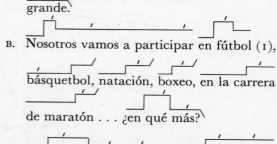

A. En nada más, pero desgraciadamente

to lose in everything. With countries like the United States, Brazil, and Argentina, the competition is too stiff.

B. I bet we at least win in football. By the way, why is it that the Americans aren't any good at football?

A. Because in the United States that game isn't played very much. There they play another kind of football quite different from ours.

* * *

A. Another thing I'd like to see, if I go to the games, is a good bullfight.

B. In Peru? Isn't it just Spain and Mexico where they have bullfights?

A. No sir! In Peru, Colombia, Ecuador, Venezuela, and Panama they also have them.

B. That's one sport I don't know beans about [about which . . . potato].

A. It's something terrific. And don't say sport. Bullfighting is considered a real art.

B. That's the nice thing about my job; every day you learn something new. Shall I put brilliantine on your hair?

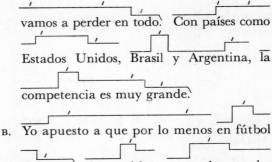

vamos a perder en todo. Con países como Estados Unidos, Brasil y Argentina, la competencia es muy grande.

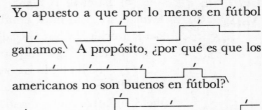

B. Yo apuesto a que por lo menos en fútbol ganamos. A propósito, ¿por qué es que los americanos no son buenos en fútbol?

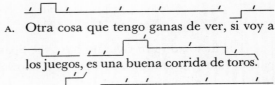

A. Porque en los Estados Unidos se practica muy poco ese deporte. Allá se juega otra clase de fútbol muy diferente del nuestro.

* * *

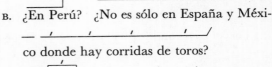

A. Otra cosa que tengo ganas de ver, si voy a los juegos, es una buena corrida de toros.

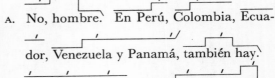

B. ¿En Perú? ¿No es sólo en España y México donde hay corridas de toros?

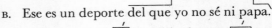

A. No, hombre. En Perú, Colombia, Ecuador, Venezuela y Panamá, también hay.

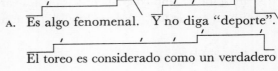

B. Ese es un deporte del que yo no sé ni papa.

A. Es algo fenomenal. Y no diga "deporte". El toreo es considerado como un verdadero arte (2).

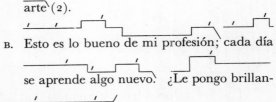

B. Esto es lo bueno de mi profesión; cada día se aprende algo nuevo. ¿Le pongo brillantina en el pelo?

A. No, thanks. Lend me the comb. Let me comb it myself.

A. No, gracias. Présteme el peine. Déjeme peinarme yo mismo.

Cultural Notes (1) Baseball is highly popular in Mexico and Cuba, whereas **fútbol** is the favorite sport in most South American countries. **Fútbol,** as played in the Hispanic world, is what we call *soccer.* In Spain, this kind of football has even come to rival the bullfight in popularity.

(2) The bullfight is not considered a sport in the sense that **fútbol, jai-alai,** and baseball are. It is rather a combination of pageant, ritual, and art, dramatizing the Spaniard's courage and feeling for the tragedy of life in the face of brute force.

● PRONUNCIATION EXERCISE

A. The stops [p] and [b]. INSTRUCTIONS: Repeat the following pairs of words just as you hear them.

[p]	[b]	[p]	[b]
paño	baño	peso	beso
pago	vago	pida	vida
peca	beca	pino	vino
pelo	velo	poca	boca
pena	vena	pesar	besar

The first and third columns have the Spanish stop [p], which differs from its English counterpart in that it is unaspirated (i.e., not followed by a puff of breath). Thus Spanish [p] is often heard by English speakers as [b].

B. The stops [t] and [d]. INSTRUCTIONS: Repeat the following pairs of words just as you hear them.

[t]	[d]
tos	dos
tía	día
teja	deja
trama	drama
tomar	domar

The first column has the Spanish stop [t], which differs from its English counterpart in that it is unaspirated, and consequently is often heard by English speakers as [d]. Both Spanish [d] and Spanish [t] are dental, whereas English [d] and [t] are alveolar.

C. The stops [k] and [g].

[k]	[g]
callo	gallo
casa	gasa
coma	goma
cura	gura
cordura	gordura

The first column has the Spanish stop [k], which differs from its English counterpart in that it is unaspirated. Thus Spanish [k] is often heard by English speakers as [g].

33   The infinitive after another verb

EXAMPLES

1. No necesitas plata. *You don't need money.*
   No necesitas **saber** inglés.
2. ¿Desea unas vacaciones? *Do you desire a vacation?*
   ¿Desea **dejar** algún recado?
3. ¿No quiere la oportunidad? *Don't you want the opportunity?*
   ¿No quiere **venir** conmigo?
4. Prefiero una corrida de toros. *I prefer a bullfight.*
   Prefiero **usar** las tijeras. *I prefer to use the scissors.*

5. Espera más dinero. *He expects more money.*
   Espera **trabajar.** *He expects (hopes) to work.*
6. Si consigo el empleo. *If I get (manage to get) the job.*
   Si consigo **entrar.** *If I manage to enter.*
7. ¿Recordaste la lista? *Did you remember the list?*
   ¿Recordaste **hacerlo?** *Did you remember to do it?*
8. Ellas saben español.
   Ellas saben **hablar.** *They know (how) to talk.*

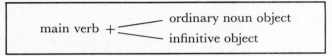

main verb + — ordinary noun object
              — infinitive object

As in English, a verb may take an infinitive object
just as it may take a noun object.

● ITEM SUBSTITUTION DRILL

1. *Desea* tomar unas vacaciones.
   (necesita, prefiere, quiere, espera, piensa)
2. *Queremos* hacer un viaje.
   (sabemos, deseamos, esperamos, pensamos)
3. *Esperan* participar en fútbol, natación y boxeo.
   (quieren, piensan, prefieren, desean, necesitan, saben)

4. Si *prefieres* volver a la profesión, está bien.
   (piensas, recuerdas, quieres, consigues, necesitas, deseas, esperas, sabes)
5. No *quiero* apostar a la carrera de maratón.
   (necesito, espero, pienso, deseo, sé)

● CONSTRUCTION SUBSTITUTION DRILL

INSTRUCTIONS: Repeat each sentence just as you hear it.   Then insert the infinitive in the sentence after the verb form.

1. Espero unas vacaciones.
   (tener, conseguir, pasar, tomar)
2. No queremos una competencia de esta clase.
   (hacer, traer, organizar, quitar)
3. Necesita el peine.
   (usar, llevar, conseguir, prestar)
4. Prefieren el equipo de básquetbol.
   (ver, llevar, mandar, conocer)
5. ¿Desea brillantina en el pelo?
   (poner, ver, tener, dejar)

6. ¿Recordaste la lista?
   (pasar, mostrar, mirar, conseguir)
7. Si consigo el empleo, está bien.
   (pedir, entender, explicar, estudiar)
8. El sabe la noticia.
   (arreglar, dar, exigir, cortar)
9. Ellas no piensan ahora.
   (entrar, celebrar, jugar, pelear)

● TRANSLATION DRILL

A. 1. He wants to bring the record player.
   2. He hopes to bring the record player.
   3. He prefers to bring the record player.

4. He needs to bring the record player.
5. He wishes to bring the record player.
6. He plans to bring the record player.

B. 1. Do you want to study the system?[1]
   2. Do you need to study the system?
   3. Do you plan to study the system?
   4. Do you hope to study the system?
   5. Do you wish to study the system?
   6. Do you prefer to study the system?

C. 1. If he remembers to come, O.K.
   2. If he plans to come, O.K.
   3. If he hopes to come, O.K.
   4. If he manages to come, O.K.
   5. If he prefers to come, O.K.
   6. If he wants to come, O.K.
   7. If he needs to come, O.K.

D. 1. I want to go to the coming Pan-American Olympic Games.
   2. I expect to go to the coming Pan-American Olympic Games.
   3. I plan to go to the coming Pan-American Olympic Games.
   4. I prefer to go to the coming Pan-American Olympic Games.
   5. I need to go to the coming Pan-American Olympic Games.

E. 1. They expect to see the traffic chief.
   2. They need to see the traffic chief.
   3. They plan to see the traffic chief.
   4. They know how to see the traffic chief.
   5. They wish to see the traffic chief.

EXAMPLES   1. **Debe estar** en la cocina.
   2. Arriba **puede cortarme** un poco.
   3. **Déjeme peinarme** yo mismo.

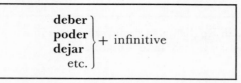

These verbs also take infinitive objects,
but in English the *to* does not appear.

● ITEM SUBSTITUTION DRILL

1. *Déjeme* ver la maquinilla.
   (puedo, debo)
2. *Debe* entrar al país.
   (déjelo, puede)
3. *Podemos* mandar saludos a la familia.
   (debemos, déjenos)
4. *Piensa* trabajar como el año pasado.
   (puede, debe, déjelo)
5. *Quieren* enseñar el toreo como un verdadero arte.
   (deben, pueden, déjelos)
6. *Esperamos* ir juntos al Teatro Nacional.
   (podemos, debemos, déjenos)

● TRANSLATION DRILL

1. I can comb my own hair (comb myself).
   I must comb my own hair (comb myself).
   Let me comb my own hair (comb myself).
2. At least he can calm down the boss.
   At least he must calm down the boss.
   At least let him calm down the boss.
3. It's something terrific; they can get the job in the Ministry.
   It's something terrific; they must get the job in the Ministry.
   It's something terrific; let them get the job in the Ministry.

EXAMPLES

1. Viene gente **a la casa.** *People are coming to the house.*
   Viene gente **a comer.** *(People are coming to eat.)*
2. Ve **al jardín.** *Go to the garden.*
   Ve **a jugar.** *(Go to play.)*
3. El profesor los invita **a la clase.** *The teacher invites them to the class.*
   El profesor los invita **a entrar.**
4. Pasaron **a la casa.** *They went on to the house.*
   Pasaron **a vernos.** *They went on (in) to see us.*
5. Entró **a mi cuarto.** *He came in my room.*
   Entró **a llamarme.** *He came in to call me.*

---
[1] *the system* **el sistema**

$$\boxed{\text{main verb} + \text{preposition} + \begin{cases} \text{noun object} \\ \text{infinitive object} \end{cases}}$$

Where the main verb would call for a preposition
before a noun object, it calls for the same preposition before an infinitive. Typical examples are
verbs of motion, calling for *to* (**a**).

● ITEM SUBSTITUTION DRILL

1. *Llegaron* a ver el patio.
   (pasaron, regresaron, entraron, salieron,
   volvieron)
2. Los *invitaron* a comer frijoles.
   (llevaron, llamaron)

3. *Viene* la pareja extranjera a pasar unos días.
   (llega, entra, regresa, sale, vuelve)
4. *Ve* a jugar al jardín.
   (sal, ven, pasa, vuelve)

● TRANSLATION DRILL

A. 1. They came in to see the race.
   2. They came back to see the race.
   3. They went out to see the race.
   4. They invited them to see the race.

B. 1. They're arriving to see us this afternoon.
   2. They're coming to see us this afternoon.
   3. They're coming by to see us this afternoon.
   4. They're coming back to see us this afternoon.
   5. They're leaving to see us this afternoon.
   6. They're inviting them to see us this afternoon.

● DISCUSSION

The infinitive (the form of the verb that appears after *to* in English) functions as a noun. Like
other nouns, it may serve as object of a verb (examples in this unit), subject or predicate noun
(**Ganar a veces es perder** *To win is sometimes to lose*), and object of a preposition (object of **a** in
this unit, other prepositions in Unit 8).

While English does not distinguish between *He wants to see me* and *He comes to see me,* using *to*
with the infinitive in both, Spanish does distinguish between **Quiere verme** and **Viene a verme,**
inserting an **a** in the latter. This **a** is the same directional *to* that is used with **venir** and other similar verbs to link them to a following noun, as in English *come* (*go, run, walk, hurry, crawl,* etc.) *to the*
house. English *He wants the house* vs. *He comes to the house* is like Spanish **Quiere verme** vs. **Viene a**
verme. We might say that **Viene a verme** means *He is heading **toward** the act of seeing me.*

When in addition to an infinitive after the verb of motion there is also a place-to-which, Spanish normally repeats the **a: Ve *a* jugar *al* jardín.** This is true whether the corresponding English
is *Go play **in** the yard* or *Go **to** the yard to play.*

34   *Ir a* plus infinitive

EXAMPLES

A. 1. **Ve a jugar** al jardín.
   2. Si **vamos a verlos** hoy, podemos traer a
      mamá a casa con nosotros. *If we go to*
      see them today, we can bring Mother home
      with us.

B. 1. **Voy a arreglar** esto.
   2. ¿Quién cree usted que **va a ganar** los
      Juegos?
   3. **Vamos a perder** en todo.
   4. **Van a estar** fantásticos.

C. **Vamos a hablar** con ellas.

Three uses of **ir a** *plus infinitive*

MEANING	EXAMPLES	POSSIBLE FORMS OF **ir**
To go to	**Ve a jugar** **Vamos a verlos**	Unlimited
To be going to (future time)	**Voy a ir** **Vamos a perder** **Van a estar fantásticos**	Present tense[1]
Let's	**Vamos a hablar con ellas**	**Vamos** only; affirmative sentences[2]

Besides the basic *to go to* meaning (§33 above), **ir a** is used like English *to be going to* to indicate future time. Also, in the one form **vamos a,** it can mean *let's.*

● PERSON-NUMBER SUBSTITUTION DRILL

1. *Ellos* van a traer muy buenos atletas.
   (Chile, nosotros, usted, los Estados Unidos, yo)
2. *El* va a quererlo muy corto atrás.
   (ustedes, nosotros, Pablo, yo, tú, ellos)
3. Mañana voy a estar a sus órdenes.
   (él, nosotros, ella, ellos, Rafael y yo, el barbero)
4. Esta tarde vas a ver esa bendita esquina.
   (usted, nosotros, él, yo, María, ustedes)
5. *Tú* vas a trabajar con mucho gusto en el Ministerio.
   (Francisco, yo, el señor Alonso, nosotros, ellos, usted, Patricio y don Rosario)
6. En realidad, voy a estar encantado de participar.
   (Pepe, tú, los muchachos, nosotros, él, ustedes, ellos)
7. *El* va a cortarlo a los lados.
   (nosotros, ellos, tú, el barbero, yo)

● CONSTRUCTION SUBSTITUTION DRILL

INSTRUCTIONS: Repeat the following sentences just as you hear them. Then repeat them again, substituting an appropriate **ir a** construction for the verb of the original sentence. (If there are two verbs in the sentence, the one to be changed is in italics.)

A. 1. TEACHER: Probablemente *cree* que vale la pena. *Repita.*
   STUDENT: **Probablemente cree que vale la pena.**
   TEACHER: *Cambie.*
   STUDENT: **Probablemente va a creer que vale la pena.**
2. Sólo el viaje cuesta muy caro.
3. Estoy algo escaso de dinero.
4. Olga está encantada de conocerlo.
5. Todos están presentes excepto mi sobrina.
6. *Hace* cuatro años que vive en México.
7. La puerta está abierta a las nueve y media.
8. Los juegos están fantásticos, ¿eh?
9. El jefe está ocupado toda la tarde.
10. ¿Y qué *sucede* si ese bruto no cree que es cosa seria?
11. De esto yo no sé ni papa.
12. Paquito siempre sale con permiso.

B. 1. TEACHER: Sea lo que sea, el policía le *exigió* una multa. *Repita.*
   STUDENT: **Sea lo que sea, el policía le exigió una multa.**
   TEACHER: *Cambie.*
   STUDENT: **Sea lo que sea, el policía le va a exigir una multa.**
2. Le quitaron todos los documentos.
3. El habló perfectamente bien.
4. Pero desgraciadamente perdieron en todo.
5. Es que me *metí* en una calle en contra del tránsito.
6. Pero hombre, ¿no viste la flecha?
7. ¡Qué bueno que llamaste!
8. Me mostraron una flecha, como a cinco metros en una pared.

---

[1] *Was going to* is treated in Unit 10. [2] *Let's not* is treated in Unit 17 §99.

● TRANSLATION DRILL

1. The boss is furious.
   The boss is going to be furious.
2. Don Rafael's hair seems very long.
   Don Rafael's hair is going to seem very long.
3. Rosa's going to the market.
   Rosa's going to go to the market.
4. He's going to talk with them.
   We're going to talk with them.
   Let's talk with them.
5. She's going to leave tomorrow.
   We're going to leave tomorrow.
   Let's leave tomorrow.

6. He's going to eat now.
   We're going to eat now.
   Let's eat now.
7. He's going to study afterwards.
   We're going to study afterwards.
   Let's study afterwards.
8. She's going to put that on the list.
   We're going to put that on the list.
   Let's put that on the list.
9. He's going to do something different.
   We're going to do something different.
   Let's do something different.

● DISCUSSION

In place of the future tense (*I'll buy it*), English often substitutes the verb *go* (*I'm going to buy it*). Spanish uses **ir a** in the same way.

35 *Al* plus infinitive

EXAMPLES

1. Hay que cerrar la puerta **al entrar.** *You have to shut the door when you go in.*
2. **Al pasar** por el parque, miramos los juegos. *As we passed through the park, we looked at the games.*
3. **Al llegar** a la Calle Veinte, doblaron a la derecha. *When they got to Twentieth Street, they turned right.*

on, at the moment of	–ing

al	infinitive

Al plus the infinitive expresses an action simultaneous with another action. The closest English equivalent is the literary *on* plus *–ing*, e.g., *on arriving at Twentieth Street, . . .*

● ITEM SUBSTITUTION DRILL

1. Al *salir*, te llamo.
   (llegar, acabar, regresar)
2. Al *entrar a* la casa, recordé la dirección.
   (salir de, volver a, pensar en)
3. Al *llegar a* la escuela, me lo explicaron.
   (salir de, llamar a, entrar a)

4. Al *mandar el café*, me llamaron.
   (doblar la esquina, pasar por ahí, abrir la puerta)
5. Al *decir eso*, algo pasó.
   (hablar fuerte, volver a la casa, recibir la noticia)

● TRANSLATION DRILL

A. 1. TEACHER: When he arrived at the school, he paid me.
      STUDENT: **Al llegar a la escuela, me pagó.**
   2. When he left the school, he paid me.
   3. When he sold the house, he paid me.
   4. When he saw me, he paid me.

B. 1. As we passed through the park, we looked at the games.
   2. As we walked along the street, we looked at the races.
   3. As we returned through the garden, we saw the car.
   4. As we turned the corner, we stopped the traffic.

Appearing with the infinitive, the contraction **al** for **a + el** (Unit 6 §29) means *at the (moment of)*. It is used under the same conditions as English *on* plus *–ing* (*on arriving, on getting up, on discovering the mistake,* etc.), though the conversational English equivalent is normally with *when, as,* or *as soon as.* This is to say that it refers to an action viewed as virtually simultaneous with another action and relatively brief.

36 The verb *haber*, there to be

EXAMPLES

1. En México **hay** corridas de toros. *In Mexico there are bullfights.*
2. ¿**Hay** huevos? *Are there any eggs?*

3. Debe **haber** un teléfono aquí. *There must (ought to) be a telephone here.*
4. ¿Cuántos números puede **haber?** *How many numbers can there be?*

there is there are	**hay**

there		to be		**haber**	
"	seems	"		**parece**	"
"	has	"		**tiene que**	"
"	ought (must)	"		**debe**	"
"	is able (can)	"		**puede**	"
			etc.		etc.

Haber has the form **hay** *there is, there are* in the present tense. It is regarded as a third-person singular, and this is the form that any other verb assumes when combined with it.

● CONSTRUCTION SUBSTITUTION DRILL

INSTRUCTIONS: Repeat each sentence just as you hear it. Then repeat it again, substituting **está el** (**están los**) for **hay un** (**hay unos**) or vice versa.

A. 1. TEACHER: Aquí hay un libro. *Repita.*
   STUDENT: **Aquí hay un libro.**
   TEACHER: *Cambie.*
   STUDENT: **Aquí está el libro.**
2. Aquí hay una lista.
3. Aquí hay unos documentos.
4. Aquí hay unas noticias.

B. 1. ¿Dónde está el restorán?
2. ¿Dónde está la ensalada?
3. ¿Dónde están los frijoles?
4. ¿Dónde están las verduras?

C. 1. Ya hay un profesor aquí.
2. Ya hay una profesora aquí.
3. Ya hay unos alumnos aquí.
4. Ya hay unas criadas aquí.

D. 1. ¿Está el café a la izquierda?
2. ¿Está la casa a la izquierda?
3. ¿Están los teatros a la izquierda?
4. ¿Están las flechas a la izquierda?

• TRANSLATION DRILL

A. 1. There's a telephone here.
    2. There seems to be a telephone here.
    3. There ought to be a telephone here.
    4. There has to be a telephone here.
    5. There can be a telephone here.

B. 1. There's a book in the school.
    2. There seems to be a book in the school.
    3. There ought to be a book in the school.
    4. There has to be a book in the school.
    5. There can be a book in the school.

C. 1. How many numbers are there?
    2. How many numbers do there seem to be?
    3. How many numbers do there have to be?
    4. How many numbers must there be?
    5. How many numbers can there be?

D. 1. There isn't [a] restaurant in the block.
    2. There doesn't seem to be [a] restaurant in the block.
    3. There doesn't have to be [a] restaurant in the block.
    4. There shouldn't be [a] restaurant in the block.
    5. There can't be [a] restaurant in the block.

37 Reflexives with nonpersonal subjects

EXAMPLES

A. 1. Cada día **se aprende** algo nuevo.
    2. Cada día **se aprenden** cosas nuevas.
       Every day new things are learned (you learn, one learns, new things).
B. 1. **Se está organizando** un grupo para ir.
    2. **Se están organizando** grupos para ir.
       Groups are being organized (they're getting up groups) to go.

C. 1. Allá **se juega** otra clase de fútbol.
    2. Allá **se juegan** otras clases de fútbol.

D. 1. **Se practica** muy poco ese deporte.
    2. **Se practican** muy poco esos deportes.

	ENGLISH MEANINGS	SPANISH EQUIVALENT
LITERAL: NORMAL:	The game organizes itself The game is (gets) organized	**Se organiza el juego**
LITERAL: NORMAL:	The games organize themselves The games are (get) organized	**Se organizan los juegos**
LITERAL: NORMAL:	A cup of coffee sent itself (up) A cup of coffee was sent (up) They sent (up) a cup of coffee	**Se mandó una taza de café**
LITERAL: NORMAL:	Two cups of coffee sent themselves (up) Two cups of coffee were sent (up) They sent up two cups of coffee	**Se mandaron dos tazas de café**
LITERAL: NORMAL:	The door opened itself The door came open The door opened	**Se abrió la puerta**
LITERAL: NORMAL:	The doors opened themselves The doors came open The doors opened	**Se abrieron las puertas**

continued on p. 114

ENGLISH MEANINGS		SPANISH EQUIVALENT
LITERAL:	The wall dirtied itself	
NORMAL:	The wall got dirtied	**Se ensució la pared**
	The wall got dirty	
LITERAL:	The walls dirtied themselves	
NORMAL:	The walls got dirtied	**Se ensuciaron las paredes**
	The walls got dirty	
LITERAL:	The traffic stopped itself	
NORMAL:	The traffic was (got) stopped	**Se paró el tráfico**
	The traffic stopped	

To show an action performed on something without regard to who or what performs it, Spanish uses **se** with the third person, singular or plural, of the verb.

Emphasis

STRESS IN ENGLISH	POSITION IN SPANISH
Here is where the **games** are organized	**Aquí es donde se organizan los juegos**
Here is where the games are **organized**	**Aquí es donde los juegos se organizan**

As with questions (see Unit 3 §9), the element which is emphasized tends to be placed last.

● NUMBER SUBSTITUTION DRILL

INSTRUCTIONS: Repeat the following sentences just as you hear them. Then repeat them again, substituting a plural (or singular) noun as subject of the reflexive verb.

A. 1. TEACHER: Se ensució el cuarto. *Repita.*
STUDENT: **Se ensució el cuarto.**
TEACHER: *Cambie.*
STUDENT: **Se ensuciaron los cuartos.**

2. Se cerró la puerta.
3. Se oyó un joropo.
4. Se paró el juego.

B. 1. Se va a organizar un grupo.
2. Se va a hacer un viaje.
3. Se va a aprender una cosa nueva.
4. Se va a necesitar una casa nueva.

C. 1. Se ve la flecha.
2. El teatro se usa mucho.
3. La multa se paga aquí.
4. Se practica mucho ese deporte.

D. 1. Se mandaron dos tazas de café.
2. Se abrieron los libros.
3. Se dejaron los recados.
4. Se vieron las calles.

E. 1. Se van a llevar los zapatos.
2. Se van a necesitar unos muebles nuevos.
3. Se van a enseñar los oficios.
4. Se van a vender unas docenas de huevos.

F. 1. Se celebran los días feriados.
2. Se barren los cuartos de arriba.
3. Se comen muchas frutas.
4. Se sacuden los muebles.

● TRANSLATION DRILL

A. 1. You say "Thank you."
Se dice "Gracias".
2. You say "You're welcome."
3. You say "Excuse me."
4. You say "Of course."
5. You say "My gosh."
6. You say "At your service."

B. 1. They say he's coming.
Se dice que viene.
2. They say he's arriving.
3. They say he's leaving.
4. They say he's returning.
5. They say he's studying.
6. They say he's speaking.
7. They say he's participating.

C. INSTRUCTIONS: Translate the following paired sentences, showing emphasis by placing the equivalents of the italicized English items last in the Spanish sentence.

1. The *traffic* was stopped.
   The traffic was *stopped*.
2. The *door* opened.
   The door *opened*.
3. A *group* is being organized.
   A group is being *organized*.
4. The *message* was left.
   The message was *left*.
5. The *document* was taken away.
   The document was *taken away*.

6. The *arrow* was lost.
   The arrow was *lost*.
7. The *restaurant* was closed.
   The restaurant was *closed*.
8. Every day *new things* are learned.
   Every day new things are *learned*.
9. Here is where the *game* is played (practiced).
   Here is where the game is *played*.

EXAMPLES

1. Sólo de eso **se habla.**
2. **Se vive** bien en Cuba. *You can live well (one lives well) in Cuba.*
3. **Se sigue** por esta calle. *You keep on down this street.*

4. No **se juega** con él. *You don't fool with him (one doesn't play with him).*
5. No **se regatea** aquí. *There's no bargaining here (you can't bargain here, one doesn't bargain here).*

Action-going-on

se + third-person singular of any verb

To show an action as merely going on, without any grammatical subject, **se** is used with the third-person singular of the verb.

● TRANSLATION DRILL

A. 1. One eats well here.
   2. One lives well here.
   3. One walks well here.
   4. One works well here.

B. 1. One studies a lot here.
   2. One plays a lot here.
   3. One haggles a lot here.
   4. One argues a lot here.
   5. One learns a lot here.
   6. One talks a lot here.

● DISCUSSION

The uses of the reflexive pronoun **se** (*yourself, yourselves, oneself, himself, herself, itself, themselves*) are complex.

One highly frequent use is equivalent to a variety of indefinite expressions in English. The doer of the action is disregarded. In fact, the purpose is often to picture the action as happening of itself. We sometimes find a parallel use of *itself* in English: *The bullet **flattened itself** (got flattened, was flattened, flattened) against the stone where it struck.*

Where English takes an object and turns it into a subject, leaving the verb exactly the same, Spanish adds **se:**

Something opened the door—The door *opened:* **se abrió.**
Something stopped the traffic—The traffic *stopped:* **se paró.**
Someone combs hair—Straight hair *combs* well: **se peina.**
Someone dusts furniture—It *dusts* easily: **se sacude.**

A special case is that of **se** with the third person singular (never plural) of any verb to indicate merely action-going-on: **se habla** *there is talking,* **se regatea** *there is bargaining,* **se come** *there is eating* (**Se come bien aquí** *There's good eating here, One eats well here, Good food is served here*).

A.
1. **Necesito salir dentro de diez minutos.**
2. Voy _____
3. _____entrar _____
4. _____un_____
5. _____hora
6. Debemos _____
7. _____media _____
8. _____comer _____
9. Vienen _____
10. _____después de _____
11. Quieres _____
12. _____volver _____
13. _____dos _____
14. _____semanas
15. Necesito _____
16. _____regresar _____
17. _____mes
18. Preferimos _____
19. _____año
20. Pienso _____
21. _____dos _____
22. _____invitarlos _____

B.
1. **Aquí hay un libro que puede estudiar.**
2. _____está el _____
3. _____necesito _____
4. _____hay un _____
5. _____usar
6. _____voy _____
7. Ahí _____
8. _____radio _____
9. _____vender
10. _____está el _____
11. _____pienso _____
12. En mi cuarto _____
13. _____hay un _____
14. _____traer
15. _____lista _____
16. _____espero
17. _____mandar
18. Allá _____
19. _____conseguir
20. _____debo _____
21. _____documento _____
22. _____está el _____
23. _____mostrar
24. _____noticia _____

● REVIEW DRILLS

Some additional verbs with stem changes.

A. Substitution drill.

1. Ahora le muestro el jardín.
   (usted, nosotros, ella, tú, los abuelos, Mercedes, ellas)
2. Le apostamos a que ganamos en fútbol.
   (yo, Pablo, Julio y Pablo, Julio y yo, tú, ella, ustedes)
3. Por lo menos juegas fútbol.
   (ellos, Francisco, nosotros, usted, yo, los muchachos, él)
4. Siempre vuelve dentro de diez minutos.
   (Elena y María, tú, ella, nosotros, usted, yo, Paquito)
5. Es que nunca perdemos.
   (Rafael, Patricio y Rosario, nosotros, él, yo, tú, las chicas)
6. *Roberto* prefiere no pagar la multa.
   (nosotros, usted, tú, Fernando y él, yo, mi padre, ellos)
7. Nunca consigo ganar en las carreras.
   (Cecilia, ellos, tú, ustedes, nosotros, él, mis hermanos)

B. Translation drill.

1. The trip costs a lot.
2. The boy plays a lot.
3. The man bets a lot.
4. My nephew loses a lot.
5. I prefer the brunette.
6. I return with the blonde.
7. I play with the team.
8. I bet with the boss.

Paquito y la relatividad

PAQ. *Paquito*   P. *Papá*

PAQ. Papá, voy a escribir una composición sobre los deportes. ¿Quieres ayudarme?[1]

P. Muy bien, Paquito. ¿Cuáles deportes?

PAQ. Todos, papá: fútbol, básquetbol, beisbol, boxeo, toreo . . .

P. ¡Por Dios, Paquito, no vas a describirlos todos! ¿Por qué no tratas[2] sólo uno o dos?

PAQ. Porque si hablo de todos no es necesario saber tanto de cada uno . . .

P. Hmm. . . . Bueno, vamos a trabajar.

PAQ. Pues aquí tengo algo que quiero leerte.[3] (*Lee.*) "El juego de fútbol es muy conocido[4] en Latinoamérica. También en los Estados Unidos. Pero allá se juega una clase de fútbol muy diferente del nuestro. En Sudamérica se toca[5] el balón[6] sólo con los pies y la cabeza.[7] En los Estados Unidos se pueden usar también las manos. Pero en los Estados Unidos el juego es muy cruel, tan cruel que los jugadores tienen que llevar ropa especial como protección, porque en los Estados Unidos, en vez de dar puntapiés al[8] balón, se dan puntapiés a los atletas del otro equipo . . ."

P. ¡Ja, ja, ja! . . . Ejem. Pero, hijo, ¿de dónde te vienen tales ideas?

PAQ. De mi primo Roberto, que vive en El Paso. El ve muchos juegos de fútbol.

P. Pues, es verdad que el fútbol americano es muy diferente del nuestro, pero . . .

PAQ. Sí, sí, papá. Roberto me dice también que sufren tantos golpes[9] que muchas veces hay que llevarlos al hospital.

P. Mira, Paquito. Eso de la crueldad es muy relativo. Hay millones de norteamericanos que creen que nuestro toreo es cruel.

PAQ. Eso es una tontería, papá. El toro no es más que un animal.

P. Muy bien, Paquito: eso decimos nosotros, pero los norteamericanos consideran al toro como algo humano . . . que vive, que tiene un corazón . . .[10] Nosotros también somos animales . . . animales humanos.

PAQ. Entonces, papá, nosotros creemos que los norteamericanos son crueles, y ellos creen que nosotros somos crueles. ¿Quiénes tienen razón?[11]

P. Los dos, digo,[12] ni unos ni otros.

PAQ. No entiendo, papá.

P. Yo tampoco, Paquito. Para entender esto, hay que ser filósofo.

---

[1] **ayudar** *to help* [2] *treat, discuss* [3] **leer** *to read* [4] *well-known* [5] **tocar** *to touch* [6] *ball* [7] *head* [8] *kicking* [9] *injuries* [10] *heart* [11] *are right* [12] *I mean*

8

A Respectable Man

A. *Alfredo* B. *Bernardo, friend of Alfredo*

A. What are you doing with those tools?

B. I'm changing the tires on the car.

A. But that's a very complicated job.

B. Nonsense. It's very simple.

A. But very dirty.

B. Phooey. I'll wash afterwards.

Hombre respetable

A. *Alfredo* B. *Bernardo, amigo de Alfredo*

A. 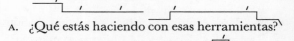 ¿Qué estás haciendo con esas herramientas?

B. Estoy cambiando las llantas del auto.

A. 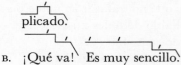 Hombre, pero eso es un trabajo muy com-

plicado.

B. ¡Qué va! Es muy sencillo.

A. Pero muy sucio.

B. Bah, después me lavo.

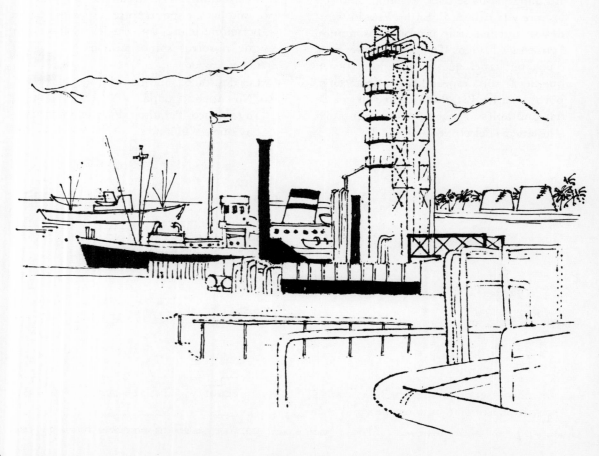

A. Are you crazy! You, a respectable, professional man.

B. Those are old-fashioned ideas.

A. O.K., O.K., let's not argue.

       *   *   *

A. Incidentally, you know that tomorrow's the official opening of the petroleum refinery?

B. Sure; I'd really like to go. You going?

A. I have two invitations; do you want to go along? They say it's a magnificent plant.

B. Too bad it's costing the country such a lot of money in dollars.

A. What of it [does it matter]? It'll be the most up-to-date plant in Latin America.

B. But, listen, man . . .

A. You've got to think about progress once in a while.

       *   *   *

B. I suppose a lot of important people are going.

A. Yes, of course: doctors, lawyers, and professors, and also some business men and tech-

---

A. ¡Qué cosa más ridícula! Tú que eres hombre respetable . . . profesional . . . (1)

B. Esas son ideas anticuadas.

A. Bueno, bueno, no discutamos.

       *   *   *

A. Pasando a otro tema, ¿sabes que mañana es la inauguración de la refinería de petróleo?

B. Sí, hombre; tengo muchas ganas de ir. ¿Tú vas?

A. Yo tengo dos invitaciones; ¿quieres ir conmigo? Dicen que es una planta magnífica.

B. Lástima que al país le cuesta una cantidad astronómica de dólares (2).

A. Y eso ¿qué importa? Va a ser la planta más moderna de Latinoamérica (3).

B. Pero, hombre . . .

A. Hay que pensar en progresar alguna vez.

       *   *   *

B. Supongo que va a ir mucha gente importante.

A. Sí, claro: médicos, abogados y profesores, y también algunos hombres de negocios y

nicians, not to mention high government officials.

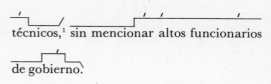

técnicos,¹ sin mencionar altos funcionarios de gobierno.

B. If you want, we can go in my car, since there's always something wrong with yours: the battery, the carburetor, the brakes, the steering . . .

B. Si quieres, vamos en mi coche, ya que el tuyo siempre tiene algo malo: la batería, el carburador, los frenos, la dirección . . .

A. Nonsense! Don't exaggerate. In any case the horn never fails and that's the main thing.

A. ¡Qué va! No exageres. En todo caso la bocina, que es lo principal, nunca falla.

B. One of these days [any day] you'll kill yourself, depending on the horn so much.

B. Por depender tanto de la bocina cualquier día te matas.

A. No, sir! With my luck . . .

A. No, hombre, con la suerte que tengo yo . . .

Cultural Notes

(1) The middle- and upper-class Spaniard and Spanish American have traditionally regarded manual labor as a symbol of lower-class status. As the dialog suggests, the pattern is changing.

(2) An important index of the economic health and growth of other nations is the amount of foreign exchange, especially of American dollars, which they have. For countries whose economies depend upon exporting raw materials, dollars are essential for buying the machinery and manufactured goods that they do not produce themselves.

(3) Latin Americans view industrialization as a *symbol* of progress.

● PRONUNCIATION EXERCISE

A. Alveolar [n] and bilabial [m]. INSTRUCTIONS: Repeat the following pairs just as you hear them.

[n]	[m]	[n]	[m]	[n]	[m]
ni	mi	nodo	modo	cana	cama
napa	mapa	nudo	mudo	lana	lama
noche	moche	nene	neme	gana	gama
note	mote				

Spanish /n/ is normally alveolar except when it assimilates to the following consonant. The bilabial nasal is [m].

B. Dental [n] and bilabial [m]. INSTRUCTIONS: Repeat the following pairs of words just as you hear them.

[n]	[m]	[n]	[m]	[n]	[m]	[n]	[m]
canto	campo	contar	comprar	un tío	un pío	sin dar	sin par
contra	compra	entender	emprender	un tomo	un pomo	cintra	cimbra
ponto	pompo	un taco	un paco	un tuerto	un puerto	en tiento	en viento
entero	empero	un techo	un pecho	ronda	rompa	indicar	invitar

---

¹ The first **c** of **técnicos** is pronounced [g].

Spanish /n/ assimilates to a following dental consonant ([t], [d]) and itself becomes dental. The Spanish nasal consonant which precedes a bilabial consonant ([p], [b], [m]) is always [m], no matter how it is spelled (i.e., the spelling may be **m** or **n**). Note also that the voiced bilabial stop [b] may be spelled either **b** or **v**.

C. Dental [n] and velar [ŋ]. INSTRUCTIONS: Repeat the following pairs of words just as you hear them.

[n]	[ŋ]	[n]	[ŋ]
cinto	cinco	un tope	un cope
junto	junco	un tubo	un cubo
monta	monja	anda	anca
en taza	en casa	banda	banca
un tarro	un carro	ronda	ronca
un teso	un queso	mando	manco
un tío	un quío		

Spanish /n/ becomes velar [ŋ] before a velar consonant ([k], [g], [w], [x]). The striking characteristic of /n/ is its readiness to assimilate to any consonant that follows it.

D. English and Spanish [nt]. INSTRUCTIONS: Listen for the difference between the English and the Spanish [nt] as an English speaker and a Spanish speaker say alternately the English and Spanish words.

English [nt]	*Spanish* [nt]
canto	canto
junta	junta
pinto	pinto
Santa	santa
Tonto	tanto

The above pairs of similar-sounding words illustrate the difference between English [nt] and Spanish [nt]. In English, the [nt] combination is usually yoked so that the [t] sounds almost like [d]. In Spanish, both the [n] and the [t] are clearly pronounced, the [n] being resonated through the nose before the [t] begins, and the [t] retaining its voiceless quality.

38 The infinitive after prepositions

EXAMPLES

1. ¿Por qué lo trae usted **en vez de mandar**lo?
2. **Sin mencionar** altos funcionarios de gobierno. *(Without mentioning high government officials.)*
3. Hay que pensar **en progresar**. *(It is necessary to think about progressing.)*
4. Tenga cuidado **de no romper** nada. *(Be careful about not breaking anything.)*
5. Tengo muchas ganas **de ir**. *(I have many desires of going.)*
6. **Por depender** tanto de la bocina. *(Because of depending so much on the horn.)*
7. Usted sigue derecho **hasta llegar** a la Calle Veinte. *(You keep straight ahead until arriving at Twentieth Street.)*

ENGLISH		SPANISH	
preposition + *–ing*	=	preposition + infinitive	
without	*mentioning*	**sin**	**mencionar**

English preposition plus verb ending in *–ing* corresponds to Spanish preposition plus infinitive.

1. En realidad, tengo muchas ganas de *ir*.
   (salir, venir, volver, seguir, participar, comer, ganar)
2. Tenga cuidado de no *romper* nada.
   (perder, dejar, prestar, traer, vender, ensuciar)
3. No puede hacerlo sin *trabajar* un poquito.
   (estudiar, saber, pagar, apostar, perder, exigir, pelear)
4. Hay que pensar en *progresar* alguna vez.
   (cambiar, practicar, participar, jugar, pagar, vender, vivir)
5. Por *hablar* tanto, no oyes nada.
   (discutir, pelear, llamar, regatear, pedir, mirar, celebrar)

6. Siga usted hasta *acabar*lo.
   (alcanzar, arreglar, conseguir, recibir, ver, oir, traer)
7. ¿Por qué no lo haces, en vez de *pensar* tanto?
   (jugar, organizar, discutir, hablar, escribir, exagerar, esperar)
8. Para *regatear,* Rosa es muy buena.
   (explicar, organizar, exagerar, apostar, pelear, discutir, vender)
9. Después de *traer* el auto, va a la nueva refinería de petróleo.
   (conseguir, pedir, mostrar, arreglar, usar, lavar, pagar)

● TRANSLATION DRILL

A. 1. Bring the coffee instead of sending it.
   2. Bring the coffee instead of selling it.
   3. Bring the coffee instead of waiting for it.
   4. Bring the coffee instead of looking at it.

B. 1. Without seeing the doctor, I can't.
   2. Without speaking to the professor, I can't.
   3. Without depending on the lawyer, I can't.
   4. Without paying the businessmen, I can't.

C. 1. Be careful about arriving at six.
   2. Be careful about changing the battery.
   3. Be careful about fixing the steering wheel.
   4. Be careful about using the brakes.

D. 1. They can't bet without losing.
   2. They can't win without practicing.
   3. They can't progress without organizing.
   4. They can't sell without bargaining.

E. 1. I don't like the idea of lending my comb.
   2. I don't like the idea of losing my scissors.
   3. I don't like the idea of selling my tools.
   4. I don't like the idea of celebrating my birthday.

F. 1. I don't have time for studying.
   2. I don't have time for learning.

3. I don't have time for waiting.
4. I don't have time for walking.

G. 1. After eating, he goes to the plant.
   2. After studying, he goes to the park.
   3. After working, he goes to the café.
   4. After playing, he goes to the patio.

H. 1. Don't leave until you see (until seeing) the marathon race.
   2. Don't leave until you explain the inauguration of the Olympic Games.
   3. Don't leave until you congratulate the football team.
   4. Don't leave until you get a job with the government.

I. 1. Because of being a professional athlete, he can't come.
   2. Because of depending on his old-fashioned car, he can't come.
   3. Because of practicing basketball, he can't come.
   4. Because of participating in (the) boxing, he can't come.

EXAMPLES

A. 1. ¿De parte de quién, **para decir**le?
   2. Le escribo **para felicitar**la.
   3. Dame diez centavos **para dar**le a un pobre.

B. 1. Dice un señor si hay ropa vieja **para vender.**
   2. Es una herramienta **para cambiar** llantas. *It's a tool for changing tires.*

ENGLISH		SPANISH	
(in order) to for	congratulate changing	**para** **para**	**felicitar** **cambiar**

(*In order*) *to* plus the infinitive and *for* (*the purpose of*) plus verb ending in *–ing* are both equivalent to **para** plus infinitive in Spanish.

1. Mamá, ven acá para *enseñar*te una cosa.
   (decir, explicar, dar, mostrar)
2. Viene mañana para *dejar* los muebles.
   (arreglar, cambiar, pagar, sacudir)
3. ¡Qué mejor oportunidad para *tomar*las!
   (mostrar, usar, traer, conseguir)
4. Dice un señor que si hay ropa para *vender*.
   (lavar, llevar, mandar, prestar)
5. Se está organizando un grupo para *ir*.
   (jugar, participar, practicar, estudiar)

● CHOICE-QUESTION RESPONSE DRILL

1. TEACHER: ¿Viene usted para estudiar o para celebrar?
   STUDENT: **Para estudiar.**
2. ¿Quiere usted la ropa para usarla o para mostrarla?
3. ¿Vienen los técnicos para organizar la planta o para hacer competencia?
4. ¿Quiere los juguetes para mostrarlos o para venderlos en el mercado?
5. ¿Va al ministerio para hablar o para oir?
6. ¿Quieres a tu mamá para decirle algo o para enseñarle algo?
7. ¿Le escribe a su sobrina para felicitarla o para calmarla?

● DISCUSSION

English has two verbal nouns (forms of verbs used in noun functions), the infinitive and the *–ing* form.[1] In most situations there is little practical difference between them, as may be seen in the virtual identity of meaning in *I prefer **to wait*** and *I prefer **waiting***. The main difference is in *where* the two forms are permitted to occur. After prepositions only the *–ing* is found.

The one exception to this is the preposition *to* itself, when used in the sense of "purpose." Thus we may say either *a tool **to change** tires* or *a tool **for changing** tires*. The *to* here is more than the sign of the infinitive; it is equivalent to the *for* of purpose, and is so translated to Spanish: **una herramienta *para cambiar* llantas.** (That *to* can actually be dropped from the infinitive we see by comparing *You don't need **to worry*** and *You needn't **worry***.) We must therefore watch out for the difference between *to* as merely the sign of the infinitive and *to* indicating purpose.

39 The infinitive with verb-plus-relator

EXAMPLES

1. **Tengo que estar** con mi tía.
2. Mañana **tiene que pagar** una multa.
3. Ahora **hay que trabajar.**
4. María Elena **acaba de salir.**
5. **Acabo de tener** un tremendo lío.

$$
\left.\begin{array}{l}
\textbf{tener que} \\
\textbf{haber que} \\
\textbf{acabar de}
\end{array}\right\} + \text{infinitive}
$$

Certain combinations of verb and relator words (**que** and prepositions) function as units.

---

[1] The *–ing* form has other uses, however: adverbial, as in *You can't make friends arguing (by arguing) all the time*, and adjectival, as in *a losing fight*.

1. Tiene una multa que pagar. *He has a fine to pay.*
2. Hay unos papeles que arreglar. *There are some papers to arrange.*
3. Me da verduras que comer. *She gives me vegetables to eat.*

	VERB	NOUN	que + INFINITIVE
Me	Tiene Hay da	una multa unos papeles verduras	que pagar que arreglar que comer

VERB		NOUN	INFINITIVE
He has There are She gives	me	a fine some papers vegetables	to pay to arrange to eat

In expressions of obligation with **que,** the noun may come directly after the verb, as in English.

● ITEM SUBSTITUTION DRILL

1. *Acaban de* cortarle el pelo.
   (tienen que, piensan en, hay que)
2. *Tienen que* discutir la profesión del toreo.
   (piensan en, hay que, acaban de)
3. *Piensan en* hacer un viaje a Perú.
   (hay que, acaban de, tienen que)
4. *Hay que* dejarlo corto atrás y a los lados.
   (acaban de, tienen que, piensan en)
5. Desgraciadamente *acaban de* salir.
   (tienen que, piensan en, hay que)

● TRANSLATION DRILL

1. In any case one must study.
   In any case I've got to study.
   In any case I'm thinking about studying.
   In any case I've just studied.
2. One of these days one must take a vacation.
   One of these days we've got to take a vacation.
   One of these days we're thinking about taking a vacation.
   We've just taken a vacation.
3. Nonsense, one must pay such a lot (an astronomical amount) in dollars.
   Nonsense, he has to pay such a lot in dollars.
   Nonsense, he's thinking about paying such a lot in dollars.
   Nonsense, he's just paid such a lot in dollars.
4. He has a bill to pay.
   There's a bill to pay.
   I'll give him a bill to pay.
5. I have some papers to arrange.
   There are some papers to arrange.
   I give him some papers to arrange.
6. She always has vegetables to eat.
   There are always vegetables to eat.
   She always gives me vegetables to eat.
7. I have to pay a fine.
   I have a fine to pay.
8. He has to write a book.
   He has a book to write.
9. He has to take a package.
   He has a package to take.
10. We have to change a tire.
    We have a tire to change.
11. They have to organize a group.
    They have a group to organize.
12. We have to say something.
    We have something to say.
13. Must one sell something?
    Is there something to sell?
14. Must one bring more plates?
    Are there more plates to bring?
15. Must one dust other furniture?
    Is there other furniture to dust?
16. One must arrange some documents.
    There are some documents to arrange.
17. It is necessary to turn off the radio.
    There is a radio to turn off.
18. It is necessary to wash the car.
    There is a car to wash.
19. It is necessary to celebrate the holiday.
    There is a holiday to celebrate.

● DISCUSSION

Like the auxiliary verbs of Unit 7, certain combinations of verb plus relator take infinitive objects. They must be separately learned.

Que as an indicator of obligation admits of two arrangements, **Tiene que comer verduras**

He has to eat vegetables and **Tiene verduras que comer** *He has vegetables to eat,* as in English. (If there is no obligation, **que** is not used: **Tiene verduras para comer** *He has vegetables to eat* means that he has them for food, not that his mother expects him to eat them.)

40   The *–ndo* form

EXAMPLES

A. 1. **Hablando** de fechas, el 4 de octubre es día feriado.
   2. **Pasando** a otro tema.
   3. Me tiró del pelo **cortando** con la maquinilla.   *He pulled my hair cutting with the clippers.*
   4. Vimos dos equipos **jugando.**   *We saw two teams playing.*
   5. **Volviendo** a casa vi a Josefina.   *Returning home (when I was returning home, on my way home) I saw Josefina.*
   6. **Viviendo** en los Estados Unidos nunca vamos a tener la oportunidad de ver una corrida de toros.   *Living (since, if we live) in the United States, we're never going to have a chance to see a bullfight.*

B. 1. **¿Diciendo** qué?   *Saying what?*
   2. No **pudiendo,** no entré.   *Not being able to, I didn't go in.*

C. 1. **Yendo** contigo, veo más.   *Going (by going) with you, I see more.*
   2. **Oyendo** eso, recordamos.   *Hearing that, we remembered.*

regular verbs	hablar comer vivir	habl– com– ⎱ viv– ⎰	–ando –iendo
irregular verbs	venir decir poder	vin– ⎱ dic– pud– ⎰	 –iendo
the verb **ir**	ir		yendo
verbs with stem ending in a vowel	traer caer creer oir incluir	tra– ca– cre– o– inclu–	 –yendo

Nearly all verbs that are irregular elsewhere are regular in the **–ndo** form; e.g., **hacer—haciendo, ser—siendo.** The three irregulars listed above are among the few exceptions.[1]

● ITEM SUBSTITUTION DRILL

1. *Pensando en* esta clase de competencia, no podemos hacer otra cosa.
   (pasando a, hablando de)
2. *Hablando de autos,* éstos nunca fallan.
   (mencionando baterías, pasando a frenos, hablando de llantas)
3. *Volviendo a casa,* pensé en una magnífica idea para el trabajo.
   (caminando a la escuela, jugando en el jardín, doblando la esquina, oyendo esos discos)

4. ¿Qué importa?   *Viviendo en Cuba,* se aprende mucho.
   (haciendo un viaje a Chile, apostando en la última carrera, arreglando este trabajo complicado, incluyendo estas ideas)
5. *Participando en las próximas carreras panamericanas,* vamos a tener unas vacaciones fantásticas.
   (viendo los Juegos Olímpicos, yendo con los funcionarios principales, cambiando a otro auto nuevo)

---

[1] The **y** in the forms that have it is merely a variant spelling for some speakers, while for others it indicates a more fricative sound than that of the **i** in **–iendo.**

The –**ndo** form of the verb points to a *happening* that is actually *taking place* at the time referred to. If either of these conditions is not met, we do not normally have an –**ndo**:

1. No happening: In *a house* **standing** *on the corner, a box* **containing** *paper, the figure* **leaning** *against the wall,* we have verbs which, at least as used in these phrases, denote a steady state, not a happening or a potentially fluctuating condition. They do not normally take –**ndo** in Spanish.

2. A happening, but not tied to a time and a place: In **Working** *is good for the health, He's fond of* **playing** *golf, People* **living** *in the tropics are more exposed to disease,* we have hypothetical or nonspecific actions. The first two examples we recognize as verbal nouns—these are infinitives in Spanish. The third is a restrictive modifier; here Spanish uses the equivalent of *People* **who live.** Neither admits an –**ndo**.

This leaves us with two kinds of English –*ings* that equate with Spanish –**ndo**. The first is adverbial, and covers all the examples given above the box. It shows something going on, usually at the same time as the action of the main verb. The two actions are loosely associated, just as in English, with a *when, because of, if,* etc., frequently implied in their relationship. The second is the –*ing* of the progressive, which is given in the next section.

41 The present progressive

EXAMPLES

A. 1. **Estoy cambiando** las llantas del auto.
2. ¿Qué **estás haciendo** con esas herramientas?
3. Ya se **está organizando** un grupo para ir.
4. **Estamos aprendiendo** español. *We are learning Spanish.*
5. **Están llegando.** *They are arriving.*

B. 1. Esta noche **viene** gente a comer.
2. ¿Le **escribe** a alguien, don Rafael?
3. Entonces, ¿qué **esperamos?**

C. 1. **Sigue sucediendo.** *It keeps on happening.*
2. Para **seguir participando,** necesitamos otro equipo. *To keep on taking part, we need another team.*

FORM OF **estar**	–**ndo** FORM OF VERB
estoy estás está estamos están	hablando comiendo viviendo durmiendo trayendo

The present progressive is used for a portrayal of *action* in *progress*.

FORM OF **seguir**	–**ndo** FORM OF VERB
sigo sigues sigue seguimos siguen	hablando comiendo viviendo durmiendo trayendo

Seguir is typical of several verbs of motion which combine with the –**ndo** form to make a kind of progressive that is colored with the meaning of the verb of motion.

● PERSON-NUMBER SUBSTITUTION DRILL

1. Estoy cambiando las llantas del auto.
   (Bernardo, tú, ellos, usted, nosotros, él, Pablo y yo)
2. Por lo menos *Julio* está trabajando.
   (yo, Elena, tú, las chicas, nosotros, Alfredo, ellas)

3. Están comiendo en la cocina.
   (nosotros, María, las criadas, Patricio, tú, ellos, yo)
4. ¿Ellas? Están sacudiendo los muebles.
   (Josefina, nosotros, ella, yo, tú, las criadas, Rosa)

● CONSTRUCTION SUBSTITUTION DRILL

INSTRUCTIONS: Repeat the following sentences just as you hear them. Then repeat them again, making the verbs progressive.

1. TEACHER: *Hablo* con un hombre respetable.
   Repita.
   STUDENT: **Hablo con un hombre respetable.**
   TEACHER: *Cambie.*
   STUDENT: **Estoy hablando con un hombre respetable.**
2. *Haces* una cosa ridícula.
3. *Pensamos* en algo diferente.
4. *Participan* en un verdadero arte.
5. *Estudiamos* para la clase de español.
6. Le *escribo* a mi tío que está en Chile.
7. *Hablo* con la casa del Dr. Arjona.
8. ¿Por qué lo *trae* usted?
9. Paquito *camina* con las manos.
10. Ya se *organiza* un grupo para ir.
11. Ellos *mandan* un equipo muy grande.
12. Le *pongo* brillantina en el pelo.
13. Bernardo *hace* un trabajo muy sencillo.
14. Lástima que al país le *cuesta* una cantidad astronómica de dólares.
15. Tú *exageras* mucho.

● PATTERNED RESPONSE DRILL

A. 1. TEACHER: ¿Qué está haciendo Bernardo?
      STUDENT: **Está cambiando las llantas del auto.**
   2. ¿Qué están haciendo ellos?
   3. ¿Qué estás haciendo tú?
   4. ¿Qué están haciendo ustedes?
   5. ¿Qué está haciendo usted?
   6. ¿Qué estoy haciendo yo?
   7. ¿Qué estamos haciendo nosotros?

B. 1. ¿Qué está vendiendo Olga?
      Está vendiendo unos discos nuevos.
   2. ¿Qué está vendiendo Pepe?
   3. ¿Qué están vendiendo los chicos?
   4. ¿Qué está vendiendo usted?
   5. ¿Qué están vendiendo ustedes?
   6. ¿Qué estás vendiendo tú?
   7. ¿Qué estoy vendiendo yo?
   8. ¿Qué estamos vendiendo nosotros?

● TRANSLATION DRILL

1. He's playing in the garden.
   Está jugando en el jardín.
   He keeps on playing in the garden.
   Sigue jugando en el jardín.
2. She's bargaining in the market.
   She keeps on bargaining in the market.
3. The brakes are failing.
   The brakes keep on failing.
4. I'm working in the Ministry.
   I keep on working in the Ministry.
5. We're studying Spanish.
   We keep on studying Spanish.
6. They're selling furniture.
   They keep on selling furniture.
7. My younger brother is celebrating his birthday.
   My younger brother keeps on celebrating his birthday.

● DISCUSSION

English uses its "simple present" tense only for those happenings that are viewed as more or less fixed or habitual, for example, *He lives in New York, He smokes a pipe;* if the happening is viewed as unsettled or as going on at the moment, English requires the present progressive, for example, *He is living in New York, He is smoking a pipe.* The present progressive in English is further extended to indicate a *planned future* action, for example, *They are coming to dinner tonight.*

Most uses of the progressive in Spanish emphasize what is *going on* at the *moment.* It is not used in reference to future time (see Unit 4 §17 for the simple present here), and even in reference to present time one finds the simple present tense, as in example *B*2, as readily as the progressive (**¿Le está escribiendo a alguien, don Rafael?**). The Spanish progressive is normally avoided in instances like the following: *He is wearing a blue tie* (he merely has it on, there is no happening; the progressive here would suggest that the speaker had been caught by surprise—he expected the man to be wearing a red tie); *He is teaching Spanish* (in the sense *He is a Spanish teacher;* the progressive again would suggest a temporary job, surprise, or something of the kind); *I am asking him for an* *immediate reply* (referring to what one has written in a letter; it is not going on now). Such instances call for the simple present in Spanish.

The progressive shares with previously studied uses of **estar** (see Unit 3 §14) the notion of comparison, change, instability.

42 The position of the with-verb pronouns in verb constructions

EXAMPLES

A. 1. **Fuimos a verla.** } *We went to see her.*
  2. **La fuimos a ver.** }

  3. **Vamos (van) a hablarle.** } *We (they) are going to speak to him.*
  4. **Le vamos (van) a hablar.** }

  5. **Puede cortarme** un poco. } *(You can cut a little for me.)*
  6. **Me puede cortar** un poco. }

  7. **¿Piensa celebrarlo?** } *(Do you expect to celebrate it?)*
  8. **¿Lo piensa celebrar?** }

  9. **Acaba de hacerlo.** } *He has just done it.*
  10. **Lo acaba de hacer.** }

  11. **Tengo que decirlo.** } *I have to say it.*
  12. **Lo tengo que decir.** }

B. 1. **Están haciéndolas.** } *They're making them.*
  2. **Las están haciendo.** }
  3. Ya **se está organizando** un grupo para ir.

C. 1. **Vamos a hablarle.** *Let's speak to him.*
  2. **Hay que mostrarlos.** *It is necessary to show them.*

Most common verbs that are coupled with infinitive or **–ndo**

PRONOUN	CONJUGATED FORM OF VERB	RELATOR IF ANY	INFINITIVE OR **–ndo**	PRONOUN
La	**Fuimos** fuimos	a a	ver– ver	**–la**
Lo	**Piensa** piensa		celebrar– celebrar	**–lo**
Lo	**Acaba** acaba	de de	hacer– hacer	**–lo**
Las	**Está** está		**haciéndo–** haciendo	**–las**

In most constructions with infinitive and **–ndo** (progressive), the pronoun may go with either verb.

Vamos a (*let's*) *and* **hay que**

CONJUGATED FORM OF VERB	RELATOR	INFINITIVE	PRONOUN
Vamos	a	**hablar–**	**–le**
Hay	que	**mostrar–**	**–los**

With **hay que**, and with **vamos a** when it means *let's*, the pronoun goes with the infinitive.

INSTRUCTIONS: Repeat the following sentences just as you hear them. Then repeat them again, changing the position of the with-verb pronoun as indicated by the models.

A. 1. TEACHER: Le vamos a hablar. *Repita.*
    STUDENT: **Le vamos a hablar.**
    TEACHER: *Cambie.*
    STUDENT: **Vamos a hablarle.**

2. Las van a traer.
3. Esta tarde lo voy a esperar.
4. Lo voy a cortar a los lados.
5. Lo vamos a perder entonces.
6. La van a quitar de aquí.
7. Lo vamos a estudiar después.
8. Me van a mostrar la flecha.

B. 1. ¿Me puede cortar un poco arriba?
    ¿Me puede cortar un poco arriba?
    ¿Puede cortarme un poco arriba?

2. ¿Lo piensa celebrar este año?
3. ¿Lo acaban de mandar?

4. ¿Lo piensa discutir?
5. Los esperamos ver.
6. La quiero invitar.
7. Le acaba de escribir.

C. 1. Están organizándolo.
    Están organizándolo.
    Lo están organizando.

2. Estoy cambiándolas.
3. Está sacudiéndolos.
4. Estamos escribiéndole.
5. Estás haciéndolo.
6. Estoy trayéndolo.
7. Está ofreciéndola.

INSTRUCTIONS: Repeat the following sentences just as you hear them. Then repeat them again substituting a verb construction for the verb, as indicated by the models.

D. 1. TEACHER: Le hablo todos los días. *Repita.*
    STUDENT: **Le hablo todos los días.**
    TEACHER: *Cambie.*
    STUDENT: **Vamos a hablarle todos los días.**

2. Las traen mañana.
3. Lo dejo en la escuela.
4. La quitan dentro de diez minutos.
5. Lo estudiamos más tarde.
6. Los tienen en casa.
7. Las venden ahora.

E. 1. Los organizan ahora.
    Los organizan ahora.
    Los están organizando ahora.

2. Le escribo una carta.
3. Me hace un favor.
4. Me cierran las puertas.
5. Nos traen dos tazas de café.
6. Lo pierden entonces.
7. Los aprende muy bien.

● DISCUSSION

Constructions in which an infinitive or an –ndo form depends on a preceding verb allow some freedom in placing the object pronoun. In general, it may go with either verb, according to the norms of placement explained in Unit 4 §18 (**Lo puedo decir** or **Puedo decirlo** *I can say it;* **para poderlo decir** or **para poder decirlo** *in order to be able to say it*). There are, however, a few constructions that permit only end-position of the pronoun. Among these are **hay que** (**Hay que mostrarlos** *It is necessary to show them*) and **vamos a** with the meaning *let's* (**Vamos a verla** *Let's go see her*). With other meanings of **ir a,** either position is possible (**Vamos a verla** or **La vamos a ver,** both meaning either *We're going to see her* or *We go to see her*).

The difference in meaning is subtle. Putting the pronoun at the end makes it exclusively the object of the second verb. The speaker's attitude toward it is more impersonal, detached, off-hand. Putting it in front makes it partly the object not only of the second verb (the infinitive) but also of the main verb. Thus **Lo quiero conocer** *I want to know (meet) him* not only says *to know him* but also suggests *I want him.* The result is added warmth, interest, or vigor, and less detachment. **Lo debo hacer** *I ought to do it* not only says *to do it* but also suggests *I owe it,* which makes the expression of obligation more forceful. An example where this contrast may also be appreciated in English is *I have to do it* (**Tengo que hacerlo**) versus *I have it to do* (**Lo tengo que hacer**)—in the latter, *it* is object both of *do* and of *have.*

Both positions are also possible with the progressive. In **Estoy arreglándolo** *I'm arranging it,* the **lo** is associated exclusively with the going-on-now meaning of the **–ndo,** and the suggestion is that the action is carried through without interruption. In **Lo estoy arreglando** the **lo** is associated also with **estoy,** whose tense form we have seen to cover more than just going-on-now time, and the suggestion is that of an action more strung out, with possible interruptions and a longer period required for its accomplishment.

43 The cardinal numerals above ten

Counting forms, 11–99

11 once	20 veinte	30 treinta		uno
12 doce	21 veintiuno	40 cuarenta		dos
13 trece	22 veintidós	50 cincuenta		tres
14 catorce	23 veintitrés	60 sesenta		cuatro
15 quince	24 veinticuatro	70 setenta	y	cinco
16 dieciséis	25 veinticinco	80 ochenta		seis
17 diecisiete	26 veintiséis	90 noventa		siete
18 dieciocho	27 veintisiete			ocho
19 diecinueve	28 veintiocho			nueve
	29 veintinueve			

Within the tens from 30 up, the units are merely added with **y;** for example, 35 **treinta y cinco;** 78 **setenta y ocho.**

Counting forms, 100–999

100 cien		
200 doscientos		uno
300 trescientos	100 ciento	dos
400 cuatrocientos	200 doscientos	veintiuno
500 quinientos	300 trescientos	cuarenta
600 seiscientos	etc.	noventa y cinco
700 setecientos		etc.
800 ochocientos		
900 novecientos		

The units and tens are added directly to the hundreds without **y.** When a smaller number is added to 100, the special form **ciento** is used.

Counting forms, 1000–999,999

1.000[1] mil	uno
2.000 dos mil	dos
21.000 veintiún mil	veintiuno
44.000 cuarenta y cuatro mil	cincuenta y seis
100.000 cien mil	cien
300.000 trescientos mil	trescientos sesenta y cinco
etc.	quinientos cuatro
	etc.

Smaller numbers are added to 1000 and its multiples. The word **mil** is not pluralized here.

---

[1] Arabic numerals are usually punctuated with the period in Spanish where the comma is used in English. The comma is used as a decimal point.

A. 1. Cuente de uno a veinte.
   2. Cuente de veintiuno a cuarenta.
   3. Cuente de cuarenta y uno a sesenta.
   4. Cuente de sesenta y uno a ochenta.
   5. Cuente de ochenta y uno a cien.
B. Cuenten en rotación.[1]

C. 1. Cuente de dos en dos[2] hasta veinte.
   2. Cuente de tres en tres hasta treinta.
   3. Cuente de cinco en cinco hasta cincuenta.
   4. Cuente de diez en diez hasta cien.
D. 1. Cuente de cien en cien hasta mil.
   2. Cuente de mil en mil hasta veinticinco mil.

EXAMPLES

A. 1. ¿Cuántos años tiene?—**Veintiuno.** *How old is she? (How many years does she have?) —Twenty-one.*
   2. ¿Cuánto cuesta?—**Veintiún** dólares. *How much does it cost?—Twenty-one dollars.*
   3. ¿Cuántas veces lo hizo?—**Veintiuna.** *How many times did you do it?—Twenty-one.*
   4. Lo hice **veintiuna** veces. *I did it twenty-one times.*

B. 1. ¿Cuántos dólares cuesta?—**Doscientos.** *How many dollars does it cost?—Two hundred.*
   2. ¿Cuántas pesetas cuesta?—**Doscientas.** *How many pesetas does it cost?—Two hundred.*
   3. Cuesta **doscientos** dólares, **doscientas** pesetas. *It costs two hundred dollars, two hundred pesetas.*

Modifying forms of **uno** *and* **–cientos** *before noun*

21 years	veintiún años	200 years	doscientos años
21 hours	veintiuna horas	200 hours	doscientas horas
31 years	treinta y un años	320 years	trescientos veinte años
31 hours	treinta y una horas	320 hours	trescientas veinte horas
101 years	ciento un años	721 years	setecientos veintiún años
101 hours	ciento una horas	721 hours	setecientas veintiuna horas

Numerals ending in *one* and multiples of 100 agree in gender with the noun they modify. When a number ending in *one* precedes the noun it modifies, **uno** shortens to **un.**

Multiple-numeral modifying forms

21,000 years	**veintiún mil años**
21,000 hours	**veintiún mil horas**
200,000 years	**doscientos mil años**
200,000 hours	**doscientas mil horas**

When a number terminating in *one* multiplies a following number, the masculine **un** is always used, regardless of the noun modified. But when one of the **–cientos** numbers multiplies a following thousand, the feminine **–cientas** is used if the noun modified is feminine.

● TRANSLATION DRILL

1. We need twenty-one hours more.
   We need twenty-one years more.
2. It's necessary to wait 101 hours.
   It's necessary to wait 101 years.
3. It costs 200 pesos.
   It costs 200 pesetas.
4. It costs 521 pesos.
   It costs 521 pesetas.
5. It costs 761 pesos.
   It costs 761 pesetas.
6. It costs 991 pesos.
   It costs 991 pesetas.
7. I have to do 21,000 things.
   I have to make 21,000 records.
8. We need 300,000 tires.
   We need 300,000 books.

[1] *Count off*   [2] *Count by twos*

1. ¿Cuántos **millones** tiene? *How many million(s) does he have?*
2. Tiene veinte **millones de** pesos. *He has twenty million pesos.*

Counting forms, 1,000,000–

1.000.000 un millón	uno
2.000.000 dos millones	dos
21.000.000 veintiún millones	veintiuno
200.000.000 doscientos millones	ochenta y seis
etc.	cien
	mil
	dos mil seiscientos tres
	etc.

The multiples of **millón,** unlike those of **mil,** use a plural, **millones.** Where English *million* modifies a noun directly, Spanish **millón** adds **de.**

● TRANSLATION DRILL

A. 1. He has a million dollars.
2. He has three million dollars.
3. He has ten million dollars.
4. He has a hundred million dollars.

B. 1. They have two million pesos.
2. They have eleven million pesos.
3. They have twenty-one million pesos.
4. They have two hundred million pesos.

C. 1. 1,000,223
2. 1,001,500
3. 1,020,700
4. 1,050,986
5. 1,111,654
6. 2,654,275
7. 10,275,837

● COMBINED PATTERN REPLACEMENT DRILL

A.

1. **Pensamos hacer una cosa importante.**
2. _____ fenomenal
3. _____ unas _____
4. Queremos _____
5. _____ trabajo _____
6. _____ profesional
7. _____ organizar _____
8. _____ sistema _____
9. Preferimos _____
10. _____ moderno
11. _____ arreglar _____
12. Podemos _____
13. _____ mencionar _____
14. _____ idea _____
15. _____ unas _____
16. _____ importantes
17. _____ traer _____
18. Tenemos que _____
19. _____ documento _____
20. Acabamos de _____
21. _____ largo
22. _____ conseguir _____

B.

1. **Pasando a otro tema, tengo que salir mañana.**
2. _____ volver _____
3. _____ esta tarde
4. _____ acabo de _____
5. _____ regresar _____
6. Hablando de otra cosa, _____
7. _____ pagar _____
8. _____ hay que _____
9. _____ pronto
10. _____ seguir _____
11. _____ alguna vez
12. Pensándolo bien, _____
13. _____ progresar _____
14. _____ debemos _____
15. _____ ahora
16. _____ celebrar _____
17. Cambiando de tema, _____
18. _____ esta noche
19. _____ vamos a _____
20. _____ jugar _____
21. _____ a las seis
22. _____ pensamos _____

The function of stress in differentiating verb forms.

A. 1. TEACHER: Speak the way I spoke.
STUDENT: **Hable usted como yo hablé.**
2. Walk the way I walked.
3. Teach the way I taught.
4. Turn the way I turned.
5. Come in the way I came in.
6. Study the way I studied.
7. Explain the way I explained.
8. Win the way I won.
9. Call the way I called.
10. Bargain the way I bargained.
11. Work the way I worked.
12. Stop the way I stopped.
13. Pay the way I paid.
14. Practice the way I practiced.
15. Change the way I changed.

B. 1. I don't talk the way he talked.
No hablo como él habló.
2. I don't celebrate the way he celebrated.
3. I don't teach the way he taught.
4. I don't come in the way he came in.
5. I don't wait the way he waited.
6. I don't explain the way he explained.
7. I don't bargain the way he bargained.
8. I don't delay the way he delayed.
9. I don't work the way he worked.
10. I don't argue the way he argued.
11. I don't participate the way he participated.
12. I don't exaggerate the way he exaggerated.
13. I don't progress the way he progressed.

READING

Juanito en la barbería

B. *Barbero* J. *Juanito*
S. *Señor Suárez, padre de Juanito*

B. Muy bien, Juanito, tú sigues. Siéntate aquí, por favor. ¿Lo quieres corto, como siempre?

J. Esta vez, señor Alonso, lo quiero largo a los lados y atrás, como los actores en el cine mexicano, ¿verdad?

B. (*al padre de Juanito*) ¿Está bien, señor Suárez, si se[1] lo corto como quiere?

S. (*que está muy ocupado mirando las fotos de una revista*[2]) Sí, Pablo; hágalo como él quiere.

J. Pero en la coronilla,[3] señor Alonso, lo quiero como el pelo de papá, con un círculo en medio.

S. ¡Juanito, el señor Alonso sabe cortar el pelo! No digas tonterías.

B. Ya sé, señor Suárez; Juanito siempre . . .

J. ¡¡Ay!!

B. ¿Qué te pasa?[4]

J. ¡Que me tiró del pelo!

B. Lo siento, Juanito. Esta maquinilla no funciona muy bien; voy a usar las tijeras. . . . Bueno, Juanito, ¿quién va a ganar los Juegos Olímpicos?

J. . . . Señor Alonso.

B. ¿Eh?

J. ¿Por qué no tienen barba[5] las mujeres?[6]

B. Pues . . . hmm . . . No es fácil explicarte eso.

J. Es que tienen más pelo en la cabeza, ¿verdad? Mi tío tiene una barba muy larga pero no tiene pelo en la cabeza. Su cabeza brilla[7] como un melón.

B. (*que también tiene cabeza que brilla como un melón*) Bueno, Juanito, esto de no tener pelo tiene sus ventajas;[8] por ejemplo, no hay que peinarse . . .

J. Es verdad, señor Alonso, pero vea usted[9] que hay una gran desventaja en no tener pelo en la cabeza.

B. ¿Y cuál es, Juanito?

J. ¡Es que cuando uno se lava la cara no sabe dónde parar!

---

[1] **se = le** = *for him* (Unit 11 §57)   [2] *magazine*   [3] *on top*   [4] *What's the matter?*   [5] *a beard*   [6] *women*   [7] *shines*   [8] *advantages*   [9] *bear in mind*

In a Café

A. *Alvaro* F. *Felipe* C. *Chalo*

A. This is a first-rate café!

F. You're right. For good coffee there's no place like this one. Hey, pst, pst! Two black coffees, good and hot.

A. There comes Carlos Francisco. What a glum look he has! What's new, Chalo? Sit down.

En un café

A. *Alvaro*[1] F. *Felipe* C. *Chalo*

A. ¡Qué buen café es éste!

F. Tienes razón. Para café bueno no hay como este lugar. ¡Mire, pst, pst! Dos cafés negros bien calientes.

A. Ahí viene Carlos Francisco. ¡Qué mala cara trae! ¿Qué hay, Chalo? (1) Siéntate.

---

[1] [álbaro]

F. Why didn't you go to school yesterday? We had an exam in philosophy.

C. I meant to go, but I couldn't. I had a bad day. I was sick.

* * *

C. How was the exam?

A. Pretty good. I got almost everything.

F. I memorized all that stuff about Socrates, but they only asked questions about Plato. I don't even know when he died.

C. What a break I didn't go, then! The only thing I know about Plato is that he was a great philosopher.

F. It's just that philosophy is a useless subject, and also too hard.

A. It's just like all other subjects. It's a question of learning them by heart.

C. I don't know what I'm going to do. We still have algebra, geometry, physics, chemistry, and biology.

F. Where are you putting history, geography, Spanish, psychology, and religion?

* * *

F. ¿Por qué no fuiste al colegio ayer? Tuvimos examen en filosofía.

C. Quise ir, pero no pude. Tuve un mal día. Estuve enfermo.

* * *

C. ¿Cómo estuvo el examen?

A. Bastante bien. Supe casi todo.

F. Yo aprendí de memoria lo de Sócrates, pero sólo hicieron preguntas sobre Platón. No sé ni cuándo murió.

C. ¡Qué suerte que no fui, entonces! Yo, lo único que sé de Platón es que fue un gran filósofo.

F. Es que la filosofía es una cosa inútil y también demasiado difícil.

A. Es igual que todas las demás materias. Es cuestión de aprenderlas de memoria.

C. Yo no sé qué voy a hacer. Todavía nos quedan álgebra, geometría, física, química y biología (2).

F. ¿Dónde dejas historia, geografía, castellano (3), psicología y religión?

* * *

A. By the way, did you know there was a big meeting of the Student Council yesterday? They came from all the schools.

A. A propósito, ¿supiste que ayer hubo una reunión muy grande del Consejo Estudiantil? Vinieron de todos los colegios (4).

F. And what did they say? Was anything done?

F. ¿Y qué dijeron? ¿Se hizo algo?

A. They asked to have the number of courses per year reduced.

A. Se pidió acortar el número de materias por año.

C. And what if the Ministry of Education doesn't accept?

C. ¿Y si el Ministerio de Educación no acepta?

F. Then there's no other way out except a general strike.

F. Entonces, no hay más remedio que hacer una huelga general (5).

C. Well, let's go; here's the bill.

C. Bueno, vámonos; aquí está la cuenta.

A. Where'd I put my wallet? Did either of you bring any money?

A. ¿Dónde puse mi cartera? ¿Alguno de ustedes trajo plata?

C. I didn't even bring a dime.

C. Yo no traje ni un diez.

F. Well, I'll pay, as usual.

F. Bueno, yo pago, como de costumbre.

Cultural Notes

(1) **Chalo** is a nickname for several given names, especially for **Carlos,** and is sometimes equivalent to *Mac,* as in *Hey, Mac.*

(2) The curriculum of the Latin-American secondary school (variously called **colegio, liceo, escuela secundaria, instituto**) is basically academic and aims to prepare the student for the university. Learning is primarily verbal, and memorization of much factual material rather than manipulation is emphasized. Though sciences form part of the curriculum, laboratory and field work are not stressed. On the other hand, the emphasis upon the traditional humanities and the handling of ideas and abstractions enable the Latin-American student at the secondary school level to discuss philosophical and literary matters with a skill which American students of the same age can rarely match.

(3) **Castellano** is widely used as a synonym of **español** in the sense of *Spanish language.*

(4) **Colegio** here refers to the secondary school with the rigidly prescribed academic curriculum mentioned in the second Note. Upon graduation from a **colegio,** a student receives the **bachillerato** or bachelor's degree. In some countries, the **bachillerato** is a university entrance examination. The **colegio** roughly corresponds to an American high school plus the first two years of college in the sense

that both are primarily concerned with general education rather than specialized training.

(5) Latin-American students have gone out on strike in protest against certain professors, a politically appointed rector (president), courses, and methods of instruction. Their strikes have often resulted in changes.

● PRONUNCIATION AND WRITING EXERCISE

A. Vowels and consonants in similar-sounding words. INSTRUCTIONS: Listen for the difference between the sounds indicated as an English speaker and a Spanish speaker say alternately the English and Spanish words.

English /a/	Spanish /o/	English /æ/	Spanish /a/	English /z/	Spanish /s/
October	octubre	admirable	admirable	rose	rosa
occupied	ocupado	attack	ataque	use	usar
office	oficina	class	clase	result	resultar
opportunity	oportunidad	pass	pasa	present	presente
doctor	doctor	Spanish	español	president	presidente

B. Writing drill. INSTRUCTIONS: Write the following lists of words from dictation.

1	2	3	4	5
cara	codo	cura	que	quipos
casa	como	curso	queso	quince
cama	copo	cuna	quebrar	quise
carta	cosa	cuyo	quedar	química
casi	corto	culpa	quemar	quitar
cada	comer	culto	querer	quizá
campo	común	cubrir		
carne	contar	cumplir		
cabo	cortar	cubano		
caso	costar	cuñado		

You have noted that the Spanish sound [k] is written **qu** when followed by the sounds [e] or [i], and written **c** in all other positions (except for a few words borrowed by Spanish from other languages, in which **k** is written, as in **kilo,** for example). The different spellings have no effect upon the pronunciation, but the Spanish writing system, like that of many other languages, contains a number of spelling conventions which must be observed.

44 Irregular preterits

EXAMPLES

A. 1. **Estuve** enfermo.
2. **Tuve** un mal día.
3. ¿Dónde **puse** mi cartera?
4. **Supe** casi todo.
5. **Quise** ir pero no **pude.**
6. No **traje** ni un diez.

B. ¿**Supiste** que ayer hubo una reunión?

C. 1. ¿Cómo **estuvo** el examen?
2. ¿Se **hizo** algo?
3. ¿Alguno de ustedes **trajo** plata?

D. **Tuvimos** examen en filosofía.

E. 1. **Anduvieron** hasta el parque. *They walked as far as the park.*
2. Sólo **hicieron** preguntas sobre Platón.
3. **Vinieron** de todos los colegios.
4. ¿Qué **dijeron?**
5. **Produjeron** más ese año. *They produced more that year.*

The unstressed –e, –o preterits

estar	estuv–	
andar	anduv–	
tener	tuv–	–e
poder	pud–	–iste
poner	pus–	–o
saber	sup–	–imos
querer	quis–	–ieron
hacer	hic–[1]	
venir	vin–	
		–e
traer	traj–	–iste
decir	dij–	–o
producir	produj–	–imos
		–eron

Both stem and ending are irregular in these verbs.
Note that the –e and –o endings are not stressed
as in the regular verbs.

EXAMPLES   A. ¿Por qué no **fuiste** al colegio ayer?

         B. 1. **Fue** una tontería.
             2. **Fue** un gran filósofo.

The preterit of **ser** *and* **ir**

fui	fuimos
fuiste	
fue	fueron

These two verbs are identical in the preterit.

EXAMPLES   1. Ayer **hubo** una reunión.
             2. No **hubo** Juegos Olímpicos en ese año.
                There were no Olympic Games in that year.

> The preterit of **haber** *there to be* is **hubo**

● PERSON-NUMBER SUBSTITUTION DRILL

1. *Yo* estuve equivocado.
   (usted, tú, ellos, mi profesor, nosotros, Susana, mis padres)
2. *Pablo* anduvo en el parque todo el día.
   (ellos, María Elena, tú, nosotros, yo, él, Pepe y yo)
3. Hoy tuvimos exámenes en álgebra, química y psicología.
   (yo, Betty y Susana, Julio y yo, tú, Carlos Francisco, ellos, usted)
4. ¿Dónde pusiste el libro de física?
   (yo, Josefina, ellos, mamá, nosotros, usted, ustedes)
5. No pudieron aceptar el honor en ese caso.
   (el Ministerio de Educación, los profesores, yo, nosotros, usted, ustedes)
6. No supe ni lo de Sócrates ni lo de Platón.
   (nosotros, Alvaro, las chicas, tú, Felipe, ustedes, él)

---

[1] Spelled **hiz–** in the form **hizo.**

7. Sin embargo, *nosotros* no quisimos acortar esa parte.

(el Consejo Estudiantil, yo, ellos, tú, los técnicos, Patricio y yo, usted)

8. *Mi Mamá* hizo la comida, como de costumbre.

(tú, ellos, yo, usted, nosotros, ella, mis padres)

9. Por eso *los señores* vinieron a la inauguración.

(yo, usted, los funcionarios de gobierno, nosotros, él, tú, ellos)

10. ¿Por qué no trajo una nueva batería, entonces?

(ustedes, tú, ellos, nosotros, él, los chicos, Bernardo)

11. *Yo* no dije nada sobre una huelga general.

(él, nosotros, ella, ustedes, el Consejo Estudiantil, ellos, tú)

12. Produjeron más arroz que frutas.

(nosotros, tú, él, estos países, usted, yo, ellos)

13. *Mi abuelo* fue un gran filósofo.

(tú, él, yo, usted)

14. ¿Por qué no fuiste a la refinería de petróleo ayer?

(usted, ustedes, él, ellos, nosotros, los abogados, yo)

15. Quise ir pero no pude.

(nosotros, ellos, usted, los alumnos, ella, tú, ellas)

● TENSE SUBSTITUTION DRILL

INSTRUCTIONS: Repeat the following sentences just as you hear them. Then repeat them again, substituting a preterit for the present-tense verb form, or vice versa.

A. 1. El carburador y la dirección están descompuestos.

El carburador y la dirección están descompuestos.

El carburador y la dirección estuvieron descompuestos.

2. Arreglar los frenos *es* demasiado complicado.
3. La bocina no *puede* fallar.
4. Yo nunca *tengo* razón en esto.
5. ¿Qué *puede* importar lo de Platón?
6. No *hay* más remedio que hacer una huelga.
7. Esta tarde *tengo* exámenes en biología e historia.
8. *Es* cuestión de aprenderlos de memoria.
9. Esas *son* ideas modernas.
10. Yo no *sé* nada de negocios.

11. ¿De dónde *trae* ese tocadiscos portátil?
12. ¿Quién *dice* "Si me hace el favor"?
13. No *quiero* ir a ver al médico.

B. 1. Mi hermano *estuvo* enfermo.
2. ¿Por qué no *fuiste* al colegio hoy?
3. Yo *tuve* un examen en geometría.
4. No *supimos* nada de castellano.
5. No *hubo* nadie en la reunión.
6. Ellos no *pudieron* faltar a la clase de religión.
7. Sólo *hicieron* preguntas sobre Sócrates.
8. *Anduvieron* hasta la esquina.
9. ¿Dónde *puse* mi cartera?
10. Yo no *quise* ir a geografía.
11. ¿Alguno de ustedes *trajo* plata?
12. ¿Quién *dijo* "Vámonos"?
13. Eso *fue* una cosa inútil.
14. ¿Quiénes *vinieron* a la planta?

● CHOICE-QUESTION RESPONSE DRILL

A. 1. ¿Fuiste a biología o no tuviste clase hoy?
2. ¿Pudiste pagar o no trajiste plata?
3. ¿Estuviste en el examen o no pudiste ir?
4. ¿Viniste a la escuela o anduviste en el parque?
5. ¿Hiciste la comida o no quisiste hacerla?
6. ¿Anduviste en el parque o fuiste a la casa?

B. 1. ¿Fue usted a ver al médico o no quiso?
2. ¿Hizo usted lo mismo o dijo que no?
3. ¿Trajo usted la cartera o la puso en la mesa?
4. ¿Tuvo el examen o no fue a clase hoy?
5. ¿Estuvo usted aburrido o pudo ir al teatro?
6. ¿Vino usted ayer o hubo otra reunión?

● DISCUSSION

The unstressed –e, –o preterits all have the same endings except that those with preterit stem ending in j have –**eron** rather than –**ieron** in the third-person plural.

Numerous derivatives are identical except in the prefix. For example, all verbs ending in –ducir are like **producir: reducir** *to reduce* is **reduje, redujimos,** etc.; **detener** *to stop* is like **tener: detuve, detuvimos,** etc.

The verb **hubo** *there was, there were* is normally found only in the third person singular. See Unit 7 §36.

45 The preterit and *–ndo* form of *–ir* stem-changing verbs

EXAMPLES

A. 1. No sé ni cuándo **murió.**
   2. Se **pidió** acortar el número de materias.

B. 1. **Durmieron** siete horas. *They slept seven hours.*
   2. **Siguieron** hablando. *They kept on talking.*

C. Lo vi **durmiendo.** *I saw him sleeping.*

	dormir	pedir
Preterit	dormí dormiste **durmió** dormimos **durmieron**	pedí pediste **pidió** pedimos **pidieron**
–ndo form	**durmiendo**	**pidiendo**

All the –**ir** verbs that have stem changes in the present tense (See Unit 4 §16) also have the **o → u** and **e → i** changes in the above three forms.

● PERSON-NUMBER SUBSTITUTION DRILL

1. *El* murió el año pasado.
   (ellos, ella, mis abuelos, ellas, la profesora)
2. *Nosotros* no dormimos bien anoche.
   (ella, tú, Francisco, yo, ellos, Chalo y yo, los otros)
3. *Yo* preferí un trabajo profesional.
   (usted, nosotros, ellos, Julio y yo, Pablo, tú, ustedes)
4. No le pedimos una cosa difícil ni ridícula.
   (ustedes, tú, Carlos, yo, Betty y Susana, nosotros, ella)
5. *Yo* seguí diez minutos después.
   (ellos, Mercedes y yo, ella, tú, ustedes, nosotros, usted)
6. Conseguimos una criada magnífica.
   (mamá, yo, ellos, Beatriz y yo, doña Mercedes, tú, usted)

● TENSE SUBSTITUTION DRILL

INSTRUCTIONS: Repeat the following sentences just as you hear them. Then repeat them again changing each present-tense verb to preterit or vice versa.

A. 1. Se *muere* de hambre.
   2. Ellos nunca *duermen* ocho horas en total.
   3. ¡Qué va! Ella *prefiere* una clase de filosofía.
   4. Pero ustedes *piden* el único documento.
   5. Usted *sigue* hasta llegar a la Avenida Norte.
   6. Probablemente ellos *consiguen* un empleo en la refinería.

B. 1. Se *murieron* de hambre.
   2. Paquito *durmió* en el patio.
   3. Los altos funcionarios de gobierno *prefirieron* no hacer nada.
   4. Roberto *pidió* un trabajo más importante.
   5. Ellos *siguieron* esa costumbre anticuada.
   6. Por depender de su padrino, no *consiguió* el puesto.

INSTRUCTIONS: Repeat the following sentences just as you hear them. Then repeat them again, changing the present-tense verb forms to progressive.

A. 1. Aquí no se *muere* nadie.
2. Mi hermana casada *duerme* en la sala.
3. Una señorita muy amable me *pide* un favor ahora.
4. El *sigue* derecho hasta llegar al Parque Central.
5. Alvaro *consigue* autos caros sin pagar.

B. 1. ¿Qué *dice* el profesor?
2. *Vienen* de Perú para participar en los juegos.
3. *Dicen* la verdad exacta.
4. *Viene* el amigo de Felipe.

46 Limiting adjectives

EXAMPLES

A. 1. Tengo **dos** invitaciones.
2. Con muy **poquito** azúcar.
3. No es **ninguna** molestia.
4. Es igual que todas las **demás** materias.

B. 1. Me hizo **otras tres** preguntas. *He asked me three other questions.*
2. Me hizo **otras muchas (muchas otras)** preguntas. *He asked me many other questions.*

C. Los **cien primeros (primeros cien)** días. *The first hundred days.*

D. 1. Tengo dos invitaciones **más**. *I have two more invitations.*
2. Cuesta un dólar **menos**. *It costs one dollar less.*

E. 1. Estuve aquí **todo el** día. *I was here all day (the whole day).*
2. **Todo el** examen fue así. *The whole exam was like that.*
3. Es igual que **todas las** demás materias.

Otros may either precede or follow **muchos,** but may only precede a cardinal numeral.

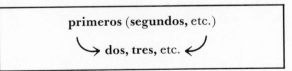

Ordinal numerals may either precede or follow cardinal.

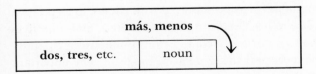

Más and **menos** must come after the combination of cardinal numeral plus noun.

| the whole | todo el, toda la |
| all the | todos los, todas las |

Todo precedes the article, as in English, and also precedes in the sense of *whole.*

A. 1. **Es tanta molestia.**
    2. ___ mucha _____
    3. _____ dinero
    4. ___ algún _____
    5. _____ plata
    6. ___ tanta _____
    7. _____ fruta
    8. ___ muchas _____
    9. _____ recados
  10. ___ algunos _____
  11. _____ recado

B. 1. **Hay otros dos chicos en la clase.**
    2. _____ tres _____
    3. _____ chicas _____
    4. ___ otros _____
    5. _____ alumnas _____
    6. _____ cinco _____
    7. ___ otros _____
    8. _____ muchas _____
    9. ___ muchas otras _____

C. 1. **Hay muchos otros libros.**
    2. _____ algunos _____
    3. _____ otro _____
    4. _____ lista
    5. _____ algunas _____
    6. _____ documentos
    7. ___ tantos _____

D. 1. **Las dos últimas casas.**
    2. ___ últimas dos _____
    3. ___ primeras _____
    4. _____ tres _____
    5. ___ tres primeras _____
    6. _____ papeles
    7. ___ cuatro _____
    8. ___ primeros cuatro _____
    9. ___ próximos _____
  10. _____ cosas
  11. ___ cuatro próximas _____
  12. ___ cinco _____

E. 1. **Todas las demás noches yo estaba ahí.**
    2. _____ días _____
    3. _____ mismos _____
    4. ___ el _____
    5. _____ tarde _____
    6. Todas _____
    7. _____ semana _____

A. 1. There are two more kilos.
    2. There are three more meters.
    3. There are five more pesos.
    4. There are ten more chickens.
    5. There's one more egg.
    6. There's one dozen more.

B. 1. He was here all day.
    2. He was here all night.
    3. He was here all month.
    4. He was here all week.
    5. He was here the whole day.
    6. He was here the whole night.
    7. He was here the whole month.
    8. He was here the whole week.
    9. He was here all the time.

● DISCUSSION

    Adjectives that relate the noun to its environment (to its possessor, as with *my, his;* to its position relative to other things, as with *this, that, third, last;* to itself, as with *other, same,* etc.), and adjectives that quantify the noun (*more, many, some, eight,* etc.), normally come before the noun in Spanish. Their positions relative to each other are for the most part the same as in English. The important exceptions involve **otro,** the numerals, and **más:**

    1. Cardinal numerals come *after* **otro,** but **mucho** may either precede or follow **otro.**
    2. Ordinal numerals usually come *after* cardinal, but may come before.
    3. **Más** takes the position of English *more* in *two times more* rather than in *two more times.*

47 The ordinal numerals

EXAMPLES

A. 1. ¿Barro **primero** aquí abajo?
2. Es la **primera** clase del día. *It's the first class of the day.*
3. Fue el **primer** ruido que oí. *It was the first noise I heard.*
4. Los veinte **primeros** días fueron típicos. *The first twenty days were typical.*
5. Fue el **primer** buen día que tuvimos. *It was the first good day we had.*

B. 1. El **segundo** escándalo fue casi tan malo. *The second scandal was almost as bad.*
2. Mi **segunda** dirección está en la lista. *My second address is on the list.*

C. 1. ¿Cuál examen? ¿El **tercero?** *Which exam? The third (one)?*
2. La **tercera** cuenta se perdió. *The third bill got lost.*
3. El **tercer** recado fue de Pablo. *The third note was from Paul.*
4. Fue el **tercero** o cuarto cónsul que fue allá. *He was the third or fourth consul who went there.*

D. El **tercer** Felipe; Felipe **Tercero.** *The third Philip; Philip the Third.*

E. 1. El cuarto **doce.** *Room Twelve, the twelfth room.*
2. La casa **veintiuna.** *The twenty-first house.*

*The ordinals, **first** to **tenth***

| | MASCULINE | | FEMININE | |
	BEFORE NOUN	ELSEWHERE		
first	**primer**	**primero**	**primera**	
second		**segundo**	**segunda**	
third	**tercer**	**tercero**	**tercera**	
fourth		**cuarto**	**cuarta**	
fifth		**quinto**	**quinta**	plurals regularly formed with **–os, –as**
sixth		**sexto**	**sexta**	
seventh		**séptimo**	**séptima**	
eighth		**octavo**	**octava**	
ninth		**noveno**	**novena**	
tenth		**décimo**	**décima**	

These are uniformly –o for masculine and –a for feminine, except for the two shortened forms **primer** and **tercer** used before masculine singular nouns when nothing more than another adjective intervenes.

● ITEM SUBSTITUTION DRILL

1. Mi número está en la *primera* lista.
   (segunda, tercera, cuarta, quinta, sexta, séptima, octava, novena, décima)
2. El *primer* auto es de Julio.
   (segundo, tercero, cuarto, quinto, sexto, séptimo, octavo, noveno, décimo)
3. Estoy en la primera *clase.*
   (juego, clases, juegos)
4. Yo vi la segunda *pregunta.*
   (toro, preguntas, toros)
5. Caminamos la tercera *noche.*
   (día, cuadra, domingo)
6. Supongo que el cuarto *examen* vale la pena.
   (chica, caso, idea)
7. Es el quinto *cónsul* que viene hoy.
   (muchacha, señor, señora)
8. Es la sexta *puerta* a la derecha.
   (cuarto, casa, número)
9. Es la séptima *semana.*
   (mes, hora, día)
10. ¿Dónde está el octavo *libro?*
    (lista, juguete, calle)
11. ¿Cuál es la novena *cosa?*
    (color, cuadra, estado)
12. Vaya usted a la décima *cuadra.*
    (cuarto, calle, jardín)

1. Which is the first?
2. Where is the second?
3. Who has the third?

4. First, dust down there.
5. Second, sweep up here.

● DISCUSSION

The ordinal numerals from *first* to *tenth* are among the adjectives that normally precede rather than follow the noun. But for emphasis, and especially in titles, they may follow.

Most speakers of Spanish are agreed on the ordinal numerals from *first* to *tenth*. From *eleventh* on, however, there is considerable variation with different speakers and in different contexts.[1] A safe compromise is to use the cardinal numerals and put them after the noun, for example, **el cuarto trece** *Room Thirteen*, substituting for *the thirteenth room*. Numerals that can differentiate the feminine normally do so with feminine nouns; thus *the thirty-first list* and *the two-hundredth list* are respectively **la lista treinta y una** and **la lista doscientas**.

48 Days, months, years

EXAMPLES

A. 1. ¿Qué día es hoy, **jueves** o **viernes?**
   2. Cae **miércoles.**

B. 1. El domingo es **primero,** lunes **dos.**
   2. **Estamos a primero (dos, tres,** etc.). *It's the first (second, third, etc.).*
   3. **¿A cuántos (del mes) estamos?** *What day (of the month) is it?*

C. 1. El 4 de **octubre.**
   2. Fue el 23 (veintitrés) de **agosto** de 1771 (mil setecientos setenta y uno). *It was the 23rd of August, 1771.*

Sunday	**domingo**	January	**enero**
Monday	**lunes**	February	**febrero**
Tuesday	**martes**	March	**marzo**
Wednesday	**miércoles**	April	**abril**
Thursday	**jueves**	May	**mayo**
Friday	**viernes**	June	**junio**
Saturday	**sábado**	July	**julio**
		August	**agosto**
		September	**setiembre**
		October	**octubre**
		November	**noviembre**
		December	**diciembre**

● TRANSLATION DRILL

A. 1. The first Sunday in (of) May.
   2. The second Thursday in August.
   3. The third Saturday in January.
   4. The fourth Tuesday in March.

B. 1. Friday, July 4, 1776.
   2. Monday, October 12, 1492.
   3. Wednesday, August 15, 1588.
   4. Thursday, November 11, 1918.
   5. Sunday, February 22, 1732.

C. 1. December 25, 1965.
   2. April 29, 1958.
   3. June 10, 1951.
   4. September 18, 1938.
   5. March 11, 1923.
   6. April 1, 1899.

[1] *Eleventh,* for example, may be **undécimo, décimo primero, onceavo,** or simply **once.**

The days of the month are designated by cardinal numerals (**diez, doce, veintiuno,** etc.), except for the first (**primero**).

The standard formula for asking the day of the month is **¿A cuántos (del mes) estamos?,** literally *At how many [days] (of the month) are we?* The reply is **Estamos a siete** (**veintiséis,** etc.).

Normally the preposition **de** appears twice in a complete date: **el 23 de agosto de 1771** *August 23, 1771.* Thousands are not represented as multiples of hundreds: *eighteen twenty-six* is **mil ochocientos veintiséis.**

49 The plural of nouns with singular ending in [s]

EXAMPLE

Practican los **jueves** y juegan los **viernes.** *They practice (on) Thursdays and play (on) Fridays.*

SINGULAR				PLURAL			
one	birthday record player Thursday Monday	un	cumpleaños tocadiscos jueves lunes	two	birthdays record players Thursdays Mondays	dos	cumpleaños tocadiscos jueves lunes
one	Saturday Sunday	un	sábado domingo	two	Saturdays Sundays	dos	sábados domingos
one	Englishman country month	un	inglés país mes	two	Englishmen countries months	dos	ingleses países meses

Almost all nouns whose last syllable is a weak-stressed syllable ending in [s] in the singular, have the same form for the plural.

● TRANSLATION DRILL

1. I celebrate my birthday here.
   I celebrate my birthdays here.
2. I haven't got my record player here.
   I haven't got my record players here.
3. I'm here on Monday.
   I'm here on Mondays.
4. I'm busy on Tuesday.
   I'm busy on Tuesdays.
5. He comes on Wednesday.
   He comes on Wednesdays.
6. I see her on Thursday.
   I see her on Thursdays.
7. It's going to happen on Friday.
   It's going to happen on Fridays.
8. We don't go to (the) school on Saturday.
   We don't go to (the) school on Saturdays.
9. The market's not open on Sunday.
   The market's not open on Sundays.

50 Shortened adjectives

EXAMPLES

A. 1. ¡Qué **buen** café es éste!
   2. Para café **bueno,** no hay como este lugar.
   3. **Buena** idea.

B. 1. Tuve un **mal** día.
   2. El suyo siempre tiene algo **malo.**
   3. ¡Qué **mala** cara trae!

C. 1. Fue un **gran** filósofo.
2. Como **gran** cosa me concedieron hasta mañana.
3. Ayer hubo una reunión muy **grande.**

D. 1. ¿Desea dejar **algún** recado? *(Do you wish to leave some message?)*
2. ¿Quieres traerme **algún** buen libro? *Will you bring me some good book?*
3. ¿**Alguno** de ustedes trajo plata?
4. Hay que pensar en progresar **alguna** vez.

E. 1. **Ningún** extranjero puede. *No foreigner is able to.*
2. No es **ninguna** molestia. *(It isn't any trouble.)*

F. 1. **Cualquier** día te matas.
2. ¿Cuál desea usted?—**Cualquiera.** *Which do you wish?—Any (any one).*

	Before singular noun		Elsewhere
	MASCULINE	FEMININE	
	buen	buena	bueno, –a, –os, –as
	mal	mala	malo, –a, –os, –as
	gran		grande, –s
	algún	alguna	alguno, –a, –os, –as
	ningún	ninguna	ninguno, –a, –os, –as
	un	una	uno, –a, –os, –as
	primer	primera	primero, –a, –os, –as
	tercer	tercera	tercero, –a, –os, –as

Except for **grande,** the shortening takes place only in the masculine singular when the adjective precedes the noun and nothing more than another adjective intervenes.

Before noun, either gender		Elsewhere	
SINGULAR	PLURAL	SINGULAR	PLURAL
cualquier	**cualesquier**	**cualquiera**	**cualesquiera**

Besides being shortened like the other adjectives, this one has an interior plural.

● ITEM SUBSTITUTION DRILL

1. Aquí no hay ninguna *profesora.*
(profesor, tijeras, frijoles)
2. ¿Desea dejar algún *recado?*
(cosa, libros, herramientas)
3. ¡Qué buena *carne!*
(café, frijoles, verduras)
4. Tuve una mala *idea.*
(día, preguntas, exámenes)
5. Aquí hay un *médico.*
(planta, funcionarios, refinerías)
6. No puedo venir la primera *semana.*
(día, tarde, mes)
7. ¿Dónde está el tercer *libro?*
(noticia, documento, cuenta)
8. Es un gran *filósofo.*
(señora, jefes, profesores)
9. Deme cualquier *libro* de éstos.
(cartera, libros, carteras)
10. La *batería* está mala.
(carburador, llantas, frenos)
11. Este *café* es muy bueno.
(carne, huevos, frutas)
12. La *muchacha* ya está muy grande.
(muchacho, muchachas, muchachos)
13. Primero vienen *Susana y Betty.*
(Julio, Cecilia, Pablo y Roberto)
14. No es una *señorita* cualquiera.
(señor, señoras, señores)

● DISCUSSION

Only a limited number of adjectives, the majority of which are listed above, undergo shortening. Shortening characteristically occurs in the masculine singular, when the adjective stands directly before the noun it modifies (or with nothing more than some additional adjective between it and its noun). A very few adjectives are shortened under other circumstances. Among these are certain of the numerals studied in this unit: **cien** is the regular form for *one hundred,* shortened from **ciento,** the latter being used only when some smaller numeral follows, as in **ciento dos,** and in the plural multiples **doscientos,** etc.; **veintiún** (**treinta y un,** etc.) is shortened from **veintiuno** (**treinta y uno,** etc.), and is used under conditions like those of the other shortened adjectives except that it is, of course, always plural in meaning (there is no such form as **veintiunos**).

Cualquier(a) means *any* in the sense *any whatsoever* when it precedes the noun and *just any, any old* when it follows. **Deme cualquier libro** *Give me any book (whatsoever);* **No me dé un libro cualquiera** *Don't give me just any old book.*

● COMBINED PATTERN REPLACEMENT DRILL

A.

1. **Cualquier día viene la cuestión.**
2. _____ huelga
3. _____ semana _____
4. _____ pasa _____
5. Esta _____
6. _____ las _____
7. _____ suceden _____
8. _____ lío
9. _____ vez _____
10. _____ inauguración
11. _____ vuelve _____
12. _____ las _____
13. _____ año _____
14. _____ vacaciones
15. _____ siguen _____
16. El próximo _____
17. _____ enero _____
18. _____ llegan _____
19. _____ noticia
20. _____ las _____

B.

1. **Los primeros señores supieron trabajar después.**
2. _____ quisieron _____
3. _____ dos _____
4. _____ ayer
5. _____ últimos _____
6. _____ señor _____
7. _____ dormir _____
8. _____ pudo _____
9. Los _____
10. _____ buenos _____
11. _____ llegar _____
12. _____ señor _____
13. _____ tarde
14. _____ consiguió _____
15. _____ filósofo _____
16. _____ gran _____
17. Los _____
18. _____ prefirieron _____
19. _____ pronto
20. _____ venir _____
21. _____ tuvieron que _____
22. _____ otro _____
23. _____ abogado _____

● TRANSLATION REVIEW DRILL

Contrasts of **ser** and **estar.**

A. 1. He's serious, but he's wrong (mistaken) now.
2. He's strong, but he's sick now.
3. He's old, but he's sad now.
4. He's simple, but he's furious now.
5. He's typical, but he's alone now.
6. He's respectable, but he's dirty now.
7. He's nice, but he's busy now.
8. He's different, but he's married now.

B. 1. It's black, but it's not hot.
2. It's big, but it's not open.
3. It's magnificent, but it's not here.
4. It's expensive, but it's not out of order (bad).
5. It's antiquated, but it's not there.

C. 1. It's not portable, but it's okay.
2. It's not modern, but it's dirty.
3. It's not important, but it's here.
4. It's not serious, but it's broken.

Lección de aritmética[1]

J. *Juanito*   PAQ. *Paquito*
P. *papá de Paquito*

J. ¡Hola, Paquito! ¿Qué estás haciendo?

PAQ. Papá me está enseñando las lecciones de aritmética.

P. ¿Qué tal, Juanito? . . . Sí, hay que estudiar para progresar en la escuela . . . Vamos a ver, Paquito, si tienes un peso, y te doy tres pesos más, ¿cuántos pesos vas a tener en total?

PAQ. Tres, papá.

P. ¿Tres no más?

PAQ. Sí.

P. Mira, Paquito: ya tienes un peso que te di . . .

PAQ. ¡No, papá! No me diste nada.

P. ¡Suponlo, suponlo! . . . Ahora, ¿cuántos pesos tienes?

PAQ. Cuatro.

P. ¿Cuatro qué?

PAQ. Cuatro no más.

P. Mira, hijo: pesos y pesos son pesos; huevos y huevos son huevos; gatos y gatos son gatos. Para ser exacto, hay que dar la unidad . . . es decir, hay que mencionar la cosa de que se trata.[2] ¿Entiendes?

PAQ. Sí, papá.

P. Bueno: otra vez . . . Si tengo dos coches y compro tres coches más, ¿cuántos tengo?

PAQ. (*contando con los dedos*[3]) Cinco.

P. ¡¿Cinco qué, por Dios?!

PAQ. ¡Ah, cinco autos!

P. Cinco coches, sí . . . y si tomo dos cafés negros y más tarde cuatro cafés negros, ¿cuántos cafés negros tomo en total?

PAQ. Seis . . . cafés negros . . . Pero la última vez que tomaste tanto café, no dormiste en toda la noche, y mamá dijo que . . .

P. (*con prisa*[4]) A Juanito no le puede interesar lo que dijo mamá . . . Bueno, vamos a tomar un helado.

J. No traigo dinero, don Rafael.

P. Yo pago, Juanito . . . como de costumbre.

---

[1] The first **t** in **aritmética** is pronounced [d]. [2] *in question* [3] *fingers* [4] *hastily*

10

The Country and the City

M. *Mario*   L. *Luis, friend of Mario*

M. I heard you were going to work in the country. How awful! I can't even stand looking at a picture of it [to me not even in painting].

L. Why? I'm crazy about the country: fresh air, mountains, clouds, blue sky, trees, simple people . . .

M. Yes? And what about the rain and the

El campo y la ciudad

M. *Mario*   L. *Luis, amigo de Mario*

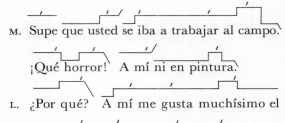

M. Supe que usted se iba a trabajar al campo.

¡Qué horror! A mí ni en pintura.

L. ¿Por qué? A mí me gusta muchísimo el campo: aire puro, montañas, nubes, cielo azul, árboles, gente sencilla . . .

M. ¿Sí? ¿Y qué me dice de la lluvia y el

mud in the winter and the wind and the
dust in the summer?

L. When you're working, that's the least of
your troubles, don't you think?

M. Could be, but it's pretty sad to see nothing
but farm [farmers'] houses with straw roofs,
without drinking water, light, or other
conveniences. It's all right to have the
country, but live in the city, like Don
Pepe . . . .

L. I see you prefer the noise of the streetcars
and this hectic life in the city. At least I'm
not going to die of ulcers or a heart attack.

* * *

M. Which of Don Pepe's ranches are you
going to?

L. The Hacienda El Alamo, about forty kilo-
meters from here, more or less.

M. And what do they grow there?

L. Wheat, lentils, corn, potatoes, onions, and
things like that.

M. I hear Don Pepe had a lot of cattle on that
ranch.

L. Yes, he still does. There are imported cows

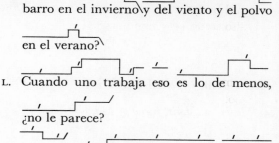
barro en el invierno y del viento y el polvo
en el verano?

L. Cuando uno trabaja eso es lo de menos,
¿no le parece?

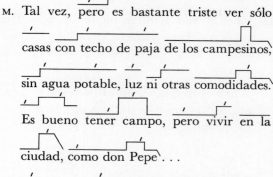
M. Tal vez, pero es bastante triste ver sólo
casas con techo de paja de los campesinos,
sin agua potable, luz ni otras comodidades.
Es bueno tener campo, pero vivir en la
ciudad, como don Pepe . . .

L. Veo que usted prefiere el ruido de los
tranvías en las calles y esta vida agitada de
la ciudad. Por lo menos yo no voy a morir
de úlceras ni de ataque al corazón.

* * *

M. ¿A cuál de las fincas de don Pepe va?

L. A la Hacienda El Alamo, como a cuarenta
kilómetros de aquí, más o menos.

M. ¿Y qué producen allí?

L. Trigo, lentejas, maíz, papas, cebollas y cosas
por el estilo.

M. Me dijeron que don Pepe tenía mucho
ganado en esa finca.

L. Sí, todavía tiene. 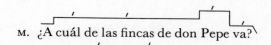 Hay vacas y toros

and bulls for breeding and dairy stock, and also some very fine horses.

importados (1) para crianza y lechería, y también caballos muy finos.

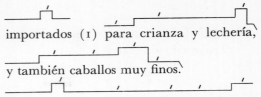

M. I imagine they must have sheep and hogs, too.

M. Me imagino que deben tener ovejas y cerdos, también.

L. Yes, mainly for wool, hides, and meat. The hogs bring in a lot [leave plenty of profit] at the fair.

L. Sí, principalmente para lana, cueros y carne. Los cerdos dejan bastante ganancia en la feria.

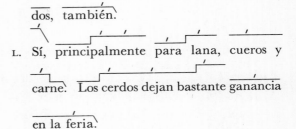

* * *

* * *

M. And when did you accept that job? As manager, right?

M. ¿Y cuándo aceptó ese trabajo? De administrador (2), ¿verdad?

L. Yes. Just the night before last we met at the Union Club. While we were eating, Don Pepe told me he needed someone.

L. Sí. Sólo anteanoche nos encontramos en el Club de la Unión. Mientras comíamos, don Pepe me contó que necesitaba a alguien.

M. And then he offered you the job, I suppose.

M. Y entonces le ofreció el puesto, me imagino.

L. That's how it was. I was very excited and I promised to give him an answer the next day.

L. Así fue. Yo me entusiasmé y le prometí contestarle al otro día.

M. And what did your wife say to all this?

M. Y su señora, ¿qué dijo a todo esto?

L. She said it was fine, if it was necessary, but that she and the children had to stay here this winter on account of school.

L. Dijo que estaba bien, si era necesario, pero que ella y los niños tenían que quedarse aquí este invierno por el colegio.

M. What's it like? Good salary?

M. ¿Y qué tal? ¿Buen sueldo?

L. It sure is! *And* what's more, he promised to give me one fourth of the wheat crop.

L. Ya lo creo. Además prometió darme una cuarta parte de la cosecha de trigo.

M. Well, I congratulate you! Apparently farmers don't do so bad, eh?

L. A little better than a bank clerk, my friend, a little better . . .

M. Hombre, lo felicito. Por lo visto, los agricultores (3) no la pasan mal (4), ¿eh?

L. Algo mejor que un empleado de banco, mi amigo, algo mejor . . .

Cultural Notes

(1) A livestock breeder may import purebred stock as much for prestige as for building up his herd.

(2) Only a man of fairly high social position is eligible for the post of tenant administrator of a large ranch.

(3) *Farmer,* in the sense of peasant or one who cultivates ground as a tenant, is **campesino** in Spanish; a landed farmer, one who owns or manages a farm, is **agricultor.**

(4) The feminine object pronoun **la** is used in a number of idiomatic expressions without reference to a definite antecedent. Sometimes it is equivalent to an indefinite *it* in English (e.g., *Now you're going to catch it!*), but often there is no specific equivalent.

● PRONUNCIATION AND WRITING EXERCISE

A. Identical vowel fusion. INSTRUCTIONS: Repeat the following phrases and sentences just as you hear them.

1. *Fusion of /e/'s*	2. *Fusion of /a/'s*	3. *Fusion of /e/'s and of /a/'s*
la clase de español	Va a hablar.	el hombre que está aquí
¿Qué es eso?	Se lo doy a aquel hombre.	¿Le escribe a alguien?
un ejemplar de este libro	Llega a la puerta.	un pobre que está ahí
porque es la verdad	¿Qué va a hacer?	Decían que era a mediodía.
Tengo que estudiar.	Está abierta.	
compañera de escuela	la puerta abierta	
Vive en México.	Voy a arreglar esto.	
¿Qué edad tiene ella?	Va a ir mucha gente.	
que ensucias la pared	esta vida agitada	
Habla el cuñado de él.	necesitaba a alguien	
Ya se está organizando.	La cuenta está algo baja.	
¿Qué mejor oportunidad que ésta?	Va a aceptar.	
porque en los Estados Unidos	La acompaño en su pena.	
¿Qué estás haciendo?	Llama a la policía.	
Tú que eres hombre respetable.	Mira a los artilleros.	
Dicen que es una planta magnífica.	Están mirando hacia acá.	
el lugar sagrado donde estaban	las recomendaciones necesarias	
¿Dónde está María Elena?	a ambos países	
¡Qué suerte tiene ese tipo!		

When two or more like vowels of different words come together in a breath group they contract so that only one vowel is pronounced. In the great majority of instances, the vowels which are found at the end and at the beginning of words in the same breath group are /e/ and /a/. In an earlier period in the history of the Spanish language, some contractions were shown in writing;

e.g., **de este** was written **deste,** and **de él** was written **dél.** Today only the contraction of **de** and **el** (definite article) is represented in writing (the only other contraction shown in written Spanish, namely the fusion of **a** and **el** to **al,** involves unlike vowels; see Unit 6 §29).

B. Writing drill.   INSTRUCTIONS: Write the following lists of words from dictation.

1.	2.	3.	4.		5.
gana	goma	gusto	pagué	pague	guía
gato	golfo	gula	negué	niegue	guija
ganga	gota	gura	regué	riegue	guincho
ganso	gorra	gustar	vagué	vague	guiño
ganar	golpe	gusano	jugué	juegue	guisa
gastar	gordo	gutural	llegué	llegue	guiar
ganado	gorila		entregué	entregue	guión
garganta	gobierno				guitarra
ganancia	gozar				Guillermo
garrafa	gobernar				

You have noted that the Spanish phoneme /g/ with its two variants [g] and [g] is written **gu** when followed by the sounds [e] or [i], and written **g** in all other positions.   Initial **gu** before [e] is found in very few words in Spanish (principally **guerra** *war* and its derivatives).   The different spellings do not represent different pronunciations.   See the treatment of **c** and **qu** in Unit 9.

51   The imperfect

EXAMPLES

1. Dijo que **estaba** bien, si **era** necesario, pero que ella y los niños **tenían** que quedarse aquí.
2. Mientras **comíamos,** don Pepe me contó que **necesitaba** a alguien.
3. Don Pepe **tenía** mucho ganado.
4. Se **iba** a trabajar al campo.
5. Yo no **sabía** que usted **hablaba** español. *I didn't know that you spoke Spanish.*

Imperfect of regular verbs

hablar habl–		comer com–	vivir viv–
–aba	–ábamos	–ía	–íamos
–abas		–ías	
–aba	–aban	–ía	–ían

The imperfect indicates "unstopped action" in the past.   English *I used to work* (*play, live,* etc.) and *I was working* (*playing, living,* etc.) are among its equivalents.

Imperfect of **ser,** **ir,** *and* **ver**

ser		ir		ver	
era	éramos	iba	íbamos	veía	veíamos
eras		ibas		veías	
era	eran	iba	iban	veía	veían

These three verbs are the only ones that are irregular in the imperfect.

1. Antes *usted* hablaba español, ¿verdad?
   (ustedes, nosotros, Luis, tú, yo)
2. *Don Pepe* necesitaba a alguien.
   (ellos, yo, tú, nosotros, él)
3. *Yo* trabajaba en el Ministerio de Educación.
   (nosotros, ella, tú, ustedes, Mario)
4. Siempre comíamos en ese restorán.
   (ellos, yo, tú, él, Fernando y yo)
5. Antes vivían en el extranjero.
   (yo, nosotros, ella, tú, el administrador)

6. *Los niños* tenían que volver a la ciudad.
   (el consejo estudiantil, nosotros, Rosa, usted, alguien)
7. *Yo* veía los árboles en las montañas.
   (tú, ellos, usted, nosotros, los campesinos)
8. *Yo* iba al campo todos los días excepto los domingos.
   (nosotros, ellos, usted, tú, los agricultores)
9. En esos días *él* era considerado como un gran filósofo.
   (tú, yo, nosotros, ellos, Pablo y yo)

● TENSE SUBSTITUTION DRILL

INSTRUCTIONS: Repeat the following sentences just as you hear them. Then repeat them again, changing the present tense verb forms to imperfect.

A. 1. Carlos siempre *contesta* mis preguntas fáciles.
   2. Sólo *faltan* tres días, ¿verdad?
   3. Por lo visto los empleados de banco no la *pasan* mal.
   4. Como de costumbre me *da* una cuarta parte de la cosecha de trigo.
   5. Siempre *dobla* a la derecha en esa esquina.
   6. *Estudiamos* álgebra, biología y castellano.

B. 1. *Producen* cebollas, lentejas y maíz.
   2. *Vivimos* cerca de la Hacienda El Alamo.
   3. No *hay* bastante agua potable allá.
   4. Las casas *tienen* techo de paja.
   5. Yo no *quiero* morir de úlceras ni de ataque al corazón.

6. Siempre *trae* ovejas y caballos importados a la feria.
7. No *hay* más remedio que hacer una huelga general.
8. La casa *tiene* luz, agua y otras comodidades.

C. 1. Lo *veo* casi todos los días en el Club de la Unión.
   2. *Voy* a tener exámenes en física, geografía y religión.
   3. Mi cuñado *va* a su finca en el campo casi todos los días.
   4. Eso *es* lo de menos, hombre.
   5. Las vacas *son* para crianza y lechería.
   6. *Es* cuestión de aprenderlas de memoria.

● CHOICE-QUESTION RESPONSE DRILL

A. 1. Antes de entrar a la clase, ¿usted estudiaba o dormía?
   2. Antes de entrar a la clase, ¿usted escribía o jugaba?
   3. Antes de vivir aquí, ¿ustedes trabajaban o estudiaban?
   4. Antes de vivir aquí, ¿usted tenía auto o tomaba el tranvía?
   5. Antes del invierno, ¿le gustaba el campo o tenía que trabajar demasiado?
   6. Antes del verano, ¿producían leche o vendían carne?
   7. Antes de la huelga, ¿usted tenía un puesto o le prometían uno?

B. 1. Cuando usted vivía ahí, ¿comía en la casa o iba a un restorán?
   2. Cuando usted vivía ahí, ¿aprendía o enseñaba español?

3. Cuando ustedes vivían ahí, ¿estudiaban o trabajaban?
4. Cuando ustedes vivían ahí, ¿les gustaba el aire puro del campo o preferían las comodidades de la ciudad?
5. Cuando ustedes vivían ahí, ¿les gustaba el cielo azul del campo o preferían el ruido de la ciudad?

C. 1. ¿Usted no tenía hambre o no quería volver a la casa?
   2. ¿Ustedes no tenían dinero o no querían pagar?
   3. ¿Usted estudiaba química o prefería psicología?
   4. ¿Usted era amigo de Pablo o no lo conocía?

52 Imperfect versus preterit

EXAMPLES

1. No sé ni cuándo **murió.**
2. Me **tiró** del pelo.
3. **¿Recibiste** alguna mala noticia?
4. Me **quitaron** los documentos.

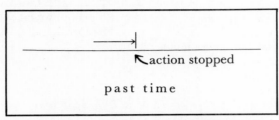

↖action stopped

past time

To report an action as "happening and then over with," the preterit is used.

EXAMPLES

A. 1. **Tuvimos** examen en filosofía.
2. Don Pepe **tenía** mucho ganado.

B. 1. ¿Por qué no **fuiste** al colegio ayer?
2. Se **iba** a trabajar al campo.

C. 1. ¿Cómo **estuvo** el examen? *(How did it* ***turn out?****)*
2. Dijo que **estaba** bien.

D. 1. **Estuve** allí a las seis. *I was (=* ***got****) there at six.*
2. **Estaba** allí a las seis. *I was (already) there at six.*

E. 1. **Fue** una tontería. *(**What happened** was only a trifle.)*
2. Dijo que estaba bien, si **era** necesario.

F. 1. Quise ir pero no **pude.** *(I **failed** to.)*
2. Dijo que no **podía.** *He said he couldn't (lacked the power or ability).*

G. 1. **Tuvieron** que quedarse aquí. *They had to stay here (and did).*
2. **Tenían** que quedarse aquí. *(They felt obliged to.)*

H. 1. **Costó** mucho. *It cost a lot (there was an actual purchase).*
2. **Costaba** mucho. *The price was high.*

I. 1. ¿Supiste que ayer **hubo** una reunión? *(A meeting **took place**.)*
2. **Había** mucha gente en el comedor. *There were a lot of people in the dining room (they were on hand, doing whatever they were doing).*

Preterit ⟶ ↖outcome

Imperfect ⟶ outcome disregarded

The preterit concentrates on the *outcome*. The imperfect ignores it.

INSTRUCTIONS: Repeat the following sentences just as you hear them. Then repeat them again, substituting the words or phrases suggested and changing the verb from imperfect to preterit, or vice versa.

1. TEACHER: *Antes* producía mucho trigo.
   Repita.
   STUDENT: **Antes producía mucho trigo.**
   TEACHER: El año pasado _____
   STUDENT: **El año pasado produjo mucho trigo.**

2. Yo pagaba la cuenta *como de costumbre.*
   _____una vez.

3. *Siempre* me ofrecía un puesto con buen sueldo.
   Anteanoche _____

4. *Muchas veces* él salía encantado.
   Después de un rato _____

5. *Antes* yo lo veía con horror.
   Anteanoche _____

6. *Ayer* tuvimos examen en geometría e historia.
   Casi todos los días _____

7. *El año pasado* tuve una vida agitada.
   En esos días _____

8. Comió pollo *todo el día.*
   _____ todos los días.

9. *Ayer* comimos en el Club de la Unión.
   Siempre_____

● TRANSLATION DRILL

INSTRUCTIONS: The following paired sentences are designed as equivalents of Spanish sentences requiring preterit in the first and imperfect in the second sentence of the pair. Since context beyond the sentence frequently gives the cue that determines the choice, these cues are occasionally presented here parenthetically; the hints in parentheses are not to be translated.

1. How was the exam (did it turn out)?
   How was the professor?

2. He went to do it.
   He was going to do it.

3. They had to stay home (and did).
   They had to stay home (felt they should).

4. It cost too much (but was purchased).
   It cost too much (and therefore was not purchased).

5. Then I learned about the saint's day.
   I already knew about the saint's day.

6. I managed to win.
   I was able to win.

7. Then I caught on to the idea.
   I understood the idea.

8. I worked at the Ministry (for a time).
   I was working at the Ministry (at that time).

9. I went to the theater (once).
   I went to the theater (customarily).

10. Did you get the invitation?
    Did you have the invitation?

11. Yesterday there was a meeting.
    Many times there used to be meetings.

12. I got very enthusiastic (when she told me).
    I was very enthusiastic (whenever she told me).

13. I wrote very little (that time).
    I wrote very little (as a rule).

14. There was a lot of rain and mud (that summer).
    There was a lot of rain and mud (in the summertime).

15. I preferred the other horse (picked out).
    I preferred the other horse (liked most).

EXAMPLES

1. Nos **encontramos** en el club. Mientras **comíamos,** don Pepe me **contó** que **necesitaba** a alguien.
2. **Dijo** que **estaba** bien.
3. Como **estaba** algo escaso de dinero, yo mismo **cambié** las llantas y después **lavé** el auto. *As I was a little short of money, I changed the tires myself and then washed the car.*

Preterit ——————→| ————→| ————→| ——————————
successive events, each brought to an end

Imperfect ——————————→ ————————→ ————————→
"unstopped" events, providing background

In combinations of preterit and imperfect, the preterit pictures the successive events while the imperfect gives the background or the unfinished business.

● PERSON-NUMBER SUBSTITUTION DRILL

INSTRUCTIONS: Repeat the following sentences just as you hear them. Then repeat them again, substituting the subjects suggested. Note that in these sentences both verbs (in preterit and imperfect) have the same subject.

1. *Don Pepe* le contó que necesitaba a alguien.
   (yo, ellos, nosotros, tú, él)
2. *¿Ellos* dijeron que estaban bien?
   (él, yo, tú, nosotros, usted)
3. Dijo que iba a hablar sobre lentejas y cosas por el estilo.
   (nosotros, tú, ellos, yo, él)
4. *Yo* no quería, pero tuve que hacerlo.
   (ella, nosotros, ustedes, Mario, tú)
5. Cuando tenía once años, fui a las montañas.
   (ella, ellos, tú, María Elena, nosotros)
6. Hablé con la chica que quería conocer.
   (Luis, tú, mis sobrinos, nosotros, él)
7. Mientras comíamos, hablamos sobre las demás cosas.
   (ellos, yo, él, tú, Alfredo)
8. Cuando yo estaba en México, fui a ver al Dr. Arjona.
   (nosotros, ella, ellos, tú, usted)

● TENSE SUBSTITUTION DRILL

INSTRUCTIONS: Repeat each sentence just as you hear it. Then repeat it again changing the present-tense verbs in the first group to preterit and imperfect, and in the second group to imperfect and preterit.

A. 1. TEACHER: Dice que va a hablar más tarde. *Repita.*
      STUDENT: **Dice que va a hablar más tarde.**
      TEACHER: *Cambie.*
      STUDENT: **Dijo que iba a hablar más tarde.**
   2. Dice que hay muchas nubes.
   3. Veo una casa que está a dos kilómetros de aquí más o menos.
   4. Josefina barre el cuarto que está sucio.
   5. Salgo con una chica que no habla inglés.
   6. Vemos a la señora que quiere la casa.

B. 1. Como estoy algo escaso de dinero, yo mismo lavo el auto.
   2. Ya que tengo la oportunidad, consigo acortar el número de materias.
   3. Como voy para arriba en todo caso, llevo los zapatos.
   4. Cuesta mucho; por eso no la compro.

EXAMPLES

A. 1. Entre enero y junio, le **escribí** todos los días. *Between January and June, I wrote him every day (and then I stopped writing).*
   2. Eramos amigos. Le **escribía** todos los días. *We were friends. I wrote (used to write) him every day.*

B. 1. Al principio la **llamé** cada dos o tres días y luego fui a verla unas pocas veces. *At first I called her every two or three days and then I went to see her a few times.*
   2. **La llamaba** cada dos o tres días. *I called (used to call, was calling) her every two or three days.*

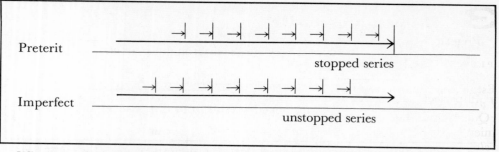

Preterit — stopped series

Imperfect — unstopped series

When a series of repeated acts (each terminated within itself) is viewed by the speaker as terminated, the preterit is used. If the series is not viewed as terminated, the imperfect is used.

● TRANSLATION DRILL

1. I wrote him every day (until Christmas, when I stopped).
   I wrote (used to write) him every day.
2. I called her every three days (until she left the hospital).
   I called her every three days (at that time).
3. We went four times.
   We used to go often (often = many times).
4. They argued every week (last year).
   They were arguing every week.

● DISCUSSION

The preterit and imperfect represent two different ways of looking at events in the past. The preterit is like an on-off switch, while the imperfect just lets things run. The preterit focuses on the termination; whatever the event is, however long it lasted or however many times it was repeated, we picture it as having come to an end. Since actions of brief duration are the ones that we most typically think of in these terms—an act like *it burst,* for example, is hard to view in any other way than as happening and terminating at once—these are the ones most commonly met in the preterit: *he said, it fell, I sneezed, the ship sank,* etc. Nevertheless, any event may be so viewed, and is then preterit: *I lived thirty years in Palma and then went to Rome* **Viví treinta años en Palma y después fui a Roma.** The example **Estuve enfermo** implies that I got over it or at least that that particular period of illness came to an end; **Estaba enfermo** tells us that at a certain time in the past I was ill, but is noncommittal about the outcome.

English makes similar contrasts but organizes them differently. The English past-tense forms listed in Unit 6 §26 give us no clue—without context they can be equivalent to either preterit or imperfect. But when English uses *used to* (*He used to have cattle there* **Tenía ganado allí**), *would* as a synonym of *used to* (*When we played, I would lose in order to please him* **Cuando jugábamos, yo perdía para darle gusto**), and generally when it uses *was* (*were*) . . . *-ing* (*I was working for Don Pepe* **Trabajaba para don Pepe**), Spanish uses the imperfect. These are the English devices for picturing a past action as in progress and disregarding its termination.

What Spanish accomplishes by a change of tense, English is sometimes obliged to express by an entirely different verb:

sabía	*I knew* (a fact)	**supe**	*I learned* (a fact)
podía	*I could* (was able, had the ability)	**pude**	*I managed*
comprendía	*I understood* (had an understanding)	**comprendí**	*I realized* (caught on)

These equivalents are approximate, but illustrate the use of the preterit to imply that a cutoff point was reached. **Lo supe** might mean *I knew it and then I forgot it,* or it might mean *I learned (grasped) it;* in either case the action is carried through to its finish.

53　The past progressive[1]

EXAMPLES

A. 1. **Estaba comiendo,** y no podía[2] hablar. *I was eating, and couldn't talk.*
   2. ¿Qué **estaban haciendo** con esas herramientas? *What were they doing with those tools?*

B. 1. **Estuve trabajando** allí hasta ayer. *I was working there until yesterday.*
   2. **Estuviste hablando** muy fuerte ahí por un minuto, amigo. *You were talking pretty loud there for a minute, friend.*

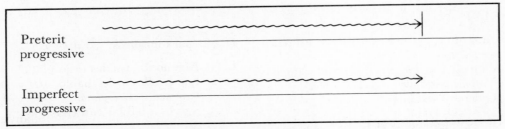

Preterit progressive

Imperfect progressive

The preterit of **estar** shows the action continuing up to a cutoff point. The imperfect shows it merely continuing.

● TRANSLATION DRILL

INSTRUCTIONS: These drill sentences are designed to elicit preterit progressive in the first sentence and imperfect progressive in the second.

1. He was celebrating until 1 o'clock.
   He was celebrating at 1 o'clock.
2. We were waiting on the corner until six.
   We were waiting on the corner yesterday.

3. I was studying bullfighting until yesterday.
   I was studying bullfighting in Spain.

● TENSE SUBSTITUTION DRILL

INSTRUCTIONS: Repeat each sentence just as you hear it. Then repeat it again, substituting imperfect progressive for present progressive.

A. 1. TEACHER: *Estoy* estudiando para la clase de castellano. *Repita.*
      STUDENT: **Estoy estudiando para la clase de castellano.**
      TEACHER: *Cambie.*
      STUDENT: **Estaba estudiando para la clase de castellano.**
   2. *Estamos* hablando con el Dr. Fernández.
   3. Tampoco *está* trabajando hoy.

4. Paquito *está* caminando con las manos.
5. *Están* pensando en algo igual.

B. 1. Le *estoy* escribiendo a mi tío.
   2. ¿Por qué *están* comiendo en la cocina?
   3. *Está* haciendo otra pregunta inútil.
   4. Le *están* poniendo brillantina en el pelo.
   5. *Estamos* haciendo una cosa ridícula en vez de estudiar.

● DISCUSSION

The past progressive with the imperfect of **estar** differs from the simple imperfect in the same way that the present progressive differs from the simple present. (Reread Unit 8 §41.) It is not used for something future to the past time referred to, that is, for something *planned*. **Se iba a trabajar al campo** cannot be expressed with **estaba yendo.** But elsewhere it may replace the simple imperfect whenever the speaker wishes to emphasize comparison or instability; **mientras comíamos**

---

[1] See also present progressive Unit 8 §41.
[2] **No pude hablar** would mean that I *failed* to speak when the impulse hit me or at the moment I was expected to.

could appear as **mientras estábamos comiendo,** hinting more strongly that the persons involved might be, or would presently be, doing something else. *He was wearing a blue tie* would be unlikely in the progressive unless the speaker had expected something else.

The preterit of **estar** does here just what the preterit does elsewhere: brings the action to a conclusion.

54 The with-preposition pronouns

EXAMPLES

A. 1. **A mí,** ni en pintura. *([To] me, not even in a painting.)*
   2. **A mí,** me gusta muchísimo el campo. *([To] me, the country pleases me a lot.)*
   3. ¿Quieres ir **conmigo?**

B. 1. Nosotros pasamos **por ti.**
   2. ¿Cuándo puedo hablar **contigo?**

C. 1. No tengo nada **en contra de usted.** *I don't have anything against you.*
   2. Todo por culpa **de él.**
   3. No puede vivir **sin él.** *She can't live without it (coffee).*
   4. Vamos **sin ella.** *We're going without her (or without it).*

D. ¿Es **para nosotros?** *Is it for us?*

E. 1. Alguno **de ustedes** trajo plata?
   2. Fue **a ellos** y les habló. *He went up to them and spoke to them.*
   3. Vamos a hablar **con ellas.**

	AFTER **con**	AFTER ANY OTHER PREPOSITION
	–migo	mí
	–tigo	ti
	usted	
	él	
	ella	
	nosotros, –as	
	ustedes	
	ellos	
	ellas	

Aside from the special forms **conmigo** and **contigo,** and **mí** and **ti** used with other prepositions, the pronouns used after prepositions are identical to those used as subjects.

● ITEM SUBSTITUTION DRILL

1. A *mí,* ni en pintura.
   (él, ellos, nosotros, ti, usted)
2. Y todo por culpa de *él.*
   (ella, ellos, nosotros, mí, ustedes)
3. Pablo no tiene nada en contra de *usted.*
   (ellos, nosotros, ti, ella, mí)
4. Pasan por *ti* a las ocho.
   (ustedes, usted, mí, ellas, nosotros)
5. ¿El postre es para *nosotros?*
   (mí, él, ustedes, ellas, ti)
6. Van a salir sin *ella.*
   (nosotros, ti, ustedes, mí, nosotras)
7. Quieren ir *con nosotros.*
   (con ellos, con ella, con usted, conmigo, contigo)

A. 1. ¿Fue esa tontería por culpa de él o de ella?
   2. ¿Fue a verlos a ellos o a él?
   3. ¿Vas a pasar por él o por ella?
   4. ¿Vamos a hablar con ella o con ellos?
   5. ¿Salieron sin ella o sin él?

B. 1. ¿Los saludos son para mí o para ella?
   2. ¿Va usted conmigo o con ellos?
   3. ¿Esto es para mí o para ti?
   4. ¿Quieres hablar conmigo o con todos nosotros?
   5. ¿Ellos quieren comer con nosotros o con ustedes?

● TRANSLATION DRILL

A. 1. We're going without her.
   2. We're going without you all.
   3. We're going without him.
   4. We're going without them.

B. 1. Do you want to go with them?
   2. Do you want to go with us?
   3. Do you want to go with her?
   4. Do you want to go with me?

C. 1. The bread is from us.
   2. The bread is from her.
   3. The bread is from them.
   4. The bread is from you.

55 With-preposition pronouns as objects with *a*

EXAMPLES 1. —¿Quieres traer a Olga y a José María? *"Will you bring Olga and José María?"*
—Sí, y **a ti** también. *"Yes, and you too."*
2. —¿La profesora? La vimos ayer. (Vamos a verla hoy.)
"The teacher? We saw her yesterday. (We're going to see her today.)"
—¿Y los alumnos? *"And the students?"*
—Sí, **a ellos** también. *"Yes, them too."*
3. **A mí,** ni en pintura.

	la	vimos
ver–	–la	

a ella

With-verb pronouns are used only with verbs; therefore, when no verb is present, the with-preposition pronoun (introduced by **a**) is used.

● RESPONSE DRILL

INSTRUCTIONS: Answer the following questions according to the models given.

1. TEACHER: A mí me gusta muchísimo el campo. ¿Y a ella?
   STUDENT: **A ella también.**

   ¿Y a ellos?
   ¿Y a usted?
   ¿Y a ustedes?
   ¿Y a nosotros?
   ¿Y a mí?

2. A ella no le gusta nada la psicología.
   ¿Y a él?
   A él tampoco.
   ¿Y a ellos?
   ¿Y a ellas?
   ¿Y a ustedes?
   ¿Y a usted?
   ¿Y a nosotros?
   ¿Y a mí?

1. **A mí me** gusta muchísimo el campo.
2. **Me** gusta **a mí.** *I like it.*

3. Para regatear, **a mí** nadie **me** gana.
4. De los dos, **lo** prefiero **a él.** *Of the two, I prefer* **him.**

a	WITH-PREP. PRON.		WITH-VERB PRON.	VERB		a	WITH-PREP. PRON.
A	**mí**		**me**	**gusta**		a	**mí**
			Me	**gusta**			

The with-verb pronouns are always weak-stressed. Therefore, when the speaker wishes to add emphasis, he gives the with-preposition pronoun (introduced by **a**) *in addition to* the with-verb pronoun.

● PERSON-NUMBER SUBSTITUTION DRILL

1. Para regatear, a *ella* nadie le gana.
   (mí, las señoras, nosotros, ustedes, ti)
2. A *él* le falta dinero para el viaje.
   (mí, nosotros, ella, ti, ustedes)
3. A *nosotros* nos pasó exactamente lo mismo.
   (ellos, él, ustedes, ti, mí)

4. A *mí* me parece un poco caro.
   (ella, ustedes, ti, ellos, nosotros)
5. Pero no la veo a *ella.*
   (él, ellas, ellos, usted, ti)
6. Los prefiere a *ellos.*
   (ellas, ella, ti, nosotros, mí)

● DISCUSSION

Stress is achieved by adding the with-preposition pronoun to the with-verb pronoun. As in English, whether it is put before the verb or after the verb depends on where the speaker wants his stress. Thus **A mí me gusta** is similar to *As for* *me, I like it* (answering the question *What about* **you?**), while **Me gusta a mí** is similar to *The one who likes it is* **me** (answering the question *Who likes it?*).

56 With-verb pronouns that repeat noun objects

EXAMPLES

A. 1. **A mi sobrina la** dejo con usted. *My niece I leave with you.*
   2. **Esas materias las** encuentro muy difíciles. *Those subjects I find too hard.*

B. 1. **A un muchacho amigo mío le** quitaron los documentos.
   2. **Al país le** cuesta una cantidad astronómica.

(a)	noun	with-verb pronoun	verb

When a noun object, either direct or indirect, precedes the verb, the corresponding with-verb pronoun is usually added.

EXAMPLES 1. Tengo que ver a **la nueva criada.**
          2. Los cerdos dejan **bastante ganancia.**

verb	(a)	direct-object noun

Direct-object nouns that come after the verb do not call for any added with-verb pronoun.

1. Esas *materias* las encuentro muy difíciles.
   (materia, exámenes, examen)
2. Los *cerdos* los llevo a la feria.
   (cerdo, ovejas, oveja)
3. La *ropa* la tengo aquí.
   (tijeras, libro, exámenes)
4. Los *frijoles* los llevé a la cocina.
   (pan, verduras, harina)
5. A mi *sobrino* lo dejo con su abuelo.
   (sobrina, hijo, hija)
6. A un *muchacho* le quitaron los documentos.
   (muchachos, muchacha, muchachas)
7. A la *alumna* le dieron los discos.
   (alumnas, alumno, alumnos)
8. Al *país* le cuesta una cantidad astronómica.
   (países, planta, plantas)
9. Le dio al *pobre* diez centavos.
   (pobres, muchacho, niños)
10. Le hice un favor a mi *amigo*.
   (tíos, jefe, sobrinas)

● TRANSLATION DRILL

1. TEACHER: These courses I find very easy.
   STUDENT: **Estas materias las encuentro muy fáciles.**
   TEACHER: I find these courses very easy.
   STUDENT: **Encuentro estas materias muy fáciles.**
2. The class I teach (give) every day.
   I teach the class every day.
3. The bulls I see every afternoon.
   I see the bulls every afternoon.
4. The wool I have here.
   I have the wool here.
5. This coffee I send at 6:00 A.M.
   I send this coffee at 6:00 A.M.
6. Her age she doesn't tell.
   She doesn't tell her age.
7. The fine I pay later.
   I pay the fine later.
8. The address I don't remember.
   I don't remember the address.
9. The holiday we celebrate tomorrow.
   We celebrate the holiday tomorrow.
10. The green house I can't see.
   I can't see the green house.
11. The wind we don't want.
   We don't want the wind.

EXAMPLES

1. ¿Qué **le** parece (a ella)? *What does she say to it? (How does it seem to her? How does she like it?)*
2. No **les** gusta (a ellos). *They don't like it (it is not pleasing to them).*
3. **Le** gané a Juan. *I beat John.*

indirect with-verb pronoun	+	gustar parecer ganar

With the meanings given, these verbs take indirect objects.

EXAMPLES

1. ¿Qué **le** parece a **María?** *What does María say to it? (How does it seem to María? How does María like it?)*
2. No **les** gusta a **los otros.** *The others don't like it (it is not pleasing to the others).*
3. **Le** gané a **Juan.**

indirect with-verb pronoun	+	gustar parecer ganar	+	a	+	indirect-object noun

When these verbs have a noun object, they add the with-verb pronoun object as well.

1. A *Felipe* le parece muy bien.
   (los muchachos, Olga, las chicas)
2. ¡Cuidado! A los *señores* no les gusta discutir.
   (policía, pareja extranjera, señoritas)
3. No le falta nada a mi *amigo*.
   (cuñados, sobrina, tíos)
4. A los *otros* les parece un poquito lejos.
   (jefe, profesoras, cónsul)

5. Vámonos; nadie les gana a las *criadas*.
   (empleado, agricultores, abogado)
6. ¿Le pasó algo al *profesor?*
   (médicos, barbero, técnicos)
7. Ya lo creo; le gusta muchísimo a *Mario*.
   (Luis y Mario, todo el equipo, los viejos)

EXAMPLES

A. 1. Dame diez centavos para dar**le** a un pobre.
   2. Enséñe**le** la casa a ese señor. *Show the house to that gentleman* (real estate agent referring to client).

B. 1. Dio diez centavos a Rockefeller. *He gave ten cents to Rockefeller.*
   2. Enseñe la casa a ese señor. *Show the house to that gentleman* (householder referring to policeman with a warrant).

Doing the customary, familiar, relaxed thing

with-verb pronoun	verb + **a** + indirect-object noun

Doing the unfamiliar, unusual, or standoffish thing

	verb + **a** + indirect-object noun

Adding the with-verb pronoun brings the act within the range of normal operations of the subject.

● TRANSLATION DRILL

A. 1. TEACHER: I'm going to write my father.
      STUDENT: **Voy a escribirle a mi padre.**
   2. TEACHER: I'm going to write the consul.
      STUDENT: **Voy a escribir al cónsul.**
B. 1. Show your papers to the policeman.
   2. Show your papers to the servant.
C. 1. He gave ten dollars to his son.
   2. He gave ten dollars to Rockefeller.
D. 1. (To) John I showed the house.
      A Juan le enseñé la casa.
   2. I showed the house to John.
      Le enseñé la casa a Juan.
   3. (To) The policeman I showed the house.
      Al policía le enseñé la casa.
   4. I showed the house to the policeman.
      Enseñé la casa al policía.

E. 1. To the doctor I mentioned my aches.
   2. I mentioned my aches to the doctor.
   3. To the consul I mentioned my aches.
   4. I mentioned my aches to the consul.
F. 1. To the students the teacher explained the examination.
   2. The teacher explained the examination to the students.
   3. To the teacher the students explained the examination.
   4. The students explained the examination to the teacher.
G. 1. The employees the boss fined.
   2. The boss fined the employees.
   3. The boss the employees fined.
   4. The employees fined the boss.

● DISCUSSION

Noun objects usually follow their verbs, but sometimes, when we want to treat them as the topic or logical subject of the sentence, we put them ahead of the verb: *My niece I leave with you* implies *As for my niece, I leave her with you*—*niece* is the topic. In English we often have to make an additional change, going from active to passive: *A friend of mine **was relieved of** his papers* (in place of *A friend of mine they relieved of his papers*). In Spanish, however, the rearrangement is enough and there is no need to change to passive. The important structural fact is that the with-verb pronoun is added: *My niece I leave with you* **A mi sobrina *la* dejo con usted;** *A friend of mine was relieved of his papers* **A un amigo mío *le* quitaron los documentos.**

When the noun object *follows* the verb, the with-verb pronoun is not added except under certain circumstances with *indirect* objects:

1. There is a small class of verbs, represented by **gustar** *to be pleasing*, **parecer** *to seem*, and **ganar** *to beat*, which, carrying special meanings, calls for indirect objects. Thus **Le gané** means *I beat him* (got-the-advantage over-him, won-out on-him), while **Lo gané** means *I won it*. When a noun object accompanies one of these verbs with its special meaning, the with-verb pronoun is added: **Le gané a Juan** *I beat John* (in the competition).

2. The with-verb pronoun is also added when the act is one that the speaker would regard as within the normal range of operations. Not adding it then gives the impression of unfamiliarity or standoffishness to the act. Thus **Enséñele la casa a ese señor** *Show the house to that gentleman* would be normal referring to a familiar house and a person who might well be there, such as a real-estate prospect or a new renter or a visiting friend. But a householder faced by a policeman with a search warrant would say **Enseñe la casa a ese señor. Voy a escribir al jefe** *I'm going to write to the boss* might refer to someone with whom you are not on easy terms. **Voy a escribirle al jefe** implies a kind of closeness; perhaps you are doing him a favor; at any rate, there is nothing unusual in your writing to him. The **le, les** is a kind of handle, attached to what one is used to handling.

● COMBINED PATTERN REPLACEMENT DRILL

A.

1. **Cuando estaba aquí, llamé al Ministerio.**
2. _____en México_____
3. _____fui_____
4. _____inauguración
5. Ya que_____
6. _____ vivía_____
7. _____carreras
8. _____ Perú_____
9. _____campo
10. Mientras_____
11. _____teatro
12. _____los_____
13. _____ trabajaba_____
14. _____ Panamá_____
15. _____juegos
16. _____ regresé_____
17. _____ estudiaba_____
18. _____ Cuba_____
19. Como_____
20. _____hacienda
21. _____ Venezuela_____
22. _____ volví_____

B.

1. **Después le prestó el dinero al agricultor.**
2. _____ les _____
3. _____herramienta_____
4. _____ dio_____
5. _____técnico
6. _____cuestión_____
7. _____ explicó_____
8. Entonces_____
9. _____administrador
10. _____tema_____
11. Luego_____
12. _____abogados
13. _____documentos_____
14. _____ prometió_____
15. Además_____
16. _____tijeras_____
17. _____barbero
18. _____ ofreció_____
19. Por eso_____
20. _____ les _____
21. _____auto_____
22. _____a nosotros
23. _____ vendió_____
24. _____llantas_____
25. _____a mí_____
26. _____ mostró_____
27. _____flecha_____

Theme vowels in present-tense verb forms.

A. 1. He works and eats a lot.
   2. He studies and learns a lot.
   3. He talks and writes a lot.
   4. He enters and leaves a lot.
   5. He bargains and sells a lot.
   6. He waits and offers a lot.
   7. He celebrates and sleeps a lot.
   8. He bets and loses a lot.

B. 1. We work and eat a lot.
   2. We study and learn a lot.
   3. We bargain and sell a lot.
   4. We wait and offer a lot.
   5. We bet and lose a lot.
   6. We celebrate and sleep a lot.
   7. We talk and write a lot.
   8. We enter and leave a lot.

READING

La familia Alvarez va a la feria[1]

P. *Papá*   M. *Mamá*   PAQ. *Paquito*   L. *Luisa*

P. Bueno, aquí estamos en la feria. Mucha gente, muchos animales, muchas cosas que ver . . .

M. Sí, y mucho polvo, mucho viento . . . y apuesto a que va a llover. ¡Uf!

P. No fue idea mía, María, que . . .

PAQ. ¡Mamaaa! Quiero un helado.

M. Ay, Paquito, acabamos de llegar. Siempre estás pensando en el estómago. Tuvimos una buena comida y . . .

L. ¡Mamaaa! Quiero ver las ovejas.

P. Sí, sí: vamos a ver los animales. Están por allá, a la derecha. Empezamos con las vacas y toros importados, ¿eh? . . . Aquí están. Me dijeron que había mucho ganado fino en esta feria . . . Sí, mira a este toro, Paquito. ¡Qué cabeza tan grande, no? ¡Qué . . . !

L. ¡Quiero ver las ovejas! ¡Quiero ver las ovejas!

M. Paciencia, hija; no se puede ver todo a la vez.

* * *

P. Y ahora, aquí están las ovejas, Luisa. ¡Mira qué bonitas y qué blancas!

L. ¡Ah sí! ¿Puedo tocarlas, papá?

P. } ¡Claro que sí!
M. } ¡Claro que no!

P. Mira, María, no van a hacerle daño.

M. ¡No se trata de eso! Es que se va a ensuciar. . . . ¡Ay Jesús, Luisa, tócalas con las manos, pero no con la cara! ¡Vámonos!

L. ¿Adónde, mamá?

M. Vamos a . . . ¿Dónde está Paquito? *(llamando)* ¡Paquitoo! ¡Paquitooo!

PAQ. *(gritando)* ¡Aquí estoy, mamá!

M. ¿Qué estás haciendo?

PAQ. Estoy jugando con los cerdos. ¿No son . . . ?

M. *(escandalizada)* ¿Con los cerdos? ¿Con esos sucios animales? Ay, ¡ese chico va a volverme loca!

L. Yo lo voy a buscar, mamá. *(Va corriendo adonde está su hermano. Corto silencio. Entonces se oye un grito formidable.)* ¡Mamaaa! ¡Papaaa! ¡Paquito me tiró del vestido y me caí . . . !

PAQ. ¡No le hice nada, no le hice nada! ¡Fue culpa de Luisa! ¡Me tiró del pelo!

P. ¡LUISA! ¡PACO!

M. ¡Jesús, María y José! ¡Denme paciencia! *(Con un poco de dificultad separan a los dos chicos ya muy sucios y se van en busca de los baños.)*

---

[1] From this point on, only the more unusual words will be annotated. Before looking up a word in the end vocabulary, however, you should make every effort to figure out its meaning from the context in which it occurs. For the most part, this was the way in which you acquired your basic vocabulary in English. You will be surprised at how often an intelligent inference will give you the meaning of the word you are confronted with.

Las lenguas de América

El español se habla en España y también es la lengua oficial de dieciocho naciones independientes del Hemisferio Occidental. Estas dieciocho naciones comprenden "la América española".[1]

La América hispánica incluye hoy diecinueve naciones. Una—Brasil—es de lengua portuguesa y es la tercera nación en área del Hemisferio Occidental. (Canadá y los Estados Unidos son más grandes.) Con la pequeña república de Haití, donde se habla francés, hay un total de veinte naciones que comprenden Latinoamérica o la América latina.

Se habla español no sólo en España y en la América española sino también en varios estados de los Estados Unidos. Aunque en los Estados Unidos de Norte América la lengua oficial es el inglés, en buena parte de Nuevo México, Colorado, Arizona, Texas y California la lengua española se mantiene viva al lado del inglés. Además, hay muchas personas que hablan español en las ciudades grandes; por ejemplo, en Nueva York hay más de medio millón.

Así se ve que hay cuatro lenguas oficiales de América: español y portugués, inglés y francés.

Puerto Rico es un estado libre asociado a[2] los Estados Unidos pero la cultura es española y allí se habla español. En las dieciocho naciones de la América española, en Puerto Rico y en España es notable la uniformidad con que se habla el español y se entiende por todos. Bien se sabe que entre una y otra nación hay ciertas diferencias de pronunciación, de entonación, de sintaxis y de vocabulario, pero hay tal vez más diferencias entre una y otra región de España y también entre el inglés de Londres, de Nueva York, de Atlanta, de Minneapolis y de Los Angeles.

La América española no es una sola nación, sino muchas. Las repúblicas de origen español, dice Angel Ganivet[3]—aun las más pequeñas—tienen un sello peculiar que distingue admirablemente las unas de las otras. Cuando un hombre dice que es mexicano, argentino, venezolano, chileno, peruano, uruguayo, paraguayo, boliviano, ecuatoriano, colombiano, guatemalteco, cubano, hondureño, costarricense, salvadoreño, nicaragüense o dominicano, dice algo que le[4] redondea, que le da un aire personal, que le marca en el espíritu de su territorio. Sin embargo, entiende perfectamente bien lo que dice su vecino, tal vez mejor que a otros paisanos suyos.[5] Estos son los indios que mantienen sus propias lenguas. Muchos no hablan español.

Una de las diferencias principales entre las varias zonas[6] procede de su distinto porcentaje racial. Esto ha tenido[7] gran influencia, no sólo en la lengua que se habla sino también en el desarrollo político-cultural y socioeconómico.

---

[1] The designations used in the readings are those of Henríquez Ureña and other Spanish-American scholars. Henríquez Ureña prefers **América hispánica** to **América latina,** to include all the Spanish-speaking and Portuguese-speaking nations (19). **La América española** refers to the eighteen countries in the New World where Spanish is spoken. **La América latina** refers to all the nations of the New World, south of the United States (20). These with the U.S. comprise the **Organización de los Estados Americanos** (21).

[2] **estado libre asociado a** *commonwealth of*

[3] Angel Ganivet (1865–1898), the Spanish author of a significant critical study called *Idearium español* (1897), in which the author urges Spain to revive the best of her past and to incorporate into it modern ideas of the rest of the world.

[4] **le** *him.* Many Spaniards use **le** as a masculine direct object referring to a person.

[5] **suyos** *of his.* This is explained in Unit 11 §60.

[6] The five zones are: (1) Mexico and Central America; (2) the Caribbean (Cuba, Dominican Republic, a good part of Venezuela, and the Atlantic Coast of Colombia); (3) the mountainous zone of the Andes (a good part of Colombia, the mountainous part of Venezuela, Peru, Bolivia, Ecuador, and the northwest of Argentina); (4) Chile; (5) the Río Plata zone (most of Argentina, Uruguay, and Paraguay).

[7] **ha tenido** *has had*

Las veintiuna repúblicas americanas (la América latina con los Estados Unidos) forman la Organización de los Estados Americanos.[8]

En conjunto, más de ciento cincuenta millones usan el idioma español.[9] Así se ve que para todos los americanos (del norte y del sur) es indispensable saber al menos dos idiomas: inglés y español.

Se habla español en	México	(Norte América)
	Guatemala Nicaragua Honduras El Salvador Costa Rica y Panamá	(Centroamérica)
Se habla también en	Cuba la República Dominicana y Puerto Rico	(Islas del Mar Caribe)
También se habla en	Venezuela Colombia Ecuador Perú Bolivia Chile Argentina Uruguay Paraguay	(Sud América) *Total:* 19

● CUESTIONARIO

1. ¿Cuál es la diferencia entre (a) América española, (b) América hispánica, (c) América latina?
2. ¿En qué estados de los Estados Unidos de Norte América se habla español además de inglés?
3. ¿Cuántas lenguas oficiales hay en América?
4. Mencione un estado libre asociado a los Estados Unidos de cultura y lengua españolas.
5. ¿Por qué es notable el español que se habla en la América española, en Puerto Rico y en España?
6. ¿Qué diferencias hay entre una nación y otra en cuanto a la lengua española?
7. ¿Cómo se llaman los habitantes de (a) Guatemala, (b) Honduras, (c) Ecuador, (d) Costa Rica, (e) Nicaragua?
8. ¿Qué importancia tiene el porcentaje racial en la lengua y el desarrollo político-cultural y socio-económico de una nación?
9. ¿Cuántas zonas hay en la América española?
10. ¿Quiénes forman la Organización de los Estados Americanos?
11. ¿Por qué es indispensable para todos los americanos hablar el inglés y el español?

● SUGGESTED READINGS

Entwistle, William, *The Spanish Language,* Macmillan, New York, 1938: Ch. 6, "Standard Spanish"; Ch. 7, "The Extension of Spanish to Spanish America."

Moehlman, Arthur Henry, and Joseph S. Roucek, *Comparative Education,* Dryden, New York, 1951: Ch. 3 "Education in Latin America" (by George Sánchez).

Tomlinson, Edward, *The Other Americans,* Scribner's, New York, 1943; pp. 1–6.

Whitaker, John T., *Americas to the South,* Macmillan, New York, 1940; pp. 1–12, pp. 279–300.

---

[8] See Unit 24, Cultural Note 1.

[9] According to recent estimates, Latin America has the fastest-growing population in the world. Dr. Calvert Dedrick, of the U.S. Census Bureau, stated in June, 1950, that when the 1960 census is taken Latin America will be ahead of the U.S. In 1950, they were about evenly divided, each with roughly 150,000,000. Latin America is increasing its population at the rate of three million a year, while the U.S. is growing by about two million annually.

11

At the Cleaner's

C. *Clerk* M. *Maid* A. *Doña Ana*

C. What can I do for you?

M. I've got a bundle of clothes here.

C. That one?

M. No, these are shoes; *this* one. It's three shirts, five pairs of socks, six pairs of shorts, six undershirts, four sheets, and four pillowcases.

C. How soon do you want them?

M. The underwear and the socks by Tuesday and the bed linen by Saturday.

C. All right. Anything else?

M. Oh, this lady's dress and this man's suit. Can you have them ready for me by tomorrow?

En la tintorería (1)

D. *Dependiente* C. *Criada* A. *Doña Ana*
DA. *Dependienta*

D. ¿Qué se le ofrece?

C. Aquí traigo un paquete con ropa.

D. ¿Ese?

C. No, éstos son unos zapatos; éste. Son tres camisas, cinco pares de calcetines, seis calzoncillos y seis camisetas, cuatro sábanas y cuatro fundas.

D. ¿Para cuándo los quiere?

C. La ropa interior y los calcetines para el martes y la de cama para el sábado.

D. Muy bien. ¿Nada más?

C. Ah, este vestido de la señora y este traje del señor (2). ¿Me los puede tener para mañana?

c. Of course. We'll send them to you at five o'clock.

M. Can I count on that [without fail]?

c. Yes, yes. Don't worry.

* * *

(two days later)

A. Young lady, we didn't get back a suit and a dress that you promised to send yesterday.

c. Impossible, ma'am. Did you bring them in yourself?

A. No, the maid did.

c. Oh, then she didn't say it was for yesterday.

A. But here are the receipts.

c. Can I see them? —But there's no address here.

A. And why didn't you ask her for it?

c. I don't know, ma'am. I wasn't the one that took these clothes.

A. How ridiculous!

* * *

c. Is this your suit and dress?

A. No, they're not mine. That green one and that blue one over there.

c. All right, wait until I wrap them up for you. That's four seventy-five.

A. This is the first and last time I come here.

c. I'm sorry, ma'am, but it isn't our fault.

D. Cómo no. Se los mandamos a las cinco.

c. ¿Sin falta?

D. Sí, sí, no tenga cuidado.

* * *

(dos días después)

A. Señorita, no recibimos un traje y un vestido que ustedes quedaron en mandar ayer.

DA. Imposible, señora. ¿Usted misma nos los trajo?

A. No, vino la criada.

DA. Ah, entonces ella no dijo que era para ayer.

A. Pero aquí están los recibos.

DA. ¿A ver? . . . Pero aquí no hay dirección.

A. ¿Y por qué no se la preguntaron?

DA. Quién sabe, señora. Yo no fui la que recibí esta ropa.

A. ¡Qué barbaridad!

* * *

DA. ¿Son éstos los trajes suyos?

A. No, ésos no son míos; aquel (3) verde y aquel azul que están allá.

DA. Muy bien, espere para envolvérselos. Son cuatro setenta y cinco.

A. Primera y última vez que vengo aquí.

DA. Lo siento, señora, pero no es culpa nuestra.

Cultural Notes

(1) This dialog illustrates the casualness of certain business relationships.

(2) In this context, **señora** and **señor** refer to the mistress and the master of the house.

(3) In the Spanish spoken in Spain, there are two commonly used demonstratives corresponding to English *that*: **ese** and **aquel** (the forms of **aquel** are: **aquel** *m. sing.,* **aquella** *f. sing.,* **aquellos** *m. pl.,* and **aquellas** *f. pl.*). **Ese** refers to something near the person addressed or not far from either speaker in a conversation; **aquel** suggests greater remoteness from both speakers. Thus the distinction between **ese** and **aquel** is merely a matter of comparative distance. The tendency in Spanish America has been to disregard this distinction, as English does, with **ese** crowding out **aquel** so that for the most part the meaning *that* is translated by **ese**. See Unit 6 §27 on the demonstratives and Unit 3, Cultural Note 6.

● PRONUNCIATION AND WRITING EXERCISE

A. The variants [s] and [z].[1] INSTRUCTIONS: Repeat the following pairs of words and phrases just as you hear them.

---

[1] Note that we are now talking about *sounds,* not spellings. The spelling of letter z is treated in Unit 12.

[s]	[z]	[s]	[z]
esposo	esbozo	de este	desde
rascar	rasgar	estado	es dado
buscar	juzgar	este	es de
fisco	fisgo	es francés	es mexicano
descaro	desgarro	es todo	es lodo
discurso	disgusto	es té	es rey
escribir	esgrimir	es falso	es verdad
desteñir	desdeñar	es paca	es vaca
asco	asno	es Paco	es Baco
misto	mismo	es paqueta	es baqueta

Spanish [s] and [z] are variants of a single phoneme /s/; consequently, they do not distinguish words as they do in English (cf. *seal* and *zeal*). The voiced variant [z] occurs in Spanish when /s/ is final in a syllable before a voiced consonant /b, d, g, m, n, l, ʀ/. Everywhere else, the voiceless variant [s] occurs. The occurrence of the voiced variant [z] before a voiced consonant is an instance of *assimilation*. See pp. 10, 15, 16, 18, 20, 23 for other examples of *assimilation*.

B. The variants [s] and [h]. INSTRUCTIONS: Listen to the variant pronunciations of /s/ in the following pairs of words:

[s]	[h]	[s]	[h]
ese	este	mesa	mesta
esa	esta	misa	mista
asa	hasta	pasa	pasta
casa	caspa	pisa	pista
quiso	quisto	pese	peste
cosa	costa	pose	poste

In some dialects of Spain and Spanish America, /s/ at the end of a syllable becomes a mere aspiration, represented phonetically [h]. It is not quite the same as the voiceless velar fricative [x], which is represented in writing by **j** or **g**.

C. Writing drills. INSTRUCTIONS: Write the following lists of words from dictation.

1.		2.	3.
guapo	Gualterio	amenguo	amengüe
guante	guanaco	apaciguo	apacigüe
guardia	Guatemala	averiguo	averigüe
guagua	guajolote	antiguo	pingüe
guardar	guacamole	ambiguo	bilingüe
guadaña	aguantar	exiguo	güiro
Guaraní	agua		vergüenza
Guadalupe	lengua		lingüístico

The sound sequence [gw] is written **gu** when followed by [a] or [o], and is written **gü** when followed by [e] or [i]. Note that **gu** without the dots over the **u** represents in writing the sound [g] or [g] before [e] or [i], and **gü** represents the sound [gw]. Compare **guerra** with **güiro**. The [gw] sequence occurs mostly before [a].

57 Two with-verb pronoun objects

EXAMPLES

1. ¿**Me los** puede tener para mañana?
2. ¿Usted misma **nos los** trajo? *(Did you yourself bring them to us?)*
3. Quiero enseñár**telo**. *I want to show it to you.*

● CONSTRUCTION SUBSTITUTION DRILL

INSTRUCTIONS: Repeat the following sentences just as you hear them.   Then repeat them again, substituting an appropriate with-verb pronoun for the direct-object noun (and any modifiers it has).

A. 1. TEACHER: Mario me mostró *la finca* ayer.
       Repita.
       STUDENT: **Mario me mostró la finca ayer.**
       TEACHER: *Cambie.*
       STUDENT: **Mario me la mostró ayer.**
    2. Don Pepe me mostró *el trigo* ayer.
    3. Luis me mostró *los cerdos* ayer.
    4. Francisco me mostró *las cebollas.*
    5. El campesino me enseñó *el ganado.*
    6. El dependiente me vendió *el arroz.*

    7. La dependienta me vendió *la mantequilla.*
    8. La dependienta me prometió *las sábanas*
        para mañana.
    9. ¿Me puede tener *estos vestidos* para mañana?
   10. ¿Me puede tener *estas fundas* para el martes?
   11. ¿Me puede tener *los calzoncillos* para el
        sábado?
   12. ¿Me puede tener *estas camisas* sin falta?
   13. La dependienta no me dio *el recibo.*
   14. La dependienta no me dijo *la verdad.*

B. 1. Mario nos mostró *la hacienda* ayer.
    2. Don Rosario nos mostró *el maíz* ayer.
    3. Ricardo nos mostró *la cosecha.*
    4. El empleado nos vendió *la manteca.*
    5. Josefina nos va a traer *el rosbif.*
    6. Rosa nos va a mandar *las lentejas.*
    7. Don Rafael nos consiguió *un buen puesto.*

    8. Alberto nos dio *estos cueros.*
    9. Antonio nos dejó *esta lana.*
   10. Las ovejas nos dejaron *esta ganancia* en la
        feria.
   11. El viento nos trajo *esta mala suerte.*
   12. Las nubes negras nos trajeron *esta lluvia.*
   13. La empleada nos vendió *esta harina.*

C. 1. ¿Mario te mostró *el Club de la Unión?*
    2. ¿Antonio no te quitó *el polvo?*
    3. Por lo visto el administrador te prestó *un
        peso.*
    4. A ver, ¿quién te dio *el caballo?*
    5. ¿Quién te explicó *el oficio?*
    6. ¿Quién te mostró *los tranvías?*

    7. ¿Quién te arregló *el techo?*
    8. Quiero enseñarte *las paredes.*
    9. ¿El ruido te dio *esa úlcera?*
   10. Queremos darte *este traje.*
   11. Sea lo que sea, queremos mostrarte *este
        árbol.*

EXAMPLES

1. **Se los** mandamos a las cinco.
2. Espere para envolvér**selos.**
3. ¿Por qué no **se la** preguntaron?   *(Why didn't you ask it of her, address the question to her?)*

INSTRUCTIONS: Repeat the following sentences just as you hear them. Then repeat them again, substituting an appropriate with-verb pronoun for the direct-object noun (and any modifiers it has), which will cue the substitution of the with-verb pronoun **se** for **le** or **les**.

A. 1. TEACHER: Le mandamos los trajes a las cinco. *Repita.*
   STUDENT: **Le mandamos los trajes a las cinco.**
   TEACHER: *Cambie.*
   STUDENT: Se los mandamos a las cinco.

   2. Le traemos *las papas* esta tarde.
   3. ¿Le muestro *las ovejas* el próximo verano?
   4. Le vendo *la paja* en octubre.
   5. Yo le mostré *este árbol viejo* a Paquito.

   6. Pobre Mario; la lluvia le dejó *todo este barro.*
   7. Entonces le presté *el peine.*
   8. Después le explicamos *la profesión.*
   9. Le vendí *el carro* al señor ahí afuera.
   10. Le ofrecimos *el puesto* a Luis.
   11. Le di *las maquinillas* al barbero.
   12. Le traje *los helados* a mi mamá.
   13. Le mencioné *la idea* al consejo estudiantil.

B. 1. Les di *los centavos* a los pobres.
   2. Les explicaron *la pintura* a los alumnos.
   3. Yo les arreglé *el carburador.*
   4. ¿Les mandaste *los paquetes* a tus padres?
   5. Les dieron *un baile* a los estudiantes.
   6. Les prestaron *las tijeras* a las señoras.

   7. Les prometí *un caballo* a los niños.
   8. Les ofrecimos *las comodidades* a los campesinos.
   9. El policía les mostró *la flecha* a los hombres.
   10. Les concedimos *esta semana* a los empleados.
   11. Les quitamos *los juguetes* a los niños.

● PATTERNED RESPONSE DRILL

A. 1. ¿Le presté el libro?
   Sí, me lo prestó.
   ¿Cuándo se lo presté?
   Me lo prestó ayer.

   2. ¿Le presté los centavos?
   ¿Cuándo se los presté?
   3. ¿Le presté las herramientas?
   ¿Cuándo se las presté?
   4. ¿Le expliqué la idea?
   ¿Cuándo se la expliqué?
   5. ¿Le mostré la flecha?
   ¿Cuándo se la mostré?
   6. ¿Le apagué la luz?
   ¿Cuándo se la apagué?
   7. ¿Le prometí los documentos?
   ¿Cuándo se los prometí?
   8. ¿Le di la invitación?
   ¿Cuándo se la di?
   9. ¿Le di el examen?
   ¿Cuándo se lo di?
   10. ¿Le vendí los autos?
   ¿Cuándo se los vendí?
   11. ¿Le vendí el arroz?
   ¿Cuándo se lo vendí?
   12. ¿Le traje los paquetes?
   ¿Cuándo se los traje?
   13. ¿Le traje el recado?
   ¿Cuándo se lo traje?

B. 1. ¿Me prestó el libro?
   Sí, se lo presté.
   ¿Cuándo me lo prestó?
   Se lo presté ayer.

   2. ¿Me prestó las herramientas?
   ¿Cuándo me las prestó?
   3. ¿Me prestó los pesos?
   ¿Cuándo me los prestó?
   4. ¿Me explicó el tema?
   ¿Cuándo me lo explicó?
   5. ¿Me mostró la pintura?
   ¿Cuándo me la mostró?
   6. ¿Me apagó el radio?
   ¿Cuándo me lo apagó?
   7. ¿Me dio la invitación?
   ¿Cuándo me la dio?
   8. ¿Me dio la orden?
   ¿Cuándo me la dio?
   9. ¿Me prometió los documentos?
   ¿Cuándo me los prometió?
   10. ¿Me vendió la lana?
   ¿Cuándo me la vendió?
   11. ¿Me trajo las llantas?
   ¿Cuándo me las trajo?
   12. ¿Me hizo el favor?
   ¿Cuándo me lo hizo?

INSTRUCTIONS: Indicate with appropriate gestures that the questions in the following two sections, although intended to be answered by one individual, are actually directed to a group of two or more.

C. 1. ¿Les presté el libro?
   Sí, nos lo prestó.
   ¿Cuándo se lo presté?
   Nos lo prestó ayer.

   2. ¿Les pasé los frijoles?
   ¿Cuándo se los pasé?

   3. ¿Les llevé las noticias?
   ¿Cuándo se las llevé?

   4. ¿Les pagué la cuenta?
   ¿Cuándo se la pagué?

   5. ¿Les vendí los caballos?
   ¿Cuándo se los vendí?

   6. ¿Les traje el dinero?
   ¿Cuándo se lo traje?

   7. ¿Les dije la pregunta?
   ¿Cuándo se la dije?

E. 1. ¿Te presté el libro, Juan?
   Sí, me lo prestaste.
   ¿Cuándo te lo presté?
   Me lo prestaste ayer.

   2. ¿Te pasé la leche, María?
   ¿Cuándo te la pasé?

   3. ¿Te acorté las materias, Luis?
   ¿Cuándo te las acorté?

   4. ¿Te prometí el coche, Cecilia?
   ¿Cuándo te lo prometí?

   5. ¿Te vendí la vaca, Alberto?
   ¿Cuándo te la vendí?

   6. ¿Te rompí los platos, Elena?
   ¿Cuándo te los rompí?

   7. ¿Te traje la invitación, Roberto?
   ¿Cuándo te la traje?

D. 1. ¿Nos prestó el libro?
   Sí, se lo presté.
   ¿Cuándo nos lo prestó?
   Se lo presté ayer.

   2. ¿Nos arregló los frenos?
   ¿Cuándo nos los arregló?

   3. ¿Nos pasó el azúcar?
   ¿Cuándo nos lo pasó?

   4. ¿Nos prometió los helados?
   ¿Cuándo nos los prometió?

   5. ¿Nos vendió las ovejas?
   ¿Cuándo nos las vendió?

   6. ¿Nos prometió la cuenta?
   ¿Cuándo nos la prometió?

   7. ¿Nos trajo las frutas?
   ¿Cuándo nos las trajo?

F. 1. ¿Me prestaste el libro, Susana?
   Sí, te lo presté.
   ¿Cuándo me lo prestaste?
   Te lo presté ayer.

   2. ¿Me explicaste la cosa, Bernardo?
   ¿Cuándo me la explicaste?

   3. ¿Me ofreciste el puesto, Olga?
   ¿Cuándo me lo ofreciste?

   4. ¿Me prometiste las ovejas, Alfredo?
   ¿Cuándo me las prometiste?

   5. ¿Me trajiste la noticia, Mercedes?
   ¿Cuándo me la trajiste?

INSTRUCTIONS: Indicate with appropriate gestures that the questions in the following two sections are asked (in *G*) or answered (in *H*) by one individual who is speaking for a group of two or more.

G. 1. ¿Le prestamos el libro?
   Sí, me lo prestaron.
   ¿Cuándo se lo prestamos?
   Me lo prestaron ayer.

   2. ¿Le mostramos la pintura?
   ¿Cuándo se la mostramos?

   3. ¿Le escribimos las preguntas?
   ¿Cuándo se las escribimos?

   4. ¿Le conseguimos el auto?
   ¿Cuándo se lo conseguimos?

   5. ¿Le hicimos la comida?
   ¿Cuándo se la hicimos?

H. 1. ¿Me prestaron el libro?
   Sí, se lo prestamos.
   ¿Cuándo me lo prestaron?
   Se lo prestamos ayer.

   2. ¿Me mostraron las fincas?
   ¿Cuándo me las mostraron?

   3. ¿Me lavaron el coche?
   ¿Cuándo me lo lavaron?

   4. ¿Me vendieron la lana?
   ¿Cuándo me la vendieron?

   5. ¿Me ofrecieron el oficio?
   ¿Cuándo me lo ofrecieron?

INSTRUCTIONS: Indicate with appropriate gestures that the questions in the two sections following are exchanges between two groups of two or more individuals each.

I. 1. ¿Les prestamos el libro?
   Sí, nos lo prestaron.
   ¿Cuándo se lo prestamos?
   Nos lo prestaron ayer.

   2. ¿Les pagamos la cuenta?
   ¿Cuándo se la pagamos?

   3. ¿Les vendimos las casas?
   ¿Cuándo se las vendimos?

   4. ¿Les trajimos los toros?
   ¿Cuándo se los trajimos?

   5. ¿Les prometimos la paz?
   ¿Cuándo se la prometimos?

J. 1. ¿Nos prestaron el libro?
   Sí, se lo prestamos.
   ¿Cuándo nos lo prestaron?
   Se lo prestamos ayer.

   2. ¿Nos mostraron la ciudad?
   ¿Cuándo nos la mostraron?

   3. ¿Nos prometieron los trajes?
   ¿Cuándo nos los prometieron?

   4. ¿Nos dieron la plata?
   ¿Cuándo nos la dieron?

   5. ¿Nos trajeron los vestidos?
   ¿Cuándo nos los trajeron?

58 Meaning of the indirect object

EXAMPLES

A. 1. Yo tampoco, excepto **a esta sobrina.**
   2. **¿Le** pongo brillantina en el pelo? *(Shall I put brilliantine on the hair **for you?**)*
   3. Arriba puede cortar**me** un poco también.
   4. ¿Por qué no **se** la preguntaron?

B. 1. **A un muchacho amigo mío** le quitaron los documentos.
   2. **Me** exigieron una multa. *(They required a fine **from me.**)*

   3. ¿Qué **te** pidieron? *What did they ask **of you?***
   4. No **me** entendió nada. *(He didn't understand anything **for me, from me.**)*
   5. **Le** compré una casa. *I bought a house **from him** (or **for him**).*

C. 1. **Nos** apagaron las luces. *They turned the lights off **on us.***
   2. No **me** los pierda. *Don't lose them **for me (on me).***

VERB	INDIRECT OBJECT
Action	Person (rarely thing) who is interested in the action, or who stands to gain or lose by it

The indirect object includes meanings that are translated by English *from, off, on,* etc., as well as the more usual *to* and *for.* (See Unit 4 §18.)

● TRANSLATION DRILL

A. 1. TEACHER: He gave the money to me.
   STUDENT: **Me dio el dinero.**
   2. He changed the money on me.
   Me cambió el dinero.
   3. He took the money from me.
   Me quitó el dinero.
   4. He won the money off me.
   Me ganó el dinero.
   5. He arranged the money for me.
   Me arregló el dinero.

B. 1. She gave the book to me.
   2. She changed the book on me.
   3. She took the book from me.
   4. She won the book off me.
   5. She arranged the book for me.

C. 1. They gave the horse to me.
   2. They changed the horse on me.
   3. They took the horse from me.
   4. They won the horse off me.
   5. They arranged the horse for me.

D. 1. They gave the suits to me.
   2. They changed the suits on me.
   3. They took the suits from me.
   4. They won the suits off me.
   5. They arranged the suits for me.

E. 1. They gave the car to us.
   2. They changed the car on us.
   3. They took the car from us.
   4. They won the car off us.
   5. They arranged the car for us.

EXAMPLES

A. 1. No puedo ir **al mercado** hoy.
   2. Me llevaron **a ella.** *They took me to her (to where she was).*

B. 1. Compré un tocadiscos **para mi sobrina.** *I bought a record player for my niece.*
   2. Trabajo **para la refinería.** *I work for the refinery.*

C. Nosotros pasamos **por ti.**

D. El recado es **de Rafael.** *The message is from Rafael.*

	POINT OF VIEW	TARGET OR SOURCE
to (terminus of motion) = **a**	● —————————————→	■
for (aim) = **para**	● ————→	■
for (to get) = **por**	● ←————	◖
from (source) = **de**	● ←————	■

The more literal meanings of *to, for,* and *from* do not call for the indirect object in Spanish.

● TRANSLATION DRILL

1. TEACHER: They passed the money to us.
  STUDENT: **Nos pasaron el dinero.**
  TEACHER: The money passed to us.
  STUDENT: **El dinero pasó a nosotros.**
2. They passed the plate for us.
  They passed by for us.

3. I bought a record player from her.
  I bought a record player (intended) for her.
4. I took her a book.
  They took me to her.
5. The professor called the roll on us.
  The list passed to us.

● DISCUSSION

    Although *to* and *for* are the meanings most commonly associated with the indirect object (Unit 4 §18), actually the range of meanings is much wider. Except in a few relics like *He played **us** a dirty trick* (played a trick *on us*), *His recklessness cost **him** his life* (took his life *from him*), *It took **me** an hour* (took an hour of my time *from me*), English must use prepositions for these broader meanings. Spanish, however, is free to use the indirect object to indicate a loose sort of involvement in the action not necessarily implying anything more than an interest in it. A more accurate translation of **Le quitaron los documentos** is *They took the papers where-he-was-concerned,* or *with-respect-to-him.* One who loses as well as one who benefits may therefore appear as an indirect object. **Le compré una casa** means only that he was involved in the purchase, and covers the more specific meanings of *from,* i.e., *I bought the house from him* (he benefited by getting the money) or *for,* i.e., *I bought the house for him* or *I bought him the house* (he benefited by the service I performed for him, or even by getting the house). The precise meaning depends on the context. The meaning of the verb is usually enough to tell us in what sense to take the indirect object; thus **quitar,** *to take* in the sense of *remove,* suggests *from* or *off:* **Le quitaron el dinero** *They took the money from him.*

The underlying meaning of **para** is *toward.* For this reason **para** is used, rather than the indirect object, if the speaker implies nothing as to whether the person at the receiving end derives any benefit (or loss). English makes this distinction, rather loosely, with some verbs: *I brought my niece a record player* **Le traje a mi sobrina un tocadiscos,** versus *I brought a record player for my niece* **Traje un tocadiscos para mi sobrina.** In the first we imply that she benefited, but in the second nothing is implied as to whether she received it or even knew about it. With other verbs, English has to express both ideas with *for,* but Spanish continues to make the distinction: *I wrapped the package for them* is either **Les envolví el paquete** (I did them this favor, they benefited) or **Envolví el paquete para ellos** (the package was for them, or the act was aimed in their direction, but nothing is implied as to whether they wanted the favor, received the package, or otherwise benefited).

Para is required in two special cases: (1) Employment (impersonal; no favor or disfavor is done): **Trabajo para la refinería** *I work for the refinery;* **Estudio para mis clases** *I study for my classes.* (2) If no *act* is mentioned, from which a benefit (or loss) can be derived: **Es un tocadiscos para mi sobrina** *It's a record player for my niece.*

59 Nominalization

EXAMPLES

A. 1. **La rubia** se llama Betty y **la morena** Susana.
2. Yo soy **la menor.**
3. Había calcetines en el primer paquete y camisas en **el segundo.** *There were socks in the first bundle and shirts in the second (one).*
4. Estas refinerías no son **las principales.** *These refineries are not the main ones.*

B. 1. La ropa interior para el martes y **la de cama** para el sábado. *(The underclothing by Tuesday and the [clothing] of bed by Saturday.)*
2. Los empleados del club y **los del banco.** *The employees of the club and those of the bank.*

C. 1. Ella no fue **la que recibió esta ropa.** *She wasn't the one who received these clothes.*
2. **Los que me gustan más** son importados. *The ones I like best are imported.*

Nominalization with the article

NOUN EXPRESSED		NOUN OMITTED	
the blonde girl	**la muchacha rubia**	the blonde	**la rubia**
the youngest sister	**la hermana menor**	the youngest	**la menor**
the second bundle	**el segundo paquete**	the second (one)	**el segundo**
the main refineries	**las refinerías principales**	the main ones	**las principales**
the bedclothing	**la ropa de cama**	that of the bed	**la de cama**
the bank employees	**los empleados del banco**	those of the bank	**los del banco**
the employee who received . . .	**la empleada que recibió**	the one who received . . .	**la que recibió**
the horses I like	**los caballos que me gustan . . .**	the ones I like . . .	**los que me gustan**

Modifiers of nouns (these include adjectives, **de** phrases, and **que** clauses) may function as nouns when combined with the definite article. Thus **las principales** is an abbreviated way of saying **las refinerías principales,** the **refinerías** being understood from context.

● CONSTRUCTION SUBSTITUTION DRILL

INSTRUCTIONS: Repeat the following sentences just as you hear them. Then repeat them again, omitting the noun indicated, thus nominalizing the accompanying modifiers.

A. 1. TEACHER: La *muchacha* rubia se llama Betty. *Repita.*
STUDENT: **La muchacha rubia se llama Betty.**
TEACHER: *Cambie.*
STUDENT: **La rubia se llama Betty.**

2. Yo soy la *hermana* menor.
3. El *señor* americano está en la sala.
4. ¿Dónde están los *alumnos* españoles?
5. La próxima *semana* no puedo ir.
6. La *muchacha* bonita es mi hermana.
7. Alvaro es el *hombre* bruto.
8. El *muchacho* furioso soy yo.
9. El segundo *libro* es mejor.
10. Salió la *señora* enferma.
11. ¿Dónde está el *disco* venezolano?
12. ¿Tiene usted el mismo *libro?*
13. Es el mejor *equipo* de Perú.
14. Esta es la *casa* más moderna que tenemos.
15. ¿Quién tiene el *tocadiscos* portátil?
16. Es el único *documento* que tenemos.
17. El *señor* viejo me dijo que estaba a mis órdenes.
18. Me gustan más los *caballos* finos.
19. El pobre *policía* paró el tráfico.
20. Los *hombres* importantes comieron juntos.
21. Los nuevos *juguetes* están abajo.
22. El *ataque* primero fue el peor.
23. Me gustó más el *viaje* largo.
24. La *señora* amable es mi profesora.
25. La *casita* verde es mía.
26. Es el *plato* típico de este país.
27. Las mejores *fincas* de don Pepe están cerca.
28. Los *vestidos* cortos son nuevos este año.

B. 1. Quiero la *ropa* de cama para el sábado.
2. Los *empleados* del banco están celebrando el día feriado.
3. La *chica* del vestido azul es mi compañera de clase.
4. El *techo* de la casa verde es diferente.
5. Los *funcionarios* de gobierno no la pasan mal.
6. Los *empleados* del mercado me dieron gato por liebre.
7. Los *alumnos* de Colombia celebraron un día feriado.
8. Los *campesinos* de la montaña llegaron a la ciudad.
9. El *muchacho* del colegio tuvo un tremendo lío con la policía.
10. El *señor* del Ministerio dijo que no era nada serio.

C. 1. Ella fue la *empleada* que recibió esta ropa.
2. Los *caballos* que me gustan más son importados.
3. ¡Caramba! éste es el *paquete* que perdí en el patio.
4. Estas son las *tijeras* que me prestó el barbero.
5. El no fue el *señor* que murió de un ataque al corazón.
6. Esta es la *finca* que produce arroz, trigo y cosas por el estilo.
7. El es el *empleado* que quedó en mandar el traje ayer.
8. Y tú eres el *muchacho* que dijo "imposible".
9. Lo siento, pero yo no soy el *empleado* que tiene la culpa.

● CHOICE-QUESTION RESPONSE DRILL

A. 1. ¿Cuál traje quiere, el negro o el azul?
2. ¿Cuál profesor es, el americano o el mexicano?
3. ¿Cuál lista tiene, la nueva o la vieja?
4. ¿Cuál hijo es, el segundo o el menor?
5. ¿Cuál pregunta tiene, la fácil o la difícil?
6. ¿Cuál casa compró, la moderna o la anticuada?
7. ¿Cuál auto es más caro, el verde o el negro?

B. 1. ¿Cuál funcionario es, el del ministerio o el de la escuela?
2. ¿Cuál agricultor viene, el de la Hacienda El Alamo o el de la montaña?
3. ¿Cuál muchacha es, la del restorán o la de la tintorería?

4. ¿Cuáles días son más cortos, los del verano o los del invierno?
5. ¿Cuáles ciudades le gustan más, las de México o las de Panamá?
6. ¿Cuál clase es más difícil, la de física o la de química?

C. 1. ¿Cuál cuarto es más grande, el que está arriba o el que está abajo?
2. ¿Cuál profesor le gusta más, el que acaba de salir o el que viene ahora?
3. ¿Cuál coche es más nuevo, el que está aquí o el que está allí?
4. ¿Cuál árbol es más alto, el que está en el patio o el que está en la calle?

A. 1. Give me the green dress and the blue one.
   2. Give me the new book and the old one.
   3. Give me the first number and the second one.
   4. Give me the easy question and the hard one.

B. 1. Bring us the long document and the short one.
   2. Bring us the new list and the old one.
   3. Bring us the short dress and the long one.
   4. Bring us the first horse and the last one.

C. 1. Take them the complicated toys and bring me the simple ones.
   2. Take them the new tools and bring me the old ones.
   3. Take them the bad news and bring me the good.
   4. Take them the old-fashioned furniture and bring me the modern.

EXAMPLES

A. 1. No, **éstos**[1] son unos zapatos; **éste.**
   2. ¿Pero qué mejor oportunidad que **ésta?**
   3. ¿A **cuál** de las fincas de don Pepe va?

B. 1. **Aquel verde** y **aquel azul** que están allá.
   2. **¿Cuál verde?   ¿Ese que usted tiene?**
      Which green one?   That (one) that you have?

*Nominalized demonstratives and **¿cuál?***

this (one)	**éste** **ésta**	that (one)	**ése (aquél)** **ésa (aquélla)**
these (ones)	**éstos** **éstas**	those (ones)	**ésos (aquéllos)** **ésas (aquéllas)**
which (one)?	**¿cuál?**	which (ones)?	**¿cuáles?**

The demonstratives and **¿cuál?** function like nouns without adding the equivalent of the nominalizing *one* in English.

*Nominalization with demonstratives and **¿cuál?***

NOUN EXPRESSED		NOUN OMITTED	
that green suit this invitation from Olga those papers I lost which green suit?	**ese traje verde** **esta invitación de Olga** **esos papeles que perdí** **¿cuál traje verde?**	that green one this one from Olga those I lost which green one?	**ese verde** **esta de Olga** **esos que perdí** **¿cuál verde?**

The demonstratives and **¿cuál?** may be used to nominalize in the same way as the article.

● CONSTRUCTION SUBSTITUTION DRILL

INSTRUCTIONS: Repeat the following sentences just as you hear them.   Then repeat them again, omitting the noun indicated, thus nominalizing the accompanying demonstrative or other adjective.

A. 1. TEACHER: Esa *muchacha* es mi prima.
   Repita.
   STUDENT: **Esa muchacha es mi prima.**
   TEACHER: *Cambie.*
   STUDENT: **Esa es mi prima.**

   2. Este *barro* es lo de menos.
   3. Esa *docena* es para nosotros.
   4. Esta *criada* nunca tarda mucho.
   5. Este *dinero* alcanza para toda la semana.

---

[1] When they are themselves nominalized, the demonstratives are written with the accent mark.   The neuter forms **esto, eso,** and **aquello,** however, are never written with the accent mark.   See Unit 6 §27.

6. Estos *muchachos* tienen las manos muy sucias.
7. Esta *chica* quiere comprar un par de zapatos.
8. Ese *deporte* es un verdadero arte.
9. Me imagino que estos *toros* son importados.
10. ¡Qué horror! Esta *vida* no es para mí, ni en pintura.
11. ¿Cuál *hombre* es el venezolano?

B. 1. Esa *muchacha* rubia es mi prima.
   Esa muchacha rubia es mi prima.
   Esa rubia es mi prima.
2. Este *traje* negro es para mí.
3. Esos *hombres* pobres no tienen nada.
4. Déme ese *traje* azul.
5. ¿De quién es este *vestido* negro?
6. ¿Dónde está esa *señora* extranjera?
7. Ese último *muchacho* es mi hijo.
8. Esas *muchachas* tristes son mis compañeras.
9. Ya lo creo; estos *señores* americanos van a salir pronto.

10. Ese mismo *señor* me lo contó mientras comíamos.
11. ¿Cuál *señor* extranjero quiere verme?

C. 1. Esta *invitación* de Olga acaba de llegar.
2. Ese *señor* del traje negro le está esperando.
3. Esa *chica* del vestido azul es mi sobrina.
4. ¿Cuál *camisa* de las dos quiere?

D. 1. Esta *invitación* que acaba de llegar es de Olga.
2. Ese *señor* que está ahí quiere hablar con usted.
3. Esos *papeles* que perdí eran para ustedes.
4. Esa *criada* que está en la cocina se llama Josefina.

● DISCUSSION

The adjectives in English that can be freely used like nouns, without the addition of something to show the noun function, are comparatively few. The most familiar examples are the demonstratives (*This book is new:* **This** *is new*), the adjectives of order (*Here is the last copy: Here is the* **last**), and the superlatives (*The biggest fellow was over two hundred pounds: The* **biggest** *was over two hundred pounds*). Normally it is necessary to add the word *one, ones,* or replace with *that, those: The pretty girl was elected queen,* repeated without *girl,* calls for *one: The pretty one was elected queen. The cards you gave me* repeated without *cards* calls for *ones* or *those: the ones you gave me, those you gave me.*

In Spanish, almost any adjective can be nominalized without adding anything, provided there is an accompanying definite article, demonstrative, or **¿cuál?** *The pretty one,* referring to *girl,* is **la bonita,** and *the pretty ones,* referring to *girls,* is **las bonitas;** *the pretty ones,* referring to *shoes,* is **los bonitos.** *Those portable ones,* referring to *tools,* is **esas portátiles.** *Those I lost,* referring to *books,* is **los que perdí** if *those* is just another way of saying *the ones* (*the ones I lost*), or is **esos que perdí** if *those* has its full demonstrative meaning (*those-over-there,* as if pointing at them).

60 Possessives that do not precede nouns

EXAMPLES

A. No, ésos no son **míos.**

B. La culpa no es **nuestra.** *The fault isn't ours.*

C. ¿Es **tuyo** éste? *Is this one yours?*

D. 1. Creo que es **suyo.** *I think it's yours (his, hers, theirs).*
2. Creo que es **de usted** (**de ustedes, de él, de ellos, de ella, de ellas**). *I think it's yours* [singular] (*yours* [plural], *his, theirs* [masculine], *hers, theirs* [feminine]).

Possessives before nouns	Possessives not before nouns	
SHORT FORM	LONG FORM	ALTERNATE CONSTRUCTION WITH **de**
mi	**mío, –a, –os, –as**	
nuestro, –a, –os, –as	**nuestro, –a, –os, –as**	
tu	**tuyo, –a, –os, –as**	de usted de ustedes de él de ellos de ella de ellas
su	**suyo, –a, –os, –as**	

In all positions except before the noun, the forms in the second and third columns are used. The forms with **de** are sometimes needed where **suyo** would be ambiguous.

● ITEM SUBSTITUTION DRILL

1. Esa *camiseta* no es mía.
   (traje, camisas, calzoncillos)
2. ¿Es tuyo este *vestido?*
   (ropa, paquetes, sábanas)

3. Lo siento, pero la *culpa* no es nuestra.
   (dinero, ideas, papeles)
4. ¿Son suyas estas *fundas?*
   (zapatos, plata, coche)

● PERSON-NUMBER SUBSTITUTION DRILL

1. *Yo* digo que este libro no es mío.
   Yo digo que este libro no es mío.
   El _____
   El dice que este libro no es suyo.
   (nosotros, ellos, tú, usted, ustedes)

2. *Usted* dice que tampoco es suyo.
   (yo, ellos, nosotros, ella, tú)
3. *Pablo* dice que la lista no es de él.
   (ellos, ella, ellas, usted, ustedes, yo, tú, nosotros)

● PATTERNED RESPONSE DRILL

A. 1. ¿Es tuyo este libro?
      No, no es mío.
   2. ¿Es tuya esta cartera?
   3. ¿Es tuyo este auto?
   4. ¿Son tuyas estas llantas?
   5. ¿Son tuyos estos papeles?

B. 1. ¿Es suya esta refinería?
      Sí, es nuestra.
   2. ¿Son suyas estas plantas?
   3. ¿Es suyo este mercado?
   4. ¿Es suyo este jardín?
   5. ¿Son suyos estos discos?
   6. ¿Son suyas estas tijeras?
   7. ¿Es suya esta idea?

EXAMPLES   1. Un amigo **mío** quiere conseguir un empleo.
           2. No es culpa **nuestra**. *It isn't **our** fault (It's no fault of ours).*

*Position for **of mine, of his,** etc.*

noun	possessive

Where English has *of mine, of his,* etc.,
Spanish puts the possessive after the noun.
See Unit 4 §20.

1. Es un *amigo* mío.
   (compañera, primos, sobrinos)
2. Son unas *casas* nuestras.
   (restoranes, finca, jardín)

3. ¿Un *pariente* tuyo está en México?
   (tía, alumnos, profesores)
4. Es una *prima* nuestra.
   (sobrino, tías, cuñados)

● DISCUSSION

The essential difference between the **mi-tu-su** possessives and the **mío-tuyo-suyo** possessives is one of stress. The short forms are normally weak-stressed; they correspond to the weak-stressed possessive in an English phrase such as *my **brother**,* where the only strong stress occurs on the noun. (There is one situation in which they may be stressed: where the possessive is contrastive, and the noun, being merely repeated from what has been said before, is de-stressed: *She wants to be close to **her** family [not mine]* **Ella quiere estar cerca de *su* familia.**)

In the usual positions of stress, the longer forms are required. The two most frequent are after the verb **ser,** as in **Es mío** *It's mine,* and in the sense *of mine, of his,* etc., as in **un hermano mío** *a brother of mine.* But other occasions of stress (apart from the contrastive one above) also call for the longer forms, as in **Todo por culpa de él,** which could also be said **Todo por culpa suya,** corresponding to English *It was **his fault**,* with strong stress on both possessive and noun.

There are sizable areas of the Spanish-speaking world in which **de nosotros** replaces **nuestro.** To use **de mí** for **mío,** or **de ti** for **tuyo,** however, is regarded as substandard.

For many speakers of Spanish the **su, suyo** forms are more normally taken in the sense *your, yours,* than in the sense *his, her(s), its, their(s).* For the latter meanings, the **de** constructions are more usually substituted by these speakers, and do not necessarily indicate emphasis: **Habla el cuñado de él.**

61 Nominalized possessives

EXAMPLES

1. Si tu café no está caliente, toma **el mío.** *If your coffee isn't hot, take mine.*
2. Allá se juega otra clase de fútbol muy diferente **del nuestro.**
3. **El tuyo** siempre tiene algo malo.

4. Estas herramientas son mías. ¿Dónde están **las suyas?** *These tools are mine. Where are yours?*
5. Nuestra madre no es como **la de ellos.** *Our mother isn't like theirs.*

mine (my one) mine (my ones)	**el mío, la mía** **los míos, las mías**
yours (your one) yours (your ones) etc.	**el suyo, la suya (el, la de usted)** **los suyos, las suyas (los, las de usted)** etc.

The long possessives (**mío, tuyo, nuestro, suyo,** and the forms with **de**) nominalize in the same way as other adjectives (see above, §59). When English *mine, ours,* etc. function as nouns, the nominalized form must be used in Spanish.

1. Si tu *café* no está aquí, toma el mío.
   (leche, helados, frutas)
2. Ahí está mi *camisa,* pero ¿dónde está la tuya?
   (traje, camisetas, calcetines)
3. No tengo mis *papeles,* pero los suyos están en la sala.
   (camisas, documento, invitación)
4. Mi *dinero* está aquí, pero el de ella no llegó.
   (plata, zapatos, tijeras)
5. Nuestro *coche* está aquí, pero no sé dónde está el de ustedes.
   (batería, caballos, vacas)

● PATTERNED RESPONSE DRILL

A. 1. ¿Es tuyo este libro?
       No, el mío está en la sala.
    2. ¿Es tuya esta cartera?
    3. ¿Es tuyo este peine?
    4. ¿Son tuyos estos papeles?
    5. ¿Es tuyo este plato?
    6. ¿Son tuyos estos documentos?
    7. ¿Es tuya esta lista?

B. 1. ¿Son suyos estos discos?
       No, ya tenemos los nuestros.
    2. ¿Son suyas estas tijeras?
    3. ¿Es suyo este libro?
    4. ¿Son suyos estos trajes?
    5. ¿Es suya esta plata?
    6. ¿Son suyos estos zapatos?
    7. ¿Es suya esta invitación?

● TRANSLATION DRILL

A. 1. My car is the green one; how about yours?
       Mi coche es el verde; ¿y el suyo?
    2. My shirts are the blue ones; how about his?
    3. My shoes are the old ones; how about yours?

B. 1. Here's your comb; where's mine?
    2. Here's your invitation; where's his?
    3. Here's your ice cream; where's ours?
    4. Here's your dessert; where's hers?
    5. Here's your chicken and rice; where's mine?

62   Telling time

EXAMPLES

A. 1. ¿Qué hora es?
    2. Son las tres y media.
    3. Es la una y cuarto. *It's a quarter past one.*
    4. Son las cinco menos veinte. *It's twenty minutes to five (five minus twenty).*
    5. Eran las doce y diez. *It was ten past twelve.*

B. 1. **¿A qué hora** llegan? *When do they arrive?*
    2. Llegan **a la una menos cuarto.** *They arrive at a quarter to one.*
    3. Llegan **a las nueve de la mañana (noche).** *They arrive at nine in the morning (at night).*
    4. Llegan **por la tarde.** *They arrive in the afternoon.*

| Verb | | Hour | Fraction before the hour | Fraction after the hour | Period of day |
PRESENT	PAST				
Es	**Era**	**la una**	**menos diez**	**y diez**	**de la mañana**
Son	**Eran**	**las dos**	**menos cuarto**	**y cuarto**	**de la tarde**
		las tres	**menos veinte**	**y veinte**	**de la noche**
		etc.	etc.	etc.	
				y media	

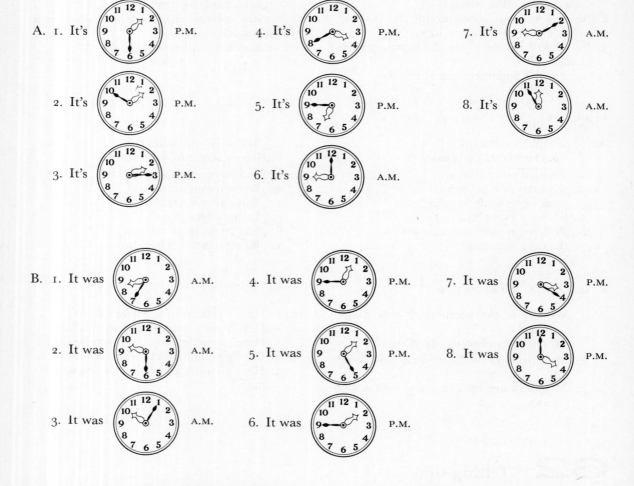

A. 1. It's ___ P.M.   4. It's ___ P.M.   7. It's ___ A.M.

2. It's ___ P.M.   5. It's ___ P.M.   8. It's ___ A.M.

3. It's ___ P.M.   6. It's ___ A.M.

B. 1. It was ___ A.M.   4. It was ___ P.M.   7. It was ___ P.M.

2. It was ___ A.M.   5. It was ___ P.M.   8. It was ___ P.M.

3. It was ___ A.M.   6. It was ___ P.M.

C. 1. They arrived at six o'clock in the morning.
   They arrived in the morning.
 2. They arrive at five-thirty in the afternoon.
   They arrive tomorrow (in the) afternoon.
 3. He came back at eight-fifteen in the evening (night).
   He came back in the evening (night).

● DISCUSSION

It is and *It was* appear in the forms **es, son,** and **era, eran** (the time is almost always "background," and therefore the preterit is rarely used here). One o'clock (plus or minus fractions) calls for the singular, and hours later than one call for the plural.

The feminine article (agreeing with **hora, horas** understood) is required with the numeral.

Fractions appear as simple addition (**y** *plus,* hence *past*) and subtraction (**menos** *minus,* hence *before, to, till, of*).

Period of the day is introduced by **de** when the hour is specified, otherwise by **por.**

Spanish does not recognize a period corresponding to *evening;* it may be translated, according to the lateness of the hour, by either **tarde** or **noche.** Just as in English many speakers do not make a precise division (compare *I'll see you at five tonight*), there is no clear-cut division between **tarde** and **noche;** but generally **tarde** corresponds to daylight hours.

63 Anticipation of number and person

A. 1. **Son** las tres y media.
2. Vea que **son** cincuenta pesos.
3. **Son** tres camisas, cinco pares de calcetines. . .
4. **Son** cuatro setenta y cinco.
5 La cuestión principal **eran** las huelgas.   *The main problem was the strikes.*

B. 1. El hombre que lo hace mejor **eres** tú.   *The man who does it best is you.*
2. No **fui** yo.   *It wasn't me.*

	Singular noun	ser be	Plural noun
ENGLISH	problem	was (singular)	strikes
SPANISH	**cuestión**	**eran** (plural)	**huelgas**

Ser is normally plural if it has a plural predicate noun.

	Third-person noun	ser be	First- or second-person pronoun
ENGLISH	man	is (3rd person)	you
SPANISH	**hombre**	**eres** (1st or 2nd)	**tú**

Ser is normally first or second person if it has a first- or second-person predicate pronoun.

● TRANSLATION DRILL

A. 1. The main thing was the strike.
   La cosa principal era la huelga.
2. The main thing was the strikes.
   La cosa principal eran las huelgas.
3. The main thing was the attack.
4. The main thing was the meetings.
5. The main thing was the plant.
6. The main thing was the refineries.
7. The main thing was the inauguration.

B. 1. The package?   It was the socks.
   ¿El paquete?   Eran los calcetines.
2. The package?   It was the shirt.
3. The package?   It was the shorts.
4. The package?   It was the underwear.
5. The package?   It was the pillow cases.
6. The package?   It was the dress.
7. The package?   It was the sheets.
8. The package?   It was the suit.
9. The package?   It was the shoes.

C. 1. The difficult part is the document.
   La parte difícil es el documento.
2. The difficult part is the papers.
3. The difficult part is the car.
4. The difficult part is the streetcars.
5. The difficult part is the wheat.
6. The difficult part is the beans.
7. The difficult part is the traffic.
8. The difficult part is the street.

D. 1. It's three shirts.
   Son tres camisas.
2. It's one suit.
3. It's six pairs of socks.
4. It's one pair of shoes.
5. It's five undershirts.
6. It's one dress.
7. It's four o'clock.
8. It's one o'clock.
9. It's eight o'clock.
10. It's one-thirty.
11. It's fifty pesos.
12. It's one peso.
13. It's four seventy-five.

E. 1. It wasn't me.
    No fui yo.

  2. It wasn't him.
  3. It wasn't you (**tú**).
  4. It wasn't you.
  5. It wasn't us.
  6. It wasn't them.
  7. It wasn't her.

F. 1. The lawyer was Francisco.
    El abogado fue Francisco.

  2. The lawyer was me.

  3. The lawyer was you.
  4. The lawyer was you (**tú**).
  5. The lawyer was him.
  6. The lawyer was Don Rafael.

G. 1. The one who does it best is you.
    El que lo hace mejor eres tú.

  2. The one who does it best is him.
  3. The one who does it best is Rosario.
  4. The one who does it best is me.
  5. The one who does it best is you.

● DISCUSSION

At an earlier period of English, constructions like *It am I, That man **wert** thou* (modern *It's me* or *It's I, That man was you*) were regular, the verb *be* taking its *person* not from the subject but from the predicate. The Spanish equivalents parallel this older form in English: **Soy** yo (note absence of an equivalent of *it*—Unit 2 § 2), **Ese hombre eras** tú.

Similarly, in Spanish, with *number:* where English says *Your life **is** all the things you do,* Spanish says **Tu vida *son* todas las cosas que haces.** (English sometimes wavers: *The only thing I never forget **is** (**are**) the keys.*)

● COMBINED PATTERN REPLACEMENT DRILL

A.

1. **¿El dinero? Te lo voy a dar a ti mañana.**
2. _____ a usted ____
3. La plata _____
4. _____ prestar _____
5. _____ a ustedes ____
6. _____ vamos _____
7. _____ traer _____
8. Las noticias _____
9. _____ el domingo
10. _____ a él _____
11. _____ van _____
12. _____ a mí _____
13. Los muebles _____
14. _____ vender _____
15. _____ la otra semana
16. _____ a nosotros ____
17. _____ mandar _____
18. _____ va _____
19. _____ el otro mes
20. Las herramientas _____
21. _____ conseguir _____
22. _____ después

B.

1. **Mi auto y el tuyo estaban en la próxima esquina.**
2. _____ calle
3. ____casa _____
4. _____ suya _____
5. _____ segunda _____
6. ____ministerio _____
7. _____ avenida
8. Tu _____
9. _____ nuestro _____
10. _____ tercera _____
11. ____coche _____
12. _____ mío _____
13. _____ misma _____
14. ____escuela _____
15. _____ ciudad
16. Su _____
17. _____ están _____
18. _____ lugar
19. ____colegio _____
20. _____ tuyo _____
21. Mi _____
22. _____ cuadra
23. ____café _____
24. _____ otra _____

● TRANSLATION REVIEW DRILLS

Possessive constructions.

A. 1. Julio's sister just arrived.
  2. Pablo's aunt just arrived.
  3. Susana's grandfather just arrived.
  4. Mercedes' son just arrived.

  5. Francisco's niece just arrived.
  6. Fernando's brother-in-law just arrived.
  7. Patricio's friend just arrived.

B. 1. Elena's furniture is here.
    2. Alvaro's books are here.
    3. Josefina's cups are here.
    4. Paquito's toys are here.

    5. Rosa's plates are here.
    6. Antonio's papers are here.
    7. Olga's things are here.

READING

Fragmento de una conferencia[1]
sobre la etimología hispánica

... La mayor parte de las palabras españolas vienen del latín. Puedo demostrárselo a ustedes sin ninguna dificultad. Por ejemplo, voy a leerles algunas líneas de la primera parte del diálogo "En la tintorería", que acabamos de estudiar. Se las voy a leer, como digo, pero si llego a una palabra *no* latina, en vez de la palabra voy a hacer una pausa. Escuchen ustedes con mucho cuidado (*leyendo*):

—¿Qué se le ofrece?
—Aquí traigo un ... con ...
—¿Ese?
—No, éstos son unos .... ; éste. Son tres camisas, cinco pares de calcetines, seis calzoncillos y seis camisetas, cuatro sábanas y cuatro fundas.
—¿Para cuándo los quiere?
—La ... interior y los calcetines para el martes y la de cama para el sábado. Ah, este vestido de la señora y este traje del señor. *Etcétera etcétera.*

Si ustedes siguen leyendo hasta el final, y buscan los orígenes de las otras palabras en el gran diccionario de Corominas,[2] van a hallar solamente una palabra de origen no latino: la palabra *azul,* que deriva del árabe. ... Es una demostración ... ejem ... muy clara, ¿verdad? Y hay que notar también que las palabras no latinas son todas, o casi todas, sustantivos, o nombres. *Paquete,* por ejemplo, es palabra tomada directamente del francés; la palabra francesa es de origen neerlandés. *Ropa* tiene el mismo origen que *robar,* de origen germánico; su sentido primitivo era "despojos,[3] botín.[4]" *Zapato* es de origen incierto: puede ser árabe. Se puede añadir[5] que *cama, camisa* y *sábado,* aunque pasando al español por medio del latín, tienen orígenes diferentes: el de *cama* es oscuro; *camisa* viene del céltico; y *sábado* es hebreo en su origen más remoto. *Traje* no es una forma del pretérito de *traer;* es más bien[6] un préstamo[7] del portugués, aunque la forma portuguesa está relacionada con el verbo español ...

---

[1] *lecture*
[2] J. Corominas is the author of the *Diccionario crítico etimológico de la lengua castellana,* in four volumes, which appeared successively from 1954 to 1957.
[3] *spoils*   [4] *booty*   [5] *add*   [6] *rather*   [7] *loanword*

READING

Dos triángulos americanos

El Nuevo Mundo es un magnífico cuadro que comprende dos grandes continentes, Norte América y Sud América, enlazados por una extensión de tierra muy estrecha, que se llama Centroamérica. El istmo de Panamá es la parte más estrecha del hemisferio, pero es de grandísima importancia porque allí se abren los miradores del Canal para dar libre paso entre los dos océanos, Atlántico y Pacífico.

La América del Norte y la América del

Sur son continentes de forma triangular. Se parecen en muchos aspectos, especialmente en la columna vertebral que se extiende por las montañas Rocosas y los Andes. Las montañas Alleghanys y Apalaches[1] en el norte, las Sierras de las Guayanas y la Sierra del Mar en Brasil son similares, pero son pequeñas comparadas con las Rocosas y los Andes. Estos sistemas montañosos determinan la dirección de todos los grandes ríos. El San Lorenzo[2] y el Misisipí-Misurí en el norte, el Magdalena, el Orinoco, el inmenso Amazonas y el Plata en el sur fluyen todos hacia el Océano Atlántico en el este. Los ríos Frazer, Columbia, Guayas y Bío-Bío, que fluyen hacia el Pacífico, son ríos pequeños comparados con los otros. En efecto, el orden simétrico y similar de la geografía de las Américas es extraordinario.

Latinoamérica va desde más allá del paralelo 30°[3] norte al 56°[4] sur, es decir, en términos generales, unos 90°,[5] un cuarto de círculo.

Algunos norteamericanos creen que toda Latinoamérica es una sola nación y que tiene un clima tropical. Esto es tan falso como creer que Maine tiene el mismo clima que la Florida y California simplemente porque son estados del mismo país y están en el mismo continente. Los que no saben nada de la geografía no observan que el continente sudamericano se extiende hasta las regiones subantárticas. Si estamos en la latitud ecuatorial cerca de la ciudad de Quito, Ecuador, y viajamos hacia el sur, vemos que la temperatura desciende: más fría en Perú, mucho más fría en el sur de Chile, hasta llegar al eterno hielo del polo antártico. (Y lo mismo ocurre si viajamos hacia el norte.) La latitud sur máxima del continente es de 56° en el Cabo de Hornos,[6] al sur de la ciudad chilena de Magallanes.[7] Si doblamos el papel por la línea del ecuador y ponemos un triángulo sobre el otro, vemos que el Cabo de Hornos corresponde al Océano Ártico y Magallanes corresponde a la Bahía Mackenzie. Por eso, en el sur de Argentina y

Chile hay enormes glaciares como en Alaska y Canadá. En el invierno (junio, julio y agosto) podemos ver esquiar a mucha gente.

Los productos agrícolas de Argentina, Chile y Uruguay son los mismos que los del oeste central de los Estados Unidos. ¿Por qué? Es porque esos países están en latitudes correspondientes y tienen el mismo clima. Allí es imposible cultivar bananas y café, como es imposible cultivarlos en los Estados Unidos.

Si las dos Américas se parecen en muchos aspectos, en otros son muy diferentes. Una de las grandes diferencias entre las dos Américas es el clima. La mayor parte de los Estados Unidos está situada en la zona subártica, de clima moderado y estaciones distintas que facilitan los cultivos y el desarrollo económico. La mayor parte de la América hispánica está en las zonas tropicales y subtropicales que son obstáculos para cultivos buenos y comunicación fácil. Puesto que la geografía y el clima son relativamente permanentes, es necesario considerar esto para comprender la historia y conocer los pueblos.

El clima y la geografía influyen en la división política y lingüística del continente y la capacidad del hombre depende de ellos en gran parte. En las zonas montañosas todavía viven muchos indios que no hablan español. En Chile, Argentina y Uruguay hay pocos indios.

Otra diferencia entre las dos Américas es el *mestizaje,* pues en casi todas las regiones tropicales ha surgido[8] un nuevo tipo de hombre: el mestizo, fusión de blancos e indios. Los mestizos no son uniformes en las varias razas ni en el modo de hablar. Todo depende del porcentaje, y también de la tribu indígena. Algunas personas creen que los pueblos hispanoamericanos poseen un profundo e íntimo sentido regionalista que atribuyen a diversos factores. El gran humanista mexicano Alfonso Reyes dice: "Hay choques de sangres, problemas de mestizaje, esfuerzos de adaptación y absorción. Según las regiones, domina el tinte

---

[1] *Allegheny* and *Appalachian*   [2] *Saint Lawrence*   [3] 30° = **treinta grados**   [4] 56° = **cincuenta y seis grados**   [5] 90° = **noventa grados**
[6] Spanish equivalent of the geographical designation "Horn" or "Hoorn." This cape was discovered by the Dutch explorer Willem Schouten in 1616. He named it after his birthplace, Hoorn, in the Netherlands.
[7] **Magallanes** was formerly called **Punta Arenas.** It is situated on the Pacific entrance of the Strait of Magellan (Lat. 53° S.) named for the Portuguese navigator Fernando de Magallanes who undertook to sail around the world in 1520. He died, however, in 1521 before he was able to complete the journey. Magallanes is known as the southernmost city in the world.
[8] **ha surgido** *there has emerged*

indio, el ibérico, el gris del mestizo, el blanco de la inmigración europea general, y el negro africano traído por las antiguas administraciones coloniales. La gama admite todos los tonos . . . y poco a poco está mezclándose la heterogeneidad." [9]

La mano del hombre (es decir, la ingeniería moderna) ha construido[10] ferrocarriles a través de las montañas y selvas, está construyendo canales y grandes puertos de mar y aeropuertos. En fin, la ciencia está conquistando el aire y la tierra y tal vez el clima también. Algunos picos de los Andes tienen nieve perpetua en la región ecuatorial. El pico de Aconcagua, entre Chile y Argentina, es el pico más alto de América (pasa de los 7.000 metros), pero vuelan cerca de él aviones enormes y trenes lo bordean. De los tres grandes océanos del mundo, dos bañan las costas de América. El Atlántico, siluetado por Europa, Africa y América, presenta una escena de vida intensa sobre las aguas y por el aire. El Pacífico empieza a ser un centro de grandes actividades a todo lo largo de ambas Américas, de Alaska a Patagonia.

De veras, la ciencia está venciendo las distancias y todas las Américas se preocupan de estas maravillosas conquistas.

● CUESTIONARIO

1. ¿Cuáles son los dos grandes continentes que comprende el Nuevo Mundo?
2. ¿A qué se llama Centroamérica?
3. ¿Cuál es la importancia del istmo de Panamá?
4. ¿Qué forma tienen la América del Norte y la del Sur?
5. ¿En qué aspectos se parecen los dos continentes?
6. ¿Qué determina la dirección de todos los grandes ríos?
7. ¿Qué ríos fluyen hacia el Océano Atlántico (a) en la América del Norte y (b) en la América del Sur?
8. ¿Hacia dónde fluyen los ríos (a) Frazer, (b) Columbia, (c) Guayas, (d) Bío-Bío?
9. ¿Entre qué paralelos se extiende Latinoamérica?
10. ¿Qué ideas falsas tienen algunos norteamericanos sobre Latinoamérica?
11. ¿Por qué es importante saber geografía?
12. ¿Cómo es la temperatura en (a) Ecuador, (b) Chile, (c) las regiones antárticas?
13. ¿Dónde está la latitud máxima del continente sudamericano? ¿Cuál es?
14. ¿En qué país está Magallanes?
15. ¿Qué países latinoamericanos están en latitudes correspondientes con el oeste central de los Estados Unidos?
16. ¿En qué aspectos son diferentes las dos Américas?
17. ¿De qué depende la división política y lingüística del continente?
18. ¿Qué es un mestizo?
19. ¿Cuáles son algunos de los adelantos construidos por la ingeniería moderna en América?
20. ¿Cuál es el pico más alto de los Andes?
21. ¿Qué océanos bañan las costas de América?

● SUGGESTED READINGS

Arciniegas, Germán, ed., *The Green Continent,* Knopf, New York, 1944: pp. xiv-xxii, "Our Little Big World"; Part I: "Landscape and Man."

Humphreys, Robin A., *The Evolution of Modern Latin America,* Oxford University Press, New York, 1946: Ch. 1, "The Setting and the People."

James, Preston E., ed., *Latin America,* Odyssey, New York, 1942: Preface, pp. vii-xii; General Introduction, pp. 1-42.

Menéndez Pidal, Ramón, *The Spaniards in their History* (tr. by Walter Starkie), Norton, New York, 1950: Ch. 3, "Individualism"; Ch. 4, "Centralism and Regionalism."

Reyes, Alfonso, *The Position of America* (selected and tr. by Harriet de Onís), Knopf, New York, 1950.

Schurz, William L., *This New World,* Dutton, New York, 1954; Ch. 1, "The Environment."

Wilgus, A. Curtis, *The Development of Hispanic America,* Farrar and Rinehart, New York, 1941: Ch. 1, "The Ethnological Background."

[9] Alfonso Reyes, *Ultima Tule,* "Notas sobre la inteligencia americana," Ed. Imprenta Universitaria, Mexico, 1942, p. 133. Alfonso Reyes (1889-1959) was Director of *El Colegio de México,* a publishing company and group of Mexican scholars.
[10] **ha construido** *has built*

12

A Medical Appointment

R. *Ricardo* N. *Nurse* D. *Doctor*

R. Good morning.

N. Good morning; do you want to see the doctor?

R. Yes, ma'am. I have an appointment with him for eleven o'clock.

N. Your name, please?

R. Ricardo Mendoza.

N. Of course. Now I remember. Come right in.

* * *

D. Come in [forward, ahead], Mr. Mendoza. How are you?

R. Just so-so.

Una visita al médico

R. *Ricardo* E. *Enfermera* M. *Médico*

R. Buenos días, señorita.

E. Buenos días. ¿Quiere ver al doctor?

R. Sí, señorita. Tengo hora con él para las once.

E. ¿Su nombre, por favor?

R. Ricardo Mendoza.

E. Ah, claro. Ahora me acuerdo. Pase usted.

* * *

M. Adelante, Sr. Mendoza. ¿Cómo está usted?

R. Así, así, regular.

D. Please [have the goodness to] sit down. Tell me what seems to be the trouble [you feel].[1]

R. I think I've got the flu, doctor. I ache all over [all the body].

D. With this winter weather everybody's got a cold. They've all got a headache and a sore throat [to them all the head and the throat ache].

R. What should I do, doctor?

D. Let's see. First tell me how long [how much time it makes that] you've been feeling this way.

R. About three days.

D. Are you taking anything?

R. Yes, aspirin. Yesterday I took five.

D. Take off your shirt and tie. Put this thermometer under your tongue.

* * *

R. Do I have a fever?

D. Just a little. You must go home and go to bed. Take this prescription with you.

R. Go to bed!

D. Yes, and when you get home, take these pills with a hot lemonade. And don't take a bath tomorrow.

R. But doctor, I have to get up tomorrow.

D. My friend, there're no buts about it [there's no but that counts].

M. Tenga la bondad de sentarse. Dígame qué siente.

R. Creo que tengo gripe, doctor. Me duele todo el cuerpo.

M. Con este invierno todo el mundo está resfriado. A todos les duele la cabeza y la garganta.

R. ¿Y qué debo hacer, doctor?

M. A ver. Primero dígame cuánto tiempo hace que se siente así.

R. Como tres días.

M. ¿Está tomando algo?

R. Sí, aspirinas. Ayer me tomé cinco.

M. Quítese la corbata y la camisa. Póngase este termómetro debajo de la lengua.

* * *

R. ¿Tengo fiebre?

M. Sí, un poquito. Tiene que irse a su casa y acostarse. Llévese esta receta.

R. ¡¿Acostarme?!

M. Sí, y al llegar, tómese estas pastillas con una limonada bien caliente. Y mañana no se bañe.

R. Pero doctor, tengo que levantarme mañana.

M. Mi amigo, no hay pero que valga.

● WRITING EXERCISE

The written representation of /s/ by **c** and **z**.[1] INSTRUCTIONS: Write the following lists of words from dictation.

A.					B.				
	zanco	cinco	caza	cace		faz	faces	cruz	cruces
	zona	cena	plaza	place		haz	haces	tez	teces
	zumo	cimo	gozo	goce		paz	paces	pez	peces
	zurdo	cerdo	trozo	trece		hoz	hoces	juez	jueces
	zarzuela	ciruela	empieza	empiece		voz	voces	vez	veces
	zurrido	cerrado	rezó	recé		luz	luces	lápiz	lápices

In Spanish, the letter **z** represents the same sound as the letter **s**. The letter **c** represents this same sound before [e] or [i]. Note that in the examples in *B* above, the final **z** of a noun or adjective is changed to **c** before adding the plural ending.

That Spanish spelling is not always consistent may be shown by the existence of such variants as the following: **zinc** or **cinc, zenit** or **cenit, zimo** or **cimo,** etc.

---

[1] Note that we are now talking about the letter **z**, not the sound [z]. The latter was treated in Unit 11.

64 Descriptive adjectives

EXAMPLES

1. El nuevo cónsul **americano.**
2. Unos joropos **venezolanos.**
3. Los Juegos **Olímpicos.**
4. El Consejo **Estudiantil.**
5. Sin agua **potable.** *(Without drinkable water.)*
6. La ropa **interior.**
7. Una huelga **general.**
8. Una casita **verde.**
9. Dos cafés **negros.**
10. Dice un señor si hay ropa **vieja.**
11. Esas son ideas **anticuadas.**
12. Los invitados son una pareja **extranjera.**
13. No recuerdo la dirección **exacta.**
14. La filosofía es una cosa **inútil.**
15. Aire **puro,** cielo **azul,** gente **sencilla.**
16. Va a ir mucha gente **importante.**
17. Una cantidad **astronómica.**
18. Esta vida **agitada.**
19. Es una planta **magnífica.**
20. Tiene unos discos **nuevos.**
21. Para café **bueno,** no hay como este lugar.

$$\boxed{\text{noun}} \quad + \quad \boxed{\text{differentiating adjective}}$$

Descriptive adjectives, when used to differentiate, follow the noun. Differentiation ranges from *classification* according to nationality, position, official status, etc., to *contrast,* i.e., "x rather than y" —new rather than old, good rather than bad, etc. The examples above are roughly scaled from classification, (1 . . .) to contrast (. . . 21).

● REPLACEMENT DRILL

A.

1. **Es un cónsul americano.**
2. _____ venezolano
3. _____ joropo _____
4. _____ nuevo
5. _____ disco _____
6. _____ fantástico
7. _____ planta _____
8. _____ importante
9. _____ huelga _____
10. _____ general
11. _____ idea _____
12. _____ anticuada
13. _____ coche _____
14. _____ verde
15. _____ casita _____
16. _____ sencilla
17. _____ vida _____
18. _____ inútil
19. _____ cosa _____
20. _____ vieja

B.

1. **¿Hay gente importante?**
2. _____ extranjera
3. _____ muebles _____
4. _____ viejos
5. _____ ropa _____
6. _____ negra
7. _____ café _____
8. _____ caliente
9. _____ arroz _____
10. _____ bueno
11. _____ leche _____
12. _____ pura
13. _____ agua _____
14. _____ potable

C.

1. **Este juego es fenomenal.**
2. _____ fantástico
3. _____ vida _____
4. _____ agitada
5. _____ viento _____
6. _____ fuerte
7. _____ batería _____
8. _____ regular
9. _____ finca _____
10. _____ grande
11. _____ refinería _____
12. _____ diferente
13. _____ tocadiscos _____
14. _____ complicado
15. _____ cosa _____
16. _____ sucia
17. _____ ciudad _____
18. _____ imposible
19. _____ competencia _____
20. _____ buena
21. _____ equipo _____

EXAMPLES

1. Hay vacas y toros **importados** para crianza y lechería.
2. Arboles y plantas **extranjeros.** *Foreign trees and plants.*
3. El carburador y la batería están **descompuestos.** *The carburetor and battery are out of order.*

```
┌─────────────────────────────────────────────────┐
│      noun + noun + plural masculine adjective     │
│              ↖    ↗                                │
│           one or both                             │
│        masculine, singular                        │
│             or plural                             │
└─────────────────────────────────────────────────┘
```

When an adjective modifies and follows
two or more nouns of different genders, it
is plural and masculine.

● REPLACEMENT DRILL

1. **Hay vacas y toros importados.**
2. _____ vacas y ovejas _____
3. _____ cerdos y ovejas _____
4. _____ sucios
5. _____ cerdos y pollos _____
6. _____ grandes
7. _____ caballos y ganado _____
8. _____ tremendos
9. _____ caballos y toros _____

10. _____ típicos
11. _____ carne y frutas _____
12. _____ café y verduras _____
13. _____ diferentes
14. _____ agua y leche _____
15. _____ puras
16. _____ manteca y helados _____
17. _____ fenomenales
18. _____ frijoles y huevos _____

EXAMPLES

1. Caballos **muy finos.**
2. Prefiero un plato **más típico.**
3. Esa cara **tan triste.**

4. Este policía **medio bruto.**   (*This half-brute policeman.*)
5. Una limonada **bien caliente.**   (*A thoroughly hot lemonade.*)

```
┌─────────────┐         ┌─────────────────────────┐
│    noun     │    +    │    modified adjective    │
└─────────────┘         └─────────────────────────┘
```

Descriptive adjectives that are themselves modified normally follow the noun.

● REPLACEMENT DRILL

1. **Son caballos muy finos.**
2. _____ vacas _____
3. _____ tan _____
4. _____ típicas
5. _____ ganado _____
6. _____ bien _____
7. _____ caro
8. _____ ovejas _____
9. _____ más _____
10. _____ bruta
11. _____ toro _____

12. _____ medio _____
13. _____ bueno
14. _____ cerdo _____
15. _____ menos _____
16. _____ fino
17. _____ café _____
18. _____ igualmente _____
19. _____ bueno
20. _____ papas _____
21. _____ casi _____

EXAMPLES

A. 1. El **nuevo** cónsul americano.
   2. Tengo que ver a la **nueva** criada.

B. 1. Tuve un **mal** día.
   2. ¿Recibiste alguna **mala** noticia?
   3. Esa **bendita** esquina del Teatro Nacional.
   4. Acabo de tener un **tremendo** lío con la
      policía.

C. 1. ¿**Buen** sueldo?
   2. ¿Qué **mejor** oportunidad que ésta?
   3. El toreo es considerado como un **verda-
      dero** arte.
   4. Sin mencionar **altos** funcionarios de
      gobierno.
   5. Fue un **gran** filósofo.

$$\boxed{\text{enhancing adjective}} \; + \; \boxed{\text{noun}}.$$

Descriptive adjectives that enhance rather than classify or contrast normally precede. Typically these adjectives express value judgments, referring to badness (*B* examples) or goodness (*C* examples).

● TRANSLATION DRILL

1. I had a big *row*.
   I had a *big* row.
2. I have a good *group*.
   I have a *good* group.
3. It's considered a real *art*.
   It's considered a *real* art.
4. We had a bad *day*.
   We had a *bad* day.
5. There were high *officials*.
   There were *high* officials.
6. There goes the new *maid*.
   There goes the *new* maid.
7. He's a good *student*.
   He's a *good* student.
8. He's my old *friend*.
   He's my *old* friend.
9. We sold our best *bed*.
   We sold our *best* bed.
10. It was the worst *bullfight* of the month.
    It was the *worst* bullfight of the month.
11. Where are the new *sheets?*
    Where are the *new* sheets?
12. I lost that dirty *receipt*.
    I lost that *dirty* receipt.
13. This is my first *winter* here.
    This is my *first* winter here.
14. I lost my only *socks*.
    I lost my *only* socks.

● DISCUSSION

Descriptive adjectives are typically those which tell something about the nature of the thing they describe. In this they differ from the adjectives treated in Unit 9 §46: **mi coche** *my car* relates the car to its environment (specifically, to me), but tells nothing about the car itself—its make, color, size, efficiency, etc. On the other hand, **buen coche** *good car,* **coche negro** *black car,* **coche fenomenal** *wonderful car,* etc., do tell something about the nature of the car.

Descriptive adjectives include some, such as those of nationality (*American, Costa Rican*), affiliation in society (*Masonic, Methodist, social, medical, Democratic, financial*), scientific or technical classification (*oxalic, radioactive, metrical*), etc., that almost always follow the noun in Spanish. They also include many which may appear in Spanish either after the noun (the more usual position) or before it.

The basis for the distinction is what might be termed the "relative informativeness" of the noun and the adjective. When we say, for example, **No es leal amigo** *He isn't a loyal friend,* we are saying, essentially, that he is not a *friend,* loyalty being something one expects of friends. But when we say **No es amigo leal** *He isn't a loyal friend,* we are not denying that he is a friend—he may be a fair-weather friend—but we are denying that he is loyal; **leal** here is essential and differentiating.

English (and Spanish also) does much the same with verb and adverb as Spanish does with noun and adjective. The contrast in English between *Can we safely wait?* ("Can we wait?") and *Can we wait safely?* ("Will it be safe?") parallels the contrast between **leal amigo** and **amigo leal**.

Most instances of descriptive adjective before noun are those in which the adjective is used for enhancement, to suggest a good quality or a bad quality; the speaker is being complimentary or uncomplimentary about the thing described. In **bendita esquina** the adjective **bendita** tells us little about **esquina** but a lot about the speaker's feelings. This is why **buen(o)** and **mal(o)** (see Unit 9 §50 for loss of –o) more often precede the noun than follow it, even sometimes when **bueno** or **malo** is itself modified (**Tienen muy buenos atletas**); but when used in a differentiating sense—**para café bueno no hay como este lugar** *for **really good** coffee there's no place like this one*—they follow the noun.

65 The reflexive with-verb pronouns

EXAMPLES

1. **Me** escribí un recado. *I wrote myself a message.*
2. ¿**Te** cortaste? *Did you cut yourself?*
3. Siénten**se**. *(Seat yourselves.)*
4. Siénte**se,** por favor. *(Seat yourself, please.)*

myself, to (for) myself	**me**
ourselves, to (for) ourselves	**nos**
yourself, to (for) yourself	**te**
yourself, to (for) yourself yourselves, to (for) yourselves himself, to (for) himself herself, to (for) herself itself, to (for) itself themselves, to (for) themselves	**se**

Except for **se,** the reflexive pronouns are the same as the nonreflexive.

● PERSON-NUMBER SUBSTITUTION DRILL

1. ¿Cómo se llama *usted?*
   (tú, él, ellas, ella, ustedes)
2. *Yo* me llamo Mario (María).
   (él, nosotros, ellos, tú, ella)
3. ¿Dónde puedo sentarme?
   (él, tú, ellas, nosotros, usted)
4. ¿Por qué te preocupas tanto?
   (ellos, usted, yo, ella, nosotros)
5. *Rosa* no se dejó dar gato por liebre.
   (las criadas, tú, ustedes, yo, nosotros)
6. *Yo* me metí en una calle en contra del tránsito.
   (ustedes, nosotros, Roberto, ellos, tú)
7. *El muchacho* no pudo calmarse.
   (nosotros, ella, tú, ellos, yo)
8. *Yo* me puedo imaginar el gran lío que sucedió.
   (ustedes, tú, usted, nosotros, ellas)
9. *La pobre señora* casi se volvió loca.
   (nosotras, ellas, yo, usted, tú)
10. Si la comida no llega pronto, *yo* me muero de hambre.
    (Paquito, nosotros, ustedes, tú, María Elena)
11. *Las chicas* se acostaron muy tarde anteanoche.
    (Pablo, ustedes, nosotros, tú, yo)
12. No vale la pena, pero me levanto a las seis.
    (nosotros, ellos, tú, ella, ustedes)
13. *Las criadas* no quieren bañarse por la mañana.
    (la muchacha, tú, ella, nosotros, usted)
14. En realidad, no me acordé de la competencia de natación.
    (el equipo, los atletas, nosotros, él, tú)
15. Es que *Paquito* no sabe peinarse bien ni atrás ni a los lados.
    (las niñas, el chico, tú, yo, nosotros)
16. *Yo* me siento así así, regular.
    (Olga, Pablo y yo, las alumnas, tú, usted)
17. Desgraciadamente se cayeron en esa bendita esquina.
    (yo, mi abuela, tú, ellos, nosotros)
18. Tuvo que quitarse hasta los calzoncillos.
    (nosotros, los chicos, tú, yo, él)
19. Probablemente tenemos que irnos al campo.
    (ustedes, tú, usted, yo, ellos)
20. *Ellos* se quedaron a ver el boxeo y el juego de básquetbol.
    (usted, los muchachos, yo, tú, nosotros)
21. *Ricardo* se tomó las pastillas con mucho gusto.
    (yo, ellos, nosotros, usted, tú)

The –*self* words in English to which the Spanish reflexives correspond are unemphatic: the English to which **¿Te cortaste?** corresponds is *Did you **cut** yourself?*, with strong stress on the verb but weak stress on –*self*. The emphatic –*self* word in Spanish is **mismo, –a, –os, –as,** as in the example **Déjeme peinarme yo mismo** *Let me comb myself* **I myself.**

The multiple meanings of **se** given here do not cause confusion because **se** merely repeats the subject, and the subject may always be expressed; thus **El se cortó** means *He cut himself* and **Usted se cortó** means *You cut yourself.*

In the reflexive pronouns there is no difference between direct and indirect objects. Example 1 above is indirect (**me** *to myself*), while Example 2 is direct.

66 Reflexive constructions, direct object

1. **¿Por qué no llamamos a María Elena?**
   La rubia **se llama** Betty. *(The blonde calls herself Betty.)*
2. **Lo mataron.** *They killed him.*
   Cualquier día **te matas.**
3. El barbero **me peinó.** *The barber combed me (combed my hair).*
   Déjeme **peinarme** yo mismo. *(Let me comb myself I myself.)*

4. **Metí la plata** en la cartera. *I put (stuck) the money in the wallet.*
   Me metí en una calle en contra del tránsito.
5. La madre **acostó a sus hijos.** *The mother put her children to bed (put-to-bed her children).*
   ¡¿Acostarme?! *(Put-to-bed myself?)*
6. La madre **bañó a sus hijos.** *The mother bathed her children.*
   Mañana no **se bañe.** *(Tomorrow don't bathe yourself.)*

	DIRECT OBJECT, REFLEXIVE OR NONREFLEXIVE	VERB
I wash them	los	lavo
I wash (myself)	me	lavo
we seat them	los	sentamos
we seat ourselves (sit down)	nos	sentamos
he raises it	lo	levanta
he raises himself (gets up)	se	levanta

Any verb that may take a nonreflexive direct object may take a reflexive direct object, as in English. The best English translation, however, does not always have a reflexive pronoun.

● TRANSLATION DRILL

1. We call her Betty.
   She calls herself Betty.
2. They killed him.
   He killed himself.
3. The barber combs my hair (combs me).
   I comb my hair (comb myself).

4. We seated them at one side.
   They sat down (seated themselves) at one side.
5. The mother put them to bed.
   The mother went to bed.
6. She bathed her.
   She took a bath (bathed herself).

7. I put them in their place.
   I put myself in their place.
8. He raises it.
   He gets up (raises himself).
9. She cut it.
   She cut herself.
10. We washed it.
    We washed ourselves.

EXAMPLES   1. ¡**Cálmate,** chico!
   2. Yo **me entusiasmé.**
   3. No **te preocupes.**

to calm (someone or something)	**calmar**
to calm down	**calmarse**
to thrill, excite (someone)	**entusiasmar**
to be thrilled, excited	**entusiasmarse**
to worry (someone)	**preocupar**
to worry, be (get) worried	**preocuparse**

Most verbs signifying a change in the subject's state are reflexive. The English equivalent often carries the verb *get: get worried, get sore, get upset, get scared, get worse.*

EXAMPLES

A. 1. ¡Ese hombre **me pone** tan furiosa! *That man makes me so furious!*
   2. La noticia **nos puso** tristes. *The news made us sad.*

B. 1. ¡No **te pongas** tan furiosa! *Don't get so furious!*
   2. **Se pusieron** muy tristes. *They got very sad.*
   3. ¿Qué hacemos si no **se pone** mejor? *What do we do if he doesn't get better?*

to make (him)	furious sad better	**poner (lo)**	**furioso** **triste** **mejor**
to get	complicated bigger etc.	**ponerse**	**complicado** **más grande** etc.

Poner is used for *make* in the sense of "bring about a change of state" (in someone else); **ponerse** is used for *get* when the change is within oneself.

● TRANSLATION DRILL

1. Calm him down, boy!
   Calm down, boy!
2. Don't worry her!
   Don't worry!
3. They thrilled me.
   They were thrilled.
4. Then I calmed her down.
   Then I calmed down.
5. He didn't thrill us.
   He wasn't thrilled.
6. She doesn't worry me.
   She doesn't get worried.
7. They made (put) him furious.
   They got (put themselves) furious.
8. She made (put) him sad.
   She got (put herself) sad.
9. She drove me crazy.
   She went (drove herself) crazy.
10. He made me furious.
    He got furious.
11. She made me sad.
    She got sad.
12. He made me sick.
    He got sick.
13. He made me serious.
    He got serious.
14. The class got boring.
    The exam got complicated.
    The boss got ridiculous.
    The strike got serious.
    The teacher got sad.

67 Reflexive constructions, indirect object

EXAMPLES

1. **Le quité** la corbata. *I took off the (his) tie for him.*
   Quítese la corbata. *(Take off the tie for yourself.)*
2. **Te** voy a **poner** este termómetro debajo de la lengua. *I'm going to put this thermometer under your tongue (under the tongue for you).*
   Póngase este termómetro debajo de la lengua. *(Put this thermometer under the tongue for yourself.)*

3. Mi madre **me ponía** la corbata. *My mother used to put my tie on for me.*
   Voy a **ponerme** la corbata. *I'm going to put on my tie.*
4. El médico **le lavó** las manos. *The doctor washed his hands (for him).*
   El médico **se lavó** las manos. *The doctor washed his (own) hands.*

On him ⟶	Le Me	⟵ On myself
I put	**puse**	I put
the	**los**	the
shoes	**zapatos**	shoes
(I put his shoes on for him)		(I put my shoes on)

On me ⟶	Me Se	⟵ On himself
he cut	**cortó**	he cut
the	**la**	the
face	**cara**	face
(He cut my face)		(He cut his face)

A service or disservice done to oneself or to someone else takes the indirect-object pronoun, reflexive or nonreflexive. English generally uses a possessive for this meaning.

● TRANSLATION DRILL

1. I washed his hands.
   I washed my hands.
2. He pulled my hair.
   He pulled his (own) hair.
3. He put on my socks (for me).
   He put on his socks.
4. He cut my face.
   He cut his face.

5. She took off my shoes (for me).
   She took off her shoes.
6. Wash his face.
   Wash your face.
7. Put on my shirt (for me).
   Put on your shirt.
8. Take off my tie (for me).
   Take off your tie.

EXAMPLES

A. 1. **¿Está tomando** algo?
   2. Sí, aspirinas. Ayer **me tomé** cinco. *(Yesterday I took five for myself.)*
   3. **Tómese** estas pastillas.

B. 1. **Lleve** el paquete. *Carry the package.*
   2. **Llévese** esta receta. *(Take this prescription for yourself.)*

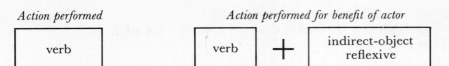

Action performed	Action performed for benefit of actor	
verb	verb $+$	indirect-object reflexive

To emphasize the benefit that the actor gets from his action, a reflexive pronoun may be added; compare English *I'm going to eat **me** a sandwich.*

EXAMPLES

A. 1. —¿Tomó las aspirinas? *Did you take the aspirins?*
   2. —Sí, **me las** tomé anteanoche. *Yes, I took them night before last.*
B. 1. —¿Me llevo los paquetes? *Shall I take the packages?*
   2. —Sí, lléve**selos**. *Yes, take them.*

INDIRECT-OBJECT REFLEXIVE	OTHER PRONOUN, DIRECT OBJECT
me nos te se	lo la los las

The reflexive pronoun precedes the other pronoun.

● CONSTRUCTION SUBSTITUTION DRILL

INSTRUCTIONS: Repeat the following sentences just as you hear them. Then repeat them again, substituting an appropriate with-verb pronoun for the direct-object noun and modifiers, if any.

1. TEACHER: Ella se comió *la fruta. Repita.*
   STUDENT: **Ella se comió la fruta.**
   TEACHER: *Cambie.*
   STUDENT: **Ella se la comió.**

2. Nos comimos *cuatro huevos.*
3. Me lavé *la cabeza.*
4. María se compró *el traje.*

5. Se comieron *la carne.*
6. El se lavó *los pies.*
7. Me corté *el pelo.*
8. Nos tomamos *la limonada.*
9. Se compraron *los zapatos.*
10. Me tomé *dos tazas de café.*

● TRANSLATION DRILL

1. TEACHER: He ate the meal up.
   STUDENT: **El se comió la comida.**
   TEACHER: I ate it up too.
   STUDENT: **Yo me la comí también.**

2. She drinks two cups of coffee every day.
   I drink them too.

3. I ate the eggs.
   He ate them too.
4. We bought us a car.
   We bought [us] it yesterday.
5. He took along the shoes.
   He took them this morning.

EXAMPLES

A. 1. **Cae** la lluvia. *The rain falls.*
   2. **Cayeron** muchos en ese ataque. *Many fell in that attack.*
   3. **Me caí.** *I (lost my balance and) fell.*

B. 1. **Muere** el día. *The day is dying.*
   2. Los policías a veces tienen que **morir**. *Policemen sometimes have to die.*
   3. **Se muere** mi padre. *My father is dying.*

C. 1. Así el aire no **entra**. *That way the air doesn't get in.*
    2. **Entró** por la puerta. *He came in through the door.*
    3. La lluvia **se entró** por el techo. *The rain worked its way in through the roof.*

D. 1. **Quedé** muy triste. *I remained (the experience left me) very sad.*
    2. La pared **quedó** sucia. *The wall was left (came out as a result) dirty.*
    3. **Nos quedamos** aquí. *We're staying here.*

E. 1. **Iba** a trabajar. *He was going (was on his way) to work.*
    2. Supe que usted **se iba** a trabajar al campo. *(I heard you were going off to work in the country.)*

Action with personal involvement of actor

verb	+	reflexive pronoun

To show the participation (interest, effort, pleasure, pain, restraint, etc.) of the actor in the action, a reflexive pronoun is added.

● TRANSLATION DRILL

1. TEACHER: He took aspirins.
   STUDENT: **Tomó aspirinas.**
   TEACHER: He took those aspirins.
   STUDENT: **Se tomó esas aspirinas.**
2. He carried the package.
   He carried off the package.
3. He ate a plate of beans.
   He ate himself a plate of beans.

4. The rain fell.
   The man fell down.
5. The day is dying.
   The man is dying.
6. I remained sad.
   I stayed a week.
7. He's going to work.
   He's going off to work.

● DISCUSSION

The last set of examples contains verbs without direct objects ("intransitive verbs") accompanied by reflexive pronouns. Certain verbs, such as **caer** and **morir,** are more often than not used in this way. The difference that adding the reflexive pronoun makes is rather subtle:

An action may be viewed as a historical unit, with the actor being carried along as part of it. Or the action may be viewed as a developing something, with the actor in a position to affect the course of developments: to make them inevitable by his carelessness, slower by his resistance, possible by his efforts, pathetic by his suffering, etc. To express the latter view, Spanish adds a reflexive pronoun; for example, to imply that a body is affected by gravity or is swept down by force, we use the simple verb **caer;** but to imply that the body, in the act of falling, fails to keep erect, or fights to hold its balance, or gives in to an impulse to fall, we use the reflexive **caerse:** the body is a partner in what happens to it or in what it causes to happen. English has no single device that is parallel to this, but certain rough approximations can be listed: **ir** *to go,* **irse** *to get on one's way, pick up and go, go off, go away;* **quedar** *to remain,* **quedarse** *to stay;* **caer** *to fall,* **caerse** *to go (come) tumbling down.*

Now that the last of the with-verb pronouns have been introduced, we can summarize their position with respect to one another when two occur in sequence (see Unit 11 §57):

se	me nos te	lo la los las le les

The **se** here is either the reflexive **se** (direct or indirect) or the **se** for **le, les.** Rarely do more than two of these appear in combination.

68 The reflexive for unplanned occurrences

1. **Se me** olvidó su nombre. *I forgot his name (his name slipped my mind [forgot itself on me]).*
2. **Se me** ocurrió la idea. *The idea popped into my head.*
3. ¿**Se te** cayeron (rompieron) las tazas? *Did you drop (break) the cups (did the cups fall [break] for you)?*
4. **Se nos** quedaron las herramientas en casa. *We left our tools at home (the tools stayed [got left] home on us).*

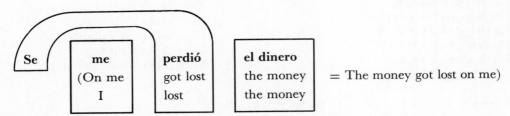

| Se | me
 (On me
 I | perdió <br> got lost <br> lost | el dinero <br> the money <br> the money | = The money got lost on me) |

Where English has *It fell, It broke, It got away from me,* etc., to make a happening appear to occur on its own, without any premeditation, Spanish uses a reflexive construction for the verb and adds an indirect object referring to the person.

● PERSON-NUMBER SUBSTITUTION DRILL

1. *A mí* se me olvidó la dirección.
   (a él, a nosotros, a ellos, a ti, a usted)
2. *A Juan* se le cayó una taza de café.
   (a ellos, a mí, a ti, a ella, a nosotros)
3. Se le rompió la taza.
   (a ellos, a mí, a ti, a ella, a nosotros)
4. Se me ofreció una buena oportunidad.
   (a él, a ellos, a nosotros, a usted, a ti)

5. Se nos quedó el libro en casa.
   (a mí, a Pablo, a ustedes, a ti, a ella)
6. *A mí* se me rompió la camisa.
   (a ustedes, a ti, a usted, a nosotros, a ellos)
7. Se me ocurrió una idea magnífica.
   (a nosotros, a usted, a ti, a ellos, a ella)

● ITEM SUBSTITUTION DRILL

1. Se me rompió la *camisa*.
   (zapatos, libro, camiseta, discos, plato, juguetes, flecha)
2. Se nos olvidó el *número*.
   (recados, lista, noticias, edad, colores, fecha, cuentas)
3. Se le cayó una *taza*.
   (platos, paquete, fundas, postre, helados, pan, frijoles)

4. Se les quedaron las *pastillas* en la sala.
   (receta, papeles, termómetro, cheques, recibo, cuenta, lista)
5. Se me vino un *hambre* tremenda.
   (ideas, lluvia, huelgas, suerte)
6. Se le ofreció un *puesto* nuevo.
   (temas, idea, remedios, oficio, negocio)
7. Se me ocurre *una cosa*.
   (algo, una idea, otra cosa, algo diferente, un tema)

● TRANSLATION DRILL

A. 1. TEACHER: I forgot my tie.
      STUDENT: **Se me olvidó la corbata.**

   2. I forgot my books.
   3. I forgot my comb.
   4. I forgot my papers.
   5. I forgot my receipt.

   6. I forgot my checks.
   7. I forgot my prescription.

B. 1. My plate got broken.
      Se me rompió el plato.
   2. My records got broken.

3. My arrow got broken.
4. My furniture got broken.
5. My egg got broken.
6. My scissors got broken.
7. My shirt got torn.
8. My socks got torn.
9. My pillowcase got torn.
10. My sheets got torn.

C. 1. He dropped his bread.
   Se le cayó el pan.
   2. He dropped his vegetables.
   3. He dropped his lemonade.
   4. He dropped his ice cream.
   5. He dropped his dessert.
   6. He dropped his beans.
   7. He dropped his salad.

D. 1. We forgot the prescription.
   Se nos olvidó la receta.
   2. We forgot the money.
   3. We forgot the aspirins.
   4. We forgot the pills.
   5. We forgot the sheets.
   6. We forgot the pillowcases.
   7. We forgot the suits.

E. 1. They broke their thermometers.
   Se les rompieron los termómetros.
   2. They broke their scissors.
   3. They broke their clippers.
   4. They broke their eggs.
   5. They broke their plates.
   6. They broke their cups.
   7. They broke their furniture.

● COMBINED PATTERN REPLACEMENT DRILL

A. 1. **Ay, se me olvidó la ropa sucia.**
   2. _____ nueva
   3. _____ disco _____
   4. _____ los _____
   5. _____ nos _____
   6. Caramba, _____
   7. _____ plato _____
   8. _____ rompió _____
   9. _____ grande
   10. _____ le _____
   11. Dios mío, _____
   12. _____ platos ____
   13. _____ viejos
   14. _____ cayó _____
   15. _____ les _____
   16. _____ tijeras ____
   17. _____ largas
   18. _____ me _____
   19. _____ quedaron _____
   20. A ver, _____
   21. _____ lista _____
   22. _____ corta

B. 1. **Ellos se iban a quedar en la ciudad.**
   2. _____ van _____
   3. Ella _____
   4. _____ campo
   5. _____ ir a _____
   6. _____ van _____
   7. Yo _____
   8. _____ hacienda
   9. _____ nos _____
   10. El _____
   11. _____ montaña
   12. _____ las _____
   13. _____ salir de _____
   14. _____ van _____
   15. Tú _____
   16. _____ auto
   17. _____ meter en _____
   18. _____ me _____
   19. _____ iba _____
   20. _____ tranvía
   21. Nosotros _____
   22. _____ vamos _____
   23. _____ coche
   24. Usted _____

● TRANSLATION REVIEW DRILL

Masculine demonstratives.

1. That paper is mine.
   Those papers are mine.
2. That toy is mine.
   Those toys are mine.
3. That book is mine.
   Those books are mine.
4. That car is mine.
   Those cars are mine.
5. That bull is mine.
   Those bulls are mine.

6. That comb is mine.
   Those combs are mine.
7. That theater is mine.
   Those theaters are mine.
8. This child is mine.
   These children are mine.
9. This horse is mine.
   These horses are mine.
10. This document is mine.
    These documents are mine.

11. This plate is mine.
    These plates are mine.
12. This record is mine.
    These records are mine.
13. This shoe is mine.
    These shoes are mine.

READING
Una visita al médico

P. *Pablo* R. *Ricardo, amigo de Pablo*

P. Buenos días, Ricardo. ¿Qué tal?

R. Hola, Pablo, ¿cómo estás?

P. Muy bien, ¿y tú?

R. Así, así; tenía gripe hace unos cuantos días, pero ya estoy recobrando la salud.

P. ¡Qué lástima! ¿Viste al médico?

R. Sí, pero tú conoces a esos matasanos.[1] Le hacen a uno esperar en una antesala elegantemente adornada y ricamente amueblada;[2] le preguntan a uno qué siente . . . si sé lo que siento, ¿para qué debo ir al médico, eh?

P. Yo me acuerdo de una visita . . .

R. *(con el aire insistente de un hombre que va a decirlo todo)* Cuando entré, estaba la enfermera sentada en la antesala . . .

P. ¿Era bonita?

R. ¡Ni en pintura! Bastante vieja, demasiado gorda . . . De todos modos, me preguntó si quería ver al doctor . . . ¡qué diablos! ¿Para qué creía que estaba allí? . . . Le dije que sí, y le recordé que tenía hora con él para las once. Entonces me preguntó cómo me llamaba. ¡Caramba! Si tengo gripe, fiebre, dolor de cabeza o cualquier otra cosa, ¿qué puede importar mi nombre? Pero al fin se acordó de que yo tenía hora con el médico, y me admitió a la presencia de Su Señoría[3] . . .

P. ¿Y entonces?

R. ¡No me apures![4] . . . — Tenga la bondad de sentarse, me dijo. Así que tuve la bondad de sentarme. Me preguntó cómo me sentía. Le dije que tenía gripe, que me dolía todo el cuerpo. Me contestó que con este invierno todo el mundo está resfriado, y que a todos les duele la cabeza y la garganta. — ¿Qué debo hacer? le dije. Entonces me preguntó que cuánto tiempo llevaba sintiéndome[5] así, que si estaba tomando algo y otras cosas por el estilo. Me quité la corbata y la camisa y me puse un termómetro debajo de la lengua.

P. ¿Tenías fiebre?

R. Sí, pero sólo un poquito. Tuve que irme a casa y acostarme, lo que no quería hacer; tomé unas pastillas con una limonada bien caliente. ¡Una limonada caliente, figúrate! No pude protestar; no hay pero que valga —con estos médicos. Y además, hay que pagar la cuenta. La vida es dura, ¿verdad?

---

[1] *charlatans, quacks:* The word is derived from **mata-sanos;** the first part of this compound you know already, and **sanos** means *healthy.*
[2] Cf. **mueble.**   [3] *His Lordship*   [4] *hurry*   [5] *how long I'd been feeling*

READING
España y la formación de la lengua española

España es una antigua nación de Europa y ocupa con Portugal una península: la Península Ibérica (o hispánica),[1] en el extremo sudoeste de Europa. Aunque es más pequeña que Texas, es la tercera nación de Europa en área: la superficie es de 504.000 kilómetros cuadrados.[2] España tiene casi treinta millones de habitantes; pero realmente esto es poco en comparación con otros países de Europa.

España es uno de los países más monta-

---

[1] **hispánica,** from **Hispania,** the old name for the Iberian Peninsula, which includes Spain and Portugal.
[2] **quinientos cuatro mil kilómetros cuadrados** = *190,000 sq. miles*

ñosos de Europa. (Suiza es la única que tiene más montañas.) Casi toda España está cruzada de cordilleras: la Sierra Nevada y la Sierra Morena, la Cordillera Cantábrica y la Ibérica, y los montes Pirineos. Hay llanuras en la Mancha, Castilla la Vieja y las provincias de Valladolid y Zamora. Los principales ríos son: el Duero, el Tajo, el Guadiana, el Guadalquivir y el Ebro. Todos, menos el Ebro, fluyen hacia el Atlántico. Los límites de España en el norte son el Mar Cantábrico y los montes Pirineos, que la separan de Francia. En el sur la limitan el mar Mediterráneo y el Estrecho de Gibraltar; en el este también el Mediterráneo y al oeste Portugal y el Océano Atlántico. El Estrecho de Gibraltar, de unos quince kilómetros de anchura, separa España de Africa.

El clima de España, como el de la América hispánica, no es parejo: en unos lugares hace frío; en otros hace calor; llueve mucho en algunos lugares; en otros llueve poco; hace viento; no hace viento. Cerca de los Pirineos hace frío; en las orillas del mar el clima es templado y en el sur hace calor. Llueve mucho en Galicia y casi nada en Murcia y gran parte de Andalucía. En la meseta central el clima es parecido al de los estados centrales de los Estados Unidos. La costa del Mediterráneo disfruta de un clima como el de California, y Galicia como el del estado de Washington. Andalucía se parece a la Florida en su clima. En Madrid, la capital, nunca hace tanto calor como a veces en Texas ni tanto frío como a veces en Wisconsin. Sin embargo, los españoles gozan de fama internacional de no jactarse del clima de su país. Más bien les gusta repetir estos versos que se refieren a la meseta central:

Nueve meses de invierno
y tres de infierno.

España es predominantemente agrícola. Ocupa el primer lugar del mundo en la producción de aceite, aceitunas y naranjas, y el tercero en la producción de vino. Produce también arroz, trigo, caña de azúcar, corcho, almendras, avellanas, limones, melones y otras frutas. Tiene minas de hierro, carbón, plata, plomo, mercurio y sal. Hay también cría[3] de ovejas, caballos, burros, cerdos y toros. Estos últimos son muy numerosos.

El español es uno de los idiomas neolatinos o románicos. (Otros son el francés, el italiano, el portugués, el rumano, etc.) El español se llama a veces *castellano,* por ser la lengua hablada en el antiguo reino de Castilla, en la Península Ibérica. Cuando los romanos empezaron la conquista de la península en el siglo III a. de J.C.,[4] trajeron con ellos su propia lengua, el latín hablado o vulgar.[5] Con el transcurso de los años, esta lengua fue reemplazando[6] a las lenguas indígenas, pero los habitantes la hablaban de una manera *españolizada.*[7] Fue este latín españolizado el que hallaron los visigodos cuando se apoderaron del país hacia fines del siglo V d. de J.C.,[8] y cuando los árabes invadieron la península en 711, parece probable que la lengua allí hablada era más bien español que latín. Los árabes vivieron con los españoles ocho siglos, unas veces en paz y otras en guerra, hasta el año 1492. Dejaron muchas huellas de su dominación en la lengua, y también en otras formas de cultura. (Ejemplos: algodón, aceite, alfombra, alcalde, alcohol, naranjo, azafrán, almohada.) Al conversar los españoles con los moros se les *pegaron* muchos de sus vocablos . . .

---

[3] **cría** *raising*   [4] **a. de J.C.** = **antes de Jesucristo** *B.C.*

[5] Vulgar Latin was the speech of the Roman masses (*vulgus*). Propagated by the Roman soldiers, colonists, traders, and (later) missionaries, throughout the Empire, it became, in increasingly altered forms, the languages of what we may now term the Romance-speaking countries—Spain, France, Italy, etc. Classical Latin, the literary medium of Cicero, Virgil, Horace, Martial, Quintilian, and others, was a refined artistic instrument used by the polished writers and educated speakers. It differed from popular speech in pronunciation, forms, syntax, and vocabulary just as the prose of Hemingway and Faulkner, and the prepared utterances of eminent politicians, ministers, and Phi Beta Kappa speakers, differ from the colloquial English of the man on the street.

[6] **fue reemplazando** *gradually replaced* (a progressive tense with **ir** as the auxiliary verb).

[7] **de una manera españolizada** *in a Hispanized manner.* We are all familiar with the fact that when foreigners are learning English they carry over their own speech habits and superimpose them upon English patterns. This accounts for what we loosely term "a foreign accent." English-speaking persons, of course, make comparable mistakes in learning a foreign language. When a subjugated people, like the pre-Roman inhabitants of Spain, gradually acquired a new language over a period of time, the language acquired was accordingly altered in varying degrees by the previous speech habits of the speakers, as well as by other factors.

[8] **d. de J.C.** = **después de Jesucristo** *A.D.*

Pero con todas estas mezclas la lengua latina es el principal fundamento del castellano.

De todos los elementos que forman el léxico español (palabras iberas, celtas, latinas, griegas, germanas, árabes), el elemento latino predomina en un ochenta por ciento de sus palabras. También han influido[9] en el léxico muchos neologismos de las lenguas modernas: anglicismos (ejemplos: fútbol, rosbif, yate, vagón, repórter, líder, sport), americanismos (ejemplos: béisbol, jonrón, nilón) y muchísimas palabras indias de las naciones del Nuevo Mundo (ejemplos: chocolate, cacao, tomate, canoa, sabana, tabaco, barbacoa, batata o patata).

Menéndez Pidal, el gran investigador y filólogo español,[10] cree que todas las lenguas y culturas en contacto influyen las unas en las otras.[11] "Toda lengua", dice, "es una mezcla de múltiples elementos venidos[12] de los otros idiomas con que se ha comunicado el pueblo que la habla."

La eminente poetisa chilena Gabriela Mistral[13] dice: "Una lengua completa . . . tiene que ganar clientela entre los extraños. Un idioma es una verdadera pieza comercial, lo mismo que el cheque, y pide agentes extranjeros que le den[14] estimación y entera confianza."

En 1492 la lengua castellana—es decir, el español—fue traída por los españoles al Nuevo Mundo. Hoy el español es la lengua oficial de dieciocho naciones del Nuevo Mundo y es una de las lenguas oficiales de la O.N.U.[15]

● CUESTIONARIO

1. ¿Qué países ocupan la Península Ibérica?
2. ¿Qué superficie y número de habitantes tiene España?
3. ¿Cuáles son los dos países más montañosos de Europa?
4. ¿Qué característica tienen casi todos los ríos de España?
5. ¿Con qué países limita España al norte y al oeste?
6. ¿Qué océanos bañan las costas de España?
7. ¿Qué continente está al sur de España?
8. ¿Por qué se dice que el clima de España no es parejo?
9. ¿Qué regiones de España y Estados Unidos tienen clima parecido?
10. ¿Puede usted explicar los versos:

    Nueve meses de invierno
    y tres de infierno?

11. Mencione algunos de los productos agrícolas de España.
12. ¿Por qué hay muchos toros en España?
13. ¿A qué se llama idiomas neolatinos o románicos?
14. ¿Quiénes invadieron la península Ibérica en el siglo III a. de J. C.? ¿Qué lengua trajeron los invasores?
15. ¿Cuándo se apoderaron los visigodos de España?
16. ¿Cuánto tiempo vivieron los árabes en España? ¿Qué influencias dejaron?
17. ¿Qué elementos forman el léxico español? ¿Cuál de estos elementos predomina en el castellano?
18. Mencione algunos neologismos que han influido en el léxico español.
19. Explique por qué se habla español en el Nuevo Mundo.

● SUGGESTED READINGS

Adams, Nicholson B., *The Heritage of Spain,* Holt, rev. ed., New York, 1959: Ch. 2, "Spain is Romanized"; Ch. 4, "The Moors Enrich Spain"; Ch. 5, "Christian Spain to 1252."

Brenan, Gerald, *The Face of Spain,* Grove, New York, 1956.

Entwistle, William J., *The Spanish Language, Together with Portuguese, Catalan and Basque,* Macmillan, New York, 1938: Ch. 1, "The Languages of the Spanish Peninsula"; Ch. 5, "The Rise of Castilian"; Ch. 6, "Standard Spanish"; Ch. 7, "The Extension of Spanish to Spanish America."

Kany, Charles E., *American-Spanish Syntax,* University of Chicago Press, 2nd ed., Chicago, 1951: Introduction, pp. v–xii.

Spaulding, Robert K., *How Spanish Grew,* University of California Press, Berkeley, 1943.

---

[9] **han influido** *have influenced*
[10] Ramón Menéndez Pidal (born in Madrid in 1869) is the dean of Spanish philologists.
[11] **las unas en las otras** *each other* (This is explained in Unit 15 §85.)
[12] **venidos** *that have come*
[13] Gabriela Mistral (pseudonym of Lucila Godoy de Alcayaga), winner of the Nobel prize in literature in 1945, was born in Chile in 1889 and died on Long Island, New York, in 1956.
[14] **que le den** *to give (to) it*
[15] **Organización de las Naciones Unidas** *the United Nations*

13

The University and Politics

A. *Don Antonio*   R. *Ricardo*   P. *Paper boy*

A. Ricardo, Ricardo! Come here. What's going on? Why's everybody running?

R. The police fired on a student demonstration; it was something awful.

A. How terrible! Did they kill anyone?

R. I don't know if there were any killed, but I know there are more than ten wounded, several of them seriously.

A. Murderers! Cowards! There's never been a government as bad as this one. But they'll pay for it all right.

R. Sh . . . calm down, Don Antonio, somebody'll hear you. Let's go inside and talk.

* * *

La universidad y la política

A. *Don Antonio*   R. *Ricardo*   V. *Vendedor*

A. ¡Ricardo! ¡Ricardo! Venga acá, ¿qué pasa? ¿Por qué anda toda la gente corriendo?

R. La policía disparó contra una manifestación de estudiantes (1), algo horrible.

A. ¡Qué barbaridad! ¿Mataron a alguno?

R. No sé si hubo muertos pero sé que hay más de diez heridos, varios de ellos gravemente.

A. ¡Asesinos! ¡Cobardes! ¡Un gobierno tan malo como éste jamás ha existido! Pero ya la pagarán (2).

R. Sh . . . ., cálmese, don Antonio, que lo pueden oir. Vamos a hablar adentro.

* * *

R. You know that today is the anniversary of the death of the university leader and martyr, Gustavo Díaz.

A. Yes, sure, and his comrades went to put flowers on his tomb. What's so bad about that?

R. Nothing, an admirable gesture. But it was also a pretext for speeches against the President.

A. Very well done. That tyrant deserves them. And then what? I suppose the police made one of their dastardly attacks upon them.

R. Yes, and without respecting the sacred place they were in, they broke up the demonstration with clubs and guns [shots].

A. Scoundrels! I tell you things can't go on like this. Something's got to be done.

R. The elections are coming up soon. And don't forget that the opposition has a much stronger party than the government.

A. But is it possible you still believe in free elections? Don't be so simple-minded. Only a revolution can carry us to power.

* * *

P. Extra! Extra! All about the trouble [events] this morning at the cemetery! Eeextra! Extra, sir?

R. Which is it, *El Independiente* or the Government paper?

P. I've got both, take your pick.

A. Both, just so we can see the lies put out by the government. Look at these headlines, Ricardo: POLICE ATTACKED BY STUDENTS. COMPELLED TO DEFEND THEMSELVES.

R. *El Independiente* says: TWELVE STUDENTS WOUNDED, HUNDREDS IN JAIL. STUDENTS DECLARE NATIONWIDE STRIKE!

R. Usted sabe que hoy es el aniversario de la muerte del líder universitario y mártir, Gustavo Díaz.

A. Sí, claro, y sus compañeros fueron a ponerle flores a su tumba. ¿Qué hay de malo en eso?

R. Nada, un gesto admirable. Pero fue también un pretexto para discursos contra el Presidente.

A. Muy bien hecho. Ese tirano se los merece. Y entonces ¿qué? La policía los atacó infamemente.

R. Sí, y sin respetar el lugar sagrado donde estaban, disolvió la manifestación a palos y a tiros.

A. ¡Infames! Yo le digo a usted que esta situación no puede seguir así. Hay que hacer algo.

R. Las elecciones vienen pronto y no olvide que la oposición tiene un partido mucho más fuerte que el del gobierno.

A. ¿Pero es que usted todavía cree en elecciones libres? No sea tan inocente. Sólo una revolución puede llevarnos al poder.

* * *

V. ¡Extra! ¡¡Extra!! ¡Con los acontecimientos de esta mañana en el cementerio! ¡¡¡Eeextra!!! ¿Extra, señor?

R. ¿De cuál es, de *El Independiente* o del periódico del gobierno?

V. Traigo de los dos, usted escoja.

A. Los dos, no más para ver las mentiras del gobierno. Mire usted, Ricardo, estos titulares: POLICIA ATACADA POR ESTUDIANTES. OBLIGADA A DEFENDERSE.

R. *El Independiente* dice: DOCE ESTUDIANTES HERIDOS, CIENTOS EN LA CARCEL. ESTUDIANTES DECLARAN HUELGA GENERAL EN TODO EL PAIS.

Cultural Notes

(1) Latin-American university students play a much more active role in the political life of their countries than do American college students, as the university is regarded as an institution which provides for informal apprenticeship in politics. Political leaders seek the support of the students. Students often co-operate with workers in labor strikes; and at times student demonstrations and uprisings have led to the fall of dictatorial regimes.

(2) See Unit 10 Cultural Note 4 for an explanation of indefinite **la**.

A. The written representation of /s/ by **s** or **c** before **e** or **i**. INSTRUCTIONS: As the teacher dictates the following list, write each word in two ways (note that **z** does not occur in any of these words).

sien	cien	sebo	cebo	sera	cera	segar	cegar
seso	ceso	siervo	ciervo	sidra	cidra	coser	cocer
sima	cima	seda	ceda	sierra	cierra	sesión	cesión
sena	cena	sepa	cepa	serrar	cerrar	resiente	reciente
siento	ciento						

B. The written representation of /s/ by **s** or **z** before **a, o,** or **u**. INSTRUCTIONS: As the teacher dictates the following list, write each word in two ways (note that **c** does not occur in any of these words).

vos	voz	tasa	taza	rosa	roza	sueco	zueco
ves	vez	baso	bazo	poso	pozo	sonado	zonado
rasa	raza	laso	lazo	saga	zaga	asar	azar
masa	maza			sumo	zumo		

You have noted that the pairs of words in both columns of the exercises above are identical in pronunciation, though spelled differently. Consequently, without a context there is no way of knowing how to spell them when you hear them.

In Castilian pronunciation, however, the letter **c** before **e** or **i**, and the letter **z** wherever it occurs, represent the voiceless interdental fricative [θ], corresponding to the voiceless *th* in English *thin*. Therefore, the pairs of words in both columns of *A* and *B* are pronounced differently in Castilian and can be correctly differentiated in spelling when heard, whether or not a context is provided.

Before a consonant, the variant [s] may be spelled **s** or **z** (e.g., **viscoso, vizconde, mescal, mezcla**) and the variant [z] may also be spelled **s** or **z** (e.g., **lesna, lezna, resma, rezno**). Whatever the spelling, the variant that occurs before a voiceless consonant is [s], and the variant that occurs before a voiced consonant is [z]. This is another instance of *assimilation*. See also the discussion of the variants [s] and [z] in Unit 11.

That Spanish spelling is not always consistent may be shown by the existence of such variants as the following: **mesquite** or **mezquite, bisnieto** or **biznieto, cusma** or **cuzma, piesgo** or **piezgo,** etc. See also Unit 12, page 191.

C. The written representation of /s/ before a consonant by **s** or **x**. INSTRUCTIONS: As the teacher dictates the following list, remember that /s/ before a consonant in the first word of each pair is written **s**, and in the second word of the pair it is written **x**.

esperar	explicar	estreno	extremo
espuela	expuesto	estraperlo	extranjero
espeso	expreso	escarpa	excava
espejar	expeler	misto	mixto
espolada	explanada		

The letter **x** in Spanish is found normally before a voiceless consonant or between vowels. Before a voiceless consonant, **x** usually represents the sound [s]; between vowels **x** represents the sound group [ǵs] or [ks] as in **examen, existencia, taxi**. In a few words, **x** between vowels represents the sound [s], e.g., **exacto** and **auxilio**.

To sum up, the phoneme /s/ in Spanish is written **s, z, c,** or **x**; the variant [z] may be written **s** or **z**.

69 The position of negative words other than *no*

EXAMPLES

A. 1. A mí **nadie** me gana. } *Nobody gets the better of me.*
   2. A mí **no** me gana **nadie.** }

B. 1. **Nunca** les escribo. } *I never write to them.*
   2. **No** les escribo **nunca.** }

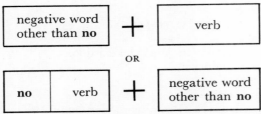

The negative word other than **no** may be placed either before or after the verb that it negates. If after, **no** is placed before the verb (see Unit 3 §10).

● ITEM SUBSTITUTION DRILL

INSTRUCTIONS: Repeat the following sentences just as you hear them. Then repeat them again, substituting **nunca** for **no**.

A. 1. *No* tengo gripe.
   2. *No* estoy equivocado.
   3. *No* puedo ir al mercado.
   4. *No* participamos en natación.
   5. *No* piensas en progresar.
   6. *No* se la preguntaron.
   7. *No* hay pero que valga.

B. 1. Paquito *no* me deja en paz.
   2. Yo *no* voy a morir de úlceras.
   3. Los agricultores *no* la pasan mal, ¿eh?
   4. La bocina *no* falla.
   5. Los americanos *no* son buenos en fútbol.
   6. Yo *no* les escribo.
   7. Ellos *no* hablan inglés.
   8. La vida universitaria *no* es muy fácil.

● CONSTRUCTION SUBSTITUTION DRILL

INSTRUCTIONS: Repeat the following sentences just as you hear them. Then repeat them again, moving **nunca** to a position after the verb, which requires adding **no** before the verb.

A. 1. TEACHER: Ellos *nunca* atacan. *Repita.*
     STUDENT: **Ellos nunca atacan.**
     TEACHER: *Cambie.*
     STUDENT: **Ellos no atacan nunca.**
   2. Yo *nunca* corrí.
   3. *Nunca* disparamos.
   4. Tú *nunca* llamas.
   5. Usted *nunca* trabaja.

B. 1. La dirección *nunca* falla.
   2. El abogado *nunca* exagera.
   3. Los alumnos *nunca* duermen.
   4. La policía *nunca* ataca.
   5. Los profesores *nunca* discuten.

● DISCUSSION

The negative words other than **no**, unlike **no** itself (which occupies a fixed position in front of the verb, see Unit 3 §10), are relatively free as to position. For effects similar to those in English, for example *I never write to them* vs. *I don't write to them ever (at any time)*, the negative words may precede or follow the verb. When they follow, **no** is placed before the verb.

70   Negative words (other than *no*) and their affirmative counterparts

EXAMPLES

I. A. 1. Me contó que necesitaba a **alguien.**
        2. Para regatear, a mí **nadie** me gana.
   B. 1. Hay que hacer **algo.**
        2. No oigo **nada.**
   C. 1. Es **algo** fenomenal.
        2. No es **nada** serio.
   D. 1. **Algún día** voy allá. *Some day I'm going there.*
        2. La bocina **nunca** falla.
        3. Un gobierno tan malo como éste **jamás** ha existido.
   E. 1. ¿Recibiste **alguna** mala noticia?
        2. No es **ninguna** molestia.
   F. 1. ¿Pongo eso en la lista **también?**
        2. Yo tengo muchos parientes en el extranjero, pero nunca les escribo. —Yo **tampoco.**
   G. 1. ¿Con **o** sin leche?
        2. Ya casi no queda manteca **ni** harina. *(There almost doesn't remain lard or flour.)*

II. A. 1. **Ninguna** otra profesión es posible. ⎫
        2. No es posible **ninguna** otra profesión. ⎬ *No other profession is possible.*
   B. 1. **Nada** puede entrar. ⎫
        2. No puede entrar **nada.** ⎬ *Nothing can get in.*
   C. 1. **Ni** Juan **ni** Pablo pueden[1] hacerlo. ⎫
        2. No puede hacerlo **ni** Juan **ni** Pablo. ⎬ *Neither John nor Paul can do it.*
   D. 1. **Tampoco** lo creo yo. *Neither do I believe it.*
        2. No lo creo yo **tampoco.** *I don't believe it either.*

AFFIRMATIVE		NEGATIVE	
*some*one	**alguien**	no one, not *any* one	**nadie**
*some*thing	**algo**	nothing, not *anything*	**nada**
some day	**algún día**	never, not ever, not at *any* time	{ **nunca** **jamás**
some, either (one)	**alguno(s),–a(s)**	no, none, not *any*, neither (one)	**ninguno,–a**[2]
also	**también**	neither, not either	**tampoco**
either . . . or	**o** . . . **o**	neither . . . nor	**ni** . . . **ni**

The affirmative-negative contrast in Spanish is like the *some-any* contrast in English. All these Spanish negative words have the choice of positions discussed in §69 above.

● CONSTRUCTION SUBSTITUTION DRILL

INSTRUCTIONS: Repeat the following sentences just as you hear them. Then repeat them again, substituting the negative counterpart of the italicized form, which will require adding **no** before the verb.

A. 1. TEACHER: Hay *alguien* adentro. *Repita.*
      STUDENT: **Hay alguien adentro.**
      TEACHER: *Cambie.*
      STUDENT: **No hay nadie adentro.**
   2. La manifestación es *algo* serio.

3. Vamos al cementerio *algún día*.
4. ¿Es *alguna* molestia?
5. Yo tengo un discurso *también*.
6. El presidente es *o* tirano *o* mártir.

---

[1] Singular nouns joined by **o** or **ni** and preceding the verb normally take a plural verb.

[2] The plurals **ningunos, –as** rarely appear except in reference to mass plurals such as *leaves, grains, hairs,* or plural stereotypes such as *trousers, shears, pliers, etc.:* **ningunas tijeras** *no scissors.* For *no lessons* Spanish prefers *no lesson:* **ninguna lección.**

B. 1. Necesitaban a *alguien*.
   2. Pero se puede hacer *algo*.
   3. Debe conocer al presidente *algún día*.
   4. ¿Recibiste *alguna* mala noticia?
   5. Pongo flores en la lista *también*.
   6. Ellos son *o* cobardes *o* asesinos.

● ITEM SUBSTITUTION DRILL

INSTRUCTIONS: Repeat the following sentences just as you hear them. Then repeat them again, making the negative words affirmative.

A. 1. TEACHER: Los frenos nunca fallan.
     Repita.
     STUDENT: **Los frenos nunca fallan.**
     TEACHER: *Cambie.*
     STUDENT: **Los frenos algún día fallan.**
   2. *Ninguno* pudo defenderse.
   3. *Nada* horrible va a pasar.
   4. *Nadie* está resfriado.
   5. *Tampoco* tenemos elecciones libres.
   6. *Ni* Carlos *ni* Pablo son inocentes.
   7. *Jamás* va a haber un gobierno tan malo.

B. 1. *Tampoco* fue un gesto admirable.
   2. *Nadie* tiene el poder.
   3. *Ninguno* fue atacado infamemente.
   4. *Jamás* hay que pensar en progresar.
   5. *Nada* puede disolver esta manifestación.
   6. Los estudiantes *ni* declararon la huelga *ni* atacaron al gobierno.

● TRANSLATION DRILL

INSTRUCTIONS: Translate the following paired sentences placing the emphasized (italicized) elements last in the Spanish.

1. TEACHER: Nobody *deserves it.*
   STUDENT: **Nadie lo merece.**
   TEACHER: *Nobody* deserves it.
   STUDENT: **No lo merece nadie.**
2. Neither Alfredo nor Roberto *depends on the party.*
   Neither Alfredo nor Roberto depends on the party.

3. Nothing *can happen to you.*
   Nothing can happen to you.
4. None of you *want to come tomorrow?*
   None of you want to come tomorrow?
5. Neither did *the leader* say it.
   The leader didn't say it *either.*
6. Never do I see *the headlines.*
   I don't *ever* see the headlines.

● DISCUSSION

   The negative words in the above table are not permitted after the verb unless a negative also precedes the verb.

   While changing the position of the negative word produces effects similar to those in English (§69 above), the restrictions on word order in English often make the comparison difficult to see. The second sentence in II *C* above, for example, requires us to say something like *It can't be done by either John or Paul* in order to maneuver *John or Paul* to the end so as to get a parallel contrast with *Neither John nor Paul can do it.*

   Ninguno differs from **cualquier(a)** (Unit 9 §50) in that it is merely the negative of *some*, whereas **cualquier(a)** means *just any*: **No compre ninguna pintura** *Don't buy any painting (Buy no painting)*, **No compre cualquier pintura** *Don't buy any (just any) painting (Be particular about what painting you buy)*. English makes this distinction by means of intonation, using a terminal fall plus rise when the sense is **cualquier(a)**.

71   Negatives other than *no* both before and after the verb

EXAMPLES   A. 1. **Nadie** dijo **nada.** *Nobody said anything.*
          2. **Tampoco** vi a **nadie.** *I didn't see anybody either.*
          3. **Nadie nunca** dice **nada.** *Nobody ever says anything.*

B. 1. Casas **sin** agua potable, luz **ni** otras comodidades.
   2. **Sin** llamar a **nadie.**   *Without calling anyone.*

C. 1. No dijo **nadie nada.**   *Nobody said anything.*
   2. No vi a **nadie tampoco.**   *I didn't see anybody either.*
   3. No dice **nadie nunca nada.**   *Nobody ever says anything.*

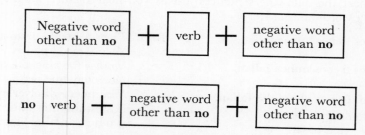

It is necessary to add **no** before the verb if the other negative words follow the verb, but not if at least one precedes the verb.   For the latter purpose an implied negative such as **sin** is sufficient.

● TRANSLATION DRILL

1. Nobody said anything.
2. Never does anything happen.
3. Neither of you is going to come, ever.
4. Neither of them saw anybody.

5. Nobody believes that either.
6. Neither is there any employee.
7. Nobody left any message for you.
8. Never is there anything bad there.

● DISCUSSION

The "implied negatives" referred to under the table are parallel to the words in English that call for *any* rather than *some:* compare We **hardly** *need* **anything** and We **surely** *need* **something.**

72   Position of *no* in contradictions and reservations

A. 1. —Sí, pero tu papá . . .
     —No, él **no;** ella, mi mamá.
   2. —¿Qué le parece una ensalada, rosbif y helados?
     —Rosbif **no.**

B. —¿Quieres ir conmigo al restorán?
   —Sí, pero esta vez **no** sin plata, hombre.
   "Do you want to go to the restaurant with me?"
   "Yes, but this time not without money, old boy."

Contradictions		
FIRST SPEAKER	X	
SECOND SPEAKER	X	**no**

Reservations		
FIRST SPEAKER		X
SECOND SPEAKER	**no**	X

To repeat and contradict something that another has just said, **no** is normally placed after it; to express a reservation, **no** is placed before.

1. TEACHER: Is he coming?
   STUDENT: **¿Viene él?**
   TEACHER: No, he's not, she is.
   STUDENT: **No, él no; ella.**

2. Does your throat hurt?
   No, not my throat; my head.

3. Do you want wheat?
   No, not wheat; rice.

4. Do I have to sit down?
   No, not sit down; go to bed.

5. And was it a meeting?
   No, not a meeting; a demonstration.

6. Did you eat roast beef?
   No, not roast beef; chicken and rice.

7. Did she go upstairs?
   No, not upstairs; downstairs.

8. Is he up ahead?
   No, not ahead; behind.

9. Shall we go inside?
   No, not inside; outside.

10. Shall we have dessert?
    ¿Tomamos postre?
    Yes, but not ice cream.
    Sí, pero no helados.

11. Shall I bring my brothers?
    Yes, but not the youngest.

12. Do you want the books?
    Yes, but not the green one.

13. Tomorrow is your saint's day?
    Yes, but not my birthday.

14. Is that your party?
    Yes, but not my group.

15. Do you like the idea?
    Yes, but not the excuse.

● DISCUSSION

End position is favored for things that are new to the context. In **Rosbif no,** the **rosbif** has already been mentioned. (**No rosbif** would put extra emphasis on **rosbif,** perhaps implying "Roast beef won't do at all," or "Maybe some other kind of meat, but not roast beef.") In **no sin plata,** the **sin plata** is new to the context.

73 The personal *a* with indefinites

EXAMPLES

A. 1. Mataron **a alguno?**
   2. No mataron **a ninguno.** *They didn't kill anyone.*
   3. Necesitaba **a alguien.**
   4. No vi **a nadie.** *I didn't see anybody.*

B. 1. Necesito **un médico.** *I need a doctor (any doctor).*
   2. Trajeron **muchos heridos.** *They brought in a lot of wounded.*
   3. Van a mandar **un equipo** muy grande.

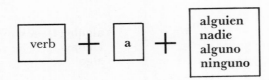

verb + a + alguien / nadie / alguno / ninguno

As object of a verb, the indefinite words **alguien, nadie, alguno,** and **ninguno** call for the personal **a.**

verb | indefinite or depersonalized noun

When a noun that does not refer to a particular person or persons, or one that refers to people in the mass as if they were things, is direct object of a verb, no personal **a** is used.

A. 1. I don't see anybody.
   2. I see someone.
   3. I don't see any of them.
   4. I see some of them.
   5. Do you need anybody?
   6. I don't need anyone.
   7. Do you want to meet some of them?
   8. I don't want to meet any of them.

B. 1. I need a doctor.
   2. I need a lawyer.
   3. I need a business man.
   4. I need a technician.

   5. I need a maid.
   6. I need a manager.
   7. I need a leader.

C. 1. They're going to send a big team.
   2. They're going to send a big group.
   3. They're going to send a big class.
   4. They're going to send a big family.
   5. They're going to choose a Ministry.
   6. They're going to choose a profession.
   7. They're going to choose a government.
   8. They're going to choose a union.

• DISCUSSION

Indefiniteness in general makes it possible to use a personal noun as direct object of a verb without introducing it with the personal **a.** The four indefinites **alguien, nadie, alguno,** and **ninguno,** however, do call for the **a.**

The **alguien-nadie** pair differs from the **alguno-ninguno** pair in that the latter normally refers to a member of a group already held in mind. For example, ¿**Alguno de ustedes trajo plata?** refers to a member of the known **ustedes** group; ¿**Mataron a alguno?** refers to a member of the known group of demonstrators: *any one **of them.***

Since **alguno** may refer to one of a group of two as well as one of a group of more than two, it may be translated by *either* (e.g., *either of you two*) as well as by *some* or *any* (*some one of you three, any of you three*).

74   The indefinites in affirmative questions

EXAMPLES   1. ¿Mataron a **alguno?**
   2. ¿Le escribe a **alguien,** don Rafael?
   3. ¿Vio usted a **alguien?** *Did you see someone (anyone)?*
   4. ¿Tiene usted **algo?** *Do you have something (anything)?*
   5. ¿Va usted allí **alguna** vez? *Are you going there sometime? (any time? ever?)*

some
  –one
  –body
  –thing
    etc.
any
  –one
  –body
  –thing
    etc.
	alguno(s),–a(s)
	alguien
	algo
	   etc.

Spanish does not make the distinction in affirmative questions that we find between *some* and *any* in English.

• TRANSLATION DRILL

A. 1. Did you see some of them?
   2. Did you write to someone?

   3. Did you leave something?
   4. Did you ever go there (Did you go there sometime)?

B. 1. Did you see any of them?
   2. Did you write to anyone?

3. Did you leave anything?
4. Did you go there any time?

75   The definite article for "definite wholes"

EXAMPLES

A. 1. ¿Tengo **fiebre?**
   2. **La fiebre** está muy alta.   *The fever is too high.*

B. 1. Un poco menos **cebolla,** si me hace el favor.   *A little less onion, please.*
   2. ¿Dónde puse **las cebollas?**   *Where did I put the onions?*

C. —A mí me gusta muchísimo el campo: **aire puro, montañas, nubes, cielo azul, árboles, gente sencilla . . .**
   —¿Sí?   ¿Y qué me dice de **la lluvia** y **el barro** en **el invierno** y del **viento** y **el polvo** en **el verano?**

el, la, los, las	all of a single thing or set of things

English and Spanish are alike in using the definite article to specify a single thing or set of things and in omitting it to suggest *some, any,* or an indefinite mass.

EXAMPLES

1. **Los agricultores** no la pasan mal, ¿eh?
2. **La filosofía** es una cosa inútil.
3. **La cebolla** es buena con **el rosbif.**   *Onion is good with roast beef.*
4. No discutamos **del dinero.**   *Let's not argue about money.*
5. **Las casas sin luz ni otras comodidades** son bastante tristes.   *Houses without light or other conveniences are pretty sad.*

el, la, los, las	an entire mass or collectivity

Spanish, unlike English, uses the definite article to refer to all of something.

● TRANSLATION DRILL

A. 1. Meat is expensive.
   2. Rice is good.
   3. Money is necessary.
   4. Death is horrible.
   5. Life is hectic.
   6. People are simple.
   7. Petroleum is important.

B. 1. Philosophy is a useless subject.
   2. History is a required (obligatory) subject.
   3. Psychology is a difficult subject.
   4. Geometry is a complicated subject.
   5. Geography is a typical subject.
   6. Algebra is an exact subject.
   7. Spanish is an easy subject.

C. 1. Students are independent.
   2. Situations are different.
   3. Children are innocent.
   4. Cemeteries are sacred.
   5. Ideas are important.
   6. Tombs are sacred.
   7. Streetcars are antiquated.
   8. Anniversaries are ridiculous.
   9. Tyrants are infamous.

D. 1. Elections should be free.
   2. Newspapers should be respectable.
   3. Lawyers should be serious.
   4. Doctors should be professional.
   5. Schools should be modern.
   6. Friends should be true.
   7. Nurses should be kind (amiable).

EXAMPLES

1. **Toda la carne** cuesta mucho. *All meat costs a lot.*
2. **Todas las huelgas** fueron inútiles. *Every strike (all the strikes) was useless.*
3. **Toda huelga** es inútil. *Every strike is useless.*

all			**todo(s),–a(s)**	**el, los, la, las**	
every (all of a limited number)	noun		**todo(s),–a(s)**	**los, las**	noun
every (unlimited totality)			**todo,–a**		

When *every* is used in a universal sense, the Spanish equivalent is **todo, –a** (singular) without the article. The equivalent of *all* is normally **todo, –a, –os, –as,** with the article.

● TRANSLATION DRILL

A. 1. All meat is expensive.
   2. All rice is good.
   3. All money is useless.
   4. All opposition is difficult.

B. 1. Every class was difficult.
   2. Every day was long.
   3. Every hour was necessary.
   4. Every school is modern.
   5. Every receipt was important.

C. 1. Every subject is important.
   2. Every professor is half crazy.
   3. Every religion is sacred.
   4. Every election is different.
   5. Every man is complicated.
   6. Every new idea is admirable.
   7. They forgot every comfort.
   8. They accepted every opportunity.

● DISCUSSION

In most respects the definite article has the same uses in Spanish as in English.

In both languages it is used to specify particular things; note the difference between *They threw it in the water* (a particular body of water) and *They threw it in water*. But Spanish goes farther in calling for the definite article also to specify all of something. English does this sporadically (*He likes the movies* vs. *He likes television*), Spanish consistently.

More often than not, when a noun would be used in English without the article but in Spanish with the article, it will be found to be a subject noun rather than an object noun. This is because we ordinarily do not operate on wholes but on parts: in **Como carne** *I eat meat,* one eats only as much meat as he has within reach. One can *discuss* meat as a whole, but not *eat* it as a whole, and most verbs are like *eat* rather than like *discuss*. When a noun is subject, there is no such problem: **La carne es buena** *Meat is good* readily refers to the whole.

Since *all* normally specifies wholes, it normally calls for the article in Spanish whether it has it (*all the money*) or does not have it (*all money*) in English. But Spanish **todo** translates not only *all* but also *every*. In the latter sense, we must distinguish between a limited *every* (*Every member present voted* = *All the members present voted*) and an unlimited *every* (*Every election should be honest*). The latter calls for **todo, –a** in the singular, without the article.

76 The definite article with days and places

EXAMPLES A. 1. Hoy es **viernes.** *Today is Friday.*
  2. Ayer fue **jueves.** *Yesterday was Thursday.*
  B. 1. **(El) domingo** es primero, [**el**] **lunes** dos.
  2. ¿Qué fecha fue **(el) domingo?** *What day of the month (what date) was Sunday?*
  C. 1. Terminamos **el lunes.** *We finish (on) Monday.*
  2. Me gusta ir **los lunes.** *I like to go (on) Mondays.*
  3. La ropa interior para **el martes** y la de cama para **el sábado.**

	ENGLISH	SPANISH
predicate of *to be* **ser** subject of *to be* **ser**	Today is Friday Sunday is the first	**Hoy es viernes** **(El) domingo es primero**
elsewhere	It's for Tuesday I go (on) Mondays	**Es para el martes** **Voy los lunes**

When the day of the week answers the question *What day is it?* the article is not used. When the day of the week is itself identified (as by the day of the month), the article may be used or omitted. Elsewhere the article is used.

● TRANSLATION DRILL

1. Today is Monday.
   I'll see you (on) Thursday.
2. Today is Saturday.
   I'll see you (on) Wednesday.
3. Tomorrow is Tuesday.
   I'll see you (on) Friday.
4. Tomorrow is Sunday.
   I'll see you (on) Tuesday.
5. It's Thursday.
   He comes (on) Saturdays.
6. It's Friday.
   He comes (on) Sundays.
7. It's Wednesday.
   He comes (on) Tuesdays.
8. It's Monday.
   He comes (on) Fridays.

EXAMPLES A. 1. ¿Por qué no fuiste **al colegio** ayer?
  2. Cientos en **la cárcel.**
  3. Voy **al mercado.** *I'm going to (the) market.*
  4. Viene de**l trabajo.** *He's coming from work.*
  B. 1. Voy a **clase.** *I'm going to class.*
  2. Está en **casa.** *He's (at) home.*

from —(and other prepo-sitions)	*the*	*country* *ranch* *club* —(and most other nouns)	de —(and other prepo-sitions)	el, la	**campo** **finca** **club** —(and most other nouns)
	——	*school* *jail* *market* —(and a few other nouns)			**colegio** **cárcel** **mercado**
		class *home*		——	**clase** **casa**

In prepositional phrases with most nouns indicating place, such as *office, store, club,* etc., both English and Spanish require the article. With the few where English omits it, such as *jail, town, school,* Spanish usually requires it. *Class* and *home* are exceptions in that both English and Spanish omit the article.

A.
1. I'm going to the country.
2. I'm going to the ranch.
3. I'm going to the club.
4. I'm going to the inauguration.
5. I'm going to the refinery.
6. I'm going to the cleaner's.
7. I'm going to the ministry.
8. I'm going to the bullfight.
9. I'm going to the restaurant.
10. I'm going to the park.
11. I'm going to the café.
12. I'm going to the bank.
13. I'm going to the meeting.
14. I'm going to the theater.
15. I'm going to the cemetery.
16. I'm going to the demonstration.
17. I'm going to the speech.

B.
1. I'm going to school.
2. I'm going to jail.
3. I'm going to market.

C.
1. He's coming from class.
2. He's coming from home.

● DISCUSSION

Both English and Spanish have nouns of the *home, school, class* type, where one or the other language, or both languages, do not require the article. They are nouns which refer to places where some activity goes on, and the reference is as much to the activity as to the place; for example, *to go to church* refers to the *service* at the church; *to go to class* means to participate in the class *session*, etc. The difficulty is that English and Spanish do not usually agree on which nouns to regard in this way. Except for **casa** and **clase,** therefore, it is safer to add the article.

The definite article was traditionally used with certain geographical names in Spanish (compare English *the Argentine, the Hague, the Yukon*): **el Canadá, el Brasil, la Argentina,** etc. This practice is fading, with the result that instances both with and without the article may be found; for example, in the dialogs we have both **países como Estados Unidos** and **en los Estados Unidos.**

● COMBINED PATTERN REPLACEMENT DRILL

A.
1. **Hay estudiantes que siempre quieren ir al campo.**
2. _____ gente _____
3. _____ reunión
4. _____ piensa _____
5. _____ alumnos _____
6. _____ alguna vez _____
7. _____ colegio
8. _____ pueden _____
9. _____ nunca _____
10. _____ finca
11. _____ trabajar en _____
12. _____ jamás _____
13. _____ campesinos _____
14. _____ prefieren _____
15. _____ siempre _____
16. _____ hacienda
17. _____ vivir en _____
18. _____ agricultores _____
19. _____ volver a _____
20. _____ esperan _____
21. _____ administradores _____
22. _____ ahora _____
23. _____ desean _____

B. 1. **¡Qué va! Es un buen pretexto para los discursos.**
   2. Cómo no _____
   3. _____ manifestaciones
   4. Ya lo creo _____
   5. _____ mal _____
   6. _____ ataques
   7. _____ fue _____
   8. _____ fantástico _____
   9. En realidad _____
   10. _____ huelgas
   11. _____ situación _____
   12. _____ ridícula _____
   13. Por lo visto _____
   14. _____ elecciones
   15. _____ magnífica _____
   16. _____ hay _____
   17. _____ oportunidad _____
   18. En todo caso _____
   19. _____ vacaciones
   20. _____ tremenda _____
   21. Cualquier día _____
   22. _____ va a haber _____
   23. _____ inauguraciones
   24. _____ importante _____

• TRANSLATION REVIEW DRILL

Word order in information questions.

A. 1. When did *he* come?
    2. Where did *he* go?
    3. Why did *he* leave?
    4. How did *he* eat?
    5. How much did *he* pay?
    6. How many did *he* bring?
    7. Which did *he* finish?
    8. What did *he* do?

B. 1. When did John come?
    2. Where did John go?
    3. Why did John leave?
    4. How did John eat?
    5. How much did John pay?
    6. How many did John bring?
    7. Which did John finish?
    8. What did John do?

READING

Dos puntos de vista

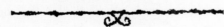

I

Todo el mundo sabe ahora los tristes resultados de la manifestación de estudiantes que se hizo anteanoche en el cementerio. Con el pretexto de celebrar el aniversario de la muerte de su "líder martirizado" Gustavo Díaz, cuyas actividades eran bien conocidas de la policía de la ciudad, cientos de estos estudiantes, en vez de quedarse en sus casas estudiando para sus carreras, fueron a poner flores en la tumba de Díaz, según dijeron. No sabemos exactamente cómo empezó el lío, pero parece que[1] algunos estudiantes llevaban palos y revólveres, y que[2] se enfrentaron a[3] la policía en el propósito de[4] ejercer su deber de mantener el orden público. Al ser atacada la policía,[5] tuvo que defenderse y unos pocos estudiantes resultaron levemente heridos. También fue necesario llevar a unos cuantos estudiantes a la cárcel para

---

[1] *apparently (it seems that)*   [2] Repeats the **que** of two lines above.   [3] *interfered with*   [4] *attempts to*   [5] *When the police were attacked*

aclarar detalles del acontecimiento. En fin, creemos que un gobierno tiene que gobernar y que la policía debe mantener el orden. De otra manera no puede existir ninguna democracia. (Editorial tomado de *El Conservador,* 17 de agosto de 1960.)

II

La brutal acción de la policía, al disparar anteanoche contra una manifestación de estudiantes en el cementerio, donde se hallaban reunidos para celebrar el aniversario de la muerte del héroe y mártir Gustavo Díaz, casi no tiene paralelo en los anales históricos de nuestra patria. Fue acción de cobardes y asesinos. Los estudiantes estaban allí sólo para rendir homenaje a la memoria de un gran hombre. Sin respetar el sagrado lugar donde estaban, la policía los atacó infamemente y disolvió la manifestación a palos y a tiros. Doce estudiantes quedaron gravemente heridos y tres de ellos están para morir.[6] Cientos fueron llevados a la cárcel. Acabamos de oir que los otros están declarando una huelga general en todo el país.

La situación no puede seguir así. El gobierno debe poner en libertad a los estudiantes que están en la cárcel. A los heridos hay que darles las mejores atenciones médicas, a costa del gobierno. Por último recordamos a nuestros lectores que las elecciones vienen pronto. El partido liberal va a ser bastante más fuerte a consecuencia de estos acontecimientos, y el triunfo de este partido es necesario para la restitución de nuestras instituciones democráticas. (Editorial tomado de *El Liberal,* 17 de agosto de 1960.)

III

BUENCLIMA, Andivia, August 20 (Overseas Press Association). —The government of Andivia has announced the suspension of the world-famous newspaper *El Liberal,* in the interest of peace and order. It further announces the postponement of the general elections originally scheduled for next month, so as to avoid possible bloodshed at the polls. The editor of *El Liberal,* Alvaro Fernández Lucientes, has been taken into protective custody by the government, and could not be reached for comment. (News item from the New York *Herald-Times,* August 20, 1960.)

---

[6] *on the point of death*

READING

Entrevista de dos periodistas

(En un hotel de una ciudad universitaria de los Estados Unidos. Un periodista argentino y su esposa esperan la hora de la comida. Un periodista del lugar acaba de obtener una entrevista con la pareja extranjera y dice:)

G. *González, periodista argentino* SRA. *su esposa*
S. *Smith, periodista americano*

S. Buenas tardes, señor González. Mucho gusto de[1] conocerlo. *(Se estrechan la mano.)*

G. El gusto es mío, señor Smith. Quiero presentarle a mi señora, Maruja Anderson de González.

S. Ah, ¿es norteamericana la señora?

G. No, es argentina. Pertenece a una antigua familia angloargentina. Por eso, el apellido Anderson.

S. Mucho gusto de conocerla, señora.

SRA. Thank you very much, Mr. Smith.

S. Encantado de conocerla. Usted habla inglés muy bien.

SRA. Muchísimas gracias, señor Smith. Y usted habla muy bien el español. ¿Dónde lo aprendió?

S. Gracias, señora. Lo aprendí aquí en la universidad. Me especialicé en periodismo y español. Además, durante la guerra, estuve en Panamá. Trabajé en nuestro Departa-

---

[1] **Mucho gusto de** is the preferred form in most Spanish American countries, while **Mucho gusto en** is used in Spain.

mento de Censura . . . Con su permiso voy a hacerles algunas preguntas para mi crónica. Vamos a empezar por sus impresiones de la llegada a los Estados Unidos.

G. Pues, es un poco difícil coordinar nuestras impresiones. Viajamos rápidamente en avión. Nuestro viaje de Buenos Aires a Miami duró sólo unas cuantas horas. En Miami tomamos el tren para ver un poco del país y llegamos aquí ayer por la mañana. Salimos de B. A.[2] pocos días antes de la llegada del verano, que es en diciembre: campos verdes, flores, las primeras frutas de la estación templada. Invierno aquí y verano allá en el lejano sur y el avión llegó en menos de un día.

S. ¿Le gusta el invierno? Hace dos días que nieva casi continuamente. ¿Les gusta a ustedes la nieve?

SRA. Estamos acostumbrados al invierno con nieve. Mi familia vivía en Magallanes de Chile. El periódico de Guillermo lo envió a Magallanes de corresponsal y allí nos conocimos.

S. ¡Qué buena suerte la suya, señor!

G. ¡Ya lo creo! Muchísimas gracias . . . Para nosotros fue una experiencia agradable notar la facilidad con que en este país se hacen amistades entre los viajeros.

SRA. *Yes,* Mr. Smith. Todo el mundo aquí quiere trabar nuevas amistades.[3] En esto nos parecemos todos los americanos de ambas Américas.

G. Pero sin ánimo de criticar, déjeme decir algo que nos preguntaban durante el viaje: "¿Qué idioma se habla en Brasil?" "Siempre hace calor en Sud América, ¿verdad?" "¿Se pueden entender ustedes con los mexicanos cuando visitan el país?" "¿Es verdad que todas sus comidas son muy picantes?" "Los trenes en Argentina, ¿tienen coche-comedor?"

S. Desafortunadamente esto pasa muy a menudo, pero nosotros no tenemos toda la culpa. Anoche yo leía un libro interesante escrito por el autor mexicano Urquizo. En una de sus charlas describe una visita suya a Madrid. Dice que muchos españoles saben muy poco de México. Con su permiso voy a leer unas líneas. *(Saca el libro y lee.)* "Las gentes que yo iba conociendo[4] me miraban con simpatía; *un americano* siempre cae bien en la Madre Patria, es como de la familia. '¿Usted de dónde es?, porque usted no es español.' 'No, señor, soy de México.' 'De México, ¿eh? Va usted muy a menudo a Buenos Aires, ¿eh?' 'Cada ocho días; ¡está tan cerca!'" *(Se ríen.)* "O si no: '¡¿Conque de México?! ¡Vaya, vaya! ¿Y qué me cuenta usted de Pancho Villa?[5] 'Bien, gracias; por ahí anda como siempre.'"[6]

SRA. ¡Qué lindo!

S. Pero hablando en serio, señor González, quiero hacerle algunas preguntas sobre Argentina. No voy a decir nada del trigo ni de la carne, porque leemos esto muy a menudo. Yo pienso escribir algo nuevo: algo sobre los subterráneos de B. A. Creo que muchas personas aquí tienen una gran curiosidad por conocer Buenos Aires. He leído de las bonitas estaciones de los subterráneos con los cuadros murales hechos de azulejos de colores, de las escaleras mecánicas, de los puestos de libros y periódicos en varios idiomas . . . ¿qué me dice sobre esto?

G. Pues, hay tres sistemas de subterráneos que pertenecen a tres compañías distintas. El *Chadopyf,*[7] en que nosotros viajamos mucho, es el más nuevo y tiene las estaciones más artísticas con motivos murales que representan escenas de España y Argentina. El *Chadopyf* tiene también escaleras mecánicas

---

[2] **B.A.** *Buenos Aires* (The abbreviation is frequently used here and in Argentina. The letters are pronounced [be a].)

[3] **trabar . . . amistades** *to make . . . friends*

[4] **iba conociendo** *was getting to know.* **Ir** is one of the verbs of motion, like **seguir,** referred to in Unit 8 §41 used in making a kind of progressive.

[5] Pancho Villa (?–1923), the pseudonym of Doroteo Arango, a leader of the revolutionary forces in the Mexican Army of the North, during the Social Revolution of 1910. Although ruthless in his methods, he has become a popular hero, because of his strong fight for the peon.

[6] Urquizo, Francisco L., *Ahora charlemos,* Talleres Gráficos de la Nación, México, 1949, pp. 95–96.

[7] This subway system, the newest in B.A., begins in the Retiro railroad station and runs southwest to the Plaza Constitución. Another subway is the *Lacrozo,* built in 1930, which runs under Corrientes Street and on to the suburbs. The first subway in B.A. was constructed in 1912.

para comodidad de los viajeros. Estas escaleras mecánicas funcionan intermitentemente. El primer pasajero que sale del tren y va hacia la escalera eléctrica proyecta su sombra en una "célula fotoeléctrica" que abre un circuito y hace funcionar la escalera. Cuando no hay pasajeros, entre tren y tren, no funcionan y así se ahorra corriente eléctrica.

s. Pero la palabra Chadopyf, ¿qué significa?

G. *Compañía Hispana-Argentina de Obras Públicas y Finanzas*. Es la más grande de Argentina. Los puestos de libros son muy interesantes. Por ejemplo, a un lado se puede ver un estante con algunos libros traducidos del inglés: *Hamlet, Romeo y Julieta,* o *La Cabaña del Tío Tom,* o *Lo que se llevó el viento*.[8] Hay otros de autores rusos, franceses y alemanes. También hay clásicos españoles: *La vida es sueño,*[9] *Don Quijote de la Mancha,*[10] *Fuente Ovejuna,* [11] y muchísimos otros.

(*Suena el teléfono y llaman al Sr. González.*)

G. Con permiso. Debe ser la colonia latinoamericana que viene a buscarnos para comer juntos.

s. Pues, el fotógrafo nos espera y, si ustedes no tienen inconveniente, vamos a sacar una foto de ustedes.

G. Con mucho gusto, Sr. Smith.

● CUESTIONARIO

1. ¿Qué es una entrevista?
2. ¿En dónde habla el periodista norteamericano al Sr. González y Sra.?
3. Explique el apellido de la Sra. de González.
4. ¿Cuál es la profesión del Sr. González?
5. ¿Cuál es la manera correcta de presentar a una persona?
6. ¿Dónde aprendió español el Sr. Smith?
7. Explique la abreviatura *B. A.*
8. ¿Cómo es el clima de Argentina en comparación con el de Estados Unidos?
9. ¿Qué quiere decir el modismo "trabar amistades"?
10. Mencione algunas de las preguntas que hacían a los esposos González en Norteamérica.
11. ¿Qué dice el Sr. González sobre los subterráneos en Argentina?
12. ¿Por qué son interesantes los puestos de libros en Argentina?

● SUGGESTED READINGS

Arciniegas, Germán, ed., *The Green Continent* (tr. by Harriet de Onís), Knopf, New York, 1944: Part V, pp. 448–465.

Crow, John A., *Mexico Today,* Harper, New York, 1957: Ch. 23, "Some Differences in our Cultures."

Greenup, Ruth and Leonard, *Revolution before Breakfast,* University of North Carolina Press, Chapel Hill, 1947.

Hanson, Earl, *Chile, Land of Progress,* Reynal and Hitchcock, New York, 1941: Ch. 1, "The Land"; Ch. 4, "Culture"; Ch. 9, "Chile and the Visitor."

Strode, Hudson, *South by Thunderbird,* Random House, New York, 1937; "Interlude," pp. 185–197; Ch. 5, "Argentina."

Subercaseaux, Benjamín, *Chile, A Geographic Extravaganza* (tr. by Angel Flores), Macmillan, New York, 1943: Part III, "The Land of the Interrupted Path"; Part IV, "The Land of the Snow-Capped Wall"; Part VII, "The Land of the Twilight Night."

---

[8] **Lo que se llevó el viento** *Gone With the Wind*
[9] By Calderón de la Barca (1600–1681), author of many philosophical dramas as well as comedies. (Calderón, Cervantes, and Lope de Vega will be discussed in Unit 23.)
[10] By Cervantes (1547–1616).
[11] By Lope de Vega (1562–1635).

14

Problems of a Tourist

c. *Clerk*   t. *Ted*   b. *Bob, friend of Ted's*
f. *Argentine friend*

c. Sir, it's three *nacionales*. Tell the gentleman
he gave me *guaraníes*.

t. He says that what you gave him isn't Argentine money, but Paraguayan.

b. Yes, yes. I understand. Here. This business of going around with *nacionales, bolivianos, sucres, colones, soles, quetzales* has me half
crazy.

t. How do we get downtown from here?

c. Take a *colectivo* at this corner . . .

b. A what?

t. A *colectivo*, a bus.

b. But, aren't they called *micros?*

Problemas de un turista

d. *Dependiente*   t. *Ted*   b. *Bob, amigo de Ted*
a. *amigo argentino*

d. Señor, son tres nacionales (1).   Dígale al
señor que él me dio guaraníes (2).

t. Dice que lo que tú le diste a él no es plata
argentina, sino paraguaya.

b. Sí, sí, comprendo. Tome. Esto de andar
con nacionales, bolivianos, sucres, colones,
soles, quetzales, me tiene medio loco (3).

t. ¿Cómo vamos de aquí al centro?

d. Tome un colectivo (4) en esta esquina . . .

b. ¿Un qué?

t. Un colectivo: un bus.

b. Pero, ¿no se llaman micros? (4)

T. No, that's in Chile.   Sort of complicated, isn't it?

B. You're telling *me!*

*   *   *

F. We go down this street to get to the Plaza de Mayo.

B. Did you hear the way he pronounced his *elles?*

T. Here in the Argentine they talk almost the same as in Paraguay and Uruguay.

F. Okay, don't rub it in [overbearing, deprecatory]. In Latin America we don't speak as well as in Spain, but so what?

T. Don't get mad, fellow.   We're just comparing, that's all.   And this business of speaking better or worse is a relative matter.

B. It seems every time I open my mouth, I put my foot in it.

T. That's the tough part of it, old boy.

*   *   *

T. The photos, did you send them to be developed?

B. Yes, and I also bought these postcards. I don't know . . . I had hardly gotten in the door when they asked me, "You're North American, aren't you?"

T. I went to the bank to cash some personal checks.   The president, Alberto Rodríguez, is a nice fellow; he okayed them for me right away.

B. What was the exchange?

T. Thirty to one. Well, I've got a ferocious appetite.   Shall we go have lunch?

B. Very good idea.   What do you suggest?

T. A nice juicy steak.

T. Eso es en Chile, hombre.   Un poco enredado, ¿verdad?

B. A mí me lo dices.

*   *   *

A. Vamos por esta calle para llegar a la Plaza de Mayo (5).

B. ¿Oíste la pronunciación de las elles?

T. Aquí en la Argentina hablan casi igual que en el Paraguay (6) y el Uruguay.

A. Bueno, no sean cargantes.   En Latinoamérica no hablamos tan bien como en España, pero, qué.

T. No te enojes, hombre.   Estamos comparando no más.   Y lo de hablar mejor o peor es algo muy relativo (7).

B. Parece que cada vez que abro la boca, meto la pata.

T. Eso es lo malo, viejo . . .

*   *   *

T. Las fotos, ¿las mandaste a revelar? (8)

B. Sí, y también compré estas tarjetas postales. Yo no sé . . . apenas entré me preguntaron: Usted es norteamericano, ¿no?

T. Yo fui a cambiar unos cheques personales al banco.   El Director, Alberto Rodríguez, es muy buena persona; me dio el visto bueno inmediatamente (9).

B. ¿A cómo estaba el cambio?

T. A treinta por uno.   Bueno, tengo un hambre feroz.   ¿Vamos a almorzar?

B. Muy buena idea.   ¿Qué sugieres?

T. Un churrasco bien jugoso.

Cultural Notes (1) The monetary unit of Argentina is the **peso,** but in order to differentiate it from the **peso** of Argentina's neighbors, Chile and Uruguay, **nacionales** are used in this context.

(2) The monetary unit of Paraguay is the *guaraní.*

(3) The following are the monetary units of the countries listed: **nacional** i.e., **peso** (Argentina), **boliviano** (Bolivia), **sucre** (Ecuador), **colón** (Costa Rica), **sol** (Perú), **quetzal** (Guatemala), **escudo** (Chile).   The **peso** is the monetary unit of the following Latin-American countries: Argentina, Colombia, Cuba, Dominican Republic, Mexico, and Uruguay, each with its own value.   The monetary unit of Spain is the **peseta.**

(4) The **colectivo** (in Argentina) or **micro** (in Chile) is a bus which travels a regular route.

(5) The point here is the typical Argentine pronunciation of the sound spelled **ll** or **y** (note **calle, llegar,** and **Mayo** in the sentence). For discussion of this point, see Unit 17, Writing Exercise.

(6) Reference here is to the Spanish and not the Guaraní language, both of which are officially recognized languages in Paraguay.

(7) The Spanish of Spain, more particularly that of Castile, enjoys high cultural prestige among many segments of the population of Spanish America. Deference to authority in matters of language is widespread. In some countries (e.g., Spain, France, several in Spanish America), the Academy of the Language is an official body of scholars who set standards of language and whose decisions are respected. For this reason, a conscious effort is made to follow them. The principal types of publications through which the Spanish Academy (**Real Academia Española de la Lengua**) attempts to establish standards are a dictionary, a grammar, and a treatise on prosody and orthography. The highly centralized educational system under a Minister of Public Instruction, which is typical of such countries as Spain and France, makes it possible for the Academies to gain acceptance of their precepts.

(8) When used after the preposition **a,** the infinitive may have passive force. Compare English *send pictures for developing = send pictures for being developed.* See Unit 5, Cultural Note 2.

(9) Here is another example of the part played by personal contacts in the Hispanic world in conducting business or in expediting service.

● WRITING EXERCISE

The written representation of /x/ by **g** or **j.** INSTRUCTIONS: Write the following lists of words from dictation.

A.	B.	C.
jarra	joven	junto
jaula	jota	jugo
jarabe	jobo	julio
jarana	joya	junio
jalea	joropo	jueves
jamás	jornada	jurar
jardín	joroba	jugar
jabón	jocoso	justicia
jamón	jornal	judío
Japón	José	

D.	E.
gente	gis
gesto	Gil
genio	giro
género	gigante
gerente	ginebra
gemelo	gitano
geografía	giralda
geometría	ginesta
general	gimnasio
gestión	girasol

You have noted that the Spanish phoneme /x/ is written **j** before **a, o,** or **u,** and written **g** before **e** or **i.**

That Spanish spelling is not always consistent may be shown by a number of words in which the [x] sound before **e** or **i** is written **j,** for example, **jefe, jinete,** and **jifa.** There are also variant spellings of certain words, such as **gira** and **jira, giga** and **jiga,** etc.

77 Nominalization with the neuter article *lo*

EXAMPLES

A. 1. No podemos hacer **lo imposible.** *We can't do the impossible.*
   2. **Lo poco** que hice. *The little (that) I did.*

B. 1. Hay que respetar **lo sagrado.** *One must respect what is sacred.*
   2. **Lo mío** es mío. *What's mine is mine.*

C. 1. **Lo triste** del campo son las casas de los campesinos. *The sad part of the country is the houses of the farmers.*
   2. **Lo inútil** de la filosofía es **lo peor.** *The useless nature (uselessness) of philosophy is the worst part.*

D. 1. Esto es **lo bueno** de mi profesión.
   2. **Lo único** que sé de Platón es que fue un gran filósofo.
   3. La bocina, que es **lo principal,** nunca falla.
   4. **Lo primero** es trabajar. *The first thing is to work.*

the	impossible little			imposible poco
what is	sacred mine			sagrado mío
the	sad } useless }	part –ness (nature)	lo	triste inútil
the	nice } only } main } first }	thing		bueno único principal primero

To nominalize an adjective that refers to a known noun, the articles **el, la, los,** and **las** are used (Unit 11 §59); to nominalize an adjective that does not refer to a known noun, the neuter article **lo** is used. The English equivalent usually adds a cover word such as *part, side, aspect, thing,* or the suffix *–ness.*

● ITEM SUBSTITUTION DRILL

1. Lo *mejor* de la casa es la sala.
   (bueno, malo, típico, peor, moderno)
2. No nos gusta nada lo *ridículo.*
   (sucio, extranjero, complicado, anticuado, cargante)
3. Hay que respetar lo *sagrado.*
   (profesional, fino, viejo, fuerte, bueno)
4. Lo *bonito* de la casa son los muebles.
   (fino, admirable, caro, viejo, horrible)
5. Espere un momentito; ahora viene lo *importante.*
   (fantástico, serio, triste, bueno, enredado)
6. Lo *primero* es defenderse.
   (difícil, necesario, próximo, imposible, último)
7. Lo *pasado* se debe olvidar.
   (personal, equivocado, presente, fácil, horrible)
8. Eso es lo *infame* de la situación.
   (tremendo, grave, feroz, principal, grande)
9. Esto es lo más *probable.*
   (posible, inútil, desgraciado, fenomenal, relativo)

● TRANSLATION DRILL

A. 1. This is the good thing about my profession.
   2. This is the main thing about my profession.
   3. This is the new part of my profession.
   4. This is the innocent aspect of my profession.
   5. This is the sad side of my profession.

B. 1. The important thing is not to get mad.
   2. The necessary thing is not to get mad.
   3. The difficult thing is not to get mad.
   4. The best thing is not to get mad.
   5. The admirable thing is not to get mad.

EXAMPLES 1. **Lo de** hablar mejor o peor es algo muy relativo.
   2. Aprendí de memoria **lo de** Sócrates.
   3. ¿Y qué me dices de **lo de** ayer?   *And what do you say about yesterday's business?*
   4. **Lo de** Juan fue peor.   *That John thing (business) was worse.*

the business matter affair concern stuff etc.	of about		lo	de

Prepositional phrases with **de** may also be nominalized.   Again English uses cover words.

EXAMPLES 1. **Lo de usted** es sencillo; **lo mío** no.   *Your part is easy; mine isn't.*
   2. Esto es **lo de Juan.**   *This is John's part.*
   3. **Lo de ellos (lo suyo)** no es mucho.   *What's theirs (their part) isn't much.*

my part what is mine	**lo mío**
your part what is yours etc.	**lo tuyo** etc.
x's part what is x's	**lo de x**

Possessives with **de**, as well as the other possessives of Unit 11 §61, may be nominalized with **lo**.   The usual English cover words are *what is* and *part*.

● TRANSLATION DRILL

A. 1. That business about eating lunch is very important.
   2. That business about understanding is very important.
   3. That stuff about comparing is very important.
   4. That matter of getting up at six is very important.
   5. That matter of taking a bath every day is very important.

B. 1. That stuff about John is a lie.
   2. That stuff about the salesman is a lie.
   3. That stuff about the director is a lie.
   4. That business about the check is a lie.
   5. That business about the salary is a lie.

C. 1. And what do you say about yesterday's affair?
   2. And what do you say about Sunday's affair?
   3. And what do you say about the affair of night before last?
   4. And what do you say about that pronunciation stuff?
   5. And what do you say about that "extra" business?

D. 1. This is Alvaro's part.
   2. This is my part.
   3. This is our part.
   4. This is your stuff.
   5. This is their stuff.

1. Sea **lo que** sea. *(Let be that which may be.)*
2. Haga **lo que** yo. *Do what I do.*
3. **Lo que** dices es ridículo. *What you're saying is ridiculous.*

what that which	**lo que**

What (noninterrogative) and *that which,* when they have no specific noun as their referent, are equivalent to **lo que.**

● TRANSLATION DRILL

A. 1. This is what I said.
   2. This is what I did.
   3. This is what I mentioned.
   4. This is what I explained.
   5. This is what I suggested.

B. 1. What you are saying is phenomenal.
   2. What you are saying is useless.

   3. What you are saying is impossible.
   4. What you are saying is a lie.
   5. What you are saying is a pity.

C. 1. Take (along) what you have.
   2. Bring what you have.
   3. Send what you have.
   4. Sell what you have.
   5. Forget what you have.

● DISCUSSION

Like the definite articles **el, la, los, las** which show number and gender (see Unit 11 §59), the neuter article **lo** is used to nominalize adjectives. English has something similar in phrases like *the good, the true,* and *the beautiful,* but Spanish extends the process to virtually all adjectives.

Attaching **lo** to an adjective amounts to giving your hearer these instructions: "Treat this adjective as a noun, and make its meaning cover as broad an area as the context will permit." So in **lo sagrado,** without further qualification, the meaning covers *everything* that is sacred. But in **lo sagrado de este lugar** the meaning is *whatever-is-sacred about this place,* or *the sacredness of this place,* or *the sacred part of this place,* depending on context, for now **lo sagrado** is limited.

Since **de** phrases and **que** clauses are used as adjectives (they modify nouns), attaching **lo** to them is a part of the same nominalizing process as attaching **lo** to any other adjective. But it is convenient to treat **lo de** and **lo que** as units, **lo de** with the meaning *the business (concern,* etc.) *of* (or *the part of, 's part* when the **de** is possessive), and **lo que** with the meaning *what* or *that which.* Remember that **lo** is neuter, whence *that which* when equivalent to **lo que** cannot refer to anything already mentioned in the form of a specific noun. If we say *The money I have and that which (what) you have, that which* or *what* refers to *money,* **el dinero,** a masculine singular noun, and consequently **el que,** not **lo que,** is the equivalent. *Do only that which (what) is right* has **lo que** in the Spanish.

78 Comparatives

EXAMPLES

A. 1. ¿Qué **más** sucedió?
   2. A cuarenta kilómetros de aquí, **más** o **menos.**

B. 1. Hay **más camisetas** en este paquete. *There are more (most) undershirts in this package.*
   2. **Menos elecciones, menos manifestaciones.** *Fewer elections, fewer demonstrations.*

C. 1. Va a ser la planta **más moderna** de Latinoamérica.
   2. La oposición tiene un partido mucho **más fuerte.**
   3. Ahora la reunión es **menos aburrida.** *Now the meeting is less (least) dull.*

D. 1. Lo voy a explicar **más adelante.** *I'm going to explain it later on.*
   2. En esta religión, Dios parece **menos cerca.** *In this religion, God seems less (least) near.*

Comparatives with **más** *and* **menos**

more (—) } −er } most (—) } −est }	**más** (—)	less (—) } fewer (—) } least (—) } fewest (—) }	**menos** (—)

The usual way of showing a greater or lesser degree or amount of something (verb, noun, adjective, adverb) is with the words **más** and **menos,** corresponding to English *more* (*most*) and *less* or *fewer* (*least, fewest*), respectively.

● ITEM SUBSTITUTION DRILL

1. No puedo *comer* más.
    (hablar, prometer, contestar, comprar, faltar)
2. Ya no tengo más *quetzales.*
    (soles, sucres, bolivianos, plata, colones)
3. Es la planta más *moderna* de Latinoamérica.
    (típica, independiente, complicada, importante, grande)
4. Explíquelo más *exactamente.*
    (pronto, tarde, adelante)

5. Después *comió* menos.
    (peleó, concedió, alcanzó, tardó, salió)
6. Ahora hay menos *micros.*
    (buses, competencia, mártires, ganado, ganancia)
7. Esta huelga es menos *interesante.*
    (enredada, horrible, libre, necesaria, personal)
8. Hoy habló más *perfectamente.*
    (exactamente, pronto, tarde)

● TRANSLATION DRILL

A. 1. This exam is easier.
    2. His hair is shorter.
    3. His body is stronger.
    4. This roof is higher.
    5. These horses are finer.

B. 1. Biology is more difficult.
    2. Wool is more expensive.
    3. Education is more important.

4. Religion is more sacred.
5. Bullfighting is more respectable.

C. 1. These post cards are less expensive.
    2. The total is less ridiculous.
    3. The headlines are less fantastic.
    4. The events are less complicated.
    5. The situation is less serious.

EXAMPLES

1. Lo de hablar **mejor** o **peor** es algo muy relativo.
2. ¿Qué **mejor** oportunidad que ésta?
3. Yo soy la **menor.**
4. Es mi hermano **mayor.** *He's my older (oldest) brother.*

The **−or** *comparatives*

better, best	**mejor**
worse, worst	**peor**
older, oldest (greater, greatest; bigger, biggest)	**mayor**
younger, youngest (smaller, smallest; lesser, least[1])	**menor**

These are the only comparatives not formed with **más** or **menos:** Spanish **mejor** is like English *better* in place of *more good.* In place of **mayor** and **menor, más grande** and **más pequeño** are preferred when physical size is emphasized.

───────────

[1] *Least* in size or importance; *least* in amount is **menos** (see the preceding table).

A. 1. He works better now.
   2. I feel worse today.
   3. Luis is my younger brother.
   4. Elena is my elder sister.

B. 1. They use the best bulls.
   2. They sell the worst cows.
   3. She is the youngest.
   4. I am the oldest.

● DISCUSSION

English has two ways of forming comparatives, the words *more* and *less* (with verbs, nouns, adjectives, and adverbs) and the suffixes *–er* and *–est*. In Spanish, virtually all comparatives are formed with **más** and **menos**. There is only a remnant of four forms, **mejor** and **peor** (which may be either adjectives or adverbs) and **mayor** and **menor** (adjectives), that are exceptions.

English has two distinct forms, with divided functions: — *er, more* ——— and — *est, most* ———. Spanish has only the comparatives listed in the boxes above, relying on context, where necessary, for the difference in meaning. Sometimes this means adding a bit of context. To distinguish between *He does it better* and *He does it best,* for example, the latter may appear as **El lo hace mejor que nadie** (*He does it better than anyone,* i.e., *best*).

The words **mayor** and **menor,** when referring to age, are relative, not absolute. To imply that someone is "really old" or "really young," the words **viejo** and **joven** are used. **Soy más viejo que usted** *I am older than you* means that we are both along in years; **Soy mayor que usted** *I am older than you* might be spoken equally by a five-year-old or by a seventy-year-old.

Both **menor** and **menos** translate *least.* **Menor** refers to importance or size, as in **No es la menor molestia** *It isn't the least (slightest, smallest) bother,* or in **El menor ruido me preocupa** *The least (smallest, slightest) noise worries me.* **Menos** refers to amount, as in **¿Cuál va a ser menos molestia?** *Which is going to be least (or less) bother?* or **Prefiero el cuarto con menos ruido** *I prefer the room with least (or less) noise.*

79 The comparison of inequality

EXAMPLES

A. 1. Hay más **de** diez heridos.
   2. Me prometió menos **de** una cuarta parte. *He promised me less than a fourth.*
   3. No quiere trabajar más **de** lo poco que le exigimos. *He won't work more than the little that we require of him.*

B. 1. El puede hacer más **que** yo. *He can do more than I (can).*
   2. Ella es más bonita **que** usted. *She is prettier than you (are).*
   3. La oposición tiene un partido mucho más fuerte **que** el del gobierno.
   4. ¿Qué mejor oportunidad **que** ésta para tomar unas vacaciones? *(What better opportunity than this to take a vacation?)*
   5. Algo mejor **que** un empleado de banco.

C. 1. No hay más remedio **que** hacer una huelga general. *(There's no more [other] remedy than to call a general strike.)*
   2. No tengo más **que** seis pesos. *I have only (no more than) six pesos.*
   3. Necesito algo más **que** dinero. *I need something more than money.*
   4. Estoy más **que** furioso. *I'm more than furious.*

*Comparing different amounts or degrees of the **same thing***

	COMPARATIVE AMOUNT OR DEGREE		AMOUNT OR DEGREE THAT IT IS COMPARED WITH
Hay	**más [heridos]**		**diez heridos**
Me prometió	**menos**	***de***	**una cuarta parte**
No quiere trabajar	**más**		**lo poco . . .**

When both the amount or degree compared and the amount or degree that it is compared with are specifically mentioned, and both refer to amounts or degrees of the same thing (wounded, quantity of work, etc.), the equivalent of *than* is **de.**

Comparisons in which the primary amount or degree (the amount or degree with which the comparison is made) is left out

	COMPARATIVE AMOUNT OR DEGREE		AMOUNT OR DEGREE THAT IT IS COMPARED WITH	
Puede hacer	**más**			**yo**
Ella es	**más bonita**			**usted**
Tiene un partido mucho	**más fuerte**	***que***		**el del gobierno**
¿Qué (oportunidad)	**mejor**			**ésta . . . ?**
Algo	**mejor**			**un empleado de banco**

When one pole of the comparison is left out, the equivalent of *than* is **que.** For example, in the second sentence there is no word (or words) telling *how pretty* you are; in the fourth sentence there is no word (or words) telling *how good* the present opportunity is.

*Comparing **different** things*

	WHAT IS COMPARED		THE DIFFERENT THING THAT IT IS COMPARED WITH
No hay	**más remedio**		**hacer una huelga general**
No tengo	**más**	***que***	**seis pesos**
Necesito	**algo más**		**dinero**
Estoy	**más**		**furioso**

Where the comparison is between two different things, the equivalent of *than* is **que.** For example, *something more* (than money) probably refers to *love* or something of the kind: *more = other than.*

● TRANSLATION DRILL

A. 1. TEACHER: There are more than ten photos.
STUDENT: **Hay más de diez fotos.**
2. There are more than twenty employees.
3. There were more than fifteen clubs.
4. There were more than a dozen shots.

B. 1. There's more than one tyrant in this world.
2. There are more than three clerks at the cleaner's.
3. There are less than fifteen unions in the country.
4. There were less than thirty students in the room.

C. 1. I have more than ten pesos.
   2. I have less than ten pesos.
   3. I have more than a hundred dollars.
   4. I have less than a hundred dollars.

D. 1. I don't have more than ten dollars; I
      have eight.
      **No tengo más de diez dólares; tengo
      ocho.**
   2. I don't have less than ten dollars; I have
      twelve.
   3. He doesn't have more than a thousand
      dollars; he has seven hundred.
   4. He doesn't have less than a thousand
      dollars; he has three thousand.

E. 1. Her clothing is more expensive than
      mine.
      Su ropa es más cara que la mía.
   2. His car is newer than Carlos'.
   3. His sister is younger than Josefina.
   4. My brother is older than Francisco.

F. 1. He always arrives later than Felipe.
   2. He never leaves later than Alberto.
   3. I eat earlier than the family.
   4. I go to bed earlier than Rosa.

G. 1. We work fewer hours than you.
   2. I have fewer books than you.
   3. I have less money than Olga.
   4. We have less time than Cecilia.

H. 1. When he goes to the fair, he sells more
      than anyone (no one).
   2. When he goes downtown, he buys more
      than anyone (no one).
   3. When she goes to the market, she hag-
      gles more than anyone (no one).
   4. When she goes to the plaza, she talks
      more than anyone (no one).

I. 1. To work is better than to wait.
   2. To talk is better than to argue.
   3. To be a coward is worse than to die.
   4. To be a tyrant is worse than to lose.

J. 1. There's more cattle for milk than for
      meat.
   2. There's more cattle for dairy than for
      breeding [purposes].
   3. There's more time for sleeping than for
      studying.
   4. There's more opportunity for betting
      than for winning.

K. 1. I'm more than furious.
   2. I'm more than sad.
   3. He's more than serious.
   4. He's more than dumb (brutish).

L. 1. He lost more than money.
   2. He lost more than time.
   3. I need more than documents.
   4. I need more than papers.

M. 1. That coward is more than [a] tyrant.
   2. That assassin is more than infamous.
   3. His house was not more than a jail.
   4. His speech was no more than an excuse.

N. 1. All they did was (they did nothing
      more than) ask what the exchange was.
   2. All they did was give me an O.K.
   3. All he did was put his foot [in it].
   4. All he offered was a gesture.

O. 1. I have only (no more than) ten cows.
   2. I have only four hides.
   3. She has only one tongue.
   4. She has only a fourth part of the harvest.

P. 1. There's only one plaza.
   2. There's only one university.
   3. There's only one bus today.
   4. There's only one *micro* today.

Q. 1. We only celebrate our anniversary once
      a (per) year.
   2. We only go to class once a week.
   3. We only go to the café once a day.
   4. We only go to the cleaner's once a month.

• DISCUSSION

The chief problem in the comparison of inequality is the choice of **que** or **de** for *than*. In the following we take the diagrams, above, in reverse order:

1. **Que** is used when the comparison is between two *different* things, that is, when the phrase *more than* implies *other than* (as we might expect from this, *other than* is **otro que**). **No hay más remedio** means *There is no other remedy* (there is nothing else to do). There are places where **que** and **de** contrast in this sense of *other* and the more usual sense of *more*: In **Perdió más de mil dólares** *He lost more than a thousand dollars* we infer that he lost, say, a thousand plus two hundred; we are comparing two different amounts of the same thing: dollars. But in **Perdió más que mil dólares** we infer *He lost [something] more [important] than a thousand dollars*—in addition to losing the money, he lost, say, his reputation. He lost something *other than* dollars. A common use of the

que for "otherness" is in negative sentences with quantities, in the sense of *only:* **No tengo más que seis** means *I have no other amount than six,* that is, *I have only six* (but I do have six). **No tengo más de seis** means *I don't have more than six* (maybe I have only four—I don't necessarily have six).

2. **Que** is used where the primary amount or degree, that is, the amount or degree with which the comparison is made, that serves as the standard of the comparison, is not embodied in an explicit word. In *I have more than John,* the *more* that I have is measured against *what* John has, but there is no word—*fifty, a hundred, several,* or just the word *what* itself—to make this measuring stick explicit. In *You have a longer workday than I* (*have*), the comparative *longer* is included, but there is no other explicit word referring to an amount of *length.*

3. **De** is used when this primary amount or degree is explicitly given. In *I have less than fifty* the comparative *less* is included, and so is the amount against which it is measured: *fifty.* The amount or degree need not be precise, so long as there is a word for it. Thus *I have more than that amount* is **Tengo más de esa cantidad,** using just the noncommittal word *amount* itself. The **de** actually has its fundamental meaning of *from* or *of,* for we are saying *I have upwards of* (an amount *up from*) *that amount.*

80   *Lo* with compared adverbs

EXAMPLES
1. Vuelva **lo** más pronto **posible.**
2. Lo expliqué **lo** más claro **que pude.**
   I explained it as clearly as I could (the most clearly I could).

	COMPARED ADVERB	FURTHER MODIFICATION
lo	**más pronto**	**posible**

When a superlative adverb (one with *–est* or *most* in English) is further modified, **lo** precedes it.

● TRANSLATION DRILL

A. 1. TEACHER: He came back as soon as possible.
     STUDENT: **Volvió lo más pronto posible.**
2. She came back as late as possible.
3. He spoke as clearly as possible.
4. He came as near as possible.
5. I went as far as possible.

B. 1. I put it as high as I could.
     Lo puse lo más alto que pude.
2. I put it as low as I could.

3. I put it as far away as I could.
4. I put it as near as I could.
5. I put it as [far] ahead as I could.
6. I put it as [far] back as I could.
7. I put it as [far] inside as I could.
8. I put it as [far] outside as I could.

C. 1. He did it the best he could.
     Lo hizo lo mejor que pudo.
2. He did it the worst he could.
3. He did it the soonest he could.

81   The comparison of equality

EXAMPLES

A. 1. Tengo **tantos** nacionales **como** guaraníes. *I have as many nacionales as guaraníes.*
2. Lo hice **tantas** veces **como** él. *I did it as many times as he (did).*
3. ¿Es **tanta** molestia **como** antes? *Is it as much bother as before?*
4. No trabajan **tanto como** nosotros. *They don't work as much as we (do).*

B. 1. El es **tan** buena persona **como** su hermano. *He's as good a guy as his brother (is).*
   2. Un gobierno **tan** malo **como** éste jamás ha existido.
   3. No hablamos **tan** bien **como** en España.

as many . . . as	**tantos,–as . . . como**
as much . . . as	**tanto,–a . . . como**
as . . . as	**tan . . . como**

The first *as* is **tan(to),** the second **como.** As in the comparison of inequality, the tagged *is, do,* etc. normally has no equivalent in Spanish.

● ITEM SUBSTITUTION DRILL

1. Pero no debes *comer* tanto como tu papá.
   (hablar, discutir, pelear, trabajar, dormir)
2. Yo no tengo tanto *dinero* como Bernardo.
   (plata, tiempo, ropa, poder, suerte)
3. Hay tantos *problemas* aquí como en Latino-américa.
   (barbaridades, vendedores, comodidades, abogados, profesoras)
4. Perdí tantas *camisas* como calzoncillos.
   (calcetines, camisetas, trajes, sábanas, vestidos)

5. El director no es una persona tan *buena.*
   (mala, seria, difícil, inocente, admirable)
6. Un gobierno tan *malo* como éste nunca ha existido.
   (bueno, fuerte, horrible, equivocado, independiente)
7. No hablamos tan *bien* como en España.
   (mal, perfectamente, infamemente, desgraciadamente)

● TRANSLATION DRILL

A. 1. TEACHER: Relatives? I have as many as he does.
      STUDENT: **¿Parientes? Tengo tantos como él.**
   2. Ideas? I have as many as he does.
   3. Holidays? I have as many as he does.
   4. Photos? I have as many as he does.
   5. Suits? I have as many as he does.
   6. Shirts? I have as many as he does.

B. 1. Money? We have as much as they do.
   2. Education? We have as much as they do.
   3. Petroleum? We have as much as they do.
   4. Good luck? We have as much as they do.
   5. Time? We have as much as they do.
   6. Power? We have as much as they do.

7. University life? We have as much as they do.
8. Wheat? We have as much as they do.
9. Wool? We have as much as they do.
10. Cattle? We have as much as they do.
11. Straw? We have as much as they do.

C. 1. There are as many extras as regulars.
   2. There are as many old ones as new ones.
   3. There are as many *bolivianos* as *nacionales.*
   4. There are as many ranches as haciendas.
   5. There are as many streets as avenues.
   6. There are as many cowards as assassins.
   7. There are as many excuses as attacks.

82 The comparison of identity

EXAMPLES

A. 1. Yo tengo la misma cantidad. *I have the same amount.*
   2. Estos joropos no son los **mismos que** en los discos. *These joropos are not the same as on the records.*
   3. Llegó a la **misma** hora **que** ayer. *He arrived at the same time as yesterday.*
   4. Ellos van a morir lo **mismo que** nosotros. *They are going to die the same as we are.*

B. 1. Yo tengo igual cantidad. *I have the same amount.*
   2. Estos joropos no son iguales **que** en los discos. *These joropos are not the same as on the records.*
   3. Es igual **que** todas las demás materias. *(It's the same as all the other subjects.)*
   4. Hablan casi igual **que** en el Paraguay.

ABSOLUTE IDENTITY		
the	same	as
el la los las lo	mismo misma mismos mismas mismo	que

CLOSE SIMILARITY		
the	same	as
	igual iguales	que

When two things are matched as identical, **mismo** is used. When they are compared for similarity, **igual** is used. Often it is possible to view the comparison either way. As adverbs, the forms are **lo mismo** and **igual,** without inflection for number or gender.

● TRANSLATION DRILL

A. 1. TEACHER: His name is the same as mine.
STUDENT: **Su nombre es el mismo que el mío.**
2. His idea was the same as mine.
3. Her hair is (of) the same color as mine.
4. Her house is (of) the same color as mine.
5. These records are the same as mine.
6. This prescription is the same as mine.
7. His group is the same as mine.
8. Her language (tongue) is the same as mine.
9. His party is the same as mine.

B. 1. His car is just like mine.
Su auto es igual que el mío.
2. His tie is just like mine.
3. These records are just like mine.
4. This prescription is just like mine.
5. This group is just like mine.
6. Her pronunciation is just like mine.
7. His party is just like mine.
8. He brought some photos just like mine.
9. He developed some photos just like mine.

● DISCUSSION

English blends two senses of the word *same:* absolute identity, as in *It's the same man I saw yesterday* ($x = x$), and close similarity, as in *He's the same as his brother* ($x = y$). Spanish distinguishes them, using **mismo** for the first and **igual** for the second.

Mismo and **igual** overlap somewhat. **La misma cantidad** and **igual cantidad** are practically equivalent: in the first, the speaker thinks of your amount, say *five,* being identical with my five ($x = x$); in the second, he thinks of two separate things, *yours and mine* ($x = y$). But when there is real identity, as in the example *It's the same man I saw yesterday,* only **mismo** may be used.

83 Certain uses of the indefinite article: identification and individualization

EXAMPLES

A. 1. Es pariente del Jefe. *(He's a relative of the Chief.)*
2. Eres hombre respetable.
3. Usted es norteamericano.

B. 1. Dicen que es **una** planta magnífica.
   2. Fue **un** gran filósofo.
   3. Ese viaje fue **un** maratón.   *That trip was a marathon.*

MERE IDENTIFICATION	
John is a philosopher	John is an athlete
Juan es filósofo	**Juan es atleta**

John is a philosopher or athlete by profession: we are merely identifying him as a member of a class by tagging him with this label.

INDIVIDUALIZATION	
John is a philosopher	John is an important athlete
Juan es un filósofo	**Juan es un atleta importante**

John is being philosophical. This is not a standard label for John, but is something exceptional. Similarly, while "athletes" are a class, "important athletes" are not—this is an individualizing term.

● TRANSLATION DRILL

1. Rafael is a philosopher.
   Rafael is *a philosopher.*
2. Luis is an administrator.
   Luis is *an administrator.*
3. Chalo is a student.
   Chalo is *a student.*
4. Alberto is a doctor.
   Alberto is a good doctor.
5. Antonio is a lawyer.
   Antonio is an innocent lawyer.
6. Don Francisco is a Spaniard.
   Don Francisco is an old Spaniard.
7. Don Carlos is Latin American.
   Don Carlos is a typical Latin American.
8. José is a friend of María Elena's.
   José is a real friend of María Elena's.
9. Olga is a cousin of Pepe's.
   Olga is a pretty cousin of Pepe's.
10. Felipe is a companion of Bernardo's.
    Felipe is a bad companion of Bernardo's.
11. Rodríguez is a tyrant.
    Rodríguez is a ferocious tyrant.
12. Mr. Romero is a clerk.
    Mr. Romero is a good clerk.
13. Mr. Fernández is a tourist.
    Mr. Fernández is a typical tourist.

EXAMPLES

A. 1. Tuvimos examen en filosofía.
   2. Es bueno tener campo.
   3. Tengo hora con él.
   4. ¿Tengo fiebre?
   5. Busco casa.   *I'm house-hunting.*
   6. ¿Hay médico aquí?   *Is there a doctor here?*
   7. Salió sin corbata.   *He went out without a tie.*
   8. Necesito una casa con cocina.   *I need a house with a kitchen.*

B. 1. Tome **un** colectivo.
   2. Tengo **un** hambre feroz.
   3. ¿Qué sugieres?   —**Un** churrasco bien jugoso.
   4. Aquí traigo **un** paquete con ropa.
   5. No recibimos **un** traje y **un** vestido que ustedes quedaron en mandar.
   6. Ayer hubo **una** reunión muy grande.
   7. Es considerado como **un** verdadero arte.

STRESSING THE MERE EXISTENCE OF SOMETHING		
tener **haber** **buscar** **sin** **con** etc.		noun

When the question is merely about the existence or nonexistence (occurrence or nonoccurrence) of something, the indefinite article is not used.

FOCUSING ON AN INDIVIDUAL THING OR THINGS		
verb preposition (or other relator)	**un, –a**	noun

In the sense *one of those,* or *a certain,* where the thing is individualized, the indefinite article is used.

● TRANSLATION DRILL

1. I'm looking for a maid.
   I'm looking for help (maid).
2. I have to find a job.
   I have to find work.
3. I need a clerk.
   I need clerical help.

4. I'm looking for a house.
   I'm house-hunting.
5. Do you have a paper?
   Are you supplied with paper?
6. Do I have a very high fever?
   Do I have a fever?

7. He has a good heart.
   He has a heart.
8. Is there a good doctor here?
   Is there a doctor here?
9. Can you wrap a package here?
   Do you wrap packages here?

● DISCUSSION

After the verb **ser,** Spanish does not use the indefinite article when the purpose is merely to identify a person or thing by attaching some conventional label. It does use the article when the purpose is not merely to identify, but to make the person or thing stand out. A noun used as a figure of speech (e.g., *She is an angel,* or *He is a pirate* meaning he is a sharp businessman) therefore calls for the article, as do most combinations where there is an enhancing adjective such as *great, wonderful, despicable,* etc.

Similarly, the indefinite article is not used in Spanish when a noun in object position is considered merely in the light of its existence or nonexistence. The verbs whose meaning refers fundamentally to existence, **tener** and **haber,** and the prepositions that refer to presence or absence, **con** and **sin,** are the commonest situations where the article is not used. But if the purpose is to focus on something already considered to be in existence (*one of those*), and to make it stand out, the indefinite article is used.

English has this identical contrast in the plural, though not, as we have seen, in the singular. Thus if we say *We have examinations* we mean merely that examinations take place (where we are concerned)—we refer to the existence, or occurrence, of the examinations. But if we say *We have some examinations,* the attention is immediately drawn to particular examinations. Likewise, though in the singular we require *a* in *John is a lawyer,* nothing similar is required in the plural: *John and Henry are lawyers.*

Unos is simply the plural of **un.** Both **unos** and **algunos** are translated *some.* Their difference in meaning is the same as the difference between their respective singulars: just as **un hombre** *a man* makes a more specific reference than **algún hombre** *some man* (none in particular), so **unos hombres** is more specific than **algunos hombres.**

A. 1. **Mi primo desgraciadamente habla más que yo.**
   2. Mis _____
   3. _____cuñado _____
   4. _____ tanto _____
   5. _____ella
   6. _____ discute _____
   7. _____ casi _____
   8. _____profesor _____
   9. _____nosotros
  10. _____ más _____
  11. Nuestros _____
  12. _____ pelean _____
  13. _____amigos _____
  14. _____usted
  15. _____ siempre _____
  16. Nuestro _____
  17. _____ compra _____
  18. _____ tanto _____
  19. _____ustedes
  20. _____ nunca _____
  21. _____compañera _____
  22. _____tú

B. 1. **Aquí tenemos tantas comodidades como en la ciudad.**
   2. _____campo
   3. _____ más _____
   4. Allá _____
   5. _____ competencia _____
   6. _____hay _____
   7. _____ tanta _____
   8. _____ cosas _____
   9. _____colegio
  10. _____ huelgas _____
  11. _____tienen _____
  12. _____ más _____
  13. _____universidad
  14. _____ manifestaciones _____
  15. _____había _____
  16. Ahí _____
  17. _____ discursos _____
  18. _____dan _____
  19. _____ministerio
  20. _____ tantos _____
  21. _____ plata _____
  22. _____ganan _____
  23. _____banco
  24. _____ más _____
  25. _____ dinero _____

● TRANSLATION REVIEW DRILL

Theme vowels in imperfect-tense verb forms.

A. 1. He used to work and eat a lot.
   2. He used to study and learn a lot.
   3. He used to talk and write a lot.
   4. He used to enter and leave a lot.
   5. He used to buy and sell a lot.
   6. He used to win and ask a lot.
   7. He used to celebrate and sleep a lot.
   8. He used to bet and lose a lot.
   9. He used to walk and run a lot.

B. 1. We used to work and eat a lot.
    2. We used to study and learn a lot.
    3. We used to buy and sell a lot.
    4. We used to wait and ask a lot.
    5. We used to bet and lose a lot.
    6. We used to walk and run a lot.
    7. We used to celebrate and sleep a lot.
    8. We used to talk and write a lot.
    9. We used to enter and leave a lot.

READING

Problema de pronunciación

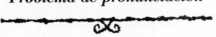

P. *Profesor*   M. *Señor Moreno, estudiante*

P. Todos ustedes saben la historia del norte-americano que fue a cazar[1] a una selva[2] de Sud América. (*En efecto, la clase ya la ha oído[3] dos veces durante el semestre, pero es la historia favorita del profesor.*) Este cazador se detuvo delante de una casa situada cerca de la selva y llamó a la puerta. Apareció el dueño de la casa, y le preguntó al cazador qué deseaba. Este respondió: ¿Aquí se caza, señor? El dueño, señalando a sus tres hijas, de edad avanzada para el matrimonio, contestó rápido: Sí, señor, elija usted a cualquiera. (*risa complaciente[4] de parte de la clase*) Muy bien, señores, ¿quién puede explicarme esta historia? . . . ¿Señor Moreno?

M. Pues se trata de la pronunciación de la zeta.[5] Las palabras *casar* y *cazar* se pronuncian del mismo modo en Hispanoamérica. Nosotros decimos [kasár] en vez de [kaθár], como debemos . . .

P. No, no, señor Moreno, nada de[6] "como debemos". En primer lugar, nadie tiene que disculparse del modo de hablar de[7] su propia lengua. Si el español de Puerto Rico, por ejemplo, es un poco diferente, en algunos aspectos, del de Castilla, eso no quiere decir que sea[8] inferior. El de Puerto Rico es tan "correcto" para los que lo hablan como el de Castilla para los castellanos. En segundo lugar, en cuanto a diferencias de pronunciación tales como [kaθár] en la mayor parte de España y [kasár] en Andalucía e Hispanoamérica, tales detalles han sido muy discutidos por los eruditos. Sólo puedo decir que se trata de consideraciones históricas y sociales muy complejas, y debemos dejar tales asuntos para los especialistas . . . que no siempre están de acuerdo.

---

[1] *went hunting*   [2] *forest*   [3] *heard*   [4] *obedient*   [5] *letter* **z**   [6] *let's not have any of that stuff about*   [7] *to apologize for*   [8] *it is*

READING

En la sala de matrícula en una universidad de los Estados Unidos

P. *Pepe*   R. *Ramón*   M. *María*   C. *Catalina*
T. *Todos juntos*

P. Hola, Ramón. ¿Cómo estás? ¿Cuándo regresaste?

R. ¡Tengo muchas dificultades! Ya no hay lugar para más estudiantes en ninguno de los cursos que quería seguir.

P. Yo también tengo dificultades. Debo estudiar una lengua extranjera y no quiero hacerlo. Exige mucho tiempo y no se puede faltar a clase . . . Ahí está María.

¡Hola! ¿Cómo estás? ¿Qué vas a estudiar?

M. Estoy disgustada. Ya no hay más lugar en la clase de español de las once . . .

P. ¿Para qué estudiar lenguas extranjeras?

R. Sí. ¿Para qué?

P. Eso se contesta muy fácilmente. Tengo que estudiar una lengua extranjera para graduarme. ¿Quién es el profesor menos exigente?

M. Tonto. Yo creo que las lenguas extranjeras son muy interesantes. Quiero viajar por todas partes, hablar con los extranjeros guapos y leer periódicos y libros.

R. ¡Bah!

C. (uniéndose al grupo) ¿Quién dice "Bah"? Ah, Ramón, ¡eres tú de nuevo! Déjame decirte algo. Hace cuatro años que estudio el español en esta universidad. Voy a graduarme en junio y tengo muchas oportunidades de empleo en las que[1] puedo usar el español: el FBI,[2] el Servicio de Información de los Estados Unidos, el Departamento de Estado, y también puedo enseñar español aquí o inglés en Hispanoamérica.

P. ¿Qué más?

C. Puedo ser traductora, o una secretaria bilingüe, o bibliotecaria, o . . .

R. ¡Qué dicha! Acaban de decir que hay clases adicionales de español . . . Con permiso. ¡Adiós! Un buen puesto me espera en Sud América. (Todos se ríen.)

C. Buena suerte, Ramón.
   (Más tarde, los estudiantes toman café en la "Unión" y hablan sobre sus programas de clase.)

C. Muchachos, ya que estamos juntos, ¿quieren saber algo de las clases en la primera universidad del Nuevo Mundo, la Universidad Nacional de México? Yo sé mucho acerca de ella.

T. Sí. ¡Dinos![3]

P. Pues, esperen ustedes. Yo voy a pedir otras tazas de café. ¿Cuántos lo toman con leche y azúcar? ¿Cuántos lo quieren negro? Está bien. Con permiso.
   (más tarde)

C. Pues, la primera apertura solemne de clases en el Nuevo Mundo tuvo lugar en la Universidad de México el 25 de enero de 1553.[4] Sólo treinta años después de la fundación de escuelas primarias en la Nueva España[5] los virreyes querían fundar una institución de estudios superiores como la universidad española de Salamanca.

P. Hace más de cuatrocientos años. ¡Figúrate!

C. Sí. Y el infatigable Virrey, don Antonio de Mendoza, propuso la fundación de una Universidad "en donde los naturales y los hijos de españoles fueren[6] industriados en las cosas de nuestra fe católica y en las demás facultades . . ." y luego se nombraron personas en todas las facultades para enseñar las materias entonces más estimadas.

R. Todo en español, ¿verdad?

C. No. El latín era la lengua oficial de las clases. Esta tradición era tan fuerte que los médicos usaban el latín para recetar, los abogados lo usaban en sus alegatos y los profesores también ponían letras latinas para calificar.

P. ¿Por ejemplo?

C. Una C era "condenado" o F. Una A era "aprobado" y NL[7] significaba en latín non liquet, esto es "no está claro".

P. ¡Caramba!

C. Algunos estudiantes trataban de hablar latín aunque sólo lo sabían de oídas. Querían pasar por latinistas ante sus padres al regresar a casa y saludaban al perro de su casa de este modo:

> Perritiquis miquis,
> ¿no me conociorum?
> Ego sum amicus,
> el estudiantorum.[8]

R. Esto quiere decir: "Perro mío, ¿no me

---

[1] **las que** *which,* referring to **oportunidades**   [2] The letters are pronounced [efe, be, i].   [3] **Dinos** *tell us*

[4] On September 21, 1551, Charles V solemnly declared that two pioneer American universities should be founded "to honor and favor our Indies and to dissipate the clouds of ignorance." The Royal and Pontifical University of Mexico was the first active major university in the New World, inaugurating its courses in 1553. The first classes in the University of San Marcos, Peru, were begun in 1576.

[5] **Nueva España** was the name given to the part of the New World which is now Mexico.

[6] **fueren** *may be* (**fueren** is the future subjunctive, now archaic). The Viceroy Antonio de Mendoza was so anxious to see classes begun in New Spain that he made a donation of land and cattle to the proposed university as a symbol of his faith. This gift became known as the first "endowment" in the New World.

[7] The letters are pronounced [ce, efe, a, ene, ele].

[8] Vicente T. Mendoza, *Vida y Costumbres de la Universidad de México,* Instituto de Investigaciones Estéticas, Mexico, 1951, p. 18.

conoces? Yo soy tu amigo, el estudiante."
Es latín macarrónico.[9]

C. ¡Claro que sí! Otros estudiantes cantaban debajo de las ventanas de sus novias—en español. (*Canta.*)

La ca - pa del es - tu - dian - te   pa - re - ce un jar - dín de   flo - res;

to - da lle - na de re - mien - dos y   de dis - tin - tos co - lo - res.

La capa del estudiante
parece un jardín de flores:
toda llena de remiendos
y de distintos colores.

El amor del estudiante
es como un terrón de azúcar;
las jóvenes que lo prueban
hasta los dedos se chupan.

La joven que no ha sido
la novia de un estudiante
no sabe lo que es cajeta,
ni ha probado el chocolate.[10]

(aplausos de todos)

T. ¡Hurra! ¡Bis, bis, bis!

C. Gracias. Esto es bastante para hoy. Voy a continuar con cosas más serias. Para obtener grados y diplomas en la Universidad los estudiantes tenían que dar exámenes[11] (para el Bachillerato, la Maestría, la Licenciatura y el Doctorado). Las veinticuatro horas que precedían a los exámenes eran de horrible angustia y desvelo para los estudiantes, que se llamaban "aspirantes". Cada estudiante tenía que señalar, con anticipación, los puntos que iba a "defender" en su examen. Para esto un niño con una urna llena de papeletas entraba en la sala de clase. Luego cada estudiante escogía sus "puntos" para defenderlos al día siguiente ante cinco profesores. Algunos exámenes eran de noche y duraban dos horas. Los estudiantes decían que pasaban una "Noche Triste", peor que la de Cortés.[12]

R. Como aquí.

C. Se llamaba también a los exámenes "pique de puntos".[13] Probablemente todos los estudiantes fueron aprobados, pues recibían buena instrucción. Según las antiguas crónicas de la Universidad "los profesores debían leer con puntualidad durante una hora justa, haciéndolo a gusto de los estudiantes, con riesgo de pagar multas o aun de perder la cátedra".

R. ¡Buena idea!

P. Pero no se hace aquí.

C. ¡No me interrumpas más!

R. Sí; no seas majadero.

C. Pues, escuchen ustedes. Los estudiantes eran vigilados aun fuera de la universidad y en sus propias casas, pues tenían que vivir en casas honestas y sin sospecha. Les era absolutamente prohibido comportarse mal y dar escándalos, o entrar en las clases con armas ofensivas o defensivas. Si esto acontecía, un estudiante debía estar ocho días en la cárcel y si no entregaba las armas, perdía el curso.

R. y P. ¡Caramba!

C. Hay mucho más que decir sobre esta cuestión tan interesante. Por ahora sólo voy a decirles que la actual Universidad Nacional de México ya ha celebrado el cuarto centenario de su fundación. La Ciudad Universitaria, cuya construcción se ha terminado[14] en el Pedregal de San Angel,[15] es la nueva sede de la universidad. Invitan a todos los estudiantes de español y a sus profesores a inscribirse en las varias Facultades.

M. Este ha sido uno de los descansos[16] más interesantes que hemos tenido en todo el año. ¿Por qué no podemos hacerlo más a menudo?

C. Podemos hacerlo.

P. Bueno, ya es hora de ir a clase.

---

[9] **latín macarrónico** *"fractured Latin"*   [10] Mendoza, *op. cit.*, p. 18.   [11] **dar exámenes** *to take exams*

[12] **La Noche Triste de Cortés** refers to the night of July 1, 1520, when Cortés was defeated by the Mexicans and, sitting down under a large tree in the town of Popotla, wept for his dead comrades. The tree is preserved today as a precious relic of the struggle of the Indians to keep their land.

[13] **pique de puntos** *drawing,* a term used in card games.

[14] **se ha terminado** *has been finished*   [15] A suburb of Mexico City.   [16] **descansos** *"coffee breaks"*

1. ¿Cuáles son algunas de las dificultades que tienen los estudiantes al matricularse?
2. ¿Por qué debe Pepe estudiar una lengua extranjera?
3. ¿Qué oportunidades de empleo ofrece el estudio de las lenguas extranjeras?
4. Diga dónde y cuándo tuvo lugar la apertura de la primera universidad del Nuevo Mundo.
5. ¿En qué idioma se enseñaron las materias?
6. ¿Quiénes usaban también la lengua oficial?
7. ¿Cómo se divertían los estudiantes de la universidad?
8. ¿Qué quiere decir "pique de puntos"?
9. ¿Cómo enseñaban sus materias los profesores?
10. ¿Cuáles son algunas de las restricciones que tenían los estudiantes?
11. Cuando un estudiante se comportaba mal, ¿qué sucedía?
12. ¿Dónde está actualmente la nueva sede de la Universidad Nacional de México?

● SUGGESTED READINGS

Booth, George, *Mexico's School-Made Society,* Stanford University Press, California, 1941.

Diffie, Bailey W. and Justine W., *Latin-American Civilization,* Stackpole Sons, Harrisburg, Pa., 1945.

Johnston, Marjorie C., *Education in Mexico,* U.S. Government Printing Office, no. 1, Washington D.C., 1956.

Lanning, John Tate, *Academic Culture in the Spanish Colonies,* Oxford University Press, New York, 1940: Ch. 2, "University Life and Administration."

Northrop, F. S. C., *The Meeting of East and West,* Macmillan, New York, 1946: Ch. 2, "The Rich Culture of Mexico."

15

Early at the Office

s. *Secretary* B. *Boss*

s. Mrs. Méndez called about a raffle or something [for a matter of a raffle]. How that woman can talk!

B. Yes, she'll talk your head off.

s. She's raffling off a fur coat at a hundred pesos a ticket, for the benefit of her neighborhood church.

B. What?! A hundred pesos! If she calls again, tell her I'm not in and you don't know when I'll be back.

s. The mail's finally come. Here it is, two magazines and several bills. Oh, and a letter for me.

Temprano en la oficina

s. *Secretaria* J. *Jefe*

s. Llamó la Sra. Méndez para un asunto de una rifa. ¡Cómo habla esa señora!

J. Sí, hasta por los codos.

s. Está rifando un abrigo de pieles a cien pesos el número, a beneficio de la capilla de su barrio.

J. ¡¿Qué?! ¡Cien pesos! Si vuelve a llamar, dígale que no estoy y que usted no sabe cuándo regreso.

s. Por fin llegó el correo; aquí está, dos revistas y varias cuentas. Ah, y una carta para mí.

B. Let me see those bills: rent, electricity, doctor, dentist . . . My gosh! Well, there's nothing else to do but pay them.

S. Your bank account is a bit low. Shall I just pay the rent? That's the most important for now.

B. And the electric bill too. If we don't, they'll shut it off on us. The others can wait.

* * *

S. Do you know who wrote me? Ana Guadalupe Martínez, the girl who worked here two years ago.

B. Oh yes, of course, Lupita, the girl with the green eyes. We sure do miss her. What does she have to say?

S. She's getting married to Lorenzo, that Spanish fellow who was her boy friend for so long.

B. Really? I'm delighted to hear it. What a lucky guy! He's getting a fine girl.

S. She says he's already asked her father.

B. And when's the wedding? I'd like to send them a nice present.

S. They wanted to get married this month, but since it's Lent now they're going to wait until after Holy Week.

* * *

B. By the way, I must go to communion one of these days. If I don't, my wife will raise the roof.

S. She's right. You've got to do your duty by the Church at least once a year.

B. Do you go to communion often?

S. Almost every Sunday. Communion is extremely important.

B. I agree. And to think that I almost never go to mass.

S. How awful!

B. Forget it. My wife goes all the time and prays for both of us. Well, let's get to work.

J. Déjeme ver esas cuentas: alquiler, electricidad, el médico, el dentista . . . ¡Caramba! Bueno, no hay más remedio que pagarlas (1).

S. La cuenta del banco está algo baja. ¿Pago sólo la del alquiler, que es la más importante por ahora?

J. Y la de la electricidad. Si no, nos la cortan (2). Las demás pueden esperar.

* * *

S. ¿Sabe quién me escribió? Ana Guadalupe Martínez, la que trabajó aquí hace dos años.

J. Ah, claro, Lupita, la de los ojos verdes. ¡Cómo la echamos de menos! ¿Qué cuenta?

S. Que se casa con Lorenzo, el español, su novio de años (3).

J. ¡De veras! ¡Cuánto me alegro! ¡Qué suerte de hombre! Se lleva a una gran muchacha.

S. Dice ella que él ya le pidió la mano a su padre.

J. ¿Y cuándo es la boda? Quisiera mandarles un buen regalo.

S. Querían casarse este mes, pero como ahora estamos en Cuaresma, van a esperar hasta después de Semana Santa.

* * *

J. A propósito, debo ir a comulgar uno de estos días. Si no, quién vería a mi mujer.

S. Tiene razón ella. Hay que cumplir con la iglesia por lo menos una vez al año.

J. ¿Usted comulga muy a menudo?

S. Casi todos los domingos. La comunión es algo muy importante.

J. De acuerdo. Y pensar que yo casi nunca voy a misa (4).

S. ¡Qué barbaridad!

J. ¡Qué va! Mi mujer va siempre y reza por los dos. Bueno, señorita, vamos a trabajar.

Cultural Notes

(1) Personal matters, such as domestic bills, often form part of the routine in Latin-American business offices.

(2) The American concept of credit, with its period of grace within which to pay an overdue bill, is not usual in Latin America. Hence the need to pay promptly in order to maintain service.

(3) Long courtships are quite general, since young men usually wait until they become established before they marry.

(4) Latin-American women take religion more seriously than do men, who are often only nominal church members. An illustration of this difference of attitude is the long tradition of anticlericalism among Hispanic men, addressed mainly against the temporal power of the Church.

● WRITING EXERCISE

The use of the letter **h**. INSTRUCTIONS: Write the following lists of words from dictation.

A.	B.	C.	D.	E.
haber	ahora	hiedra	hueco	hijo
hablar	ahito	hielo	hueso	hoja
hacer	deshonra	hiena	huevo	hijuelo
hambre	dehesa	hierba	huelgo	higiene
hombre	rehusar	hierro	huerta	ahijado
hasta	rehacer	hiel	huésped	héjira
himno	ahondar			
hora	ahogar			
historia	inhalar			
hermano	inhumano			

The letter **h** represents no sound at all, its use in the Spanish spelling system being an inheritance from Latin (e.g., Spanish **h** may represent a Latin *h* as in **haber** from Latin *habere,* or it may represent a Latin initial *f* as in **hacer** from Latin *facere*).

Note that in the examples in *E,* the letters **j** and **g** have the value [x], but that **h** in these words has, of course, no sound value.

Variant spellings of some words are a further indication of the absence of sound value for the letter **h**; e.g., **harmonía** and **armonía, hujier** and **ujier, harpa** and **arpa,** etc.

84 Nominalization of indefinites

EXAMPLES

A. 1. Ella tiene **uno** portátil. *(She has a portable [one].)*
2. Necesito **unas** más grandes. *I need some bigger ones.*

B. 1. ¿No tiene usted **otro** azul? *Don't you have a blue one (another [that is] blue)?*
2. Tráeme **otras** mejores. *Bring me some better ones (others [that are] better).*

C. 1. ¿Mataron a **alguno?**
2. ¿Conoce usted **alguno** menos complicado? *Do you know some less complicated one?*

D. No hay **ninguno** peor. *There's no worse one.*

E. Hay **pocos** modernos. *There are few modern ones.*

F. Encontré **muchos** más fáciles. *I found many easier ones.*

a some another (some) other some (any) no few many } portable bigger blue better etc.	one(s)

uno,–a unos,–as otro,–a otros,–as alguno,–a, –os, –as ninguno,–a[1] pocos,–as muchos,–as }	portátil,–es más grande,–s azul,–es mejor,–es etc.

In Spanish, indefinites are nominalized directly, without the addition of any equivalent of *one* (but when *one* itself is nominalized, the equivalent **uno, –a, –os, –as** is required, as in *I have one* **Tengo uno,** *I have a good one* **Tengo uno bueno**).

● ITEM SUBSTITUTION DRILL

1. Ella tiene uno *portátil.*
   (diferente, regular, complicado, sencillo, anticuado)
2. Necesito unas más *grandes.*
   (modernas, importantes, profesionales, típicas, fuertes)
3. ¿No tiene usted otros *azules?*
   (negros, verdes, mejores, finos, nuevos)
4. No hay ninguno *mejor.*
   (peor, fácil, importado, nacional, viejo)

5. ¿Tiene alguno menos *complicado?*
   (enredado, difícil, grande, sucio, ridículo)
6. Hay pocos *profesionales.*
   (heridos, independientes, infames, inocentes, libres)
7. Encontré muchos más *fáciles.*
   (bajos, altos, puros, horribles, juntos)

● TRANSLATION DRILL

A. 1. I have a portable one at home.
   2. I have a better one at home.
   3. I have a new one at home.
   4. I have a magnificent one at home.

B. 1. There's another married one.
   2. There's another wounded one.
   3. There's another invited one.
   4. There's another rude one.

C. 1. In this world there are few innocent [ones].
   2. In this world there are few simple [ones].
   3. In this world there are few respectable [ones].
   4. In this world there are few free [ones].

EXAMPLES

1. Disparó contra una manifestación de estudiantes, **algo** horrible.
2. La cuenta del banco está **algo** baja.

something good	**algo bueno**

Algo *something,* like the other indefinites, may be modified by an adjective, which then takes the same form as the masculine singular.

somewhat (rather) good	**algo bueno, –a, –os, –as**

Algo *somewhat, rather,* being an adverb, modifies the adjective, which in turn agrees with its noun (e.g., **baja** with **cuenta,** example 2).

---

[1] See Unit 13 §70 for the plurals **ningunos, –as.**

1. TEACHER: The letter is something typical.
   STUDENT: **La carta es algo típico.**
   TEACHER: The letter is somewhat typical.
   STUDENT: **La carta es algo típica.**
2. The matters are something fantastic.
   Los asuntos son algo fantástico.
   The matters are somewhat fantastic.
   Los asuntos son algo fantásticos.
3. The chapel is something new.
   The chapel is somewhat new.
4. Electricity is something necessary.
   Electricity is somewhat necessary.
5. Communion is something serious.
   Communion is somewhat serious.
6. The wedding is something sacred.
   The wedding is somewhat sacred.
7. This neighborhood is something old-fashioned.
   This neighborhood is somewhat old-fashioned.
8. This business of speaking better or worse is something relative.
   This business of speaking better or worse is somewhat relative.
9. This magazine is something modern.
   This magazine is somewhat modern.
10. This raffle is something ridiculous.
    This raffle is somewhat ridiculous.
11. This church is something old.
    This church is somewhat old.

EXAMPLE

Trajo algo para **cada uno (cada una)** de ustedes.   *He brought something for each (one) of you.*

each (one)	cada uno cada una

The adjective **cada** cannot be nominalized.
In the example above it modifies the nominalized **uno,–a.**

● TRANSLATION DRILL

1. I have a gift for each one of the boys.
   I have a fur coat for each one of the girls.
2. The director saw each one of the checks.
   The woman saw each one of the photos.
3. Each of the post cards was short.
   Each of the letters was long.
4. Each of the receipts was necessary.
   Each of the prescriptions was important.
5. I saw each one of the races.
   I saw each one of the sports.

● DISCUSSION

The nominalization of indefinites is like that of the definites (Unit 11 §59) in that no equivalent of *one* is used (**cada** is an exception).   It differs, however, when an adjective is added.   With the definites, it is the adjective that is nominalized: **el nuevo** means *the new-one*.   With the indefinites, it is the indefinite word that is nominalized: **uno nuevo** means *one that-is-new;* **otros nuevos** means *others (other-ones) that-are-new*.   This is why we find **uno nuevo** and not **un nuevo, alguno nuevo** and not **algún nuevo,** etc.   (When an adjective has become a noun in its own right, then we do find the shortened forms: **un general** means *a general,* while **uno general** means *one that-is-general, a general one*.   Note the example with **portátil:** since this adjective has not, unlike the English *portable*, become a noun in its own right, we must say **uno portátil** *a portable one* rather than the literal equivalent of *a portable*.)

85   The *each-other* construction

EXAMPLES

A. 1. Llegó este policía y **nos peleamos.** *(We fought each other.)*
   2. Sea lo que sea, no **nos entendimos.**
   3. **Nos encontramos** en el Club de la Unión. *(We met each other at the Union Club.)*
   4. ¿Van a **verse** mañana? *Are you going to see each other tomorrow?*
   5. **Nos compramos** regalos. *We buy each other presents.*

B. 1. **Se ofrecen** regalos **uno al otro.** *They offer each other presents.*
   2. **Se ofrecen** regalos **unos a otros.** *They offer one another presents.*

C. 1. No queremos hablar mal **uno del otro.** *We don't want to speak ill of each other.*
   2. No pueden hacer nada **uno sin el otro.** *They can't do anything without each other.*
   3. Hablaron **unas con otras.** *They (women) talked with one another.*

verb +	*each other* *one another*	NORMAL UNEMPHATIC	ADDITION FOR EMPHASIS OR CLARITY
		nos + verb **se**	**uno al otro** **(una a la otra)** **unos a otros** **(unas a otras)**

Except for emphasis or, especially with **se,** for clarity, the meanings of *each other* (two persons) and *one another* (more than two) are carried simply by the reflexive. There is no difference between direct and indirect objects. When both sexes are involved, the masculine is used.

preposition	*each other* *one another*	**uno** **(una)** **unos** **(unas)**	preposition	**el otro** **(la otra)** **otros** **(otras)**

Where *each other (one another)* is object of a preposition rather than object of a verb, the preposition separates the two halves in Spanish.

● TRANSLATION DRILL

1. TEACHER: Finally we understood each other.
  STUDENT: **Por fin nos entendimos.**
  TEACHER: Finally we understood *each other.*
  STUDENT: **Por fin nos entendimos uno al otro.**
2. The engaged couple offer each other presents.
  The engaged couple offer *each other* presents.
3. The ladies are going to see each other tomorrow.
  The ladies are going to see *each other* tomorrow.
4. We bought each other presents.
  We bought *each other* presents.
5. Why did they kill one another?
  Why did they kill *one another?*

6. The children showed their toys to one another.
  The children showed their toys *to one another.*
7. They can't do anything without each other.
  They can't study without each other.
  They can't go to communion without each other.
  They can't eat lunch without each other.
8. They don't want to speak ill against one another.
  They don't want to say anything against one another.
  They don't want to argue against one another.
  They don't want to fight against one another.

86 The equivalents of *that, which, who,* and *whom*

EXAMPLES

A. 1. ¿Pago sólo la del alquiler, **que** es la más importante por ahora? *(Shall I pay just that of the rent, which is the most important for now?)*
2. Primera y última vez **que** vengo aquí.
3. Mi sobrina **que** vive en México.
4. En casa de Olga, **que** tiene unos discos nuevos. *(At the house of Olga, who has some new records.)*
5. El papel en **que** escribo. *The paper I write on (on which I write).*
6. El dentista **que** escogieron. *The dentist (that, whom) they picked.*

B. 1. ¿Ella es la muchacha de **quien** me hablabas? *She's the girl (that, whom) you were telling me about?*
2. Yo no soy la persona a **quien** se lo dio. *I'm not the person he gave it to (to whom he gave it).*

IN MOST SITUATIONS	
that which who whom	**que**

The word which most frequently carries the meanings of *that, which, who,* and *whom* is **que.** But see exception below. **Que** is not normally omitted as the English equivalents often are.

AFTER A PREPOSITION	
that (person) *whom*	**quien**

Under these conditions, **quien** is used rather than **que.** This includes **a quien** as an indirect object.

● TRANSLATION DRILL

A. 1. Where are the *sucres* that I gave you?
2. Where are the *quetzales* that I gave you?
3. Where are the *soles* that I gave you?
4. Where are the *guaraníes* that I gave you?
5. Where are the *colones* that I gave you?

B. 1. First and last time that I come here.
2. First and last time that I stop here.
3. First and last time that I pass here.
4. First and last time that I turn here.

C. 1. Which is this magazine that you mentioned?
2. Which is this benefit that you mentioned?
3. Which is this mass that you mentioned?
4. Which is this exchange that you mentioned?
5. Which is this row that you mentioned?

D. 1. This is the bus which goes downtown.
2. This is the *colectivo* which goes to the plaza.
3. This is the *micro* which goes to the park.
4. This is the car which goes to the cemetery.

E. 1. Olga is the clerk that sold me the bed.
2. Rosa is the employee that gave me the pillowcases.
3. Elena is the girl that showed me the pair of shoes.
4. Lupe is the secretary that we miss.
5. Mercedes is the woman that talks your head off.

F. 1. There goes the secretary who got married.
   2. There goes the boss who got mad.
   3. There goes the employee who developed the films.
   4. There goes the tourist who put his foot in it.

G. 1. He's the barber (whom) I want.
   2. He's the doctor (whom) I need.
   3. He's the vendor (whom) I wait for.
   4. He's the student (whom) I teach.
   5. He's the president (whom) I respect.

H. 1. She's the girl (whom) we were speaking of.
   2. She's the person (whom) we were writing about.
   3. He's the martyr (whom) we were studying about.

I. 1. He's the person she used to have lunch with.
   2. He's the person she used to go to communion with.
   3. He's the person she used to come with.
   4. He's the person she used to play with.
   5. He's the person she used to go out with.

J. 1. The lawyer we gave it to is Venezuelan.
   2. The tourist we sold it to is American.
   3. The administrator we spoke to is Spanish.
   4. The vendor we paid is Mexican.

4. He's the director (whom) we were arguing about.
5. He's the leader (whom) we were depending on (of).

EXAMPLES

1. Las dos chicas **que están** en la sala.
2. Una casita verde **que está** en la esquina.
3. El periódico **que está** debajo del paquete. *The newspaper (that is) under the package.*

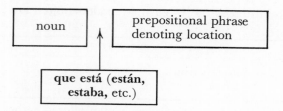

Where English may modify a noun directly by means of a prepositional phrase denoting location, Spanish normally adds **que** plus a form of **estar**.

● TRANSLATION DRILL

A. 1. Who are the two girls in the living room?
   2. Who are the two maids in the kitchen?
   3. Who are the two boys in the patio?
   4. Who are the three boys on the corner?

B. 1. The newspapers under the package.
   2. The papers under the plate.
   3. The documents under the picture.
   4. The tools under the car.
   5. The horse under the tree.

● DISCUSSION

Que covers most instances of the English relatives *that, which, who,* and *whom.* An exception is *that* or *whom,* referring to a person as the object of a preposition, where **quien** must be used instead of **que.** The same is true when *that* or *whom* is an indirect object.

Spanish almost never omits relative words as English does: *The man (   ) I saw* **El hombre que vi.** And prepositions are joined directly to relatives: *The house (that) I live in* **La casa en que vivo.**

87 Word order

A. 1. Llamó la señora **Méndez.**
   2. Por fin llegó el **correo.**
   3. Llegó este **policía.**
   4. Vino la **criada.**
   5. ¿Por qué anda toda la gente **corriendo?**
   6. Y eso ¿qué **importa?**

B. 1. Sólo de **eso** se habla. *(Only of **that** do they speak.)*
   2. Se practica muy **poco** ese deporte.
   3. ¡Qué buen **café** es éste! *(What a good **café** this is!)*
   4. Cómo **habla** esa señora. *(What a **talker** that woman is.)*

---

x' = the center of attention or most informative element, carrying the major stress of the sentence
y = some other informative element
z = an element with very little attention, already spoken about or obvious from the context, carrying least stress

CLIMACTIC WORD ORDER		ANTICLIMACTIC WORD ORDER		
y	x'	(y)	x'	z

Corresponding to the type *A **police-man** came up, The **telephone** rang, The **mail** arrived,* with order $x'y$ in English, Spanish normally has order yx': *Came a **policeman.*** These are examples *A* above.

As in English, a sentence may be made more "relaxed" by putting some unstressed element at the end and uttering it at a low pitch. These are examples *B* above.

● PATTERNED RESPONSE DRILL

1. TEACHER: ¿Quién llamó?
   STUDENT: **Llamó la señora Méndez.**
   TEACHER: ¿Qué hizo la señora Méndez?
   STUDENT: **La señora Méndez llamó.**

2. ¿Quién salió?
   ¿Qué hizo la señora Méndez?

3. ¿Quién terminó?
   ¿Qué hizo la señora Méndez?

4. ¿Quién se enojó?
   ¿Qué hizo la señora Méndez?

5. ¿Quién almorzó?
   ¿Qué hizo la señora Méndez?

6. ¿Quién comió?
   ¿Qué hizo la señora Méndez?

● TRANSLATION DRILL

INSTRUCTIONS: Translate the following sentences, placing the emphasized (italicized) words last.

1. The pronunciation *changed.*
   The pronunciation changed.

2. The steak *arrived.*
   The steak arrived.

3. The steering *failed.*
   The steering failed.

4. The consul *understood.*
   The consul understood.

5. The government *defended itself.*
   The government defended itself.

6. The police *arrived.*
   The police arrived.

7. The maid *swept.*
   The maid swept.

● FRAME SUBSTITUTION DRILL

INSTRUCTIONS: Repeat the following sentences just as you hear them. Then repeat them again following the intonation shift illustrated by the model.

A. 1. TEACHER: Es difícil la filosofía. *Repita.*

STUDENT: **Es difícil la filosofía.**
TEACHER: *Cambie.*

STUDENT: **Es difícil la filosofía.**

  2. Es feroz el tránsito.
  3. Es importante la Cuaresma.
  4. Es ridículo el discurso.
  5. Es necesario cumplir.
  6. Es anticuada la casa.
  7. Es bueno sugerir.
  8. Es imposible terminar.

B. 1. Sin falta se lo traigo.
  2. ¡Cuánto lo siento!
  3. De veras lo digo.
  4. A menudo los compara.
  5. Inmediatamente se lo presto.
  6. Seguí sus órdenes.

C. 1. Por eso lo digo.
  2. Por eso lo menciono.
  3. Por eso lo explico.
  4. Por eso lo exagero.

● DISCUSSION

The fact noted in connection with questions (Unit 3 §9) is true to some extent of most other sentences in Spanish: emphasis is achieved both by stressing the item that is the center of attention and by shifting it to the end.

English does this too, to some extent: *There came a blinding **flash*** is more vivid and forceful than *A blinding **flash** came.* But English is hampered by the fact that word order must serve another purpose at the same time, that of showing grammatical relationships. If we were to say *Called Mrs. Méndez* it would sound as if *Mrs. Méndez* were the object rather than the subject of the verb; so we are not free to put *Méndez* at the end in order to make the sentence more climactic. In Spanish, the presence or absence of the personal **a** tells us whether **la señora Méndez** is object or subject, and sentence order is free to arrange itself according to climax and anticlimax. Normally it is the climactic order that is preferred, and the difference between Spanish and English shows up most sharply in brief sentences where in English the subject is stressed and precedes the verb but in Spanish the subject is stressed and follows the verb. If Spanish had the same order as English in a sentence like *The **telephone** rang,* the hearer would feel like asking "What else can a telephone do?" or "What else would one expect to be ringing except the telephone?"

Where something other than the subject is the *x'*, Spanish and English usually agree in word order. In example *A*5 *running* is the center of attention, and gets major stress and end position in both languages. Such sentences are in the majority.

The speaker may, however, not *want* a climactic order. In place of *How that woman **talks!*** we might prefer to say *What a **talker** that woman is!* or in place of *They talk about nothing but **that*** to say *It's only **that** that they talk about.* Notice that to accomplish this in English we have to change the words. In Spanish we merely change their position: **Sólo de *eso* se habla** instead of **Sólo se habla de *eso*.**

Though less so than in English, word order in Spanish is restricted in certain ways. The sentence **Cómo habla esa señora** would not be normal with the subject **esa señora** between **Cómo** and **habla,** since interrogative words (Unit 3 §9) are normally followed by the verb.

88 The position of adjectives with *qué*

EXAMPLES A. 1. ¡Qué **buen** café es éste!
      2. ¡Qué **mala** cara trae!

B. 1. ¡Qué cosa más **ridícula!** *What a ridiculous thing!* (*What thing more ridiculous!*)
  2. ¡Qué tío tan **bueno** es usted! *What a good uncle you are!* (*What uncle so good you are!*)

$$\boxed{\textbf{qué} \quad + \quad \begin{cases} \text{adjective} + \text{noun} \\ \text{noun} + \textbf{más (tan)} + \text{adjective} \end{cases}}$$

Exclamations containing **qué** and an adjective may take either of the above forms.

● REPLACEMENT DRILL

A. 1. **¡Qué buen café es éste!**
   2. _____ leche _____
   3. _____ magnífica _____
   4. _____ pollo _____
   5. _____ bonito _____
   6. _____ rosbif _____
   7. _____ mal _____
   8. _____ mantequilla _____
   9. _____ buena _____
 10. _____ papas _____

B. 1. **¡Qué mala cara trae!**
   2. _____ tiene
   3. _____ bonita _____
   4. _____ pelo _____
   5. _____ largo _____
   6. _____ pies _____
   7. _____ grandes _____
   8. _____ manos _____
   9. _____ fuertes _____
 10. _____ cuerpo _____
 11. _____ perfecto _____
 12. _____ vida _____
 13. _____ inútil _____
 14. _____ educación _____
 15. _____ mala _____
 16. _____ costumbre _____

C. 1. **¡Qué cosa más ridícula!**
   2. _____ costumbre _____
   3. _____ anticuada
   4. _____ idea _____
   5. _____ típica
   6. _____ plato _____
   7. _____ sencillo
   8. _____ gente _____
   9. _____ moderna
 10. _____ señor _____
 11. _____ importante
 12. _____ persona _____
 13. _____ fantástica
 14. _____ invitación _____
 15. _____ aburrida
 16. _____ cuestión _____
 17. _____ difícil
 18. _____ caso _____

D. 1. **¡Qué tío tan bueno es usted!**
   2. _____ padre _____
   3. _____ malo _____
   4. _____ profesor _____
   5. _____ amable _____
   6. _____ abogado _____
   7. _____ bruto _____
   8. _____ médico _____
   9. _____ anticuado _____
 10. _____ administrador _____
 11. _____ serio _____
 12. _____ empleado _____
 13. _____ fino _____
 14. _____ abuelo _____
 15. _____ respetable _____
 16. _____ hombre _____
 17. _____ moderno _____
 18. _____ técnico _____

E. 1. **¡Qué carrera tan fenomenal!**
   2. _____ cantidad _____
   3. _____ astronómica
   4. _____ número _____
   5. _____ horrible
   6. _____ escándalo _____
   7. _____ grande
   8. _____ persona _____
   9. _____ equivocada
 10. _____ jefe _____
 11. _____ malo
 12. _____ tránsito _____
 13. _____ diferente

F. 1. **¡Qué cosa más ridícula!**
   2. _____ tremenda
   3. _____ vida _____
   4. _____ agitada
   5. _____ juego _____
   6. _____ complicado
   7. _____ materia _____
   8. _____ exacta
   9. _____ sistema _____
 10. _____ diferente

89   Singular for "one each"

PLURAL OF POSSESSOR			SINGULAR OF THING POSSESSED
A	todos les	**duele**	la cabeza y la garganta
	Nos ponemos		la corbata[1]
Lo	tuvieron	**en**	la mano derecha[2]

When the speaker brings together (1) more than one possessor with (2) a single thing possessed by each one, normally the thing appears in the singular.

PLURAL OF POSSESSOR	PLURAL OF THING POSSESSED
Levantaron	**las manos**[3]

If the speaker relates the possessors to more than one thing apiece, the thing appears in the plural.

● TRANSLATION DRILL

A. 1. TEACHER: All the students have cars.
    STUDENT: **Todos los alumnos tienen coche.**
  2. All the men have blue suits.
  3. All the nurses have thermometers.
  4. All the barbers have clippers.

B. 1. The three boys have appointments with the doctor tomorrow.
  2. Please (be so kind as to) raise your left hands.
  3. Put on your shirts and ties.

90   Idioms with *tener* and *dar*

EXAMPLES

A. 1. **Tiene razón** ella. Hay que cumplir con la Iglesia.
  2. **Tienes razón.** Para café bueno no hay como este lugar.
  3. Otra cosa que **tengo ganas** de ver es una buena corrida de toros. (*Another thing that I have desires of seeing.*)
  4. **Tengo hambre;** voy a ir a comer algo.

B. 1. **Tengo muchas ganas** de ir.
  2. **Tengo un hambre feroz.**
  3. —¿**Qué edad tiene** ella? (*What age does she have?*)
    —Debe **tener unos veintiún años.**
  4. ¡Ella **tiene tanta suerte!** *She's so lucky!*

to be right	**tener razón**
to be eager	**tener ganas**
to be hungry	**tener hambre**
to be ten years old	**tener diez años**
How old are you?	{ **¿Cuántos años tienes?** { **¿Qué edad tienes?**

The English equivalents of the **tener** idioms usually contain the verb *to be*.

---

[1] *We put on our ties.*   [2] *They held it in their right hands.*   [3] *They raised (both) their hands.*

FORM OF *be*	ADVERB MODIFYING THE ADJECTIVE	ADJECTIVE
I am	very	eager
I am	ferociously	hungry

FORM OF *tener*	ADJECTIVES MODIFYING THE NOUN	NOUN	
Tengo	muchas	ganas	
Tengo	un	hambre	feroz

Where the adjectives on the English side are modified by adverbs, the nouns on the Spanish side are modified by adjectives.

● PERSON-NUMBER SUBSTITUTION DRILL

1. *Ella* tiene razón en eso.
   (usted, nosotros, tú, ustedes, yo, ellos, él)
2. *Yo* tengo ganas de ver una buena corrida de toros.
   (nosotros, ella, ellos, ustedes, usted, tú, él)
3. Tenemos unas ganas tremendas de ir.
   (él, yo, ellas, ustedes, tú, usted, ellos)
4. Tengo muchísima hambre.
   (ella, nosotros, ellos, tú, ustedes, usted)
5. *Ella* tiene unos veintiún años.
   (tú, él, ustedes, ella, usted, ellos, Susana)

● TRANSLATION DRILL

1. TEACHER: She's right.
   STUDENT: **Ella tiene razón.**
   TEACHER: She's very right.
   STUDENT: **Ella tiene mucha razón.**
2. I'm eager to go.
   I'm very eager to go.
3. We're hungry.
   We're very hungry.
4. She's twenty years old.
   She's approximately twenty years old.
5. I'm hungry.
   I'm so hungry.
6. She's eager.
   She's so eager.
7. He's hungry.
   He's ferociously hungry.

EXAMPLES

A. 1. **Tenga cuidado** de no romper nada.
   2. Tú **tienes** más **suerte** que yo. *You're luckier than I am.*

B. 1. No **tenga cuidado,** doña Beatriz.
   2. No, hombre, con la **suerte** que **tengo** yo . . .
   3. ¿Quién **tiene** la **culpa?** *Whose fault is it? (Who is to blame?)*
   4. **Tenga** la **bondad** de sentarse.

to be careful, to worry	**tener cuidado**
to be lucky, to have luck	**tener suerte**
It's my fault	**Yo tengo la culpa**

Not all **tener** idioms are matched by *to be* expressions in English.

● TRANSLATION DRILL

A. 1. Be careful not to break anything.
   2. I'm always careful not to break anything.
   3. We're always careful not to break anything.

B. 1. You're never very lucky.
   2. We're never very lucky.
   3. I'm never very lucky.

C. 1. Don't worry, Doña Beatriz.
   2. Don't worry, ladies.
   3. Don't worry, sir.
   4. Don't worry, gentlemen.
   5. Don't worry, Paquito.

D. 1. No, sir, with my luck . . .
   2. No, sir, with our luck . . .
   3. No, sir, with his luck . . .
   4. No, sir, with their luck . . .

E. 1. It's his fault.
   2. It's their fault.
   3. It's our fault.
   4. It's your fault.

F. 1. Please sit down, sir.
   2. Please sit down, gentlemen.
   3. Please sit down, ma'am.
   4. Please sit down, ladies.

EXAMPLES

1. Ese rosbif **da hambre** a toda la familia.   *That roast beef makes the whole family hungry.*
2. Los exámenes me **dan ganas** de quedarme en casa.   *Exams make me feel like staying home.*
3. El ser fuerte no te **da razón**.   *Being strong doesn't make you right.*

FORM OF *make*	OBJECT	ADJEC-TIVE
It makes	the family	hungry
It makes	you	right

INDIRECT OBJECT	FORM OF **dar**	NOUN	
	Da	hambre	a la familia
Te	da	razón	

Most of the nouns used with **tener** may also follow **dar** with the meaning *make.*

● ITEM SUBSTITUTION DRILL

1. Ese *rosbif* le da hambre a toda la familia.
   (frijoles, carne, verduras, pan)
2. Estos *exámenes* me dan ganas de quedarme en casa.
   (examen, manifestaciones, huelga, discursos)

3. El *ser moderno* no te da razón.
   (ser pobre, estar aburrido, ser extranjero)

● TRANSLATION DRILL

1. TEACHER: I'm hungry.
   STUDENT: **Tengo hambre.**
   TEACHER: It makes me hungry.
   STUDENT: **Me da hambre.**
2. He's right.
   It makes him right.

3. We're very eager.
   It makes us very eager.
4. I'm very lucky.
   That makes me very lucky.
5. It's not my fault.
   That doesn't make it my fault.

● DISCUSSION

In a number of expressions where English has *to be* plus an adjective, Spanish has **tener** plus a noun. English, too, often uses its verb *have* in ways that compare with *be: He has all the luck* is similar to *He is always lucky,* and *Have courage* is like *Be brave;* the problem is one of remembering the particular expressions where English uses one form and Spanish the other.[1] An additional problem is the modifiers: in English they are adverbs (*I am **very** hungry*); in Spanish they are adjectives (**Tengo *mucha* hambre,** literally *I have **much** hunger*).

---

[1] Included are those of the examples, plus the Spanish equivalents of *to be warm, cold, in a hurry, ashamed, afraid, thirsty, successful, sleepy,* and a very few others. Elsewhere, English *be* matches Spanish **ser-estar:** *He is sick* is matched with **Está enfermo,** not with a literal equivalent of *He has sickness.*

Tener cuidado normally means *to be careful;* i.e., to have care in the sense of taking pains. **No tener cuidado** means *to be carefree;* i.e., not to have cares or worries, hence *not to worry.*

Many of the same nouns that serve as objects of **tener** are also found with **dar;** here the person *acquires* the quality or state referred to. **Tengo hambre** (*I have hunger, I'm hungry*) refers to being in the condition or having it; **Me da hambre** (*It gives me hunger, It makes me hungry*) refers to getting that way.

91 *Hacer* in expressions of time

EXAMPLES

A. 1. **Hace** como **cuatro años que vive** allá. (**Vive** allá **hace** como **cuatro años.**)
  2. Dígame **cuánto tiempo hace que se siente** así.

B. 1. Llegó **hace una hora.** (**Hace una hora que** llegó.) *He arrived an hour ago.* (*It's been an hour since he arrived.*)
  2. Ana Guadalupe Martínez, la que trabajó aquí **hace dos años.**

FORM OF *have*	−ed FORM OF VERB		PERIOD OF TIME
She has	lived	there	four years

hace	PERIOD OF TIME	**que**	PRESENT TENSE OF VERB	
Hace	**cuatro años**	**que**	**vive**	**allá**

To express the time during which something has been going on (*y has been going on for x time*), Spanish uses the equivalent of *It makes x time that y goes on.*

x time	*ago*

hace	*x* time

For the meaning *ago,* Spanish uses the equivalent of *it makes:* e.g., *two years ago = it makes two years* **hace dos años.**

● CONSTRUCTION SUBSTITUTION DRILL

INSTRUCTIONS: Repeat the following sentences just as you hear them. Then repeat them again, reorganizing the order of the elements of the sentence in the pattern of the model given.

A. 1. TEACHER: Vive allá hace cuatro años. *Repita.*
    STUDENT: **Vive allá hace cuatro años.**
    TEACHER: *Cambie.*
    STUDENT: **Hace cuatro años que vive allá.**
  2. Está aquí hace dos semanas.
  3. Está en México hace seis meses.
  4. Vive en Argentina hace unos años.
  5. Trabaja en la planta hace unos días.
  6. Existe ese problema hace años.
  7. Enseña castellano hace tiempo.
  8. Espero en esta esquina hace una hora.
  9. Me siento así hace como tres días.
  10. Está enferma hace una semana.

B. 1. Hace tres años que Guadalupe trabajó aquí.
    Hace tres años que Guadalupe trabajó aquí.
    Guadalupe trabajó aquí hace tres años.
  2. Hace una hora que Lorenzo llegó.
  3. Hace un año que volví de Colombia.
  4. Hace mucho tiempo que entró en el país.
  5. Hace dos meses que celebré mi aniversario.
  6. Hace ocho días que me prometió el puesto.
  7. Hace quince días que encontré un trabajo.
  8. Hace años que hubo una revolución.

A. 1. I've been here for a week.
    Hace una semana que estoy aquí.
    (Estoy aquí hace una semana.)
    2. We've been here for two months.
    3. They've been here for eight days.
    4. He's lived here for ten years.
    5. You've lived here for years.
    6. She's lived here for five years.
    7. I've lived here for a few days.

B. 1. I arrived a week ago.
    Llegué hace una semana.
    (Hace una semana que llegué.)
    2. They arrived two days ago.
    3. She arrived ten minutes ago.
    4. He came half an hour ago.
    5. We came a long time ago.
    6. You entered a few minutes ago.
    7. I went by for him an hour ago.

● DISCUSSION

Hacer is found in two different contexts referring to time.   The first has to do with how long something that is now going on has been going on.   Where English looks at the past duration and says *She **has lived** there four years,* Spanish looks at the present continuation and says **Hace cuatro años que *vive* allá,** literally *It makes four years that she **lives** there,* with the verb in the present.   The second context is with the meaning *ago: He arrived an hour ago* **Llegó hace una hora,** literally *He arrived it makes an hour.* (While the word order as given in the examples is slightly more usual, the position of **hacer** can be reversed in both contexts: **Vive allá hace cuatro años** and **Hace una hora que llegó.**   Note that **que** is used only when the **hacer** phrase comes first.)

● COMBINED PATTERN REPLACEMENT DRILL

A.

1. **¿Esa revista?   No hay una mejor.**
2. _____ ninguna __
3. ___ periódico _____
4. _____ hubo _____
5. _____ nunca _____
6. _____ otro _____
7. _____ más ridículo
8. ___ titulares _____
9. _____ jamás _____
10. ___ pretexto _____
11. _____ no _____
12. _____ más inocente
13. _____ uno _____
14. _____ hay _____
15. ___ persona _____
16. _____ más enredada
17. _____ otra _____
18. ___ ministerio _____
19. _____ apenas _____
20. _____ tan __
21. _____ independiente

B.

1. **¡Cuánto me alegro de verlos en esta casa!**
2. _____ nos _____
3. _____ verla _____
4. _____ la _____
5. _____ campo
6. _____ alegran _____
7. _____ verlo _____
8. _____ ciudad
9. _____ me _____
10. Tanto _____
11. _____ esta _____
12. _____ encontrar _____
13. _____ lugar
14. _____ estos ___
15. _____ alegramos _____
16. Cuánto _____
17. _____ encontrarlos _____
18. _____ barrio
19. _____ organizar _____
20. _____ me _____
21. _____ planta
22. _____ nos _____
23. _____ estas ___

● PATTERNED RESPONSE REVIEW DRILL

The **usted** command forms.

A. 1. TEACHER: ¿Llego mañana?
        STUDENT: **No, no llegue.**
    2. ¿Enseño mañana?
    3. ¿Llamo mañana?
    4. ¿Estudio mañana?
    5. ¿Pago mañana?
    6. ¿Trabajo mañana?
    7. ¿Corro mañana?

8. ¿Discuto mañana?
9. ¿Barro mañana?
10. ¿Escribo mañana?
11. ¿Salgo mañana?
12. ¿Sigo mañana?
13. ¿Vuelvo mañana?
14. ¿Vengo mañana?

B. 1. ¿La apago?
   No, no la apague.
2. ¿La arreglo?
3. ¿Las cambio?
4. ¿Lo celebro?
5. ¿Los invito?
6. ¿Los llevo?
7. ¿Los mando?
8. ¿Lo paso?
9. ¿La abro?

10. ¿La barro?
11. ¿Lo discuto?
12. ¿Lo prometo?
13. ¿Los rompo?
14. ¿Los sacudo?

C. 1. ¿Le doy el termómetro?
   No, no me lo dé.
2. ¿Le presto la maquinilla?
3. ¿Le llevo el café?
4. ¿Le mando la comida?
5. ¿Le abro la puerta?
6. ¿Le digo la verdad?
7. ¿Le ofrezco pan?
8. ¿Le prometo la oportunidad?
9. ¿Le traigo el coche?
10. ¿Le vendo la casa?

R E A D I N G

Orden de las palabras

E. *Estudiante*   P. *Profesor*   S. *Segundo estudiante*
T. *Tercer estudiante*

E. Señor profesor, usted nos dijo ayer algo sobre el orden de las palabras. A mi parecer, los libros de gramática nos enseñan muy poco acerca de esto, y yo lo encuentro algo enredado.

P. Usted tiene razón, y voy a repetir algunas de mis observaciones de ayer, usando ejemplos nuevos. Vamos a empezar con frases sencillas, o independientes. Por ejemplo, en una afirmación el orden común es sujeto-verbo-complemento, ¿no es verdad? Si le pregunto a usted: "¿Qué hizo la señora Méndez?", ¿qué me responde?

E. Pues, digo: "La señora Méndez hizo tal cosa."

P. Muy bien: La señora Méndez llamó, o habló, o rifó un abrigo, o volvió a llamar, etc. Lo importante en estos casos es lo que *hizo* la señora Méndez, en contestación a la pregunta "¿Qué hizo?" Pero si le pregunto: "¿Quién llamó?", ¿qué me contesta?

E. "Llamó la señora Méndez."

P. Exactamente. Es decir, que la información nueva que se busca se halla al final[1] de la frase, ¿cierto? Miren ustedes la primera frase del diálogo. Lo fundamental es la señora Méndez, y no la acción de llamar... Ahora... Miren la segunda. Una vez más, lo importante es que *la señora Méndez,* concretamente *esa señora,* habla mucho... ¿Quién puede mostrarme otros ejemplos en el diálogo?

S. La secretaria, en su tercer discurso, dice: "Por fin llegó el correo." La cosa más importante es *el correo,* y no la llegada.

P. Bien. ¿Otros ejemplos?

T. Hacia el final del diálogo la secretaria dice: "Tiene razón ella." Esto quiere decir que es la esposa la que tiene razón, y no el jefe, ¿no es así?

P. ¿Comprenden todos?

---

[1] *end* (e.g., of something written)

Los estudiantes hispanos y sus actividades políticas

Leemos a menudo en la prensa referencias a las actividades políticas de los estudiantes de las universidades en los países hispanos. Casi siempre la oposición más decidida a los regímenes de tiranía es capitaneada[1] por los estudiantes. De las filas de los grupos estudiantiles salen grandes agitadores. Los estudiantes con frecuencia pagan con su libertad y hasta con su vida el derecho de protesta contra los dictadores. Así que[2] resulta tan difícil para esos estudiantes el comprender[3] la indiferencia política de sus compañeros en las universidades norteamericanas, aun durante las campañas electorales, como para éstos el entender[3] la pasión por la política de los estudiantes hispánicos.

La juventud es naturalmente idealista y generosa, y ¿qué causa más digna de despertar los anhelos más elevados que la mejora de la Patria y sus destinos? Y la política señala estos destinos. En los Estados Unidos, la filiación política se hereda muchas veces de la familia, o está tradicionalmente vinculada con el estado donde uno vive. Un partido determinado no puede alterar radicalmente la vida de la nación. Pero en países no tan sólidamente estratificados, es muy distinto. Así como el estudiante norteamericano y el ciudadano en general tienen la impresión de que no pueden influir decisivamente en los destinos de su país, el estudiante de los países hispanos está convencido de que el futuro está en sus propias manos y que puede cambiarlo. La educación es para él un privilegio que de momento, por una serie de circunstancias, está negado a la mayoría. Por lo tanto, como sólo unos pocos disfrutan de ella, el que pertenece a esta minoría privilegiada se siente particularmente responsable ante su conciencia y la sociedad.

Naturalmente al estudiante hispano también le interesan los deportes, las diversiones en general, las citas[4] y las fiestas. También le interesan las actividades literarias y artísticas. Pero estos intereses y aficiones no son específicamente estudiantiles. Los comparte con la juventud en general. No le distinguen como estudiante sino como joven. Pero, como estudiante, sabe que puede ser la voz de su generación. Voz articulada, porque su misión es aprender a pensar y expresarse. Voz organizada, porque en sus clases se halla en contacto constante con otros que comparten los mismos ideales y aspiraciones. El miembro activo de un partido político es un militante, según la terminología aceptada. Es un convencido,[5] uno que está seguro de la verdad y uno que está comprometido emocional e intelectualmente.[6]

Esta actitud de un sector importante de la juventud que no está todavía madura, ni intelectual ni emocionalmente, y que carece de experiencia, lleva naturalmente tras sí muchos peligros. Muchas veces políticos profesionales sin escrúpulos explotan el idealismo y el entusiasmo de los jóvenes universitarios para lanzarlos al combate. También es verdad que muy a menudo es fácil para los políticos asegurarse del apoyo leal y generoso de una juventud exaltada por el entusiasmo patriótico para defender un programa de oposición. Lógicamente abundan los ejemplos de cómo los desengaños inevitables de la realidad y las lecciones de la política concreta vuelven prematuramente cínicos a algunos jóvenes. Pero lo innegable[7] es que en cada generación de estudiantes surge un puñado de idealistas que dan esperanzas y sirven de ejemplo a la generación más madura, tentada a resignarse y a conformarse con fatalismo suicida con la corrupción y la opresión.

---

[1] **capitaneada** *led*   [2] **Así que** *Thus*
[3] **el comprender** *to comprehend;* **el entender** *to understand* (See Unit 16, Cultural Note 1.)
[4] **citas** *dates* (i.e., appointments, not "persons" as in the American sense)
[5] **un convencido** *a zealot, a person with convictions*
[6] **emocional e intelectualmente.** *—mente* is understood with both **emocional** and **intelectual**. This is treated in Unit 16 §96.
[7] **lo innegable** *the undeniable fact*

Al estudiante norteamericano parece que le preocupa principalmente el provecho que va a sacar de sus estudios, económica y socialmente. Sabe que un diploma académico, casi automáticamente, le abre las puertas al mundo económico y social de sus aspiraciones. En la universidad el estudiante quiere ante todo ajustarse, quiere hacer los contactos útiles para el futuro. También quiere disfrutar de la vida y de su juventud antes de tomar mayores responsabilidades mientras trabaja para obtener un diploma.

El estudiante hispano se prepara para una sociedad más competitiva. Es verdad que el solo hecho de ser estudiante le hace miembro de una clase privilegiada. Pero sabe que las oportunidades son limitadas y que después de la graduación va a luchar para abrirse paso. Entre el sueño y la realidad hay un gran trecho. Muchas veces la competencia va a ser feroz. Si no tiene el futuro asegurado por sus padres—caso que puede ser menos frecuente en el futuro—sabe que tiene que luchar a brazo partido, tal vez por largo tiempo. Sabe que por lo tanto tiene que equiparse. Sabe que como maestro, como médico, como ingeniero, no sólo van a considerarlo como un especialista que ocupa un puesto determinado en el organismo social, sino que como persona educada está llamado a ejercer una función de guía. Las masas que no gozan del privilegio de la educación miran siempre a la persona de carrera como aquel que, sabiendo más, ha de ir adelante para mostrarles el camino y dar ejemplo. El estudiante hispano durante su carrera ya se ensaya para esta función dirigente, porque si no la cumple, se hunde.

El estudiante norteamericano gasta gran parte de su tiempo libre en actividades que no están relacionadas ni con sus estudios académicos ni con su futura responsabilidad social. Se forma, se prepara como individuo para tener éxito y lograr sus aspiraciones. Hasta una parte de sus estudios en la escuela superior y en la universidad puede consistir en asignaturas extraacadémicas en que aprende habilidades o conocimientos que puede fácilmente adquirir por su cuenta o practicar en sus horas libres. También está desorientado. La desorientación del estudiante hispano se produce más bien del lado de la sociedad y de la nación. Se siente ciudadano con responsabilidades particulares y toma ya posiciones en la arena política, porque en ella se deciden los destinos de su país en los que[8] siente que está inescapablemente llamado a participar. Se cree investido de una misión salvadora, se considera responsable del futuro de su patria y a veces, quijotescamente,[9] de toda la humanidad.

[8] **los que** *which,* referring to **destinos.**
[9] **quijotescamente** *quixotically* (*i.e.,* like Don Quixote, determined to right the wrongs of the world)

● CUESTIONARIO

1. ¿Cómo se paga con frecuencia el derecho de protesta contra los dictadores?
2. ¿Cuál es la actitud del estudiante norteamericano sobre la política?
3. ¿Qué intereses y aficiones comparte el estudiante hispanoamericano con la juventud en general?
4. Mencione algunos intereses del estudiante hispano.
5. ¿Qué peligros puede llevar tras sí esta actitud del estudiante hispano sobre la política?
6. ¿Qué influencia tienen los jóvenes idealistas en las generaciones más maduras?
7. ¿Qué diferencia hay entre la actitud del estudiante norteamericano y la del estudiante hispano respecto a los fines de la educación universitaria?
8. ¿A quiénes miran las masas que no gozan del privilegio de la educación?
9. ¿Cómo gasta gran parte de su tiempo libre el estudiante norteamericano?
10. ¿A qué se debe la desorientación del estudiante hispano?

● SUGGESTED READINGS

Beals, Carleton, *Lands of the Dawning Morrow,* Bobbs-Merrill, Indianapolis, New York, 1948: Ch. 10, "The March of Books"; Ch. 13, "Democratic Profiles."

Green, Philip Leonard, *Our Latin American Neighbors,* Hastings House, New York, 1941: Ch. 12, "Leaders in the Making"; Ch. 13, "How Latin Americans Think."

Moehlman, Arthur Henry, and Joseph S. Roucek, *Comparative Education,* Dryden Press, New York, 1951: Ch. 3, "Education in Latin America"; Ch. 4, "Education in Mexico."

Romanell, Patrick, *Making of the Mexican Mind,* University of Nebraska Press, Lincoln, 1952: Ch. 1, "A Character Sketch of the Two Americas."

16

Problems of Growing Up

P. *Pedrito*   M. *Mom*   D. *Dad*

P. Pass me the meat, Mom.

M. Just a minute, Pedrito; your father hasn't been served.

D. Where's María Elena?

M. She ate early and went to the movies with Luis Alberto.

D. Again? They've already been twice this week. Who's with them?

M. I let them go alone since all of us here have already seen that picture.

* * *

D. I don't know, Alicia, but it seems to me that girls shouldn't be allowed to go out alone at night, especially to the movies.

Problemas del crecer (1)

P. *Pedrito*   M. *Mamá*   PA. *Papá*

P. Pásame la carne, mamá.

M. Un momentito, Pedrito, tu papá no se ha servido.

PA. ¿Y dónde está María Elena?

M. Comió temprano y se fue al cine con Luis Alberto.

PA. ¿Otra vez? Ya han ido dos veces esta semana. ¿Con quién andan?

M. Los dejé ir solos porque ya aquí todos hemos visto esa película.

* * *

PA. No sé, Alicia, pero me parece que las muchachas no deben salir solas de noche, y menos al cine.

M. Don't worry. They'll be back early. Anyway, Luis Alberto is a fine boy and comes from a fine family.

D. I know, it's not that. It's just that I've never gone along with these modern customs.

M. But, Jorge, it's ridiculous nowadays for girls to have to take a chaperon everywhere.

D. Call it ridiculous or anything you like, but in my day . . .

M. Yes, yes, yes, I know . . . in your day. But times change and customs change. Only you don't change.

* * *

D. But remember when you and I were going together, we weren't allowed to go out alone even as far as the front door.

M. Yes, and how you fumed.

D. That has nothing to do with it. Maybe you don't remember that you were a good deal older then than María Elena.

M. All right, all right, let's not get on [touch] that subject, we've already discussed it many times.

P. Mommy, will you pass me a little bit of meat, please?

M. No te preocupes, vuelven temprano. Además, Luis Alberto es un buen muchacho y de muy buena familia (2).

PA. Ya lo sé (3), no es eso; es que yo nunca he estado de acuerdo con estas costumbres modernas.

M. Pero Jorge, hoy día es ridículo que las muchachas tengan que llevar chaperón a todas partes.

PA. Puede ser ridículo o lo que tú quieras, pero en mis tiempos . . .

M. Sí, sí, sí, ya lo sé . . . en tus tiempos. Pero los tiempos cambian y las costumbres también cambian. Sólo tú no has cambiado.

* * *

PA. Pero acuérdate que cuando tú y yo éramos novios, no nos dejaban salir solos ni a la puerta.

M. Sí . . . y cómo rabiabas.

PA. Eso no tiene nada que ver. Tal vez ya no recuerdes que entonces tú eras bastante mayor que María Elena.

M. Bueno, bueno, no toquemos ese tema; ya lo hemos discutido muchas veces (4).

P. Mamacita . . . ¿me pasas un poquito de carne, por favor?

Cultural Notes

(1) The article accompanies the infinitive here as it accompanies any other noun to emphasize "all-of-something": *Problems of Growing-up-in-General* (see Unit 13 §75). Remember that the infinitive is a verbal noun (Unit 7 §33).

(2) The reference to Luis Alberto's family is an instance of the prevalent social stratification and the tendency among Spaniards and Latin Americans to regard family background as an important factor in the evaluation of people.

(3) The object pronoun **lo,** referring to an idea expressed in a preceding clause, is often used after such verbs as **saber, decir, preguntar,** and **creer.** Sometimes **lo** may be rendered by English *it* or *so* (*He's sick but he doesn't look it, If you want them say so*), but often there is no equivalent.

(4) Except for the respect she receives in her home and as a mother, the Spanish-American woman generally remains in the background. Though old customs are giving way, the typical family is still patriarchal; but the wife often gets her way indirectly.

● WRITING EXERCISE

The written representation of /b/ by **b** or **v.** INSTRUCTIONS: Write the following lists of words from dictation, remembering that those in the first column are written with **b,** those in the second column with **v.**

	A.		B.		C.
basta	vasta	cabo	cavo	embastar	envasar
baso	vaso	nabo	nave	combinar	convidar
baca	vaca	toba	tova	embestir	investir
Baco	vaco	sabia	savia	embicar	enviar
bello	vello	libar	livor	combatir	convertir
biga	viga	gabán	gavilán	imberbe	inverne
bino	vino	cibal	civil	Amberes	anverso
bagar	vagar	cabal	cavar		
bocal	vocal	rebotar	revotar		
botar	votar	pábilo	pávido		
bocear	vocear	obeso	overo		
balaca	valaca	dibujo	divulgo		

The letters **b** and **v** represent both the stop and fricative variants of /b/ in modern Spanish. The distinction, which is merely orthographic, is generally due to the etymology of the word (e.g., **beber** derives from Latin *bibere,* and **vivir** from Latin *vivere*).

Up to the sixteenth century, **b** and **v** indicated two different sounds for many writers, but this distinction was later lost.

Note that the pairs of words in column *A* are pronounced alike. In *B* the fricative [ƀ] is spelled **b** and **v,** and in *C* the groups **mb** and **nv** are pronounced alike.

92   The *–do* form as an adjective

EXAMPLES

A. 1. Es un trabajo muy **complicado.**
    2. Esas son ideas **anticuadas.**
    3. Claro que podemos; **encantados.**

B. 1. Fue un árbol **caído.**[1] *It was a fallen tree.*
    2. ¿Cuál es la religión **preferida?** *Which is the preferred religion (the religion preferred)?*
    3. Tiene un patio **cubierto.** *It has a covered patio.*

The –do form of regular verbs

hablar: habl– –ado	comer: com– vivir: viv– } –ido

Most verbs are regular in the **–do** form.

Verbs irregular in the –do form

escribir	escrito	romper	roto
abrir	abierto	ver	visto
cubrir	cubierto	poner	puesto
morir	muerto	suponer	supuesto
volver	vuelto	hacer	hecho
envolver	envuelto	decir	dicho
disolver	disuelto		

These are the verbs thus far encountered in the dialogs which have irregular **–do** forms.

---

[1] The same verbs have the accent mark on **–ido** that have it on **–iste** and **–imos.** See Unit 6 §26, footnote 1.

a broken arrow	una flecha rota
the leader chosen	el líder escogido
the work done	el trabajo hecho
my lost pills	mis pastillas perdidas

Used as an adjective, the –**do** form agrees with the noun like any other adjective. It follows the noun almost without exception, regardless of the position in English.

● ITEM SUBSTITUTION DRILL

1. Tiene un *sistema* muy complicado.
   (receta, corazón, educación, empleo, filosofía)
2. Esas son *ideas* anticuadas.
   (asuntos, revistas, trajes, capillas, techos)
3. Esto fue el *mes* pasado.
   (semana, año, vez, lunes, cuaresma)
4. ¡Qué *clase* más aburrida!
   (correo, elecciones, acontecimientos, revolución, grupo, persona, barrios)

5. ¡Qué *acuerdo* tan enredado!
   (situación, titulares, secretarias, partido, boda, periódicos, clases)
6. Don Pepe tiene unos *toros* importados.
   (vacas, cerdo, oveja, trajes, camisas, abrigo, corbata)
7. Mire. Aquí hay una *flecha* rota.
   (termómetro, tazas, zapatos, camisa, juguete, herramientas, discos)[1]
8. Es un *líder* escogido.
   (profesora, pieles, vacas, cueros, ovejas)

EXAMPLES

A. 1. **Los invitados** son una pareja extranjera.
   2. ¿Cuál puerta, **la abierta** o **la cerrada**? *Which door, the open one or the closed one?*

B. 1. **Lo conseguido** fue bastante poco. *What was accomplished was mighty little.*
   2. No voy a recibir ni un centavo de **lo pagado.** *I'm not going to get even a cent of what was paid.*

definite article + –**do** form
The –**do** form may be nominalized like any other adjective. With **lo,** the English equivalent is usually *what was (is, has been)* –*ed.*

● CONSTRUCTION SUBSTITUTION DRILL

INSTRUCTIONS: Repeat the following sentences just as you hear them. Then repeat them again, omitting the noun indicated, thus nominalizing the accompanying –**do** form.

A. 1. TEACHER: Los señores invitados están aquí. *Repita.*
   STUDENT: **Los señores invitados están aquí.**
   TEACHER: *Cambie.*
   STUDENT: **Los invitados están aquí.**
   2. Aquí están las *lentejas* importadas.
   3. Los *estudiantes* heridos se defendieron.
   4. Las *novias* preocupadas no duermen bien.
   5. Los *hombres* casados ya la pagarán.

B. 1. El *líder* preferido llegó.
   2. Estos son los *nombres* mencionados.
   3. El *viaje* organizado nos gustó más.
   4. La *señorita* respetada es la profesora.
   5. El *señor* equivocado es el dentista.
   6. La *señora* enojada es la cuñada.

---

[1] With shoes, **roto** means *worn, worn out;* with other articles of clothing, *torn.*

A. 1. What's sacred is important.
   Lo sagrado es importante.
   2. What's united is strong.
   3. What's written is scarce.
   4. What's sold isn't worthwhile.
   5. What's promised isn't worthwhile.

B. 1. This is what's mixed up.
   Esto es lo enredado.
   2. This is what's bought.
   3. This is what's declared.
   4. This is what's produced.
   5. This is what's arranged.

● DISCUSSION

The **–do** form, traditionally called the "past participle," parallels in almost all respects the related *–ed* form in English:

1. As an adjective: *imagined earnings* **ganancias imaginadas;** *written documents* **documentos escritos.**

2. As a "passive voice" (explained in the next section): *The city was attacked* **La ciudad fue atacada.**

3. As part of the constructions termed "perfect tenses" (§94 below): *They have come* **Han venido.**

As an adjective the **–do** form readily nominalizes. In addition, quite a number of words that now are nouns in their own right have come from it; among those encountered thus far in the dialogs are **entrada** (from **entrar**), **ganado** (from **ganar**),[1] **empleado** (from **emplear** *to employ:* the English *–ee* suffix corresponds to Spanish **–do**), **helados** (from **helar** *to freeze*), and **visto bueno** (from **ver** *to see,* "seen and approved").

93 The *–do* form with *estar* and *ser*

EXAMPLES

A. 1. La puerta **está abierta.**
   2. Sí, pero **está descompuesto.**
   3. Las luces **están apagadas.** *The lights are out (extinguished).*
   4. El radio **estaba puesto.** *The radio was on (turned-on).*

B. 1. El toreo **es considerado** como un verdadero arte.
   2. ¿Cómo **fueron heridos** tus padres? *How were your parents wounded?*
   3. Un gobierno como ése nunca va a **ser aceptado** por nadie. *A government like that is never going to be accepted by anyone.*
   4. La policía **fue atacada** por los estudiantes. *The police were attacked by the students.*

Action ended *(its result continuing)*	*Action happening*
estar + **–do** form	**ser** + **–do** form

Where English has *is* (*was,* etc.) *–ed,* Spanish may use **ser –do** if the reference is to the happening of an action, but must use **estar –do** if the happening is over and only the result is referred to.

● ITEM SUBSTITUTION DRILL

1. Mi *tío* está enojado conmigo.
   (tía, primo, novia, cuñado, amigas, abuelos, compañeras, padres)

2. La *muchacha* está resfriada.
   (alumno, inglesa, cónsul, alumna, señoras, señores, profesoras, agricultor)

---

[1] For a similar semantic shift compare English *capital–chattel–cattle.*

3. El *tocadiscos* está descompuesto.
   (maquinilla, radio, bocina, coches, plantas)
4. Por fin la *sala* está ocupada.
   (cuarto, cocina, patio, campos, fincas)
5. El *banco* está abierto ahora mismo.
   (puerta, cine, flor, colegios, clases)
6. El *cónsul* fue herido.
   (española, tirano, criada, asesino, estudiantes, líder, chicas)
7. El *policía* fue atacado a tiros.
   (oposición, presidente, iglesia, campesinos, escuelas)
8. El *toreo* es considerado como un arte.
   (natación, boxeo, pintura, cine, religión, deporte)
9. La *policía* fue obligada a defenderse a palos.
   (jefe, chica, administrador, latinoamericanos, infame, estudiantes, director)
10. La *misa* fue ofrecida.
    (regalo, comunión, libros, dinero, vacaciones, empleo, cheques)
11. La *carta* fue escrita por él.
    (libro, lección, noticias, periódico, revista, cheque, invitaciones)

● DISCUSSION

English *is* (*was*, etc.) plus *–ed* has two distinct functions: *The chair was cracked* may mean that the chair was in a cracked state (*I didn't sit on the chair because it was cracked*) or that it got cracked (*The chair was cracked by the weight that was put on it*). These two functions call for **estar** and **ser** respectively. Sometimes English does not use its *–ed* form but some other word corresponding to Spanish **–do** with **estar,** e.g., *The door is open* (rather than *opened*) or *The meeting was over* (rather than *finished*).

Example B1 means that people are actively considering bullfighting in this way; the considering is going on. With **estar** it would mean that people took this view when the question first came up, and then just held on to it—there is no active thinking about it now. (It is rather seldom that something can be viewed, like this, in two ways.)

The construction with **ser** competes with the reflexive (see Unit 7 §37), and is somewhat infrequent in speech. It is usually limited to subjects that are not viewed as being so helpless or unimportant that they can be easily pushed around. In *The door was opened (came open)*, there is very little that the door can do about it, and we normally find **se abrió.** Also, in *The wounded were taken to the hospital* **Se llevaron los heridos al hospital,** we readily find **se llevaron** because the wounded are viewed impersonally, as more or less inert. But in *We weren't invited* **No fuimos invitados** and in *Religion is respected* **La religión es respetada,** the **ser** construction is normal because the subject is important to the speaker. More often than not, such subjects are persons.

94 The present perfect

EXAMPLES

A. Nunca **he estado** de acuerdo.

B. Sólo tú no **has cambiado.**
   (*Only you haven't changed.*)

C. 1. Tu papá no se **ha servido.**
   2. Un gobierno tan malo como éste jamás **ha existido.**

D. 1. Todos **hemos visto** esa película.
   2. Ya lo **hemos discutido** muchas veces.

E. Ya **han ido** dos veces.

he has ha hemos han	–do form

The present perfect is composed of the present-tense forms of **haber** plus the **–do** form, with nothing else between them. The feminine and plural of the **–do** form never appear in this construction.

1. *Yo* nunca he estado de acuerdo.
   (ellos, nosotros, ustedes, tú, él, él y yo, usted)

2. Ya han tomado una limonada bien caliente.
   (nosotros, él, tú, yo, ella, ustedes, mi hermano mayor)

3. Todavía no he pagado la electricidad.
   (ellos, nosotros, usted, tú, ella, ustedes, los otros)

4. No hemos comido en este restorán.
   (usted, él, yo, él y yo, tú, nosotros, los estudiantes)

5. *Yo* no he escogido los muebles.
   (ella, tú, nosotros, ustedes, él, usted, ellos)

6. ¿*El* ha cumplido alguna vez con la iglesia?
   (ustedes, tú, ella, ellos, nosotros, yo, el jefe)

7. No hemos ido a ponerle flores a su tumba.
   (ellos, yo, usted, ella y yo, ustedes, tú, esos cobardes)

8. Ya hemos hecho la comida.
   (ella, ustedes, tú, usted, yo, ellos, la criada)

9. *Ellos* no han visto esa película.
   (yo, usted, nosotros, ella, tú, ellos, mi novia)

10. Nunca he visto ojos tan verdes.
    (nosotros, él, ellas, tú, ustedes, usted, mi hermano)

11. Han puesto la flecha como a cinco metros en una pared.
    (yo, él, tú, nosotros, usted, el Jefe de Tránsito)

● CONSTRUCTION SUBSTITUTION DRILL

INSTRUCTIONS: Repeat the following sentences just as you hear them. Then repeat them again, changing the present-tense form of the verb to present perfect.

A. 1. ¡Ay, que me tira del pelo!
      ¡Ay, que me tira del pelo!
      ¡Ay, que me ha tirado del pelo!

   2. Nosotros comulgamos casi todos los domingos.
   3. Mandan las fotos a revelar.
   4. Yo corro en la carrera de maratón.
   5. El no merece otra cosa.
   6. No celebran el aniversario.
   7. Siempre vivimos en el norte.
   8. Pablo no me deja en paz.
   9. Mario sigue derecho por la avenida.

B. 1. La cuenta del banco está algo baja.
   2. Esa mujer habla hasta por los codos.
   3. ¡Cómo la echamos de menos!
   4. El barbero siempre me pone brillantina.
   5. ¿A cómo está el cambio?
   6. Todos van excepto mi sobrina.
   7. ¡Cómo rabia mi hermano mayor!
   8. Me duelen la cabeza y la garganta.

C. 1. Siempre me acuesto a las diez.
   2. Nos levantamos a las siete.
   3. Alfredo se baña todos los días.
   4. Nunca se acuerdan de mí.
   5. No me siento muy bien hoy.

● PATTERNED RESPONSE DRILL

A. 1. TEACHER: ¿Ya almorzó usted?
      STUDENT: **No, todavía no he almorzado.**

   2. ¿Ya terminó usted?
   3. ¿Ya comulgó usted?
   4. ¿Ya aceptó usted?
   5. ¿Ya contestó usted?
   6. ¿Ya esperó usted?
   7. ¿Ya ganó usted?
   8. ¿Ya jugó usted?
   9. ¿Ya pagó usted?

B. 1. ¿Ya comió usted?
      No, todavia no he comido.

   2. ¿Ya durmió usted?
   3. ¿Ya escribió usted?
   4. ¿Ya pidió usted?
   5. ¿Ya siguió usted?
   6. ¿Ya volvió usted?

C. 1. ¿Ensució los trajes?
      No, no los he ensuciado.

   2. ¿Rifó el abrigo?
   3. ¿Celebró el aniversario?
   4. ¿Cambió el cheque?
   5. ¿Mencionó la idea?

D. 1. ¿Envolvió la ropa?
      No, no la he envuelto.

   2. ¿Escribió la carta?
   3. ¿Trajo el auto?
   4. ¿Metió la pata?
   5. ¿Recibió el paquete?

E. 1. ¿Se cayó la taza?
      No, no se ha caído.

   2. ¿Se entusiasmó el jefe?
   3. ¿Se arregló la rifa?
   4. ¿Se discutió el escándalo?
   5. ¿Se peinó el señor?
   6. ¿Se disolvió la manifestación?

The present perfect is a two-word construction as in English: the forms of **haber** correspond to English *have,* and Spanish **–do** corresponds to English *–ed.* The chief difference is that English sometimes divides the construction (*Have **they** gone? They have **never** gone*), but Spanish does not (**¿Han ido** *ellos?* **Ellos** *nunca* **han ido**). With-verb pronouns precede the inflected form of **haber**: *Lo* **hemos discutido**.

Where English makes a dual use of its verb *have* (*have* in *I have gone* does not mean the same as *have* in *I have money*), Spanish has two different verbs:

I have gone = I've gone	**He ido**
I have money = I've got money	**Tengo dinero**

English and Spanish use the present perfect in similar ways. It may safely be used in Spanish wherever English has it.

95 Forms of the present subjunctive; subjunctive or indicative with *tal vez*

EXAMPLES OF SUBJUNCTIVE FORMS

1. Tal vez ya no **recuerdes**.
2. No **toquemos** ese tema.
3. Es ridículo que las muchachas **tengan** que llevar chaperón.

Regularly formed present subjunctive

	INFINITIVE	FIRST PERSON SINGULAR PRESENT		SUBJUNCTIVE ENDINGS
regular –ar	hablar	habl–	–o	–e –es –e –emos –en
regular –er and –ir	comer vivir	com– viv–	–o	
verbs irregular in the first-person singular	conocer parecer[1] producir[2] tener venir poner[3] valer salir caer traer hacer decir oir incluir ver	conozc– parezc– produzc– teng– veng– pong– valg– salg– caig– traig– hag– dig– oig– incluy– ve–	–o	–a –as –a –amos –an

In almost all verbs the present subjunctive is based on the first-person singular of the present indicative (its **usted, ustedes** forms are the same as the **usted, ustedes** commands; see Unit 5 §22).

[1] Similarly most other –ecer verbs, e.g., **ofrecer** and **merecer**. [2] Similarly all other –ducir verbs.
[3] Similarly all other –poner verbs, e.g., **suponer**.

PRESENT SUBJUNCTIVE OF VERBS WITH CHANGES IN THE STEM	
recordar	**pensar**
recuerde	piense
recuerdes	pienses
recuerde	piense
recordemos	pensemos
recuerden	piensen
poder	**querer**
pueda	quiera
puedas	quieras
pueda	quiera
podamos	queramos
puedan	quieran
dormir[1]	**sentir**[2]
duerma	sienta
duermas	sientas
duerma	sienta
durmamos	sintamos
duerman	sientan
	pedir[3]
	pida
	pidas
	pida
	pidamos
	pidan

The stem changes in the present subjunctive resemble those in the present indicative (Unit 4 §16) except in the first-person plural of **-ir** verbs. Endings are regular.

IRREGULARLY FORMED PRESENT SUBJUNCTIVES	
dar	dé des dé demos den
estar	esté estés esté estemos estén
ser se– **ir** vay– **haber** hay– **saber** sep–	–a –as –a –amos –an

These verbs do not base the present subjunctive on the first-person singular of the present indicative. Endings, however, are regular.

---

[1] Similarly **morir.**   [2] Similarly **mentir, preferir,** and a few other verbs.
[3] Similarly **seguir, conseguir, servir,** and a few other verbs.

EXAMPLES OF **tal vez**

A. 1. Tal vez ya no **recuerdes.**
   2. Tal vez no **hayan** contestado. *Maybe they haven't answered.*
   3. Tal vez **haya** algún beneficio. *Maybe there'll be some benefit.*

B. 1. Tal vez **puedo** ir.
   2. Tal vez no le **entendiste** tú.

C. 1. **Viene** mañana, tal vez. *He's coming tomorrow, maybe.*
   2. No le **entendiste** tú, tal vez.

	INDICATIVE	SUBJUNCTIVE
tal vez precedes the verb	√	√
tal vez follows the verb	√	

When **tal vez** appears after the verb, the verb is in the indicative; when it appears before the verb, the verb may be either indicative or subjunctive.

● PERSON-NUMBER SUBSTITUTION DRILL

1. Tal vez trabajemos aquí.
   (él, ellos, yo, tú, usted, ustedes)
2. Tal vez *ella* enseñe ahí.
   (tú, yo, ellos, nosotros, ustedes, él)
3. Tal vez no olvidemos nada.
   (yo, ellos, usted, tú, ella, ustedes)
4. Tal vez llame ahora.
   (tú, yo, ustedes, nosotros, él, ellos)
5. Tal vez ganen otra vez.
   (nosotros, usted, tú, yo, ustedes, él)
6. Tal vez paguemos algo.
   (él, ustedes, yo, tú, ella, ustedes)

7. Tal vez *yo* venda la casa.
   (ellos, nosotros, él, ustedes, tú, mis padres)
8. Tal vez aprendamos algo.
   (yo, ustedes, ella, tú, ellos, usted)
9. Tal vez metamos la pata.
   (usted, ellos, tú, ella, ustedes, yo)
10. Tal vez reciba una carta.
    (nosotros, yo, ellos, tú, usted, ustedes)
11. Tal vez abra un restorán.
    (nosotros, ellos, usted, tú, él, ellos)
12. Tal vez escriban esta noche.
    (yo, tú, usted, ellas, nosotros, ustedes)
13. Tal vez no discuta ese asunto.
    (nosotros, ellos, él, tú, usted, ustedes)

14. Tal vez *yo* conozca a alguien.
    (él, tú, nosotros, usted, ellos, el jefe)
15. Tal vez produzcan más.
    (él, ustedes, tú, yo, usted, nosotros)
16. Tal vez *él* no tenga tiempo.
    (ellos, tú, usted, nosotros, ella, ustedes)
17. Tal vez *Juan* venga mañana.
    (ellas, nosotros, tú, yo, él, los otros)

18. Tal vez no tengamos que llevar chaperón.
    (ella, tú, ellas, yo, usted, las muchachas)
19. Tal vez salgamos esta noche.
    (yo, ustedes, ella, él y yo, ellos, tú)
20. Tal vez hagamos una comida.
    (tú, ellos, ella, ustedes, yo, nosotras)
21. Tal vez digas la verdad.
    (usted, ellos, ella, ustedes, nosotros, él)
22. Tal vez oiga mejor.
    (ustedes, tú, él, nosotros, ellos, yo)
23. Tal vez puedan ir.
    (yo, tú, él, ustedes, nosotros, usted)
24. Tal vez *tú* ya no recuerdes.
    (usted, ustedes, nosotros, ella, ellas, yo)
25. Tal vez pierdan hoy.
    (él, ustedes, nosotros, tú, yo, ellos)
26. Tal vez no quiera venderlo.
    (ellos, usted, tú, nosotros, ustedes, yo)
27. Tal vez no piensen lo mismo.
    (nosotros, él, ustedes, yo, tú, usted)

28. Tal vez durmamos en casa.
    (yo, ellos, tú, él y yo, ustedes, él)
29. Tal vez se sientan mejor hoy.
    (usted, ellos, ella, ustedes, tú, yo, nosotros)
30. Tal vez pidamos leche.
    (él, ustedes, tú, ellos, yo, él y yo)
31. Tal vez sirva bien.
    (ustedes, tú, él, nosotros, ellos, yo)
32. Tal vez no estén ahí.
    (ella, ellos, él, tú, yo, nosotros)
33. Tal vez no vayan mañana.
    (nosotros, él, ustedes, tú, ella, yo)
34. Tal vez no hayan entendido bien.
    (ustedes, usted, ellos, tú, nosotros, yo)
35. Tal vez no sepamos todo.
    (yo, tú, usted, él, ustedes, ellos)

● CONSTRUCTION SUBSTITUTION DRILL

INSTRUCTIONS: Repeat the following sentences just as you hear them.   Then repeat them again, shifting **tal vez** to the end of the sentence and changing the verb from subjunctive to indicative.

A. 1. TEACHER: Tal vez llegue mañana. *Repita.*
     STUDENT: **Tal vez llegue mañana.**
     TEACHER: *Cambie.*
     STUDENT: **Llega mañana, tal vez.**

  2. Tal vez no necesites una corbata.
  3. Tal vez esté adentro.
  4. Tal vez desee la muerte.
  5. Tal vez cambie el viento.
  6. Tal vez no la preste.
  7. Tal vez no lo exijan.

B. 1. Tal vez no salgan extras.
  2. Tal vez haya algún beneficio.
  3. Tal vez no sea tan independiente.
  4. Tal vez la conozcan.
  5. Tal vez no produzcan maíz.
  6. Tal vez no diga la verdad.
  7. Tal vez no valga la pena.

● PATTERNED RESPONSE DRILL

A. 1. TEACHER: ¿Viene Juan?
     STUDENT: **No sé, tal vez venga.**

  2. ¿Estudia Elena?
  3. ¿Participa don Rosario?
  4. ¿Sale Felipe?
  5. ¿Vuelve Carlos?
  6. ¿Espera Fernando?
  7. ¿Gana Rosa?
  8. ¿Sigue el señor Alonso?

B. 1. ¿Vino Cecilia?
     No sé, tal vez haya venido.

  2. ¿Estudió Susana?
  3. ¿Participó don Pepe?
  4. ¿Salió Patricio?
  5. ¿Volvió Roberto?
  6. ¿Esperó doña Mercedes?
  7. ¿Ganó Josefina?
  8. ¿Discutió el barbero?

● TRANSLATION DRILL

1. Perhaps he'll come today.
  Tal vez viene hoy.
  Perhaps he may come today.
  Tal vez venga hoy.
2. Maybe he's mistaken.
  Just possibly he may be mistaken.
3. Perhaps it'll arrive too late.
  Perhaps it may arrive too late.

4. Maybe he'll do it.
  He just may do it.
5. Perhaps it's the other one.
  Perhaps it may be the other one.
6. Maybe it's not ridiculous nowadays.
  Could be it's not ridiculous nowadays.
7. Perhaps he has an appointment.
  Perhaps he may have an appointment.

● DISCUSSION

The "subjunctive" is a set of verb forms contrasting with the "indicative."   All the verb forms thus far studied, except the infinitive, the –ndo, the –do, and commands, have been forms of the indicative.   The **usted, –es** commands (Unit 5 §22) are special uses of the subjunctive.

The subjunctive endings are, roughly, the reverse of those in the indicative, in the way they are associated with –**ar** verbs on the one hand and –**er, –ir** verbs on the other: the indicative –**ar** endings are now attached to –**er, –ir** verbs, and the indicative –**er** endings are now attached to –**ar** verbs.   The exception is the first person, which in the subjunctive is the same as the third.

As in the indicative, stem changes, in the verbs that have them, are associated with stress (Unit 4 §16).   The changes occur when the vowel is stressed.   In addition, –**ir** verbs have the same changes in the first-person plural that they have in the third-person preterit and the –**ndo** (Unit 9 §45), namely, **o→u** and **e→i: durmamos, sintamos, pidamos.**

The present subjunctive of **haber** (**haya, hayas,** etc.) is used to form the present perfect subjunctive exactly as the present perfect indicative is formed (§94 above).   In addition, its third singular, **haya,** is the equivalent of *there is, there are,* and *there will be* in the subjunctive; compare Unit 7 §36.

After **tal vez,** Spanish uses the subjunctive to express greater uncertainty than is expressed by the indicative in a similar sentence.   English usually makes this distinction by tone of voice or by using other qualifying words like *possibly, just:* **Es hoy tal vez** *It's today, maybe;* **Tal vez es hoy** *Perhaps it's today, Quite possibly it's today;* **Tal vez sea hoy** *Perhaps it's today, Possibly it's today.*

As the example **Tal vez haya algún beneficio** indicates, the present subjunctive includes future meanings. Thus **Tal vez no valga más** may mean, depending on context, either *Maybe it isn't worth more* or *Maybe it won't be worth more.*

96 The equivalents of –ly

EXAMPLES

1. Lo llamaron cobarde, y **con razón.** *They called him a coward, and no wonder (and rightly).*
2. Hágalo **con cuidado.** *Do it carefully.*
3. Me lo ofreció **con mucha bondad.** *He very kindly offered it to me.*

(very)	adjective	–ly

con	(**mucho, –a**)	noun

Spanish frequently prefers a noun with **con** where English has an adjective with –ly. The equivalent of *very* is then **mucho, –a** before the noun.

EXAMPLES

A. 1. **Exactamente,** una casita verde que está en la esquina.
  2. —Saludos a todos.
    —**Igualmente.**
  3. **Desgraciadamente** vamos a perder en todo.
  4. —¿Quién va a ganar los Juegos? ¿Los americanos?
    —**Probablemente.**
  5. **Principalmente** para lana.
  6. Me dio el visto bueno **inmediatamente.**

B. 1. Lo conozco **personal y profesionalmente.** *I know him personally and professionally.*
  2. **¿Regular o necesariamente?** *Regularly or necessarily?*

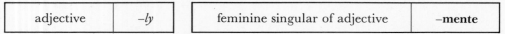

adjective	–ly

feminine singular of adjective	–**mente**

The usual equivalent of the English –ly is –**mente,** attached to the feminine singular of the adjective.

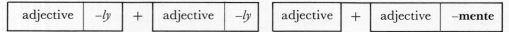

adjective	–ly	+	adjective	–ly

adjective	+	adjective	–**mente**

Where English repeats –ly with each member of a series, Spanish attaches –**mente** only to the last member.

● TRANSLATION DRILL

A. 1. He said it, and rightly (with reason).
  2. He did it, and carefully (with care).
  3. He accepted it, and pleasurably (with pleasure).
  4. He ate it, and hungrily (with hunger).
  5. He fixed it, and competently (with competence).
  6. He mentioned it, and pityingly (with pity).

B. 1. It's exactly the same thing.
  2. It's unfortunately the same thing.
  3. It's probably the same thing.
  4. It's principally the same thing.
  5. It's necessarily the same thing.
  6. It's generally the same thing.
  7. It's truly the same thing.
  8. It's clearly the same thing.
  9. It's possibly the same thing.

C. 1. He speaks perfectly.
   2. He speaks immediately.
   3. He speaks amiably.
   4. He speaks easily.
   5. He speaks madly.
   6. He speaks typically.
   7. He speaks professionally.
   8. He speaks seriously.
   9. He speaks sadly.
   10. He speaks horribly.
   11. He speaks innocently.
   12. He speaks freely.
   13. He speaks regularly.

D. 1. She's equally respectable.
   2. She's totally respectable.
   3. She's newly respectable.
   4. She's impossibly respectable.
   5. She's perfectly respectable.
   6. She's strongly respectable.
   7. She's typically respectable.

E. 1. They attacked fiercely and furiously.
   2. They attacked uselessly and ridiculously.
   3. They attacked openly and freely.
   4. They attacked easily and professionally.
   5. They attacked regularly and personally.

● DISCUSSION

The usual equivalent of *–ly,* with which English makes adverbs out of adjectives, is **–mente,** attached to the feminine singular of an adjective. Where two or more occur in a coordinate series, **–mente** is attached only to the last.

In writing, any accent mark that occurs on the adjective is retained when **–mente** is added, e.g., **fácil** *easy,* **fácilmente** *easily.* This reflects the fact that **–mente** was historically an independent word (compare English *contrary wise, contrariwise*) and in speech still has the typical characteristic of an independent word: strong stress, occurring on the syllable **–men–.** There are thus two strong stresses in **fácilmente, exactamente,** etc., one on the adjective and one on **–mente.**

Rather more than in English, one finds phrases with **con** used instead of adverbs with **–mente.** (This is not unknown to English, of course; we say *easily* but cannot say *difficultly*—for the latter, we use *with difficulty.*) Thus there are two equivalents for *carefully:* **cuidadosamente** (**cuidadosa** *careful* + **–mente**) and **con cuidado** *with care,* of which the latter is probably heard oftener.

● COMBINED PATTERN REPLACEMENT DRILL

A. 1. **Tal vez él ha escrito la carta hoy.**
   2. _____ haya _____
   3. _____ tarjetas __
   4. _____ ellas _____
   5. _____ contestado _____
   6. _____ han _____
   7. _____ esta semana
   8. _____ recibido _____
   9. _____ hayan _____
   10. _____ documento ____
   11. _____ ustedes _____
   12. _____ han _____
   13. _____ los _____
   14. _____ enviado _____
   15. Desgraciadamente _____
   16. _____ este mes
   17. _____ nosotros _____
   18. _____ lista _____
   19. Por supuesto _____
   20. _____ visto _____
   21. _____ he _____
   22. _____ las _____

B. 1. **Don Pepe tiene un toro importado.**
   2. _____ unos _____
   3. _____ tenía _____
   4. _____ vacas _____
   5. _____ importada
   6. ___ Rosario _____
   7. _____ cosas _____
   8. _____ traía _____
   9. ___ Mercedes _____
   10. _____ envueltas
   11. _____ vestidos ____
   12. _____ un _____
   13. _____ dio _____
   14. _____ anticuado
   15. _____ pintura _____
   16. _____ enseña _____
   17. ___ Rafael _____
   18. _____ aburrida
   19. _____ ofrece _____
   20. _____ preferida
   21. _____ la _____
   22. ___ Rosa _____
   23. _____ comida _____
   24. _____ pedida
   25. _____ ofreció _____

Unemphatic *some, any.*

A. 1. TEACHER: Give me some rice.
   STUDENT: **Déme arroz.**
   2. Give me some sugar.
   3. Give me some coffee.
   4. Give me some salad.
   5. Give me some butter.
   6. Give me some milk.
   7. Give me some bread.
   8. Give me some chicken.
   9. Give me some corn.
   10. Give me some potatoes.

B. 1. Have you got any meat?
   ¿Tiene carne?
   2. Have you got any beans?
   3. Have you got any fruit?
   4. Have you got any lard?
   5. Have you got any flour?
   6. Have you got any ice cream?
   7. Have you got any eggs?
   8. Have you got any roast beef?
   9. Have you got any vegetables?
   10. Have you got any onions?
   11. Have you got any wheat?
   12. Have you got any aspirins?

READING

A la mesa

PAQ. *Paquito*   E. *Elena, su hermana mayor*
M. *Madre*   P. *Padre*   ABUELA   ABUELO

PAQ. Elena, pásame los frijoles.

E. (*como hermana mayor*) Paquito, ya te he dicho muchas veces cómo se deben pedir las cosas. Tienes que decir: Ten la bondad de pasarme la carne, o bien[1] ¿Quieres pasarme el pan? o bien: Haz el favor de pasarme la mantequilla; o bien . . .

PAQ. Pero no quiero carne ni pan ni mantequilla; quiero los frijoles na más.[2]

E. Esa palabra es *nada,* no *na: na–da.* ¿Cuándo vas a hablar correctamente? A tu edad . . .

PAQ. A tu edad Tía Julia estaba casada y tenía tres hijos. ¿Cuándo te vas a casar tú?

M. Niños, niños, por favor: dejen de pelearse. Paquito, come tu comida. Elena, no atormentes[3] a tu hermanito . . . Y pásale los frijoles, por favor. . . . ¿Sales?

E. Sí, madre, con permiso. Tengo que ver a alguien.

PAQ. ¿A quién?

E. Si es que te importa, a Rodney Ramsbottom, un joven inglés que conocí la semana pasada.

PAQ. ¿Ese tipo?[4]

E. (*No dice nada, pero la mirada que da a su hermanito es muy expresiva. Sale.*)

ABUELA ¿Adónde va Elena con su amigo?

M. Al cine. Hay una película que no han visto.

ABUELA ¿Quién los acompaña?

M. (*Tenemos la impresión de que la familia ya ha discutido este asunto muchas veces, puesto que Elena es una joven muy bonita.*) Nadie, abuela.

ABUELA Ay, estas costumbres modernas no me gustan. Cuando yo era joven . . .

PAQ. ¿Cuántos años tienes, abuelita?

P. (*escandalizado*) ¡Paquito! ¡A tu abuelita no tienes que hacerle esa pregunta! Y mira, a las señoras nunca se les pregunta la edad. (*Habla tan fuerte que despierta al abuelo, que se ha caído dormido en su silla, y ha empezado a roncar.*)[5]

ABUELO (*despertando de un salto*[6]) ¿Eh? ¿Qué fue eso?

ABUELA Abuelo, ¿cuántas veces he tenido que decirte que no debes roncar cuando duermes, y que no debes dormir cuando comes?

ABUELO ¡Pobre de mí! No puedo roncar, no puedo dormir . . . ¡tan pocos placeres que tiene un viejo!

ABUELA (*con ironía*) ¡Qué lástima, sí! ¡Y tú que eres el hombre más rico de la ciudad! ¡Pobre de ti!

---

[1] *or else*   [2] *just*   [3] *tease*   [4] *fellow, guy, creep*   [5] *to snore*   [6] *with a start*

READING

Las riquezas de la América hispánica

(En la Student Union, varios estudiantes están sentados en sillas grandes y cómodas pasando el tiempo entre períodos de clase.)

J. *Jaime*   E. *Eduardo*   R. *Rafael*   T. *Todos juntos*

J. A ver, muchachos. Si quieren hacerle preguntas a nuestro nuevo compañero de clase sobre su país, él dice que tendrá mucho gusto de[1] contestarlas.

E. ¿Quién es él?

J. Es Rafael Cuervo, de Venezuela. Está en esta Universidad por un año siguiendo cursos graduados de Ingeniería de Minas. El es . . . Hola, Rafael, ¿cómo está usted?

R. *(Responde en un inglés perfecto.)* Very well, thanks, and you?

J. O.K. Pues, quiero que conozca[2] a estos amigos. Este señor es Rafael Cuervo, venezolano. Tengo mucho gusto de presentarlo a Eduardo Lance, Enrique Everett y Carlos Murray.

R. Mucho gusto de conocerlos.

T. Igualmente. Gracias.

R. Es un placer para mí visitar su maravilloso país y conocer a su gente tan simpática.

J. Gracias. Nosotros también estamos muy contentos de conocerlo a usted. Les dije a nuestros amigos que usted iba a hablarles

---

[1] **tendrá mucho gusto de** *he will be glad to* (See footnote 1, p. 220.)
[2] **quiero que conozca** *I want you to meet.* This is treated in Unit 17 §97.

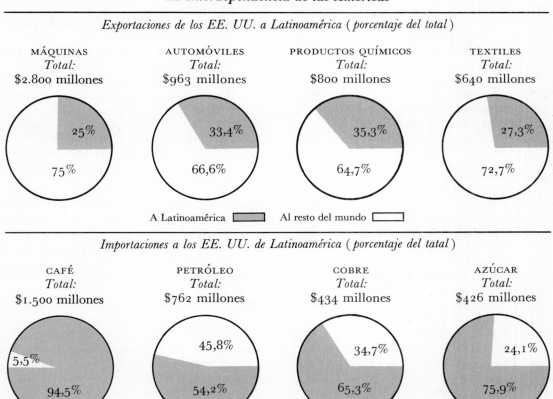

La Interdependencia de las Américas

Exportaciones de los EE. UU. a Latinoamérica (porcentaje del total)

MÁQUINAS	AUTOMÓVILES	PRODUCTOS QUÍMICOS	TEXTILES
Total: $2.800 millones	*Total:* $963 millones	*Total:* $800 millones	*Total:* $640 millones
25% / 75%	33,4% / 66,6%	35,3% / 64,7%	27,3% / 72,7%

A Latinoamérica ▨   Al resto del mundo ☐

Importaciones a los EE. UU. de Latinoamérica (porcentaje del tatal)

CAFÉ	PETRÓLEO	COBRE	AZÚCAR
Total: $1.500 millones	*Total:* $762 millones	*Total:* $434 millones	*Total:* $426 millones
5,5% / 94,5%	45,8% / 54,2%	34,7% / 65,3%	24,1% / 75,9%

De Latinoamérica ☐   Del resto del mundo ☐

de las riquezas de su país. Como todos saben, el continente americano es inmensamente rico. Los países al sur del Río Grande son una reserva para el mundo entero.

R. Encantado. Y solamente conocemos una pequeña parte de la riqueza mineral. Chile, México y Perú tienen gran cantidad de cobre. En México, Perú, Honduras, el Salvador y Bolivia hay muchas minas de plata. Bolivia tiene casi todos los minerales que existen y posee la mayor parte del estaño del mundo. ¿Me entienden ustedes?

T. Sí, señor, siga, por favor.

R. En Chile hay muchos nitratos, que se usan no sólo para explosivos sino también para abonos. En las montañas de México, Guatemala, Honduras, el Salvador, Nicaragua, Costa Rica, Venezuela, Colombia (*va indicando en un mapa todos los países que menciona*), Perú, Bolivia y Chile se hallan minerales: oro, plomo, tungsteno, antimo-

nio y muchos más. Mi país Venezuela exporta petróleo. México, Colombia, Perú y Ecuador también exportan petróleo . . . Voy a mostrarles un cuadro que hicimos hace algunos meses, en la clase de economía. Se titula "La Interdependencia de las Américas" y está basado en un informe publicado hace unos meses.

J. Muchas gracias, Rafael. Es hora de ir a clase. ¿Tendremos el placer[3] de escucharlo de nuevo otro día? ¿Podemos servirle en algo?

R. Sí. Mi esposa, que está conmigo, no habla bien el inglés. ¿Tendría su esposa la amabilidad de[4] llevarla a la tienda de comestibles? Se lo agradeceríamos mucho.[5]

J. Con mucho gusto. Pueden ir juntas mañana si su esposa quiere. Ann puede pasar por ella en el automóvil.

R. Muchas gracias. Ha sido un placer hablar con ustedes.

T. Gracias a usted. El placer ha sido nuestro.

● CUESTIONARIO

1. ¿Qué importancia tiene la Unión de Estudiantes en la vida del estudiante norteamericano?
2. ¿Quién es Rafael Cuervo?
3. ¿Qué piensa Rafael Cuervo de los EE. UU.?
4. ¿Qué desean saber los estudiantes americanos sobre Venezuela?
5. ¿Dónde se produce gran cantidad de cobre?
6. ¿En qué países hay muchas minas de plata?
7. ¿Por qué es famosa Bolivia?
8. ¿Para qué se usan los nitratos?

9. ¿Qué otros minerales se producen en el continente americano?
10. ¿Cuál es la principal fuente de exportación de Venezuela?
11. ¿Qué nombre recibe el estudio de los diferentes minerales?
12. ¿Por qué se dice que los países al sur del Río Grande son una reserva para el mundo entero?
13. ¿Qué usa Rafael Cuervo para explicar la interdependencia de las Américas?
14. ¿Qué favor pide Rafael Cuervo a Jaime?

● SUGGESTED READINGS

Aikman, Duncan, *The All-American Front,* Doubleday, New York, 1940: Ch. 19, "Neighbors, or Else."

Arciniegas, Germán, *The State of Latin America,* Knopf, New York, 1952: Ch. 18, "Latin America's Hopes and Fears."

Beals, Carleton, *America South,* Lippincott, Philadelphia, 1937: Ch. 20, "The Struggle for the Market."

Castañeda, Jorge, *Mexico and the United Nations,* Manhattan Pub. Co., New York, 1958.

Padilla, Ezequiel, *Free Men of America,* Ziff-Davis, New York, 1943.

Palmer, Thomas W., *Search for a Latin-American Policy,* University of Florida Press, Gainesville, 1957: Ch. 13, "Reflections on the Future."

Quintanilla, Luis, *A Latin American Speaks,* Macmillan, New York, 1943: Ch. 10, "Trade for Democracy."

Soule, George, David Efron, and Norman Ness, *Latin America in the Future World,* Rinehart, New York, 1945: Part I, "Purchasing Power, Economic Activity, etc."

Tomlinson, Edward, *New Roads to Riches in the Other Americas,* Scribner's, New York, 1942.

Uruguay and the United Nations (prepared under the auspices of the Uruguayan Institute of International Law), Manhattan Pub. Co., New York, 1958.

Wythe, George, *Industry in Latin America,* Columbia University Press, New York, 1949.

---

[3] **¿Tendremos el placer?** *Will we have the pleasure?*
[4] **¿Tendría la amabilidad de . . . ?** *Would . . . be so kind as to . . . ?*
[5] **Se lo agradeceríamos mucho.** *We would appreciate it very much.*

17

Politics in the Home

s. *Son*   f. *Father*   m. *Mother*

s. Well, no matter what they say, Vargas Campo is the man of the hour.

f. Don't talk foolishness. He's an idealistic fool who wants to change everything. Our people will never accept such radical changes.

s. In spite of what you say, dad, I don't agree with you.

m. Please don't talk about politics any more. Let's change the subject.

s. What do you want us to talk about, mom? Clothes?

m. You two never agree. You always end up in an argument.

* * *

La política en la casa

h. *Hijo*   p. *Padre*   m. *Madre*

h. Pues digan lo que digan, Vargas Campo es el hombre del día.

p. No digas tonterías. Es un loco idealista que todo lo (1) quiere cambiar. Nuestro pueblo (2) jamás va a aceptar cambios tan radicales.

h. A pesar de lo que tú digas, papá, no estoy de acuerdo contigo (3).

m. Les ruego que no discutan más de política. Cambiemos de tema.

h. ¿De qué quieres que hablemos, mamá? ¿De vestidos?

m. Es que ustedes dos nunca se ponen de acuerdo. Siempre terminan en un pleito.

* * *

F. Let's drop the subject. Anyway, I wanted to talk to you about something more important, your studies.

S. Please, don't insist that I study medicine.

F. Then pick some other career with the same prestige; engineering, for example.

M. The only thing we ask is that you don't study law.

S. What's so bad about that? You don't think it's a good profession?

F. It's not that, son, but there are so many lawyers that it's difficult to get ahead in that field.

M. Unless one gets into politics, and we hope you won't do that. Let somebody else do it.

* * *

F. Nevertheless, you're the one to decide. Study what you like best.

M. Of course, we can only give you advice. We won't stand in the way of your choice.

S. Don't think I'm not grateful for that advice. It's just that it's so hard for me to decide.

F. But you should try to make up your mind soon. Time flies.

M. Well, talk it over. I've got to go see how dinner's coming.

S. . . . Look, Dad, about that other matter, what do you really have against Vargas Campo? Why do you hate him?

F. Because I don't want to see our country ruined. And let's not discuss it any further. No one can convince you young people.

P. Dejemos ese tema. De todos modos, quería hablarte de otra cosa más importante, tus estudios.

H. Por favor, no insistan en que estudie medicina.

P. Entonces sigue alguna otra carrera de igual prestigio (4); ingeniería, por ejemplo.

M. Lo único que te pedimos es que no estudies para abogado.

H. ¿Qué hay de malo en eso? ¿Que no es una buena profesión?

P. No, hijo, pero es que hay tantos abogados que es muy difícil destacarse en ese campo.

M. A menos que uno se meta en la política; y ojalá (5) que tú no te dediques a eso. Que lo hagan otros.

* * *

P. Sin embargo, tú eres el que decides. Estudia lo que más te guste.

M. Claro, nosotros sólo podemos darte consejos y no nos vamos a oponer a lo que tú escojas.

H. No crean que no les agradezco esos consejos. Lo que pasa es que me cuesta tanto decidirme (6).

P. Pero debes tratar de llegar a esa decisión pronto. El tiempo vuela.

M. Bueno, sigan ustedes hablando de eso. Yo tengo que ir a ver cómo anda lo de la comida.

H. . . . Mira, papá, volviendo a lo otro, sinceramente, ¿qué tienes tú en contra de Vargas Campo? ¿Por qué lo odias?

P. Porque no quiero ver a nuestra patria en la ruina. Y no discutamos más. A ustedes los jóvenes no los convence nadie.

Cultural Notes   (1) The pronoun **lo** is generally used with **todo** *everything*, when **todo** is the object of a verb. It makes the *everything* more concrete and emphatic. When the **todo** comes before the verb (this position makes it still more emphatic), the accompanying **lo** shows that **todo** is the object of the verb and not its subject. See Unit 10 §56 for a related construction, with-verb pronouns that repeat noun objects, and compare English *He knows everything* vs. *He knows it all.*

(2) *People* in the sense of "group of persons" (e.g., *There were many people at the meeting*) is **gente** in Spanish; in the sense of "nation, race, body of persons united by a common culture" (e.g., *A characteristic trait of the Spanish people is individualism*), **pueblo** is used.

(3) The transition from childhood to adulthood in Spanish America is abrupt. Children in their teens become acquainted with adult problems and decisions, including those of politics, where their combination of idealism and inexperience may lead them to extremes.

(4) The professions with the greatest prestige in Latin America are medicine, engineering, and law, although others, such as architecture and economics, are gaining ground. The field of law, which is overcrowded, is one of the avenues to a political career. Many students have no intention of practicing their profession and a large number aspire to government positions which in some countries afford considerable security and always confer prestige. The fact that professions as a whole are held in higher esteem than trades accords with the Latin American's view of manual labor as menial (see Unit 8, Cultural Note 1).

(5) **Ojalá** is derived from Arabic [wàšalá] and literally means *May God grant*. The long occupation of Spain or parts of Spain by the Moors (A.D. 711–1492), with its many cultural contacts between Christians and Moslems, gave many Arabic words to Spanish.

(6) In contrast to American students, who enter professional schools of law, medicine, and the like at around the age of twenty-one, after a three- or four-year undergraduate preparation, the Latin-American student, at the age of seventeen or eighteen, goes directly to a professional school after completing secondary-school education (see Unit 9, Cultural Notes 2 and 4). He thus has to decide upon a career several years before his American counterpart.

● WRITING EXERCISE

The written representation of /y/ by **ll** or **y**. INSTRUCTIONS: Write the following lists of words from dictation, remembering that those in the first column are written with **ll** and those in the second column, with **y**. Note also that the pairs of words in group *A* are pronounced identically.

A.				B.	
halla	haya	sallo	sayo	llaga	yaba
valla	vaya	pollo	poyo	llano	yambo
malla	maya	bollo	boyo	llave	yate
falla	faya	olla	hoya	lluvia	yuyuba
ralla	raya	bullo	buyo	llena	yema
salla	saya	tulla	tuya	llora	yola
gallo	gayo	calló	cayó	taller	ayer
rallo	rayo			llegar	yeguar

In most dialects of Spanish, both **ll** and **y** represent the voiced palatal semiconsonant /y/. The distinction, which is merely orthographic, is generally due to the etymology of the word; e.g., Spanish **caballo** derives from Latin *caballus,* Spanish **llave** from Latin *clavis,* Spanish **llama** (*flame*) from Latin *flamma,* and Spanish **llorar** from Latin *plorare;* Spanish **mayo,** however, derives from Latin *maius.*

In some parts of Spain and in a few dialects of Spanish America, a distinction is made, **ll** representing in those areas a voiced palatal lateral, and **y** representing a voiced palatal fricative. In such areas, there is a phonetic difference between the pairs of words in group *A* and likewise **ll** and **y** in the words in group *B* represent different sounds.

It is clear, then, that in the greater part of the Hispanic world, where **ll** and **y** represent the same sound, there is no way of knowing how to spell the words in group *A* without context when the words are first heard. Also, there is no way of knowing whether the words in column *B* are spelled with **ll** or **y** when they are heard unless one has become familiar with them in their written form.

97 Indicative and subjunctive in noun clauses

EXAMPLES

A. 1. Es que **hay** tantos abogados. *(It's that there are so many lawyers.)*
   2. Lo que pasa es que me **cuesta** tanto decidirme.
   3. ¿Por qué es que los americanos no **son** buenos en fútbol?

B. 1. Sé que **hay** más de diez heridos.
   2. Yo sé que **viven** cerca del Parque Central.
   3. ¿Sabes que mañana **es** la inauguración?

C. 1. Veo que usted **prefiere** el ruido de los tranvías.
   2. ¿No ve que **soy** su padrino?

D. 1. Dice que no **es** plata argentina.
   2. Dígale que no **estoy.**

E. 1. Acuérdate que no nos **dejaban** salir solos.

   2. Recuerde que esta noche **viene** gente a comer.
   3. No olvide que la oposición **tiene** un partido mucho más fuerte.

F. 1. Creo que **tengo** gripe.
   2. ¿Quién cree usted que **va** a ganar? *(You think that who is going to win?)*
   3. No crean que no les **agradezco** esos consejos.

G. Me parece que las muchachas no **deben** salir solas.

H. Apuesto a que en fútbol **ganamos.**

I. Supongo que **va** a ir mucha gente importante.

J. Me imagino que **deben** tener ovejas y cerdos.

VIEWING WHAT FOLLOWS AS INFORMATION		THE INFORMATION
Es	que	hay tantos abogados
Sé	que	viven
Dígale	que	no estoy
Me parece	que	no deben salir
Apuesto a	que	ganamos

When what the noun clause says is viewed as straight *information*, its verb is in the indicative.   Usually the main verb gives the point of view, whether the information is held (e.g., *know, believe*), found out (e.g., *see, discover, learn*), or given (e.g., *say, predict*).

● TRANSLATION DRILL

A. 1. I know that he's an idealist.
   2. It seems to me that he's an idealist.
   3. They say that he's an idealist.
   4. I'll bet that he's an idealist.
   5. It's just that he's an idealist.
   6. Tell him that he's an idealist.

B. 1. I know time flies.
   2. It seems to me time flies.
   3. They say time flies.
   4. I'll bet time flies.
   5. It's just that time flies.
   6. Tell him that time flies.

EXAMPLES

A. 1. Les ruego que no **discutan** más de política. *(I beg you that you do not argue more about politics.)*
   2. Lo único que te pedimos es que no **estudies** para abogado.
   3. No insistan en que **estudie** medicina.
   4. ¿De qué quieres que **hablemos**? *(About what do you want that we speak?)*
   5. Merece que lo **odiemos.** *He deserves that we hate him.*

   6. ¿Qué sugieres que **hagamos**? *What do you suggest that we do?*
   7. Prefiero que **rifes** otra cosa. *I'd rather you raffled (I prefer that you raffle) something else.*
   8. Es muy temprano para que **lleguen** ahora. *It's too early for them to arrive now.*
   9. Me dice que lo **haga** después. *She tells me to do it later.*

B. 1. Me gusta que **sigas** mis consejos. *It pleases me that you are following my advice.*

   2. Sentimos que no **hayas** decidido. *We're sorry you haven't decided.*

   3. Me alegro que te **haya** dado el visto bueno. *I'm glad he's given you his O.K.*

C. 1. Ojalá que tú no te **dediques** a eso.

   2. Es ridículo que las muchachas **tengan** que llevar chaperón. *(It's ridiculous that girls have to take a chaperon.)*

   3. Se oponen a que lo **cambiemos** tanto. *They're opposed to our changing it so much.*

   4. No creo que **haya** nada de malo en eso. *I don't think there's anything wrong in that.*

   5. No están convencidos de que **sea** importante. *They're not convinced that it's important.*

AN INFLUENCE BROUGHT TO BEAR		WHAT IS INFLUENCED
Les ruego	que	no discutan
Prefiero	que	rifes
Es muy temprano para	que	lleguen ahora

Where the main idea tends to affect the course of what happens in the clause (to cause it, encourage it, prevent it, discourage it), the verb of the clause is in the subjunctive.

AN ATTITUDE OF LIKE-DISLIKE OR ACCEPTANCE-REJECTION		WHAT IS LIKED OR DISLIKED, ACCEPTED OR REJECTED
Me gusta	que	sigas mis consejos
Sentimos	que	no hayas decidido
Es ridículo	que	tengan que llevar chaperón
No creo	que	haya nada de malo

Where the main idea shows a positive or negative bias, often tinged with emotion, the verb in the clause is subjunctive.

● PERSON-NUMBER SUBSTITUTION DRILL

INSTRUCTIONS: Repeat the following sentences just as you hear them. Then repeat them again, substituting the suggested subjects for the second verb.

1. ¿De qué quieres que hablemos, mamá?
   (yo, ellos, ella, él y yo, él)

2. Susana quiere que *yo* le compre tarjetas postales.
   (ellas, nosotros, ustedes, tú, usted, Lorenzo)

3. ¿Desean los señores que *yo* entre?
   (nosotros, ellas, él, ellos, ella, el vendedor)

4. Prefiero que no exageres tanto.
   (ustedes, él, ellos, usted, tú, las señoras)

5. El merece que *nosotros* lo odiemos.
   (yo, ellos, ella, tú, tú y yo, el pueblo)

6. Mis padres sugieren que *yo* siga otra carrera.
   (nosotros, él, tú, ustedes, él y yo, mi hermano mayor)

7. Mi madre se opone a que *yo* estudie ingeniería.
   (él, ustedes, nosotros, ellos, tú, ella)

8. No aceptan que *ustedes* discutan la decisión.
   (nosotros, yo, tú, usted, ellas, él)

9. Por favor, no pidan que salgamos otra vez.
   (yo, ellos, él, Alberto y yo, ella, los señores)

10. Yo no dejo que *mis hijas* vayan ahí.
    (ella, ustedes, Elena, las chicas, tú, ellas)

11. El profesor dice que abramos el libro.
    (usted, ustedes, tú, yo, ellos, ella)

12. Ellos necesitan que *yo* les haga la comida.
    (nosotros, él, tú, ella, ustedes, usted)

13. Ella espera que llegues a una decisión pronto.
    (yo, ustedes, usted, ellos, él, nosotros)

14. Siento que *usted* no pueda cambiar mis bolivianos.
    (ustedes, él, ellos, tú, el empleado)

15. Me alegro que no tenga que comprar otra batería.
    (nosotros, ustedes, él, tú, ellos, Ricardo)

16. Me gusta que *tú* sigas mis consejos.
    (él, ellos, usted, ustedes, mi sobrina)
17. Ojalá que *tú* no te dediques a la política.
    (él, ellos, usted, ustedes, nosotros, yo)
18. Ojalá que *Rosa* reciba esa carta.
    (usted, yo, tú, ellos, ella, nosotros)
19. Ojalá que *yo* pueda ir.
    (nosotros, él, tú, usted, ustedes, Antonio)
20. Es ridículo que *las muchachas* tengan que llevar chaperón.
    (ella, nosotras, ellas, tú, usted, ustedes, yo)
21. Es mejor que no rabies tanto.
    (yo, ustedes, usted, nosotros, ellos, él)
22. Es bueno que *Olga* estudie el español.
    (ustedes, tú, usted, yo, ellos, nosotros)
23. Es difícil que *Pablo* haga eso.
    (yo, nosotros, tú, ellos, ella, ustedes)
24. Es importante que pasemos lista.
    (el profesor, ellas, yo, tú, ustedes, usted)
25. Es probable que *ellos* salgan esta noche.
    (yo, ustedes, tú, nosotros, ella, los muchachos)
26. Es necesario que esperes un momento.
    (nosotros, ella, ustedes, usted, ellos, yo)
27. Lástima que *yo* no sepa jugar.
    (usted, ellos, nosotros, tú, él, ustedes)
28. No importa que no paguen ahora.
    (usted, tú, yo, ellos, nosotros, él)
29. El paquete es muy grande para que *Paquito* lo lleve.
    (tú, usted, ustedes, nosotros, ellas, el niño)
30. Son muy jóvenes para que *nosotros* los dejemos salir de noche.
    (ella, yo, ellos, tú, usted, mis padres)

INSTRUCTIONS: Repeat the following sentences just as you hear them. Then substitute the phrase given for the one in italics, or simply use the phrase given as a cue to determine the correct form of the indirect with-verb pronoun. This pronoun will have the same person and number as the subjunctive verb form in the noun clause.

1. *Les* ruego *a ustedes* que no dependan tanto de la bocina.
    (a usted, a ellos, a ella, a los jóvenes, al muchacho)
2. *Nos* dice que tomemos un colectivo.
    (a ustedes, a mí, a usted, a ti, a ellos, a él)
3. *Me* sugiere que cambie los sucres.
    (a nosotros, a usted, a ti, a ustedes, a ella, a ellas)
4. *Les* pide que estén ahí sin falta.
    (a mí, a usted, a ti, a ustedes, a nosotros, a él)
5. *Te* mando que no vayas sin permiso.
    (a usted, a ustedes, a él, a ellos, a ella, a ellas)
6. *Me* escribe que vaya la otra semana.
    (a ellas, a él, a nosotros, a ellos, a ti, a ella)

● CONSTRUCTION SUBSTITUTION DRILL

INSTRUCTIONS: Repeat the following sentences just as you hear them. Then repeat them again, preceded by the expressions indicated, which will change the verb of the model from indicative to subjunctive.

1. Me cambian los guaraníes en el banco.
    (quiero que, prefiero que, espero que)
2. Vendo el ganado en el invierno.
    (me exigen que, me sugieren que, me piden que)
3. Las chicas viven allí.
    (me alegro que, me preocupa que, me opongo a que)
4. Mueren de úlceras o de un ataque al corazón.
    (es ridículo que, es difícil que, es probable que)
5. Dormimos nueve horas en el verano.
    (es bueno que, es importante que, es ridículo que)
6. Entiende bien la pronunciación de Betty.
    (deseo que, espero que, me gusta que)
7. Seguimos otra carrera de igual prestigio.
    (es importante que, es mejor que, es necesario que)
8. Pides un churrasco bien jugoso.
    (sugiero que, prefiero que, quiero que)
9. Los muchachos tienen un hambre feroz.
    (lástima que, no importa que, es probable que)
10. Don Rafael conoce bien el centro.
    (espero que, me alegro que, ojalá que)
11. Nosotros salimos para el Club de la Unión.
    (ruegan que, insisten en que, no les gusta que)
12. No digo nada de mis estudios.
    (quieren que, sugieren que, prefieren que)

13. Aquí no hay agua potable.
   (es probable que, es difícil que, es ridículo que)
14. Mi patria está en la ruina.
   (siento que, no creo que, lástima que)
15. Este amigo no es cargante.
   (me alegro que, espero que, ojalá que)
16. Hoy día no hay pleitos.
   (insisten en que, prefieren que, esperan que)

17. Yo no sé nada de quetzales, soles, colones y cosas por el estilo.
   (lástima que, no es bueno que, es ridículo que)
18. No hay más remedio que callarse.
   (es imposible que, lástima que, parece fantástico que)
19. Ellas salen solas de noche.
   (me preocupa que, no estoy de acuerdo que, parece fantástico que)

● CHOICE-QUESTION RESPONSE DRILL

A. 1. ¿Quiere que salgamos en bus o prefiere que tomemos el coche?
   2. ¿Quiere que le demos una parte de la cosecha o prefiere que le paguemos un sueldo?
   3. ¿Desea que nos vayamos al cementerio o prefiere que nos quedemos aquí?
   4. ¿Desea que busquemos otras vacas para crianza o prefiere que compremos éstas para lechería?

B. 1. ¿Quiere que yo vaya al cine o prefiere que me quede en casa?
   2. ¿Quiere que yo estudie química o prefiere que busque un empleo?
   3. ¿Quiere que yo sirva la carne ahora o prefiere que espere un rato?
   4. ¿Desea que yo mande los documentos a la casa o sugiere que los lleve a la escuela?

*English infinitive or –**ing** form becoming a clause in Spanish*

		USUAL ENGLISH FORM	ENGLISH CLAUSE FORM EQUIVALENT TO SPANISH
to want, and message-carrying verbs	She { wants tells writes wires phones etc. }	me to do it	that I do it
preposition before infinitive or –*ing*	It's too late	for you to go	for that you go
	They're opposed	to our changing	to that we change
	They're not convinced	{ of its being that it is }	of that it is

In general, where English has an infinitive or an –*ing* with its own subject, the Spanish equivalent is a clause. (Spanish keeps the preposition before the clause just as it keeps it before the infinitive. See Unit 8 §38.)

● TRANSLATION DRILL

A. 1. Tell him to come early.
   2. Tell him to go to the plaza.
   3. Tell him to bring the straw.
   4. Tell him to sell the wool.
   5. Tell him to adjust (arrange) the carburetor.
   6. Tell him to use another example.
   7. Tell him to turn off the light.

B. 1. She wants me to come early.
   2. She wants me to go to the plaza.
   3. She wants me to study physics.
   4. She wants me to fly tomorrow.
   5. She wants me to do it now.
   6. She wants me to leave immediately.
   7. She wants me to eat more.

C. 1. They're opposed to our coming.
   2. They're opposed to our going to the movies.
   3. They're opposed to our betting so much.
   4. They're opposed to our working all day.
   5. They're opposed to our studying psychology.
   6. They're opposed to our opening a restaurant.
   7. They're opposed to our comparing everything.

● DISCUSSION

The most important uses of the subjunctive in Spanish (apart from its use in the **usted,–es** commands) are in subordinate clauses. A subordinate clause is a sentence-like group of words with its own subject and verb, which fits into a larger sentence where it occupies the same place that might be occupied by some nonsentence element. In the following pairs, note how the sentence-like clause performs the same function, essentially, as the nonsentence element directly beneath it:

1) He deserves *that people hate him.* (Subject *people,* verb *hate.*)
   He deserves *hatred.* (No subject, no verb.)
2) Do you admire someone *who works hard?* (Subject *who,* verb *works.*)
   Do you admire someone *industrious?*
3) I saw him *when he came.*
   I saw him *yesterday.*

The first of these clauses occupies the position of a noun, and is therefore called a noun clause; just like the single word *hatred,* it is the object of the main verb *deserves.* The second clause is like the adjective *industrious,* and is called an adjective clause. The third clause is like the adverb *yesterday,* and is called an adverb clause.

Noun clauses are more frequent in Spanish than in English; in English the infinitive and *–ing* form occupy much the same semantic area. It takes a little practice to adapt the English infinitive or *–ing* to a clause in Spanish. There are two situations where it is necessary to make this change: (1) where the main verb is *tell* (someone to do something) or one of its synonyms, or the verb *want,* and (2) where the English infinitive or *–ing* has its own subject, and follows a preposition.

The subjunctive has been all but lost in noun clauses in English. The few remnants resemble Spanish; for example, *I recommend that he try harder, I insist that he stop, I move that it be tabled* has the subjunctive forms *he try, he stop, it be* rather than the indicative forms *he tries, he stops, it is* and correspond to Examples *A,* where an influence is brought to bear.

Spanish organizes its indicative-subjunctive contrast in noun clauses around the point of view that the main part of the sentence takes toward the content of the clause. If the main part of the sentence, especially the main verb, is one of the expressions that we use when we report information—*to know, to be sure, to say, to tell, to find out, to reveal, to state, to assert, to think, to assume, to realize, to conclude, to decide, it seems, it is true, it is a fact, it is evident*—then the content of the clause is generally viewed as information, and its verb is indicative. If the main part of the sentence, especially the main verb, is one of the expressions that we use to show our desires, hopes, or feelings toward the content of the clause, then its verb is subjunctive. It does not matter that the content actually is to some extent informative. For example, *I am sorry that you are sick* (**que estés malo**) would inform a third party that the person in question is sick, but the verb is nevertheless subjunctive, because *to be sorry* does not convey a report but an emotion; *I hear that you are sick* (**que estás malo**) uses an expression, *I hear,* that is common in straight reporting, and the verb of the clause is indicative.

Whether the information in the clause is true or false, real or imagined makes no difference so long as the main idea is one of *conveying* it. In **Apuesto a que ganamos,** the speaker uses *I bet* as a way of conveying a prediction; he does not say how he feels about it, or try to make it happen, but simply foresees it. In *I dreamed that I was queen,* the speaker reports the content of the dream; the verb is indicative despite its unreality. Furthermore, the speaker may be quite vehement in his assertion of the information. He may thump his fist and say *I declare,* but this does not affect the verb: it is still indicative. The kind of emotion that does call for subjunctive is one that views the idea in the noun clause as something to be welcomed or spurned. *To accept, be glad, approve, applaud* are notions of welcoming; *to disapprove, be sorry, disbelieve, dislike* are notions of spurning.

The "influence" notion admits of no alternative: the verb of the clause here is always subjunctive. But certain expressions in the "welcoming-spurning" group sometimes express the "conveying information" point of view. In *I didn't know that he was here* (**que estaba aquí**), the speaker reports his ignorance of a piece of information, and **estaba** is indicative; in *Oh, I don't know that it's so good* (**que sea tan bueno**), the speaker spurns the idea of its being good, and **sea** is subjunctive. In *I don't think it's true,* the indicative will be used if the speaker implies "This item of information is conveyed as false" (positive denial): **No creo que es la verdad;** but the subjunctive will be used if he implies "I'm dubious about the idea (I'm inclined to reject it)": **No creo que sea la verdad.** The subjunctive is generally used here for politeness' sake: such statements usually occur when contradicting someone else, and a positive denial might be rude.

98 Indirect commands

EXAMPLES

1. Que lo **hagan** otros.
2. **Digan** lo que digan. *(Let them say what they may say.)*
3. Que **espere.** *Let him wait (he can just wait).*
4. Que **pasen.** *Have them come in.*
5. Que se **vaya.** *Let him go (he can go for all I care).*
6. Que ella los **lleve** (que los **lleve** ella). *Let her carry them.*
7. Que no **estudie** medicina. *Don't let (have) him study medicine.*

Let Have	him her them	do it	
Que	(él) (ella) (ellos, –as)	lo haga lo hagan	(él) (ella) (ellos, –as)

Indirect commands, like **usted, –es** commands, use the present subjunctive, third-person singular and plural. Except in a few set phrases (example 2), they are introduced by **que.** With-verb pronouns precede the verb, and subject pronouns, as usual, are normally included only for emphasis.

● PATTERNED RESPONSE DRILL

A. 1. TEACHER: ¿Rosa va a comprar la carne?
   STUDENT: **Sí, que la compre.**
  2. ¿Patricio va a pedir el cambio?
  3. ¿Don Pepe va a contar la ganancia?
  4. ¿Fernando va a arreglar el aire?
  5. ¿Chalo va a discutir la cuestión?
  6. ¿Alvaro va a traer los libros?
  7. ¿El profesor va a explicar las costumbres?
  8. ¿La criada va a llevar los vestidos?
  9. ¿Josefina va a traer los libros?
  10. ¿Víctor va a explicar lo de las nubes?
  11. ¿El padre va a discutir lo del cielo?

B. 1. Barra usted la sala.
   Yo no; que la barra otro.
  2. Apague usted el radio.
  3. Traiga usted las sábanas.
  4. Lave usted los platos.
  5. Haga usted la ensalada.
  6. Mande usted el paquete.
  7. Conteste usted las preguntas.
  8. Sacuda usted los muebles.
  9. Envuelva usted la ropa.

C. 1. ¿No salen ustedes ahora?
   Nosotros no; que salgan otros.

   2. ¿No entran ustedes ahora?
   3. ¿No regresan ustedes ahora?
   4. ¿No vienen ustedes ahora?
   5. ¿No vuelven ustedes ahora?
   6. ¿No pagan ustedes ahora?
   7. ¿No abren ustedes ahora?
   8. ¿No almuerzan ustedes ahora?
   9. ¿No comulgan ustedes ahora?

D. 1. Acuéstense ustedes.
   Nosotros no; que se acuesten otros.

   2. Váyase usted.
   Yo no; que se vaya otro.

   3. Levántense ustedes.

4. Siéntese usted.
5. Duérmanse ustedes.
6. Acuérdese usted.
7. Alégrense ustedes.
8. Quédese usted.
9. Cálmense ustedes.

E. 1. Tráigame el libro.
   Yo no; que se lo traiga otro.

   2. Véndame la camisa.
   3. Lléveme los paquetes.
   4. Mándeme las fotos.
   5. Láveme el coche.
   6. Muéstreme la tarjeta.
   7. Déme los recibos.
   8. Cómpreme las pastillas.

● CHOICE-QUESTION RESPONSE DRILL

A. 1. TEACHER: ¿Vengo yo o viene él?
   STUDENT: **Que venga él.**

   2. ¿Corro yo o corre él?
   3. ¿Disparo yo o dispara él?
   4. ¿Escojo yo o escoge él?
   5. ¿Pregunto yo o pregunta él?
   6. ¿Rezo yo o reza él?
   7. ¿Termino yo o termina él?
   8. ¿Sigo yo o sigue él?

B. 1. Vamos nosotros o van ellos?
   Que vayan ellos.

   2. ¿Comemos nosotros o comen ellos?
   3. ¿Hablamos nosotros o hablan ellos?
   4. ¿Rifamos nosotros o rifan ellos?
   5. ¿Escribimos nosotros o escriben ellos?
   6. ¿Jugamos nosotros o juegan ellos?
   7. ¿Pedimos nosotros o piden ellos?
   8. ¿Volvemos nosotros o vuelven ellos?

● TRANSLATION DRILL

A. 1. Have Rosa wash the cups.
   Que Rosa lave las tazas.

   2. Have Josefina sweep the living room.
   3. Have Ana dust the furniture.
   4. Have Alfredo bring the car.
   5. Have the barber use the scissors.

B. 1. See that they buy the bread.
   Que compren el pan.

   2. See that they develop the photos.
   3. See that they pay the fine.
   4. See that they work tomorrow.
   5. See that they come early.

C. 1. Let her go to the movies.
   Que vaya al cine.

   2. Let her eat in the kitchen.
   3. Let her wait in the rain.
   4. Let her count the books.
   5. Let her come back tomorrow.

● DISCUSSION

To convey an indirect command or permission, Spanish uses the present subjunctive. The English equivalents *let* and *have* are somewhat stronger than the Spanish implies. The *let* of *Let him go,* when in the Spanish form **Que se vaya,** does not suggest releasing him from restraint (this would be **Deje que se vaya,** with **dejar** for *let*) but merely *He may go if he wants to. Have them come in* in the form **Que pasen** does not necessarily imply compulsion, but only *They may come in,* anywhere between urging and permitting.

English at one time abounded in such expressions of commanding, permitting, or wishing, and a number of idiomatic expressions still survive, especially those with religious associations. The words *may* and *let* are frequent: *(May) God bless you; May they rest in peace; May (let) the best man win; Heaven help us; Those whom God hath joined together, let no man put asunder.*

99 Present subjunctive for *let's*

EXAMPLES

A. 1. **Cambiemos** de tema.
2. **Dejemos** ese tema.
3. **Sentémo**nos   *Let's sit down.*
4. **Hagámos**lo ahora.   *Let's do it now.*

B. 1. No **discutamos** más.
2. No **toquemos** ese tema.
3. No nos **sentemos**.   *Let's not sit down.*
4. No lo **hagamos** ahora.   *Let's not do it now.*

C. Bueno, **vámonos**.

	LET'S	LET'S NOT
with –**nos** with other with-verb pronouns	**discutamos** **sentémo**– –**nos** **hagámos** –**lo**	**no discutamos** **no nos sentemos** **no lo hagamos**

The present subjunctive, first-person plural, is used for *let's*. As with the direct commands (Unit 5 §24), the with-verb pronouns precede when the verb is negative, follow when it is affirmative. When –**nos** follows the verb, the final **s** of the verb is dropped.

● PATTERNED RESPONSE DRILL

A. 1. TEACHER: Hable usted.
   STUDENT: **No; hablemos nosotros.**
2. Entre usted.
3. Termine usted.
4. Espere usted.
5. Pague usted.
6. Coma usted.
7. Escriba usted.
8. Salga usted.
9. Siga usted.
10. Venga usted.
11. Vuelva usted.

B. 1. Acuéstese usted.
   No; acostémonos nosotros.
2. Quédese usted.
3. Acuérdese usted.
4. Levántese usted.
5. Siéntese usted.
6. Duérmase usted.
7. Defiéndase usted.
8. Sírvase usted.
9. Váyase usted.

C. 1. ¿Pagamos la cuenta?
   Sí, paguémosla. No, no la paguemos.
2. ¿Acortamos el discurso?
3. ¿Tomamos la casa?
4. ¿Rifamos el abrigo?
5. ¿Miramos a las chicas?
6. ¿Dejamos los zapatos?
7. ¿Discutimos el asunto?
8. ¿Traemos la receta?
9. ¿Vendemos los libros?
10. ¿Escribimos las cartas?

D. 1. ¿Le prestamos la plata?
   Sí, prestémosela.[1] No, no se la prestemos.
2. ¿Le llevamos el tocadiscos?
3. ¿Le contamos las mentiras?
4. ¿Le mostramos los titulares?
5. ¿Le apagamos la luz?
6. ¿Le quitamos el abrigo?
7. ¿Le enseñamos las cartas?
8. ¿Le arreglamos los frenos?

● CHOICE-QUESTION RESPONSE DRILL

A. 1. TEACHER: ¿Estudiamos o hablamos?
   STUDENT: **Hablemos.**
2. ¿Entramos o regresamos?

3. ¿Regateamos o salimos?
4. ¿Seguimos o volvemos?
5. ¿Contestamos o esperamos?

---

[1] = **prestémossela**. The –**ss**– is reduced to –**s**–.

B. 1. ¿Nos quedamos o nos vamos?
   Quedémonos.

   2. ¿Nos sentamos o nos levantamos?
   3. ¿Nos defendemos o nos vamos?
   4. ¿Nos lavamos o nos bañamos?

C. 1. ¿Vendemos la casa o la arreglamos?
   Vendámosla.

2. ¿Traemos a los niños o los dejamos?
3. ¿Mencionamos la invitación o la olvidamos?
4. ¿Llevamos las cartas o las mandamos?
5. ¿Servimos los huevos o los cambiamos?
6. ¿Cerramos la puerta o la abrimos?
7. ¿Usamos el coche o lo prestamos?

● DISCUSSION

In addition to **vamos a** plus infinitive (Unit 7 §34), Spanish uses the present subjunctive, first-person plural, to express the meaning *let's*.

The subjunctive is the only way of saying *let's not* (while **Vamos a hacerlo** may mean *Let's do it*, **No vamos a hacerlo** can only mean *We aren't going to do it*). This gives the clue to the slight difference in meaning between the two constructions. We may readily say in English *Come on, let's do it,* but not (at least in the same sense) *Come on, let's not do it.* **Vamos a** suggests this livelier notion of movement: **Vamos a hacerlo** *Come on, let's do it,* or *Let's go do it.* **Hagámoslo** *Let's do it* proposes the action as something desirable or worth doing, in the direction of *What do you say we do it,* though stronger.

Vámonos is the form used for the meaning *let's get going, let's go*.

100 Colors

EXAMPLES
1. **Negro,** con muy poquito azúcar.
2. Montañas, nubes, cielo **azul.**
3. Una casita **verde** que está en la esquina.

NEUTRALITY	
white	**blanco**
gray	**gris**
black	**negro**

INTENSITY	
light	**claro**
dark	**oscuro**

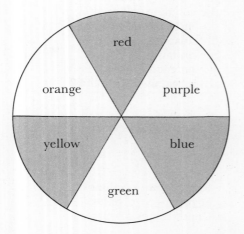

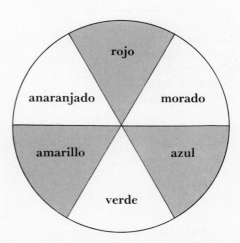

The primary colors are **rojo, amarillo,** and **azul.** The secondary colors are **anaranjado** (from **naranja** *orange*), **verde,** and **morado.**

1. Aquí hay varios libros *negros*.
   (amarillos, rojos, azules, anaranjados)
2. ¿Dónde está mi camisa *blanca?*
   (azul, gris, verde, morada)
3. ¡Qué bonitas son esas flores *rojas!*
   (moradas, amarillas, anaranjadas, azules)
4. Vivimos en una casita *verde*.
   (blanca, gris, amarilla, azul)
5. Mi vestido nuevo es *amarillo*.
   (morado, rojo, gris, negro)
6. Me gusta el color *verde* claro.
   (azul, rojo, morado, anaranjado)
7. Ana prefiere el *rojo* oscuro.
   (azul, anaranjado, verde, morado)

● TRANSLATION DRILL

A. 1. That black overcoat is mine.
   2. That red necktie is mine.
   3. That white shirt is mine.
   4. That gray suit is mine.
   5. That blue house is mine.
   6. That green car is mine.

B. 1. Where's the blue post card?
   2. Where's the yellow bus?
   3. Where's the red wool?
   4. Where's the green room?
   5. Where's the white cow?
   6. Where's the black bull?
   7. Where's the gray horse?

101   Nouns and *todos* with first- and second-person verbs

EXAMPLES

A. 1. **(Nosotros) los americanos** no pensamos así.   *We Americans don't think that way.*
   2. **Ustedes los abogados** discuten demasiado.   *You lawyers argue too much.*

B. Ya aquí **todos hemos visto** esa película.

C. 1. A **ustedes los jóvenes** no los convence nadie.
   2. Creen que casa y comida son bastantes para **nosotras las viejas**.   *They think that room and board are enough for us elderly women.*

SUBJECT PRONOUN	DEFINITE ARTICLE	SUBJECT NOUN	VERB
(Nosotros) Ustedes	los los	americanos abogados	pensamos discuten

		Todos	hemos visto

As subject in this construction, **nosotros, –as** is optional, since the verb identifies the meaning as *we*, but **ustedes** is required. With nouns the definite article must be used in any case because of the meaning *all* (see Unit 13 §75).

	OBJECT PRONOUN	DEFINITE ARTICLE	OBJECT NOUN
para a	nosotras ustedes	las los	viejas jóvenes

As object, both **ustedes** and **nosotros, –as** are required.

● TRANSLATION DRILL

A. 1. TEACHER: We technicians drink too much coffee.

STUDENT: **Nosotros los técnicos tomamos demasiado café.**

2. We government officials work hard.
3. We paper boys don't earn much.
4. We barbers talk a lot.
5. We tourists buy lots of things.

B. 1. You lawyers argue too much.
Ustedes los abogados discuten demasiado.
2. You dentists work hard.
3. You farmers eat well.
4. You students need to study more.
5. You idealists shouldn't exaggerate so much.

C. 1. We have all seen that film.
Todos hemos visto esa película.
2. We are all from the United States.

3. We all live in Colombia.
4. We all work in the same plant.
5. We all eat at the same restaurant.

D. 1. There's not much for us elderly women.
No hay mucho para nosotras las viejas.
2. There's not much for us country people.
3. There's very little for us athletes.
4. No one expects much from us servants.
5. No one expects much from us housewives.

E. 1. No one can convince you young people.
A ustedes los jóvenes no los convence nadie.
2. No one can convince you idealists.
3. No one can understand you philosophers.
4. No one can comprehend you administrators.
5. No one can teach you maids.

● DISCUSSION

The Spanish equivalent of the type *you soldiers, we doctors, us students* differs in two ways from the English: First, the definite article is required with the noun, since **We doctors** *have licenses* generalizes in the same way as **Practicing doctors** *have licenses*. Second, whereas in English both *we* (*us*) and *you* always accompany the noun, in Spanish **nosotros,–as** as subject of an explicit verb is not required, unless for emphasis, because the verb ending tells that *we* is the meaning (see Unit 2 §2): **Los americanos no pensamos así.** But **nosotros,–as** as object is expressed as in English and **ustedes** is expressed regardless of its grammatical function.

● COMBINED PATTERN REPLACEMENT DRILL

A. 1. **Por ejemplo, los abogados se destacan mucho.**
2. Qué va _____
3. _____ idealistas _____
4. _____ preocupan _____
5. _____ el _____
6. Sin embargo _____
7. _____ demasiado
8. _____ independientes _____
9. _____ entusiasman _____
10. Qué barbaridad _____
11. _____ jefe _____
12. _____ los _____
13. _____ alegran _____
14. _____ bastante
15. Ya lo creo _____
16. _____ director _____
17. _____ opone _____
18. _____ todavía
19. _____ presidente _____
20. En realidad _____
21. _____ defiende _____
22. _____ policía _____
23. _____ la _____

B. 1. **Yo sé que el niño juega bien.**
2. _____ mi _____
3. ___espero que _____
4. _____ mucho
5. _____ estudie _____
6. _____ niños _____
7. ___veo que _____
8. _____ las _____
9. _____ ahora
10. ___prefiero que _____
11. _____ chica _____
12. _____ trabaje _____
13. ___creo que _____
14. _____ los _____
15. _____ temprano
16. _____ llegan _____
17. ___siento que _____
18. _____ alumnos_____
19. _____ tarde
20. _____ la _____
21. _____ salga _____
22. ___sugiero que _____
23. _____ mañana
24. _____ grupo _____

The required relator **que**.

A. 1. I think she is American.
   2. I think she speaks Spanish.
   3. I think she goes to this school.
   4. I think she wants to leave immediately.

B. 1. It seems to me she is Spanish.
   2. It seems to me she speaks English.
   3. It seems to me she studies philosophy.
   4. It seems to me she wants to participate in politics.

C. 1. She says she is Venezuelan.
   2. She says she speaks English.
   3. She says she went to the university.
   4. She says there's nothing bad in that.
   5. She says she spoke against a demonstration.
   6. She says no.
   7. She says not even in a painting.
   8. She says it's a horror.

READING

Escojamos una carrera

E. *Estudiante* P. *Su profesor*
S. *Secretaria del profesor*

E. Profesor, quiero que usted me dé unos consejos.

P. Con mucho gusto. Pasemos a mi oficina... Aquí estamos... Sentémonos... Bueno, ¿en qué puedo servirle?

E. Profesor, mis padres me han dicho que empiece a pensar en escoger una carrera.

P. Y tienen razón. ¿Cuántos años tiene usted?

E. Diecinueve, señor.

P. ¿Ah?... Yo siento una corriente de aire aquí. ¿Le molesta si cierro una ventana?

E. De ninguna manera. ¿Quiere usted que le ayude?

P. Gracias... ¿Por qué no es posible, en esta época de progreso científico, que los constructores hagan una ventana que funcione? (*Llaman a la puerta.*) ¡Pase!

S. (*entrando*) Hay una señorita aquí afuera que quiere hablarle.

P. Que vuelva. ...¿Una señorita, dice?... Pues, que espere. No voy a tardar mucho. Que espere, que espere.

S. Muy bien, señor. (*Sale.*)

P. ¿En dónde estábamos?

E. Mi carrera, profesor.

P. Ah, sí. Su carrera. ...Pues, ¿no quiere ser ingeniero? Puede inventar una ventana que se cierre y se abra con facilidad. ¿Cómo van las matemáticas?

E. Muy mal. Salí reprobado[1] en álgebra el año pasado.

P. Entonces no debe ser ingeniero. ... Usted puede perder su regla de cálculo.[2] ¿Por qué no escoge usted la carrera de abogado?

E. Ay, señor, hay tantos abogados ahora que es difícil destacarse en ese campo.

P. Pero el abogado puede meterse en la política, ¿no?

E. Sí, señor, pero no toquemos ese tema. Yo soy muy idealista para meterme en la política.

P. Hmm. ... Pues usted es el que decide. ¿Qué quiere ser usted?

E. (*corta pausa*) Poeta, señor.

P. ¡Dios mío!... Pero, mire: lo de ser poeta ...no es carrera, ¡es una condición de la mente!... Usted sí que es[3] un idealista. Pero, si quiere escribir, si sabe escribir... entonces... escriba.... Dios sea[4] contigo, hijo mío.... Yo también quise ser poeta...

---

[1] *I failed*   [2] *slide rule*   [3] *You are indeed*   [4] **sea** rather than **esté** because more than location is involved: "May God be active on your behalf."

READING
De compras

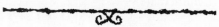

(En el supermercado, Ana, esposa de Jaime, la que[1] entiende muy bien el español, acompaña a Concha, la esposa de Rafael Cuervo, a una de las grandes tiendas de comestibles de la ciudad para servirla de intérprete.)

c. *Concha*   a. *Ana*

c. ¡Qué limpias y bien surtidas están las tiendas norteamericanas!

a. Es verdad. Y es una tarea fácil ir de compras si uno tiene bastante dinero.

c. Veo que tienen ustedes productos de todos los países, especialmente de este continente. Un gran mercado es una lección práctica de interdependencia y solidaridad continental. ¡Mire a nuestro alrededor! Café, azúcar, chocolate, piñas, avocados, o aguacates...

a. Sí, vamos a ver cuántas cosas de otros países pongo en mi carrito. ¿Quiere usted ayudarme, Concha? Y al mismo tiempo vamos a llenar el carrito de usted con comestibles de este país. ¿O.K.?

c. Muy bien. Aquí está una lata de carne de Argentina. Con la salsa "tabasco"[2] mexicana es muy rica.

a. Ahora, necesitamos pensar en la ensalada. Vamos a ver: aceitunas sevillanas, aceite español, tomates mexicanos y lechuga... lechuga internacional...

c. Pues, en mi país, hay muy pocos supermer-

cados. Las criadas hacen la mayoría de las compras y van de tienda en tienda, de la panadería a la carnicería o a la fiambrería y de ahí a la lechería. Pero a ellas les gusta porque pueden hablar y comentar muchas cosas durante toda la mañana mientras hacen las compras.

a. ¡Mire! Ya tenemos los carritos llenos y yo estoy muy cansada. Usted también, ¿no? Vámonos. Pero, primero debemos comprar un poco de café colombiano y de azúcar cubano.

c. ¡Qué chiste! Y ¿también chicle guatemalteco?

a. Usted aprende muy pronto.

c. Ahora, vamos a una farmacia de su país donde hay de todo. Allí vamos a tomar un helado con chocolate ecuatoriano y nueces brasileñas, ¿eh? Y vamos a comprar tabaco cubano para nuestros esposos.

a. Con mucho gusto. La invito.

c. Muchas gracias.

a. Y mañana vamos a comprar la ropa que me decía que quería comprar, ¿eh?

c. ¡Qué amable es usted! Pero no necesita molestarse tanto. Rafael quiere acompañarme a la tienda pero tiene miedo de entrar. Yo voy a hacer las compras sola. ¿Nos vemos más tarde para tomar té?

Otro día

(Se ve que Concha Romero de Cuervo va acostumbrándose muy fácilmente a la vida de los Estados Unidos. Está en el primer piso de una tienda con su esposo. La ascensorista es una señorita puertorriqueña muy bonita.)

c. *Concha*   a. *Ascensorista*   r. *Rafael*   e. *Empleada cubana*   o. *Otra empleada*

c. *(A la ascensorista.)* Señorita, ¿en qué piso venden ropa de señoras?

---

[1] **la que** *who* (referring to **esposa**)

[2] **tabasco** Tabasco is one of the states of Mexico, famed for its beautiful forests. A native shrub, the tabasco, yields a small red fruit which is used to make tabasco sauce.

A. En el cuarto piso, señora. La ropa blanca está hacia la derecha y a la mano izquierda están los vestidos y sombreros. Aquí hay varias empleadas que hablan español. (*Suben.*) Aquí están ustedes.

C. Muchas gracias.

A. De nada, señora.

C. ¿Vas a acompañarme, Rafael?

R. No. Aquí te dejo sola. Aquí se habla español, dice el cartel. En tu cartera tienes dinero y un diccionario. Adiosito.[3]

C. Dentro de una hora nos vemos en el quinto piso para tomar té. Ana va a acompañarnos.

R. Muy bien. Mientras tanto yo me voy a comprar un traje de gabardina. Anda con ojo tú y no gastes mucho, ¿eh? No olvides que tenemos que comprar un baúl, maletas y otras cosas.

C. No tengas cuidado. No soy gastadora. Hasta lueguito.[4]
(*Una empleada cubana se dirige a la señora.*)

E. ¿En qué puedo servirla, señorita?

C. Yo quisiera comprar primero ropa interior y después vestidos, un sombrero, zapatos y medias de nilón.

E. Un momentito,[5] señorita. Señorita Delgado, esta señora desea comprar ropa interior . . .

O. Buenas tardes, señorita . . . ¿Qué medida[6] tiene?

C. No sé exactamente. En mi país mi medida es cuarenta y dos; aquí una amiga me dijo que mi medida es catorce. Mi estatura es de un metro sesenta y cinco centímetros. Peso cincuenta y seis kilos.[7]

E. Sí, su talla[8] debe ser catorce.

C. Espere usted un momento. Voy a buscar en este diccionario español-inglés los nombres de la ropa interior de señoras. (*Busca las palabras en el diccionario.*) En mis clases de inglés no aprendí estas cosas. (*Y la señora Romero de Cuervo compra muchas cosas que los estudiantes curiosos pueden hallar en los diccionarios.*)

E. Muchas gracias, señora, aquí tiene usted el vuelto.

C. Bueno, ¿dónde está la sección de vestidos y sombreros?

E. Por ahí.
(*La señora se prueba varios vestidos y compra cuatro, pero necesitan algunas alteraciones en los hombros y en el largo de la falda. Pasa otra hora gastando más dinero.*)

O. ¿En qué puedo servirla, señora?

C. Quisiera comprar unos guantes y una cartera, y unos zapatos y medias de nilón. ¿Tiene usted guantes de nilón?

O. Sí, señora.

C. Me han dicho que los zapatos aquí son buenos. Necesito por lo menos cinco pares . . .

O. ¿Qué más desea la señora?

C. Un impermeable.

O. Pues, los impermeables están en el primer piso, donde están también los paraguas y los zapatos de goma.

C. ¿Qué hora es? Tenía que reunirme con mi esposo a las cinco en el salón de té.

O. Son las seis menos veinte, señora.

C. Pues, voy a pagar la cuenta.

O. El total de la cuenta es doscientos noventa y dos dólares y con el impuesto. . . .

C. ¡Ay, por Dios!, no tengo más que . . .

O. ¿Ha gastado demasiado, señora?

C. Sí, pero aquí viene mi esposo a buscarme. Tú tienes más dinero, ¿eh, querido?

R. Ya me lo imaginaba. Te compraste toda la tienda, ¿eh? (*Paga la diferencia a la empleada.*) ¿Hubo liquidación[9] hoy?

C. No importa. Vas a ver lo que compré . . . compré sólo lo indispensable . . . y no tenía absolutamente nada que ponerme . . . y

---

[3] **Adiosito** *Good-bye now* (The ending **–ito** is explained in Unit 19 §108. It implies smallness or affection.)

[4] **Hasta lueguito** *Bye-bye*

[5] **Un momentito** *Just a moment* (This diminutive shows both interest and shortness of time.)

[6] **medida** *size (measure)*

[7] She is approximately 5′ 4″ tall and weights about 123 pounds. In all Latin countries the size for men's and women's clothing is often confusing to the shopper from the United States. Shoe sizes are arbitrary both here and in Latin countries. 32 is the key number for shoes in most of the Latin American stores. To ascertain your size abroad add 32 to your size; *i e.,* if you wear a 6, your size is 38, etc. Widths are usually the same: A, B, etc. Since most Latin Americans have small feet, a woman who wears 9 AAAA could hardly buy shoes in Latin America. 17 is the key number for children's shoes. Size 10 here would be 27. Dresses and underwear go by size 44 (16 in the U.S.), 42 (14), 40 (12), 38(10). Socks are based on the length of the foot: size 10 here = 25 in Latin America (2.54 centimeters = 1 inch). Gloves are based on the circumference of the hand: size 7 here = 18.

[8] **talla** *size (stature)*   [9] **liquidación** *clearance sale*

mañana voy al salón de belleza para que me hagan un permanente.[10]

R. ¡Pero, mujer! Yo no tengo fábrica de billetes.

C. Ya lo sé, querido. Ahora vamos al salón donde sirven el té. ¿Dónde está Ana?

Tengo hambre. Vamos.

R. ¿Dónde está Ana? ¡Dios mío! ¡Qué mujer tan gastadora!

C. La pobre Ana nos espera. Vamos. Se hace tarde.

R. Sí, vamos.

● CUESTIONARIO

1. ¿Adónde acompaña Ana a Concha, la esposa de Rafael Cuervo?
2. ¿Qué piensa Concha de las tiendas norteamericanas?
3. ¿Qué es un intérprete?
4. Nombre usted algunos de los productos del mercado que representan la interdependencia y solidaridad continental.
5. ¿Cómo es el sistema de compras de comestibles en Venezuela?
6. ¿Qué diferencia hay entre una farmacia norteamericana y una farmacia sudamericana?

7. ¿Qué artículos de ropa quiere comprar Concha?
8. ¿Por qué no sabe Concha cuál es su medida exacta?
9. ¿Qué debía hacer Concha a las cinco ese día?
10. ¿Cuánto dinero gasta en la tienda? ¿Qué compra?
11. ¿Cuál fue la reacción de Rafael al saberlo?
12. ¿Qué piensa hacer Concha al día siguiente?
13. ¿Por qué pregunta Rafael si hubo liquidación?

● SUGGESTED READINGS

Beals, Carleton, *Lands of the Dawning Morrow,* Bobbs-Merrill, New York, 1948: Ch. 9, "New Vitamins."

Reid, William A., "Economic Gifts of America to the World" (pamphlet), Pan American Union, Washington, D.C.

Verrill, A. H., *Foods America Gave the World,* Page, Boston, 1937.

---

[10] **para que me hagan un permanente** *to get a permanent*

18

A Businessman

(It's eleven a.m.; Mr. Suárez has just arrived at the office.)

s. *Mr. Suárez*   j. *Juanita, his secretary*
v. *Víctor*

s. Anything new, Juanita?
j. Two gentlemen came. They said they'd come back later.
s. I have to go in half an hour. Oh, before I forget, I have a letter to dictate to you, for Córdova and Company.
j. All right, Mr. Suárez.
s. "Dear Sirs, colon. We received your letter of the 21st of this month . . ."
j. The 22nd, Mr. Suárez.

Un hombre de negocios

(Son las once de la mañana; el señor Suárez acaba de llegar a la oficina.)

s. *Señor Suárez*   j. *Juanita, su secretaria*
v. *Víctor*

s. ¿Alguna novedad, Juanita?
j. Vinieron dos señores. Dijeron que iban a volver después.
s. Tengo que irme dentro de media hora. Ah, antes que me olvide, tengo una carta que dictarle, para la firma Córdova y Compañía.
j. Muy bien, Sr. Suárez.
s. "Muy señores míos, dos puntos. Recibimos su atenta (1) del 21 del presente. . . ."
j. Del 22, Sr. Suárez.

s. Oh, yes. ". . . and in regard to your order we are pleased to advise you that . . ." When will the spare parts arrive?

J. Maybe they'll be here next week.

s. ". . . that as soon as the parts reach us, we will send them to you immediately."

J. Anything else?

s. "I am, yours very truly, etc." You know.

* * *

(Mr. Suárez goes out to the street.)

v. Hello, Don Domingo. Don't get away from me again. I've never seen anybody as busy as you are.

s. Hi there, Víctor. Say, I'm sorry. I had completely forgotten that you were coming to see me.

v. That's all right, Don Domingo; don't worry.

s. I had it so much on my mind. Why just last night I was thinking, "When Víctor comes . . ."

v. It doesn't matter, Don Domingo.

s. You know, social obligations . . . first one thing, then another.

* * *

v. Do you have just a minute?

s. Well, right now I'm on my way over to the Exchange Commission, but if you want to, come along.

v. All right. I'll go along with you and we can talk on the way.

s. Let's see . . . Oh, I still have time for a cup of coffee. Let's look for a place that's not so noisy.

v. Wonderful, provided it's no bother to you, Don Domingo.

s. No, no, not at all. Let's go to the Café Brasil.

s. Ah, sí. ". . . y con respecto a su pedido tenemos el gusto de informarles que . . ." ¿Cuándo llegan los repuestos?

J. Tal vez estén aquí la otra semana.

s. ". . . que tan pronto nos lleguen los repuestos vamos a enviárselos de inmediato."

J. ¿Nada más?

s. "Quedo de ustedes su atento y seguro servidor (2) . . . etc., etc." Usted sabe.

* * *

(El señor Suárez sale a la calle.)

v. ¡Hola, don Domingo! ¡No se me escape otra vez! ¡Parece que no hay nadie que sea tan ocupado como usted! (3)

s. ¡Qué hubo, Víctor! Hombre, perdóneme. Se me había olvidado totalmente que iba a venir a verme.

v. Está bien, don Domingo; no se preocupe.

s. Lo tenía tan presente . . . Anoche no más estaba pensando, "Cuando venga Víctor . . ."

v. No tiene importancia, don Domingo.

s. Usted sabe, los compromisos sociales . . . esto, lo otro.

* * *

v. ¿Tiene un minutito?

s. Hombre, ahora voy a la Comisión de Cambios (4), pero si quiere, venga conmigo.

v. Muy bien, lo acompaño y vamos hablando.

s. ¿A ver? Ah, todavía tengo tiempo para un cafecito. Vamos a buscar un lugar que sea más tranquilo.

v. Magnífico, pero con tal que no le sea molestia, don Domingo.

s. No, no, hombre. Vamos al Café Brasil.

Cultural Notes

(1) **Atenta** is the feminine form of an adjective meaning "kind, courteous." In letter writing, **atenta,** which stands for **atenta carta,** means a letter of which one acknowledges receipt. This use of **atenta** is restricted to business or professional correspondence.

(2) The use of ceremonious formulas, especially in the complimentary close of a letter, has long been characteristic of Spanish commercial and social correspondence (in the formula used here, **atento y seguro servidor** is sometimes abbreviated **atto. y S. S.**). The meaning of the expressions is just as conventional as *Yours truly* etc. in English.

(3) By using **ser ocupado,** Víctor classifies Mr. Suárez as a *busy man;* **estar ocu-pado** would suggest being busy now.

(4) The **Comisión de Cambios** is a governmental agency which regulates foreign exchange and the issuance of export and import permits.

102 Indicative and subjunctive in adverb clauses

EXAMPLES

A. 1. **Como** ahora **estamos** en Cuaresma van a esperar. *(Since we are now in Lent, they're going to wait.)*
2. Prefiero un plato más típico **porque** los invitados **son** una pareja extranjera.
3. Llegamos después de las cinco, **pues** no **salimos** hasta las doce. *We got there after five, since we didn't leave until twelve.*
4. **Puesto que vale** tanto, no lo vamos a vender. *Since it is worth so much, we aren't going to sell it.*
5. **Ya que va,** ¿puede mandarme una taza de café?
6. **Ahora que** lo **conocemos** mejor, lo respetamos más. *Now that we know him better, we respect him more.*
7. No lo he visto **desde que** le **presté** mi coche. *I haven't seen him since I lent him my car.*
8. **Aunque esperamos** dos horas, no nos llamaron. *Though we waited two hours, they didn't call us.*

B. 1. **A menos que** uno se **meta** en la política.
2. **Antes que** me **olvide.**
3. Bueno, **con tal que** no le **sea** molestia.
4. Trabajemos **para que haya** más comodidades. *Let's work so that there will be more comforts.*
5. ¿Puede hacerlo **sin que** lo **sepamos?** *Can he do it without our knowing it?*

CONJUNCTIONS THAT TAKE INDICATIVE		
expressing cause	since, as = since because since since, inasmuch as since, now that	como[1] porque pues[2] puesto que ya que
	now that since [time] though, although	ahora que desde que aunque

These Spanish conjunctions take indicative when they have the meanings listed above.

CONJUNCTIONS THAT TAKE SUBJUNCTIVE	
before provided so that, in order that without unless	antes (de) que con tal (de) que para que sin que a menos que

[1] **Como** in this sense is usually at the beginning of the sentence.
[2] **Pues** in this sense is usually in the middle of the sentence.

1. Antes que *yo* me olvide, es necesario dictar la carta.
   (tú, usted, nosotros, él, ellos, ella, ustedes)
2. No, a menos que *uno* se meta en la política.
   (yo, ustedes, usted, tú, él, nosotros, ellos)

3. Con mucho gusto, con tal que no estudiemos biología.
   (yo, ustedes, él, ellos, tú, usted, ellas)
4. Y temprano, para que llegues a tiempo.
   (ustedes, yo, ella, nosotros, usted, ellos, él)
5. No es posible ir sin que *él* lo sepa.
   (nosotros, ella, tú, ustedes, yo, ellos, usted)

● CONSTRUCTION SUBSTITUTION DRILL

INSTRUCTIONS: Repeat the following sentences just as you hear them.   Then repeat them again substituting the expressions indicated for the italicized prepositions.

1. Llámeme *antes de* salir.
   _____ antes que Julio _____
2. Voy a hacer lo posible *para* volver mañana.
   _____para que Cecilia _____
3. No podemos ganar *sin* jugar.
   _____ sin que usted _____
4. *Con tal de* venir, no hay problema.
   Con tal que Rafael _____

5. Comemos temprano *para* ir al cine.
   _____ para que las chicas ___
6. Estoy esperando *para* participar.
   _____ para que tú _____
7. No podemos progresar *sin* trabajar.
   _____ sin que todo el mundo ___

● PATTERNED RESPONSE DRILL

A. 1. TEACHER: ¿Van a discutirlo con él?
   STUDENT: **Sí, antes que se vaya.**

   2. ¿Van a discutirlo con ellos?
   3. ¿Van a discutirlo con ella?
   4. ¿Van a discutirlo con nosotros?
   5. ¿Van a discutirlo con usted?
   6. ¿Van a discutirlo contigo?
   7. ¿Van a discutirlo conmigo?
   8. ¿Van a discutirlo con ustedes?

B. 1. ¿Se lo han dicho a él?
   Sí, para que se informe.

   2. ¿Se lo han dicho a ellos?
   3. ¿Se lo han dicho a ella?
   4. ¿Se lo han dicho a usted?
   5. ¿Te lo han dicho a ti?
   6. ¿Se lo han dicho a ustedes?

C. 1. ¿El se va mañana?
   Sí, a menos que no se sienta bien.

   2. ¿Ellos se van mañana?
   3. ¿Ella se va mañana?
   4. ¿Nosotros nos vamos mañana?
   5. ¿Usted se va mañana?
   6. ¿Tú te vas mañana?
   7. ¿Yo me voy mañana?
   8. ¿Ustedes se van mañana?

D. 1. ¿Lo supo él?
   No, lo han arreglado sin que lo sepa.

   2. ¿Lo supieron ellos?
   3. ¿Lo supo ella?
   4. ¿Lo supieron ellas?
   5. ¿Lo supo usted?
   6. ¿Lo supiste tú?
   7. ¿Lo supieron ustedes?

E. 1. ¿Va a pedir él los repuestos?
   Sí, con tal que los necesite.

   2. ¿Van a pedir ellos los repuestos?
   3. ¿Va a pedir ella los repuestos?
   4. ¿Vamos a pedir nosotros los repuestos?
   5. ¿Va a pedir usted los repuestos?
   6. ¿Vas a pedir tú los repuestos?
   7. ¿Voy a pedir yo los repuestos?
   8. ¿Van a pedir ustedes los repuestos?

F. 1. ¿Van a discutir la cuestión con él?
   Sí, para que pueda hacer algo.

   2. ¿Van a discutir la cuestión con ellos?
   3. ¿Van a discutir la cuestión contigo?
   4. ¿Van a discutir la cuestión con usted?
   5. ¿Van a discutir la cuestión con nosotros?
   6. ¿Van a discutir la cuestión conmigo?
   7. ¿Van a discutir la cuestión con ustedes?

● TRANSLATION DRILL

1. They're coming to study.
   They're coming so we can study.[1]
2. Call me before eating.
   Call me before the children eat.
3. I'm not going without knowing.
   I'm not going without my family knowing.

4. They're coming to practice.
   They're coming so we can practice.
5. Before deciding, write me.
   Before they decide, write me.
6. We get up early to go to school.
   We get up early so the girls can go to school.

---

[1] The meaning of *can* is included in the Spanish subjunctive form.

A. 1. **Cuando** uno **trabaja** eso es lo de menos.
   2. **Cuando** tú y yo **éramos** novios no nos dejaban salir solos.
   3. **Cuando venga** Víctor.

B. 1. Toman las pastillas **hasta que** se **sienten** mejor.   *They take the pills until they feel better.*
   2. Siga tomando las pastillas **hasta que** se **sienta** mejor.   *Keep on taking the pills until you feel better.*

C. 1. Escribe **mientras come.**   *He writes while he eats.*
   2. **Mientras comíamos** don Pepe me contó que necesitaba a alguien.
   3. Vienen mañana; **mientras estén** aquí, llevémoslos al teatro.   *They're coming tomorrow; while they're here, let's take them to the theater.*

D. 1. **Tan pronto como** nos **llegaron** los repuestos, se los enviamos.   *As soon as the parts arrived, we sent them to them.*
   2. **Tan pronto** (**como**) nos **lleguen** los repuestos vamos a enviárselos.

E. 1. Lo voy a hacer **según** me **dice.**   *I'm going to do it the way (according to what) he tells me.*
   2. Lo voy a hacer **según** me **diga.**   *I'm going to do it the way (according to what) he tells (may tell) me.*

F. 1. Explícalo **como** lo **entiendes.**   *Explain it as you understand (do understand) it.*
   2. Explícalo **como** lo **entiendas.**   *Explain it as (however) you may understand it.*

G. 1. Compra **donde dan** más.   *Buy where they give more.*
   2. Compra **donde den** más.   *Buy wherever they give more.*

H. 1. Me gusta, **aunque es** inútil.   *I like it, even though it's useless.*
   2. Me gusta, **aunque sea** inútil.   *I like it, even though it may be useless (even if it's useless).*

Conjunctions that take indicative or subjunctive

		INDICATIVE	SUBJUNCTIVE
when until while as soon as	**cuando** **hasta que** **mientras** **tan pronto** (**como**) **en cuanto**	something that has happened, is happening, or happens regularly	something yet to happen
the way, as the way, according to what where	**como** **según** **donde**	something known	something unknown
even though even if	**aunque**	something conceded as true	something unproved or not conceded as true

The indicative covers real happenings and things regarded as factual; the subjunctive covers things that are pending and regarded as nonfactual.

● PERSON-NUMBER SUBSTITUTION DRILL

1. El Consejo Estudiantil lo va a decidir cuando llegue *Felipe.*
   (tú, usted, ellos, yo, nosotros, ustedes, ella)
2. Van a esperar aquí hasta que *nosotros* vengamos.
   (él, tú, usted, usted y yo, ella, ustedes, yo)
3. Hágalo mientras *ella* estudie geografía.
   (ellos, nosotros, usted, ellas, yo, los chicos, él)
4. Sí, señor, tan pronto como nos escapemos.
   (tú, él, ellos, usted, don Domingo y yo, ella, yo)
5. En cuanto vuelvas, va a estar todo arreglado.
   (yo, ustedes, usted, nosotros, él, ellos, el tirano)
6. Lo voy a hacer según me digan *ellos.*
   (usted, tú, él, ustedes, ella, ellas)
7. Es verdad, aunque *tú* no lo creas.
   (ustedes, nosotros, usted, ellos, yo, ellas, el filósofo)

INSTRUCTIONS: Repeat the following sentences just as you hear them. Then repeat them again with an **ir a** future for the verbs indicated and change the other verb from indicative to present subjunctive.

1. Lo compré cuando lo vi.
   ——voy a comprar ——

2. No le mandaron el pedido hasta que lo pidió otra vez.
   ——— van a mandar ————————————

3. Estudié mucho mientras estaba aquí.
   Voy a estudiar ——————————

4. Lo hice tan pronto como acabé mi carrera de ingeniería.
   ——voy a hacer ——————

5. Lo convencimos en cuanto le dijimos lo de la huelga.
   ——vamos a convencer ——————————

6. Aprendí de memoria lo de Sócrates cuando terminé de estudiar historia.
   Voy a aprender ——————————————

7. No aceptaron esa decisión aunque vieron a su patria en la ruina.
   —— van a aceptar ————————————

8. La rubia no fue hasta que le dijeron.
   ————va a ir ——————

9. Tan pronto como lo declararon un mártir, el pueblo lo respetó.
   ———————————————— va a respetar.

10. Lo vieron cuando fue a la Comisión de Cambios.
    ——van a ver ——————————

11. El tirano salió del país aunque tuvo que hacerlo de noche.
    ————va a salir ——————————

12. Visité a Enrique aunque no me dejó entrar.
    Voy a visitar ——————————

13. En cuanto se terminó el pleito, el partido de la oposición se destacó.
    ————————————————— va a destacar.

14. No aceptó cambios tan radicales aunque lo atacaron.
    —— va a aceptar ——————————

15. Llegó al poder, aunque fue a palos y a tiros.
    Va a llegar ——————————

16. Nunca salgo hasta que estoy totalmente seguro.
    ———— voy a salir ——————————

17. Cuando algo de importancia sucede, sale una extra.
    ————————————————, va a salir ——

18. Compro zapatos tan pronto como los necesito.
    Voy a comprar ——————————

19. Aunque no lo pagas, te lo doy.
    ———————————— voy a dar.

20. Cuando hay una novedad, me la cuentan.
    ———————————— van a contar.

21. Ese cobarde nunca me convence aunque sale con gestos admirables.
    ———————————— va a convencer ——————————

● PATTERNED RESPONSE DRILL

A. 1. TEACHER: ¿Cuándo viene Víctor?
      STUDENT: **Viene cuando pueda.**

   2. ¿Cuándo vienen las compañeras?
   3. ¿Cuándo viene la hermana menor?
   4. ¿Cuándo vienen los de la firma Córdova y Compañía?

   5. ¿Cuándo viene usted?
   6. ¿Cuándo vienen ustedes?
   7. ¿Cuándo vienes tú?
   8. ¿Cuándo vengo yo?
   9. ¿Cuándo venimos nosotros?

B. 1. ¿Cuándo van ustedes a arreglar lo de anoche?

   Tan pronto como decidamos.

   2. ¿Cuándo va usted a arreglar lo de anoche?

   3. ¿Cuándo van los señores a arreglar lo de anoche?

   4. ¿Cuándo va él a arreglar lo de anoche?

   5. ¿Cuándo vamos a arreglar lo de anoche?

   6. ¿Cuándo vas a arreglar lo de anoche?

C. 1. ¿Pablo va a ser médico?

   No, no puede, aunque se dedique a estudiar medicina.

   2. ¿Ellos van a ser médicos?

   3. ¿Usted va a ser médico?

   4. ¿Ustedes van a ser médicos?

   5. ¿Tú vas a ser médico?

   6. ¿El va a ser médico?

● TRANSLATION DRILL

A. 1. Leave it wherever you want.

   Déjelo donde quiera.

   2. Leave it whenever you want.

   3. Leave it any way (however) you want.

   4. As you wish.

B. 1. Work the way he tells you.

   Trabaje como le diga él.

   2. Work where he tells you.

   3. Work when he tells you.

   4. Work until he tells you [to stop].

C. 1. Study while they're [here].

   Estudie mientras estén ellos.

   2. Study as soon as they arrive.

   3. Study until they come.

   4. Study even though they don't want [you to].

● DISCUSSION

The indicative or subjunctive in adverb clauses is determined by whether or not the content of the clause squares with the facts. In *When he comes I'm going to see him* the clause states *he comes;* but this is not a fact, for he has not come and may not come; so Spanish uses the subjunctive: **Cuando venga lo voy a ver.** But in *When he came I saw him* the clause states *he came,* and this squares with the facts as the speaker knows them; the Spanish equivalent has indicative, **Cuando vino lo vi.** Similarly in *When he comes I see him* the *he comes* is something that he regularly does, so that this squares with the facts; the Spanish equivalent again has indicative, **Cuando viene lo veo.**

Similar to clauses with **cuando** are all clauses of time in which the content of the clause refers (1) to something unaccomplished or unfulfilled, something that has not happened or is yet to happen: here the verb is subjunctive; (2) to something that has already happened or is happening now or happens regularly: here the verb is indicative. The conjunction **antes (de) que** always takes the first point of view, and is followed by the subjunctive. The other temporal conjunctions lend themselves to either point of view.

Adverb clauses that do not refer to time follow the same general principle. The expression of purpose, for example, is always contingent: our purpose may not be carried out; so in the type **para que haya más comodidades** the subjunctive is always encountered. The reason one gives for one's actions, however, is regarded as real, and clauses with **puesto que,** for example, always call for the indicative, even when the meaning is future: *Since I'm not going to like it* **Puesto que no me va a gustar.**

The entire situation may be moved into the past without altering the conditions that call for indicative or subjunctive. In *I wanted to see him as soon as he came,* the *he came* does not square with any facts: from the past point of view it is something unfulfilled, yet to happen, and the verb is subjunctive. But in *I was there when he came,* the *he came* does square with the facts.

Both conjunctions and prepositions are relator words that link subordinate elements to the rest of the sentence. Conjunctions perform this function for the elements that we term *clauses* (containing, among other things, a verb form other than the infinitive, –**ndo,** or command); prepositions perform it for the elements termed *phrases* (without a verb form other than the infinitive). The conjunctions that begin adverb clauses are closely related to prepositions; many are derived from prepositions by adding **que:**

before eating	antes de comer
before he eats	antes (de) que coma

until six	hasta las seis
until it is six	hasta que sean las seis

in order to open it (for opening it)	para abrirla
in order that it may open	para que se abra

without waiting	sin esperar
without their waiting	sin que esperen

since yesterday	desde ayer
since I arrived	desde que llegué

according to Paul	según Pablo
according to what Paul said	según dijo Pablo

103   Indicative and subjunctive in adjective clauses

	THE THING DESCRIBED IS PREDETERMINED		THE VERB IS INDICATIVE	
A. 1. Llegan a la	puerta que		está	abierta.
2. Las dos	chicas que		están	en la sala.
3. Es un loco	idealista que	todo lo	quiere	cambiar.
4. Lo	único que	te	pedimos.	
5. ¿Pago sólo	la del alquiler, que		es	la más importante?
6. Con la	suerte que		tengo	yo.
7. Este	policía que	no me	entendió.	
8. En casa de	Olga, que		tiene	unos discos nuevos.
B. 1. Primera y última	vez que		vengo	aquí.
2. Cada	vez que		abro	la boca.
C. 1. Tú eres	el que		decides.[1]	
2. Ana Guadalupe Martínez,	la que		trabajó	aquí.
3.	Lo que	tú le	diste	no es plata argentina.
D. 1. Es un	deporte del que	yo no	sé	ni papa.
2. El	lugar sagrado donde		estaban.	

When the speaker has in mind a particular thing or things to which he applies his description, the verb of the clause is indicative.

	THE THING DESCRIBED IS UNDETERMINED		THE VERB IS SUBJUNCTIVE	
1. Vamos a buscar un	lugar que		sea	más tranquilo.
2. A pesar de	lo que	tú	digas,	papá.
3. Estudia	lo que	más te	guste.	
4. No nos vamos a oponer a	lo que	tú	escojas.[2]	
5. No hay	nadie que		sea	tan ocupado.

When the speaker does not have in mind a particular thing or things to which his description applies, the verb of the clause is subjunctive.

---

[1] *(You're the one who decides.)*   [2] *(We're not going to oppose what you choose.)*

1. No hay nada aquí que *él* pueda entender.
   (yo, nosotros, ellas, usted, tú, ella, ustedes)
2. ¿Hay aquí una iglesia que *yo* no conozca?
   (nosotros, él, ellos, ella, ustedes, usted, tú)
3. Busco una película que *nosotros* entendamos.
   (yo, ellos, ella, él y yo, tú, ustedes, usted)
4. No se van a oponer a lo que *tú* escojas.
   (yo, ustedes, usted, ellos, nosotros, ellas, él)
5. No se puede terminar hoy, a pesar de lo que *él* diga.
   (ellos, usted, tú, ella, ustedes, nosotros, yo)

● CONSTRUCTION SUBSTITUTION DRILL

INSTRUCTIONS: Repeat the following sentences just as you hear them.   Then repeat them again substituting the expressions indicated for those in italics, and changing the second verb from indicative to present subjunctive.

1. Necesito encontrar *la compañía* que vende autos importados.
   _____ una compañía _____
2. Llamemos *al estudiante* que se dedica a estudios sociales.
   _____ un estudiante _____
3. Invitemos *a los alumnos* que son buenos atletas.
   _____ unos alumnos _____
4. Vamos a escoger *los que* producen más.
   _____ unos que _____
5. Voy *al restorán* donde sirven comida mexicana.
   _____a un restorán _____
6. Vamos *al país* donde hay corridas de toros.
   _____ a un país _____
7. Quiero conocer *a la morena* que habla castellano.
   _____ una morena _____
8. Busco *al profesor* que entiende geometría.
   _____ un profesor _____
9. ¿Dónde encuentro *a la secretaria* que habla inglés?
   _____ una secretaria _____
10. ¿Cuándo me presentas *a la muchacha* que comulga todos los días?
    _____ una muchacha_____

11. *Hay una calle* que es demasiado larga.
    No hay calle _____
12. *Hay un abogado* que dice la verdad.
    No hay abogado _____
13. *Hay una cosa* que sirve.
    No hay cosa _____
14. *Hay algo* que yo puedo usar.
    No hay nada _____
15. *Hay alguien* aquí que compra ropa vieja.
    No hay nadie _____
16. *Hay algo* que merece respeto.
    No hay nada _____
17. *Hay alguien* aquí que sabe volar.
    No hay nadie _____

● PATTERNED RESPONSE DRILL

A. 1. TEACHER: ¿Qué busca?
      STUDENT: **Busco una casa que sea bastante grande.**
   2. ¿Qué quiere?
   3. ¿Qué necesita?
   4. ¿Qué desea?
   5. ¿Qué espera encontrar?
   6. ¿Qué quiere comprar?

B. 1. ¿Tiene un peine?
      No, no tengo ninguno que sirva.
   2. ¿Tiene una maquinilla?
   3. ¿Tiene unas tijeras?
   4. ¿Tiene un periódico?
   5. ¿Tiene una revista?

1. TEACHER: They're going to take the ones that are here.
   STUDENT: **Van a llevar los que están aquí.**
   TEACHER: They're going to take whichever ones are here.
   STUDENT: **Van a llevar los que estén aquí.**

2. We pay the one that works best.
   We'll pay whichever one works best.

3. We invite the ones that come first.
   We'll invite whichever ones come first.

4. In spite of what you are saying, no.
   In spite of what you may say, no.

5. Do what he says.
   Do whatever he says.

6. No matter what they say, it's O.K.
   Digan lo que digan, está bien.
   No matter what they bring, it's O.K.
   No matter what they want, it's O.K.
   No matter what they ask for, it's O.K.
   No matter what they do, it's O.K.
   No matter what they think, it's O.K.
   No matter what they have, it's O.K.

7. Be that as it may, I don't agree.
   Sea lo que sea, no estoy de acuerdo.
   Let come what may, I don't agree.
   Let follow what may, I don't agree.
   Let happen what may, I don't agree.

● DISCUSSION

Adjective clauses pose a choice between indicative and subjunctive. This is true regardless (1) of whether the clause is found attached to a noun, as in **la puerta que está abierta,** or in a nominalization, as in **lo que tú le diste;** (2) of whether the noun to which the clause is attached refers to a thing, as in **la puerta que está abierta,** or is used adverbially, as in **primera y última vez que vengo aquí;** (3) of what the connecting words are: **que, donde,** etc.

The most obvious clue to indicative or subjunctive is whether the speaker has in mind something predetermined or something undetermined to which the clause is to apply. The situation that calls for indicative is this: "The description applies squarely to x (or to xs, plural)." The situation that calls for subjunctive is this: "The description applies maybe to x, maybe to y, or maybe to nothing." In the latter case, the speaker may have in mind certain specifications that he *wants* the thing to meet, but is unable (at least as yet) to point to thing x or thing y that meets them.

Examples of indicative: *I'm buying a house that has ten rooms* **Compro una casa que tiene diez cuartos**—assuming that this is house x, which the speaker could locate for you on such-and-such a corner if you asked him. *I know someone who is going to the inauguration* **Conozco a alguien que va a la inauguración**—person x, the speaker's brother (or friend, or other identifiable individual). *The one who wins deserves the prize* **El que gana merece el premio**—assuming that the speaker has in mind the winners in his experience, any or all of whom he can point to. *In spite of what you say* **A pesar de lo que tú dices**—assuming that the speaker refers to what you have just said or are saying.

Examples of subjunctive: *I want a house that has ten rooms* **Quiero una casa que tenga diez cuartos**—assuming that the speaker sets up these specifications but does not know whether house x or house y will turn out to meet them. *Let's find someone who's going to the inauguration* **Busquemos a alguien que vaya a la inauguración**—this is perhaps in hopes of asking for a ride there, and the speaker does not know whether person x or person y will turn out to be the one. *The one who wins deserves the prize* **El que gane merece el premio**—the speaker now is referring to a particular contest in which contestants x, y, and z are taking part; he implies "Whichever one of this group (and I have no way of knowing whether it will be x, y, or z) turns out to be the winner, deserves the prize." *In spite of what you say* **A pesar de lo que tú digas**—assuming now that the person addressed has not yet said it, and the speaker therefore cannot point to remark x or remark y that the other has made; he implies "In spite of whatever you may say."

Fundamentally, the choice of indicative or subjunctive in adjective clauses is the same as in adverb clauses. In the example *In spite of what you say* **A pesar de lo que tú dices** the speaker implies **Tú lo dices**—you are really saying or have said something; it squares with the facts. In the example *In spite of what you (may) say* **A pesar de lo que tú digas** the speaker does not imply that you are really saying or have said anything—there is no action to square with any facts.

104 Mass nouns and countables

EXAMPLES
1. Sólo podemos darte **consejos**.
2. Sacuda todos los **muebles**.
3. Un Hombre de **Negocios**.
4. ¿Recibiste alguna mala **noticia**?
5. No digas **tonterías**.

SINGULAR MASS	=	PLURAL COUNTABLE	MASS WITH COUNTER	=	SINGULAR COUNTABLE
advice		**consejos**	piece (bit) of advice		**consejo**
furniture		**muebles**	piece of furniture		**mueble**
business		**negocios**	piece of business		**negocio**
news		**noticias**	piece (item) of news		**noticia**
foolishness		**tonterías**	piece of foolishness		**tontería**

In the above nouns, as well as in certain others, the English singular matches the Spanish plural, while the English with *piece of, bit of,* and similar counters, matches the Spanish singular.

● TRANSLATION DRILL

A. 1. TEACHER: There's another piece of furniture.
STUDENT: **Hay otro mueble.**
2. There's another item of news.
3. There's another bit of advice.
4. There's another piece of business.
5. There's another piece of foolishness.
6. There's another serving of ice cream.

B. 1. There's more furniture.
Hay otros muebles.
2. There's more news.
3. There's more advice.
4. There's more business.
5. There's more foolishness.
6. There's more ice cream.

● DISCUSSION

In English we say *this popcorn* but *these beans,* to refer to a mass or quantity, and *this grain of popcorn* but *this bean,* to refer to a single item. We have concepts that can be referred to in either way:

machinery	machines	piece of machinery	machine
poetry	poems	piece of poetry	poem
jewelry	jewels	piece of jewelry	jewel
anger	flareups	fit of anger	flareup
strife	quarrels	outbreak of strife	quarrel

The mass noun is singular in form but akin to plural in meaning. To make it singular in meaning, we prefix a counter such as *piece of, bit of, grain of, item of,* etc.

In matching words across languages, it often happens that mass nouns fail to line up with mass nouns, and countables with countables. Then, just as we can "translate" *machinery* to *machines* and *piece of machinery* to *machine,* we are obliged to equate the mass noun in one language with the plural countable of the other, and the mass with counter in the one with the singular in the other. With English and Spanish, the commonest problem is that of English mass noun corresponding to Spanish countable in the plural, and English with *piece of* and the like corresponding to Spanish countable in the singular.

A.

1. **Puesto que vale tanto, lo vamos a llevar.**
2. _____ vender
3. _____ mucho _____
4. A menos que _____
5. _____van _____
6. _____ comprar
7. Ahora que _____
8. _____ menos _____
9. _____vas _____
10. _____ la _____
11. _____valen _____
12. _____voy _____
13. Con tal que _____
14. _____ enviar
15. _____cuesten _____
16. _____ los _____
17. Ya que _____
18. _____van _____
19. _____ lo _____
20. _____ olvidar
21. _____ tanto _____
22. _____vamos _____
23. _____sucede _____

B.

1. **Es un loco idealista que todo lo quiere cambiar.**
2. _____ quieren _____
3. Hay _____
4. _____varios _____
5. _____exagerar
6. _____unos _____
7. Son _____
8. _____funcionario _____
9. _____ nuevo _____
10. _____arreglar
11. _____piensa _____
12. _____secretaria _____
13. _____ típica _____
14. _____decidir
15. _____administrador _____
16. _____ viejo _____
17. _____estudiar
18. _____filósofo _____
19. _____ mal _____
20. _____saber
21. _____criada _____
22. _____atenta _____
23. _____espera _____
24. _____cumplir

English *verb-preposition* equivalent to Spanish *verb*.

A. 1. Let's look for the bus.
2. Let's wait for the bus.
3. Let's look at the bus.

4. Let's ask for the bus.
B. 1. I'm going to look for the book.
2. I'm going to wait for the book.

3. I'm going to look at the book.
4. I'm going to ask for the book.

¿Quiere usted empleo? (*El Universal*, México, D. F.)

ANUNCIO muy importante: Deje de buscar trabajos que no le convienen. Venga a vernos con la seguridad de que aquí se quedará.[1] Entrevistas de 8.30 a 10 y de 5 a 7 p.m. Correspondencia No. 17 "A". Colonia Postal.	SOLICITO agente de ventas,[7] conozca mercado llantas,[8] con coche. Autos Munguía, S. A.,[9] Av. Chapultepec 376.
	SOLICITO señorita que haya trabajado en café para trabajo en restaurante. Covarrubias 45, Tacubaya.
AAA.[2] Solicitamos agentes que quieran aumentar sus ingresos.[3] Radio América. Argentina No. 72.	SE solicita señorita que hable inglés, para atender niños de las 14 a las 20 horas. Teléfono 14-79-80.
NECESITAMOS dos señoritas mecanógrafas[4] que tengan velocidad y presentación. Palma Norte No. 518, despacho 503.	SOLICITAMOS joven que sepa escribir bien a máquina.[10] Claudio Bernard 43, pinturas.
SE solicitan dependientes de abarrotes[5] que sepan trabajar y con cartas de recomendación. Inútil presentarse sin estos requisitos. La Santanderina. Roldán 4.	TINTORERIA necesita planchador.[11] Iturbide No. 33.
SOLICITO empleados ágiles, jóvenes, que sepan el ramo.[6] Zapatería "Rodolfo". Argentina 6. México, D. F.	URGENNOS[12] vendedores que estén conectados con farmacias y doctores, gastos pagados. Fray Servando Teresa de Mier 505, de 9 a 1.30 y de 3 a 6.

[1] *you will remain* [2] i.e., *A–1* [3] *incomes* [4] *typists* [5] *grocery clerks* [6] *line of goods* [7] *sales* [8] Want ads in Spanish newspapers exhibit the same telegraphic style as our own. Typical here is the omission of the relative pronoun, the definite article, and the preposition (**[que] conozca [el] mercado [de] llantas**). [9] i.e., **Sociedad Anónima:** we would write *Inc.* [10] *to typewrite* [11] *ironer, presser* [12] **Urgir** patterns like **faltar, gustar,** etc. (see Unit 10 §56): translate *We need.*

Las comidas en Hispanoamérica

(Otro día la Sra. Concha Romero de Cuervo acompaña a su esposo a una charla en la Unión de Estudiantes donde siempre hay mucha animación.)

J. *Jaime*   C. *Señora Concha Romero de Cuervo*
E. *Eduardo, estudiante*   R. *Rafael, esposo de la Señora*   T. *Todos*

J. Muy buenos días, señora. ¿Qué tal la excursión al supermercado?

C. Perfectamente, gracias a su señora.

J. Encantado de poder ayudarla en algo.

E. Muy buenos, señora.

C. Buenos días, todos.

J. El otro día Rafael nos habló de las riquezas minerales de Sud América. Señora, ¿nos hará usted el favor de decirnos algo sobre las comidas en Hispanoamérica—cosa de muchísimo interés para todos nosotros?

C. Con mucho gusto . . .

R. *(Interrumpe riendo.)* Perdonen ustedes la interrupción: creer que todas las comidas de Hispanoamérica son picantes es una idea tan falsa como creer que todos los habitantes de esas naciones llevan sombreros de medio metro de diámetro y montan burros . . .

C. Hay que hablar en serio, Rafaelito . . . Pues, hay una gran variedad de comidas en los veinte países del sur como hay grandes diferencias en su cultura, en el clima y en las razas. En primer lugar, notamos cuatro influencias principales: la india, la española, la francesa y la italiana. Hay comidas picantes, especialmente entre la gente rural y pobre, en México, Guatemala, Ecuador, Perú y Bolivia porque gran parte de la población es india o mestiza. Les gusta el *chile,* como dicen en México y Centro América, o *ají,* como dicen en el sur de Sud América. Los tamales, tacos y otros platos tienen una buena cantidad de chile. Hay también muchos platos hechos con maíz y frijoles.

Toman chocolate y comen mucha fruta y verduras. En las ciudades hay bastante influencia española y francesa.

R. ¡Las comidas hispanas son un verdadero arte!

C. En otros países como Cuba, Colombia, Venezuela y Costa Rica, hay influencia española adaptada a los productos locales; comen plátanos o bananas fritas, pescado y mucho arroz: arroz con pollo, arroz con pavo y arroz con pescado, y la olla.[1] En los cafés y en los grandes hoteles sirven a un público cosmopolita y hay mucha influencia europea en la cocina.

R. Repito: ¡la cocinera es una verdadera artista!

C. En la parte sur de Sud América (en Uruguay y Argentina) hay más influencia española, italiana y francesa. Muchas personas de esa región comen tallarines, ravioles y ñoquis italianos como ustedes comen spaghetti aquí en los Estados Unidos. La influencia de la cocina francesa es también muy importante y se combina con la española. Las condiciones locales modifican un poco estas tres influencias . . . Ahora, vamos a hablarles de algunas características de la cocina y de las comidas.

R. Primero, yo quiero decirles que el consumo de carne es el más alto del mundo (más de doscientas libras por persona al año) en Uruguay y en Argentina.[2] En muchos platos típicos la carne es necesaria: el asado a la parrilla, el asado de tira, el de costado, el biftec de lomo, el famoso "puchero criollo", que tiene más de diez distintos ingredientes; el churrasco, el "bife a caballo" y los fiambres. En Chile y en Brasil comen también mucho pescado. La corbina y la langosta de Chile son especialmente buenas.

---

[1] A popular definition of the **olla** is: **Nadie sabe lo que tiene la olla más que la cuchara que la menea.** *(No one knows what is in the olla except the spoon that stirs it.)*

[2] This is because Argentina and Uruguay owe their progress chiefly to stock raising, in addition to wheat and corn growing. The typical meat dishes are listed above by Rafael.

c. Comen mucha fruta fresca.

r. Beben vino.

c. Toman café negro o mate.

r. O un amargo.[3]

c. Sólo para los gauchos, ¿eh?

r. Cierto. Pues, en las familias de los ricos y de la clase media las comidas y algunas costumbres de servirlas tienen ciertas características comunes a todos los países. Diles, Concha.

c. Toda comida empieza con una sopa sustanciosa y nutritiva. En todas las comidas sirven un plato a la vez: sopa, entremeses, pescado o huevos, el plato fuerte,[4] ensalada, postres, café. De postre sirven fruta fresca. Algunas veces sirven pasteles, dulces, flan, confituras o helados.

r. Nunca mezclan las cosas dulces con las cosas saladas. Nunca comen ensalada de frutas con mayonesa. ¡Esto sería[5] un sacrilegio! Tampoco jalea ni salsas dulces con la carne. El café es fuerte y no se sirve durante la comida. Siempre lo sirven después de la comida y en tacitas. La cantidad de azúcar que ponen es simplemente escandalosa, desde el punto de vista del norteamericano. En Cuba, donde hay mucho azúcar, ponen hasta tres o cuatro cucharaditas.

j. ¿La política del buen vecino, eh?

c. Sí. En toda la América Latina usan el maíz en la cocina y hacen muchísimos platos con este cereal que se originó en América. Al maíz tierno lo llaman *choclo* en el sur de Sud América y *elote* en México. Del maíz hacen docenas de platos: entre ellos el pastel de choclo, la mazamorra, las tortillas, y los tamales. Los indios de Bolivia y de Perú beben *chicha* hecha de maíz, pero la *chicha* chilena se hace de uvas. En Hispanoamérica la señora de la casa, no el esposo, se sienta a la cabecera de la mesa y sirve la comida. Ella sirve los platos y los da a la criada que va distribuyéndolos a todos. Por lo general, el trinchado se hace en la cocina o a veces lo hace la señora de la casa en el momento de servir.

r. La etiqueta es esencialmente europea. Jamás cambiamos el tenedor de la mano izquierda a la derecha. Cortamos con el cuchillo en la mano derecha y sin dejar el cuchillo en el plato usamos el tenedor con la mano izquierda como en Europa.

t. ¿Quién tiene hambre?

● CUESTIONARIO

1. ¿Cuál es el tema de la charla de la Sra. Concha Romero de Cuervo?
2. ¿Qué influencias pueden notarse en la cocina sudamericana?
3. ¿Dónde son comunes las comidas picantes?
4. Mencione algunos platos en que se usa el ají o el chile en gran cantidad.
5. ¿Qué países hispanos consumen mucho arroz?
6. ¿Dónde se puede apreciar la influencia europea en la cocina?
7. ¿Qué variedad ofrece la cocina de la parte sur de Sud América?
8. ¿Qué países tienen el consumo de carne más alto del mundo?

9. Mencione algunos platos típicos en que la carne es el elemento esencial.
10. ¿En qué países se consume mucho pescado?
11. ¿De dónde es originario el mate?
12. ¿Qué diferencias fundamentales hay entre la cocina hispana y la norteamericana?
13. ¿Cómo usan el maíz en la América hispana?
14. ¿Cuáles son las bebidas más comunes de Hispanoamérica?
15. ¿Quién sirve la comida en Hispanoamérica?
16. ¿En dónde se hace el trinchado?
17. ¿Cómo es la etiqueta hispanoamericana?
18. ¿Cuáles son algunos platos que a usted le gusta comer?

● SUGGESTED READINGS

Fergusson, Erna, *Mexican Cookbook,* University of New Mexico Press, Albuquerque, 1945.

Greenup, Ruth and Leonard, *Revolution Before Breakfast, Argentina, 1941–1946,* University of North Carolina Press, Chapel Hill, 1947: Ch. 3, "Picardía Criolla."

Tomlinson, Edward, *The Other Americans,* Scribner's, New York, 1943: Ch. 23, "The Estancia"; Ch. 22, "Aristocrats of the Pampa—Argentina."

---

[3] **amargo** is strong *mate* served without sugar and enjoyed by the gauchos.
[4] **el plato fuerte** *the main course* (usually meat and some green vegetables)
[5] **sería** *would be*

19

The New Manager

w. *Mr. Wright, the new manager*   d. *Mr. Delgado*
r. *Rosa*   s. *Susana*   e. *Esperanza*

w. Mr. Delgado, day before yesterday I asked
you to speak to the employees about the
matter of punctuality.   Did you do it?

d. Yes, Mr. Wright, and yesterday before they
left I reminded them again.

w. Then what's going on?   It's already twenty-
five to nine and they still haven't all arrived.

d. I don't know.   It's just that they've always
been accustomed to arriving between 8:30
and 8:45.

w. Well even if that was the custom before I
came, we're going to change it right now.

El nuevo gerente

w. *Mr. Wright, el nuevo gerente*   d. *Señor Delgado*
r. *Rosa*   s. *Susana*   e. *Esperanza*

w. Señor Delgado, anteayer le pedí a usted
que les hablara a los empleados sobre el
asunto de la puntualidad.   ¿Lo hizo?

d. Sí, Mr. Wright, y ayer antes que salieran
les volví a recordar.

w. Entonces, ¿qué pasa?   Ya faltan veinticinco para las nueve y todavía no han llegado todos.

d. No sé.   Es la costumbre que han tenido de
llegar siempre entre ocho y media y nueve
menos cuarto.

w. Pues si antes que yo viniera existía esa
costumbre, ahora vamos a cambiarla (1).

D. I wish you would speak to them personally, if you could.

W. All right, I will, because as the new manager, the first thing I require is that everybody be on time.

D. One other thing: you told me to consult the employees about the change in time schedule.

W. Yes, thanks. I don't like that business of two hours for lunch. I wish we could reduce it to one.

D. It has its advantages and disadvantages, but most of the employees are against it.

W. Why? Do they have to have a siesta?

D. It's not that, it's just that almost all of them have to go home for lunch.

W. I see. Nevertheless, I'd like for us to try it for a few days to see if it works out.

* * *

R. Mr. Wright is hopping mad because you came in ten minutes late.

S. Yes, I've already noticed it without your telling me. As if *we* were to blame! It's those awful busses.

E. Besides, what's ten minutes, more or less? What an old grouch!

R. Don't believe it; he's very nice. It's just that he's strict, and he may be right.

E. The only thing I can say is that I'm so sorry Mr. Roberts resigned.

S. Yes. Mr. Roberts didn't mind whether we were a little late as long as we did our work right.

D. Ojalá que usted les hablara directamente, si pudiera.

W. Muy bien, porque como nuevo gerente, lo primero que exijo es que todo el mundo sea puntual.

D. Otra cosa, me dijo usted que consultara con los empleados sobre el cambio de horario.

W. Sí, gracias. Eso de dos horas para el almuerzo no me parece bien. Ojalá pudiéramos reducirlas a una.

D. Tiene sus ventajas y desventajas, pero la mayoría de los empleados se oponen.

W. ¿Por qué? ¿Les hace falta la siesta? (2)

D. No es eso, es que casi todos tienen que ir a sus casas a almorzar.

W. Sí, ya comprendo. Sin embargo, quisiera que lo probáramos por algunos días a ver si resulta.

* * *

R. Mr. Wright está enojadísimo porque ustedes llegaron diez minutos tarde.

S. Sí, ya me di cuenta sin que me lo dijeras. ¡Como si nosotros tuviéramos la culpa...! Son esos cochinos autobuses.

E. Además ¿qué son diez minutos más, diez minutos menos? ¡Qué antipático es ese señor!

R. No creas, él es muy simpático. Lo que pasa es que es exigente y a lo mejor tiene razón.

E. Lo único que digo yo es que siento tanto que Mr. Roberts renunciara al puesto.

S. Sí. A Mr. Roberts no le importaba que llegáramos un poquito tarde con tal que le hiciéramos bien el trabajo.

Cultural Notes

(1) Mr. Wright is obviously eager to introduce American ideas of efficiency, which disrupt the informal nature of Latin-American business.

(2) The **siesta** traditionally was a period of about two hours during the middle of the workday when one might relax or take a nap. Today, in those places where it is still in vogue, it serves mainly to allow employees to go home for lunch; but many industrial communities have reduced the lunch period to an hour or less. The **siesta** often means closing all stores and offices for the period; but to compensate for this, the closing hour for the day is later. (The origin of **siesta** is Latin *sexta* in *hora sexta*, "sixth hour," i.e., 12:00 noon counting from 6:00 A.M.—the period when heat was greatest in Mediterranean countries and a recess from work was needed.)

105 The imperfect subjunctive

	INFINITIVE	THIRD-PERSON PLURAL PRETERIT		SUBJUNCTIVE ENDINGS
regular verbs	hablar comer vivir	habla– comie– vivie–		–ra –ras –ra –'ramos[1] –ran
verbs with stem changes in preterit	dormir pedir	durmie– pidie–	–ron	
verbs irregular in preterit	estar haber poner hacer decir	estuvie– hubie– pusie– hicie– dije–		

The imperfect subjunctive is formed from the third-person plural of the preterit, as shown. There are no exceptions.

EXAMPLES

A. 1. Quisiera que lo **probáramos** por algunos días. *(I'd like that we should try it for a few days.)*
   2. Me dijo que **buscara** otro empleado. *He told me to look for another employee.*
   3. Les rogó que no **discutieran** más de política. *She begged them not to argue about politics any more.*

B. 1. A Mr. Roberts no le importaba que **llegáramos** un poquito tarde. *(It didn't matter to Mr. Roberts that we arrived a little late.)*
   2. Era ridículo que las muchachas **tuvieran** que llevar chaperón. *It was ridiculous that girls should have to take a chaperon.*

AN INFLUENCE BROUGHT TO BEAR		WHAT WAS INFLUENCED
Les rogó	**que**	**no discutieran**

AN ATTITUDE OF LIKE-DISLIKE OR ACCEPTANCE-REJECTION		WHAT WAS LIKED OR DISLIKED, ACCEPTED OR REJECTED
Era ridículo	**que**	**tuvieran que llevar chaperón**

In noun clauses, the imperfect subjunctive is used under the same conditions as the present subjunctive, except that the point of view is in the past.

● PERSON-NUMBER SUBSTITUTION DRILL

1. Susana quería que *yo* le comprara unas tarjetas postales.
   (ellas, nosotros, usted, tú, ustedes, Víctor)
2. ¿Deseaban los señores que consultáramos *nosotros?*
   (ellos, usted, ustedes, tú, yo, ellas)
3. Preferían que *ella* no saliera sin permiso.
   (nosotros, usted, ellos, tú, yo, ustedes)
4. El mereció que *ella* lo odiara.
   (tú, ustedes, usted, ellos, nosotros, yo)
5. Quería que *yo* lo pusiera debajo del árbol.
   (usted, ellas, tú, él, nosotros, ustedes)
6. Mis padres sugirieron que *yo* siguiera otra carrera.
   (él, ustedes, nosotros, ellos, tú, ella)

---

[1] There is a written stress in the first-person plural: **habláramos, dijéramos.** The same syllable is strong-stressed in all the forms of the imperfect subjunctive, and the conventions of writing require that it be marked in first-person plural forms.

7. Mi madre se oponía a que *yo* estudiara ingeniería.
   (nosotros, él, tú, ustedes, él y yo, mi hermano mayor)

8. Insistían en que *él* siguiera adelante.
   (yo, tú, usted, ellos, él, él, y yo)

9. Rogaban que no lo metiéramos en la boca.
   (yo, tú, usted, ellos, él, él y yo)

10. Pidieron que *tú* hicieras preguntas sobre Platón.
    (ustedes, él, nosotros, usted, ellos, ella)

11. Exigió que *todo el mundo* fuera puntual.
    (nosotros, yo, ellos, ella, ustedes, él)

12. Ojalá que *usted* les hablara directamente.
    (ustedes, tú, ellos, nosotros, él, ellas)

13. Ojalá que tuviera *yo* tanta plata.
    (nosotros, usted, tú, ellos, él, ustedes)

14. Sentí mucho que *él* fuera tan exigente.
    (ustedes, usted, ellos, ella, ellas, tú)

15. No me gustó que *ella* estuviera tan enojada.
    (ellos, él, ustedes, usted, tú, ellas)

16. Me entusiasmé de que *ellos* decidieran ir sin falta.
    (usted, ustedes, tú, él, ellas, ella)

17. Se alegraron que *usted* no tuviera que conseguir otra criada.
    (ustedes, nosotros, ella, yo, tú, ellos)

18. Era necesario que fuéramos a ver la tumba del mártir.
    (yo, ustedes, usted, tú, ellos, él)

19. Fue bueno que le dieras algunas flores a la secretaria.
    (ustedes, usted, ellos, nosotros, yo, ellas)

20. Era ridículo que no respetaras la puntualidad.
    (nosotros, ustedes, usted, ellos, él, yo)

21. Fue fantástico que *él* se escapara de nuevo.
    (ellos, ella, ellas, usted, ustedes, nosotros)

22. *Le* pedí *a usted* que no hablara tan fuerte.
    (a ustedes, a él, a ellos, a ella, a ellas, a ti)

23. *A nosotros* no *nos* perdonaba que saliéramos tan temprano.
    (a él, a ellos, a mí, a ustedes, a ti, a ella)

24. *Nos* rogó que hiciéramos bien el trabajo.
    (a mí, a ellos, a ti, a ustedes, a él, a ellas)

25. *Nos* dijo que no discutiéramos más sobre la muerte.
    (a ellos, a ella, a mí, a ti, a usted, a ustedes)

● TENSE SUBSTITUTION DRILL

1. Francisco desea que yo lo haga, como de costumbre.
   _____ deseaba _____

2. Sugiero que quedemos en venir mañana.
   Sugerí _____

3. Me dice que abra la boca.
   ___ dijo _____

4. El jefe quiere que ponga dos puntos.
   _____ quería _____

5. Espero que me concedan hasta mañana para pagarla.
   Esperaba _____

6. Quiero que me pida un churrasco bien jugoso.
   Quería _____

7. No creo que venga ese cochino autobús.
   ___ creía _____

8. Me alegro que no haya ninguna novedad.
   ___ alegré _____

9. Siento que no podamos enviar los repuestos de inmediato.
   Sentí _____

10. Me alegro que el asunto no sea tan enredado.
    ___ alegré _____

11. Siento que le duela tanto la cabeza y la garganta.
    Sentía _____

12. Es ridículo que suceda una cosa tan grave.
    Fue _____

13. No es bueno que pares todo el tráfico.
    ___ fue _____

14. Es importante que vendamos pronto estas pieles.
    Era _____

15. Es necesario que paguen la cuenta de la electricidad.
    Fue _____

16. Es difícil que siempre lleguemos entre ocho y nueve.
    Era _____

17. Es necesario que cumpla con la iglesia.
    Era _____

● CONSTRUCTION SUBSTITUTION DRILL

INSTRUCTIONS: Repeat the following sentences just as you hear them. Then repeat them again, preceded by the expressions indicated, using imperfect subjunctive in place of indicative.

1. El gerente explicó las ventajas y desventajas del nuevo horario.
   (querían que, preferían que, esperaban que)

2. Siempre tomábamos el almuerzo juntos.
   (deseaba que, insistía en que, no me gustaba que)

3. La mayoría se oponía al cambio de la siesta.
   (fue imposible que, fue ridículo que, no importaba que)

4. Anteayer no metiste la pata.
   (me alegré que, esperaba que, fue bueno que)

5. Su seguro servidor no pagó el alquiler.
   (sentí que, no creí que, lástima que)

6. Esta firma no mandó el pedido.
   (preferimos que, queríamos que, no creímos que)

7. No era nada de importancia.
   (me alegré que, esperaba que, fue bueno que)

8. La señora Méndez hablaba hasta por los codos.
   (no les gustó que, no importó que, fue una lástima que)

9. Les hacía falta la misa.
   (no creía que, era probable que, sentía que)

10. No lo dijo con respecto a la pronunciación.
    (esperaban que, se alegraban que, era bueno que)

11. Ella no pudo contestar su atenta carta.
    (sintió que, fue ridículo que, fue probable que)

12. Fuimos a ver al dentista.
    (nos sugirió que, nos dijo que, insistió en que)

13. Le dolía todo el cuerpo.
    (me preocupaba que, parecía fantástico que, no creía que)

● PATTERNED RESPONSE DRILL

A. 1. TEACHER: ¿Qué fue difícil?
      STUDENT: **Fue difícil que cumpliera con tantos compromisos sociales.**

   2. ¿Qué era necesario?
   3. ¿Qué era probable?
   4. ¿Qué era ridículo?
   5. ¿Qué parecía fantástico?

B. 1. ¿Qué sentía él?
      Sentía que no llegáramos tan a menudo.

   2. ¿Qué prefería él?

   3. ¿Qué esperaba él?
   4. ¿En qué insistía él?
   5. ¿Qué sugería él?
   6. ¿Qué quería él?

C. 1. ¿Qué quería usted?
      Yo quería que usted me acompañara.

   2. ¿Qué sugería usted?
   3. ¿Qué prefería usted?
   4. ¿Qué deseaba usted?
   5. ¿En qué insistía usted?

● TRANSLATION DRILL

A. 1. TEACHER: I wanted him to come.
      STUDENT: **Quería que él viniera.**

   2. I insisted he come.
   3. I hoped he would come.
   4. I wished he would come.

B. 1. I asked him to come.
      Le pedí que viniera.

   2. I told him to come.
   3. I begged him to come.
   4. I suggested he come.

C. 1. He wanted us to come in.
      Quería que entráramos.

   2. He insisted we come in.
   3. He hoped we would come in.
   4. He wished we would come in.

D. 1. He asked us to come.
      Nos pidió que viniéramos.

   2. He told us to come.
   3. He begged us to come.
   4. He suggested we come.

	CONJUNCTION THAT TAKES SUBJUNCTIVE		IMPERFECT SUBJUNCTIVE	
Si	Antes que		salieran	les volví a recordar.
Ya me di cuenta	antes que	yo	viniera	existía esa costumbre . . .
No le importaba	sin que	me lo	dijeras.	
	con tal que		hiciéramos	bien el trabajo.

	CONJUNCTION THAT TAKES INDICATIVE OR SUBJUNCTIVE		INDICATIVE	IMPERFECT SUBJUNCTIVE
Lo iba a hacer	según	me	decía.[1]	
Lo iba a hacer	según	me		dijera.[2]

In adverb clauses, the imperfect subjunctive is used under the same conditions as the present subjunctive, except that the point of view is in the past.

● PERSON-NUMBER SUBSTITUTION DRILL

1. Tuve que dictar la carta antes que saliera *ella.*
   (ellas, él, ustedes, tú, ellos, la secretaria)
2. Volvimos temprano para que *ellos* pudieran estudiar.
   (ella, ustedes, tú, usted, ellas, yo)
3. Ya me di cuenta sin que *tú* me lo dijeras.
   (usted, ustedes, ella, ellos, él, ellas)
4. Don Domingo iba a la Comisión de Cambios con tal que *yo* fuera también.
   (ustedes, nosotros, tú, ella, ellos, el director)
5. No era posible a menos que *ellos* le dieran permiso.
   (él, ustedes, usted, tú, nosotros, el gerente)
6. Iban a decidir cuando llegara *Pablo.*
   (ellos, él, tú, yo, ustedes, nosotros)
7. Iban a esperar hasta que *yo* me sintiera mejor.
   (nosotros, ustedes, usted, tú, las chicas, Julio)
8. Tan pronto como *tú* volvieras, íbamos a tomar el bus.
   (él, ellos, ella, ustedes, usted, ellas)
9. Lo iba a hacer según me dijeran *ellos.*
   (usted, ellas, él, tú, ustedes, ella)
10. Era verdad aunque *tú* no lo creyeras.
    (ustedes, nosotros, usted, ellos, yo, ellas)
11. Roberto iba a salir en cuanto le informaran *ellos.*
    (él, tú, ustedes, yo, nosotros, usted)

● TENSE SUBSTITUTION DRILL

1. Salgo antes que llame ese antipático.
   Salía _____
2. Entro sin que ellos se den cuenta.
   Entré _____
3. Te acompaño con tal que no me lleves a una clase aburrida.
   __ acompañaba _____
4. Voy temprano para que comparemos la relativa importancia.
   Fui _____
5. Ella no viene a menos que él también venga.
   _____ venía _____
6. Voy a echar esta carta antes que salga el correo.
   Iba _____
7. Los dejo ir con tal que vuelvan temprano.
   __ dejé _____
8. No lo vamos a ver, para que no nos pregunte de nuevo.
   _____ íbamos _____
9. No voy a menos que se me quite esta fiebre.
   __iba _____

_____
[1] *I was going to do it the way he told me* (he was telling me then).
[2] *I was going to do it the way he told me* (he might turn out to tell me).

● PATTERNED RESPONSE DRILL

A. 1. TEACHER: ¿Cuándo iba a venir José María?
STUDENT: **Tan pronto como pudiera.**

2. ¿Cuándo iban a venir los señores?
3. ¿Cuándo iba a venir María Elena?
4. ¿Cuándo iban a venir las chicas?
5. ¿Cuándo iba a venir usted?
6. ¿Cuándo iban a venir ustedes?
7. ¿Cuándo ibas a venir tú?

B. 1. ¿De veras iba don Patricio?
Cómo no, con tal que no tuviera que ir solo.

2. ¿De veras iban los directores?
3. ¿De veras iba Olga?
4. ¿De veras iban las muchachas?
5. ¿De veras iba usted?
6. ¿De veras iban ustedes?
7. ¿De veras ibas tú?

C. 1. ¿Para qué vino Pepe a ver a Rosa?
Para que Rosa lo perdonara.

2. ¿Para qué vino Pepe a ver a las chicas?
3. ¿Para qué vino Pepe a ver al profesor?
4. ¿Para qué vino Pepe a ver a los técnicos?
5. ¿Para qué vino Pepe a verlo a usted?
6. ¿Para qué vino Pepe a verlos a ustedes?
7. ¿Para qué vino Pepe a verte a ti?

D. 1. ¿Iba Fernando a explicárselo a Ana?
No, a menos que Ana se lo pidiera.

2. ¿Iba Fernando a explicárselo a ellas?
3. ¿Iba Fernando a explicárselo a Chalo?
4. ¿Iba Fernando a explicárselo a los muchachos?

5. ¿Iba Fernando a explicárselo a usted?
6. ¿Iba Fernando a explicárselo a ustedes?
7. ¿Iba Fernando a explicártelo a ti?

E. 1. ¿Esperanza vio a Bernardo?
No, él entró sin que lo viera.

2. ¿Las chicas vieron a Bernardo?
3. ¿Alfredo vio a Bernardo?
4. ¿Los alumnos vieron a Bernardo?
5. ¿Usted vio a Bernardo?
6. ¿Ustedes vieron a Bernardo?
7. ¿Tú viste a Bernardo?

F. 1. ¿Guadalupe vino a ver a Lorenzo?
Sí, pero él salió antes que llegara.

2. ¿Las secretarias vinieron a ver a Lorenzo?
3. ¿Alvaro vino a ver a Lorenzo?
4. ¿Los directores vinieron a ver a Lorenzo?
5. ¿Usted vino a ver a Lorenzo?
6. ¿Ustedes vinieron a ver a Lorenzo?
7. ¿Tú viniste a ver a Lorenzo?

G. 1. ¿Y todavía iba a salir Juanita con Alberto?
Sí, aunque él no lo quisiera.

2. ¿Y todavía iba a salir Juanita con ellos?
3. ¿Y todavía iba a salir Juanita con el gerente?
4. ¿Y todavía iba a salir Juanita con los jefes?
5. ¿Y todavía iba a salir Juanita con ustedes?
6. ¿Y todavía iba a salir Juanita contigo?

EXAMPLES

1. Ibamos a buscar un lugar que **fuera** más tranquilo. *We were going to look for a place that was quieter.*
2. Le dije que estudiara lo que más le **gustara.** *I told him to study what he liked best.*
3. No había nadie que **fuera** tan ocupado como él. *There was no one who was such a busy man as he was.*

	THE THING DESCRIBED IS UNDETERMINED	THE VERB IS SUBJUNCTIVE	
Ibamos a buscar un	lugar que	fuera	más tranquilo

In adjective clauses, the imperfect subjunctive is used under the same conditions as the present subjunctive, except that the point of view is in the past.

● PERSON-NUMBER SUBSTITUTION DRILL

1. No había nada ahí que *él* pudiera entender.
(yo, nosotros, ellas, usted, tú, ellas)

2. El deseaba un negocio que *todos* aceptaran.
(usted, nosotros, ellos, tú, yo, ustedes)

3. No había un jefe que *ella* respetara.
(ustedes, usted, tú, él, nosotros, yo)

4. No se iban a oponer a lo que *tú* escogieras.
(yo, ustedes, usted, ellos, nosotros, él)

5. No se podía terminar, a pesar de lo que *él* dijera.
(ellos, usted, tú, ella, ustedes, nosotros)

● TENSE SUBSTITUTION DRILL

1. Deseo una novia que tenga ojos verdes.
   Deseaba _____
2. Necesito un tocadiscos que sea portátil.
   Necesitaba _____
3. Quiero un horario que resulte bien.
   Quería _____
4. Busco un barrio donde no haya tanto ruido.
   Buscaba _____
5. Ahí no hay empleado que no sea cargante.
   _____ había _____
6. ¿Dónde hay un micro que vaya al centro?
   _____ había _____
7. No hay nadie que tenga un hambre tan feroz como la mía.
   ___ había _____
8. Quiero encontrar un banco que cambie un cheque personal.
   Quería _____

9. Necesito un criado que no sea tan bruto.
   Necesitaba _____
10. No hay médico que no tenga gripe.
    ___ había _____
11. Busco un lugar donde sirvan limonada.
    Buscaba _____

● PATTERNED RESPONSE DRILL

A. 1. TEACHER: ¿Había alguien ahí que tuviera un auto?
      STUDENT: **No, no había nadie que tuviera.**
   2. ¿Había alguien ahí que tuviera una aspirina?
   3. ¿Había alguien ahí que tuviera un libro?
   4. ¿Había alguien ahí que tuviera una batería?
   5. ¿Había alguien ahí que tuviera un radio?

B. 1. ¿Había un profesor que fuera simpático?
      No, no había nadie que fuera simpático.
   2. ¿Había un empleado que hablara inglés?
   3. ¿Había un señor que tuviera hora con el doctor?
   4. ¿Había un jefe que le diera el visto bueno?
   5. ¿Había una secretaria que fuera a comulgar?

● DISCUSSION

The imperfect subjunctive is used in noun, adjective, and adverb clauses under the same conditions as the present (and present perfect) subjunctive, except that the point of view is in the past. Note the following parallels:

*I'm sorry you **feel** bad.*	Siento que te **sientas** malo.
*I was sorry you **felt** bad.*	Sentía que te **sintieras** malo.
*There's nobody who **knows** it.*	No hay nadie que lo **sepa.**
*There was nobody who **knew** it.*	No había nadie que lo **supiera.**
*I'm not going unless he **goes** along.*	Yo no voy a menos que él me **acompañe.**
*I wasn't going unless he **went** along.*	Yo no iba a menos que él me **acompañara.**

The English infinitive and –ing form carry no sign of tense, which must therefore be inferred from the main verb (in *He ate while working* we infer *while he worked*, not *while he works*). The Spanish equivalent shows the tense:

*He tells me **to work**.*	Me dice que **trabaje.**
*He told me **to work**.*	Me dijo que **trabajara.**
*I catch on without **your telling me**.*	Me doy cuenta sin que me lo **digas.**
*I caught on without **your telling me**.*	Me di cuenta sin que me lo **dijeras.**

There is another imperfect subjunctive, not used by all speakers but quite common in written Spanish, which is the same in form as the one described here except that –se– replaces –ra–. Examples: **dijeses** in place of **dijeras**, **hablásemos** in place of **habláramos**.

106 The present and present perfect subjunctive after a verb in the present

EXAMPLES

1. Espero que **sigas** mis consejos. *I hope you are following (will follow) my advice.*
2. Vamos a buscar un lugar que **sea** más tranquilo. *(Let's find a place that is [will be] quieter.)*

	English			*Spanish*	
PRESENT	PRESENT OR FUTURE		PRESENT		PRESENT
I hope	you're following you'll follow		**Espero**	**que**	**sigas**

In Spanish the present subjunctive covers both present and future meanings.

● TRANSLATION DRILL

1. TEACHER: I hope you are following my advice.
   STUDENT: **Espero que sigas mis consejos.**
   TEACHER: I hope you'll follow my advice.
   STUDENT: **Espero que sigas mis consejos.**
2. I prefer that she wash the clothes today.
   I prefer that she wash the clothes tomorrow.
3. I hope they are at the park.
   I hope they'll be at the park.
4. We're eating early so the girls can go to the movies.
   We're eating early so the girls will be able to go to the movies.
5. Is there someone here that buys old clothes?
   Is there someone here that will buy old clothes?

EXAMPLES

A. 1. Siento que no te **hayas sentido** bien anoche. *I'm sorry you didn't feel well last night.*
   2. Es posible que **haya estado** allí. *It's possible he was there.*
   3. Buscan a alguien que **haya estado** en Bogotá en 1902. *They're looking for someone who was in Bogota in 1902.*

B. 1. Siento que no te **hayas sentido** bien hoy. *I'm sorry you haven't felt well today.*
   2. Buscan a alguien que **haya estado** en Bogotá este año. *They're looking for someone who has been in Bogota this year.*

	English			*Spanish*	
PRESENT	PAST, OR PRESENT PERFECT		PRESENT		PRESENT PERFECT
I'm sorry	you felt you've felt		**Siento**	**que te**	**hayas sentido**

The meanings of both the present perfect and the past in English are normally carried by the Spanish present perfect, in noun and adjective clauses with verb in the subjunctive when the main verb is in the present.

1. TEACHER: I'm sorry you didn't feel well last night.
   STUDENT: **Siento que no te hayas sentido bien anoche.**
   TEACHER: I'm sorry you haven't felt well today.
   STUDENT: **Siento que no te hayas sentido bien hoy.**
2. I hope you studied a lot last night.
   I hope you've studied a lot today.
3. I'm glad you wrote yesterday.
   I'm glad you have written today.
4. It's possible he was here day before yesterday.
   It's possible he's been here today.
5. It's probable that the country progressed a lot last year.
   It's probable that the country has progressed a lot this year.
6. I'm looking for some man who was here last night.
   I'm looking for some man who has been here three hours.
7. I prefer someone who was here before.
   I prefer someone who has been here all day.

● DISCUSSION

When a main verb in the present is followed by a noun clause or an adjective clause with its verb in the subjunctive, normally the latter verb occurs in one of two tenses: present for meanings corresponding to the English present and future (**Espero que estén allí** *I hope they're there* or *I hope they'll be there*), and present perfect for meanings corresponding to the English present perfect and past (**Es posible que haya estado allí** *It's possible he has been there* or *It's possible he was there*). Context usually clears up any confusion.

Sometimes a main verb in the present is followed by a verb in the imperfect subjunctive, as in one example from the present dialog: **Siento tanto que Mr. Roberts renunciara al puesto.** The speaker momentarily adopts the point of view of the past, as if to say *I'm **still** sorry that Mr. Roberts gave up the job*—sorry about something already filed away in the past and no doubt discussed on previous occasions. For a past happening now being brought up for the first time, the present perfect would be used: **Siento tanto que Mr. Roberts haya renunciado al puesto;** this is the more usual situation.

107 The equivalents of *I wish* and *as if*

EXAMPLES

1. **Ojalá** (que) **tuviera** más. *I wish I had more.*
2. **Ojalá** (que) **supieran** lo que yo sé. *I wish they knew what I know.*
3. **Ojalá pudiéramos** reducirlas a una.
4. **Ojalá** que usted les **hablara** directamente.
5. **Ojalá** (que) **hubiera.** *I wish there might be.*

	VERB IN THE PAST OR WITH *would* OR *might*			IMPERFECT SUBJUNCTIVE
I wish	I had they knew we could you would speak there might be	**Ojalá**	(que)	tuviera supieran pudiéramos hablara hubiera

Ojalá (with or without **que**) plus the imperfect subjunctive carries the meaning of *I wish* plus the verb forms that normally follow it.

1. ¡**Como si** nosotras **tuviéramos** la culpa!
2. Anda **como si estuviera** enfermo. *He walks as if he were sick.*
3. ¡**Como si hubiera** lluvia aquí! *As if there would (might) be rain here!*

	VERB IN THE PAST OR WITH *would* OR *might*		IMPERFECT SUBJUNCTIVE
As if	we were (had) he were there would (might) be	**Como si**	**tuviéramos estuviera hubiera**

Como si plus the imperfect subjunctive carries the meaning of *as if* plus the past tense (and *would* or *might*) forms that normally follow it.

● CONSTRUCTION SUBSTITUTION DRILL

INSTRUCTIONS: Repeat the following sentences just as you hear them. Then repeat them again, preceded by the expressions **ojalá (que)** or **como si** which will change the verb from indicative to imperfect subjunctive.

1. Podíamos reducirlas a una.
   Ojalá que _____
2. Ellos sabían lo del radio descompuesto.
   Ojalá que _____
3. Tenía la bondad de invitarnos.
   Ojalá que _____
4. El se sentía por lo menos regular.
   Ojalá que _____
5. Pedrito no tenía la cara sucia.
   Ojalá que _____
6. Por fin salía del tremendo lío.
   Ojalá que _____
7. Me echaban de menos.
   Ojalá que _____
8. Tú le dabas saludos de parte de tu mamá.
   Ojalá que _____
9. El se ponía a tus órdenes.
   Ojalá que _____
10. Iba a tomar un colectivo dentro de quince minutos.
    Ojalá que _____
11. Ellos no salían furiosos de la reunión.
    Ojalá que _____
12. No estaba equivocado.
    Ojalá que _____
13. No pasaba nada malo.
    Ojalá que _____
14. Nosotras teníamos la culpa.
    Como si _____
15. Había mucha lluvia aquí.
    Como si _____
16. Le dolía todo el cuerpo.
    Como si _____
17. Apenas llegaba a la entrada.
    Como si _____
18. Por eso tenía que peinarse.
    Como si _____
19. Eso era lo de menos.
    Como si _____
20. Se moría de un ataque al corazón.
    Como si _____
21. Debía doblar a la izquierda.
    Como si _____
22. Había una flecha a cinco metros en una pared.
    Como si _____

● DISCUSSION

In both English and Spanish a past tense is frequently used not to indicate past time but to indicate something unreal or unlikely now or in the future: *Let's suppose he **died*** (should die) *tomorrow* **Vamos a suponer que se *muriera* mañana.** In Spanish the past tense used for this purpose is always the past *subjunctive,* which combines the meanings of nonfactuality and remoteness from the present, thus lending itself to notions of unreality.

When in English we use the expression *as if* (*as though, like*), we are normally "pretending" something: *He walks as if he **were** sick* (but he isn't, really). Similarly when we *wish,* we wish for something we do not actually have: *I wish I knew*—but I don't know (note the past *knew* rather than the present *know*). *As if* and the verb *wish* are typical instances that call for the past in English and past subjunctive in Spanish.

(Spanish lacks an exact equivalent for *as if* with the present tense, an expression often encountered in English when unreality is not emphasized: *He walks as if he is sick*—perhaps he really is. **Como si** always implies unreality.)

108 The diminutive suffix *–ito*

EXAMPLES   1. Un **momentito, Pedrito.**
2. Una **casita** verde.
3. Es un hombre muy **chiquito.**   *He's a very small man.*

BASE FORM	SUFFIXED FORM
Paco	Paquito
Pedro	Pedrito
momento	momentito
minuto	minutito
poco	poquito
chico	chiquito
Juana	Juanita
(Guada)lupe	Lupita
casa	casita

To indicate smallness or cuteness, or as an endearing nickname, the suffix **–ito, –ita** is attached to many words, especially nouns and adjectives.   The gender normally remains the same.

● DIMINUTIVE SUBSTITUTION DRILL

INSTRUCTIONS: Repeat the following sentences just as you hear them.   Then repeat them again, using the diminutive forms of the items indicated.

A. 1. TEACHER: Es una *casa* verde. *Repita.*
   STUDENT: **Es una casa verde.**
   TEACHER: *Cambie.*
   STUDENT: **Es una casita verde.**

2. Es un *libro* verde.
3. Es una *cama* verde.

B. 1. ¿Tiene un *minuto?*
2. ¿Tiene un *plato?*
3. ¿Tiene una *taza?*[1]
4. ¿Tiene un *disco?*

C. 1. Aquí hay dos *puntos.*
2. Aquí hay un *papel.*
3. Aquí hay una *planta.*
4. Aquí hay un *toro.*

D. 1. ¿Hay una *carta* para mí?
2. ¿Hay una *tarjeta* para mí?
3. ¿Hay un *cuarto* para mí?
4. ¿Hay una *casa* para mí?
5. ¿Hay un *regalo* para mí?

E. 1. Hola, *abuela.*
2. Hola, *amigo.*
3. Hola, *Pedro.*
4. Qué hubo, *Paco.*

F. 1. ¿Dónde está la *señora?*
2. ¿Dónde está mi *hijo?*
3. ¿Dónde está mi *sobrina?*
4. ¿Dónde están los *chicos?*
5. ¿Dónde está *Juana?*

G. 1. Es un vestido *corto.*
2. Es un vestido *azul.*
3. Es un vestido *español.*
4. Es un vestido *igual.*
5. Es un vestido *negro.*

H. 1. Vuelvo después de un *rato.*
2. *Ahora* viene.
3. Hasta *luego.*

---

[1] The diminutive is spelled **tacita.** See p. 191.

Like the English suffix of smallness and endearment in *baby, cutie, laddie, sonny, girlie*, Spanish has a suffix **–ito, –ita** with similar meanings. Some words carrying this suffix have a long history in the language, such as **bonito** *pretty* (compare English *bonny*) and **señorita** *miss* (based on **señora**), but **–ito** is rather freely used in making new derivatives.

Alternate forms of this same suffix are **–cito** and **–ecito;** e.g., **cafecito** (**café**), **mujercita** (**mujer**), and **nuevecito** (**nuevo**).

While **–ito** probably has the widest spread of all the diminutive suffixes, certain regions have their own preferences, e.g., **–ico** in Costa Rica.

Next in frequency to **–ito** is the diminutive suffix **–illo,** which is encountered in the dialogs in the words **mantequilla** *butter* (**manteca** *lard*), **maquinilla** *little machine* (**máquina** *machine*), **pastilla** *pill, tablet* (**pasta** *paste*), and **calzoncillos** *shorts* (**calzones** *breeches*). The suffix **–illo** is less freely used for new formations.

109 Singular and plural with collective nouns

EXAMPLES

A. 1. **Viene gente** a comer.
   2. **Va** a ir mucha **gente** importante.
   3. ¿Por qué **anda** toda la **gente** corriendo? *(Why are all the people running?)*
   4. Nuestro **pueblo** jamás **va** a aceptar cambios tan radicales.
   5. La **policía** los **atacó** infamemente.

B. 1. **Parte** de los **heridos murieron.** *Part of the wounded died.*
   2. La **mayoría** de los **empleados** se **oponen.**

C. 1. Buena **parte** del **pueblo** no **quiere** elecciones libres. *A good part of the people don't want free elections.*
   2. La **mayoría** se **opone.** *The majority is (are) opposed.*

gente pueblo policía	singular verb

The nouns **gente, pueblo,** and **policía**[1] regularly take a singular verb.

FRACTION		PLURAL WHOLE		PLURAL VERB
Parte **La mayoría**	de los de los	**heridos** **empleados**	se	**murieron** **oponen**

FRACTION		SINGULAR WHOLE OR NONE		SINGULAR VERB
Buena parte **La mayoría**	del	**pueblo**	no se	**quiere** **opone**

When the collective noun represents a fraction of a plural whole, and the plural whole is expressed, the verb is regularly plural; otherwise it is singular.

● TRANSLATION DRILL

A. 1. TEACHER: The people are wrong.
      STUDENT: **La gente está equivocada.**
   2. Our people are organized.
      Nuestro pueblo está organizado.

3. The police are here.
   La policía está aquí.

---

[1] Meaning *police* (see Unit 6, Cultural Note 1). We have also encountered **el policía** in the sense *the policeman;* in this sense it is pluralized, **los policías** *the policemen,* and of course takes a plural verb.

B. 1. The people of this school are very nice.
   La gente de esta escuela es muy simpática.
   2. The people of this country are very idealistic.
   3. The police of the United States are very strict.

C. 1. Nowadays people are quite sincere.
   2. Nowadays our people are quite tranquil.
   3. Nowadays the police are quite respectable.

D. 1. People are complicated.
   2. Our people are independent.
   3. The police are punctual.

E. 1. Part of the wounded died.
   2. Part of those invited came.
   3. Part of the students left.
   4. Part of the employees stayed.

F. 1. The majority of the employees are opposed.
   2. The majority of the directors are opposed.
   3. The majority of the secretaries want to leave early.
   4. The majority of the young girls want to go out without a chaperon.

G. 1. A good part of the people want Vargas Campo.
   2. The majority of the people want a new leader.
   3. The majority want a change of government.

H. 1. A good part of the police have already taken a vacation.
   2. The majority of the police have already studied the situation.
   3. The majority have already had the exam.

● DISCUSSION

Formal agreement between subject and verb is more closely followed in Spanish than in English. Collective nouns like *people* and *police* regularly take plural verbs in English (*The people **are** ready; The police **are** after him*), and many others have the option of doing so (*My family **are**, **is** all with me now*), but this is done less frequently in Spanish. One place where it may and usually does occur is with a collective noun that signifies a fraction of the whole, when the whole is expressed by means of a plural noun.

● COMBINED PATTERN REPLACEMENT DRILL

A. 1. **Creen que yo les compro unas tarjetas.**
   2. Creían _____
   3. _____ nosotros _____
   4. _____ mandábamos _____
   5. _____ cartas
   6. Querían _____
   7. _____ regalos
   8. _____ tú _____
   9. _____ enviaras _____
   10. _____ flores
   11. _____ yo _____
   12. Esperaban _____
   13. _____ trajera _____
   14. _____ le _____
   15. _____ cheques
   16. _____ un _____
   17. Sugería _____
   18. _____ nosotros _____
   19. _____ película
   20. _____ consiguiéramos _____
   21. _____ les _____
   22. _____ yo _____
   23. _____ vendiera _____

B. 1. **Ojalá que nosotros tengamos razón.**
   2. _____ tú _____
   3. _____ tuvieras _____
   4. _____ él _____
   5. _____ la bondad
   6. _____ ellos _____
   7. _____ la culpa
   8. Como si _____
   9. _____ nosotros _____
   10. _____ ella _____
   11. _____ la verdad
   12. _____ creyera _____
   13. _____ ellas _____
   14. _____ dijeran _____
   15. _____ una mentira
   16. No creíamos que _____
   17. _____ prefirieran _____
   18. _____ un tranvía
   19. _____ él _____
   20. _____ tomara _____
   21. _____ un colectivo
   22. No esperábamos que _____
   23. _____ ellos _____
   24. _____ usaran _____

Variants of the present progressive.

A. 1. TEACHER: The people are running.
STUDENT: **La gente está corriendo.**
2. The people are out running.
La gente anda corriendo.
3. The people are running along (busy running).
La gente va corriendo.
4. The people are still running.
La gente sigue corriendo.
5. The people come running.
La gente viene corriendo.

B. 1. The students are studying.
2. The students are out studying.
3. The students are studying away.
4. The students are still studying.
5. The students come studying.

C. 1. The director is organizing the business.
2. The director is out organizing the business.
3. The director is setting about organizing the business.
4. The director is still organizing the business.
5. The director comes [around] organizing the business.

D. 1. The poor [man] is begging (asking.)
2. The poor [man] is out begging.
3. The poor [man] is busy begging (begging away).
4. The poor [man] is still begging.
5. The poor [man] comes begging.

READING
La puntualidad

E. *Esperanza*   R. *Rosa*

E. ¡Rosa, figúrate!   ¿Sabes lo que ha hecho el nuevo gerente?
R. ¿Míster Wright?
E. Sí, ése.
R. No, ¿qué ha hecho?
E. Pues, te acuerdas de que el señor Delgado nos habló anteayer sobre el asunto de la puntualidad.
R. Sí, lo recuerdo.
E. Bueno, ésa no fue idea del señor Delgado.
R. Ya lo sé.
E. No, fue idea de Míster Wright. . . . Ahora, insiste en que todos lleguemos al trabajo a las ocho y media *en punto*.[1]
R. No entiendo.   Es lo que hacemos ahora.
E. No, no.   No comprendes.   Míster Wright dice que algunas veces no llegamos antes de las nueve menos cuarto.

R. Ah, eso es verdad, pero . . . ¡Qué diablo! Una no es máquina, como un reló.   Por ejemplo, si te digo que voy a encontrarte a las cinco para el té, no es como si te dijera que estuvieras allí precisamente a las cinco. Pudieras llegar a las cinco y cinco, o a las cinco y diez, o aun a las cinco y cuarto, sin que yo me preocupara de ello.[2]
E. Sí, sí, sí: todo lo que dices es verdad, y es eso lo que disgusta[3] a Míster Wright.   (*Imitando con voz muy grave.*) "Y cuando digo las ocho y media, digo las ocho y media en punto, y no las nueve menos veintinueve." . . . ¡Figúrate eso!
R. . . . ¡Ay, la pobre mujer!
E ¿Cómo?   ¿Quién?
R. Pues la señora Wright . . . si existe.
E. ¡Ojalá que no!   ¡Quién querría[4] casarse con un autómata!
R. Estoy perfectamente de acuerdo . . . ¡Ojalá que Míster Roberts volviera! . . .

[1] *sharp, on the dot*   [2] *without my worrying about it*   [3] *negative of* **gusta**   [4] *would like*

La familia

En una casa hispana típica viven a menudo varios miembros de la familia. Si no viven bajo el mismo techo, apenas pasan un día sin visitarse. Si la casa es bastante grande, lo más corriente es que a lo menos dos generaciones viven en ella. Las familias que van saliendo del tronco principal siempre conservan sus relaciones íntimas.

Si viven en la misma casa o si viven en hogares distintos, los padres siempre reciben muestras de respeto y obediencia de los hijos. Muchas veces los hijos casados y con familia propia, que en su casa ejercen una autoridad indiscutible, dan pruebas de sumisión, de reverencia y casi de temor cuando están frente a sus padres.

En esta organización de tipo patriarcal, en que la autoridad de los mayores no se discute, toda la familia se siente protegida. Algunas veces los hijos tratan de emanciparse y los mismos padres, tal vez, les animan a probar la suerte por su cuenta. Otras veces los padres ven con dolor como la nueva generación quiere emanciparse, aflojar los lazos y empezar una vida nueva en otra parte del país o del mundo. Pero el miembro de una familia hispana que se lanza a una aventura sabe siempre que tiene las espaldas guardadas. Si fracasa, si el experimento no le sale como quiere o espera, sabe que puede volver atrás. La casa siempre es la casa. En el hogar de sus padres siempre hay sitio para él: un plato en la mesa, techo para la noche y unos corazones que le permanecen fieles. ¿Quién no conoce casos en que, después de

años fuera del hogar, uno de los miembros de la familia regresa, tal vez con el cuerpo enfermo y el alma también quebrantada, arruinado y humillado? Llega a casa y se le recibe[1] como la cosa más natural del mundo. Del pasado sólo interesa lo que él quiere decir. El gozo de tenerle al lado hace olvidar las cosas tristes y desagradables. El esfuerzo económico de toda la familia, prestado con generosa naturalidad y con sentido inquebrantable de solidaridad, muy pronto hace el milagro de restaurar las fuerzas físicas y morales.

Los ancianos son siempre una parte integrante y honrosa de la familia hispana. Se dice que los viejos son la bendición de un hogar. No es que se les tolera;[1] más bien se les estima; se les ama, respeta y rodea de cariño, como a los niños. Los hijos se sienten orgullosos de sus padres; y cuando éstos están inválidos o enfermos, extreman las demostraciones de amor, las atenciones y hasta los mimos. En la sociedad hispana un buen hijo no abandona a sus padres. No sólo los mantiene en su casa, los cuida y los rodea de todo cariño, sino que los exhibe y se enorgullece de ellos y hace todo lo posible porque pasen[2] agradablemente los últimos años de la vida. Sólo si pasa lo peor[3] y no sin vergüenza y humillación, un hijo pobre se ve forzado a desprenderse de sus viejos y llevarlos a un asilo de ancianos. Prefiere sufrir en su casa, pasar mil apuros y hasta arruinarse o perder la salud, antes de[4] enviar a manos extrañas al padre o madre enfermos y sin recursos.

● CUESTIONARIO

1. ¿Cómo es la familia hispana típica?
2. ¿Cuál es la actitud de los hijos frente a los padres?

3. ¿Qué significa para el miembro de una familia hispana aquello de que "la casa siempre es la casa"?

---

[1] **se recibe** = there is receiving, **le** = for him: he is received; **se les tolera** = they are tolerated
[2] **porque pasen** that they may pass (**porque** = por que, por for "motive"; see p. 372)
[3] **si pasa lo peor** if worse comes to worse
[4] **antes de** rather than

4. ¿Cuál es la actitud hacia los ancianos en la familia hispana?
5. ¿En qué casos se ve obligado un hijo a desprenderse de sus ancianos padres y llevarlos a un asilo?
6. ¿Por qué razón es algunas veces común enviar a los ancianos inválidos o enfermos a un asilo de ancianos en Norte América?

7. ¿Qué es una organización de tipo patriarcal?
8. ¿Quiénes son los miembros de su familia de usted?

● SUGGESTED READINGS

Aikman, Duncan, *The All-American Front,* Doubleday, Garden City, New York, 1940: Ch. 19, p. 99, "Family Life"; Ch. 6, "Certain Social Values."
Green, Philip Leonard, *Our Latin-American Neighbors,* Hastings House, New York, 1941: pp. 135–6, "Women and Society"; Ch. 16, "One Family or Many?"

Hanke, Lewis, *Mexico and the Caribbean,* Van Nostrand, Princeton, 1959.
———, *South America,* Van Nostrand, Princeton, 1959.

20

The Lottery

G. *Guillermo* A. *Alberto, a friend* W. *Woman*

G. Did you hear the news about Raúl? I'd like to be in his shoes.

A. Yes, indeed. He won the grand prize in the lottery. A hundred thousand pesos. His wife told mine that now they're going to buy a house in the Miramar district.

G. What a lucky guy! And all because of a lucky break!

A. I wonder how it happened?

G. They say he was standing in the doorway of a restaurant one day when an old woman came by selling tickets.

A. I bet he bought them all.

La lotería (1)

G. *Guillermo* A. *Alberto, un amigo* M. *Mujer*

G. ¿Supo lo de Raúl? Me gustaría estar en su lugar.

A. Sí, hombre; se sacó el gordo de la lotería (2). Cien mil pesos. Su señora le contó a la mía que ahora van a comprar una casa en el barrio Miramar.

G. ¡Qué suerte tiene ese tipo! Y todo por una casualidad.

A. ¿Y cómo sería?

G. Dicen que un día estaba parado en la puerta de un café cuando pasó una vieja vendiendo billetes.

A. Apuesto que se los compró todos.

G. No, how could he? He didn't even have a dime in his pocket.

A. How was it, then?

G. Well, the old woman pestered him so much that, when a friend happened to come by, he borrowed twenty pesos from him and bought a whole ticket.

A. And now he won't even look at anybody. I can just imagine how he must feel.

G. I'd like to see how you'd be! The same thing would happen to anybody.

A. Not to me, never.

G. And why not?

A. Because I'll never play the lottery.

G. Never say never [of this water I won't drink].

A. Only if they gave me a ticket!

G. And if it turned out to be the lucky one [rewarded], what would you do with the money?

A. Perhaps we'd take a trip to Europe . . . the children would have everything, but . . .

w. Lottery! Lottery tickets for sale!

A. Look, Memo, uh . . . could you lend me twenty pesos?

G. No, qué va. No tenía ni un diez en el bolsillo.

A. ¿Y cómo, entonces?

G. Que la vieja le insistió tanto que cuando pasaba un amigo, le pidió veinte pesos y compró un entero (3).

A. Y ahora ni mirará a nadie. Me imagino cómo estará.

G. Quisiera verlo a usted. A cualquiera le pasaría lo mismo.

A. ¿A mí? Nunca.

G. ¿Y por qué no?

A. Porque yo jamás jugaré a la lotería.

G. Nunca diga "De esta agua no beberé."

A. Sólo que me regalaran el billete.

G. Y si saliera premiado, ¿qué haría con la plata?

A. Quizá haríamos un viaje a Europa . . . Los niños tendrían de todo, pero . . .

M. ¡Lotería! ¡Se juega la lotería!

A. Mire, Memo (4), este . . . ¿podría prestarme veinte pesos?

Cultural Notes

(1) The lottery is a fund-raising institution organized by the state, appealing to the gambling instinct, as a supplement to taxation. It supports public and charitable works (e.g., the construction and maintenance of a national shrine to the patron saint of Mexico, the Virgin of Guadalupe, and the construction of a vast medical center in Mexico City; in Chile, its funds are used to aid the Red Cross).

(2) **El gordo** or **el premio gordo** means *the fat prize,* i.e., the first or grand prize.

(3) The **entero** *whole ticket* is also referred to as **billete entero** or **número entero.** It is a long sheet often containing ten **décimos** *tenths,* all having the same serial number. Since a **décimo** is the usual *share* or *ticket* purchased, Raúl, in buying an **entero,** was playing for much higher stakes and was thus able to win ten times as much as if he had held only a **décimo.**

(4) **Memo** is a common nickname for **Guillermo,** of which it is the reduplicated final syllable. See Unit 3, Cultural Note 4, on the nickname **Pepe.**

110 The future tense

EXAMPLES

A. 1. Yo jamás **jugaré** a la lotería.
   2. De esta agua no **beberé.**

B. ¿Qué **dirás?** *What will you say?*

C. 1. Ahora no **mirará** a nadie.
   2. **Habrá** más tiempo mañana. *There'll be more time tomorrow.*

D. No **podremos** dormir. *We won't be able to sleep.*

E. **¿Comprenderán?** *Will they understand?*

Verbs regular in the future

INFINITIVE STEM	ENDINGS
hablar–	–é
comer–	–ás
vivir–	–á
ser–	
traer–	–emos
etc.	–án

The straight infinitive serves as the stem of the future of almost all verbs.

Verbs irregular in the future

INFINITIVE	MODIFIED INFINITIVE STEM	ENDINGS
haber	habr–	
poder	podr–	
querer	querr–	
saber	sabr–	–é
		–ás
poner[1]	pondr–	–á
tener	tendr–	
venir	vendr–	–emos
salir	saldr–	–án
valer	valdr–	
decir	dir–	
hacer	har–	

In these verbs a modified form of the infinitive serves as the stem of the future.

● PERSON-NUMBER SUBSTITUTION DRILL

1. *Yo* jamás jugaré a la lotería.
   (nosotros, él, ellos, tú, ella, ustedes)
2. Y ahora *él* no mirará a nadie.
   (ellos, ella, yo, nosotros, tú, usted)
3. *La señorita* volverá dentro de un rato.
   (ellos, nosotros, él, yo, tú, ustedes)
4. Comeremos esta noche en casa de don Patricio.
   (yo, él, tú, ellos, ella y yo, usted)
5. Un momentito, ya verás.
   (nosotros, ustedes, usted, ellos, él, yo)
6. *El gerente* tratará de reducir las horas de la siesta.
   (ellos, yo, nosotros, usted, tú, el jefe)
7. ¿Seguirán *ustedes* estudiando español?
   (ellos, usted, ellas, ella, tú, él)
8. *Ellos* participarán en básquetbol, boxeo, y en la carrera de maratón.
   (nosotros, ustedes, tú, usted, yo, él)
9. Veremos a todos los parientes de mi señora.
   (yo, ellos, usted, ellas, tú, ustedes)
10. Servirá una comida fantástica.
    (ellas, nosotros, tú, ustedes, usted, yo)
11. Tomaré unas vacaciones más tarde este verano.
    (nosotros, ellos, ella, tú, ustedes, usted)
12. Podrán organizar unos juegos típicos.
    (nosotros, usted, tú, ellos, usted y yo, yo)
13. Sí, pero ¿todavía querrá esto mañana?
    (nosotros, ellos, usted, yo, tú, ustedes)
14. No sabremos la verdad hasta el domingo.
    (yo, tú, ellos, él, ustedes, usted)
15. Pondré las flores en la sala.
    (nosotros, ellos, usted, ustedes, tú, ella)
16. Tendrá veintidós años la semana próxima.
    (yo, tú, ella, ustedes, nosotros, él)
17. Vendremos mañana en vez del jueves.
    (yo, ella, ustedes, tú, usted, ellos)
18. Saldrán para los Juegos Olímpicos el domingo.
    (ella, nosotros, yo, ellos, usted, tú)
19. No diremos nada excepto lo necesario.
    (yo, él, ellos, ella, tú, usted)
20. Harás más dinero en ese puesto.
    (usted, ustedes, él, yo, ellos, nosotros)

---

[1] Also **oponer** and other derivatives of verbs in this list.

● CONSTRUCTION SUBSTITUTION DRILL

INSTRUCTIONS: Repeat the following sentences just as you hear them. Then repeat them again, substituting an equivalent future-tense form for the **ir a** construction.

A. 1. TEACHER: No *voy a morir* de úlceras.
   Repita.
   STUDENT: **No voy a morir de úlceras.**
   TEACHER: *Cambie.*
   STUDENT: **No moriré de úlceras.**

2. Lo del horario *va a resultar* muy bien.
3. *Vamos a hablar* adentro.
4. Ese tipo se *va a sacar* el gordo de la lotería.
5. *Vamos a vivir* en el norte.
6. *Vas a ver* un cielo muy azul.
7. *Van a prometer* demasiado.
8. La *va a encontrar* parada en la puerta de un café.
9. *Voy a ver* a mi padrino el día de su santo.
10. Sí, pero le *va a costar* caro.

B. 1. *Va a haber* aire puro en el campo.
2. No *vamos a poder* oponernos a la mayoría.
3. Ellas no *van a querer* ir a una corrida de toros.
4. El *va a saber* terminar el pleito.
5. ¿No te *vas a poner* el vestido nuevo?
6. *Voy a tener* mucha suerte en este país.
7. *Vamos a venir* en un día feriado.
8. A ver; *voy a salir* a las ocho de la mañana.
9. No *va a valer* la pena.
10. Nunca *voy a decir* otra mentira.
11. *Va a hacer* mucho viento este invierno.

● TENSE SUBSTITUTION DRILL

INSTRUCTIONS: Repeat the following sentences just as you hear them. Then repeat them again substituting a future-tense form for the present or imperfect.

A. 1. TEACHER: Mañana compro un entero.
   Repita.
   STUDENT: **Mañana compro un entero.**
   TEACHER: *Cambie.*
   STUDENT: **Mañana compraré un entero.**

2. Mañana vemos una película importada.
3. Mañana explico las ventajas y las desventajas.
4. Mañana podemos encontrar agua potable.
5. Mañana hay una reunión del Consejo Estudiantil.
6. Mañana te regalo un nuevo par de zapatos.
7. Mañana compro otro billete.

B. 1. Después de eso, ella te miraba con horror.
2. ¿Tomaba usted el autobús o el tranvía?
3. Nos encontrábamos en el Club de la Unión.
4. Nos veíamos muy a menudo.
5. Ellos seguían estudiando castellano.
6. Ella nunca comprendía la importancia de la situación.
7. Yo no podía llevarla.

● CHOICE-QUESTION RESPONSE DRILL

A. 1. ¿Se levantará temprano mañana o se quedará en la cama?
2. ¿Le mandará una carta o la llamará por teléfono?
3. ¿Le exigirá una multa o lo dejará escapar?
4. ¿Trabajará todo el día o jugará por la tarde?
5. ¿Doblará en esa esquina o seguirá adelante?

B. 1. ¿Saldrá mañana o podrá esperarme?
2. ¿Vendrá conmigo o querrá quedarse a estudiar?
3. ¿Habrá mucha gente o valdrá la pena ir?
4. ¿Dirá la verdad o pondrá un pretexto?
5. ¿Sabrá arreglarlo o no tendrá tiempo?

● DISCUSSION

The future tense in Spanish is used somewhat less frequently than the future (the form with *will*) in English. In both languages the future must compete with the **ir a** *going to* construction (see Unit 7 §34); but the Spanish future must also compete, more than the English future, with the present tense used with future meanings (see Unit 4 §17).

The future is the prediction of a coming event, detached from the present. In **¿Cuándo llegan?** *When do (will) they arrive?* the speaker uses a present for future, suggesting that the time, whatever it is, has already been decided on: "When are they supposed to arrive?" In **¿Cuándo van a llegar?** *When are they going to arrive?* the speaker implies a future event growing out of present conditions or intentions: "When is it their intention to be here?" In **¿Cuándo llegarán?** *When will they arrive?* the speaker asks to have something foreseen, without tying it to the present.

The Spanish future is proper wherever English has its future with *will* (but review Unit 4 §17).

111   The conditional

EXAMPLES
1. A cualquiera le **pasaría** lo mismo.
2. Quizá **haríamos** un viaje a Europa.
3. Los niños **tendrían** de todo.

Verbs regular in the conditional

INFINITIVE STEM	ENDINGS
hablar–	–ía
comer–	–ías
vivir–	–ía
ser–	
traer–	–íamos
etc.	–ían

Verbs irregular in the conditional

INFINITIVE	MODIFIED INFINITIVE STEM	ENDINGS
haber	habr–	
poder	podr–	
querer	querr–	
saber	sabr–	–ía
		–ías
poner[1]	pondr–	–ía
tener	tendr–	
venir	vendr–	–íamos
salir	saldr–	–ían
valer	valdr–	
decir	dir–	
hacer	har–	

The stem of the conditional is the same as that of the future. The endings are the same as in the imperfect indicative of –er and –ir verbs.

● PERSON-NUMBER SUBSTITUTION DRILL

1. En ese caso, *yo* sería menos exigente.
   (ellos, usted, tú, él, nosotros, ustedes)
2. Además, *nosotros* estaríamos algo escasos de dinero.
   (yo, ellas, tú, usted, ustedes, él)
3. Si no, *él* no hablaría tanto.
   (tú, yo, ellos, nosotros, ustedes, usted)
4. De otro modo, *ellos* no venderían los cueros.
   (él, ustedes, usted, tú, nosotros, yo)

---

[1] Also **oponer** and other derivatives of verbs in this list.

5. Entonces *el gerente* no se preocuparía tanto de la puntualidad.
   (ellos, usted, ustedes, tú, yo, nosotros)
6. En ese caso *ellos* se defenderían del tirano.
   (usted, ustedes, él, nosotros, yo, tú)
7. Si no, *ella* se levantaría muy tarde.
   (ellas, usted, ustedes, tú, nosotros, yo)
8. En este caso *yo* no tendría nada en el bolsillo.
   (nosotros, usted, ustedes, tú, él, ellas)
9. De otra manera *él* no sabría defenderse.
   (ustedes, ella, nosotros, ellos, tú, yo)
10. Pero *ellos* no podrían arreglar lo de la fecha.
    (usted, ustedes, nosotros, yo, tú, él)
11. ¿En este caso vendría *usted* sin falta?
    (ustedes, tú, él, ellas, ella, ellos)
12. De todos modos *ellos* saldrían para México.
    (usted, ustedes, él, ellas, ella, tú)
13. *Yo* no pondría el radio tan fuerte.
    (usted, tú, nosotros, ella, ustedes, él)
14. Bueno, *yo* no diría eso.
    (nosotros, él, ellos, ella, ellas, él y yo)
15. Quizá haríamos un viaje a Europa.
    (yo, ustedes, él, tú, ellos, usted)

● TENSE SUBSTITUTION DRILL

INSTRUCTIONS: Repeat the following sentences just as you hear them.   Then repeat them again substituting a conditional-tense form for the present or imperfect.

A. 1. TEACHER: A cualquiera le pasa lo mismo. *Repita.*
      STUDENT: **A cualquiera le pasa lo mismo.**
      TEACHER: *Cambie.*
      STUDENT: **A cualquiera le pasaría lo mismo.**
   2. Compran una casa en el campo.
   3. No tomo ese cochino autobús.
   4. Lupe se casa con Lorenzo.
   5. Ustedes dos nunca se ponen de acuerdo.
   6. Hacemos un viaje a Europa.

B. 1. Iba a la reunión del Consejo Estudiantil.
   2. Contestaba su atenta del 21.
   3. Nos veíamos muy a menudo.
   4. Había mucha gente en la plaza.
   5. Todo lo quería cambiar.
   6. Ese barbero ponía brillantina en el pelo.

● CONSTRUCTION SUBSTITUTION DRILL

INSTRUCTIONS: Repeat the following sentences just as you hear them.   Then repeat them again substituting an equivalent conditional-tense form for the **ir a** construction.

A. 1. TEACHER: Dijo que *iba a trabajar* mañana. *Repita.*
      STUDENT: **Dijo que iba a trabajar mañana.**
      TEACHER: *Cambie.*
      STUDENT: **Dijo que trabajaría mañana.**
   2. Dijo que *iba a comprar* la leche.
   3. Dijo que *iba a preguntar* su edad.
   4. Dijo que me *iba a cortar* el pelo atrás y a los lados.
   5. Dijo que el ganado *iba a dejar* bastante ganancia en la feria.
   6. Dijo que los estudiantes *iban a ir* al parque central.
   7. Dijo que las muchachas *iban a llevar* una mujer casada de chaperón.
   8. Dijo anteayer que les *iba a hablar* directamente.

B. 1. Dijo que *iba a salir* a las siete y media.
   2. Dijo que *iba a poner* las flores en la sala.
   3. Dijo que *iba a venir* temprano.
   4. Dijo que no *iba a poder* agradecerle.
   5. Dijo que su hermano mayor no *iba a tener* tiempo.
   6. Dijo que el gerente *iba a decir* algo.
   7. Dijo que *iba a hacer* una ensalada.

● PATTERNED RESPONSE DRILL

A. 1. TEACHER: ¿Qué discutirías?
      STUDENT: **Yo discutiría la política.**
   2. ¿Qué estudiarías?
   3. ¿Qué explicarías?
   4. ¿Qué atacarías?
   5. ¿Qué preferirías?
   6. ¿Qué seguirías?
   7. ¿Qué mencionarías?

B. 1. ¿Qué traerían ustedes?
      Traeríamos el coche.
   2. ¿Qué comprarían ustedes?
   3. ¿Qué venderían ustedes?
   4. ¿Qué llevarían ustedes?
   5. ¿Qué buscarían ustedes?
   6. ¿Qué desearían ustedes?
   7. ¿Qué ofrecerían ustedes?
   8. ¿Qué prometerían ustedes?
   9. ¿Qué regalarían ustedes?

● DISCUSSION

The conditional is to the past what the future is to the present. Note the following parallels:

I know it will change	**Sé que se cambiará**
I knew it would change	**Sabía que se cambiaría**
He says it will be enough	**Dice que será bastante**
He said it would be enough	**Dijo que sería bastante**

The usual English equivalent is *would*.[1]

112 Additional progressives

EXAMPLES

1. ¿Dónde **han estado viviendo?** *Where have they been living?*
2. No **estaremos trabajando.** *We won't be working.*
3. ¿Qué **estaría pensando** ahora? *What would he be thinking now?*
4. Tal vez **estén practicando.** *Perhaps they are practicing.*
5. Dudaba que **estuviera dictando** a esas horas. *I doubted that he was dictating at that time.*
6. Espero que no **hayan estado siguiéndonos.** *I hope they haven't been following us.*

form of **estar**	**–ndo** form

Any form of **estar** may be used with the **–ndo**
form of another verb to make a progressive.
(See Unit 8 §41 and Unit 10 §53.)

● CONSTRUCTION SUBSTITUTION DRILL

INSTRUCTIONS: Repeat the following sentences just as you hear them. Then repeat them again substituting the present perfect progressive for the present progressive.

A. 1. TEACHER: ¿Dónde están viviendo?
   Repita.
   STUDENT: **¿Dónde están viviendo?**
   TEACHER: *Cambie.*
   STUDENT: **¿Dónde han estado viviendo?**

   2. ¿Dónde está trabajando?
   3. ¿Dónde estás comiendo?
   4. ¿Dónde están estudiando?
   5. ¿Dónde estás jugando?

B. 1. No estoy haciendo nada.
   2. No está viviendo aquí cerca.
   3. No estamos estudiando psicología.
   4. No están esperando a Roberto.
   5. No están trabajando en la planta.

INSTRUCTIONS: Repeat the following sentences just as you hear them. Then repeat them again substituting the future progressive for the future.

C. 1. No trabajaremos a las ocho.
   No trabajaremos a las ocho.
   No estaremos trabajando a las ocho.
   2. Esperaré aquí a las ocho.

   3. Jugarán a las ocho.
   4. Compraré un regalo para los novios a las ocho.
   5. Correrá en la carrera de maratón a las ocho.
   6. Le explicarás el oficio a las ocho.

---

[1] *Would* has several different meanings. See the discussion of Unit 10 §52 for *would = used to*. Compare also *He wouldn't (didn't want to, refused to) do it* **No lo quiso hacer,** where *would* is the past of *will (be willing)* .

INSTRUCTIONS: Repeat the following sentences just as you hear them. Then repeat them again substituting the conditional progressive for the present progressive.

D. 1. ¿Qué está pensando él ahora?
    ¿Qué está pensando él ahora?
    ¿Qué estaría pensando él ahora?
  2. ¿Qué está haciendo él ahora?

3. ¿Qué está estudiando él ahora?
4. ¿Qué está viendo él ahora?
5. ¿Qué está prometiendo él ahora?
6. ¿Qué está trayendo él ahora?

INSTRUCTIONS: Repeat the following sentences just as you hear them. Then repeat them again adding **tal vez** before the sentence and making the verb subjunctive.

E. 1. Están practicando.
    Están practicando.
    Tal vez estén practicando.
  2. Se está organizando un grupo.
  3. Está haciendo algo con esas herramientas.

4. Está trabajando en el ministerio.
5. Están lavando el auto.
6. Está escribiendo la carta.
7. Está doblando a la derecha.
8. Están viviendo lejos de aquí.

INSTRUCTIONS: Repeat the following sentences just as you hear them. Then repeat them again substituting **dudaba** for **dudo,** which will cause a change in the verb of the clause from present subjunctive progressive to imperfect subjunctive progressive.

F. 1. Dudo que estén dictando.
    Dudo que estén dictando.
    Dudaba que estuvieran dictando.
  2. Dudo que esté jugando.

3. Dudo que estén estudiando.
4. Dudo que se esté muriendo.
5. Dudo que estén escribiendo.
6. Dudo que esté sirviendo.

INSTRUCTIONS: Repeat the following sentences just as you hear them. Then repeat them again substituting the present perfect subjunctive progressive for the present subjunctive progressive.

G. 1. Espero que no estén siguiéndonos.
    Espero que no estén siguiéndonos.
    Espero que no hayan estado siguiéndonos.
  2. Espero que no esté estudiando.

3. Espero que no estén durmiendo.
4. Espero que no esté bebiendo.
5. Espero que no estén pidiendo.
6. Espero que no esté esperando.

● DISCUSSION

Any form of **estar,** including those with **haber** (**han estado, hayamos estado,** etc.), may be used in a progressive construction. Even **estando** is possible: **Estando viendo el juego** *While seeing the game* (literally *being seeing the game*).

The meaning covers what is actually going on, not what is planned. English *Tomorrow I'll be working here* may be taken in the sense "Tomorrow I plan to be working here." The Spanish for this sense is **Mañana trabajo aquí** (see Unit 4 §17). **Estaré trabajando** would be appropriate in the context *What will you be doing when I get there?—I'll be working* (engaged at that moment in the act of working).

113 Additional perfects

EXAMPLES

1. No **habíamos dicho** nada. *We hadn't said anything.*
2. Para entonces se **habrán ido.** *By then they'll have gone.*
3. Sé que **habría sido** mejor. *I know it would have been better.*
4. Dudo que **hubiera sido** mejor. *I doubt that it would have been better.*
5. ¿Dónde **habían estado** viviendo? *Where had they been living?*
6. ¿**Ha habido** huelga? *Has there been a strike?*

form of **haber**	**–do** form

All the perfect constructions in English have parallels in Spanish, in which a form of **haber** combines with the **–do** form of a verb.

● SUBSTITUTION DRILL

INSTRUCTIONS: Repeat the following sentences just as you hear them. Then repeat them again substituting the past perfect for the preterit.

A. 1. TEACHER: No dijimos nada. *Repita.*
    STUDENT: **No dijimos nada.**
    TEACHER: *Cambie.*
    STUDENT: **No habíamos dicho nada.**
  2. No hicimos nada.
  3. No trajimos nada.

4. No tuvimos nada.
5. No supimos nada.
6. No pudimos hacer nada.
7. No quisimos hacer nada.
8. No tuvimos que hacer nada.

INSTRUCTIONS: Repeat the following sentences just as you hear them. Then repeat them again substituting the future perfect for the future.

B. 1. Mañana se irán.
   Mañana se irán.
   Mañana se habrán ido.
  2. Mañana saldrá.
  3. Mañana volverán.

4. Mañana regresará.
5. Mañana comulgarán.
6. Mañana llamará.
7. Mañana consultarán.
8. Mañana discutirá.

INSTRUCTIONS: Repeat the following sentences just as you hear them. Then repeat them again substituting the conditional perfect for the present.

C. 1. Sé que es mejor.
   Sé que es mejor.
   Sé que habría sido mejor.
  2. Sé que vienen mañana.
  3. Sé que no puede.

4. Sé que lo hacen de nuevo.
5. Sé que sigue derecho.
6. Sé que saben la lengua española.
7. Sé que es una vida agitada.
8. Sé que no les hace falta la siesta.

INSTRUCTIONS: Repeat the following sentences just as you hear them. Then repeat them again substituting past perfect subjunctive for present perfect subjunctive.

D. 1. Dudo que haya sido mejor.
   Dudo que haya sido mejor.
   Dudo que hubiera sido mejor.
  2. Dudo que hayan venido el año pasado.
  3. Dudo que no haya podido.

4. Dudo que lo hayan hecho de nuevo.
5. Dudo que haya seguido adelante.
6. Dudo que hayan sabido la lengua inglesa.
7. Dudo que hayan sido muy finos.

INSTRUCTIONS: Repeat the following sentences just as you hear them. Then repeat them again substituting past perfect progressive for imperfect progressive.

E. 1. ¿Dónde estaban viviendo?
   ¿Dónde estaban viviendo?
   ¿Dónde habían estado viviendo?
  2. ¿Dónde estaba trabajando?
  3. ¿Dónde estaban enseñando?

4. ¿Dónde estaba pasando las vacaciones?
5. ¿Dónde estaban peleando?
6. ¿Dónde estaba buscando?
7. ¿Dónde estaban durmiendo?

● DISCUSSION

Any tense, indicative or subjunctive, of the verb **haber** may combine with the **–do** form of a verb (the preterit is rarely so used, however). This includes even combinations with **haber** itself in the sense *there to be* (see Unit 7 §36): **ha habido** means *there has (have) been*, **había habido** means *there had been*, **habría habido** means *there would have been*, etc.

The perfect constructions are referred to by the name of the form of **haber** used: if **haber** is in the present tense, we have the present perfect; if in the future, we have the future perfect, etc. To avoid the expression "imperfect perfect," the combination of the imperfect of **haber** with the –**do** form is called the "past perfect."

114 The future of probability; *deber*, must, ought

EXAMPLES

1. Me imagino cómo **estará.**
2. ¿Qué hora **será?** *What time do you suppose it is?*
3. **Habrá** algunas desventajas. *There probably are some disadvantages.*
4. **Estará rabiando** como siempre. *He's probably fuming as usual.*

probablemente	está es hay está rabiando	=	estará será habrá estará rabiando

The future is often used to express probability in the present. The English equivalents use expressions like *probably, do you suppose, can . . . be* (e.g., *What can he be thinking?*), etc.

EXAMPLES

A. 1. **Debe** estar en la cocina.
   2. **Debe** tener unos veintiún años.
   3. Me imagino que **deben** tener ovejas y cerdos, también.

B. 1. ¿Qué **debo** hacer, doctor?
   2. **Debes** tratar de llegar a esa decisión.
   3. Las muchachas no **deben** salir solas.

must *should* *ought*	*to*	infinitive		**deber**	infinitive

Deber plus infinitive is the equivalent of English *must, ought,* and *should* plus infinitive (without *to* except for *ought to*) to express obligation or probability.

● CONSTRUCTION SUBSTITUTION DRILL

A. INSTRUCTIONS: Repeat the following sentences just as you hear them. Then repeat them again substituting a future-tense form for **probablemente** and the present tense.

1. TEACHER: *Probablemente está en la cocina.*
   Repita.
   STUDENT: **Probablemente está en la cocina.**
   TEACHER: *Cambie.*
   STUDENT: **Estará en la cocina.**
2. *Probablemente es la criada.*
3. *Probablemente son las dos y media.*
4. *Probablemente hay algunas desventajas.*
5. *Probablemente es muy simpático.*
6. *Probablemente tiene mucha hambre.*
7. *Probablemente hace frío allá.*
8. *Probablemente están rabiando.*
9. *Probablemente está enojado.*

B. INSTRUCTIONS: Repeat the following sentences just as you hear them. Then repeat them again substituting **debe** or **deber** plus the infinitive for the future-tense form.

1. TEACHER: Julio *estará* en la cocina. *Repita.*
   STUDENT: **Julio estará en la cocina.**
   TEACHER: *Cambie.*
   STUDENT: **Julio debe estar en la cocina.**
2. *Tendrá* unos treinta años.
3. *Serán* las siete y media.
4. *Tendrá* ovejas y cerdos también.

5. *Será* muy puntual.
6. *Estarán* durmiendo a estas horas.
7. *Habrá* ciertas ventajas.
8. *Estará* en la misa.
9. *Tendrá* un recibo.
10. Tú *tendrás* un jefe muy antipático.

● TRANSLATION DRILL

TEACHER:
1. Mario must remember the address.
   Alicia should remember the address.
   Alfredo ought to remember the address.
   STUDENT:
   Mario debe recordar la dirección.
   Alicia debe recordar la dirección.
   Alfredo debe recordar la dirección.
2. Rosa must pay more.
   Pepe should pay more.
   Olga ought to pay more.
3. Bernardo must know that man.
   Alvaro should know that man.
   Felipe ought to know that man.
4. I must go now.
   I should leave now.
   I ought to return now.

5. We must sell the car.
   We should sell the house.
   We ought to sell the café.
6. They must finish the schedule.
   They should write the letters.
   They ought to send the orders.
7. I must order the wreath.
   I should call María Elena.
   I ought to leave a message.
8. You must go home.
   You should go to bed.
   You ought to take these pills.
9. We must consult with the employees.
   We should try the new schedule for a few days.
   We ought to accept some new ideas.

● DISCUSSION

English occasionally uses the future to express probability in the present: *By now they'll be worrying* themselves sick. The implication is what will turn out to be true on later verification. In Spanish this use of the future is more frequent, especially with the verbs **ser, estar, tener,** and **haber.**

A stronger probability is expressed by **deber** plus infinitive. It verges on the meaning of "obligation," and the same verb, **deber,** is used in both senses. Ordinarily, when it is used with a verb of action, e.g., **no deben salir,** the meaning is obligation; with other verbs, the meaning is probability, e.g., **Debe estar en la cocina.** English *must* shares the same range of meanings: *They mustn't go out,* obligation; *He must be in the kitchen,* probability.

115 Clauses with *si*, if

EXAMPLES

A. 1. Si **sale** premiado, ¿qué hará con la plata? *If it turns out to be the lucky one, what will you do with the money?*
   2. ¿Y si el Ministerio de Educación no **acepta?**
   3. Si **vienes,** ¿puedes traer tu tocadiscos?
   4. Si **vuelve** a llamar, dígale que no estoy.

B. 1. Si **tenía** el dinero, debe haberlo perdido. *If he had the money, he must have lost it.*
   2. Dijo que estaba bien, si **era** necesario.
   3. Si antes que yo viniera **existía** esa costumbre . . .

C. Si **llegaste** primero, ganaste.   *If you got there first, you won.*

D. Si **ha estado** en Buenos Aires, ha visto el Teatro Nacional.   *If he's been in Buenos Aires, he's seen the National Theater.*

*Neutral **if** clauses*

If	it turns	out to be the lucky one	Si	sale	premiado
If	you come		Si	vienes	
If	he had	the money	Si	tenía	el dinero
If	you arrived	first	Si	llegaste	primero
If	he's been	in Buenos Aires	Si	ha estado	en Buenos Aires

In neutral *if* clauses, Spanish uses the indicative; the tenses correspond to the meanings (present form = present meaning, past form = past meaning) as in English.

EXAMPLES

A. 1. Si **saliera** premiado, ¿qué haría con la plata?
   2. ¿Y si el Ministerio de Educación no **aceptara?**   *And what if the Ministry of Education shouldn't accept?*
   3. Si **vinieras,** ¿podrías traer tu tocadiscos?   *If you should come, could you bring your record player?*
   4. Si **volviera** a llamar, dígale que no estoy.   *If she should call again, tell her I'm not in.*
   5. Si **tuviera** el dinero lo perdería.   *If he had the money he'd lose it.*
   6. Si **llegaras** primero, ganarías.   *If you got (should get, were to get) there first, you'd win.*
   7. No hablaría así si yo **fuera** usted.   *I wouldn't talk like that if I were you.*

B. 1. Si la policía no **hubiera disuelto** la manifestación, los estudiantes no habrían declarado la huelga.   *If the police hadn't broken up the demonstration, the students wouldn't have called the strike.*
   2. ¿Lo habría ofrecido si lo **hubiera tenido?**   *Would you have offered it if you'd had it?*

*Unlikely and unreal **if** clauses*

If	it should turn out	to be the lucky one	Si	saliera	premiado
If	you should come		Si	vinieras	
If	he had	the money	Si	tuviera	el dinero
If	you arrived (were to arrive)	first	Si	llegaras	primero
If	I were	you	Si	fuera	usted
If	they hadn't broken up	the demon-stration	Si no	hubieran disuelto	la manifestación
If	you had had	it	Si lo	hubiera tenido	

To suggest something unlikely of fulfillment or something contrary to fact, English uses *should, were to,* past forms that are *nonpast* in meaning, and the past perfect.   The corresponding Spanish forms are the imperfect and past perfect subjunctive.

INSTRUCTIONS: Repeat the following sentences just as you hear them. Then repeat them again changing the verb after **si** from present to imperfect subjunctive.

A. 1. TEACHER: Si vuelve a llamar, dígale que no estoy. *Repita.*
   STUDENT: **Si vuelve a llamar, dígale que no estoy.**
   TEACHER: *Cambie.*
   STUDENT: **Si volviera a llamar, dígale que no estoy.**
2. Si sales premiado, dale gracias a Dios.

3. Si él tiene bastante dinero, véndale el coche.
4. Si puede venir, dígale que traiga su tocadiscos.
5. Si llegas primero, espérame.
6. Si viene el profesor, dele el libro.
7. Si pregunta, contéstele.

INSTRUCTIONS: Repeat the following sentences just as you hear them. Then repeat them again substituting imperfect (or past perfect) subjunctive for present (or present perfect) after **si** and changing the verb in the other clause from future to conditional (or conditional perfect).

B. 1. TEACHER: Si sales premiado, ¿qué harás con la plata? *Repita.*
   STUDENT: **Si sales premiado, ¿qué harás con la plata?**
   TEACHER: *Cambie.*
   STUDENT: **Si salieras premiado, ¿qué harías con la plata?**
2. Si llegas primero, ganarás.
3. Si vienes, ¿podrás traer tu tocadiscos?
4. Si tiene el dinero, lo perderá.
5. Si el ministerio no acepta, perderemos todo.
6. Si vuelve a llamar, me volveré loco.
7. Si es necesario, lo haré.
8. Si nos quiere, nos llamará.

C. 1. Si ha contestado la carta, la recibiremos.
   Si ha contestado la carta, la recibiremos.
   Si hubiera contestado la carta, la habríamos recibido.
2. Si ha terminado el horario, lo veremos.
3. Si ha hecho el trabajo, nos llamará.
4. Si ha lavado el auto, parecerá como nuevo.
5. Si no ha cumplido con la patria, lo sabremos.
6. Si no ha pagado el alquiler, nos dirán.
7. Si no ha pagado la electricidad, la cortarán.

● TRANSLATION DRILL

A. 1. If I had a million pesos, I'd take a trip.
   Si yo tuviera un millón de pesos, haría un viaje.
2. If he had enough money, he wouldn't work.
3. If the magazine were here, I'd give it to you.
4. If the house weren't dirty, I wouldn't be mad.
5. If I had time, I'd take a vacation.
6. If Victor were here, he'd fix it.
7. If it were upstairs, I would be able to find it.

B. 1. If I had had a million pesos, I'd have taken a trip.
   Si hubiera tenido un millón de pesos, habría hecho un viaje.
2. If he had had enough money, he wouldn't have worked.
3. If the magazine had been there, I'd have given it to you.
4. If the house hadn't been dirty, I wouldn't have been mad.
5. If I had bought a whole ticket, I'd have won ten thousand pesos.
6. If I had had time, I'd have taken a vacation.
7. If Victor had been here, he'd have fixed it.
8. If it were here downstairs, I'd have been able to find it.

A. Quién sabe **si aceptarán.** *Who knows whether they'll accept.*

B. Nos preguntó **si sería** una molestia para nosotros. *He asked us if (whether) it would be a bother to us.*

C. 1. Todavía no sé **si voy** a ir o no.
2. Dice un señor **si hay** ropa vieja para vender.
3. No **sé si** hubo muertos.

	si *if*	**si** *if, whether*
future indicative		√
conditional indicative		√
present subjunctive		
other forms of verb	√	√

When *if* has its ordinary meaning, i.e., does not mean the same as *whether*, three forms of the verb are excluded from the *if* clause: future and conditional indicative, and present subjunctive. When *if* does mean the same as *whether*, as usually happens after verbs of knowing, wondering, and asking, any form of the verb may be freely used except the present subjunctive.

● TRANSLATION DRILL

A. 1. No one knows if he will accept.
2. No one knows if he will come.
3. No one knows if he will attack.
4. No one knows if he will finish.
5. No one knows if he will resign.
6. No one knows if he will return.
7. No one knows if he will leave.

B. 1. He asked us if it would be any bother.
2. He asked us if it would be worthwhile.
3. He asked us if we would come.
4. He asked us if we would buy a ticket.
5. He asked us if we would sell the house.
6. He asked us if we would mention the matter.
7. He asked us if we would bring some plates.

● DISCUSSION

The notion of unreality often found in the imperfect subjunctive (see Unit 19 §107) is extended to sentences containing *if* clauses. All such sentences, even those with the indicative, are unreal to the extent that *if* implies something that has not happened or that is regarded as not necessarily true; but using the imperfect subjunctive increases the unreality. English uses a similar device, that of verbs past in form but nonpast in meaning: *If you talked (should talk, were to talk) that way you'd lose the position* **Si hablara así perdería el puesto** contrasts with *If you talk that way you'll lose the position* **Si habla así perderá el puesto.**

Contrary-to-fact *if* clauses are simply the extreme case of unlikelihood or unreality, and again the past subjunctive forms, imperfect or past perfect, are used. The English parallels are close: *If I were you* (but I'm not) **Si yo fuera usted;** *If he had gone* (but he didn't) **Si hubiera ido.**

Except for the form *were* (*if he were here* vs. *if he was here*), English uses the same past form of the verb where Spanish distinguishes two different meanings with two different forms, e.g. *And what if you lost it?* ("And what if you were to lose it?") **¿Y si lo perdieras?** vs. *And what if you lost it?* ("And what if you've lost it?") **¿Y si lo perdiste?**

There are certain restrictions on what forms of the verb may appear in an *if* clause. Where **si** means the *if* of condition and not *whether,* only the following appear: present, imperfect, and preterit indicative, and imperfect subjunctive (and the corresponding perfect and progressive constructions). This means that the present subjunctive and the future and conditional indicative are excluded. When something like *If you'll wait I'll go with you* appears in English, we must interpret the *will* as "willingness" and not as futurity: **Si quieres esperar, te acompaño.**

When **si** means *whether* (or *if* in the sense of *whether*), however, as it usually does after verbs like *know, ask, doubt,* and *wonder,* the future and conditional (but not, as a rule, the present subjunctive) are normal, as are all the other verb forms, including the perfect and progressive constructions in which future and conditional enter (e.g., the future progressive or the conditional perfect: *I don't know whether he'll be working at this time of day* **No sé si estará trabajando a estas horas**).

116 Softened requests and criticisms

EXAMPLES

A. 1. **¿Podría** prestarme veinte pesos?
   2. **¿Tendría** usted tiempo para almorzar conmigo?   *Would you have time to lunch with me?*
   3. Se **diría** que nos odiaba.   *You might say he hated us.*
   4. **Habría** sido mejor esperar.   *It would have been better to wait.*

B. 1. **¿Pudiera** usted aceptar menos?   *Could you possibly accept less?*
   2. **Quisiera** mandarles un buen regalo.
   3. **Quisiera** que lo probáramos por algunos días.
   4. **Quisiera** verlo a usted.
   5. No **debieras** enojarte.   *You shouldn't lose your temper.*
   6. **Hubiera** sido mejor esperar.   *It might have been better to wait.*

Two degrees of softening

the speaker is ingratiating	the conditional of any verb
the speaker is more ingratiating	the imperfect subjunctive of **deber, haber, poder,** and **querer**

Both the conditional indicative and the imperfect subjunctive are used for toning down a request or a criticism.   The imperfect subjunctive is almost apologetic, and is seldom used in this way except with the four verbs listed.

● TENSE SUBSTITUTION DRILL

INSTRUCTIONS: Repeat the following sentences just as you hear them.   Then repeat them again, replacing the present with the conditional.

A. 1. TEACHER: *¿Puede* prestarme veinte pesos? *Repita.*
      STUDENT: **¿Puede prestarme veinte pesos?**
      TEACHER: *Cambie.*
      STUDENT: **¿Podría prestarme veinte pesos?**
   2. *¿Tiene* usted tiempo para almorzar?
   3. ¿Me *acompaña* a la Comisión de Cambios?
   4. *¿Da* usted algo en beneficio de la capilla?
   5. *¿Dice* usted que es una buena idea?
   6. *¿Viven* ustedes en ese barrio?
   7. ¿Me *explica* usted la situación?
   8. ¿Me *lleva* al centro?

B. 1. Bueno, yo no *digo* esto.
   2. Bueno, yo no *hago* esto.
   3. No, yo no *traigo* al gerente.
   4. No, yo no me *enojo* por esto.
   5. Pues yo no *pago* esa cuenta.
   6. Pues yo no *juego* con ese equipo.
   7. Pues yo no *toco* ese tema.

INSTRUCTIONS: Repeat the following sentences just as you hear them. Then repeat them again, substituting an appropriate imperfect-subjunctive form in place of the present.

C. 1. TEACHER: *¿Puede* usted aceptar menos?
      Repita.
      STUDENT: **¿Puede usted aceptar menos?**
      TEACHER: *Cambie.*
      STUDENT: **¿Pudiera usted aceptar menos?**
   2. *¿Quiere* usted tener un recibo?
   3. *¿Puedes* venir a la reunión?
   4. *¿Pero debemos* esperar tanto tiempo?
   5. *¿Podemos* comer afuera esta noche?
   6. *¿Pueden* entrar pronto?
   7. *¿Quieres* prestarme cuatro fundas y cuatro sábanas?

D. 1. *Quiero* darles un buen regalo.
   2. *Podemos* comprar unos calcetines nuevos.
   3. *Debemos* mandar los calzoncillos a la tintorería.
   4. *Queremos* ver al jefe.
   5. No *debes* enojarte por eso.
   6. *Puedo* por lo menos felicitarla por su buena suerte.
   7. *Quiero* pedirte un favor.

● TRANSLATION DRILL

A. 1. Could you lend me ten pesos?
      ¿Podría prestarme diez pesos?
   2. Could you give me a newspaper?
   3. Could you permit me fifteen minutes?
   4. Would you have time to see me?
   5. Would you have an opportunity to hear it?
   6. Would you be able to do it?

B. 1. Would you lend me fifty pesos?
      ¿Quisiera prestarme cincuenta pesos?
   2. Would you accompany me downtown?
   3. Would you make me a salad?
   4. Should we finish today?
   5. Should we leave before ten?
   6. Could you finish today?

● DISCUSSION

In place of *Can I have a second helping?* one often finds, as a more polite request, *Could I have a second helping?* or, toning it down further, *Might I have a second helping?* There are two devices in Spanish for this kind of toning down: (1) the conditional for partial softening such as one might use in asking something that has a good chance of being fulfilled or in asking or criticizing something that one feels one has a right to ask or criticize; (2) the imperfect subjunctive for softening to the point of diffidence or apology, as in asking something or criticizing something which one does not have (or pretends not to have) the right to ask or criticize.

The conditional may be used as a softener with any verb. The imperfect subjunctive is normally used in this way only with the verbs **deber, haber, poder,** and **querer.** With **haber,** of course, the past perfect subjunctive of any verb becomes possible: **Hubiera perdido menos haciéndolo de otro modo** *You would (might) have lost less doing it another way;* **¿Quién lo hubiera pensado?** *Who would have thought it?,* etc.

A caution is needed about the verb **poder** when the English equivalent is *could.* Note the following parallels:

I said I could = *I said I was able* = **Dije que *podía***
I said I could = *I said I would be able* = **Dije que *podría***
I wish I could = *I wish I might be able* = **Ojalá *pudiera***

The second of these might be expanded *I said I could (would be able) if they gave me the chance.*

● COMBINED PATTERN REPLACEMENT DRILL

A.

1. **Y ahora él no mirará a nadie.**
2. Pero _____
3. _____ al jefe
4. ____ hoy día _____
5. _____ ellos _____
6. _____ directores
7. ____ mañana _____
8. _____ verán _____
9. ____ después _____
10. _____ verían _____
11. _____ gerente
12. _____ ella _____
13. _____ traería _____
14. ____ entonces _____
15. _____ profesora
16. Pues _____
17. _____ llevaría _____
18. _____ criadas
19. _____ llevaba _____
20. _____ ellas _____
21. ____ antes _____
22. _____ secretaria
23. _____ nosotros _____
24. _____ sí _____

B.

1. **Si usted sale premiado, ¿qué hará con la plata?**
2. ____ tú _____
3. _____ salieras _____
4. _____ dinero
5. ____ ustedes _____
6. _____ compraría _____
7. _____ ganando _____
8. ____ nosotros _____
9. _____ haríamos _____
10. _____ regalo
11. _____ termináramos _____
12. _____ antes _____
13. _____ tiempo
14. ____ ella _____
15. _____ auto
16. _____ viniera _____
17. _____ mañana _____
18. _____ sin _____
19. ____ ellas _____
20. _____ niños
21. _____ temprano _____
22. _____ para _____
23. ____ yo _____
24. _____ llegara _____
25. _____ traería _____

● TRANSLATION REVIEW DRILL

Theme vowels in preterit verb forms.

A.
1. He arrived and left.
2. We paid and continued.
3. We entered and returned.
4. They called and left.
5. I entered and ate.
6. I arrived and left.

B.
1. He worked and ate.
2. He waited and lost.
3. He practiced and learned.
4. We talked and drank.
5. They looked and saw.
6. They fumed and insisted.
7. They bought and sold.
8. I spoke and wrote.
9. I studied and learned.

READING

Sinfonía: Conjugación del verbo "amar"

Pedro Antonio de Alarcón[1]

CORO DE ADOLESCENTES. Yo amo, tú amas, aquél[2] ama; nosotros amamos, vosotros amáis,[3] ¡todos aman!

CORO DE NIÑAS (*a media voz*[4]). Yo amaré, tú amarás, aquélla[5] amará; ¡nosotras amaremos!, ¡vosotras amaréis![3] ¡todas amarán!

UNA FEA Y UNA MONJA[6] (*a dúo*). ¡Nosotras hubiéramos, habríamos y hubiésemos[7] amado!

UNA COQUETA. ¡Ama tú! ¡Ame usted! ¡Amen ustedes!

---

[1] Well-known Spanish novelist and playwright of the last century, best known for his delightful tale **El sombrero de tres picos,** *The Three-Cornered Hat.* [2] *he* [3] The **vosotros** verb forms, ending in **-is,** which are still used in Spain, are replaced in Spanish America by the **ustedes** forms. See Unit 2 §1 footnote. [4] *in a whisper* [5] *she* [6] *nun* [7] *Would have and might have:* any distinction in meaning among these three perfect forms is very tenuous and the choice is ordinarily one of style. It may be pointed out, however, that Alarcón uses these forms here in the order of their frequency in written Spanish: i.e., in the main clause of a contrary-to-fact sentence in the past (whether the **si** clause is expressed or not), **hubiéramos** is commoner than **habríamos,** and **hubiésemos** is the rarest of all. This suggests that the author is arranging his terms in anticlimactic order from greater to less certainty. Note that the same order is used in the statement by the dancer.

UN ROMANTICO (*desaliñándose*[8] *el cabello*). ¡Yo amaba!

UN ANCIANO (*indiferentemente*). Yo amé.

UNA BAILARINA (*trenzando*[9] *delante de un banquero*). Yo amara, amaría . . . y amase.[10]

DOS ESPOSOS (*en la menguante*[11] *de la luna de miel*[12]). Nosotros habíamos amado.

UNA MUJER HERMOSISIMA (*al tiempo de morir*). ¿Habré yo amado?

UN POLLO.[13] Es imposible que yo ame, aunque me amen.

EL MISMO POLLO (*de rodillas ante una titiritera*[14]). ¡Mujer amada, sea usted amable, y permítame ser su amante!

UN NECIO. ¡Yo soy amado!

UN RICO. ¡Yo seré amado!

UN POBRE. ¡Yo sería amado!

UN SOLTERON[15] (*al hacer testamento*). ¿Habré yo sido amado?

UNA LECTORA DE NOVELAS. ¡Si yo fuese amada de este modo!

UNA PECADORA[16] (*en el hospital*). ¡Yo hubiera sido amada!

EL AUTOR (*pensativo*). ¡Amar! ¡Ser amado!

---

[8] *disarranging* [9] *prancing* [10] *I would love . . . and might love.* [11] *wearing off* [12] *honeymoon* [13] *clever young man* [14] *female puppeteer* [15] *old bachelor* [16] *magdalene, prostitute*

READING

La rúbrica en la modalidad hispana

En todos los pueblos y en todas las civilizaciones del mundo hay ciertos modales o costumbres comunes que llegan a ser rasgos distintivos de una nación o de la gente que habla una lengua. Así es que entre los hispanos tenemos ciertos gestos y ademanes y posturas del cuerpo que reflejan la disposición de su ánimo como personas que viven en la misma corriente histórica. Un gesto o expresión de la cara y un ademán o movimiento de las manos, de la cabeza, de los hombros, puede ser señal de sentimiento que comprenden todos los que hablan español.

Así como los de habla española suelen poner después de la firma un rasgo distintivo de diversa figura que llega a ser señal de su propia personalidad, usan también gestos y ademanes que vienen siendo[1] rasgos característicos y comunes en gran parte del mundo hispánico. El rasgo que se usa después de la firma se llama "rúbrica", y los movimientos de rostro y de cuerpo que se emplean como señal de cariño, de desprecio, de saludo, de despedida, o de sorpresa son, digamos, las rúbricas del porte y de la conducta, de los sentimientos y de la modalidad, de todos los que hablan español. Para mejor conocimiento de los que tienen la "rúbrica" hispana, vamos a examinar ciertos gestos o ademanes suyos.

El ademán que quiere decir "ven acá" es todo lo contrario del que usan los de habla inglesa. Se hace con el brazo extendido pero con la palma de la mano hacia abajo. Se hace un movimiento hacia el suelo y no hacia el cielo, y como suele ser el caso, la mujer lo hace con mayor delicadeza, con la mano sola y a veces con un dedo. Este movimiento se parece al que emplean los que hablan inglés para decir "adiós".[2]

Ya que hemos examinado la cuestión de "venir acá", vamos a ver cómo se gesticula la idea de "adiós" o "hasta luego". En este caso se levanta la mano al nivel de la cara o hacia un lado, y luego se agitan los dedos.

Para decir que *no*, sin decirlo, se agita el índice de un lado a otro delante de la cara. En la corrida de toros se usa el mismo ademán pero con todo el brazo y el pañuelo en la mano para indicar a las autoridades que deben retirar el toro porque es muy manso. Así es que la gente hace la señal *no* en protesta.

Se manifiesta la actitud interrogativa con un gesto algo complicado. Primero se abren mucho los ojos, se alza la cabeza con un movimiento brusco, y se extienden las manos palma arriba a los lados del cuerpo. Para darle más énfasis a la pregunta entendida se hace otro movimiento brusco con las manos.

---

[1] **vienen siendo** *have become* (lit., *come being*). This is a progressive tense used with **venir** as the auxiliary verb.

[2] **Adiós** is also a greeting, *Hello*, used when two friends pass each other on the street.

Tal vez el gesto más complicado de los hispanos es el que significa "así así", ni muy bien ni muy mal. Se usa la cabeza, los ojos, la boca, los hombros y las manos, además de cierto tono de voz. Primero se inclina la cabeza a un lado, se hace con la boca un gesto de tristeza, se levantan las cejas pero se dejan caer los párpados. Entonces se encoge uno de hombros[3] y con la mano se imita al pez cuando nada por el agua, enseñando ya la palma de la mano, ya los nudillos; todo va dirigido a inspirar piedad. Semejante gesto es el que acompaña a "¿Quién sabe?", sólo que las manos se levantan a la altura del pecho, palmas hacia arriba y los dedos un poco encogidos. Para representar la avaricia, se dobla el brazo, mano arriba, y con la otra mano o con el puño o la palma, se dan golpecitos en el codo.

El acto de pagar o de liquidar cuentas se representa colocando el pulgar, uña arriba, sobre el lado del índice doblado, haciendo un movimiento para abajo con la mano.

Ganas de comer o el mismo acto de comer puede representarse juntando los dedos y haciendo movimiento hacia la boca. Y el beber, especialmente bebidas alcohólicas, se indica extendiéndose el pulgar hacia la cara, doblando los demás dedos, salvo el meñique.

Puede llamarse ademán ponderativo el que en algunos países parece se refiere a situación exagerada o a caso "estupendo y formidable". Se hace extendiendo la mano cerca del cuerpo y con los dedos sueltos, y luego se sacude la mano como para quitarse agua. En México este ademán puede acompañar la risa, especialmente cuando uno se burla de otro.[4]

Hay un ademán muy expresivo para dar la idea de "lejos" en el tiempo o en el espacio. Se hace levantando la mano hasta la altura de la oreja, y luego se abre la mano hacia arriba, casi como para espantar un mosquito.

Lo justo, lo delicado y lo fino se representan formando un círculo horizontal del pulgar y el índice y luego moviendo este círculo de arriba para abajo y de abajo para arriba delante del pecho.

Así es que el gesto y el ademán personalizan el carácter y el genio del hispanoparlante (como del hablante de cualquier otro idioma) así como la rúbrica puede indicar la individualidad consciente.

La interjección es una palabra interesante. Con ella, se expresan emociones o afectos súbitos. También se usa para animar o para dar avisos.

Algunas interjecciones comunes son:

¡Ah! ¡Qué bueno!—*Oh, fine!*

¡Bah! Poco importa.—*Bah! That doesn't matter.*

¡Cáspita! Se me pasó la hora.—*Gosh! The time is up.*

¡Ea! Vamos, ya es tarde.—*Come on, it's late.*

¡Eh! ¿Cómo?—*Huh? What?*

¡Guay! ¡Qué pena!—*Oh-h-h! What a pity!*

¡Hola! ¿Tú por aquí?—*Hello there! You here?*

¡Oh! ¿Qué es esto?—*Oh, what's this?*

¡Huy! ¡Qué dolor!—*Ouch! It hurts!*

¡Ojalá! ¡Oh, si pudiera!—*Oh, I wish I could!*

¡Puf! No me gusta.—*Pooh, I don't like it.*

¡Quia! o ¡Ca!—*Oh, no!*

¡Sus! ¡Anímate!—*Hey, get going!*

¡Tate! No me digas.—*Well! You're telling me!*

¡Pobre de él!—*Poor boy!*

¡Uf! ¡Qué cansado estoy!—*Oh, I'm so tired!*

¡Dios mío!—*Good Lord!*

¡Oh, cielos!—*Oh, heavens!*

¡Caramba!—*Gosh!*

¡Arre, burro!—*Get up, donkey!*

¡Bravo!—*Bravo!*

¡Calle! o ¡Cállate!—*Be still!*

¡Cómo!—*What?*

¡Cuidado!—*Be careful!*

¡Chito! Silencio.—*Sssh! Be quiet!*

¡Diablo!—*The deuce!*

¡Oiga!—*Hey!*

¡Pues!—*Well!*

¡Toma!—*Here!*

¡Vaya!—*Go on!*

¡Ya!—*Ready!*

¡Ea, ea! ¡Ven acá!—*Hey, you! Come here!*

¡Tate, tate! ¡Déjalo!—*Look out! Leave it alone!*

¡Ay de mí, qué triste estoy!—*Oh, I'm so unhappy!*

---

[3] **se encoge uno de hombros** *one shrugs one's shoulders*
[4] **uno se burla de otro** *one person laughs at another*

1. ¿Cuáles son algunos de los rasgos distintivos comunes a los hispanos?
2. ¿En qué consiste la "rúbrica"?
3. ¿Qué indica generalmente la rúbrica?
4. Haga el gesto o ademán hispano que quiere decir "ven acá".
5. ¿A qué gesto de los que hablan inglés se parece este ademán?
6. ¿Qué indica el agitar el índice de un lado a otro delante de la cara?
7. ¿Por qué es complicado el gesto que se usa para una actitud interrogativa?
8. ¿Cuáles son algunas de las partes del cuerpo que toman parte en el gesto que significa "así así"?
9. ¿Cómo representan la avaricia los hispanos?
10. Haga los ademanes que representan el acto de comer y beber.
11. ¿Qué es un ademán ponderativo? Mencione algunos.
12. ¿De qué manera se representan lo justo, lo delicado, lo fino en Hispanoamérica?
13. Mencione algunas interjecciones españolas que expresan emociones o afectos súbitos.
14. ¿Qué indican las siguientes interjecciones?
¡Bah! Poco importa.
¡Sus! Anímate.
¡Cuidado!
¡Chito! Silencio.
¡Bravo!

21

Mourning

R. *Ramírez*   F. *Alberto Fernández*   M. *Doña María*   C. *Doña Carmen*   E. *Mrs. Esparza*

R. What do you think [imagine]! Roberto Esparza just died!

F. What? I knew he was sick, but I didn't think he was that sick.

R. He had heart trouble; you know how treacherous those things [illnesses] are.

F. Just think: only last Sunday I saw him strolling on the beach! Why did the doctor let him go if he was ill?

R. He told him to go because it was good for him to be at sea level.

F. Poor Don Roberto! He had such zest for living!

De duelo

R. *Ramírez*   F. *Alberto Fernández*   M. *Doña María*   C. *Doña Carmen*   E. *Señora Esparza*

R. ¡Figúrese que se acaba de morir Roberto Esparza!

F. ¿Cómo? Yo sabía que estaba enfermo pero no creí que estuviera grave.

R. Estaba enfermo del corazón; ya sabe usted qué traicioneras son esas enfermedades.

F. ¡Imagínese que apenas el domingo lo vi paseando en la playa! ¿Cómo lo dejó ir el doctor estando enfermo?

R. Le indicó que fuera porque le convenía estar al nivel del mar.

F. ¡Pobre don Roberto! ¡Le tenía tanto apego a la vida!

R. And especially poor Marta; so young and already a widow, and with four children . . . Well . . . the time comes for every man . . .

F. When will the funeral be?

R. Tomorrow afternoon at four. That reminds me, I've got to order a wreath.

F. Then the wake is tonight. I'll give her my condolences there.

* * *

F. How is Marta?

M. Very sad. I saw her crying her eyes out [bitterly].

C. I heard her crying too, and it really broke my heart.

M. She looks so pale dressed in black!

C. And she'll have to wear mourning two years. Poor girl. Here she comes.

F. Madam, my deepest sympathy.

E. Many thanks, Alberto. Please excuse the disorderly appearance of the house.

F. Don't even think of it!

* * *

F. Pardon me for leaving, but it's very late.

E. Thanks, many thanks, Alberto . . .

C. Go ahead, Señor Fernández. Doña María and I will stay up all night.

F. You know you have my deepest sympathy, Doña Marta.

R. Sobre todo pobre Marta; tan joven y ya viuda y con cuatro hijos . . . En fin . . . a cada uno le llega el día.

F. ¿Cuándo va a ser el entierro?

R. Mañana (1) a las cuatro de la tarde. Eso me recuerda que tengo que encargar una corona (2).

F. Entonces esta noche es el velorio. Ahí le doy el pésame.

* * *

F. ¿Cómo está Marta?

M. Muy triste. La vi llorar amargamente.

C. Yo también la oí llorando y me partió el alma.

M. ¡Se ve tan pálida vestida de negro!

C. Y tendrá que estar de luto dos años. ¡Pobre señora! Ahí viene.

F. Señora, mi más sentido pésame.

E. Muchas gracias, Alberto. Le ruego que me perdone por el desorden de la casa.

F. ¡No faltaba más, señora!

* * *

F. Perdóneme que la deje, pero ya es muy tarde.

E. Gracias, muchas gracias, Alberto. . . .

C. Vaya no más, señor Fernández. Doña María y yo vamos a velar toda la noche.

F. Ya sabe que la acompaño en su pena, doña Marta.

Cultural Notes (1) Burial normally takes place the day after death.

(2) This is one of several formalized funeral procedures, which include the ordering of a wreath (**corona**), close relatives dressing in black, the widow in mourning for two years, standard expressions of sympathy (**dar el pésame; mi más sentido pésame**). The **velorio** is an all-night wake or vigil over the deceased before burial. During the **velorio,** the family usually pray and receive visitors, who offer condolences. Funeral parlors are generally not found in the Hispanic world.

117 Indicative or subjunctive in exclamations

EXAMPLES

1. Qué bueno que **llamaste** (**hayas llamado**). *(How good that you called.)*
2. ¡Qué suerte que yo no **fui** (**haya ido**)!
3. Lástima que yo no **hablo** (**hable**) inglés.
4. Gracias a Dios que nada te **ha** (**haya**) **pasado.** *Thank goodness nothing's happened to you.*

| ¡———! | indicative or subjunctive |

A noun clause after an exclamation may have its verb in the indicative or in the subjunctive.

● CONSTRUCTION SUBSTITUTION DRILL

INSTRUCTIONS: Repeat the following sentences just as you hear them. Then repeat them again, substituting present perfect subjunctive for preterit.

A. 1. TEACHER: ¡Qué bueno que llamaste! *Repita.*
STUDENT: **¡Qué bueno que llamaste!**
TEACHER: *Cambie.*
STUDENT: **¡Qué bueno que hayas llamado!**

2. ¡Qué malo que perdiste!
3. ¡Qué lástima que faltaste!
4. ¡Qué suerte que terminaste!
5. ¡Qué horror que renunciaste!
6. ¡Qué barbaridad que pagaste!
7. ¡Qué triste que peleaste!
8. ¡Qué ridículo que contestaste!
9. ¡Qué fantástico que concediste!
10. ¡Qué molestia que esperaste!
11. ¡Qué tontería que lloraste!
12. ¡Gracias a Dios que no te enojaste!

B. 1. ¡Qué suerte que no fui!
2. ¡Qué lástima que no estuve!
3. ¡Qué tontería que no terminé!
4. ¡Qué horror que no paré!
5. ¡Qué barbaridad que no gané!
6. ¡Qué molestia que no lo compré!
7. ¡Qué tontería que no lo traje!
8. ¡Qué triste que no lo envié!
9. ¡Qué ridículo que no lo envolví!
10. ¡Qué malo que no lo acepté!
11. ¡Qué bueno que no lo perdí!

C. 1. ¡Qué horror que mataron a los estudiantes!
2. ¡Qué suerte que tuvieron un día feriado!
3. ¡Qué ridículo que llevaron a los niños!
4. ¡Qué malo que rompieron el acuerdo!
5. ¡Qué lástima que murió el presidente!
6. ¡Qué triste que vino la revolución!
7. ¡Qué molestia que llegaron tantos parientes!
8. ¡Qué horror que fallaron los frenos!
9. ¡Qué barbaridad que se escapó el tirano!
10. ¡Qué bueno que se destacaron los técnicos!
11. ¡Qué tontería que se preocupó el pueblo!

● TENSE SUBSTITUTION DRILL

INSTRUCTIONS: Repeat the following sentences just as you hear them. Then repeat them again substituting present subjunctive for present indicative.

A. 1. TEACHER: ¡Qué lástima que no hablo inglés! *Repita.*
STUDENT: **¡Qué lástima que no hablo inglés!**
TEACHER: *Cambie.*
STUDENT: **¡Qué lástima que no hable inglés!**

2. ¡Qué triste que no escribo bien!
3. ¡Qué molestia que no aprendo más rápido!
4. ¡Qué horror que no recuerdo la dirección!
5. ¡Qué suerte que vamos los dos!
6. ¡Qué bueno que tenemos razón!
7. ¡Qué tontería que no comemos temprano!

B. 1. ¡Qué bueno que está aquí Guillermo!
2. ¡Qué malo que se va Alicia!
3. ¡Qué horror que vienen todos!
4. ¡Qué molestia que el tocadiscos está descompuesto!
5. ¡Gracias a Dios que terminan mañana!
6. ¡Qué bueno que tiene ojos verdes!
7. ¡Qué suerte que llega el señor Delgado mañana!
8. ¡Qué lástima que a los profesores no les pagan este mes!

● DISCUSSION

After exclamations containing expressions of the "welcoming-spurning" group (see Unit 17 §97), the indicative as well as the subjunctive may be used. Thus it is permissible to say either **Lástima que yo no *hablo* inglés** or **Lástima que yo no *hable* inglés.** The reason for this is probably that exclamations are blurted out unthinkingly, and do not form quite so integral a part of the sentence:

Lástima que yo no hablo inglés is closer to *Unfortunately, I don't speak English* or *I don't speak English, unfortunately* than to *It's too bad that I don't speak English.*

See Unit 19 §106 for the correspondence of the preterit, e.g., **llamaste,** with the present perfect subjunctive, e.g., **hayas llamado.**

118 Infinitive and subjunctive with verbs of suasion

EXAMPLES

A. 1. Los hice esperar. *I made them wait.*
    2. ¿Cómo lo dejó ir el doctor?
    3. Los dejé ir solos.
    4. Déjeme ver esas cuentas.

B. 1. Le aconsejo ir a verla. *I advise you to go see her.*
    2. Les supliqué venir. *I begged them to come.*
    3. Le exigieron pagar la multa. *They required him to pay the fine.*
    4. A los otros les mandó seguir. *The others he ordered to follow.*
    5. Les rogó no discutir. *She begged them not to argue.*

C. 1. Le aconsejo que vaya a verla. *I advise you to go see her.*
    2. Le ruego que me perdone.
    3. Le exigieron que pagara la multa. *They required him to pay the fine.*
    4. A los otros les mandó que siguieran. *The others he ordered to follow.*
    5. Les ruego que no discutan.

D. 1. Me dijo usted que consultara con los empleados.
    2. Le indicó que fuera.
    3. Te escribí que volvieras. *I wrote you to come back.*

VERB OF SUASION	INFINITIVE	CLAUSE WITH SUBJUNCTIVE	PERSONAL OBJECT DIRECT	INDIRECT
hacer **dejar**	√		√	
other verbs of suasion	√	√		√
verbs of communication used for suasion (*tell, write, phone,* etc.)		√		√

Hacer and **dejar** more usually take an infinitive than a clause with subjunctive, but other verbs whose literal meaning is *suasion* (bringing an influence to bear; see Unit 17 §97) take either infinitive or clause. Verbs of communication, such as *tell, telegraph, indicate,* take only the clause. With **hacer** and **dejar,** personal objects are direct; with the other verbs, indirect.

● CONSTRUCTION SUBSTITUTION DRILL

INSTRUCTIONS: Repeat the following sentences just as you hear them. Then repeat them again, changing the infinitive to an appropriate subjunctive construction.

A. 1. TEACHER: Le aconsejo ir a verla. *Repita.*
    STUDENT: **Le aconsejo ir a verla.**
    TEACHER: *Cambie.*
    STUDENT: **Le aconsejo que vaya a verla.**
    2. Les suplico venir temprano.

    3. Les exijo pagar la cuenta ahora.
    4. Les mando volar a México.
    5. Le ruego no discutir tanto.
    6. Les pido hacerlo mañana.
    7. Le sugiero terminarlo pronto.

B. 1. Me aconseja no mencionar esa enfermedad.
2. Nos suplica no hacer un escándalo.
3. Me exige terminar el examen.
4. Nos manda encargar una corona.
5. Me ruega traer dos kilos de cada una.
6. Nos pide comprar una docena.
7. Me sugiere ir al entierro.

C. 1. Le aconsejé dar el más sentido pésame.
2. Les supliqué acompañar a la pobre
viuda.
3. Le exigí ir al velorio.
4. Les mandé no exagerar tanto.
5. Le rogué esperar hasta después de la
cuaresma.

6. Les pedí no ir, sobretodo el domingo.
7. Le convencí no ser tan idealista.

D. 1. Me aconsejó no tener tanto apego a la
vida.
2. Nos suplicó rezar por su alma.
3. Me exigió velar toda la noche.
4. Nos mandó ir a pasear al nivel del mar.
5. Me pidió perdonarla por el desorden de
la casa.
6. Nos pidió no dejar nuestra patria en la
ruina.
7. Me convenció no hacer un cambio radical.

● PATTERNED RESPONSE DRILL

A. 1. TEACHER: ¿Ellos esperaron?
STUDENT: **Sí, los hice esperar.**
2. ¿El estudió?
3. ¿Ellas terminaron?
4. ¿Ella decidió?
5. ¿Ellos regresaron?
6. ¿El escogió?
7. ¿Ellas pagaron?
8. ¿Ella llamó?
9. ¿Ellos pararon?
10. ¿El practicó?

11. ¿Ellas durmieron?
12. ¿Ella lavó?

B. 1. ¿Fueron ellas?
No, no las dejé ir.
2. ¿Siguió ella?
3. ¿Volvieron ellos?
4. ¿Habló él?
5. ¿Entraron ellas?
6. ¿Contestó ella?
7. ¿Atacaron ellos?
8. ¿Ganó él?

● TRANSLATION DRILL

1. He told me to come.
He wrote me to come.
He indicated (to me) I should come.
2. I told them to take the exam.
I wrote them to sell the car.
I indicated they should reduce the rent.
3. They told us not to break anything.
They wrote us not to bring anything.
They indicated we should not touch any-
thing.

4. We told her to accept the schedule.
We wrote her to make the decision.
We indicated she should write the letter.
5. She told us to pay the fine.
She wrote us to buy the painting.
She indicated we should get the film.

● DISCUSSION

Nearly all verbs whose literal meaning is suasion—persuading, dissuading, helping, hindering,
urging, advising, permitting, asking, requiring, and any other that brings an influence to bear—
may take either an infinitive or a clause with subjunctive. The verbs **hacer** and **dejar** are exceptions in that while it is possible for them to take a clause (**Lo hice que viniera** *I made him come*),
normally they take infinitive. The clause makes the influence a little stronger as a rule.

Verbs of communication, while they do not literally mean suasion (*He told me that it was raining*
simply reports something), are often used for suasion (*He told me to come*). These verbs always take
clauses, in their reporting use as well as in their suasive use.

It is not always necessary to have a personal pronoun object. Thus *I advise that they go*
is **Aconsejo que vayan,** with the advice expressed to a third party. But if the advice is addressed to
the person who is supposed to take it, then the pronoun is used: **Les aconsejo que vayan** or **Les**

aconsejo ir. (Example with a noun object: **Le aconsejé a Fernández que fuera al velorio** *I advised Fernández to go to the wake.*) With **dejar** and **hacer,** the object is direct; with the other verbs, indirect.

119 Perceived actions

EXAMPLES

A. 1. La vi llorar amargamente.
   2. Vi a Marta llorar amargamente. *I saw Marta weep bitterly.*
   3. ¿Me vio cambiarlos? *Did you see me change them?*
   4. Vimos a Juan salir. *We saw John* **leave.**
   5. Vimos salir a Juan. *We saw* **John** *leave.*
   6. Mírelo andar con las manos. *Look at him walk on his hands.*
   7. Oyeron a Marta llamar a Luis. *They heard Marta call Luis.*
   8. La oyeron llamarlo. *They heard her call him.*

B. 1. Lo vi paseando en la playa.
   2. Vi a Roberto paseando en la playa. *I saw Roberto strolling along the beach.*
   3. La oí llorando.
   4. Oímos a la pobre pidiendo perdón. *We heard the poor woman begging forgiveness.*

C. 1. —¿Qué hacían? *What were they doing?*
      —Yo vi que corrían. *I saw them running.*
   2. —¿Por qué lo defiende? *Why do you defend him?*
      —Porque veo que lo atacan. *Because I see them attacking him (that they are attacking him).*
   3. Viendo que peleaban con la policía, yo me fui de allí. *Seeing them fighting with the police (that they were fighting with the police), I got out of there.*

VERB OF PERCEP-TION WITH ITS OBJECTS	INFINITIVE WITH ITS OBJECTS IF ANY	VERB OF PERCEP-TION WITH ITS OBJECTS	INFINITIVE WITH ITS OBJECTS IF ANY
I saw him I saw John Seeing him Seeing John etc.	eat eat the meat eat it *-ing* FORM WITH ITS OBJECTS IF ANY eating eating the meat eating it	**Lo vi** **Vi a Juan** **Viéndolo** **Viendo a Juan** etc.	**comer** **comer la carne** **comerla** *–ndo* FORM WITH ITS OBJECTS IF ANY **comiendo** **comiendo la carne** **comiéndola**

The common verbs of perception take infinitive and **–ndo** in Spanish corresponding respectively to infinitive and *–ing* in English.

VERB OF PERCEP-TION WITH ITS OBJECT	*–ing* FORM	VERB OF PERCEPTION	CLAUSE WITH ITS SUBJECT
I saw them	running	**Vi**	**que (ellos) corrían**

When the perceived action is central rather than incidental in importance, Spanish uses a clause rather than an **–ndo** form. The subject of the clause corresponds to the object of the verb of perception in English.

• TRANSLATION DRILL

1. TEACHER: I saw her cry.
   STUDENT: **La vi llorar.**
   TEACHER: I saw her crying.
   STUDENT: **La vi llorando.**
2. I heard him speak.
   I heard him speaking.
3. Look at him play.
   Look at him playing.
4. I saw Roberto stroll on the beach.
   I saw Roberto strolling on the beach.
5. I heard the boys run down (along) the street.
   I heard the boys running down the street.
6. Look at him walk on his hands.
   Look at him walking on his hands.
7. I heard the girls get up.
   I heard the girls getting up.

8. I saw them running.
   Yo vi que corrían.
   I saw them fighting.
   I saw them arguing.
   I saw them haggling.
   I saw them waiting.
9. We heard her coming in.
   We heard her leaving.
   We heard her arguing.
   We heard her returning.
   We heard her calling.
10. We saw him washing the car.
    We saw him talking with the policeman.
    We saw him fighting with the students.
    We saw him leaving the jail.
    We saw him returning home.

• DISCUSSION

The verbs of perception which may be followed by the infinitive or –**ndo** form in Spanish correspond closely to those that may be followed by the infinitive or –*ing* in English; they are the common ones like **ver** *see,* **oir** *hear,* and **mirar** *look at,* not the less common ones like **notar** *notice,* **contemplar** *contemplate,* etc. (we can say *I saw him come* but not *I contemplated him come*).

The infinitive constructions are practically identical in the two languages, and are used in identical circumstances. The –**ndo** form, however, is used much less than the –*ing* in English. This is because the –**ndo** form, as we saw in Unit 8 §40, is a kind of adverbial modifier, referring to an accompanying action. When we say *See them fighting with the police* we mentally classify both *them* and *fighting* as objects of *seeing:* we see *them* and we see their *fighting.* When we say **Viéndolos peleando con la policía,** however, we see them *as* they are fighting with the police. On this account, if it is important to indicate the action as properly the thing seen ("I got out of there because of their fighting with the police"), Spanish is more likely to use a clause: **Viendo que peleaban con la policía.** When Fernández says **Lo vi paseando en la playa** he refers to seeing *him,* Roberto, there alive—what he was doing was incidental. Had the remark been in answer to the question *How was he getting his exercise?* however, it would more likely have taken the form **Vi que paseaba en la playa.** (Similarly *Look at them running!* refers to looking at *their running,* and Spanish then uses the equivalent of *Look at how they run!* **¡Mire cómo corren!**)

120 *El* and *un* with feminine nouns

EXAMPLES

A. 1. Me partió **el alma.**
   2. **El álgebra** del sistema es difícil. *The algebra of the system is hard.*
   3. ¿Y si cae **al agua?** *And if it falls in the water?*
   4. En estos días hay **un hambre** de paz. *In these days there is a hunger for peace.*

B. 1. **Las almas** de los muertos. *The souls of the dead.*
   2. Es **la complicada álgebra** de estos problemas de física. *It's the complicated algebra of these physics problems.*
   3. Si es extranjero, no puede trabajar en **las aguas** nacionales de los Estados Unidos. *If he's a foreigner he can't work in the national waters of the United States.*
   4. Es **una verdadera hambre** de paz. *It's a real hunger for peace.*

	DIRECTLY BEFORE A FEMININE SINGULAR NOUN BEGINNING WITH STRONG-STRESSED [a]	BEFORE A FEMININE SINGULAR NOUN UNDER ANY OTHER CIRCUMSTANCES
the	**el**	**la**
a, an	**un**	**una**

● TRANSLATION DRILL

1. He has a hunger for peace.
   He has a true hunger for peace.
2. He has a soul.
   He has a true soul.
3. This is the water to (**para**) drink.
   This is the best water to drink.
4. I don't like algebra.
   I don't like Einstein's complicated algebra.

5. Where is the soul?
   Where is the true soul?
6. Hunger is treacherous.
   True hunger is treacherous.
7. Where is the soul of the dead [man]?
   Where are the souls of the dead?
8. We are in the water.
   We are in the national waters.

● DISCUSSION

The **el** that appears in **el alma, el hambre,** and with other feminine nouns is not, historically speaking, the "masculine" article that appears in **el hombre, el lugar,** etc., though identical with it in form. Instead, it is a separate development of the Latin demonstrative *ĭlla,* which, when it came before strong-stressed [a], preserved its first syllable rather than its second: the *–a* was, so to speak, swallowed up in what followed, leaving only *el.* A descendant of the full form of *ĭlla* is the pronoun **ella.**

121 *De* and *por* for *by,* after a *–do* form

EXAMPLES

A. 1. Llegué **acompañada de** varias amigas. *I arrived accompanied by (in the company of) several friends.*
   2. Resfriado, **seguido de** gripe—lo he tenido todo. *Cold, followed by flu—I've had everything.*
   3. La ciudad está **rodeada de** barrios pobres. *The city is surrounded by run-down suburbs.*

B. 1. Entró el cónsul **acompañado por** otros bolivianos. *The consul came in accompanied (escorted) by other Bolivians.*
   2. El asesino fue **seguido por** la policía. *The murderer was followed (chased) by the police.*
   3. El tirano fue **rodeado por** los estudiantes. *The tyrant was surrounded (hemmed in) by the students.*
   4. La refinería será **dedicada por** el presidente. *The refinery will be dedicated by the president.*

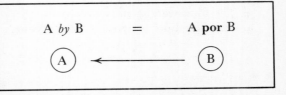

To imply that *B* is in a positional relationship to *A* but not operating on *A* (i.e., not doing anything to *A*), the equivalent of *by* is **de.**

Where *B* operates or attempts to operate on *A,* the equivalent of *by* is **por.**

A. 1. TEACHER: My niece arrived accompanied by (i.e., in the company of) her friends.
   STUDENT: **Llegó mi sobrina, acompañada de sus amigos.**

   2. My nephew arrived accompanied by his friends.
   3. My nieces arrived accompanied by their friends.
   4. My nephews arrived accompanied by their friends.

B. 1. The president arrived, followed by several high government officials.
   2. The lawyer arrived, followed by several businessmen.
   3. The traffic chief arrived, followed by several policemen.
   4. The professor arrived, followed by several students.

C. 1. He's surrounded by many friends.
   2. She's surrounded by many schoolmates.
   3. They're (*m*) surrounded by many technicians.
   4. They're (*f*) surrounded by many young men.

D. 1. The new plant will be dedicated by the president.
   La nueva planta será dedicada por el presidente.
   2. The new cemetery will be dedicated by the president.
   3. The new refineries will be dedicated by the president.
   4. The new ministries will be dedicated by the president.

E. 1. This thermometer was bought by Doña Carmen.
   2. This prescription was bought by Doña Carmen.
   3. These newspapers were bought by Doña Carmen.
   4. These pills were bought by Doña Carmen.

F. 1. The demonstration was seen by everyone.
   2. The leader was seen by everyone.
   3. The films were seen by everyone.
   4. The headlines were seen by everyone.

G. 1. The dress was made by Esperanza.
   2. The shirt was made by Rosa.
   3. The furniture was made by Carlos.
   4. The beds were made by Patricio.

H. 1. The bill was paid by Rosario.
   2. The document was bought by Alberto.
   3. The firm was sold by Domingo.
   4. The spare parts were left by Francisco.

I. 1. That man is respected by everyone.
   2. That woman is respected by everyone.
   3. Those men are respected by everyone.
   4. Those women are respected by everyone.

J. 1. That man is well known by the police.
   2. That woman is well known by the police.
   3. Those men are well known by the police.
   4. Those women are well known by the police.

K. 1. That tyrant is hated by all.
   2. That old [woman] is hated by all.
   3. Those tyrants are hated by all.
   4. Those old [women] are hated by all.

L. 1. The president arrived, escorted by the police.
   2. The consul arrived, escorted by the functionaries.
   3. The leader arrived, escorted by his companions.
   4. The widow arrived, escorted by her relatives.

M. 1. The leaders were attacked by the police.
   2. The foreigners were attacked by the people.
   3. The tyrant was attacked by the students.
   4. The president was attacked by the newspapers.

N. 1. The student was wounded by the policeman.
   2. The athlete was wounded by the arrow.
   3. The engineer was injured (wounded) by the car.
   4. The doctor was injured by the bus.

● DISCUSSION

Both **de** and **por** are equivalents of English *by*. The difference between them is that **de** is *relational* while **por** is *operational*. **De** shows position; **por** shows exertion by an active agent. To say, for example, that *A* is surrounded by *B*, **de** would be used if we merely pictured *A* with *B* around it *(Kansas is surrounded by Oklahoma, Missouri, Nebraska, and Colorado* **Kansas está rodeado de Oklahoma, Misuri,**

Nebraska y Colorado), but **por** would be used if the meaning is *hemmed in* (*The murderer was surrounded by the police* **El asesino fue rodeado por la policía**).

122   *De* as equivalent of *with* and *in*

EXAMPLES

A. 1. Llegó todo cubierto **de** barro y polvo.   *He arrived all covered with mud and dust.*
   2. Lo llenaron **de** regalos.   *They filled it with gifts.*

B. 1. ¡Se ve tan pálida vestida **de** negro!
   2. Me gusta vestirme **de** lana.   *I like to wear (dress myself in) wool.*
   3. ¿Vas a vestirte **de** otro color?   *Are you going to wear another color?*
   4. Mire las montañas envueltas **de** nubes.   *Look at the mountains wrapped in clouds.*
   5. Tendrá que estar **de** luto dos años.   *(She'll have to be in mourning two years.)*

C. 1. No quiero ensuciarlo **con** este polvo.   *I don't want to dirty it with this dust.*
   2. Algunos de los pobres tuvieron que vestirse **con** periódicos.   *Some of the poor people had to dress themselves in newspapers.*
   3. Volvió a casa envuelto **en** una sábana.   *He came back home wrapped in a sheet.*

		ENGLISH	SPANISH
The object of the preposition	a. combines with the thing	with } in }	**de**
	b. makes possible the action	with in	**con** **en, con**

To show that one thing enters into a positional relationship with another (woman has black dress *on,* box has presents *in it,* etc.), **de** is used. To show that a thing serves as the means to an action (something dirtied as a result of dust, a man clad in an emergency with whatever comes to hand), **con** or **en** is used, depending on the sense.

● TRANSLATION DRILL

1. He arrived covered with dust.
   She arrived covered with dust.
2. They filled the cup with water.
   They filled the cup with milk.
3. Let's see.   She's the lady with the red dress.
   Let's see.   He's the gentleman with the gray suit.
4. Olga is the girl with long hair.
   Pepe is the boy with short hair.
5. She filled the post card with examples.
   She filled the living room with flowers.
6. She seems so pale dressed in black.
   He seems so sad dressed in black.
7. She'll have to be in mourning two years.
   He'll have to be in mourning one year.
8. The mountain is wrapped in clouds.
   The town is wrapped in clouds.
9. Don't dirty it with that dust.
   Don't dirty it with that mud.
10. He did it with his elbow.
    He did it with his foot.
11. He stuffed (filled) his pockets with old papers.
    He stuffed (filled) his pockets with old post cards.
12. He was wrapped in a sheet.
    She was wrapped in a sheet.
13. I brought the records wrapped in paper.
    I brought the ties wrapped in paper.
14. He sent the documents written in English.
    He sent the letters written in English.

● DISCUSSION

The function of **de** in its contrast with **con** is essentially the same as in its contrast with **por,** discussed in the preceding section: **de** has to do with *positional* relationships. When we say **Llegó cubierto de barro** *He arrived covered with mud,* we mean that he had mud *on* him—the mud is in a positional relationship to the person and shares the stage with the person. When we say **Llegó cubierto con una toalla** *He arrived covered with a towel* we are not primarily referring to the fact that he had on a towel, but that he was *covered*—a sheet or anything else he might have grabbed when the telephone summoned him from his shower would have done just as well; the towel does not share the stage with him but is only a means to an end.

In the same way, **vestida de negro** means that she had a black dress *on*—the dress shares the stage in its positional relationship to the wearer. Likewise **Lo llenaron de papel** *They filled it with paper* means that when they were through, it was full *of* paper—the paper is in a positional relationship, that of contents, with the container. But **Lo llenaron con papel** would mean that paper was put in just to have the container filled with something—for example, in shipping glassware the pieces might be stuffed with paper to protect them.

De therefore relates what follows it to the thing or person, while **con** relates what follows it to the action.

123 *En* and *a* for *at*

EXAMPLES

A. 1. Los cerdos dejan bastante ganancia **en** la feria.
   2. Con los acontecimientos de esta mañana **en** el cementerio.
   3. ¿Qué hacen **en** casa? *What do they do at home?*

B. 1. Mañana **a** las cuatro puede pasar por sus papeles.
   2. Al principio la llamé cada dos o tres días.
   3. —¿**A** cómo estaba el cambio? *(At how much [what rate] was the exchange?)*
      —**A** treinta por uno.
   4. Después me mostraron una como **a** cinco metros en una pared. *(At five meters' distance.)*
   5. Le convenía estar **al** nivel del mar.

C. 1. Los alumnos llegan **a** la puerta.
   2. Llamaron **a** la puerta. *They knocked at the door.*
   3. Se sentó **al** teléfono. *He sat down at the telephone.*
   4. Está ahí, **a** la entrada del comedor. *(At the entrance of the dining room.)*
   5. ¿Lo quiere corto atrás y **a** los lados? *(At the sides.)*
   6. **A** la izquierda está el Café Brasil. *At (on, to) the left is the Brazil Café.*

	place in which (no motion toward)	**en**
at	point in space, time, or on a scale place to or toward which	**a**

En is the equivalent of *at* when the place is thought of as having dimensions within which something is located. In most other instances the equivalent of *at* is **a**.

A. 1. TEACHER: The girls are in the living room.
STUDENT: **Las chicas están en la sala.**
   2. The boys are in the patio.
   3. The children are in the garden.
   4. The teacher is in the school.
   5. The consul is in the Ministry.
   6. The widow is in the house.
   7. My aunt is in the chapel.
   8. My uncle is in the government.

B. 1. What happened at the cemetery?
¿Qué pasó en el cementerio?
   2. What happened at the theater?
   3. What happened at the meeting?
   4. What happened at the office?
   5. What happened at the church?
   6. What happened at the beach?
   7. What happened at the wake?

C. 1. Anything new at the office?
¿Alguna novedad en la oficina?
   2. Anything new at the ministry?
   3. Anything new at the plant?
   4. Anything new at the refinery?
   5. Anything new at the club?
   6. Anything new at the market?
   7. Anything new at the house?

D. 1. It was advisable for him to be at sea level.
Le convenía estar al nivel del mar.
   2. It was advisable for him to be at 200 meters.
   3. It was advisable for him to be here at one.

4. It was advisable for him to come by at four.
5. It was advisable for him to eat at six.
6. It was advisable for him to come at the beginning.
7. It was advisable for him to leave at the end (**al final**).

E. 1. He arrived at the door.
Llegó a la puerta.
   2. He called at the door.
   3. He arrived at the office.
   4. He paid at the entrance.
   5. He left it at the entrance.
   6. He waited for it at the entrance.
   7. He sat down at the table (**mesa**).

F. 1. He was in the doorway.
Estaba en la puerta.
   2. He used to sit in the doorway.
   3. He used to play in the doorway.
   4. He used to work in the doorway.
   5. He used to study in the doorway.
   6. He used to wait in the doorway.
   7. He used to sleep in the doorway.

● DISCUSSION

English and Spanish divide the *in-at* semantic range in similar ways but different proportions. Essentially, *in* and **en** refer to something having dimensions, that can be thought of as encompassing the object placed in reference to it. *At* and **a** conceptually shrink the locus to a point. Where the two languages differ is in how far they are willing to go in this mental shrinkage. We would not say *He is at England now,* for we cannot cut a whole country down, but we readily say *He is at Chicago this week end,* as if Chicago were a point on a map. Spanish cannot go this far. Where motion is involved, the place where motion stops can be thought of as a terminal point, and size does not matter: **Llegaron a Lima** *They arrived at Lima.* When something is really a point or an edge, such as a point of time or space (**a las seis** *at six,* **al principio** *at the beginning*) or a point or line on a scale (**al nivel del mar** *at sea level*), there is no problem. In between is an area where **a** may be used if one thinks of moving (oneself or just one's eyes or attention) in the given direction, or **en** if one thinks of being stationed within the place: **a la puerta, en la puerta;** compare English *at the door* (perhaps being only poised there in readiness to go in or out) vs. *in the doorway.*

An instance of **a** referring to a point of time is **al** plus infinitive; see Unit 7 §35. See also Unit 11 §62 for other instances of **a** with time.

A. 1. **¡Qué bueno que nosotros quedamos en mandarlos!**
   2. _____ quedáramos _____
   3. _____ ellos _____
   4. _____ las
   5. _____ trataran de _____
   6. _____ suerte _____
   7. _____ tratarán _____
   8. _____ enviar _____
   9. _____ la
   10. _____ ella _____
   11. _____ ridículo _____
   12. _____ tiene que _____
   13. _____ pagar _____
   14. _____ tenga _____
   15. _____ lo
   16. _____ tontería _____
   17. _____ ustedes _____
   18. _____ tuvieran _____
   19. _____ molestia _____
   20. _____ él _____
   21. _____ insistió en _____
   22. _____ comprar _____
   23. _____ insistiera _____
   24. _____ lástima _____

B. 1. **María y yo la dejamos velar toda la noche.**
   2. _____ ella _____
   3. _____ dormir _____
   4. _____ le aconsejaron _____
   5. _____ les _____
   6. Pablo _____
   7. _____ mandaron _____
   8. _____ tarde _____
   9. _____ esperar _____
   10. _____ rogaron _____
   11. _____ rogaron que _____
   12. _____ practicaran _____
   13. _____ día _____
   14. _____ le _____
   15. Pablo y yo _____
   16. _____ estudiara _____
   17. _____ suplicamos _____
   18. _____ mañana _____
   19. Mercedes y yo _____
   20. _____ rogamos _____
   21. _____ les _____
   22. _____ trabajaran _____
   23. _____ semana _____
   24. _____ aconsejamos _____
   25. Mercedes y él _____

● PATTERNED RESPONSE REVIEW DRILL

Sequence of tenses: review of preterit.

A. 1. TEACHER: ¿No va usted a estudiar?   3. ¿No va usted a jugar?   6. ¿No va usted a comer?
      STUDENT: **Ya estudié.**   4. ¿No va usted a llamar?   7. ¿No va usted a beber?
   2. ¿No va usted a almorzar?   5. ¿No va usted a preguntar? 8. ¿No va usted a escribir?

B. 1. ¿No va él a lavar el auto?
Ya lo lavó.

2. ¿No va él a dictar la carta?
3. ¿No va él a cambiar el dinero?
4. ¿No va él a pagar la cuenta?
5. ¿No va él a vender el coche?
6. ¿No va él a barrer la sala?
7. ¿No va él a escoger los periódicos?
8. ¿No va él a abrir las puertas?

C. 1. ¿Cuándo me va a mostrar las fotos?
Ya se las mostré.

2. ¿Cuándo me va a alcanzar el plato?
3. ¿Cuándo me va a terminar la pared?
4. ¿Cuándo me va a lavar la ropa?
5. ¿Cuándo me va a arreglar el bolsillo?

6. ¿Cuándo me va a traer las pieles?
7. ¿Cuándo me va a sacudir los muebles?
8. ¿Cuándo me va a vender la cartera?
9. ¿Cuándo me va a enseñar el joropo?
10. ¿Cuándo me va a contestar la carta?

D. 1. ¿Cuándo van ustedes a traerlo?
Ya lo trajimos.

2. ¿Cuándo van ustedes a hacerlo?
3. ¿Cuándo van ustedes a darlo?
4. ¿Cuándo van ustedes a tenerlo?
5. ¿Cuándo van ustedes a ponerlo?
6. ¿Cuándo van ustedes a producirlo?
7. ¿Cuándo van ustedes a decirlo?
8. ¿Cuándo van ustedes a reducirlo?

READING

El señor
ROBERTO ESPARZA ALONSO

falleció ayer a las 13.30 horas en el Seno[1] de Nuestra Madre de la Santa Iglesia Católica, Apostólica Romana, confortado con todos los auxilios espirituales.

Su inconsolable esposa, madre, hijas, hermanos, hermana, hijo político[2] y demás parientes, lo participan a usted con el más profundo dolor y le ruegan eleve sus oraciones a Dios Nuestro Señor por el eterno descanso del alma del finado.[3]

México, D. F., 4 de octubre de 1958.

[1] *bosom* [2] *son-in-law* [3] *deceased*

Muere un destacado miembro del foro[1]

Después de prolongada enfermedad dejó de existir el distinguido licenciado en Derecho[2] y Notario Público, don Roberto Esparza Alonso.

5 de octubre de 1958.—A las 13.30 horas del día 3 de octubre dejó de existir en esta ciudad, después de haberse agotado todos los recursos que la ciencia médica aconsejó,[3] el distinguido abogado Roberto Esparza Alonso, notario público Núm. 2, quien gozaba de general estimación en todos los círculos sociales.

El cadáver fue velado[4] en su domicilio calle de Providencia número 864, teniendo lugar ayer a las 15 horas las solemnes honras fúnebres, trasladándose a continuación[5] el cuerpo al Panteón[6] Americano. Debemos hacer constar que innumerables personas de todos los sectores sociales estuvieron en la velada, resultando insuficiente la amplia residencia y teniendo que estar gran cantidad de gentes en la calle y en el pequeño jardín que se encuentra frente al referido domicilio.

Por lo que respecta a[7] las ofrendas florales, han sido de igual manera numerosas, no habiendo materialmente[8] lugar donde colocarlas.

El abogado Esparza fue catedrático[9] del Instituto de Ciencias y Artes del Estado, y desempeñó[10] además las funciones de juez en distintos distritos, dedicándose finalmente a la notaría, cargo que desempeñó hasta el momento de su muerte, contando con la estimación de todos quienes lo trataron.

(Adapted from *El Universal*)

[1] *Bar* [2] *Bachelor of Laws* [3] *after . . . had been exhausted* [4] *The wake was held* [5] *immediately afterwards* [6] *Cemetery* [7] *With regard to*
[8] *literally* [9] *professor* [10] *performed, fulfilled*

La religión

Es imposible comprender la cultura de un país sin tomar en cuenta la religión. Esta afirmación tiene gran valor en España y en los países hispanos, pues la religión hace un papel muy importante no sólo en la vida personal sino también en la vida social y colectiva y en las costumbres. Se refleja en la lengua misma. La historia de esos pueblos no tiene significado si no se toman en cuenta las motivaciones religiosas que inspiran muchos de los grandes acontecimientos y empresas. La literatura hispana será un campo con muchos secretos si se ignora la religión de los hispanos.

Es más importante comprender su actitud ante la religión y las cosas religiosas que conocer en detalle cuáles son las creencias y supersticiones. En primer lugar hay que recordar que los hispanos, por muy individualistas que son,[1] se apropian de la religión, se la hacen suya, como hacen con toda idea o movimiento con que entran en contacto. La religión católica, que en todo el mundo tiene dogmas, prácticas y características comunes, es intensamente española en España, como es mexicana, cubana, argentina, colombiana en México, Cuba, Argentina y Colombia respectivamente. Es más; en el común sentir de la gente se puede decir todavía que es más regional que nacional. A un aragonés no le importa mucho el Jesús del Gran Poder, tan venerado en Sevilla, pero nunca tolera la más leve ironía o falta de respeto por su Pilarica.[2] El mexicano no venera a la Virgen María simplemente, sino a la Virgen de Guadalupe,[3] como el cubano a la Virgen del Cobre.[4]

Como cualquier concepto religioso se convierte naturalmente en el hispano en una convicción personal, tiende a menudo a la intolerancia. En la época actual, cuando para las masas la religión ha cesado de ejercer una influencia dominante como fuerza espiritual, las mismas características de adhesión personal, apasionada y resuelta se hallan aplicadas a las ideologías políticas.

Para el hispano la religión no es tanto un dogma y una teología—es de todos conocida la ignorancia y la falta de interés por las sutilezas doctrinales en la mayoría hasta de los devotos—como una necesidad de poseer un poderoso imán que una a individuos ferozmente independientes, y una sublimación de sus anhelos. La religión no se razona, se siente o no se siente, se acepta como algo profundo y consubstancial, se rechaza con la misma mística pasión, o se reconoce en general como parte de la vida nacional que dejaría un vacío difícil de reemplazar si se abandonara.

Como la religión es tan personal, tan consubstancial al espíritu hispano, se la trata muchas veces con la misma familiaridad, más o menos reverente y campechana, con que se tratan las cosas de la familia. Nada más lejos del concepto hispano que el sentido de reverencia, temor y distancia con que lo divino, lo sobrenatural y las instituciones religiosas se tratan en otras culturas. Sólo hay que recordar la forma tradicional de celebrar las Navidades, Semana Santa y Pascua y las fiestas de los Santos Patrones.[5] Esta familiaridad se nota en algunos villancicos:

Los pastores daban saltos
y bailaban de contento,
al par que los angelitos
tocaban los instrumentos.

---

[1] **por muy individualistas que son** *because they are such individualists*
[2] **Pilarica** Our Lady of Pilar ("of the Column"), in Saragossa, Spain.
[3] **La Virgen de Guadalupe** miraculously appeared to a humble Indian, Juan Diego, in 1531, on the arid Tepeyac Hill near Mexico City. In 1754 a Papal Bull declared her the Patroness and Protectress of New Spain.
[4] **la Virgen del Cobre,** national shrine of Cuba, close to Santiago.
[5] **Santos Patrones** *Patron Saints*

Caminen, pastores, ¡caramba!
que ahí viene Miguel
con la espada en la mano ¡caramba!
para Lucifer ¡ay caramba!
para Lucifer.

Tal vez este concepto de familiaridad y aceptación implícita de la religión como parte de la vida ordinaria explica las aparentes paradojas que ofrecen los pueblos latinos en sus relaciones con la Iglesia. ¿Quiénes asisten a la misa? Las mujeres. ¿Quiénes rezan? Las mujeres.

Pero, recuérdese que es el mismo pueblo— hombres y mujeres—que da generosamente sus joyas a la imagen de su devoción. Celebran procesiones y fiestas cívicas alrededor de los santos patronos, pero, en momentos de furia colectiva, provocados por injusticias sociales y políticas, se vuelven airados contra la Iglesia (entiéndase, no contra la religión). Queman edificios, saquean santuarios y persiguen a los sacerdotes. Este mismo pueblo salpica su lenguaje diario con expresiones religiosas: *Adiós,* para despedirse o para saludar; *Ave María Purísima, Virgen Santa, Jesús* para manifestar sorpresa y admiración; *Vaya con Dios, que Dios le ampare,* para no dar una limosna.[6] *Ojalá* (Alá lo quiera[7]) se dice, remedando a los musulmanes, como una confirmación a lo que escribió el gran pensador hispano Miguel de Unamuno[8] que el Cristo español es un Cristo africano. Este mismo pueblo que hace compartir sus penas y alegrías a la Virgen y a los Santos en sus expresiones corrientes es uno de los pueblos donde la blasfemia, no sólo obscena sino religiosa, es más común. No es muy agradable mencionar esto, pero es necesario para comprender la psicología de los pueblos hispanos y el lugar que la religión ocupa en su vida. ¿Es una paradoja? ¿Quién sabe?

Como la religión en los hispanos absorbe y satura, consciente o inconscientemente, toda la vida de los individuos, se han escrito en la lengua del pueblo algunos de los más grandes libros religiosos. Cuando Santa Teresa de Jesús,[9] el Fray Luis de Granada[10] y otros escriben sus libros piadosos, se dirigen a la gente devota ordinaria, de cultura simplemente media.

Si la literatura española — excepto los escritos de unos místicos—carece de gran originalidad y profundidad, teológica con todo, está saturada de sentimiento sincero, de emoción, de fuerza y realismo que le prestan cualidades únicas y perdurables. Por su abundancia, sin igual en ninguna literatura desde la Edad Media hasta nuestros días, en verso y en prosa; desde la humilde canción y el ingenioso romance *a lo divino* hasta el ambicioso poema épico religioso; desde los consejos morales y la instrucción del catecismo hasta los vuelos atrevidos hacia los misterios de la unión mística con Dios, la literatura española ofrece un conjunto de obras maestras sin par.

Vamos a leer ahora una poesía de Santa Teresa de Jesús:

> Nada te turbe,
> nada te espante,
> todo se pasa,
> Dios no se muda.
> La paciencia
> todo lo alcanza;
> quien a Dios tiene
> nada le falta:
> Sólo Dios basta.

El misticismo mexicano se nota en estos versos de Amado Nervo:[11]

> Cada día que pasa, has de decirte:
> "¡Hoy he nacido!
> El mundo es nuevo para mí; la luz
> ésta que miro,
> hiere sin duda por la vez primera
> mis ojos límpidos;
> la lluvia que hoy desfleca sus cristales
> es mi bautismo."

---

[6] A stock phrase used by beggars is **¡Una limosna por el amor de Dios!** and the answer is usually: **Que Dios le ampare** (when one does not give alms).

[7] **Alá lo quiera** *May Allah grant it.* (See Unit 17, Cultural Note 5.)

[8] Miguel de Unamuno (1864–1936), eminent Spanish philosopher.

[9] Santa Teresa de Jesús de Avila (1515–1582), Spanish mystic poet. Her best work, which in mystic language presents the soul in seven dwelling places, is *Las Moradas.*

[10] Fray Luis de Granada was a Dominican priest and writer, born in Granada in 1504. His best works are *Guía de pecadores* (Sinners' Guide) and *Símbolo de la fe* (Symbol of Faith).

[11] Amado Nervo (1870–1919), modernist Mexican poet, sought solutions for the enigmas created by the problems of life and religion.

- CUESTIONARIO

1. ¿En qué aspectos de la vida española se refleja la religión?
2. Explique por qué la religión católica tiene un sello distintivo en cada país hispano.
3. ¿A qué se debe la intolerancia que a menudo se manifiesta en los hispanos?
4. ¿Cuál es el factor que ejerce una influencia dominante como fuerza espiritual para el hispano?
5. ¿Qué representa en realidad la religión para el hispano?
6. ¿Cómo trata generalmente el espíritu hispano a la religión?
7. ¿De qué manera se trata la religión en la cultura norteamericana?
8. Mencione algunos ejemplos en que se nota la familiaridad con que el hispano trata los asuntos religiosos.
9. ¿Qué paradojas aparentes ofrecen los pueblos latinos en sus relaciones con la Iglesia?
10. ¿En qué casos se vuelve el pueblo latino contra la Iglesia?
11. ¿Qué diferencia hay entre Iglesia y religión?
12. Mencione algunas expresiones latinas comunes de carácter religioso.
13. ¿De qué origen es la expresión *Ojalá?*
14. ¿Qué escritores han dirigido sus libros a la gente devota ordinaria?
15. ¿Qué expresan los versos de Santa Teresa de Jesús y Amado Nervo?

- SUGGESTED READINGS

Crow, John A., *Mexico Today,* Harper, New York, 1957: Ch. 6, "Dawn of Empire: Government and Church."

Green, Philip Leonard, *Our Latin American Neighbors,* Hastings House, New York, 1941: Ch. 16, "One Family or Many?"

22

The Burglary

A. *Alicia*   D. *Diego*   L. *Lieutenant*   S. *Sergeant*

A. Diego! Stop snoring! Wake up!

D. What? How's that?

A. Wake up! I heard some noises downstairs.

D. It must have been the cat. Let me sleep, woman.

CRASH!

A. You see? There it is again. It's burglars. Diego, call the police.

D. Sh . . . ! I wonder where I put my pistol.

A. Where are you going? Don't leave me here alone . . .

D. Quiet, woman, you make me nervous.

*   *   *

El robo

A. *Alicia*   D. *Diego*   T. *Teniente*   S. *Sargento*

A. ¡Diego! ¡Deja de roncar! ¡Despierta!

D. ¿Qué? ¿Cómo?

A. ¡Despierta! Oí unos ruidos abajo.

D. Habrá sido el gato. Déjame dormir, mujer.

¡¡CATAPLUM!!

A. ¿No ves? Otra vez. Son ladrones. Diego, llama a la policía.

D. ¡¡Sh . . . !! ¿Dónde habré dejado la pistola?

A. ¿Adónde vas? No me dejes sola . . .

D. Cállate, mujer, que me pones nervioso.

*   *   *

A. They took the silver service that I was given for my wedding, officer.

L. Yes, yes, just one moment. Judging by these tracks, they seem to have come through here to get to the dining room.

A. Officer, they also took the clothes I left hanging in the patio.

L. All right, all right, let's begin at the beginning. What time does the patrol go by?

D. About 4 A.M., I think.

L. Hmm. How many servants are there in the house?

A. Right now, two: the cook and the maid. We let the gardener go yesterday.

D. He was with us only a few days. We didn't like him, because he was so lazy.

S. This looks suspicious. He had a key to the house?

A. Oh good Lord! Of course! Now that I think of it, I forgot to ask him for it when he left.

* * *

L. Can you give us a description of him?

D. His name is Chalo Campo, but they call him Chato on account of his flat nose. He's a man about forty, not very tall—in fact, on the short side.

A. Also dark, thin, I don't believe he weighs more than fifty-five kilos. And he had a big scar on his face.

L. Ah, I know who he is now: the famous Juan Pérez, alias "The Mouse."

A. He didn't seem like a bad sort, at least according to his references and his good conduct certificate from the police.

L. Madam, you can be sure that those documents were all forged.

A. Se llevaron la vajilla de plata que me habían regalado para mi boda, Sr. Oficial.

T. Sí, sí, un momentito. Estas huellas, parece que entraron por aquí para llegar al comedor.

A. Sr. Oficial, también se llevaron la ropa que había dejado colgada en el patio.

T. Bueno, bueno, empecemos por el principio. ¿A qué hora pasa la ronda? (1)

D. Como a las cuatro de la mañana, creo.

T. Hmm. ¿Cuántos empleados hay en la casa?

A. Por ahora, dos: la cocinera y la criada. Al jardinero lo despedimos ayer.

D. Estuvo apenas unos días con nosotros. No nos gustaba por perezoso.

S. Esto está sospechoso. ¿El tenía llave de la casa?

A. ¡Jesús María! (2) ¡Claro! Ahora que recuerdo, se me olvidó pedírsela cuando se fue.

* * *

T. ¿Puede hacernos una descripción de él?

D. Se llama Chalo Campo, pero le dicen Chato por la nariz aplastada. Es un hombre de unos cuarenta años, no muy alto, más bien bajo.

A. También moreno, delgado; no creo que pese más de cincuenta y cinco kilos. Y tenía una gran cicatriz en la cara.

T. Ah, ya sé quién es: el famoso Juan Pérez, alias "El Ratón".

A. No parecía mala persona, al menos según sus referencias y certificados de buena conducta de la policía (3).

T. Señora, tenga la seguridad de que todos eran documentos falsificados.

Cultural Notes (1) The **ronda** or night patrol is a protection provided by private agencies hired to keep watch on residences and buildings.

(2) See Unit 2, Cultural Note 2.

(3) The good conduct certificate, which might be necessary to get a job or to obtain a visa, is one of several papers a Latin American carries with him. See Unit 6, Cultural Note 4.

124   Probability in past time

EXAMPLES

A. 1. ¿Dónde **habré dejado** la pistola?
   2. **Habrá sido** el gato.   *(It was probably the cat.)*

B. 1. — ¡Qué suerte tiene ese tipo!   Y todo por una casualidad.
      — ¿Y cómo **sería?**
   2. **Serían** las dos.   *It was probably two o'clock.*
   3. **Tendría** unos veinte años.   *She was somewhere around twenty years old.*

probablemente he dejado probablemente dejé	=	habré dejado
probablemente eran	=	serían

Probability corresponding to the present perfect or the preterit is expressed by the future perfect; probability corresponding to the imperfect is expressed by the conditional.

● TENSE SUBSTITUTION DRILL

INSTRUCTIONS: Repeat the following sentences just as you hear them.   Then repeat them again substituting future perfect for present perfect, thus suggesting probability.

A. 1. TEACHER: Ha muerto el gato.   *Repita.*
      STUDENT: **Ha muerto el gato.**
      TEACHER: *Cambie.*
      STUDENT: **Habrá muerto el gato.**
   2. Ha vuelto la cocinera.
   3. Han escapado los ladrones.
   4. Ha estudiado el teniente.
   5. Han escrito los oficiales.
   6. Ha apostado el sargento.
   7. Ha terminado el jardinero.
   8. Han salido los ratones.

B. 1. ¿Ha pasado la ronda?
   2. ¿Ha dejado buenas referencias?
   3. ¿Han robado la vajilla?
   4. ¿Ha pedido un certificado de buena conducta?
   5. ¿Han tenido poca seguridad?
   6. ¿Ha despedido al señor de la cicatriz?
   7. ¿Han dado una descripción sospechosa?
   8. ¿Lo han echado de menos?
   9. ¿Han progresado bastante?
  10. ¿Ha hablado hasta por los codos?
  11. ¿La ha dejado en paz?

● CONSTRUCTION SUBSTITUTION DRILL

INSTRUCTIONS: Repeat the following sentences just as you hear them.   Then repeat them again substituting future perfect for preterit, thus suggesting probability.

A. 1. TEACHER: Rosa colgó la ropa en el patio. *Repita.*
      STUDENT: **Rosa colgó la ropa en el patio.**
      TEACHER: *Cambie.*
      STUDENT: **Rosa habrá colgado la ropa en el patio.**
   2. Roberto paseó en la playa.
   3. Memo tuvo hora para las once.
   4. Don Rafael roncó toda la noche.
   5. Carmen perdió una cantidad de dólares.
   6. Ellos encargaron una corona para el entierro.
   7. Esos fueron documentos falsificados.

B. 1. ¡Caramba! ¿Qué fue ese cataplum?
    2. ¿Qué le informaron con respecto a los compromisos sociales?
    3. ¿Qué le indicó sobre lo de estar al nivel del mar?
    4. ¿Qué dijo de la cabeza y la garganta?
    5. ¿Quién dejó esas huellas?
    6. ¿Quién tuvo la bondad de llenar mi taza?
    7. ¿Quiénes le dieron el pésame?

● TENSE SUBSTITUTION DRILL

INSTRUCTIONS: Repeat the following sentences just as you hear them. Then repeat them again substituting conditional for imperfect, thus suggesting probability.

1. TEACHER: Era Juan Pérez, alias el Ratón.
   Repita.
   STUDENT: **Era Juan Pérez, alias el Ratón.**
   TEACHER: *Cambie.*
   STUDENT: **Sería Juan Pérez, alias el Ratón.**
2. Era ese filósofo loco.
3. La viuda estaba muy nerviosa.
4. Estaban en el velorio.
5. Tenían mucho apego a la vida.
6. Tenía una fiebre bastante alta.
7. Había dos clases de biología.
8. No había más remedio.

● PATTERNED RESPONSE DRILL

A. 1. TEACHER: ¿Qué estaba comprando él?
        STUDENT: **Quién sabe. Estaría comprando un coche.**
    2. ¿Qué estaba llevando él?
    3. ¿Qué estaba vendiendo él?
    4. ¿Qué estaba buscando él?
    5. ¿Qué estaba mandando él?
    6. ¿Qué estaba pidiendo él?

B. 1. ¿A quién vio Memo?
        No sé. Habrá visto a Marta.
    2. ¿A quién llevó Memo?
    3. ¿A quién invitó Memo?
    4. ¿A quién escogió Memo?
    5. ¿A quién prefirió Memo?
    6. ¿A quién siguió Memo?
    7. ¿A quién felicitó Memo?

● TRANSLATION DRILL

1. TEACHER: I wondered what they would be wanting.
   STUDENT: **Me preguntaba qué desearían.**
2. I wondered what they would be doing.
3. I wondered what they would be thinking.
4. I wondered what they would be trying.
5. I wondered what they would be comparing.
6. I wondered what they would be believing.
7. I wondered what they would be supposing.

● DISCUSSION

In addition to probability corresponding to the perfect (*He has probably seen them* **Los habrá visto**), the future perfect is also used for probability corresponding to the preterit (*He probably saw them yesterday* **Los habrá visto ayer**). The conditional is similarly used for probability corresponding to the imperfect (*Why didn't they answer? — They probably weren't home that early* **¿Por qué no contestaron? — No estarían en casa tan temprano**).

The English equivalents are as in Unit 20 §114: *What could he be thinking?* **¿Qué estaría pensando?** *What do you suppose they did?* **¿Qué habrán hecho?** *I wondered what they would be wanting* **Me preguntaba qué desearían.**

As with the future of probability, the verbs most often encountered with the conditional of probability are **ser, estar, tener,** and **haber.** The future perfect of probability, however, may be freely used with any verb.

125   The meanings of *por*

Imprecise location	*through* *down* *along* *around* *at*	Vamos **por** esta calle. Parece que entraron **por** aquí. Anduvieron **por** la playa. *They walked along the beach.* Paseamos **por** el parque. *We strolled around the park.* Empecemos **por** el principio.
Duration	*for*	Quisiera que lo probáramos **por** algunos días. Fue a España **por** dos años. *He went to Spain for two years (for a two-year stay).*
Substitution: proxy and exchange	*for (in place of)* *to*	Mi mujer va siempre y reza **por** los dos. Estoy dictando **por** el jefe. *I'm dictating for the boss (in place of the boss).* No se deje dar gato **por** liebre. —¿A cómo estaba el cambio? —A treinta **por** uno. Le doy dos dólares **por** todo. *I'll give you two dollars for the lot.*
Correspondence	*for* *per*	Me sale un pelo blanco **por** cada día que paso allí. *I get (there comes out on me) a gray hair for every day I spend there.* Se pidió acortar el número de materias **por** año. El diez **por** ciento de los repuestos no llegaron. *Ten per cent of the parts did not arrive.*
Cause, motive, and duty	*for* *because of* *on account of* *through* *on* *after (to get)* *to*	Le ruego que me perdone **por** el desorden de la casa. *(Please excuse me for the disorder of the house.)* **Por** eso la invitación, ¿eh? Todo **por** culpa de él. *(All because of his fault.)* Tenían que quedarse aquí **por** el colegio. Y todo **por** una casualidad. Le dicen Chato **por** la nariz aplastada. No nos gustaba **por** perezoso. **Por** depender tanto de la bocina cualquier día te matas. *(Because of depending so much on the horn.)* Le escribo para felicitarla **por** su cumpleaños. Nosotros pasamos **por** ti. Puede pasar **por** sus papeles. Estudia medicina **por** su padre. *He's studying medicine for his father (because his father wants him to, as a favor to him).* Vamos a la feria **por** darles gusto a los niños. *We're going to the fair to please (because that will please) the youngsters.*
Agency	*by*	Será dedicada **por** el presidente. *It will be dedicated by the president.* (See Unit 21 §121.)

EXAMPLES

1. Es la más importante **por ahora.**
2. Ay, Paquito, **por Dios,** no hagas eso.
3. Sigue alguna otra carrera de igual prestigio; ingeniería, **por ejemplo.**
4. Trigo, lentejas, maíz, papas, cebollas y cosas **por el estilo.**
5. **Por eso** la invitación, ¿eh?

6. **Por favor,** no insistan en que estudie medicina.
7. **Por fin** llegó el correo.

8. Apuesto a que **por lo menos** en fútbol ganamos.
9. **Por lo visto,** los agricultores no la pasan mal, ¿eh?

for now, for the time being, for the present	**por ahora**
for Heaven's sake (etc.)	**por Dios**
for example	**por ejemplo**
like that, of the same sort, along those lines	**por el estilo**
that's why, therefore, for that reason	**por eso**
please	**por favor**
finally, at last	**por fin**
at least	**por lo menos**
apparently	**por lo visto**
why?—because	**¿por qué?—porque**

These are among the numerous set phrases with **por.**

● TRANSLATION DRILL

A. 1. TEACHER: Let's go down this street.
   STUDENT: **Vamos por esta calle.**
  2. Let's go along this avenue.
  3. Let's go through this door.
  4. Let's go around the park.
  5. Let's go by way of the school.
  6. Let's go along the beach.
  7. Let's go across the plaza.
  8. Let's go this way (through here).

B. 1. They strolled around the park.
   Pasearon por el parque.
  2. They walked down the avenue.
  3. They went through the house.
  4. They ran along the beach.
  5. They passed through the city.
  6. They began at the beginning.

C. 1. He went to Spain for a few days.
   Fue a España por unos días.
  2. He went to the movies for a few hours.
  3. He went to his room for a few moments.
  4. He went to the country for a few days.
  5. He went to the mountains for a few weeks.
  6. He went abroad for a few months.

D. 1. We tried it for two weeks.
   Lo probamos por dos semanas.
  2. We looked at it for an hour.
  3. We stopped traffic for ten minutes.
  4. We studied medicine for six years.
  5. We waited on the corner for half an hour.
  6. We worked at that firm for a month.

E. 1. My wife prays [enough] for the two of us.
   Mi mujer reza por los dos.
  2. My wife eats [enough] for the two of us.
  3. My wife cries [enough] for the two of us.
  4. My wife drinks [enough] for the two of us.
  5. My wife talks [enough] for the two of us.
  6. My husband thinks [enough] for the two of us.
  7. My husband fumes [enough] for the two of us.

F. 1. Don't let them give you a cat in place of a rabbit.
   No se deje dar gato por liebre.
  2. Don't let them give you lard in place of butter.
  3. Don't let them give you water in place of lemonade.
  4. Don't let them give you books in place of documents.
  5. Don't let them give you geometry in place of history.
  6. Don't let them give you geometry in place of chemistry.

G. 1. I'll give you two dollars for the book.
   Le doy dos dólares por el libro.
  2. I'll give you four pesos for the wallet.
  3. I'll give you ten *guaraníes* for the post cards.
  4. I'll give you one hundred *nacionales* for the painting.

5. I'll give you five hundred *colones* for the suit.
6. I'll give you twenty thousand *bolivianos* for the car.

H. 1. There are two busses per hour.
   Hay dos buses por hora.
2. There are five *micros* per hour.
3. There are three films per week.
4. There are two demonstrations per month.
5. There is one general strike per year.
6. There is ten per cent per year.

I. 1. Excuse me for the disorder of the house.
   Perdóneme por el desorden de la casa.
2. Excuse me for the change of the schedule.
3. Excuse us for the lack of plates.
4. Excuse us for depending so much on the horn.
5. Excuse us for bringing bad news.
6. Excuse me for having arrived late.
7. Excuse me for having broken the record.
8. Excuse me for getting nervous.

J. 1. And all because of a lucky break.
   Y todo por una casualidad.
2. And all because of an old lady selling tickets.
3. And all because of a long sickness.
4. And all because of a famous robber.
5. And all because of a bitter argument.
6. And all because of a bad philosophy.
7. And all because of a treacherous memory.

8. And all because of a lazy gardener.
9. And all because of a sincere friend.
10. And all because of an innocent person.

K. 1. He's going to go by for his papers.
   El va a pasar por sus papeles.
2. I'm going to go by for my books.
3. She's going to go by for her letter.
4. We're going to go by for our record player.
5. They're going to go by for their dresses.
6. You're going to go by for your shirts.
7. We're going to go by for you at eight o'clock.

L. 1. It was dedicated by the president.
   Fue dedicado por el presidente.
2. It was found by the technician.
3. It was explained by the lawyer.
4. It was sent by the lieutenant.
5. It was covered by the sergeant.
6. It was filled by the maid.
7. It was dissolved by the police.

M. 1. For the time being, he's not coming.
   Por ahora, no viene.
2. For goodness' sake, don't come.
3. For example, he's coming.
4. That's why he's coming.
5. Please come early.
6. At last, he's coming.
7. At least he's coming.
8. Apparently he's coming.
9. Why is he coming?

● DISCUSSION

Prepositions enter intimately into combinations with other words, in much the same way as prefixes and suffixes. They often become so stereotyped in these combinations that it is hard to trace any common core of meaning. This is strikingly true of **por** in Spanish. It has given rise to a great variety of set phrases, each of which must be learned for itself. At the same time, however, it has kept the power to make free combinations, with areas of meaning that can be outlined with some degree of precision:

1. Imprecise location. *Down* the street, *along* the beach, *through* the house, *across* the bridge, etc. are all expressed with **por**. The nature of the medium where the action takes place tells us which of the English equivalents is appropriate. Imprecise location in time also calls for **por**: *He'll be here around March* **Estará aquí por marzo.**

2. Duration. Being somewhere for an intended length of time calls for **por**: *He came for three weeks* **Vino por tres semanas.** As in English, time during which something actually lasted needs no preposition at all: *I was there (for) three weeks* **Estuve allí (por) tres semanas.**

3. Substitution. When one person acts *for* another, or one thing is given *for* another, **por** is the equivalent of *for*: **Nosotros velaremos por usted** *We'll stay up for you (in your stead).*

4. Correspondence. Where English has *for* or *per* showing two things in a kind of reciprocal relationship, Spanish uses **por**: *One dentist for every five hundred persons* **Un dentista por cada quinientas personas.**

5. Cause, motive, and duty. When something acts to bring about an effect, English uses a variety of prepositions: *for, because of, through*, etc.: *I got the job through my brother* **Conseguí el empleo**

por mi hermano. The influence toward the action is conceived as compelling, often being tinged with a suggestion of duty, for example *I went in very carefully so as not to wake them* **Entré con mucho cuidado por no despertarlos** (it was a duty not to wake them). Spanish shows here a curious merging of push and aim. If the thing that one aims at is at the same time a motive for taking aim, then (*in order*) *to* is expressed by **por.** For example, the parents in a family feel a duty to satisfy their children; so "because of satisfying the children" is the reason for going to the fair, and one gets **Vamos a la feria por darles gusto a los niños,** where purpose and cause coalesce.

6. Agency. See Unit 21 §121.

Most set phrases show their ultimate relationship to the free meanings of **por.** For example, **por lo visto** literally means *by what is seen,* i.e., the evidence of the visible, hence *apparently.*

126   The meanings of *de*

Source	*from*	¿**De** dónde son?
Possession and belonging-ness	*'s* *of* *to* *in*	En casa **de** Olga. (See Unit 4 §20.) ¿El tenía llave **de** la casa? Va a ser la planta más moderna **de** Latinoamérica. Se sacó el gordo **de** la lotería. Son las ocho **de** la mañana. (See Unit 11 §62.)
Identification	*with*	Lupita, la **de** los ojos verdes.
Theme	*about* *concerning*	¿**De** qué quieres que hablemos, mamá? ¿**De** vestidos?
Substi-tution		Cambiemos **de** tema. (*Let's-have-a-change of subject.*) Quiero cambiar **de** ropa. *I want to change clothes.*
Partitive	*of* (*or nothing*)	¿Me pasas un poquito **de** carne, por favor? Necesito un poco **de** dinero. *I need a little money.* ¿Qué hay **de** malo en eso? Hay algo **de** bueno en esta revolución? *Is there anything good about this revolution?* (Set phrases without an expressed indefinite:) Los niños tendrían **de** todo. Nunca diga "**De** esta agua no beberé."
Comparison	*than*	No creo que pese más **de** 55 kilos. (See Unit 14 §79.)
Capacity	*as* *for*	¿Y cuándo aceptó este trabajo? **De** administrador, ¿verdad? ¿Qué hacemos **de** comida? ¿Qué le parece una ensalada, rosbif y helados **de** postre? No quiero servir **de** profesor aquí. *I don't want to serve as professor here.*
Posi-tion — separation	*by*	Llegué acompañada **de** varias amigas. *I arrived accompanied by several friends.* (See Unit 21 §121.)
Posi-tion — contact	*with* *in*	Lo cubrieron **de** polvo. *They covered it with dust.* ¡Se ve tan pálida vestida **de** negro! (See Unit 21 §122.)

The central meanings of **de** are *of* and *from.* Peripheral meanings range as far as mere "connectedness."

EXAMPLES

A. 1. —La comunión es algo muy importante.
      —**De acuerdo.**
   2. No estoy **de acuerdo** contigo.
   3. Nunca se ponen **de acuerdo.**

B. Vamos a enviárselos **de inmediato.**

C. **De nada.**

D. No deben salir solas **de noche.**

E. **De todos modos,** quería hablarte de otra cosa.

F. —Se casa con Lorenzo.
   —**¡De veras!**

agreed in agreement	**de acuerdo**
immediately	**de inmediato**
you're welcome	**de nada**
at night	**de noche**
anyway	**de todos modos**
really	**de veras**[1]

These are among the numerous set phrases with **de.**

● TRANSLATION DRILL

A. 1. TEACHER: Are you from Mexico?
      STUDENT: **¿Es usted de México?**
   2. Are you from Panama?
   3. Is he from Brazil?
   4. Is he from Argentina?
   5. Is she from Spain?
   6. Is she from Colombia?
   7. Are they from Venezuela?
   8. Are they from Chile?
   9. Is Diego from Europe?

B. 1. This house is Olga's.
      Esta casa es de Olga.
   2. This book is Juanita's.
   3. This wallet is Felipe's.
   4. This bill is Alvaro's.
   5. These scissors are the barber's.
   6. These tickets are the sergeant's.
   7. These flowers are the secretary's.

C. 1. Here's the key to the house.
      Aquí está la llave de la casa.
   2. Here's the key to the car.
   3. Here's the door to the living room.
   4. Here's the door to the kitchen.
   5. Here's the entrance to the bank.
   6. Here's the ticket to the show.
   7. Here's the bus to the city.

D. 1. It's the most modern plant in the country.
      Es la planta más moderna del país.
   2. It's the best team in the competition.
   3. He's the laziest student in the world.
   4. She's the prettiest girl in the class.
   5. He's the oldest man in the city.
   6. He's the most boring teacher in the school.
   7. It's the last flower in the garden.

E. 1. Where's the girl with the green eyes?
      ¿Dónde está la chica de los ojos verdes?
   2. Where's the man with the gray suit?
   3. Where's the man with the red tie?
   4. Where's the woman with the yellow dress?
   5. Where's the boy with the flat nose?
   6. Where's the man with the new car?
   7. Where's the woman with the cat?

F. 1. Did you talk much about dresses?
      ¿Hablaron mucho de vestidos?
   2. Did you argue much about politics?
   3. Did you study much about the country?
   4. Did you worry much about the revolution?
   5. Did you mention anything about the money?
   6. Did you discuss anything about the situation?
   7. Did you say anything about the schedule?
   8. Did you find out (know) anything about the robbery?
   9. Did you understand anything about the problem?

---

[1] The equivalent of *really* uttered in the face of doubt or surprise, in situations where *really and truly* would fit.

G. 1. Let's change the subject.
Vamos a cambiar de tema.

2. Let's change the hour.
3. Let's change the date.
4. Let's change books.
5. Let's change classes.
6. Let's change teachers.
7. Let's change jobs.
8. Let's change positions.

H. 1. I'm going to change clothes.
Voy a cambiarme de ropa.

2. I'm going to change shirts.
3. I'm going to change ties.
4. I'm going to change dresses.
5. I'm going to change overcoats.
6. I'm going to change cars.
7. I'm going to change houses.

I. 1. He gave me a little sugar.
Me dio un poco de azúcar.

2. He gave me a little money.
3. I need a million pesos.
4. I need a million things.
5. We bought a dozen eggs.
6. We bought a dozen shirts.
7. I bought half a dozen ties.
8. I bought a quantity of socks.

J. 1. Is there anything bad in that?
¿Hay algo de malo en eso?

2. Is there anything good in the book?
3. Is there anything new in the house?
4. What's new?
5. There's [a little] of everything.

6. He has a little of everything.
7. He gave me a little of everything.

K. 1. He doesn't weigh more than 55 kilos.
No pesa más de 55 kilos.

2. He doesn't weigh more than 70 kilos.
3. He doesn't have more than 100 dollars.
4. He doesn't have more than 500 pesos.
5. He doesn't want more than 10 minutes.
6. He doesn't want more than 2 hours.
7. He doesn't earn more than 200 dollars.

L. 1. He works as an administrator.
El trabaja de administrador.

2. He works as a manager.
3. He serves as a technician.
4. He serves as a leader.
5. We serve chicken and rice for dinner.
6. We serve ice cream for dessert.
7. We have salad for lunch (= as our lunch).

M. 1. He goes out at night.
El sale de noche.

2. He flies at night.
3. He studies at night.
4. He practices at night.
5. He works at night.
6. He sleeps by day.

N. 1. He said, "Agreed."
Dijo: De acuerdo.

2. He said, "Immediately."
3. He said, "You're welcome."
4. He said, "Anyway."
5. He said, "Really?"

● DISCUSSION

Like English *of,* Spanish **de** cannot be assigned a clearly delimited area of meaning. The central meanings of source and belongingness fade at the edges to merely relational functions like the one in *the city of Buenos Aires* **la ciudad de Buenos Aires,** where *city = Buenos Aires,* or in *the habit of arriving late* **la costumbre de llegar tarde,** where *habit = arriving late.*

Some of the special uses of **de** have already been studied; see the references to earlier units in the table of examples above. Other special uses are the following:

1. Belongingness. English *to* and *in:* Where English has *the key to the door, the door to the house,* Spanish uses **de: la llave de la puerta, la puerta de la casa.** Where English has *in* but refers to a thing that is not merely located in a place but belongs there, Spanish uses **de:** *the students in the class* **los alumnos de la clase** (**en la clase** would suggest perhaps casual visitors, and in any case would probably be said **que están en la clase;** see Unit 15 §86); *the best team in the United States* **el mejor equipo de los Estados Unidos.**

2. Identification. English *with, in, on,* etc.: English has archaic expressions with *of;* e.g., *The House of the Seven Gables,* where nowadays we would probably say *with: the house with the blue shutters.* Spanish uses **de:** *the man with the green tie* **el hombre de la corbata verde;** *the man in (with) the big car* **el hombre del coche grande.** These are a kind of belongingness in reverse: the tie actually belongs to the man, not he to it, but we can identify him by it just as we can identify *the paint on the house* **la pintura de la casa,** where the paint does "belong to" the house.

3. Substitution. Where change involves substitution, Spanish adds **de: cambiar de ropa, cambiar de tema.** Compare English *a change of subject, a change of clothes.*

4. Partitive. In the sense *a little,* **de** is added after **poco** (and **poquito**), e.g., **un poco de azúcar** *a little sugar;* compare English *a little bit of, a lot of,* and Spanish **un millón de,** Unit 8 §43. In addition, the indefinites **¿qué?, algo,** and **nada** may take **de** before adjectives, e.g., **Tiene algo de loco** *He's a little bit cracked.* The adjectives **bueno, malo,** and **nuevo** are especially frequent: **¿Qué hay de nuevo?** *What's new?* The phrase **de todo** occurs without any expressed indefinite, especially with the verbs **haber, tener,** and **dar: Hay de todo** *There's a little bit of everything;* **Nos dio de todo** *He gave us a little bit of everything.*

5. Capacity. English *as* and *for:* Applied to the occupation or position that a person holds, this refers to official capacity. Thus **Estoy aquí de gerente** *I am here as manager* implies that this is my official job. **Trabaja allí de administrador** *He works there as administrator* means that he has been duly appointed to the position; **Trabaja allí como administrador** has a more general sense—he might be filling in temporarily, or there might exist no official position of this sort; **Trabaja allí como un administrador** means *like an administrator.* Applied to things, the **de** of capacity refers to what fills a pre-existing slot. For example, dinner is scheduled, but what is it to be?—*as* or *for* dinner there are such-and-such items. Or, dessert is scheduled, but what is to fill the dessert slot?—**helados de postre,** i.e., ice cream *as* or *for* dessert. A thing filling a slot and a person filling a job are functionally the same.

Among the set phrases, **de noche** calls for comment. We have already met **por la noche** with the meaning *at night* (Unit 11 §62). The difference is that **de noche** is like an adjective meaning *nocturnal.* **Llegó de noche** means *He made a nocturnal arrival.* The now almost obsolescent English *by day* and *by night* are close equivalents: *The owl hides by day and flies by night.* **Por la noche** normally refers to a particular night: **"Llegó ayer"—"¿Por la noche?"** *"He arrived yesterday"—"At night?"* The same contrast exists between **de día** and **por el día.**

127 The *–do* form for postures

EXAMPLES

1. Un día estaba **parado** en la puerta de un café.
2. Se llevaron la ropa que había dejado **colgada** en el patio.

3. ¿Ves aquel tipo **sentado** allá? *Do you see that fellow sitting over there?*
4. Están **acostados.** No los despiertes. *They're lying down. Don't wake them.*

standing	=	planted, erect	parado
sitting	=	seated	sentado
lying down	=	stretched out, recumbent	acostado
hanging	=	hung	colgado

When an *–ing* form in English refers to a posture already assumed that is now merely being sustained, Spanish uses a *–do* form.

● TRANSLATION DRILL

A. 1. TEACHER: My niece is sitting in the living room.
STUDENT: **Mi sobrina está sentada en la sala.**

2. My nephew is sitting in the dining room.
3. My nieces are sitting in the kitchen.
4. My nieces and nephews are sitting in the patio.

B. 1. He was standing on the corner.
    2. She was standing on the corner.
    3. They (*m*) were standing in the doorway.
    4. They (*f*) were standing in the doorway.

C. 1. He's lying down.
    2. She's lying down.
    3. They're (*m*) lying down.
    4. They're (*f*) lying down.

D. 1. He's sleeping, as usual.
    2. She's sleeping, as usual.
    3. They're (*m*) sleeping, as usual.
    4. They're (*f*) sleeping, as usual.

E. 1. The clothing's hanging in the patio.
    2. The suit's hanging in the patio.
    3. The shirts are hanging in the patio.
    4. The socks are hanging in the patio.

● DISCUSSION

English *They are seated* and *They are sitting* mean essentially the same thing.   Ordinarily, English favors an –*ing* form in referring to postures, picturing the person (or thing) as "doing something" when he maintains the posture.   Spanish, however, prefers the –*ed* view of the posture, and accordingly uses its –**do** form: once the housewife finishes hanging the clothes, they are no longer *hanging* but *hung*.   (If **colgando** were used rather than **colgado**, it would mean *swaying*—action rather than posture.)

Related meanings that call for –**do** forms are *leaning* (*She stood leaning over the crib*), *hugging* (in each other's arms), *crouching*, *huddling*, *hiding*, etc.

128   *Tener, haber,* and *estar* without complements

EXAMPLES

A. 1. —Me dijeron que don Pepe tenía mucho ganado en esa finca.
       —Sí, todavía **tiene.**
    2. —Creo que no hay más.   *I think there isn't any more.*
       —Sí **hay.**   *Yes there is.*

B. 1. —Mamá, dame diez centavos para darle a un pobre.
       —Ahora no **tengo,** estoy ocupada.
    2. —Dice un señor que si hay ropa vieja para vender.
       —Dile que no **hay.**
    3. —¿No es sólo en España donde hay corridas de toros?
       —No, hombre, en Perú, Colombia, Ecuador, Venezuela y Panamá, también **hay.**   (*In Peru etc. there are too.*)
    4. Para café bueno, no **hay** como este lugar.   (*There isn't anything like this place.*)

FORM OF *have* OR *there to be*	COMPLEMENT	FORM OF **te-ner** OR **haber**	COMPLEMENT
we have	it	**tenemos**	
	any		
there is	some	**hay**	
	anything		
etc.	something	etc.	

Spanish is free to omit the complement of **tener** or **haber** when it may be clearly inferred from the context.   English sometimes omits (examples *A*), sometimes not (examples *B*), under similar circumstances.

EXAMPLES

1. Buenas tardes, doña Mercedes.   **¿Está** Julio?
2. Si vuelve a llamar, dígale que no **estoy.**
3. Fui a verlos, pero no **estaban.**   *I went to see them, but they weren't there.*

to be	here there in around		estar	

Where a location is clearly understood from the context, Spanish is free to use **estar** without adding **aquí, allí,** etc.

● PATTERNED RESPONSE DRILL

A. 1. TEACHER: ¿Hay ropa vieja para vender?
STUDENT: **No, no hay.**

2. ¿Tiene usted ropa vieja para dar?
3. ¿Tienen ustedes algo para los pobres?
4. ¿Tienen ellos regalos para los niños?
5. ¿Había ropa vieja para vender?
6. ¿Tenía usted periódicos viejos para dar?
7. ¿Tenían ustedes dinero para la capilla?
8. ¿Tenía ella tiempo para comer?

B. 1. El tenía mucho ganado, ¿verdad?
Sí, y todavía tiene.

2. Tú tenías muchos toros, ¿verdad?
3. Ellos tenían muchas vacas, ¿verdad?
4. Usted tenía muchos caballos, ¿verdad?
5. Ellos tenían muchos gatos, ¿verdad?
6. Ustedes tenían muchos cerdos, ¿verdad?
7. Había muchas ovejas, ¿verdad?

● TRANSLATION DRILL

A. 1. TEACHER: Tell her I'm not here.
STUDENT: **Dile que no estoy.**

2. Tell her Julio's not here.
3. Tell her we're not here.
4. Tell her they're not here.
5. Tell her I haven't got any.
6. Tell her we haven't got any.
7. Tell her he hasn't got any.
8. Tell her there isn't any.

B. 1. I wanted to see them, but they weren't there.
Quería verlos pero no estaban.

2. I wanted to see her, but she wasn't in.
3. I wanted to see him, but he wasn't around.
4. I wanted to give a little, but I didn't have any.
5. We wanted to give a little, but we didn't have any.
6. They wanted to give a little, but they didn't have any.
7. I wanted to send something, but there wasn't anything.

● DISCUSSION

English restricts the omission of complements after *to have* and *there to be* to cases of *repetition*. In *Does he **have** the money?* *—Yes, he **has** (the money),* has repeats *have*.[1] Spanish restricts it to cases of *intelligibility*. When the mother replies **Ahora no tengo** to Paquito's request for ten cents, we know that the reference is to *money*. The omitted complement ordinarily refers to something indefinite or quantitative: *any(thing), some(thing), a lot, a few,* etc. (If it were pinpointed, Spanish, like English, would require a complement: *Please return that book I lent you.—I don't have **it** No lo tengo*.)

What dialectal English does occasionally, omitting an adverb of place after *to be* (*They had been and gone* for *They had been **there** and gone*), Spanish does quite commonly: *I called, but they weren't in* **Llamé, pero no estaban.**

---

[1] Not only *to be*, but also other auxiliary verbs in English show this sort of omission of something known from context: *Would you go?—Yes I would (go); Was he sick?—Well, he might have been (sick); Could you have helped them?—No, I couldn't (have [helped them])*.

A.

1. **Un señor muy tranquilo vino a verlo.**
2. _____ delgado _____
3. Unos _____
4. _____ querían _____
5. _____ hombre _____
6. _____ sincero _____
7. _____ la
8. _____ iba _____
9. _____ llamar _____
10. _____ extranjero _____
11. _____ alto _____
12. _____ trataba _____
13. _____ amable _____
14. _____ acompañar _____
15. _____ los
16. _____ turista _____
17. _____ conocer _____
18. _____ gordo _____
19. _____ algo _____
20. _____ empezó a _____
21. _____ regular _____
22. _____ vendedor _____
23. _____ seguir _____

B.

1. **¿Tú puedes hacernos una descripción del ladrón?**
2. _____ asesino
3. _____ dejar _____
4. _____ la _____
5. _____ nombre _____
6. _____ calle
7. _____ me _____
8. Usted _____
9. _____ decir _____
10. _____ quiere _____
11. _____ café
12. _____ dirección _____
13. _____ traer _____
14. _____ nos _____
15. _____ casa
16. _____ explicar _____
17. _____ acontecimientos _____
18. Ustedes _____
19. _____ van _____
20. _____ día
21. _____ problema _____
22. _____ preocuparse de _____
23. _____ los _____
24. _____ acordarse _____
25. Tú _____

● PATTERNED RESPONSE REVIEW DRILL

Sequence of tenses: review of present perfect.

A. 1. TEACHER: ¿Ya estudió usted?
    STUDENT: **No, todavía no he estudiado.**
2. ¿Ya almorzó usted?
3. ¿Ya aceptó usted?
4. ¿Ya contestó usted?
5. ¿Ya regateó usted?
6. ¿Ya habló usted?
7. ¿Ya renunció usted?
8. ¿Ya terminó usted?
9. ¿Ya disparó usted?

B. 1. ¿Ya comiste?
2. ¿Ya barriste?
3. ¿Ya dormiste?
4. ¿Ya prometiste?
5. ¿Ya saliste?
6. ¿Ya escogiste?
7. ¿Ya serviste?

C. 1. ¿Ya te peinaste?
2. ¿Ya te bañaste?
3. ¿Ya te lavaste?
4. ¿Ya te sentaste?
5. ¿Ya te casaste?

6. ¿Ya te entusiasmaste?
7. ¿Ya te defendiste?
8. ¿Ya te dormiste?

D. 1. ¿Ya lo escribieron ustedes?
2. ¿Ya lo abrieron ustedes?
3. ¿Ya lo cubrieron ustedes?
4. ¿Ya lo envolvieron ustedes?
5. ¿Ya lo disolvieron ustedes?
6. ¿Ya lo rompieron ustedes?
7. ¿Ya lo vieron ustedes?
8. ¿Ya lo hicieron ustedes?
9. ¿Ya lo dijeron ustedes?

READING

Noticia del día

M. *Marta* A. *Alicia*

M. Alicia, ¿qué es esto que oigo de un robo en tu casa hace unos días?

A. Ay, Marta, ¡qué susto tan grande![1] No pude dormir en dos noches.

M. Vi la pequeña noticia en el periódico, pero no daba los detalles. Dímelos tú.

---
[1] *I was scared speechless*

A. Pues fue así: Diego y yo estábamos acostados. El estaba roncando, pero yo no podía dormir y estaba en la cama con los ojos abiertos . . . Tú sabes que cuando una está despierta por la noche . . .

M. Sí, sí. Una oye todos los ruidos de la noche . . . y se imagina otros.

A. Eso es . . . Pues, como digo, allí estaba yo, y de repente oí unos ruidos abajo. En seguida sacudí a Diego, diciéndole que despertara. El murmuró que habría sido el gato, que yo lo dejara dormir. ¡Figúrate eso! . . . Entonces otra vez . . . ¡cataplum!

M. ¿Y te creyó Diego esta vez?

A. ¡Claro! Diego también oyó el ruido . . . Le pedí que llamara a la policía.

M. ¿Tiene Diego una pistola en la casa?

A. Sí, pero se le había olvidado dónde la había dejado . . . Sea lo que sea, las pistolas me dan miedo.

M. ¿De modo que llamaron a la policía?

A. ¡Cómo no! . . . El resto tú lo sabes por el periódico. Vinieron a casa esos dos policías, un teniente y un sargento, quienes nos hicieron preguntas sobre lo que faltaba, sobre los criados, etcétera.

M. Sí, ya sé todo eso. ¿Y crees tú que fue el jardinero . . . ¿cómo se llama?

A. Chalo Campo.

M. Sí. ¿Fue ése el ladrón?

A. Creo que sí. Es bien conocido por la policía, según su descripción, y no creo que tarden mucho en recogerlo.

M. Supongo que no. Pero me sorprendió saber que era él. Siempre me pareció buena persona.

A. Sí, yo participaba de tu buena opinión de él . . . pero no es oro todo lo que reluce . . . ¡qué lástima!

READING

El conquistador español del siglo XVI

. . . the Spanish conquest of America was far more than a remarkable military and political exploit; . . . it was also one of the greatest attempts the world has seen to make Christian precepts prevail in the relations between peoples.—LEWIS HANKE[1]

La Historia no se cultiva por el placer baldío de condenar ni exaltar. Se cultiva para aprovechar sus lecciones y atesorar experiencia para conocer el mensaje que cada época y cada raza legan a la humanidad.

Los descubridores y conquistadores de América—hoy podemos juzgarlos sin prevenciones y con exacta noción de su obra—fueron hombres maravillosos, muy de España y muy del siglo XVI.

¿Qué hicieron? Ensancharon la tierra. Descubrieron y sometieron casi la cuarta parte del planeta: un continente íntegro, antes desconocido. En ese continente poblado de razas indígenas y con naciones en diferentes etapas de evolución, sometieron en poco tiempo— menos de cincuenta años—un territorio de más de 80° al norte y sur del ecuador.

Espaciado entre dos grandes océanos y dos polos se extiende ese continente, que tocó en suerte a la actividad y al heroísmo españoles. Desde el Pacífico hasta el Atlántico ocupa en longitud unas 1600 leguas.[2]

Las conquistas se realizaban en medio de los mayores obstáculos y en proporción numérica irrisoria respecto a los conquistadores.

Este campo único en la Historia fue el desconocido continente que completó la geografía del planeta, poblado por razas antípodas de la europea; en campo único abierto a la audacia española fue la vasta América, desde el Misisipí, tumba del caballeresco Hernando de Soto,

[1] Simón Bolívar symbolized the feeling of Bartolomé de las Casas (that the Indian be treated as a human being because "All the peoples of the world are men") when he urged, at the Angostura Congress in 1819, that the new republic be called "Colombia" and its capital "Las Casas." Columbus and Las Casas belong to America, he said. Let us honor them by perpetuating forever their glorious achievement.—Lewis Hanke is a professor in the Latin American Institute at the University of Texas. See "Suggested Readings" for this Unit.

[2] Approximately 4,800 miles.

desde las tierras de la Florida donde el viejo Ponce de León busca la fuente de la Juventud, hasta la Araucania[3] de Valdivia[4] y el Estrecho de Magallanes.

Cumple el conquistador las mayores aventuras heroicas con la mayor simplicidad. Como si hiciese[5] la cosa más natural del mundo, descubre el Amazonas, descubre el Plata, descubre el Orinoco, descubre el Misisipí, cruza la pampa y los desiertos de Argentina, los llanos de Venezuela, las altiplanicies de México, de Colombia, de Bolivia; pasa por Brasil desde el Atlántico hasta Asunción; duerme entre las cálidas ciénagas, y entre la nieve de los páramos con el hielo por almohada; lucha contra la Naturaleza; vence a los indios; resiste a las fiebres; lucha con sus propios compañeros en choque de ambiciones encontradas; padece la desnudez, el hambre; vive, en suma, una vida cuyo descanso es pelear, como la del héroe cantado por el Romancero.[6]

Aquellos hombres, en presencia de lo maravilloso, sienten un dinamismo, una impetuosidad, una red de aventuras, que los hace renunciar a lo seguro por lo desconocido y lo incierto.

En el dinamismo de aquellos hombres hay algo que corresponde a la época como lo testimonió la empresa misma de Colón y otros navegantes no españoles; el encontrar Colón aventureros que le acompañasen[7] en su empresa y el ver a la América explotada en mucha parte y colonizada por portugueses, ingleses, holandeses, dinamarqueses y franceses. Pero el dinamismo en los conquistadores españoles de América fue máximo, fue, además, esencial para descubrir y someter la mayor porción del continente, desde California hasta Tierra del Fuego, en tan corto espacio de tiempo: menos de cincuenta años.

Gracias a ellos pudo España crear lo que —bueno o malo—existió durante siglos y fue raíz de lo que existe hoy y en lo futuro existirá. España, por su parte, dio lo que tenía.[8]

• CUESTIONARIO

1. ¿Qué importancia tiene el cultivo de la historia?
2. ¿Por qué decimos que los descubridores y conquistadores fueron hombres maravillosos?
3. ¿Quiénes habitaban el continente americano?
4. Mencione algunos de los descubridores españoles junto con sus descubrimientos.
5. ¿Qué país conquistó Pedro de Valdivia?
6. ¿Qué obstáculos tuvo que vencer el conquistador español?
7. ¿Por qué fue máximo el dinamismo de los conquistadores españoles?
8. ¿En qué países se encuentran los ríos Amazonas, Plata, Orinoco y Misisipí?
9. Según Simón Bolívar, ¿cómo se debía llamar la capital de Colombia?
10. ¿Quién era Blanco Fombona?

• SUGGESTED READINGS

Hanke, Lewis, *The Spanish Struggle for Justice in the Conquest of America,* University of Pennsylvania Press, Philadelphia, 1949.

————, "Aristotle and the American Indians," *The Texas Quarterly,* University of Texas, Austin, 1958, no. I.

---

[3] **Araucania,** the land of the Araucanian Indians, in Southern Chile.
[4] Pedro de Valdivia conquered Chile in 1536.
[5] **hiciese = hiciera** (See grammar discussion, Unit 19 §105.)
[6] **Romancero.** The publication of the old Spanish ballads (**romances**) began soon after the invention of printing. The **romances** from the Middle Ages on related in popular language the exploits of heroes, battles, customs, etc.
[7] **acompañasen = acompañaran**
[8] Blanco Fombona (1873–1944), a Venezuelan, has contributed much toward making Spanish American literature more widely known. The reading used here is a condensation of one of his essays in which he defends Spain's role in America.

23

Celebrating Independence

M. *Mariana*   R. *Rosalba*   S. *Second Lieutenant Ramos*   T. *Second Lieutenant Torres*

M. The parade's just now beginning, and they said it would get under way at noon!

R. Mariana, look at the artillerymen at that street corner in their brand-new uniforms.

M. What a good-looking second lieutenant, the one with the gold medal! And see the look he's giving us!

R. Here [behind] comes a bunch [corps] of paratroopers with a little dog for a mascot. —What are those funny-looking things the next ones are wearing?

M. I don't know, but they look like life jackets.

R. Look at all the flowers and streamers they're throwing at the cadets from the Military College.

Celebrando la Independencia   (I)

M. *Mariana*   R. *Rosalba*   S. *Subteniente Ramos*   T. *Subteniente Torres*

M. Ya empieza el desfile, ¡y decían que era a mediodía!

R. Mariana, mira a los artilleros por aquella bocacalle con sus uniformes nuevecitos.

M. ¡Qué subteniente tan guapo, el de la medalla de oro! ¡Y fíjate en la mirada que nos está echando!

R. Detrás viene un cuerpo de paracaidistas con un perrito de mascota. ¿Qué son esas cosas tan raras que llevan puestas esos otros?

M. No sé, pero parece que fueran chalecos salvavidas.

R. Mira todas las flores y serpentinas que les están echando a los cadetes del Colegio Militar.

M. Hope they're all going to the party at the presidential palace tonight! You going to go?

R. Am I! I wouldn't miss that dance for anything in the world. If you want we'll come by for you.

M. Thank you, but you know my parents won't let me go with anybody but them.

R. Then we'll see each other there—oh good heavens! It's starting to rain. We'd better get going; without an umbrella we'll get soaked.

* * *

R. What a lovely dance!

M. Did you see me on the dance floor with the second lieutenant we saw this morning? He told me how he won that decoration.

R. Lucky girl! —I can see him over there talking with another fellow. Say, they're looking this way [toward here].

M. I think they're coming over to the table again. Let's pretend not to notice [Let's make ourselves the pretenders].

* * *

S. Listen to the lively marches the infantry band is playing! Want to go out on the balcony?

R. All right, let's go; then we can [take the opportunity of] see the fireworks that are about to begin.

T. You go ahead; Mariana and I want to see the folk dances.

M. The dancers are forming a semicircle. I think they're going to dance a *zapateado*. What big hats they're wearing!

R. Let us know when they get ready to do the contradance, and also . . .

S. Sh . . . ! The national anthem! The president's coming in.

M. Ojalá que vayan todos esta noche a la fiesta del palacio presidencial. ¿Tú vas a ir?

R. ¡Que si voy! Ese baile no me lo pierdo por nada del mundo. Si quieres pasamos por ti.

M. Te lo agradezco, pero ya sabes que mis padres solamente con ellos me dejan ir.

R. Entonces allá nos vemos. ¡Ay Dios! Está empezando a llover. Mejor vámonos; sin paraguas nos vamos a empapar.

* * *

R. ¡Qué lindo está el baile!

M. ¿Viste que me sacó a bailar el subteniente de esta mañana? Me contó cómo se ganó esa condecoración.

R. ¡Dichosa! Allá lo veo hablando con otro. Fíjate, están mirando hacia acá.

M. Creo que vienen para la mesa otra vez. Hagámonos las disimuladas.

* * *

S. ¡Oigan qué bonitas marchas está tocando la banda de la infantería! ¿Quieren asomarse al balcón?

R. Bueno, vamos y así aprovechamos para ver los fuegos artificiales que ya van a comenzar.

T. Vayan ustedes porque Mariana y yo queremos ver los bailes típicos.

M. Los bailarines están formando un semicírculo. Creo que van a bailar un zapateado (2). ¡Qué sombrerotes llevan!

R. Avísennos cuando vayan a bailar la contradanza (3) y también . . .

S. ¡Sh . . . ! ¡El himno nacional! Viene entrando el presidente.

Cultural Notes

(1) In Latin America there is great popular esteem for a military career. This is overtly expressed in military parades which appeal to the nationalistic feelings of the people. This esteem is reflected in the political power that the army wields and in the fact that many heads of state have been generals. Many generals have been men of letters, too.

(2) The **zapateado,** which is a fast tap dance in 6/8 time performed by a pair of dancers, is common to all Latin America and comes from a popular Andalusian dance of the same name.

(3) The **contradanza,** like the French *contredanse,* derives from the seventeenth-century English *country dance.* Brought to America from Spain, the **contradanza** became the source of a number of Latin-American dances; e.g., the **habanera** and **danzón** in Cuba and the **tango** in Argentina.

129 The meanings of *para*

Direction in space and time	*toward* *for* *to* *on* } = *toward*	Creo que vienen **para** la mesa otra vez. ¿**Para** dónde va? *Where are you heading (for)?* Ya faltan veinticinco **para** las nueve. Van **para** las dos. *It's going on two.* Va **para** la una. *It's going on one.*
Action directed toward goal	*for* *to be a*	Estudia **para** (ser) médico. *He's studying to be a doctor.* Lo único que te pedimos es que no estudies **para** abogado. *(The only thing we ask is that you don't study to be a lawyer.)* Trabajo **para** otra compañía. *I work for another company.*
Object directed toward goal or recipient	*for*	Ah, y una carta **para** mí. Tengo una carta que dictarle, **para** Córdova y Compañía. La vajilla de plata que me habían regalado **para** mi boda. Fue un pretexto **para** discursos contra el Presidente. Hay vacas y toros **para** crianza y lechería. Eso de dos horas **para** el almuerzo no me parece bien.
Action or object directed toward a goal that is itself an action	*to* *in order to* *for* *so that I can* *for me to*	Concedieron hasta mañana **para** pagarla. Vamos por esta calle **para** llegar a la Plaza de Mayo. Parece que entraron por aquí **para** llegar al comedor. ¿Qué mejor oportunidad **para** tomar unas vacaciones? Una herramienta **para** cambiar llantas. *A tool for changing (to change) tires.* Dice un señor si hay ropa vieja **para** vender. (With change of subject: "so that I can . . .":) ¿De parte de quién, **para** decirle? Ven acá **para** enseñarte una cosa. Espere **para** envolvérselos. *(Wait for [me] to wrap them for you.)*
Time deadline	*for* *by*	Ella no dijo que era **para** ayer. —¿**Para** cuándo los quiere? *(By when do you want them?)* —La ropa interior y los calcetines **para** el martes y la de cama **para** el sábado. Estaré allí **para** las dos. *I'll be there by two.*
Comparison: "by the standard of"	*for*	Eres muy grande **para** tu edad. *You're very big for your age.* **Para** médico, sabe poca medicina. *For a doctor, he knows very little medicine.*

The meanings of **para** cluster about the notions of direction, destination, and goal. Review Unit 8 §38 and Unit 11 §58.

A. 1. TEACHER: I think they're coming toward the table.
   STUDENT: **Creo que vienen para la mesa.**
   2. I think they're coming toward the door.
   3. I see they're coming toward the park.
   4. I see they're coming toward the garden.

B. 1. Where are you headed? For the balcony?
   2. Where are you headed? For the palace?
   3. Where are you headed? For the corner?
   4. Where are you headed? For the intersection?

C. 1. It's already going on one o'clock.
   2. It's already going on nine o'clock.
   3. It's already going on eleven o'clock.
   4. It's already going on noon.

D. 1. He's studying to be a doctor.
   2. He's studying to be a lawyer.
   3. He's studying to be a technician.
   4. He's studying to be a dentist.

E. 1. He works for another company.
   2. He plays for another team.
   3. He teaches for another school.

F. 1. Is there a letter for me?
   2. Is there a good conduct certificate for us?
   3. Is there an umbrella for the young lady?
   4. Is there a message for Rosalba?

G. 1. They gave me a set of silverware for my wedding.
   2. They gave me a new dress for my birthday.
   3. They gave me a fur coat for my Saint's day.
   4. They gave us a famous painting for our anniversary.

H. 1. It was a pretext for a speech.
   2. It was a pretext for a meeting.
   3. It was a pretext for a demonstration.
   4. It was a pretext for a strike.

I. 1. There are new uniforms for the artillerymen.
   2. There are gold medals for the paratroopers.
   3. There are streamers for the cadets.
   4. There are life jackets for the second lieutenants.

J. 1. Two hours for lunch is enough.
   2. Four hours for the dance is enough.
   3. Six hours for the party is too much.
   4. Three days for the trip is too much.

K. 1. I have until tomorrow to pay the fine.
   2. I have until tomorrow to find the robber.
   3. We have until Saturday to arrive at a decision.
   4. We have until next week to convince the president.

L. 1. To see the fireworks you have to come out on the balcony.
   2. To see the decorations of the officers you have to come out on the balcony.
   3. To watch the parade of the cadets you have to come out on the balcony.
   4. To watch the contradance and the *zapateado* you have to come out on the balcony.

M. 1. I came to the plaza to hear the infantry band.
   2. She came to the plaza to hear the military marches.
   3. We came to the plaza to hear the presidential address.
   4. He came to the plaza to hear the national anthem.

N. 1. He's here to take advantage of the opportunity.
   2. He's here to begin his studies.
   3. She's here to dance the *zapateado*.
   4. She's here to dismiss the gardener.

O. 1. Are there any old clothes to sell?
   2. Are there any old newspapers to give?
   3. Are there any shirts to take?
   4. Is there any ice cream to eat?

P. 1. Come here so I can show you something.
   2. Come here so I can give you something.
   3. Be quiet so I can tell you something.
   4. Be quiet so I can bring you something.

Q. 1. Wait so I can wrap them for you.
   2. Wait so I can exchange them for you.
   3. Sit down so I can dictate them to you.
   4. Sit down so I can put them on you.

R. 1. When do you want them for? For tomorrow?
   2. When do you want them for? For Wednesday?
   3. When do you want them for? For two o'clock?
   4. When do you want them for? For this evening?

S. 1. I'll be there by two.
   2. I'll be there by six.
   3. We'll be there by tomorrow.
   4. We'll be there by Monday.

T. 1. You're very big for your age.
   2. You're very strong for your age.
   3. She's very tall for her age.
   4. He's very quiet for his age.

U. 1. For [a] professor he doesn't know much.
   2. For [a] technician he doesn't know much.
   3. For [a] government official he knows a lot.
   4. For [a] cook she's very thin.

V. 1. He's too (very) useless to be [a] boss.
   2. He's too nice to be [a] policeman.
   3. He's too nervous to be [a] doctor.
   4. He's too lazy to be [an] administrator.

● DISCUSSION

One of the principal uses of **para**, that of "purpose" with an infinitive, has already been studied in Unit 8 §38. We have also seen **a** used with infinitives after verbs of motion (Unit 7 §33); with these verbs, **a** is usually preferred: **Voy a ver** means *I'll go see* or *I'll go and see;* **Voy para ver** means *I'll go in order to see.*

The meanings of **para** are all related to a single fundamental meaning: that of aim, or towardness. **Para** may have as its object both things and actions. Sometimes, as in the example **Para café bueno no hay como este lugar,** the object is a thing with an action implied: *in order to get good coffee, if your aim is good coffee.*

For the meanings *to study* (*prepare oneself,* etc.) *to be a doctor* (*lawyer, technician,* etc.), Spanish may use or omit the verb **ser: Estudia para (ser) médico (abogado, técnico,** etc.) *He's studying to be a doctor* (*lawyer, technician,* etc.).

130 *Para versus por*

EXAMPLES

A. 1. Vamos **para** el parque. *Let's head for the park.*
   2. Vamos **por** el parque. *Let's go through the park.*

B. 1. Voy allá **para** mis vacaciones. *I'm going there for my vacation* (to have fun).
   2. Voy allá **por** mis vacaciones. *I'm going there for my vacation* (to spend the allotted time there; or, *because of my vacation, on account of my vacation*).

C. 1. Estaré allí **para** febrero. *I'll be there by February.*
   2. Estaré allí **por** febrero. *I'll be there around February.*

D. 1. Me dio el dinero **para** las verduras. *She gave me the money for the vegetables* (to buy them with).
   2. Me dio el dinero **por** las verduras. *She gave me the money for the vegetables* (I sold them to her).

E. 1. Hice todo ese trabajo **para** esto. *I did all that work for this (result).*
   2. Hice todo ese trabajo **por** esto. *I did all that work for this (recompense).*

F. 1. Lo hicimos **para** Juan. *We made* (or *did*) *it for John* (directed our efforts toward him).
   2. Lo hicimos **por** Juan. *We did it for John* (for his sake, from a sense of duty toward him, because of him).

G. 1. Es grande **para** su edad. *He's big for his age.*
   2. Es grande **por** su edad. *He's big because of his age.*

H. 1. Habla **para** tu papá. *Speak for your daddy* (show him how you can).
   2. Habla **por** tu papá. *Speak for your daddy* (because you owe it to him, or on his behalf, or in his place).

I. 1. Entré con cuidado **para** no despertarlos.
I came in carefully in order not to wake them (to carry out this purpose).

2. Entré con cuidado **por** no despertarlos.
I came in carefully in order not to wake them (it was a duty; my precautions were in exchange for not-waking-them).

Por penetrates or pushes; the medium is in contact with the actor.

Para aims; the goal is separated from the actor.

● TRANSLATION DRILL

1. Let's head for the avenue.
Let's go along the avenue.
2. We're headed for Panama.
We're going by way of Panama.
3. I'm leaving for the garden.
I'm leaving through the garden.
4. We're going to Europe for (to spend) our vacation.
We're going to Europe on account of our vacation.
5. He's headed for the café.
He's going for the coffee.
6. Head for the car.
Go for the car.
7. I did it for (as a favor to) my mother.
I did it because of my mother.
8. She gave me the money for (to buy) the eggs.
She gave me the money for (in exchange for) the eggs.
9. He gave me a radio for the car (to install in).
He gave me a radio for the car (in exchange for).

10. I worked for the manager.
I worked in the manager's place.
11. I worked for Diego (he paid me).
I worked for Diego (took his place).
12. I dictated a letter for (to be sent to) the boss.
I dictated a letter for (in place of) the boss.
13. Speak for your grandpa (show him you can).
Speak for your grandpa (in his place).
14. He's strong for his age.
He's strong because of his age.
15. That's the purpose (for that) you bought it for, eh?
That's why you bought it, eh?
16. I bought these flowers for Marta (to keep).
I bought these flowers for Marta (she wasn't able to).
17. I bought the pistol for my uncle (it was a gift).
I bought the pistol because of my uncle (he influenced me).

● DISCUSSION

The root of the contrast between **por** and **para** lies in the way they are used for relationships in space and time. (This is fundamental to all prepositions: *on, at, under, by, from, with,* etc. have as their primary meanings some kind of positional relationship between the things they connect.) In **Fuimos por el parque** *We went through the park,* the actor is in direct contact with the thing—he must be in order to penetrate it. In **Fuimos para el parque** *We headed for the park,* the actor is separated from the park, and only pointed in its direction. The extended, or what we might call figurative, meanings of **por** and **para** carry out this motif of "contact" versus "aim-with-separation":

1. "Proxy" and "exchange": one thing displaces another, as if pushing it out of its place. This calls for **por.** "Correspondence," two things occupying analogous places, is a further extension of this.

2. "Cause": something stimulates or is otherwise responsible for an action. This calls for **por.** We usually think of causation in terms of one thing exerting pressure on another, hence pushing, hence contact. Even where **por** is used with an infinitive as a kind of purpose, it is as if the thing aimed at had somehow got around behind the actor and given him a push. In a sense, this is also a sort of "exchange": **Vamos a la feria por darles gusto a los niños** might be thought of as "We'll

make the effort (bothering to go there) in exchange for the pleasure (that it will give the children),'' just like *I'll give a dollar for the lot,* trading *A* for *B.* On this account, **por** when used for purpose often gives the impression of being grudging: the actor does not look ahead toward doing it, as with **para,** but responds to a push.

3. "Goal," "recipient," and "purpose": these are all manifestations of the towardness of **para.** Where action is concerned, the actor, instead of being pushed, makes his way of his own volition, with a conscious aim and choice. In **Llamó la señora Méndez para un asunto de una rifa,** Mrs. Méndez was busily directing her efforts toward the goal of that raffle. Had the remark been **Llamó la señora Méndez por un asunto de una rifa,** we would have understood that she was perhaps acting just from a sense of duty; something impelled her. In **La criada está arreglando los muebles para los invitados** *The maid is arranging the furniture for the guests,* we see the maid trying to have everything in order so as to please the people who are coming; in **La criada está arreglando los muebles por los invitados** she is doing it because of the guests, that is, because of the obligation they impose; and she is quite likely grumbling at the job.

131   The equivalents of English nouns modifying nouns

	NOUN WITH NO PARTICULAR REFERENT						NOUN WITH NO MODIFIER
1. a	straw	roof	un		techo		paja
2. a	fur	coat	un		abrigo		pieles
3. the	gold	medal	la		medalla		oro
4. a	dining-room	table	una		mesa		comedor
5. high	government	officials	altos		funcionarios		gobierno
6. a	student	manifestation	una		manifestación	de	estudiantes
7. a	bank	employee	un		empleado		banco
8. the	petroleum	refinery	la		refinería		petróleo
9. the	marathon	race	la		carrera		maratón
10. some	business	men	algunos		hombres		negocios[1]
11. the	wheat	crop	la		cosecha		trigo

Where English identifies a noun by modifying it with another noun (naming what it is made of or by, or naming something with which it is regularly associated), Spanish uses a **de** phrase with the equivalent noun. In the above examples the modifying noun does not refer to any particular thing or things, and accordingly Spanish uses no article or other modifier with it (see Unit 14 §83).

	NOUN WITH A PARTICULAR REFERENT			NOUN WITH PARTICULARIZING MODIFIER
1. her neighborhood	church	la capilla		su barrio
2. the living-room	table	la mesa	de	la sala
3. our office	door	la puerta		nuestra oficina

When the modifying noun does refer to a particular thing or things, the appropriate adjective (normally article, demonstrative, or possessive) is used with it. As a rule, an article also appears with the modified noun.

---

[1] **negocio** *piece of business,* **negocios** *business.* See Unit 18 §104.

1. TEACHER: I want a fruit salad.
   STUDENT: **Quiero una ensalada de fruta.**
   TEACHER: We want a chicken salad.
   STUDENT: **Queremos una ensalada de pollo.**
   TEACHER: They want an egg salad.
   STUDENT: **Quieren una ensalada de huevo.**

2. Where does one buy a lottery ticket?
   Where does one buy a theater ticket?
   Where does one buy a streetcar ticket?

3. I prefer corn flour.
   She prefers rice flour.
   They prefer wheat flour.

4. He went with the basketball team.
   She went with the swimming team.
   They went with the boxing team.

5. Domingo is an infantry officer.
   Alberto is an infantry lieutenant.
   Antonio is an infantry sergeant.

6. She bought a country house.
   I bought a summer house.
   He bought a mud house.

7. He has a gold medal.
   They have a gold key.
   She has a gold plate.

8. He's a bank employee.
   He's a bank manager.
   It's a bank check.

9. He's a police officer.
   He's an infantry officer.
   He's a security officer.

10. I bought a wool suit.
    She bought a wool dress.
    He bought a wool tie.

11. Use the hand tool.
    Use the hand brake.
    Use the hand light.

12. We had a philosophy class.
    We had a philosophy test.
    We had a chemistry test.

13. We brought a wedding present.
    I brought an anniversary present.
    He brought a birthday present.

14. Where is there a good engineering school?
    Where is there a good infantry school?
    Where is there a good summer school?

15. Have you seen the football team?
    Have you seen the psychology exam?
    Have you seen the geometry problem?

16. I think there'll be an infantry attack.
    I think there'll be a petroleum refinery.
    I think there'll be an electricity plant.

17. I heard a pistol shot.
    I heard a car horn.
    I heard a car noise.

18. They served us a potato salad.
    Nos sirvieron una ensalada de papas.
    They served us a vegetable salad.
    Nos sirvieron una ensalada de verduras.
    They served us a bean salad.
    Nos sirvieron una ensalada de frijoles.

19. There'll be a student group.
    There'll be a student parade.
    There'll be a student meeting.

20. There was a meeting of traffic chiefs.
    There was a meeting of infantry officers.
    There was a meeting of government lawyers.

21. Where's the office manager?
    ¿Dónde está el gerente de la oficina?
    Where's the office boss?
    ¿Dónde está el jefe de la oficina?
    Where's the office secretary?
    ¿Dónde está la secretaria de la oficina?

22. He went to the Union Club.
    He went to the University club.
    He went to the Beach club.

23. He has the class list.
    She has the class documents.
    They have the class papers.

24. The school doctor is coming later.
    The school bus is coming later.
    The school cook is coming later.

25. Where's the kitchen table?
    Where's the dining-room table?
    Where's the living-room table?

26. I don't like the streetcar noise.
    I don't like the street noise.
    I don't like the traffic noise.

27. Do you know the room number?
    Do you know the house number?
    Do you know the street number?

28. Did you bring the car key?
    Did you bring the house key?
    Did you bring the office key?

29. Where's the city park?
    Where's the city cemetery?
    Where's the city school?

30. I'll meet you at (**en**) the school door.
    I'll meet you at the bank door.
    I'll meet you at the corner door.

31. I heard the infantry hymn.
    I heard the university hymn.
    I heard the school hymn.

32. He has the car (car's) tire.
    I have the bus tire.
    They have the bus schedule.

With rare exceptions, Spanish does not modify nouns directly by nouns. It has a limited number of adjectives which serve the same purpose, for example **universitario** in **los estudiantes universitarios** *university students*. But for the most part the Spanish equivalent of an English noun that modifies another noun is a phrase with **de**. This device is familiar enough in English too, of course: *roof of straw = straw roof*.

The problem is how to manipulate the number (singular or plural) of the modifying noun, and any adjective that may be present. As a rule the English parallel with *of* gives a clue. Thus in *student demonstration* we get *demonstration of students,* since obviously more than one are involved, and the Spanish equivalent is **manifestación de estudiantes**. Similarly *our office door* becomes *the door of our office,* with the Spanish equivalent **la puerta de nuestra oficina**. *An aspirin package* would probably be **un paquete de aspirinas,** since presumably it contains aspirins, plural. But *an aspirin tablet* would be **una pastilla de aspirina,** with aspirin now a substance, hence singular.

But *a bank employee* gives *an employee of a bank,* which, from the Spanish standpoint, contains an unnecessary indefinite article, the one with *bank*. Since *bank* here refers to no particular bank, Spanish simply says **de banco: un empleado de banco**. This contrast becomes clearer in *Did they bring the dining-room table that I bought?* **¿Trajeron la mesa de comedor que compré?** where the speaker refers to a dining-room table by contrast with a library table or a work table, compared with *Dust the dining-room table* **Sacuda la mesa del comedor,** where presumably he refers to the table in *the* dining room. *The car tires* for sale at the automotive supply house are **las llantas de auto;** all we need **de auto** for is to distinguish them from truck tires—they are not associated with any car; but *the car tires need replacing,* if it means the tires of *the* car that belongs to me or is otherwise particularized, calls for **las llantas del auto**. *A prison door has to be strong* calls for **una puerta de cárcel** if spoken by the manufacturer of such doors who thinks of them unattached to any prison; but it calls for **la puerta de una cárcel** if spoken by the jailer who thinks not just of the strength of the door but of how securely it is mounted and locked in a prison—the prison is now a factor in the strength.

Note the difference between *the Spanish class* **la clase de español,** where *Spanish = Spanish language* and is a noun, and *the Spanish class* **la clase española,** where *Spanish* is an adjective and the meaning is perhaps "a class in Spain, with students who are Spaniards," but in which the course studied might be mathematics or engineering.

132 Infinitive phrases and noun clauses as modifiers

EXAMPLES

A.
1. Tenga la bondad **de sentarse.**
2. Tenga cuidado **de no romper** nada.
3. Es la costumbre que han tenido **de llegar** siempre entre ocho y media y nueve menos cuarto. *(It's the habit they've had of arriving.)*
4. Otra cosa que tengo ganas **de ver.**
5. Dio la orden **de disparar.** *He gave the order to shoot.*
6. Es hora **de salir.** *It's time to leave.*

B.
1. Estas materias son imposibles **de estudiar.** *These subjects are impossible to study.*
2. Sus razones son difíciles (fáciles) **de comprender.** *Your reasons are hard (easy) to understand.*

C.
1. ¿Quién fue el primero **en mencionarlo?** *Who was the first to mention it?*
2. El es siempre el último **en decidirse.** *He's always the last to make up his mind.*
3. No quiero ser el único **en atacarlo.** *I don't want to be the only one to attack him.*

NOUN	INFINITIVE PHRASE
the order **la orden**	to shoot **de disparar**

Where English has an infinitive phrase modifying a noun, Spanish uses a phrase with **de.**

ADJECTIVE		INFINITIVE PHRASE
possible easy	impossible hard	to do
posible **fácil**	**imposible** **difícil**	**de hacer**

	INFINITIVE PHRASE
first, second, etc. only one, only man, etc.	to do it
primero, segundo, etc. **único, único hombre,** etc.	**en hacerlo**

Where an infinitive phrase in English modifies *possible* or *easy* and their synonyms and antonyms, Spanish uses a phrase with **de.** With **único** and adjectives of order, Spanish uses a phrase with **en.**

● TRANSLATION DRILL

A. 1. TEACHER: Please come in.
STUDENT: **Tenga la bondad de pasar.**
2. Please wait a minute.
3. Please let us know.
4. Please step out on the balcony.

B. 1. Be careful not to break anything.
2. Be careful not to lose anything.
3. Be careful not to accept anything.
4. Be careful not to touch anything.

C. 1. I don't like the custom of arriving late.
2. I don't like the custom of starting early.
3. I don't like the custom of wearing big hats.
4. I don't like the custom of giving condolences.

D. 1. We're eager to arrive at a decision soon.
2. They're eager to choose a career of equal prestige.
3. I'm eager to thank them for the advice.
4. She's eager to give us a description of the robber.

E. 1. He gave the order to shoot.
2. He gave the order to go to bed.
3. They gave the order to form a semicircle.
4. They gave the order to follow the footprints.

F. 1. It's time to go to the dance.
2. It's time to look for the cat.
3. It's time to serve our country.
4. It's time to pretend we don't notice.

G. 1. This argument is impossible to understand.
Este pleito es imposible de entender.
2. These problems are impossible to understand.
3. This problem was impossible to arrange.
4. This city was impossible to defend.

H. 1. The letter was hard to write.
2. The bill was hard to cover.
3. The little dog was hard to find.
4. The exam was hard to forget.

I. 1. The references were easy to get.
2. The address was easy to find.
3. The book was easy to write.
4. The mice were easy to kill.

J. 1. He was the first to leave.
El fue el primero en salir.
2. She was the first to fly.
3. He was the first to take his shirt off.
4. She was the first to get nervous.

K. 1. She was the second to arrive.
   2. He was the second to congratulate me.
   3. She was the second to suggest another meeting.
   4. He was the second to promise me a party.

L. 1. She was the last to see the mascot.
   2. He was the last to begin the dance.
   3. She would be the last to accept radical ideas.
   4. He would be the last to offer falsified documents.

M. 1. He was the only one to finish.
   2. She was the only one to remain tranquil.
   3. He was the only one to get soaked.
   4. They were the only ones to snore.

EXAMPLES

A. 1. Recibí la noticia **de** que habías salido. *I received the news that you had left (gone away).*
   2. Nunca creí la mentira **de** que hablabas contra mí. *I never believed the lie that you were talking against me.*
   3. Respetaron la orden **de** que todo el mundo se callara. *They respected the order that everyone should keep quiet.*
   4. No merecen nada por la casualidad **de** que fueron los primeros en llegar. *They don't deserve anything for the accident that they were the first to arrive.*
   5. Es hora **de** que se vayan. *It's time for them to go.*
   6. Tenga la seguridad **de** que todos eran documentos falsificados. *(Have the assurance that all were forged documents.)*

B. 1. Recibí la noticia que habías dejado. *I received the news that (which) you had left.*
   2. Nunca creí la mentira que decías contra mí. *I never believed the lie that (which) you were telling against me.*
   3. Respetaron la orden que les dimos. *They respected the order that (which) we gave them.*

NOUN			NOUN CLAUSE ATTACHED TO THE NOUN
the news		that	you had left (gone)
la noticia	**de**	**que**	**habías salido**

NOUN		ADJECTIVE CLAUSE ATTACHED TO THE NOUN	
the news		that which	you had left (left behind)
la noticia		**que**	**habías dejado**

Where English has a noun clause attached to a noun, Spanish puts **de** before its corresponding noun clause. Noun clauses may be distinguished from adjective clauses by the word *that* which normally begins the noun clause but may be changed to *which* or dropped in an adjective clause.

● TRANSLATION DRILL

A. 1. TEACHER: I received the news that you had left.
      STUDENT: **Recibí la noticia de que habías salido.**
   2. I received the news that you had arrived.
   3. I received the news that you had returned.
   4. I received the news that it had rained.

B. 1. I never believed the lie that you were talking against me.
   2. I never believed the lie that you were attacking the schools.
   3. I never believed the lie that he was defending the tyrant.
   4. I never believed the lie that he was opposing the government.

C. 1. They respected the order that everyone keep quiet.
   2. They respected the order that everyone go to bed at nine o'clock.
   3. They respected the order that everyone get up at six o'clock.
   4. They respected the order that everyone wash his hands.

D. 1. It's time that they go.
   2. It's time that they escape.
   3. It's time that they inform themselves.
   4. It's time that they get ahead.

E. 1. Be assured that all were falsified documents.
   2. Be assured that all were suspicious references.
   3. Be assured that all are sincere students.
   4. Be assured that all are lucky girls.

F. 1. I received the news that you had left.
      Recibí la noticia que habías dejado.
   2. I received the news that you had sent.
   3. I received the news that you had brought.
   4. I received the news that you had promised.

G. 1. I saw the clothing you left hanging.
   2. I saw the silver service you mentioned.
   3. We saw the letter you wrote.
   4. We saw the magazine you sent.

H. 1. I never believed the lies they told.
   2. I never believed the excuses they gave.
   3. We never believed the reason they mentioned.
   4. We never believed the headlines we saw.

I. 1. They respected the order which we gave them.
   2. They respected the schedule which we gave them.
   3. She noticed the look which we gave her.
   4. She noticed the certificate which we gave her.

● DISCUSSION

In the previous section we noted that Spanish is not free to use nouns to modify other nouns. The same is true of infinitives (which are nouns in function: see Unit 7 §33) and noun clauses: Spanish turns them into prepositional phrases, usually with **de** or **en,** to make them into modifiers. English sometimes does the same, with *–ing* instead of an infinitive: *my hope to be rewarded* is like *my hope of being rewarded.* Note the parallel use of **de** in all three of the following: **La noticia de su salida** *The news of their departure;* **La noticia de haber salido ellos** *The news of their having left;* **La noticia de que habían salido** *The news that they had left.*

With the **posible-imposible-fácil-difícil** type, it is sometimes necessary to distinguish two meanings. For example, *It is hard to understand* may have *it* as a material subject; e.g., *it = the book (the book is hard to understand),* in which case the Spanish equivalent is **Es difícil de comprender.** Or the same sequence of words may have *it* as a stopgap for *to understand;* i.e., *It is hard to understand = To understand is difficult,* in which case the Spanish equivalent is **Es difícil comprender.** Here the infinitive is the subject of the sentence, not the modifier of *hard.*

Note the use of indicative and subjunctive in the noun clauses of the illustrative sentences: **la noticia de que habías salido** conveys information, while **Es hora de que se vayan** brings an influence to bear. See Unit 17 §97.

133 The masculine referring to both sexes

EXAMPLES
   1. Buenos días, **señores.** *(Good morning, ladies and gentlemen.)*
   2. Tengo muchos **parientes** en el extranjero.
   3. Tienen muy buenos **atletas.**
   4. Los **bailarines** están formando un semicírculo.
   5. No conozco a sus **padres.** *I don't know his father and mother.*

MIXED GROUP	MASCULINE
Mr. and Mrs. Castro	**los señores Castro**
my brothers and sisters	**mis hermanos**
the father and mother ⎱ the parents ⎰	**los padres**
the (men and women) athletes	**los atletas**

Where individuals of both sexes are combined in a group that can be referred to by a single name, Spanish uses the masculine plural of that name. Compare Unit 2 §1.

● TRANSLATION DRILL

A. 1. TEACHER: How many brothers and sisters do you have?
   STUDENT: **¿Cuántos hermanos tiene usted?**
2. How many sons and daughters do you have?
3. How many uncles and aunts do you have?
4. How many nieces and nephews do you have?
5. How many cousins do you have?
6. How many relatives do you have?
7. How many servants do you have?
8. How many employees do you have?
9. How many friends do you have?
10. How many teachers do you have?

B. 1. Good morning, ladies and gentlemen.
2. Good morning, boys and girls.
3. Good afternoon, friends.
4. Good-by, fellows (companions).

C. 1. Many students live around here.
2. Many country folks live around here.
3. Many foreigners live around here.
4. Many Englishmen live around here.
5. Many Mexicans live around here.
6. Many young people live around here.
7. Many athletes live around here.
8. Many idealists live around here.
9. Many government officials live around here.

● DISCUSSION

The masculine plural referring to both sexes is a characteristic of Spanish, even in pairs or groups like **los reyes** *the king and queen,* where a single term referring to both male and female would seem odd in English.

Where it is necessary to separate the sexes, Spanish can use the masculine with exclusively male reference, as in the following: —**¿Tú tienes nueve** *hermanos?* —**Sí, cinco** *hermanos* y **cuatro hermanas.**

● COMBINED PATTERN REPLACEMENT DRILL

A. 1. **Voy a comprar el regalo para el señor.**
2. _____señores
3. _____ por _____
4. Vamos _____
5. _____ vender _____
6. _____ las flores _____
7. _____señora
8. _____ de _____
9. _____ traer _____
10. _____ los libros _____
11. _____señoritas
12. _____ estudiar _____
13. _____ con _____
14. Van _____
15. _____señorita
16. _____ sin _____
17. Va _____
18. _____ la carta _____
19. _____ contestar _____
20. _____ por _____
21. _____gerente
22. Voy _____
23. _____ dictar _____
24. _____ para _____

B. 1. **Mire, señor; parece que están durmiendo.**
2. _____ roncando
3. _____ está _____
4. _____ rabiando
5. Fíjese _____
6. _____ veo _____
7. _____ rezando
8. _____ señorita _____
9. _____ creo _____
10. _____ paseando
11. _____ supongo _____
12. _____ estén _____
13. Figúrese _____

14. _____ dudo _____
15. _____ consultando
16. _____ esté _____
17. _____ señora _____
18. Bueno _____
19. _____ comparando
20. _____ espero _____
21. _____ participando
22. _____ señores _____
23. _____ prefiero _____
24. _____ estén _____
25. _____ trabajando
26. _____ estudiando

- TENSE SUBSTITUTION REVIEW DRILL

Sequence of tenses: review of imperfect indicative and imperfect subjunctive. INSTRUCTIONS: Repeat the following sentences just as you hear them. Then repeat them again, substituting the preterit for the present of **decir**.

A. 1. TEACHER: Me dice que es Juan. _Repita._
STUDENT: **Me dice que es Juan.**
TEACHER: _Cambie._
STUDENT: **Me dijo que era Juan.**

2. Me dice que es perezoso.
3. Me dice que hay algunos beneficios.
4. Me dice que lo llaman chato.
5. Me dice que tiene la nariz aplastada.
6. Me dice que tiene una cicatriz en la cara.
7. Me dice que pesa sesenta kilos.
8. Me dice que vive detrás del parque.
9. Me dice que van hacia la ruina.

B. 1. Dicen que está muy bien hecho.
2. Dicen que está de duelo.
3. Dicen que les duele todo el cuerpo.
4. Dicen que odia a todo el mundo.
5. Dicen que está rodeado de problemas.
6. Dicen que es un caso raro.
7. Dicen que es Juan Pérez, alias el Gato.
8. Dicen que viene hacia esta bocacalle.
9. Dicen que así es, según el médico.

C. 1. Me dice que esté aquí mañana.
Me dice que esté aquí mañana.
Me dijo que estuviera aquí mañana.

2. Me dice que termine pronto.
3. Me dice que saque la lengua.
4. Me dice que me quite la camisa.
5. Me dice que me siente en la mesa.
6. Me dice que me vaya a la casa.
7. Me dice que me acueste temprano.
8. Me dice que me tome estas pastillas.
9. Me dice que no me levante mañana.

D. 1. Dicen que empecemos por el principio.
2. Dicen que no hablemos tan fuerte.
3. Dicen que lleguemos más temprano.
4. Dicen que hagamos bien el trabajo.
5. Dicen que comamos en una hora.
6. Dicen que consultemos con el gerente.
7. Dicen que no comparemos tanto.
8. Dicen que no olvidemos lo del horario.
9. Dicen que nos callemos.

READING

Un poquito sobre la derivación

PROFESOR: Voy a hablarles hoy sobre la derivación de las palabras. Ya empleamos la palabra _derivación_ con el sentido de _origen_ o _etimología_ de una palabra. Ahora voy a usar la misma palabra, _derivación,_ de una manera un poco diferente: es decir, la formación de una palabra nueva por medio de la adición de un sufijo. Ya hemos tenido muchos ejemplos en el libro que estamos estudiando.

Por ejemplo: los diminutivos. Ustedes todos saben que hay en español lo que llamamos sufijos diminutivos, como _–ito, –cito, –illo,_ etcétera, que muestran que la idea básica o fundamental de la palabra, es decir la raíz,[1] se nos presenta con una alteración de significado: la de pequeñez. Así es que una *casita* es una casa pequeña; un *perrito* es un perro pequeño; una *maquinilla* es una máquina pequeña, etc. Pero hay otras consideraciones. Veamos otras formas tales como *Paquito, Lupita, Juanita* y *Pedrito.* Aquí no se trata sólo de pequeñez; hay también la noción de juventud. Paquito no sólo es pequeño de estatura; es también un chico. Y una *señorita* no es necesariamente más pequeña que una señora: aun puede ser más grande. Pero por lo general una señorita es más joven que una señora, y casi siempre es soltera.[2] Y al fin hay que añadir que el empleo de un diminutivo lleva muchas veces una noción de cariño, de intimidad: en breve, de varios grados de expresión que reflejan el *sentimiento* del que habla. Si digo que tal o cual cosa[3] es *nuevecita,* no digo meramente que es nueva; yo digo más bien que es muy nueva, o que es de una novedad que apruebo, que me gusta. Me acuerdo de haber leído una comedia en que se describía a dos novios *juntitos en un rinconcito.* Este es un buen ejemplo de la *afectividad* en el discurso. El autor hubiera podido decir *juntos en un rincón*—pero esto podría decirse de dos muebles. El diminutivo *juntitos* sugiere un grado de intimidad personal que faltaría a la forma *juntos.* Y *rinconcito* sugiere un lugar—un lugarcito, ¿eh?—apropiado para dos novios que quieren estar solos.

Para mañana . . .

---

[1] *root*   [2] *unmarried*   [3] *this or that*

Las literaturas hispánicas

Según el humanista Alfonso Reyes[1] el panorama de las literaturas hispánicas no es fácil de abarcar. Los mejores manuales que tenemos carecen de perspectiva y en los peores la información es defectuosa. Por eso, para el que desee de veras conocer a los autores hispánicos es mejor acudir a las fuentes.[2] Es una verdad general, dice Reyes, que el conocimiento de una literatura no puede comunicarse de modo automático, como en extractos de vitaminas, sino en alimentos vivos que han de pasar por el paladar, es decir, por la conciencia del lector.

Toda literatura admite el ser estudiada en torno a unos cuantos nombres eminentes (Shakespeare, Cervantes, Dante, Goethe, etc.). Pero hay más: en España por ejemplo, desde sus primeros balbuceos (que se han descubierto recientemente en las *jarchas* mozárabes) hasta las tres mil obras literarias que anualmente se imprimen solamente en España, ésta no ha dejado de enriquecer la literatura universal con las producciones de su genio. Las *jarchas* son estribillos líricos de algunas canciones árabes, en un español deliciosamente arcaico, de la primera mitad del siglo once:

> Señor mío Ibrahim,[3]
> oh nombre dulce,
> vente a mí[4]
> de noche.
> Si no, si no quieres,
> me iré a ti:
> dime en dónde
> encontrarte.

Sabemos que más recientemente, aun a primeros del siglo pasado, los románticos de

---

[1] See page 189, footnote 9.

[2] *i.e.,* the original works and authors

[3] The original *jarcha* was a recurring refrain in a longer Arabic or Hebrew poem. The original of the above *jarcha* is: Mió sidi Ibrahim,//ya nuemne dolye,//vente mib//de nojte.// In non, si non queris,//iréme tib://garme a ob//legarte. The interesting part of these *jarchas* is that they prove that there was a popular poetry in Spain as early as the eleventh century, or even before. Ibrahim was a popular Arabic name. This may refer to Ibrahim Al-Mausili (742–804), a singer in the Caliph's court.

[4] **vente a mí** *come to me* (See Unit 12 §67 for the reflexive **vente.**)

Alemania, Francia e Inglaterra buscaban en la literatura española modelos y fuentes de inspiración.[5]

¿Cuáles son los valores más consistentes y el motivo principal de la fascinación que la literatura española ha ejercido a través de las edades y por encima de todos los gustos y estilos literarios? La razón obvia es que la literatura representa la expresión más completa y demócrata de la cultura hispana a través de los siglos, porque sus escritores reflejan las actitudes prevalecientes y se dirigen a un público que ellos creen interpretar.

La literatura española es muy distinta de las otras europeas. Es muy difícil leer una obra literaria española—ya sea en el original ya sea[6] en traducción—sin darse cuenta de su españolidad íntima. Es tan fuertemente caracterizada, y hasta cierto punto es tan exclusiva, que es muy difícil para uno que no sea hispano comprenderla perfectamente, interpretarla, clasificarla y hasta traducirla. Las razones son obvias: España, aunque parte integrante del mundo latino, bañada en su costa oriental por el mar Mediterráneo que es la cuna de la civilización occidental, ha formado siempre geográfica y espiritualmente una entidad aparte, independiente y por largos períodos aislada.

La aparente falta de consistencia en el carácter español, dividido por corrientes contradictorias, se refleja naturalmente en la literatura. El dualismo hispano, con sus poderosas corrientes individualistas e idealistas, constituye la fuente y razón de ser de una literatura que es, con mucha frecuencia, paradójica. Es *realista* en su visión del mundo y en su actitud ante la vida y los problemas esenciales, pero al mismo tiempo nunca carece del *idealismo* de una raza

que siempre quiere alcanzar las estrellas, aunque sepa que es un sueño imposible. Puede ser *amoral,* en sus pícaros, lo mismo que *mística* en sus santos: ambos, el pícaro y el santo, productos de la misma civilización, son expresiones geniales[7] del mismo pueblo. Sólo es dado a los grandes genios literarios (Cervantes, Lope de Vega, Quevedo,[8] Galdós,[9] García Lorca[10] y Juan Ramón Jiménez,[11] para citar únicamente unos pocos) alcanzar una síntesis armónica de tales cualidades que en apariencia son contradictorias.

El mismo Don Quijote y los otros caracteres de la novela: Sancho Panza, Dulcinea del Toboso[12] y hasta el mismo Rocinante,[13] son ya nombres comunes en la literatura universal. Miguel de Cervantes, con su creación genial, empieza la novela moderna y al dar expresión inmortal a todas las facetas del carácter español, produce la síntesis más acabada de los ideales que inspiran a España en su Siglo de Oro[14] y en épocas sucesivas. El Lazarillo de Tormes[15] es el pícaro por excelencia, el anti-héroe[16] de la España imperial del Siglo de Oro, simpático y a veces malicioso, pero lo perdonamos.

El teatro español del siglo diecisiete ha enriquecido la escena universal con figuras originales. Lope de Vega, a quien Cervantes llamó el "monstruo de la naturaleza", escribió más de ochocientas comedias en verso. El gran burlador, Don Juan Tenorio, creado por Tirso de Molina, es el primero de una larga dinastía que, sin interrupción, llega al teatro moderno, pues cada generación ha querido recrear la figura del clásico seductor. Calderón de la Barca creó a Segismundo, que en *La vida es sueño*[17] combina con fuerza y profundidad los

---

[5] Martin Hume's *Spanish Influence on English Literature* discusses the borrowing of Spanish plots by English and French dramatists.

[6] **ya sea . . .ya sea** *whether it be . . . or*   [7] **geniales** *of genius*

[8] Gómez de Quevedo y Villegas (1580–1645) was a satirical and humorous author whose works are full of clever puns, conceits, and quips. His religious verses, however, show a deep intensity.

[9] Benito Pérez Galdós (1843–1920) was probably the greatest novelist of Spain during the nineteenth century. His works are novels of contemporary problems as well as national episodes from 1808 on.

[10] García Lorca, one of Spain's most promising poets, was murdered during the Spanish Civil War, 1936.

[11] Juan Ramón Jiménez (1881–1958) was awarded the Nobel Prize for literature in 1956. His work *Platero y yo* was recently translated into English by Eloise Roach and published by the University of Texas Press as *Platero and I.*

[12] Dulcinea del Toboso was Don Quixote's "lady" (in reality a peasant) to whom he dedicated his victories.

[13] The famous horse of Don Quixote.

[14] **Siglo de Oro,** the 16th and 17th centuries.

[15] *Lazarillo de Tormes,* the world-famous picaresque novel, published in 1554, was translated into English by Sir Clements Markham and was published in London in 1908.

[16] **anti-héroe** *anti-hero* was a term coined by Chandler in his *Romances of Roguery* and *The Literature of Roguery,* to imply that the rogue possesses qualities the reverse of those we look for in a hero, hence "anti-hero."

[17] *La vida es sueño,* masterpiece of Calderón de la Barca, is a philosophical drama about human life and destiny.

grandes problemas del mundo. Faltaría algo si no se añadiera a esta lista de caracteres inmortales creados por la literatura española al *Gitano,* inmortalizado por el *Romancero*[18] de García Lorca, el Crispín, de *Los intereses creados,* de Benavente,[19] y ¿por qué no? Platero, el simpático burrito poetizado por Juan Ramón Jiménez.

Los países hispanoamericanos han heredado más que la lengua. Con ella toda una cultura y una riqueza de formas y matices que espiritualmente les une y les permite compartir unos con otros y con España las mismas glorias. La literatura de la Península Ibérica, especialmente la del Siglo de Oro, es la fuente en la que todavía beben algunos de los escritores que usan la lengua castellana, aunque se sabe que las naciones de la América española ya empezaban a madurar a fines de las guerras de independencia.

Bajo nuevos horizontes y distintos impulsos, la cultura se diversifica con nuevas formas, nuevos temas y nuevas inquietudes. Todo ello abre a las literaturas hispanas en ambos continentes unas perspectivas para el futuro que, en las literaturas occidentales, sólo pueden hallar paralelo en las literaturas que usan el inglés.

Citemos otra vez a Alfonso Reyes:

"Las literaturas hispanas, de Europa y de América, no representan una mera curiosidad, sino que son parte esencial en el acervo[20] de la cultura humana. El que las ignora, ignora por lo menos lo suficiente para no entender en su plenitud las posibilidades del espíritu; lo suficiente para que su imagen del mundo sea una horrible mutilación. Hasta es excusable pasar por alto algunas zonas europeas que no pertenecen al concepto goethiano[21] de la Literatura Mundial. Pero pasar por alto la literatura hispánica es inexcusable. El que la ignora está fuera de la cultura . . .

"Por lo que respecta a la sola literatura,[22] hay que analizar de cerca el fenómeno. Nuestra América no ha producido *todavía* un Dante,[23] un Shakespeare, un Cervantes, un Goethe. Nuestra literatura, como conjunto, ofrece un aspecto de improvisación y también de cosa incompleta. No nos detengamos a saber por qué. Preguntémonos simplemente si puede una literatura en tal estado aspirar a ser indispensable en el cuadro de la cultura humana. No dudamos en afirmarlo . . .

"En resumen: no somos una lengua muerta para entretenimiento de especialistas. El orbe hispano nunca se vino abajo, ni siquiera a la caída del imperio español, sino que se ha multiplicado en numerosas facetas de ensanches[24] todavía insospechados. Nuestra lengua y nuestra cultura están en marcha, y en ellas van transportadas algunas simientes de porvenir. No somos una curiosidad para aficionados, sino una porción integrante y necesaria del pensamiento universal. No somos pueblos en estado de candor, que se deslumbren fácilmente con los instrumentos externos de que se acompaña la cultura, sino pueblos que heredan una vieja civilización y exigen la excelencia misma de la cultura . . .

"No nos sentimos inferiores a nadie, sino hombres en pleno disfrute de capacidades equivalentes a las que se cotizan en plaza.[25] Y por lo mismo que han sido muy amargos nuestros sufrimientos; y por lo mismo que hoy nos defraudan los maestros que nos enseñaron a confiar en el bien, recibimos con los brazos abiertos, y con la conciencia cabal de nuestros actos, al que se nos acerca con una palabra sincera de entendimiento, de armonía y de concordia. Nuestro júbilo es grande cuando esa palabra nos viene de la gente que ha hecho del respeto humano su actual bandera . . ."[26]

---

[18] *Romancero* is a collection of ballads. García Lorca's gypsy ballad collection was published in 1927 and has gone through many editions. It is considered the best interpretation of the gypsy spirit that has ever been published.

[19] Crispín and his master, Leandro, symbolize the two sides of humanity, like Sancho and Quixote, the base and the ideal, inevitably bound together. The *Bonds of Interest* (*Los intereses creados*) helped to win for its author the Nobel Prize in literature (1922). It has been translated into English.   [20] **acervo** *storehouse*

[21] One of Goethe's notions of world literature was that the whole domain of poetry is an enchanted island like Prospero's and is enlarged by every poet. Goethe discovered the beauty of Arab and Persian poetry and said: "East and West are no more severed. They both belong to God." (From a lecture by Ernst Robert Curtius in Aspen, Colorado, 1949, at the Goethe Bicentennial Convocation.)   [22] **Por lo que respecta a la sola literatura** *As for literature alone*

[23] Dante, celebrated Italian poet, author of the *Divine Comedy,* 1265–1321.   [24] **ensanches** *expansion*

[25] **se cotizan en plaza** *are quoted in the market* (This is a common expression used in commercial Spanish.)

[26] Alfonso Reyes, *Ultima Tule,* Imprenta Universitaria, Mexico, 1942, pp. 213, *et passim.*

CUESTIONARIO

1. ¿Qué son las *jarchas?*
2. ¿Qué literaturas han influido en la literatura española?
3. ¿Qué valores y motivos persistentes hay en la literatura española?
4. ¿Por qué es algo difícil leer una obra literaria española para una persona no latina?
5. ¿Cuáles son los escritores que logran una síntesis armónica de las características del español?
6. ¿Cuál es la obra maestra de Miguel de Cervantes?
7. ¿Qué representa el *Lazarillo de Tormes?*
8. Mencione a tres escritores importantes del teatro español del siglo XVII y sus obras.
9. ¿Qué caracteres inmortales crearon García Lorca, Benavente y Juan Ramón Jiménez?
10. ¿Qué aspectos de España han heredado los países hispanoamericanos?
11. ¿Quién era Alfonso Reyes?
12. Según Alfonso Reyes, ¿por qué es inexcusable pasar por alto la literatura hispánica?
13. Resume la posición actual del orbe hispánico según Alfonso Reyes.

SUGGESTED READINGS

Arciniegas, Germán, *The Green Continent,* Knopf, New York, 1944: Part II, pp. 184–93, "Saint Rose of Lima."

Barea, Arturo, *Lorca: The Poet and His People,* Grove, New York, 1957.

Beals, Carleton, *Lands of the Dawning Morrow,* Bobbs-Merrill, Indianapolis, New York, 1948: Ch. 1, "Memories of the Future"; Ch. 5, "Dynamo"; Ch. 10, "The March of Books"; Ch. 11, "New Pictures"; Ch. 12, "New Forces"; Ch. 13, "Democratic Profiles"; Ch. 14, "Mosaic."

Benavente, Jacinto, *The Bonds of Interest* (tr. by John Garrett Underhill), Scribner's, New York, 1917, vol. I.

Calderón de la Barca, Pedro, *Life Is a Dream,* The Harvard Classics, Collier, New York, 1910, vol 26.

Flores, Angel and Dudley Poore, eds., *Fiesta in November,* Houghton Mifflin, New York, 1942. [An anthology of Spanish-American short stories]

Frank, Waldo, *Tales from the Argentine,* Farrar and Rinehart, New York, 1930: Ch. 4, "The Private Life of Facundo"; Ch. 2, "Death of a Gaucho."

Henríquez-Ureña, Pedro, *Literary Currents in Hispanic America,* Harvard University Press, Cambridge, 1945

Jiménez, Juan Ramón, *Platero and I* (tr. by Eloise Roach), University of Texas Press, Austin, 1957.

———, *Platero and I* (tr. by William and Mary Roberts), Dusches, New York, 1956.

———, *The Selected Writings of Juan Ramón Jiménez* (ed. by H. R. Hays), Grove, New York, 1957.

Johnson, Mildred E., *Spanish Poems of Love,* Exposition Press, New York, 1955.

Menéndez Pidal, Ramón, *The Spaniards in Their History* (tr. by Walter Starkie), Norton, New York, 1950.

Reyes, Alfonso, *The Position of America* (tr. by Harriet de Onís), Knopf, New York, 1950.

Sacks, Norman P., "Hispanic Literature and Civilization in English Translation," *Hispania,* XLII (December, 1959), pp. 567–70.

Torres-Ríoseco, Arturo, *The Epic of Latin-American Literature,* Oxford University Press, New York, 1946.

The OAS

SEC. *Secretary General*   R. *Rodrigo*   E. *Ernesto*
L. *Lucía*   MRS. DE L. *Mrs. de Lérida*
IST R. *First reporter*   2ND R. *Second reporter*

SEC. . . . But more than a personal honor, it is a great privilege for our republic that the OAS should have elected . . .

R. What a fine speaker Dr. de Lérida is!

E. He will do an important job [role] in Washington as Secretary General of the Organization of American States.

SEC. . . . one of her own citizens for the important task of coordinating the efforts of the American nations . . .

R. I hear the vote was unanimous.

E. That's because he turned in such a brilliant performance when he was our ambassador to the OAS.

La OEA (1)

SEC. *Secretario General*   R. *Rodrigo*   E. *Ernesto*
L. *Lucía*   SRA. DE L. *Señora de Lérida*
R.I. *Repórter 1*   R.2. *Repórter 2*

SEC. . . . Pero más que un honor personal es un alto privilegio para nuestra República que la OEA haya elegido . . .

R. ¡Qué bien habla el Dr. (2) de Lérida!

E. Hará un gran papel en Washington como Secretario General de la Organización de los Estados Americanos.

SEC. . . . a uno de sus ciudadanos para la importante tarea de coordinar los esfuerzos de las naciones americanas . . .

R. Me dijeron que la votación fue unánime.

E. Es que tuvo una brillante actuación cuando era nuestro Embajador ante la OEA.

SEC. . . . in behalf of the peace, the security, and the progress of the peoples of the Western Hemisphere. Thank you very much.

ALL (*applause and shouts*) Bravo! Magnificent!

* * *

L. Mrs. de Lérida, I congratulate you on your husband's magnificent speech.

MRS. DE L. Thanks so much, dear; you are always so kind.

L. I can imagine how many things you must have to do before leaving for the United States.

MRS. DE L. Oh, don't even mention it! Buying furniture, clothing, and all, besides the receptions and farewell parties. If we had realized it before . . .

L. Oh well, you'll settle down after you get there.

MRS. DE L. You're so right: although just looking for a house and getting settled will take us a good while. Here comes Mrs. Rodó. —Rosita, how nice to see you! I'd like to have you meet Lucía Amenábar.

* * *

1ST R. Dr. de Lérida, what is the guiding principle of the OAS?

SEC. Cooperation among all the nations of this hemisphere to solve their common problems.

1ST R. What are the areas of action in this respect?

SEC. Well, for example, better education to eliminate illiteracy, and improvement of sanitary conditions.

1ST R. Is anything being done about the farm problem and the housing shortage?

SEC. Yes. The OAS is cooperating in the improvement of techniques to raise the economic level and the standard of living in general.

2ND R. What would the OAS do in case of disagreement between two American republics?

SEC. If it should turn out that there was [this meant] a danger to the peace, the OAS Council would send an investigating commission.

2ND R. And after the commission's report?

SEC. . . . en pro de la paz, la seguridad y el progreso de los pueblos del Hemisferio Occidental. He dicho (3).

TODOS (*aplausos y voces*) ¡Muy bien! ¡Muy bien! ¡Magnífico!

* * *

L. Sra. de Lérida, la felicito por el magnífico discurso de su esposo.

SRA. DE L. Muchas gracias, linda; siempre tan amable.

L. Me imagino la de cosas (4) que tendrá que hacer antes de partir a los Estados Unidos.

SRA. DE L. Ay, no me diga. Comprar muebles, ropa, de todo; fuera de las recepciones, despedidas. Si lo hubiéramos sabido antes . . .

L. En fin, ya estarán tranquilos cuando hayan llegado.

SRA. DE L. Imagínese, aunque eso de buscar casa e instalarse nos tomará un buen tiempo. Ahí viene la Sra. de Rodó. Rosita, qué gusto de verte. Te presento a Lucía Amenábar.

* * *

R.1. Dr. de Lérida: ¿cuál es el principio operante de la OEA?

SEC. La cooperación entre todas las naciones de este hemisferio para solucionar los problemas comunes.

R.1. ¿Cuáles son los campos de acción en este sentido?

SEC. Por ejemplo, una mejor educación para eliminar el analfabetismo (5) y el mejoramiento de las condiciones sanitarias.

R.1. ¿Se hace algo en cuanto al problema de la agricultura y la escasez de viviendas?

SEC. Sí. La OEA coopera en mejorar las técnicas para elevar el nivel económico (6) y de vida en general.

R.2. ¿Qué haría la OEA en el caso de un conflicto entre dos repúblicas americanas?

SEC. Si se hubiera encontrado que esto significara un peligro para la paz, el Consejo de la OEA enviaría una Comisión Investigadora.

R.2. ¿Y después del informe de la Comisión?

SEC. The necessary recommendations would be made to both countries. We have always been successful in this. It's an example for the whole world.

SEC. Se harían las recomendaciones necesarias a ambos países. Siempre hemos tenido éxito en esto. Es un ejemplo para todo el mundo.

Cultural Notes

(1) The OEA, *Organización de los Estados Americanos* (called in English OAS, standing for Organization of American States) is a regional organization of the republics of the Western Hemisphere. The Pan-American ideal which it represents dates from Simón Bolívar, the Liberator of the northern part of South America, who first called a conference of the American republics in Panama in 1826. Since 1889, Pan-American conferences have been regularly held in various capital cities. The Pan American Union, which later became what is now known as the Organization of American States, was a forerunner of the League of Nations and the United Nations.

(2) The title of **doctor** is conferred in many Latin-American countries upon a graduate of any of several schools of a university, including law (in some countries, the graduate of a law school receives the title of **licenciado,** abbreviated **Lic.**). It is coveted because of the prestige it confers.

(3) **He dicho** (i.e., *I have said,* roughly equivalent to *I have spoken*) is a standard way of concluding an address, and is a translation of Latin *dixi,* which was used by the ancient Romans under similar circumstances.

(4) **La de cosas** is short for **la mar de cosas.** Cf. *sea of troubles,* in Shakespeare's *Hamlet.*

(5) Illiteracy is high in some Latin-American countries; in others, such as Argentina, Uruguay, and Costa Rica, it is low. Mexico has made heroic efforts to banish illiteracy among the rural folk, efforts marked by missionary zeal on the part of teachers and government alike. One of the greatest obstacles in some countries is the large Indian population whose native language is not Spanish (the languages of the Aztec and Mayan linguistic families, for example, are among the most important of those spoken by Indians in Mexico and Central America).

(6) The economic life of most Latin-American nations depends on the export of raw materials and the import of manufactured goods. Their economies are largely tied to one or two products (e.g., Brazil to coffee, Bolivia to tin, Venezuela to iron ore and petroleum, Cuba to sugar, Honduras to bananas, etc.). The United States is Latin America's principal customer for such products as coffee, copper, nitrates, bananas, sugar, cacao, chicle, cotton, silver, and other minerals. Latin America also supplies important materials which the United States lacks, such as antimony, manganese, mercury, quartz crystal, chromium, mica, tin, and tungsten.

A single-crop or single-product economy can put a country in serious difficulty if the world market for the commodity fails; for example, Chile suffers with any drop in the price of copper. This is why most suggestions for the improvement of Latin America's economy usually include a diversification of crops and an increase in industrialization.

134 Derivation

EXAMPLES

A. 1. La OEA **coopera** en mejorar las técnicas.
   2. La **cooperación** entre todas las naciones.

B. 1. Ya se está **organizando** un grupo para ir.
   2. Secretario General de la **Organización** de los Estados Americanos.

C. 1. La OEA coopera en **mejorar** las técnicas.
   2. **Mejoramiento** de las condiciones sanitarias.

D. 1. **Siento** tanto que Mr. Roberts renunciara al puesto.
   2. Lo dijo con **sentimiento.** *He said it with regret.*

E. 1. Me contó cómo se **ganó** esa condecoración.
   2. Los cerdos dejan bastante **ganancia** en la feria.

F. 1. No le **importaba** que llegáramos un poquito tarde.
   2. No tiene **importancia,** don Domingo.

VERB	NOUN
cooperar	cooperación
organizar	organización
mejorar	mejoramiento
sentir	sentimiento
ganar	ganancia
importar	importancia

The suffixes **–ción, –miento,** and **–ncia** derive nouns from verbs.

EXAMPLES

A. 1. Estaba **enfermo** del corazón.
   2. Ya sabe usted qué traicioneras son esas **enfermedades.**

B. 1. Quedo de ustedes su atento y **seguro** servidor. *(I remain your attentive and sure [dependable] servant.)*
   2. En pro de la paz, la **seguridad** y el progreso.

ADJECTIVE	NOUN
enfermo	enfermedad
seguro	seguridad

The suffix **–dad** derives nouns from adjectives.

EXAMPLES

A. 1. La cooperación entre todas las **naciones** de este hemisferio.
   2. ¡Sh . . . ! ¡El himno **nacional!**

B. 1. ¿Cómo vamos de aquí al **centro?** *(How do we go from here to the center?)*
   2. Viven cerca del Parque **Central.**

NOUN	ADJECTIVE
nación	nacional
centro	central

The suffix **–al** derives adjectives from nouns.

INSTRUCTIONS: Repeat the following sentences just as you hear them. Then substitute the items listed for the word italicized, making necessary correlated changes. Be prepared to translate the new derived forms.

1. TEACHER: Del verbo *votar* viene el sustantivo votación. *Repita.*
   STUDENT: **Del verbo votar viene el sustantivo votación.**
   TEACHER: (imaginar)
   STUDENT: **Del verbo imaginar viene el sustantivo imaginación.**

   (exagerar, terminar, declarar, informar, coordinar, instalar, organizar, cooperar, falsificar, participar, formar, indicar, invitar, felicitar, explicar, importar, presentar, eliminar, celebrar, investigar, elevar, preocupar, dedicar, significar)

2. Del verbo *casar* viene el sustantivo casamiento.

   (pensar, tratar, llamar, mandar, acompañar, levantar, aprovechar, mejorar)

3. El sustantivo *agradecimiento* viene del verbo agradecer.

   (entendimiento, conocimiento, ofrecimiento, recibimiento, cumplimiento, rompimiento, sacudimiento, merecimiento)

4. Del verbo ganar viene el sustantivo *ganancia.*

   (importancia, creencia, sugerencia, existencia, insistencia, preferencia)

● ITEM SUBSTITUTION DRILL

1. Del adjetivo *relativo* viene el sustantivo relatividad.

   (cómodo, sincero, oportuno, tranquilo, nervioso, bárbaro, seguro)

2. El sustantivo puntualidad viene del adjetivo *puntual.*

   (regular, útil, real, feroz, total, común, brutal, fatal, casual, fácil, nacional)

3. El sustantivo seriedad es del adjetivo *serio.*
   (sucio, antiguo, enfermo, solo)

4. El adjetivo igual da el sustantivo *igualdad.*
   (maldad, bondad)

5. El sustantivo *posibilidad* es del adjetivo posible.

   (probabilidad, amabilidad, imposibilidad, respetabilidad)

● ITEM SUBSTITUTION DRILL

1. Lo que es de la *profesión* se llama profesional.
   (nación, educación, flor, materia, policía, presidencia, fruta, idea, forma, medicina, secretaria, persona, semana)

2. Lo que es del *centro* es central.
   (colegio, documento, artificio, fenómeno,

   bruto, campo, ministerio, secretario, consejo, teatro, fin, común, occidente)

3. El adjetivo *invernal* viene del sustantivo invierno.

   (puntual, señorial, dominical, lateral, mortal)

EXAMPLES

A. 1. Hay que ponerlos en **orden.** *It is necessary to put them in order.*
   2. Le ruego que me perdone por el **desorden** de la casa.

B. 1. ¿Está **compuesto** ya? *Is it fixed already?*
   2. Sí, pero está **descompuesto.**

C. Tiene sus **ventajas** y **desventajas.**

D. 1. Se harían las recomendaciones **necesarias.**
   2. Son condiciones **innecesarias.** *They are unnecessary conditions.*

E. 1. Vuelva lo más pronto **posible.**
   2. **Imposible,** señora.

AFFIRMATIVE	NEGATIVE
orden	**desorden**
componer	**descomponer**
ventaja	**desventaja**
necesario	**innecesario**
posible	**imposible**

The prefixes **des–** and **in–, im–** reverse the meanings.

1. Lo contrario de *orden* es desorden.
   (acuerdo, honor, nivel, prestigio, unión, ventaja, apego, empleo)
2. Lo contrario de *atento* es desatento.
   (considerado, empleado, encantado, enredado, hecho, igual, ocupado, unido)
3. Lo contrario de *arreglar* es desarreglar.
   (colgar, conocer, contar, decir, doblar, envolver, esperar, hacer, mejorar, merecer, organizar, peinar, preocuparse)
4. Lo contrario de *acción* es inacción.
   (comodidad, competencia, decisión, oportunidad, par, puntualidad, seguridad)
5. Lo contrario de *dependiente* es independiente.
   (directo, exacto, necesario, perfecto, personal, posible, probable, puntual, puro, tranquilo)

● DISCUSSION

Most languages have elements which can be added to words of certain classes to modify the meaning in more or less definite ways (*careful-careless, red-reddish, tell-foretell*) or to shift the word from one class to another (*soft-soften-softly, devil-bedevil-devilish-deviltry*). In languages that have borrowed from other languages as extensively and over as long a period of time as English and Spanish, such devices are extremely numerous and also pretty unsystematic (for instance, what we *sell* constitutes a *sale,* but what we *buy* constitutes a *purchase; short***age***, scar***city***,* and *scant***iness*** illustrate three ways of deriving nouns from adjectives in just one semantic area in English, as do **escasez, carencia,** and **cort*edad*** in Spanish). Nevertheless, it helps in recognizing new words and in remembering old ones to have a working familiarity with the more obvious prefixes and suffixes.

The forms illustrated in this unit are only samples that come conveniently to hand from the words in the dialogs. You will add to them from your own observation, recognizing, for example, an –**or** suffix meaning *agent* in **investigador** and **administrador,** and a –**ble** suffix meaning *lending itself to* in **amable** (based on **amar** to love) and **respetable** (based on **respetar**). Also, for the sake of simplicity the samples here are presented in a way that makes them appear somewhat more regular than they really are. The suffix –**ción,** for example, works pretty well as we have schematized it for the –**ar** verbs (compare English –*ate,* –*ation* as in *relate, relation* and *exaggerate, exaggeration*), but not for –**er** and –**ir** verbs, where time has obscured the Latin models: **dirigir** *to direct* and **dirección, recibir** and **recepción, nadar** *to swim* and **natación, decidir** and **decisión.** The suffix –**al** becomes more complex in **presidente-presidencial** and **caso-casual.** Similarly the suffix –**dad** in **nuevo-novedad, posible-posibilidad, cuanto-cantidad,** and **libre-libertad.**

There are wide differences among formative elements in what we might term their chemical activity or their chemical inertness. A new verb formed with the ending –**er** or –**ir** would be an unexpected event, for these endings are chemically dead. On the other hand, a new verb formed with the ending –**ar,** such as **solucionar,** is not at all surprising, for practically all verbs now being coined have this ending. As we saw in Unit 19 §108, the suffix –**ito** is comparatively active, but the suffix –**illo** is comparatively inert.

There are also wide differences in kinship of meaning among related forms. Some are close in meaning, such as *red-reddish* in English and **rojo-rojizo** in Spanish. Others have diverged: English *intoxicate* shows little relationship to *toxic,* and *sweater* has diverged from *sweat* just as Spanish **casar** has diverged from **casa.**

Most prefixes are easily recognized from the English equivalents: **pre–** in **preocupar, anti–** in **antipático, ante–** in **anteayer, re–** in **refinería, co–** in **coordinar, sub–** in **subteniente, semi–** in **semicírculo,** etc.

Review Unit 19 §108 for the diminutives (note the new suffix –**ote** in **sombrerote,** referring to ungainliness associated with size) and Unit 16 §96 for –**mente.**

135 Compounding

A. 1. Está malo el **tocadiscos.**
   2. Parece que fueran chalecos **salvavidas.**
   3. Sin **paraguas** nos vamos a empapar.
   4. ¿Por qué no llevan los paracaidistas sus **paracaídas?** *Why don't the paratroopers carry their parachutes?*

B. 1. **Centroamérica** forma parte de **Norteamérica.** *Central America forms part of North America.*

   2. Mira a los artilleros por aquella **bocacalle.**

C. 1. **Dondequiera** que vivan, siguen siendo argentinos. *Wherever they live, they keep on being Argentineans.*
   2. A **cualquiera** le pasaría lo mismo.

VERB	NOUN	NOUN
tocar	discos	tocadiscos
salvar[1]	vidas	salvavidas
parar	aguas	paraguas
parar	caídas[2]	paracaídas

NOUN	NOUN	NOUN
centro	América	Centroamérica
norte	América	Norteamérica
boca	calle	bocacalle

INTERROGATIVE –RELATIVE	quiera[3]	INDEFINITE
donde	quiera	dondequiera
cual	quiera	cualquiera

Compound words are formed in the ways shown, in addition to other ways.

● ITEM SUBSTITUTION DRILL

1. *Tocadiscos* es un compuesto de las palabras tocar y discos.
   (paraguas, rompecabezas, salvavidas, paracaídas, cumpleaños, lavaplatos, lavamanos)

2. Las palabras *parar* y *sol* forman el compuesto parasol.
   (pasar y tiempo, cortar y papel, quitar y sol)

● TRANSLATION DRILL

A. 1. He's from North America.
   2. He's from Central America.
   3. He's North American.
   4. He's Central American.

B. 1. Go wherever you want.
   2. Go whenever you want.
   3. Go any way (however) you want.
   4. Take whichever you want.

● DISCUSSION

Spanish is less resourceful than English in forming compound words. Of the examples given, only the first, that of nouns formed of verb plus noun, is fairly free to create new words, especially

---

[1] *to save*   [2] **caída** *fall*   [3] present subjunctive of **querer: dondequiera** = *where you (one) may wish.*

in the area of the familiar mechanical operations of cutting, raising, washing, removing, destroying, etc. English has a few compounds formed in the same way, of verb plus noun; e.g., *pastime* (Spanish **pasatiempo**), *cutpurse* (Spanish **cortabolsas** with the same meaning, "thief"), *sawbones*, *breakwater*. But more usual than the *breakwater* pattern is the *circuit-breaker* pattern, with noun first, then verb plus *–er.* So Spanish **levantaválvulas, quitapintura,** and **rompecabezas** match English *valve-lifter, paint-remover,* and *head-breaker* ("puzzle"). All are masculine. See Unit 9 §49 for number.

136   Compound prepositions

EXAMPLES

A. 1. **Además,** no es ninguna molestia.
   2. **Además de** las Naciones Unidas, hay la OEA. *Besides the UN, there's the OAS.*

B. 1. Si lo hubiéramos sabido **antes** . . .
   2. La de cosas que tendrá que hacer **antes de** partir.

C. 1. El peligro está **cerca.** *The danger is near.*
   2. Viven **cerca de**l Parque Central.

D. 1. ¿Esas casas tristes con techo de paja y **debajo** los cerdos? *Those wretched houses with straw roofs and the pigs underneath?*
   2. Póngase este termómetro **debajo de** la lengua.

E. 1. **Dentro** hay un abrigo de pieles. *Inside there's a fur coat.*
   2. Regresa **dentro de** diez minutos. *(She'll be back within ten minutes.)*

F. 1. Dijeron que iban a volver **después.**
   2. ¿Y **después de**l informe de la Comisión?

G. 1. **Detrás** viene un cuerpo de paracaidistas. *(Behind comes a bunch of paratroopers.)*
   2. El perrito de mascota andaba **detrás de** los cadetes. *The little dog mascot was walking behind the cadets.*

H. 1. Se quedaron **fuera.** No forman parte de nuestro grupo. *They kept out. They don't form part of our group.*
   2. Comprar muebles, ropa, de todo; **fuera de** las recepciones, despedidas. *(Outside of receptions, farewells.)*

ADVERB	
besides	**además**
before, earlier	**antes**
near, nearby, close	**cerca**
below, underneath	**debajo**
inside	**dentro**
afterward(s), later	**después**
after, behind	**detrás**
out(side)	**fuera**

COMPOUND PREPOSITION	
besides, in addition to	**además de**
before, prior to	**antes de**
near, close to	**cerca de**
below, under, underneath	**debajo de**
inside (of), within	**dentro de**
after	**después de**
after, behind	**detrás de**
outside (of), aside from	**fuera de**

Most compound prepositions are formed by adding **de** to an adverb.

● TRANSLATION DRILL

1. The band had never played there before.
The band had never played there before noon.
2. Afterward there was lots of applause and shouting.
After the infantry hymn there was lots of applause and shouting.

3. Her husband is near.
Her husband is near that semicircle of dancers.
4. The parade's not far (off).
The parade's not far from here.
5. Inside there's an ambassador.
Inside the palace there's an ambassador.

6. They kept out.
   They kept out of the conflict.
7. The citizens danced in the street below.
   The citizens danced in the street below the balcony.
8. Both stayed behind.
   Both stayed behind the streamers.
9. Besides, he brought the fireworks.
   Besides the gold medal, he brought the fireworks.
10. Underneath he's not wearing anything.
    Underneath his shirt he's not wearing anything.

EXAMPLES

1. **A pesar de** lo que tú digas, papá, no estoy de acuerdo contigo.
2. ¿Qué tienes tú **en contra de** Vargas Campo?
3. Los esfuerzos **en pro de** la paz.
4. ¿Por qué lo trae usted **en vez de** mandarlo con la muchacha?
5. ¿Se hace algo **en cuanto al** problema de la agricultura?
6. Ella se sentó **junto a** nosotros.   *She sat down next to us.*

in spite of, despite	a pesar de
against	en contra de
for, in behalf of	en pro de
instead of	en vez de
about, regarding, concerning	en cuanto a
next to, beside	junto a

Some compound prepositions are formed differently: based on prepositional phrases, using **a** rather than **de,** etc.

● TRANSLATION DRILL

1. In spite of the success, I'm going to stay.
   In spite of the scarcity of housing, I'm going to stay.
   In spite of the illiteracy, I'm going to stay.
2. We don't have anything against the company.
   We don't have anything against the firm.
   We don't have anything against the republic.
3. There are many efforts on behalf of agriculture.
   There are many efforts on behalf of education.
   There are many efforts on behalf of progress.
4. Step out on the balcony instead of staying here.
   Dance the *zapateado* instead of staying here.
   Let the reporter know instead of staying here.
5. Is anything being done about the Investigating Commission?
   Is anything being done about the economic problems?
   Is anything being done about the peace of the hemisphere?
6. She's standing next to the table.
   She's standing next to the door.
   She's standing next to the second lieutenant.

● DISCUSSION

Like English with its *next to, aside from, out of, on top of, alongside of,* etc., Spanish uses its resources of adverbs and simple prepositions to build compound prepositions.

See Unit 18 §102 for the addition of **que** to both simple and compound prepositions to make conjunctions.

137 Forms of pronouns after relator words

EXAMPLES

A. 1. —A cualquiera le pasaría lo mismo.
   —¿**A mí?** Nunca.
   2. Hablaban **contra** (**en contra de**) **mí.**
   They were talking against me.
   3. Es **para ti.** *It's for you.*
   4. Nosotros pasamos **por ti.**
   5. No voy **sin ti.** *I'm not going without you.*
   6. **Odian** a todo el mundo, incluso **a ti.**
   They hate everybody, including you.
   7. Fueron **con él** (**con ella, con ellos, con
   ellas, con usted, con ustedes**). *They
   went with him (with her, with them, with
   them* [f]*, with you, with you* [pl]*).*

B. 1. Haga **como yo.** (*Do like me.*)
   2. —Todo el mundo ha sido invitado.
   Everybody's been invited.
   —¿**Incluso yo?** *Including me?*
   3. Nadie me quiere, **excepto tú.** *Nobody
   loves me, except you.*
   4. **Según tú,** no existe el honor personal.
   According to you, personal honor does not exist.
   5. **Entre tú** y **yo** (**usted** y **yo, tú** y **él**) no
   puede haber acuerdo. *Between you and
   me* (*you and me, you and him*) *there can be no
   agreement.*
   6. Póngase allí, **entre él** y **yo.** *Stand there,
   between him and me.*
   7. Hablan **como él** (**como ella, como ellos,
   como ellas, como usted, como ustedes**).
   They talk like him (*like her, like them, like
   them* [f]*, like you, like you* [pl]*).*

PREPOSITIONS THAT TAKE WITH-PREPOSITION PRONOUNS		RELATOR WORDS THAT TAKE SUBJECT PRONOUNS
a	hasta	como
con[1]	para	excepto
contra	por	incluso
de	sin	según
en	sobre	entre
hacia		
—and all compound prepositions		

These two lists comprise most of the prepositions that take with-preposition pronouns and the more important relator words that take subject pronouns.

● RESPONSE DRILL

A. 1. TEACHER: ¿A usted le gusta la tarea?
   STUDENT: **A mí, nunca.**
   2. ¿A ustedes les gusta la tarea?
   3. ¿A ti te gusta la tarea?
   4. ¿A él le gusta la tarea?
   5. ¿A ellos les gusta la tarea?

B. 1. ¿Viene esto para usted?
   No, para mí no.
   2. ¿Viene esto de usted?
   3. ¿Viene esto contra usted?
   4. ¿Viene esto sobre usted?

C. 1. ¿Va Rodrigo conmigo?
   No, no va contigo.
   2. ¿Va Rodrigo por mí?

3. ¿Va Rodrigo sin mí?
4. ¿Va Rodrigo hacia mí?
5. ¿Va Rodrigo antes de mí?
6. ¿Va Rodrigo después de mí?
7. ¿Va Rodrigo cerca de mí?
8. ¿Va Rodrigo detrás de mí?
9. ¿Va Rodrigo a pesar de mí?
10. ¿Va Rodrigo junto a mí?

D. 1. ¿Van todos como tú?
   Como yo no; como tú.
   2. ¿Van todos excepto tú?
   3. ¿Van todos incluso tú?
   4. ¿Van todos según tú?

---

[1] Remember the special forms **conmigo** and **contigo.** See Unit 10 §54.

A. 1. The spare parts are for me.
  2. The spare parts come with me.
  3. The spare parts are behind me.
  4. The spare parts are near me.
  5. The spare parts come from me.

B. 1. Everybody walks like you and me.
  2. Everybody walks except you and me.
  3. Everybody walks including you and me.
  4. Everybody walks according to you and me.
  5. Everybody walks between you and me.

EXAMPLES

A. 1. Es **para ti** y **para mí.** *It's for you and me.*
  2. **Con usted** y **conmigo** son más amables. *With you and me they're more friendly.*
  3. ¿Qué tienen **en contra de él** y **de ti?** *What do they have against him and you?*
  4. Me senté **junto a ella** y **a ellos.** *I sat down next to her and them.*

B. 1. ¿Cuáles son sus sentimientos **hacia Juanita** y **nosotros?** *What are his feelings toward Juanita and us?*
  2. Todo el mundo fue, **incluso Juan** y **yo.** *Everybody went, including John and me.*

PREPO-SITION	OBJECT A		OBJECT B
for	you	and	me
with	you	and	me
against	him	and	you
next to	her	and	them

PREPO-SITION	OBJECT A	PREPO-SITION	OBJECT B
para	**ti**	**y**	**para**	**mí**
con	**usted**	**y**		**conmigo**
en contra de	**él**	**y**	**de**	**ti**
junto a	**ella**	**y**	**a**	**ellos**

toward	Juanita	and	us
including	John	and	me

hacia	**Juanita**	**y**	**nosotros**
incluso	**Juan**	**y**	**yo**

If a **mí** or a **ti** would otherwise be separated from its preposition (e.g., by **y**), the preposition is normally repeated; and with compound prepositions the last element (**de** or **a**) is normally repeated regardless of what pronoun follows. Elsewhere this problem does not arise.

● TRANSLATION DRILL

A. 1. He's going for you and me.
  2. He's going against you and me.
  3. He's going with you and me.
  4. He's going without you and me.
  5. He's going in spite of you and me.
  6. He's going next to you and me.

B. 1. I plan to go with you and them.
  2. I plan to go without you and them.
  3. I plan to go for you and them.

  4. I plan to go between you and them.
  5. We plan to go against you and them.
  6. We plan to go in spite of you and them.
  7. He plans to go next to you and us.
  8. He plans to go before you and us.
  9. He plans to go after you and us.
 10. They plan to go behind you and us.
 11. They plan to go near you and us.
 12. They plan to go far from you and us.

● DISCUSSION

The counterparts of certain words or phrases which in English are regarded as prepositions and take the objective case, such as *including, except, like,* and *according to,* are not felt to be prepositions in Spanish, where they take subject rather than with-preposition pronouns. The reason with **como** is easy to see: it covers the range of both *like* and *as,* so that *Do like me* is given a form equivalent to *Do as I (do).* The other near-prepositional relator words were mostly participles to begin with, and never fully joined the ranks of prepositions: **excepto yo** *except me = I (being) excepted;*

incluso yo *including me* = *I (being) included.* (The reason for the object form **ti** in **Odian a todo el mundo, incluso a ti** is not that the **ti** is the object of **incluso,** but that it is the object of the verb **odian**—*They hate you;* it of course carries the personal **a.**)

The forms **él, ella, ellos, ellas, nosotros, nosotras, usted,** and **ustedes** cause no special problem with prepositions because they are the same whether subject or with-preposition (see Unit 10 §54). **Mí** and **ti** however, are never used except as objects of prepositions, and the bond between them and the preposition has become so close that normally nothing else can divide the two. This is why the type *for you and for me* is preferred to the type *for you and me,* so as to have *me* joined to *for* rather than to *and.* With **entre,** of course, to say *between you and between me* would be nonsense, so Spanish uses the equivalent of an English construction regarded as sub-standard, *between you and I,* with the subject forms for both *you* and *I.*

138 *¿Cuál? and ¿qué? for what?*

EXAMPLES
1. **¿Cuál** es el principio operante de la OEA?
2. —**¿Qué** es su hermano? *What is your brother?*
   —Es abogado. *He's a lawyer.*

¿Cuál	**es el día del examen?** *What is the day of the exam?* Answer: *Monday.* **es el centro de Madrid?** *What is the center of Madrid?* Answer: *The Puerta del Sol.* **es su plan?** *What is your plan?* Answer: *To leave early.*
¿Cuáles	**son los días del examen?** *What are the days of the exam?* Answer: *Monday, Tuesday, and Wednesday.* **son los centros de Madrid y de México?** *What are the centers of Madrid and Mexico City?* Answer: *The Puerta del Sol and the Zócalo.* **son sus planes?** *What are your plans?* Answer: *To leave early and take our lunch.*

English *what is (are, was,* etc.)? is equivalent to **¿cuál es** (**cuáles son, cuál fue,** etc.)? when the answer called for is the individual thing or things that fit a definition.

¿Qué	**es un joropo?** *What is a joropo?* Answer: *It's a Venezuelan dance* (it belongs to this class of things). **son esas cosas?** *What are those things?* Answer: *They're insects* (they belong to this class of things).

English *what is (are, was,* etc.)? is equivalent to **¿qué es** (**son, fue,** etc.)? when the answer called for is the definition (classifying word or words) that fits an individual thing or things.

● TRANSLATION DRILL

A. 1. TEACHER: What's your name?
      STUDENT: **¿Cuál es su nombre?**
   2. What's your age?
   3. What's your address?
   4. What's your job?
   5. What's your telephone number?

B. 1. What's the date?
   2. What's the reason?
   3. What's the question?
   4. What's the problem?
   5. What's the example?
   6. What's the solution?
   7. What's the decision?
   8. What's the message?
   9. What's the conflict?
   10. What's the surprise?
   11. What's the situation?
   12. What's the truth?

C. 1. What's her condition?
   2. What's her sickness?
   3. What's her idea?
   4. What's her political party?
   5. What's her religion?
   6. What's her excuse?

D. 1. What's a *joropo?*
      ¿Qué es un joropo?
   2. What's a *contradanza?*
   3. What's a *zapateado?*
   4. What's a cadet?
   5. What's a life preserver?
   6. What's an inauguration?
   7. What's an investigation?
   8. What's a demonstration?

   9. What's a strike?
   10. What's a patrol?
   11. What's a siesta?

E. 1. What is agriculture?
   2. What is illiteracy?
   3. What is brilliantine?
   4. What is infantry?
   5. What is psychology?
   6. What is philosophy?
   7. What is religion?
   8. What is Lent?
   9. What is football?
   10. What is luck?
   11. What is truth?

F. 1. What are conveniences?
   2. What are elections?
   3. What are artillerymen?
   4. What are paratroopers?
   5. What are streamers?
   6. What are tools?
   7. What are *guaraníes?*
   8. What are *micros?*

G. 1. What *is* the lottery?
   2. What *is* the marathon?
   3. What *is* the package?
   4. What *is* the ministry?
   5. What *is* the Union Club?

● DISCUSSION

The usual equivalent of *what?* is **¿qué?** (see Unit 3 §8), but in the combination *what is?, what are?,* etc., with a form of **ser,** it may be **¿qué?** or **¿cuál, –es?** according to meaning:
   1. If we need to know *the thing,* to have it selected for us, the equivalent is **¿cuál, –es?**
   2. If we need to know something *about* the thing, the equivalent is **¿qué?**

139   *¿De quién, -es? for whose?*

EXAMPLES

1. ¿De parte **de quién,** para decirle?
2. **¿De quiénes** son estos chalecos salvavidas? *Whose lifejackets are these? (Whose are these lifejackets?)*

3. **¿De quién** es el paraguas que llevas? *Whose umbrella are you carrying? (Whose is the umbrella you're carrying)?*
4. **¿De quién** fue el dinero con que lo compraste? *Whose money did you buy it with? (Whose was the money with which you bought it?)*

	FORM OF **ser**	THING POSSESSED
De quién, –es	son es fue etc.	estos chalecos el paraguas que . . . el dinero con que . . .

¿De quién, –es? is normally followed by a form of **ser,** with the other elements of the sentence arranged accordingly.

A. 1. TEACHER: Whose is that coat?
STUDENT: **¿De quién es ese abrigo?**

   2. Whose is that book?
   3. Whose is that dessert?
   4. Whose is that cup?
   5. Whose is that package?

B. 1. Whose are those toys?
   2. Whose are those shoes?
   3. Whose are those ties?
   4. Whose are those aspirins?
   5. Whose are those photos?

C. 1. Whose coat is that?
      ¿De quién es ese abrigo?
   2. Whose fruit is that?
   3. Whose lemonade is that?

   4. Whose dog is that?
   5. Whose horse is that?
   6. Whose record player is that?
   7. Whose money is that?
   8. Whose tomb is that?

D. 1. Whose idea was that?
   2. Whose decision was that?
   3. Whose plan was that?
   4. Whose schedule was that?
   5. Whose message was that?

E. 1. Whose cars are those?
   2. Whose shirts are those?
   3. Whose books are those?
   4. Whose letters are those?
   5. Whose shoes are those?

● DISCUSSION

English *whose?* can precede a noun: *whose hat? whose friends?* Spanish **¿de quién, –es?** has the same limitations as English *of whom?:* it calls for a form of **ser** to follow it, and an arrangement of the other elements to fit. This may mean the addition of a relative word such as **que** and perhaps also the moving of a preposition: *Whose house do you live in?* = *Of whom is the house in which you live?* **¿De quién (de quiénes) es la casa en que vives?**

● COMBINED PATTERN REPLACEMENT DRILL

A.

1. **¿Cuál es el principio operante de la OEA?**
2. ¿Cuáles _____
3. _____ filosofía _____
4. _____ social _____
5. _____ compañía
6. _____ recomendación _____
7. _____ son _____
8. _____ principales _____
9. _____ productos _____
10. _____ organización
11. Cuál _____
12. _____ fue _____
13. _____ plan _____
14. _____ presidente
15. _____ inmediato _____
16. _____ decisión _____
17. _____ embajador
18. _____ equivocada _____
19. _____ idea _____
20. _____ cónsul
21. _____ brillante _____
22. _____ solución _____

B.

1. **¿Qué haría la OEA en caso de un conflicto?**
2. _____ hace _____
3. _____ comisión _____
4. _____ revolución
5. _____ gobierno _____
6. _____ en contra de _____
7. _____ elección
8. Cuánto _____
9. _____ con respecto a _____
10. _____ república _____
11. Qué _____
12. _____ hará _____
13. _____ la _____
14. _____ en cuanto a _____
15. _____ pueblo _____
16. _____ peligro
17. _____ hizo _____
18. _____ progreso
19. _____ ciudadanos _____
20. _____ en pro de _____
21. _____ seguridad
22. _____ la policía _____
23. _____ ofrece _____
24. _____ paz
25. _____ los militares _____
26. _____ dijeron _____

The subjunctive tenses. INSTRUCTIONS: Repeat the following sentences just as you hear them. Then repeat them two more times, adding **quiero que** and **quisiera que** before each sentence.

A. 1. TEACHER: Los alumnos llegan a la puerta. *Repita.*
STUDENT: **Los alumnos llegan a la puerta.**
TEACHER: Quiero que . . .
STUDENT: **Quiero que los alumnos lleguen a la puerta.**
TEACHER: Quisiera que . . .
STUDENT: **Quisiera que los alumnos llegaran a la puerta.**
2. El profesor los invita a entrar.

B. 1. Son compañeros de escuela de mi hermana.
2. Es el nuevo cónsul americano.
3. Ellas saben español perfectamente.

C. 1. Está bueno el tocadiscos.
2. Ella tiene uno portátil.
3. Usamos el teléfono.
4. Habla con la tía.
5. María Elena regresa dentro de diez minutos.
6. Tú conoces a mamá.

D. 1. Me manda una taza de café.
2. La felicitan por su cumpleaños.
3. Viven cerca del Parque Central.
4. Usted sigue derecho por la Avenida Norte.

E. 1. No se deje dar gato por liebre.
2. A mí nadie me gana.
3. No tarde mucho.
4. Vuelva lo más pronto posible.
5. Ven acá para enseñarte una cosa.
6. Dame diez centavos para darle a un pobre.
7. Déjame en paz.

F. 1. El ve la flecha.
2. Eso no es nada serio.
3. Me conceden hasta mañana para pagarla.
4. Habla el cuñado de él.
5. Mañana a las cuatro pasa por sus papeles.

G. 1. Arriba córteme un poco también.
2. En realidad vale la pena.
3. Se dice algo de los próximos Juegos Olímpicos.
4. Ellos tienen muy buenos atletas.
5. Nosotros participamos en básquetbol.
6. Por lo menos en fútbol ganamos.
7. Allá se juega otra clase de fútbol.
8. Allí hay corridas de toros.

H. 1. Eso no es un trabajo muy complicado.
2. Tú eres hombre respetable, profesional.
3. Mañana es la inauguración de la refinería de petróleo.
4. Pensamos en progresar alguna vez.
5. En todo caso la bocina nunca falla.

I. 1. Traiga dos cafés negros bien calientes.
2. Tenemos examen en filosofía.
3. Sólo hacen preguntas sobre Platón.
4. Es igual que todas las demás materias.
5. Vienen de todos los colegios.
6. Se pide acortar el número de materias por año.

J. 1. Usted se va a trabajar al campo.
2. Los cerdos dejan bastante ganancia en la feria.
3. Me promete una cuarta parte de la cosecha.
4. Los agricultores no la pasan mal.

K. 1. Nos los mandan a las cinco.
2. Usted misma nos los trae.
3. Estos son los trajes suyos.
4. Espere para envolvérselos.

L. 1. Tenemos hora con él para las once.
2. A todos les duele la cabeza y la garganta.
3. Quítese la corbata y la camisa.
4. Llévese esta receta.
5. Mañana no se bañe.

M. 1. Es un pretexto para discursos contra el presidente.
2. La policía los ataca.
3. Disuelve la manifestación a palos y a tiros.
4. Las elecciones vienen pronto.

N. 1. Tome un colectivo en esta esquina.
2. Vamos por esta calle para llegar a la Plaza de Mayo.
3. No sean cargantes.
4. Me da el visto bueno inmediatamente.
5. Vamos a almorzar.

O. 1. Llama la señora Méndez.
2. Por fin llega el correo.
3. Déjeme ver esas cuentas.
4. Las demás pueden esperar.
5. Se casa con Lorenzo, su novio de años.
6. Se lleva a una gran muchacha.
7. Mi mujer va siempre y reza por los dos.

P. 1. Pásame la carne.
2. Las muchachas no salen solas de noche, y menos al cine.
3. Tienen que llevar chaperón a todas partes.
4. No toquemos ese tema.

Q. 1. Vargas Campo es el hombre del día.
2. Nuestro pueblo jamás acepta cambios tan radicales.
3. Ustedes dos se ponen de acuerdo.
4. No insistan en la carrera de medicina.
5. El tiempo vuela.

R. 1. El señor Suárez llega a la oficina.
2. Podemos informarles respecto al pedido.
3. Escriba "su seguro servidor".
4. No tiene importancia, don Domingo.
5. Usted sabe lo de los compromisos sociales.
6. Vamos a la Comisión de Cambios.

S. 1. El señor Delgado les habla sobre la puntualidad.
2. Hábleles directamente.
3. Todo el mundo es puntual.
4. Consultamos con los empleados sobre el horario.
5. Lo probamos por algunos días.

T. 1. Se saca el gordo de la lotería.
2. Se los compra todos.

3. A cualquiera le pasa lo mismo.
4. Jamás jugamos a la lotería.
5. Los niños tienen de todo.

U. 1. A cada uno le llega el día.
2. Perdóneme por el desorden de la casa.
3. Ahí le damos el pésame.
4. La acompañamos en su pena.

V. 1. Deja de roncar, Diego.
2. Llama a la policía, Diego.
3. Se llevan la vajilla de plata.
4. El tiene llave de la casa.
5. Háganos una descripción de él.

W. 1. Son chalecos salvavidas.
2. Empieza a llover.
3. No nos empapamos con esta lluvia.
4. Mariana es tan dichosa como linda.
5. Le da una mirada disimulada al guapo militar.
6. Los bailarines forman un semicírculo.

X. 1. Es un alto privilegio para nuestra república.
2. Tiene una brillante actuación como embajador ante la OEA.
3. Viene la señora de Rodó.
4. Hay muchos campos de acción en este sentido.
5. La OEA coopera en mejorar las técnicas.
6. Es un ejemplo para todo el mundo.

READING

La composición

P. *Profesor*   s. *Señor Sullivan*   R. *Señor Rogers*
A. *Señor Andersson*   CA. *Señor Carman*
CI. *Señorita Ciruti*

P. Hace tres o cuatro días que les hablé sobre la derivación. Hoy vamos a considerar otro fenómeno lingüístico muy interesante: la formación de vocablos nuevos mediante la composición, o la yuxtaposición de dos palabras para designar un concepto nuevo. Consideren las palabras compuestas de un verbo y de un sustantivo. El verbo *matar* es bastante común en esta clase de compuestos. Por ejemplo: la palabra *matacán* indica que se trata de un objeto para matar los canes: es una clase de veneno que se da a los perros—es decir, si no le gustan a uno los

perros. ¡Ja-ja-ja! (*La clase ríe también, aunque de una manera un poco forzada.*) —Bueno, señor Sullivan, ¿qué es un matacandelas?

s. Pues es un objeto que sirve para extinguir las candelas.

P. Muy bien. —¿Y qué es un matafuego? —¿Señor Rogers?

R. Un objeto para extinguir el fuego.

P. Bien. —Señor Andersson: ¿Qué es un matamoscas?

A. Es un instrumento para matar las moscas.

P. Bueno, bueno. Y hay otros. Todos conocemos la palabra *matasanos,* un médico de poca competencia que mata aún a los sanos. Un matasiete, o matamoros, es un valentón o fanfarrón. Un matapolvo es una lluvia ligera, o llovizna. Etcétera.

—Ahora, ¿quién puede decirme otro verbo muy usado en tales compuestos? —¿Señor Carman?

CA. El verbo *parar* es muy común en tales compuestos, ¿no?

P. Excelente. —Sí, es acaso el más común de todos. ¿Quién sabe algunos ejemplos? —¿Señorita Ciruti?

CI. Pues, el parabrisas de un auto; el paracaídas de los aviadores; todos los autos tienen parachoques; también el paraguas; el pararrayos de una casa; el parasol, etc.

P. Muy bien, señorita. —Y hay compuestos de otras clases que son muy interesantes. Quisiera darles una lista de algunos de éstos. Voy a dictarles esta lista, y para mañana ustedes estudiarán la formación y la significación de estas palabras. ¿Comprenden? Bueno, aquí está la lista. (*Dicta.*) *Vaivén; salvoconducto; camposanto; anteojos; antebrazo; aguardiente; sordomudo; mondadientes; correveidile; hazmerreir; quedirán; quehacer.* —Ahí sonó la campanilla. Hasta mañana.

READING

La Organización de los Estados Americanos (OEA)

Existía en Hispanoamérica y en los Estados Unidos gran interés por la independencia y la paz aun antes de la organización de la OEA.

En 1810, el Secretario de Estado de los EE.UU., Robert Smith, nombró a Joel R. Poinsett de South Carolina agente norteamericano en Buenos Aires y Chile. El Sr. Smith le dictó una carta: "... en el evento de una separación política de la madre patria y del establecimiento de un sistema demócrata e independiente, los Estados Unidos querrán promover las relaciones más amistosas y también el intercambio más liberal entre todos los habitantes de este hemisferio porque tendremos un común interés y obligación de mantener un sistema de paz, justicia y buena voluntad que es la única fuente de felicidad para los países."

Un año más tarde cuando James Monroe llegó a ser Secretario de Estado elevó a Poinsett al puesto de Cónsul General y le dijo:

—Como habitantes del mismo hemisferio y como vecinos, los Estados Unidos no pueden ser espectadores impasibles de un movimiento tan importante [la separación de España]. El destino de esas naciones debe depender de ellas mismas, pero nuestras relaciones con ellas serán más íntimas y nuestra amistad será más fuerte que con colonias de cualquier estado de Europa.[1]

Simón Bolívar, gran libertador de la parte norte de Sud América, escribió en su ya famosa carta al gobernador de la isla de Jamaica, hombre que tomaba interés en la causa republicana en la América del Sur:[2] "... pienso que los americanos, ansiosos de paz, ciencias, artes, comercio y agricultura preferirían las repúblicas a los reinos, y me parece que estos deseos se conforman con las miras de la Europa... Yo deseo, más que otro alguno,[3] ver formar en América la más grande nación del mundo, menos por su extensión y riquezas que por su libertad y gloria... Es una idea grandiosa pretender formar de todo el Nuevo Mundo una sola nación con un solo vínculo que ligue sus partes entre sí y con el todo... [pero] no es posible, porque climas remotos, situaciones di-

---

[1] When Poinsett was about to return to the U.S., he looked around to find some memento from Mexico to describe to his associates something of that charming land. He decided upon a beautiful flower, called **Flor de la Navidad,** which he cultivated in a hothouse in South Carolina. The beautiful flower became so popular in the U. S. that, with its new name—poinsettia— its cultivation spread through the country.

[2] This famous letter was written September 6, 1815, and was called: "Contestación de un americano meridional a un caballero de esta isla [Kingston, Jamaica]."

[3] **más que otro alguno** *more than any other person*

versas, intereses opuestos, caracteres semejantes dividen a la América. ¡Qué bello sería que el istmo de Panamá fuese[4] para nosotros lo que el de Corinto para los griegos! ¡Ojalá que algún día tengamos la fortuna de instalar allí un augusto Congreso de los representantes de las repúblicas . . . a tratar y discutir sobre los altos intereses de la paz y de la guerra, con las naciones de las otras tres partes del mundo.[5]

"Seguramente la unión es la que nos falta para completar la obra de nuestra regeneración. Sin embargo, nuestra división no es extraña, porque tal es el distintivo de las guerras civiles formadas generalmente entre dos partidos: *conservadores* y *reformadores*. Los primeros son, por lo común, más numerosos, porque el imperio de la costumbre produce el efecto de la obediencia a las potestades establecidas; los últimos son siempre menos numerosos aunque más vehementes e ilustrados. De este modo la masa física se equilibra con la fuerza moral, y la contienda se prolonga siendo sus resultados[6] muy inciertos. Por fortuna, entre nosotros, la masa ha seguido a la inteligencia . . . Cuando los sucesos no están asegurados, cuando las empresas son remotas, todos los hombres vacilan, las opiniones se dividen, las pasiones las agitan y los enemigos las animan para triunfar por este fácil medio. Luego que seamos fuertes, bajo los auspicios de una nación liberal que nos preste su protección, se nos verá de acuerdo cultivar las virtudes y los talentos que conducen a la gloria . . ."

Antes de la formación de la OEA, se celebró otra Conferencia Panamericana en Nueva York (en 1889), pero el patriota cubano José Martí[7] tenía mucho miedo. Vio muchos obstáculos en la vía de un entendimiento mutuo:

—Nuestra América corre otro peligro . . . se debe a la diferencia de orígenes, métodos e intereses entre los dos factores continentales.

En 1891 Martí asistió a una Conferencia Internacional Monetaria en Washington, D.C., y declaró:

—. . . el buen gobernante en América no es el que sabe cómo se gobierna el alemán o el francés, sino el que sabe con qué elementos está hecho su país, y cómo puede ir guiándolos en junto, para llegar, por métodos e instituciones nacidas del país mismo, a aquel estado apetecible, donde cada hombre se conoce y ejerce, y disfrutan todos de la abundancia que la Naturaleza puso para todos en el pueblo que fecundan con su trabajo y defienden con sus vidas. El gobierno ha de nacer del país. El espíritu del gobierno ha de avenirse a la constitución propia del país. El gobierno no es más que el equilibrio de los elementos del país.

La OEA es una organización internacional creada por las veintiuna Repúblicas Americanas[8] para lograr un orden de paz y de justicia, fomentar su solidaridad, robustecer su colaboración y defender su soberanía, su integridad territorial y su independencia.

Durante la Primera Conferencia Internacional Americana, celebrada en Washington en 1890, fue creada la Oficina Comercial de las Repúblicas Americanas, y en 1910 fue denominada la Unión Panamericana.[9]

En los siguientes años se celebraron varias conferencias generales y especializadas y se establecieron nuevos organismos. En 1948 fue firmada la Carta de la Organización de los Estados Americanos, a la que comúnmente se le da el nombre de Sistema Interamericano.

La OEA funciona por medio de los seis órganos:

1. La Conferencia Interamericana, que se reúne cada cinco años para decidir la acción y la política generales de la Organización;

2. La Reunión de Consulta de Ministros

---

[4] **fuese = fuera**

[5] Bolívar, as president of Colombia, did invite the presidents of the new American nations to participate in a Congress, nine years after he wrote this letter (1826). The meeting was not a great success, but it was the "first" of the meetings which developed into the Pan American Union. In July, 1956, the president of the Pan American Union invited the presidents of all the American states to attend the 130th anniversary, which was celebrated in Washington.

[6] **siendo sus resultados** *with its outcome*

[7] José Martí (1853–1895) carried on the dreams of Simón Bolívar for freedom and union of the American nations. He admired the U.S. but fought the idea that Latin America might become a vassal to it. He declared that the two Americas represent two differing concepts of life. Each one should strive to understand the other so that all Americans might live together in peace.

[8] They are: Argentina, Bolivia, Brazil, Colombia, Costa Rica, Cuba, Chile, Ecuador, El Salvador, the United States, Guatemala, Haiti, Honduras, Mexico, Nicaragua, Panama, Paraguay, Peru, the Dominican Republic, Uruguay, and Venezuela.

[9] Of course the principles of mutual collaboration and assistance existed long before the formal establishment of the system, since they were enunciated at the Congress in Panama called by Bolívar in 1826.

de Relaciones Exteriores, que se reúne cuando sea necesario para considerar problemas de carácter urgente o para tratar asuntos que amenacen la paz y la seguridad del Continente;

3. El Consejo, compuesto de un representante por cada Estado Miembro, que se reúne regularmente en la Unión Panamericana en Washington, D.C. Hay tres órganos: el Consejo Interamericano Económico y Social, el Consejo Interamericano de Jurisconsultos y el Consejo Interamericano Cultural;

4. La Unión Panamericana que es el órgano central permanente y Secretaría General;

5. Las conferencias especializadas, que tratan de materias técnicas especializadas y desarrollan aspectos determinados de cooperación interamericana;

6. Los Organismos Especializados, que tienen funciones específicas respecto de asuntos técnicos de interés común.

Con estos Organos la OEA dispone de un mecanismo eficaz para fortalecer la paz y la seguridad de los Estados Miembros; para prevenir posibles causas de dificultades y asegurar la solución pacífica de disputas; para organizar acción colectiva en caso de agresión; para encontrar solución a problemas políticos, jurídicos y económicos que puedan surgir entre ellos y promover por medio de acción cooperativa su desarrollo económico, social y cultural.

La Unión Panamericana, con sede en Washington, D.C., presta sus servicios a los demás órganos de la Organización, así como a los Gobiernos y a los pueblos de los Estados Miembros.

El Día de las Américas se celebra en todo el Continente el 14 de abril de cada año.

● CUESTIONARIO

1. ¿Qué país inició la Organización de los Estados Americanos?
2. ¿Qué instrucciones recibió Joel R. Poinsett de su gobierno?
3. En su carta al gobernador de Jamaica, ¿qué dijo Simón Bolívar que deseaba más que otro alguno?
4. ¿Qué peligros veía José Martí en el entendimiento mutuo de las Américas?
5. ¿Cuál fue la teoría de José Martí del buen gobernante?

6. ¿En qué consiste la OEA?
7. Mencione algunos organismos establecidos a partir de la organización de la OEA.
8. La OEA funciona por medio de seis órganos. ¿Cuáles son?
9. ¿Dónde está la sede del órgano central permanente (Unión Panamericana) de la OEA?
10. ¿Qué países son miembros de la OEA?
11. ¿Cuándo se celebra El Día de las Américas?

● SUGGESTED READINGS

Aikman, Duncan, *The All-American Front,* Doubleday, Garden City, New York, 1940: Ch. 19, "Neighbors, or Else."

Bolívar, Simón, *Selected Writings of Bolívar* (Vicente Lecuna, ed.), Colonial Press, New York, 1951, 2 vols.

Castañeda, Jorge, *Mexico and the United Nations* (prepared under the auspices of El Colegio de Mexico), Manhattan Pub. Co., New York, 1958.

Catalogue of Pan American Union Publications (in English, Spanish, Portuguese, and French), Pan American Union, Washington 6, D.C.

Cotner, Thomas, and Carlos E. Castañeda, *Essays in Mexican History,* University of Texas Press, Austin, 1958.

Crawford, William Rex, *A Century of Latin-American Thought,* Harvard University Press, Cambridge, 1944: Ch. 8, "The Cubans and Martí"; Simón Bolívar (see index).

Crow, John A., *Mexico Today,* Harper, New York, 1957: Ch. 5, "Some Differences between Us"; Ch. 23, "Some Differences in Our Cultures."

Guerrant, Edward O., *Roosevelt's Good Neighbor Policy,* The University of New Mexico Press, Albuquerque, 1950.

Jackson, Joseph Henry, *The Christmas Flower,* Harcourt, Brace, New York, 1951.

Pierson, William W., and Federico C. Gil, *Governments of Latin America,* McGraw-Hill, 1957: Ch. 19, "Latin America and the United States."

Quintanilla, Luis, *A Latin American Speaks,* Macmillan, New York, 1943.

Tomlinson, Edward, *Look Southward, Uncle,* Devin-Adair, New York, 1959.

Uruguay and the United Nations (prepared under the auspices of the Uruguayan Institute of International Law), Manhattan Pub. Co., New York, 1958.

Violich, Francis, *Cities of Latin America,* Reinhold, New York, 1944: Ch. 9, "Latin America and the U.S."

Wilgus, A. Curtis, *The Development of Hispanic America,* Farrar and Rinehart, New York, 1941: Ch. 49, "Pan-Americanism."

25

Una tertulia: Cervantes

Una tertulia es un grupo de personas que tienen intereses comunes. Hay tertulias de literatura, de deportes, de arte, de ciencia, de política, etc. Los miembros de la tertulia se reúnen ciertos días para hablar y cambiar impresiones. Algunas veces solamente tendrán una conversación, y otras escucharán una charla de parte de uno de los miembros de la tertulia. Las personas que pertenecen a una tertulia saben mucho de las cosas que les interesan y por esta razón, aunque la reunión no tenga pretensiones, sus opiniones tendrán mucha autoridad y serán de gran valor para los otros miembros.

(*Aquí estamos en una tertulia de confianza. La criada acaba de traer una bandeja en la cual[1] hay tortitas,*

---
[1] **la cual** *which*

café, azúcar, crema, mentas, servilletas de lienzo, tazas para café y platillos, platos, tenedores, cucharitas, una jarrita para crema, etc.)

C. *Carmen*   A. *Antonio*   T. *Todos*   J. *Jaime*
H. *Señor Herman*   M. *Miguel*

C. ¿Cómo le gusta el café, Antonio?
A. Solo . . . y fuerte, gracias. No me gusta el agua chirle.
C. Quiere tortitas, ¿verdad? Las hizo Catalina para la tertulia del día.
A. ¡Qué ricas!
T. ¡Feliz cumpleaños, Antonio! ¡Salud y pesetas, y tiempo para gozarlas!

A. Muchísimas gracias, amigos . . . ¡Qué buen café, Carmen!

J. Pues, amigos ¿no recuerdan ustedes lo que dijo el filósofo Fulano-de-Tal,[2] que el buen café debe ser fuerte como el hijo de Júpiter, negro como el diablo, puro como un ángel, dulce como el amor y caliente como el infierno?

A. ¡Ya lo creo! Ahora vamos a beber a la salud de . . .

T. De todos. (*Beben.*)

J. Ahora que ya hemos gozado de café, refresquemos el espíritu con algo interesante . . .

H. Pues, Antonio, como decíamos anoche en otra tertulia, hay algunos que juzgan a *Don Quijote* como una novela esencialmente política. Es decir, Don Quijote mismo representa a los conservadores y Sancho la democracia pura.

A. Tal vez. Podríamos discutir esta cuestión palpitante hasta el fin del mundo porque para toda discusión se pueden hallar fuentes en el *Quijote,* que es un libro universal e independiente del tiempo. Hoy todos hablamos de la democracia y en Cervantes vemos que abundan ideales democráticos.

M. ¿No recuerdan ustedes que Cervantes mismo dijo: "He dado en *Don Quijote* pasatiempo al pecho melancólico"? Yo lo considero un libro de entretenimiento y a la vez expresión del avance de la humanidad hacia el progreso.

A. No se olviden ustedes que esta novela es también un cuadro excelente que descubre en panorama la vida española del siglo dieciséis. Además de ser una parodia humorística de los libros de caballería, interesa por el vivo contraste de sus dos héroes, Quijote y Sancho, en quienes se nos representa el dualismo humano.

J. Me gusta la famosa "Letanía de Nuestro Señor Don Quijote", que compuso el gran poeta nicaragüense Rubén Darío, que . . .[3]

A. ¡Claro!

Rey de los hidalgos, señor de los tristes, que de fuerza alientas y de ensueños vistes, coronado de áureo yelmo de ilusión;[4] que nadie ha podido vencer todavía, por la adarga al brazo, toda fantasía, y la lanza en ristre, toda corazón . . .

J. Caballero errante de los caballeros, barón de varones,[5] príncipe de fieros, par entre los pares, maestro, ¡salud!

(*Se hace una pausa. Por unos momentos todos parecen transportados a un mundo de ensueño. Hay que decir algo y Carmen interrumpe con naturalidad.*)

C. ¿Quiere otra taza de café, Antonio?

A. Muchas gracias. Lo siento mucho, pero tengo que despedirme de ustedes. (*Se levanta.*) Siempre hay tantos preparativos que hacer para la conferencia de mañana. Déle mis recuerdos a su esposa, Miguel, y a la suya también, Señor Herman. Hasta luego. (*Sale.*)

T. Buena suerte y hasta la vista.

(*Los otros contertulianos siguen hablando hasta las dos de la madrugada. Se le ruega a Jaime que lea unas páginas de* Don Quijote.)

J. Con mucho gusto. Voy a leer unas páginas que me gustan mucho. Son del capítulo XLII de la Segunda Parte: "De los consejos que dio Don Quijote a Sancho Panza antes que fuese[6] a gobernar la ínsula[7] . . ." (*Lee.*)

"En esto llegó Don Quijote, y sabiendo lo que pasaba y la celeridad con que Sancho se había de partir a[8] su gobierno,[9] le tomó por

---

[2] **Fulano-de-Tal** *So-and-So*

[3] Rubén Darío (1867–1916), born in Nicaragua, is Spanish America's most famous and cosmopolitan poet—a modernist and *criollo* in that he fuses all American sources, feelings, and inspirations into one sensibility. An interesting cultural comment can be made here: at least two of these *contertulianos* can quote this well-known poem on Don Quijote.

[4] **áureo yelmo de ilusión** *golden helmet of illusion* (refers to the helmet of Mambrino—which is explained in Ch. XLV, as a barber's brass basin glittering in the sunlight)

[5] **barón** and **varón** are homonyms distinguished only by spelling, like English *past* and *passed*. The meaning is something like *lordly man.*

[6] **fuese = fuera**

[7] **la ínsula,** archaic for **la isla**

[8] **se había de partir a** *was to leave for*

[9] The governing of the "island" was a trick played on Sancho by the Duke and Duchess for the entertainment of their house guests.

la mano y se fue con él a su estancia, con intención de aconsejarle cómo se había de haber[10] en su oficio. Cerró tras sí la puerta, e hizo casi por fuerza que Sancho se sentase[11] junto a él, y le dijo:

—Primeramente ¡oh, hijo!, has de temer a Dios; porque en el temerle está la sabiduría, y siendo sabio no podrás errar en nada.

—Lo segundo, has de poner los ojos en quien eres, procurando conocerte a ti mismo que es el más difícil conocimiento que puede imaginarse. Del conocerte saldrá el no hincharte como la rana que quiso igualarse con el buey;[12] que si esto haces, vendrá a ser feos pies de la rueda[13] de tu locura la consideración de haber guardado puercos en tu tierra.

—Así es la verdad—respondió Sancho— pero fue cuando era muchacho; pero después, algo hombrecillo,[14] gansos fueron los que guardé, que no puercos. Pero esto paréceme[15] a mí que no hace al caso;[16] que no todos los que gobiernan vienen de casta de reyes.

—Así es verdad—replicó Don Quijote—; por lo cual[17] los no de principios nobles deben acompañar la gravedad del cargo que ejercitan con una blanda suavidad que, guiada por la prudencia, los libre de la murmuración maliciosa, de quien no hay estado que se escape . . .

—Haz gala, Sancho, de la humildad de tu linaje, y no te desprecies[18] de decir que vienes de labradores; porque viendo que no te corres, ninguno se pondrá a correrte, y préciate más de ser humilde virtuoso que pecador soberbio. Innumerables son aquellos que de baja estirpe nacidos, han subido a la suma dignidad pontificia e imperatoria.[19]

—Si trujeres[20] a tu mujer contigo (porque no es bien que los que asisten a gobiernos de mucho tiempo estén sin las propias), enséñala, y desbástala de su natural rudeza; porque todo lo que suele adquirir un gobernador discreto suele perder y derramar una mujer rústica y tonta . . .

—Hallen en ti más compasión las lágrimas del pobre, pero no más justicia, que las informaciones del rico . . .

—Procura descubrir la verdad por entre las promesas y dádivas del rico como por entre los sollozos e importunidades del pobre . . .

—Si alguna mujer hermosa viniere[21] a pedirte justicia, quita los ojos de sus lágrimas y tus oídos de sus gemidos, y considera de espacio la sustancia de lo que pide, si no quieres que se anegue tu razón en su llanto y tu bondad en sus suspiros.

—Si estos preceptos y estas reglas sigues, Sancho, serán luengos[22] tus días, tu fama será eterna, tus premios colmados, tu felicidad indecible, casarás tus hijos como quisieres,[23] títulos tendrán ellos y tus nietos, vivirás en paz, y en los últimos pasos de la vida te alcanzará el de la muerte en vejez suave y madura, y cerrarán tus ojos las tiernas y delicadas manos de tus terceros netezuelos. Esto que hasta aquí te he dicho son documentos que han de adornar tu alma . . ."

T. Muchas gracias.

C. Esta ha sido una lectura muy interesante. Muchísimas gracias.

J. De nada. Ha sido un gran placer para mí también.

---

[10] **se había de haber** *he should conduct himself*

[11] **hizo . . . que se sentase** *made (him) sit down* (It would not be proper for a squire to sit in the presence of his knight.) **sentase = sentara**

[12] This refers to the well-known fable of Aesop "The Ox and the Frog." The frog tried to puff herself up to the size of the ox, and, naturally, failed.

[13] This refers to the peacock that proudly spread its beautiful feathers into a wheel and then suddenly saw its own ugly feet.

[14] **algo hombrecillo** *when I was older* (Spanish peasants are very apt to use the diminutive forms for implications other than smallness. See page 295, footnote 3.)

[15] **paréceme = me parece**

[16] **no hace al caso** *has nothing to do with it*

[17] **por lo cual** *wherefore*

[18] **no te desprecies** *do not be ashamed*

[19] **imperatoria** *of being an emperor*

[20] **trujeres = traes** (**Trujeres** is an old future subjunctive form, no longer in active use.)

[21] **viniere = viene** (See footnote 20, above.)

[22] **luengos = largos**

[23] **quisieres = quieras** (See footnote 20, above.)

● CUESTIONARIO

1. ¿Qué es una tertulia?
2. ¿Qué acontecimiento celebran los miembros de la tertulia?
3. ¿Cuál es la interpretación política de *Don Quijote?*
4. ¿Por qué se considera *Don Quijote* como un libro de entretenimiento?
5. ¿Qué dualismo humano representan Don Quijote y Sancho?

6. ¿Qué expresan los versos de Rubén Darío sobre Don Quijote?
7. ¿De qué manera aconseja Don Quijote a Sancho en el capítulo XLII de la Segunda Parte?
8. ¿Cómo reacciona Sancho a los consejos de Don Quijote?
9. ¿Adónde debía partir Sancho?
10. ¿Cómo es el lenguaje de Don Quijote?
11. ¿Qué reflejan los consejos de Don Quijote?

● SUGGESTED READINGS

Adams, Nicholson B., *The Heritage of Spain,* Holt, New York, 1943; revised edition, 1959.

Cervantes, Miguel de, *Don Quixote* (tr. by Peter Motteux), Modern Library, New York, 1930.

———, *Don Quixote* (tr. by Samuel Putnam), Viking, New York, 1949.

———, *Don Quixote* (tr. and abridged by Walter Starkie), A Mentor Book, New American Library, New York, 1957.

Flores, Angel, and M. J. Benardete, eds., *Cervantes across the Centuries,* Dryden, New York, 1947.

Johnson, Mildred, *Swan, Cygnets, and Owl,* University of Missouri Studies, Columbia, 1956: pp. 84–89, "Rubén Darío."

Krutch, Joseph Wood, *Five Masters,* Jonathan Cape and Harrison, New York, 1930: Ch. 2, "Miguel de Cervantes."

Una charla: Deportes

Una charla es una conversación muy sencilla. Se pueden reunir unos amigos para tener una charla, y hablar de varias cosas, sin dar mucha importancia a ninguna de ellas.

—El señor Mateo nos ha hecho el honor de venir esta noche para hablarnos de los deportes en Latinoamérica. En otra tertulia el Sr. Herman y otros hablaron de *Don Quijote,* la obra maestra de Cervantes. Ustedes conocen muy bien las actividades del señor Mateo, su espléndida labor como profesor de inglés en la Biblioteca Benjamín Franklin en México y sus conferencias acerca de la literatura norteamericana en el Instituto Cultural Chileno-Norteamericano. Es un gran honor para nosotros tener aquí al señor Mateo. Como en estos momentos todos piensan en los partidos de fútbol de la temporada, el profesor Mateo nos hablará acerca de los deportes de Sud América.

—Muchas gracias, Sr. Martín. Al aceptar la invitación del Sr. Rafael Martín, para asistir a una charla, me he sentido satisfecho y honrado, porque me doy cuenta del interés que ustedes tienen por la cultura hispánica. Otra

vez, gracias. No voy a hablarles de las corridas de toros, como, tal vez, ustedes se imaginan. ¡Qué lástima! En primer lugar, porque las corridas de toros no son un deporte y, en segundo lugar, porque yo nunca he visto una corrida de toros.

—Tal vez ustedes saben que lo que llaman fútbol en este país es muy distinto del fútbol que se juega en Latinoamérica. Para hacerme entender mejor voy a mostrar, de acuerdo con las áreas geográficas, los deportes típicos. En primer lugar, las corridas de toros son un espectáculo popular y tienen un público entusiasta sólo en algunos países. En los países del extremo sur: Brasil, Uruguay, Paraguay, Argentina y Chile, este espectáculo no se da y está prohibido. El público de esos países parece que no revela el menor interés en él. Allí el deporte favorito es el fútbol, interés compartido por todos los países hispanos de ambos continentes. Para dar una idea de su gran popularidad, basta recordar que Uruguay, un país muy pequeño, ganó hace unos años todos los campeonatos olímpicos de fútbol, venciendo hasta los mejores equipos ingleses. (*Con orgullo.*) ¡Y fue en Inglaterra donde se originó este deporte!

—En Argentina, Uruguay y Chile hay un juego interesantísimo y muy peligroso: El Pato. Este juego es una especie de *football* norteamericano que se juega a caballo. Estuvo prohibido por muchos años porque era muy peligroso y se jugaba de una manera violenta y bárbara entre los gauchos. Cargaban contra el contrario saltando un jinete en el caballo del otro y por lo general ambos caían de sus cabalgaduras. Hasta se usaba el lazo y las boleadoras para detener al contrario y quitarle la pelota que contenía un pato en su interior. Recientemente se ha renovado el deporte con las reglas del juego hechas más humanas para evitar las fracturas graves y muchas veces mortales de otros tiempos. Ya se extiende por otros países vecinos.

—El polo se juega en casi todas partes de Latinoamérica, pero especialmente en Argentina. Este país ganó dos veces los campeonatos olímpicos. Unos jugadores argentinos de polo son conocidísimos en todo el mundo, como lo son[1] los caballos argentinos de polo que se venden a buen precio en este país.

—El *baseball* norteamericano no se practica en los países del sur de Sudamérica, pero en cambio es popularísimo en la parte norte del continente en Venezuela y Colombia. En México este deporte introducido de los Estados Unidos ha arraigado profundamente y hace unos años leímos en los periódicos que los mexicanos estaban llevándose algunos de los mejores jugadores norteamericanos para integrar los equipos al sur del Río Grande en las famosas ligas mexicanas. Ese éxodo de los jugadores de béisbol al sur del Río Bravo,[2] atraídos por las sumas astronómicas que les ofrecían en México, causó críticas en este país como ustedes saben. Algunos periodistas deportivos dijeron: "¡Los mexicanos están llevando la política del buen vecino más allá de los límites razonables!" (*Risas.*) A los cubanos también les gusta muchísimo el béisbol y tienen muy buenos jugadores, que a menudo pasan a los equipos americanos.

—Un espectáculo muy popular en Cuba y en México es el jai-alai, un espectáculo derivado del deporte tradicional de los vascongados, llamado pelota vasca. Lo juegan principalmente los famosos pelotaris venidos de aquella región de España. Se juega no sólo en México y Cuba sino también en los Estados Unidos. Ahora se juega en la Florida como resultado de la vecindad de Cuba y yo creo que en Miami se practica mucho ese deporte. ¿No es verdad? Se pueden oir allá en la Florida gritos de "Gooooool, gooooool", "Hurra, hurra", en inglés y a la vez en español.

—En fin, los otros deportes, tales como el tenis, el básquetbol o baloncesto, que los aztecas jugaban muchos años antes del nacimiento del señor Naismith (de Kansas, el inventor de este juego en los Estados Unidos), el *rugby* inglés, las regatas, el *water polo*, la natación y el *box* (o boxeo) son comunes en todos los países del sur. Las carreras de caballos tienen gran popularidad. Recientemente, en México, D.F., construyeron un hipódromo gigantesco, llamado "el Hipódromo de las Américas", donde corren muchos caballos norteamericanos.

—En la región de los lagos chileno-argentinos del sur se practican varios deportes de invierno durante la temporada. Ahí vemos muchos esquiadores y simpáticas esquiadoras haciendo *slaloms* en la nieve. Este deporte tiene gran popularidad y ha añadido un verbo más al idioma español: *esquiar*. Hay allí casinos de esquiadores con todas las comodidades modernas. A menos de una hora de viaje en auto desde Santiago está el club de esquiadores Portillo. También les gusta a todos escalar montañas. En la región de los Andes este deporte se llama "practicar el andinismo". Los que lo practican se llaman andinistas, como en Europa, alpinistas.

—En fin todos estos deportes de origen inglés y norteamericano han originado un vocabulario, o "jerga" angloespañola, que sería interesantísimo como problema de filología contemporánea: la ofensiva, el score, el teán, el tacle, un shot, un jonrón, el gol, el réferi, un penal, un match, el hockey y otras muchas palabras.

—Aquí tengo una lista de palabras anglo-

---

[1] **como lo son** *just as are* (= are it, are **conocidísimos**)
[2] **el Río Bravo** is the name of the Rio Grande frequently used by our Spanish-American neighbors.

españolas, que tal vez les interesen a ustedes como simple curiosidad.[3] (*Lee.*)

(*En esto se sirve café y dejan de hablar por unos minutos. Acabando de tomar café siguen hablando.*)

—Señor, díganos: ¿Qué hacen las muchachas? ¿Se quedan en casa bordando o tocando el piano mientras los jóvenes se divierten?

—Algunas sí, pero las jóvenes son modernas. Algunas son avanzadas, como dicen sus abuelas. Muchas pertenecen al Club Femenino de Deportes. Mi esposa es pescadora entusiasta. Ella dice que es un deporte agradable y a la vez fructífero. En casi todos los lagos de Chile hay trucha de arroyo y también trucha salmonada.

—¿Cuánto cuesta el permiso de pesca?

—Unos cinco pesos, moneda nacional, al mes.

—¿Hay canchas de golf?

—Sí. En algunas partes se juega hacia arriba y hacia abajo de la montaña. Los mejores jugadores tienen treinta y seis golpes para los nueve hoyos.

—¿De veras?

—Pero yo no.

—Sus estudiantes hacen excursiones a pie, ¿verdad?

—¡Cómo no! ¿A qué viene? Pero los excursionistas no comen *hot dogs* como aquí. En mi país comemos choclos y asado en las largas caminatas y cabalgatas.

—¿Hacen ustedes fogatas en los bosques y en las playas?

—Sí.

—Y, después de comer, ¿cantan sentados alrededor de la fogata, acurrucados y a la luz de la luna?

—Sí, cantamos. También leemos poesías. Casi todos los chilenos son aficionados a la poesía, aun los atletas.

—¡Imagínense! ¡Haciendo *touchdowns* en verso yámbico!

—¡Eso no! No llega a tanto. (*Todos se ríen.*)

—¿Por qué no nos lee una muestra?

—Con mucho gusto. "Puentes" por Pablo Neruda, chileno.[4]

Puentes—arcos de acero azul adonde vienen
a dar su despedida los que pasan,—
por arriba los trenes,
por abajo las aguas,
enfermos de seguir un largo viaje
que principia, que sigue y nunca acaba.

Cielos—arriba—cielos,
y pájaros que pasan
sin detenerse, caminando como
los trenes y las aguas.
¿Qué maldición cayó sobre vosotros?[5]
¿Qué esperáis[6] en la noche densa y larga
con los brazos abiertos como un niño
que muere a la llegada de su hermana?

¿Qué voz de maldición pasiva y negra
sobre vosotros extendió sus alas,
para hacer que siguieran
el viaje que no acaba,
los paisajes, la vida, el sol, la tierra,
los trenes y las aguas,
mientras la angustia inmóvil del acero
se hunde más en la tierra y más la clava?

---

[3] "A Glossary of Baseball Terms in Spanish," by Graydon S. DeLand, in *The Modern Language Journal,* February, 1940 and "Mexican Baseball Terminology: An Example of Linguistic Growth," by Seymour Menton, in *Hispania,* December, 1954.

[4] Pablo Neruda (1904—) is the pseudonym of Neftalí Ricardo Reyes, considered one of the most gifted of contemporary poets in the Americas. The translation of Mildred Johnson, of the University of Missouri, follows:

BRIDGES

O bridges,—arches of blue steel to which these come
To say farewell as they are passing by,—
The trains that are above,
The waters down below,
Infirm from travelling so long a journey
That starts, continues, and is never ended.

The skies—above—the skies,
And birds that pass along
And never stop, while travelling as do
The waters and the trains,
What malediction fell upon your head?

For what do you wait there through long, dense nights,
With your two arms outstretched just like a child
Who dies on the arrival of his sister?

What voice of malediction, black and passive,
Has spread its wings out wide and covered you,
To make all things continue:
The journey with no end,
The landscapes, life itself, the sun, the earth,
The waters, and the trains,—
While the immobile anguish of the steel
Sinks further in the earth and pierces more?

From *Swan, Cygnets, and Owl,* University of Missouri Studies, Columbia, Missouri, 1956.

[5] **vosotros** *you* (See page 27 footnote 1.)

[6] **esperáis** *do you wait for*

● CUESTIONARIO

1. ¿Qué diferencia hay entre una charla y una tertulia?
2. ¿Sobre qué tema habla el Sr. Mateo a sus amigos norteamericanos?
3. ¿Qué actividades desarrolla el Sr. Mateo?
4. ¿Dónde están prohibidas las corridas de toros? ¿Por qué?
5. ¿Cuál es el deporte favorito de casi todos los países hispanos?
6. ¿Dónde se originó el fútbol latinoamericano?
7. Mencione usted un ejemplo que demuestre la popularidad de que goza el fútbol en Latinoamérica.
8. ¿Por qué estuvo prohibido el juego llamado el Pato?
9. ¿Dónde se practica el béisbol norteamericano en Sud América?
10. ¿Qué reacción causó en Estados Unidos el éxodo de los jugadores de béisbol norteamericanos a México?
11. ¿En qué países se practica el jai-alai?
12. ¿Qué otros deportes son comunes en Latinoamérica?
13. ¿Cuál es el deporte que ha añadido un verbo más al idioma español?
14. ¿Qué es el andinismo?
15. Mencione algunas palabras angloespañolas que se han originado de los deportes ingleses y norteamericanos.
16. ¿Qué actividades desarrollan las muchachas latinoamericanas?

● SUGGESTED READINGS

See those for Unit 26.

Beals, Carleton, *Lands of the Dawning Morrow,* Bobbs-Merrill, Indianapolis, New York, 1948, pp. 44, 144, 305.

ARTICLES:

"Argentine Horsemen Like the Duck Game," *Scholastic,* February 9, 1942.

Bulletin of the Pan American Union, Washington, D.C.: "Sport in Latin America," September, 1926; "Water Sports in Uruguay," April, 1938; "New Ski Horizons in Chile," September, 1931; "El Pato," January, 1948; "Jai-alai," January, 1948.

Holidays and Festivals in Mexico, Pan American Union, Washington, D.C.

Inter-American, Washington, D.C.: "Caribbean Strike-out," January, 1945; "Sport in Spanish," February, 1944; "Battle of the Bases," April, 1946.

"Skiing High in the Andes," *House and Garden,* July, 1946.

"World's Most Dangerous Game," *Popular Mechanics,* October, 1941.

26

La corrida de toros

En España, y en algunos países de Hispanoamérica, se celebran corridas de toros. Pero obsérvese que los españoles y los hispanos cuando hablan de las corridas no las consideran nunca como un deporte. En España se las llama a veces *la fiesta nacional* o *la fiesta brava* y se las considera como un espectáculo y arte. Si se le pregunta a un *aficionado* cuál es su deporte favorito, contestará el fútbol, el ciclismo, la pelota, la natación, la equitación o cualquiera de los deportes que comparte con los países anglosajones.

En sus orígenes probablemente era una forma de adiestramiento para la caza. Durante la Edad Media, y hasta el siglo dieciocho, sí que fue un deporte. Lo practicaba la nobleza ante todo para demostrar su habilidad a caballo. Desde el siglo dieciséis el deporte de la nobleza pasó del palenque de justas,[1] en el castillo feudal, a la plaza pública y se hizo más espectacular al admitir al pueblo a presenciarlo. El "caballero en plaza"[2] solía hacerse ayudar por[3] varios peones que colocaban el toro ventajosamente, atrayéndolo con la capa.

En el siglo diecinueve, la aristocracia abandonó este deporte-espectáculo, y fueron formadas las cuadrillas profesionales que dieron al pueblo el espectáculo que deseaba. El torero

[1] **palenque de justas** *parade ground for jousts*   [2] **El "caballero en plaza"** *The horseman*   [3] **solía hacerse ayudar por** *usually enlisted the help of*

profesional, producto de la clase socialmente inferior, tenía que crearse un prestigio a base de valor y habilidad y trataba de sobresalir vistiendo trajes llamativos y llevando una vida extravagante. La corrida de toros, como espectáculo, requería su escenario propio y así empezaron a construirse plazas de toros. El traje de luces del torero moderno y la indumentaria y equipo de sus ayudantes se derivan directamente de los vestidos de los majos[4] de la época. Hoy día una corrida es un espectáculo tan estilizado y refinado como una representación teatral.

Principalmente desde Juan Belmonte,[5] a quien un defecto físico impedía moverse con ligereza, el toreo se convirtió en un arte, con una técnica compleja y difícil y una estética con escuelas distintas y énfasis[6] opuestos. Así existe la clásica (o de Ronda)[7] caracterizada por su valor frío, su sobriedad y su respeto a la tradición y a las normas aceptadas; y la sevillana, más espectacular, con más floreo y tendencia a la improvisación. Estas dos escuelas puede decirse que han existido siempre, desde que el toreo se hizo profesión y espectáculo y arte. Desde Belmonte el énfasis no está ya en el ataque al toro, sino en la inmovilidad del torero, en el hábil manejo de la fiera y en el balance artístico de la figura del torero, con el ritmo de una estatua clásica.

Lo dicho hasta ahora[8] nos lleva a describir brevísimamente una corrida en términos teatrales, pues al fin y al cabo son los más apropiados.

Una corrida es como una tragedia, en tres actos, precedidos de un preludio espectacular, subrayados por el coro, que en este caso es todo el público que llena la plaza y que se asocia con sus gritos de aplauso, o disgusto,[9] de alegría y de horror, a lo que ocurre en la arena. En el preludio, o paseíllo, desfilan los *toreros* que van a lidiar los toros, precedidos de los alguaciles y seguidos cada uno del resto de su cuadrilla: los *picadores*[10] y los *banderilleros;*[11] finalmente desfilan los empleados de la plaza: los *monosabios*[12] con las mulas que arrastran el toro al final de la lidia, areneros y carpinteros.

Toda la comitiva cruza la plaza al compás de un paso doble[13] brioso y se coloca frente al palco del Presidente, es decir el Gobernador de la Provincia, el alcalde de la ciudad o un delegado suyo, a quien saluda con mucha ceremonia. La autoridad que preside dirige oficialmente la lidia, sacando pañuelos de varios colores para señalar el cambio de suertes o actos. Clarines y timbales tocan para subrayar estas señales.

Después del primer toque sale con toda su fuerza el animal feroz, que ha estado encerrado en los *chiqueros,*[14] que se hallan bajo las *graderías.*[15] Unos pases[16] de los banderilleros y finalmente del matador fijan el ataque del toro y permiten al torero conocer a su enemigo y empezar a estudiar su temperamento, sus reacciones y sus hábitos. Los pases consisten en atraer al toro con una capa e inducirle[17] a que cargue contra ella,[18] y luego esquivar el cuerpo lo suficiente para que el toro pase rozándolo, pero sin herir.

El primer acto de la tragedia, no simulada sino real y a la vista de millares de espectadores, es la parte ecuestre de la corrida. Es una reminiscencia del pasado cuando sólo se lidiaba a caballo. Es la suerte de los *picadores:* el jinete incita al toro con una larga pica. Cuando el toro arremete contra el caballo, el picador hiere con la pica los grandes músculos del cuello del toro. Esta suerte sirve para estudiar la bravura del toro y también para hacerle bajar la cabeza. Los matadores se turnan en

---

[4] **majos** *dandies*

[5] Juan Belmonte was born in Seville in 1892. His most brilliant days as a bullfighter were in 1914.

[6] **énfasis** The singular is also **énfasis.** See Unit 9 §49.

[7] **de Ronda** *of the town of Ronda* (in southern Spain)

[8] **Lo dicho hasta ahora** *What has been said up to this point* (See Unit 16 §92.)

[9] **disgusto** *displeasure*

[10] The **picador** is the one on horseback who thrusts the lance in the bull's neck.

[11] The **banderillero** is the one who thrusts the darts (sometimes with firecrackers on the end).

[12] **monosabio** *wise monkey* (a kind of ring attendant, so called because a troupe of trained monkeys appeared in a burlesque of the bullfight in 1847 in Madrid)

[13] **paso doble** *two-step* (a dance)

[14] The **chiqueros** are small, dimly lighted stalls where the bulls are kept until the fight.

[15] The **graderías** are the series of steps in the grandstands.

[16] The **pases** are "passes" made at the bull. They are made sometimes to throw the bull off balance and to make him pause for a second. This gives the matador a chance to walk away.

[17] See page 167 footnote 4. The **le** personifies the bull.   [18] **a que cargue contra ella** *to charge against it*

hacer los quites[19] vistosos para apartar al toro del caballo. Si el matador no es muy perito con la capa, los banderilleros pueden sustituirle en esta suerte.

El segundo acto es el de las *banderillas*. Suena el clarín, y el banderillero, armado de dos palos con puntas de acero, incita al toro. Al mismo tiempo le sale él al encuentro y al momento preciso le clava las banderillas en la nuca. Esta faena requiere gran destreza, serenidad y piernas ágiles. Para que resulte lucida ha de practicarse con brevedad, precisión, valor y elegancia. Cuando el matador mismo pone las banderillas, la banda toca un paso doble en su honor.

Suena otra vez el clarín y empieza el tercer acto, el final de la tragedia. Sale el matador a la arena con la *muleta*:[20] un paño rojo, más pequeño que la capa, sostenido por un palo, en la mano izquierda. En la derecha lleva el estoque.[21]

Mientras sus ayudantes distraen al toro el matador va al palco del Presidente y pide su permiso para proceder. Luego le brinda la muerte del toro de una manera ceremoniosa y a menudo brinda después en forma más espontánea a otra persona distinguida que presencia la corrida o a la señora de su predilección, en cuyo palco se pone el capote de ceremonia del torero.

En seguida empieza la parte más peligrosa y emocionante de la corrida, una serie de pases coordinados en los que el torero hace alarde de su valor[22] y su dominio sobre el animal. El público demuestra su entusiasmo y su aprobación, poniéndose muchas veces de pie y gritando con todas sus fuerzas (como en los Estados Unidos durante los últimos minutos de un partido de fútbol cuando los dos equipos están empatados y uno de ellos se acerca a la línea de *goal* o durante el último *round* de un *match* de boxeo). Lo que el público aplaude con mayor entusiasmo es el valor frío, calculado e inteligente del torero, la noble fiereza del animal que ataca con bravura. El torero mueve los pies lo menos posible. Luego logra dominar el toro, frenando su ímpetu, y así le obliga a pasar exactamente por donde quiere el torero. Es el momento culminante de la corrida en el que[23] se enfrentan el valor y la inteligencia de un hombre de mediana estatura y peso, con un animal semisalvaje, criado para luchar, valeroso y fuerte, con poderosas defensas naturales y que pesa casi mil libras.

Después de diez minutos de pases, suena por última vez el clarín y el torero se dispone a dar muerte al toro con el estoque. Cuanto más instantánea sea la muerte mayor[24] mérito se concede al torero. La estocada requiere, por lo tanto, considerable valor, gran habilidad y precisión, y no poca fuerza física.

La tragedia ha terminado. El destino requiere una víctima y la ha tenido. El toro siempre es la víctima, pero muchas veces no es la única. Antes de morir puede sacrificar a otros, tal vez al ídolo de la muchedumbre, al torero arrojado y artista que les ha proporcionado unos momentos de emociones fuertes a los aficionados. La muerte está presente en una plaza de toros por lo menos seis veces, tantas como hay toros que se lidian. La atracción misteriosa que la fiesta brava ejerce en el alma española explica sin duda en parte el arraigo profundo[25] de las corridas en grandes sectores de la Península Ibérica y en algunos de los países hispanos. Pero no debe olvidarse, al juzgar este espectáculo, que lo que el público busca y aplaude ante todo son los alardes de valor, destreza y arte por parte del matador y sus ayudantes.

Y tampoco debe olvidarse que la afición a los toros dista mucho de ser compartida por todos los españoles. Lo mismo que hay entusiastas tan fanáticos como algunos graduados de las universidades americanas por sus equipos de fútbol, también hay muchos indiferentes y hasta hostiles a las corridas, unos por razones económicas, pues los toros bravos ocupan unos pastos

---

[19] **quites** is a special word used for the maneuvers of the **matadores** to attract the bulls away from the horses.

[20] The **muleta** is an oval-shaped piece of red cloth stiffened with a coarse piece of yellow cloth sewn down the middle. It is folded over a stick shaped like a baton (called **palilla** or **vara**).

[21] **estoque** *sword*

[22] **hace alarde de su valor** *shows off his bravery*

[23] **el que** *which* (referring to **momento**)

[24] **Cuanto más instantánea . . . mayor** *The more sudden the death, the greater . . .*

[25] **arraigo profundo** *deep roots*

que podrían dedicarse a reses lecheras y para carne en un país donde ambos productos esenciales son escasos. Otros se oponen a la corrida por motivos sentimentales y estéticos incomprensibles por el anglosajón.

Piense lo que piense cada uno sobre las corridas, son éstas un espectáculo tan arraigado y emocionalmente tan ligado a la vida de muchos, tan íntimamente relacionado con el arte— no sólo las artes plásticas sino la literatura en todos sus géneros—que no pueden ignorarse, y es preciso hacer un esfuerzo mental para comprenderlas.

● CUESTIONARIO

1. ¿Dónde se celebran corridas de toros?
2. ¿Cómo se transformó la corrida de toros de un deporte a un arte y un espectáculo?
3. ¿Cuál es la importancia de Juan Belmonte en el toreo?
4. ¿Qué distintos énfasis tienen las dos escuelas españolas de toreo?
5. ¿Con qué se podría comparar una corrida de toros?
6. ¿Cuál es la parte más peligrosa y emocionante de una corrida de toros?

7. ¿Cuáles son los méritos del torero que más aplaude el público?
8. Explique usted el porqué del arraigo profundo de las corridas en sectores de la Península Ibérica y en algunos de los países hispanos.
9. ¿Cuáles son algunas de las razones hostiles a las corridas de toros?
10. ¿Cuál es su opinión sobre este espectáculo?
11. ¿Puede usted nombrar algunos de los toreros famosos por su valor y destreza en los toreos?

● SUGGESTED READINGS

Buckley, Peter, *Bullfight,* Simon and Schuster, New York, 1958.
Casteel, Homer, *The Running of the Bulls,* Dodd, Mead, New York, 1953.
Conrad, Barnaby, *The Death of Manolete,* Houghton Mifflin, Boston, 1958.
———, *La fiesta brava,* Houghton Mifflin, Boston, 1953.
Hemingway, Ernest, *Death in the Afternoon,* Scribner's, New York, 1954.

Lea, Tom, *The Brave Bulls,* Little, Brown, Boston, 1949.
Smith, Rex, *Biography of the Bulls, an Anthology of Bullfighting,* Rinehart, New York, 1957.
Tynan, Kenneth, *Bull Fever,* Longmans, New York, 1955.
Note: The Runnning of the Bulls has excellent illustrations and drawings by the author, "to show what happens at a bullfight and very basically how and why."

El gaucho y el cowboy

Antes del descubrimiento de América en el año 1492 no hubo caballos en el Nuevo Mundo. Los españoles trajeron los primeros caballos a América y también ganados vacunos, gatos, perros y gallinas. Casi todos fueron importaciones españolas.

Después del descubrimiento los españoles empezaron la conquista y la colonización en una vasta zona de más de tres veces la superficie de Europa desde donde está ahora el estado de Kansas hasta Patagonia en Sud América. Con los conquistadores vinieron los caballos que causaron horror entre los primeros habitantes, los aztecas de México, los araucanos de Chile y otros. Ellos creyeron que el caballo y el jinete fueron un solo monstruo grotesco.

Después, en el período de la colonización los españoles importaron grandes cantidades de caballos y de ganado vacuno y ovejas. Muchos de esos animales se escaparon de las zonas bajo la dominación española, se multiplicaron libremente y originaron millones de rebaños salvajes de caballos y ganado vacuno en las praderas americanas, especialmente en el sudoeste de los Estados Unidos, en los llanos de Venezuela y Colombia, en las pampas de Uruguay y Argentina y en el sur de Brasil.

Se originó un nuevo tipo de hombre americano también cuyo ámbito fue la llanura: se llamaba pastor, pionero, explorador, etc. Las haciendas de estas zonas se llamaban ranchos en el sudoeste de los Estados Unidos, fundos en Chile, estancias en Uruguay y Argentina, y fincas, haciendas o ranchos en México. El dueño se llamaba ranchero, estanciero o simplemente patrón.

Algunos pioneros se llamaban "cowboys" en los Estados Unidos. Sus costumbres y su lengua muestran gran influencia de las regiones de habla española. Muchas palabras que usamos en inglés son de origen español: *buckaroo, vaquero, corral, lasso, lariat, bronco, rodeo, chaps, látigo, hombre, quirt, hoosegow, vamoose.*[1]

En Argentina, en Uruguay y en la parte sur de Brasil se llamaban gauchos, nombre de origen incierto. No puede asignársele un sentido racial, sino étnico, porque fueron gauchos también los hijos de los inmigrantes europeos, los mestizos, los negros y los mulatos que aceptaron aquel género de vida.

En los llanos de Colombia y Venezuela se llamaban *llaneros,* derivado de *llanos.* Estos jinetes americanos: cowboys, gauchos, llaneros, tenían un tipo de cultura peculiar americana con su literatura, cuentos, leyendas y canciones. Los gauchos hicieron un papel importante en las guerras de la Independencia. Los gauchos y los llaneros todos combatieron en los ejércitos de San Martín y Bolívar y cruzaron los Andes. Era el gaucho el genuino hijo del país.

Algunas veces escuchamos en la radio canciones populares: las canciones gauchescas, los corridos mexicanos, los "cowboy songs" de los Estados Unidos. También hay películas americanas en la tradición del cowboy o del gaucho. Todos son un tipo puramente americano. Todos dan inspiración para una gran parte de la literatura y de las películas modernas americanas. A principios del siglo pasado se fue modificando el significado de la palabra *gaucho.* Empezó a considerarse *hombre al margen de la sociedad.*

En Argentina y en Uruguay hay una literatura gauchesca que principió con las canciones y los cuentos relatados por los mismos gauchos. Es muy famoso el poema épico *Martín Fierro.*[2]

> Soy gaucho, y entiendaló
> como mi lengua lo explica:
> para mí la tierra es chica
> y pudiera ser mayor;[3]
> ni la víbora me pica
> ni quema mi frente el sol.

La mejor novela de este tipo es la novela criolla *Don Segundo Sombra,* escrita en 1926 por Ricardo Güiraldes. Don Segundo Sombra[4] es el gaucho ideal, símbolo de las pampas, pero una verdadera *sombra:*

> Por el camino, que fingía un arroyo de tierra, caballo y jinete repecharon la loma, difundidos, en el cardal. Un momento la silueta doble se perfiló nítida sobre el cielo, sesgado por un verdoso rayo de atardecer. Aquello que se alejaba era más una idea que un hombre.

Un gaucho muy cómico es Anastasio el Pollo, de Estanislao del Campo en su "Fausto" publicado en 1866. Este gaucho fue al teatro de Buenos Aires y trató de interpretar la famosa ópera de *Faust* a un compañero suyo.

> ¡Viera al Diablo! Uñas de gato
> flacón, un sable largote,
> gorro con pluma, capote
> y una barba de chivato.
>
> ¡Pobre rubia! Vea usté
> cuánto ha venido a sufrir:
> se le podía decir:
> ¡Quién te vido y quién te ve!
>
> —Ansí es el mundo, amigaso;
> nada dura, don Laguna,
> hoy nos ríe la fortuna,
> mañana nos da un guascaso.
>
> Bajaron el cortinao,
> de lo que yo me alegré . . .

---

[1] *vamoose* (from **vamos**), *hoosegow* (from **juzgado**), *quirt* (from **cuarta**), *chaps* (from **chaparajos**), *lariat* (from **la reata**), *lasso* (from **lazo**), *buckaroo* (from **vaquero**).

[2] By José Hernández, published in 1872. A second part was published in 1878. The poem depicts the birth and death of the gaucho, his struggle against "civilization" and his ultimate surrender to it. Note the stress on –*ló* (line 1). In emphatic speech, the with-verb pronoun attached to a command is often stressed.

[3] **y pudiera ser mayor** *and even if it were larger* (it would still be small to me)

[4] Don Segundo Sombra is to Argentinian literature what Don Quixote is to Spanish literature: an ideal of freedom and manliness. Some say that Don Segundo Sombra, even though he was a vanishing American type, initiated Argentina's commercial strength and her international meat-and-wheat business.

Tome el frasco, priéndalé.
—Sírvase no más, cuñao.[5]

El famoso pintor argentino Molina Campos pintó miles de gauchos graciosos. La compañía Minneapolis-Moline (de Minneapolis) tiene mucho interés en el pintor Molina Campos y sus gauchos porque durante muchos años publicó un calendario con reproducciones en colores de los gauchos de este pintor. Molina Campos murió en 1959.

La vida gauchesca tiene un mágico encanto y el gaucho es inmortal. Su filosofía es admirable. Dice:

Desde que aprendí a ignorar
de ningún saber me asombro.[6]

El gaucho era el "hijo de la pampa", patriótico, valiente, fuerte, independiente y leal. Su ropa era:

1) Un sombrero de alas cortas
2) Un pañuelo al cuello de colores vivos
3) Una chaqueta y un tirador cubierto de plata
4) Pantalones con flecos o bombachas
5) Un chiripá (especie de impermeable que llevaba cuando montaba a caballo)
6) Un poncho (que llevaba en el invierno)
7) Zapatos o botas de cuero con espuelas de plata
8) Un largo puñal
9) Un lazo o boleadoras[7]
10) Un facón cincelado[8]

Para todos los gauchos la posesión más preciosa era su caballo. También le gustaban sus perros y sus guitarras. Sus diversiones eran el juego de pato, la riña de gallos y las carreras de caballo. Pasaban las noches (hasta la medianoche) cantando alrededor del fogón debajo del gran árbol llamado "ombú", o en la pulpería (la antigua "general store").

En el juego del pato, los gauchos se dividían en dos partidos.[9] El árbitro[10] echaba al aire una pelota de cuero con dos asas. Dentro de la pelota había un pato. Los gauchos, a caballo, trataban de coger la pelota y de correr con ella a su rancho. Los gauchos del otro partido trataban de robar la pelota y correr con ella a su rancho. Este juego del pato se parece a nuestro juego de *polo*.

A los gauchos les gustaban también las carreras de caballos. Algunas veces corrían en parejas hasta cierto punto. Los caballos se llamaban "parejeros" también. Otras veces corrían con boleadoras (que se parecen un poco a la reata) para coger avestruces.

No es necesario describir las riñas de gallos porque todos saben lo que son.

A los gauchos también les gustaba jugar a los naipes. El juego de *canasta* es un juego de naipes de Argentina y Uruguay.

En 1921 la Junta de Historia y Numismática Americana de Argentina dio un homenaje al héroe guerrillero Güemes[11] en el centenario de su muerte y esculpió en una medalla esta inscripción: A LOS HEROICOS GAUCHOS, LA PATRIA OS LLAMO[12] A DEFENDER SUS FRONTERAS DEL NORTE.

● CUESTIONARIO

1. ¿Qué animales trajeron los españoles al Nuevo Mundo?
2. ¿Cuál es la zona que conquistaron y colonizaron los españoles?
3. ¿Qué pensaron los indios al ver los caballos y jinetes españoles?
4. ¿En qué regiones se originaron rebaños salvajes de caballos y de ganado vacuno y ovejas?
5. ¿Qué nombre recibieron las haciendas de los habitantes de la llanura en (a) el sudoeste de los Estados Unidos, (b) Chile, (c) Uruguay y Argentina, (d) México?

---

[5] The gaucho language is picturesque: **viera** *you should have seen;* **vido** for **vio;** **ansí** for **así;** **priéndalé** *drain it;* **Sírvase no más** *Just help yourself.* **Cuñao** for **cuñado, usté** for **usted,** and **cortinao** for **cortinado** are instances of the loss of fricative [ð], common throughout the Spanish-speaking world.

[6] From the epic poem *Martín Fierro* by José Hernández.

[7] The **boleadora** is a two- or three-stranded lariat with a weighted ball at the end of each strand; thrown at an animal's legs, it twists around them and throws him to the ground.

[8] The **facón,** *knife,* was considered a real treasure and was passed from father to son.

[9] **partidos** *teams*

[10] **árbitro** *umpire*

[11] A gaucho hero of the Wars of Independence. Many gauchos fought in the armies of the liberator San Martín (1778–1850).

[12] **os llamó** *called you* (See page 27 footnote 1; **os** is the with-verb pronoun corresponding to the plural **vosotros, –as.**)

6. ¿Cómo se llamaba el dueño de estas diferentes haciendas?
7. Mencione algunas palabras de origen español en las costumbres y la lengua de los "cowboys".
8. ¿A quiénes se llamaba *llaneros?*
9. ¿Qué papel desempeñaron los gauchos en las guerras de la independencia?
10. ¿Por qué es cómico el gaucho creado por Estanislao del Campo en su poema "Fausto"?
11. ¿Qué es *Don Segundo Sombra?*
12. ¿Cuáles eran las diversiones favoritas y posesiones más preciosas del gaucho?
13. ¿Cuál es el juego de naipes que se originó en Argentina y Uruguay?
14. ¿Cuál es la filosofía del gaucho?

● SUGGESTED READINGS

Amorim, Enrique, *The Horse and His Shadow* (tr. by Richard O'Connell and James G. Luján), Scribner's, New York, 1943.

Arciniegas, Germán, ed., *The Green Continent* (tr. by Harriet De Onís), Knopf, New York, 1944: pp. 339–54, "Sarmiento, the Educator."

Coester, Alfred, *A Literary History of Spanish America*, 2nd ed., Macmillan, New York, 1928.

Cunninghame-Graham, R. B., *The Horses of the Conquest*, University of Oklahoma Press, Norman, 1949.

Hernández, José, *A Fragment from Martin Fierro* (tr. by Joseph Auslander), Hispanic Society of America, New York, 1932.

———, *The Gaucho, Martin Fierro* (tr. by Walter Owen), Farrar and Rinehart, New York, 1936.

Keen, Benjamin, *Readings in Latin-American Civilization*, Houghton Mifflin, Boston, 1955: Ch. 27, "Toward a Latin-American Culture"; pp. 451–54, "Farewell to the Gaucho."

Mann, Mrs. Horace, *Life in the Argentine Republic in the Days of the Tyrants*, Hurd and Houghton, New York, 1868.

Niles, Blair, *Journeys in Time*, Coward-McCann, New York, 1946: Ch. 2, "Dedicated to Horses"; Ch. 12, "W. H. Hudson, Lover of Life"; Ch. 26, "Grand Old Scottish Gaucho" (Cunninghame-Graham).

Torres-Ríoseco, Arturo, *The Epic of Latin-American Literature*, Oxford University Press, New York, 1946: Ch. 4, "Gaucho Literature."

———, *New World Literature*, University of California Press, Berkeley and Los Angeles, 1949: Ch. 5, "Martin Fierro."

Zorilla de San Martín, Juan, *Tabaré* (an Indian legend of Uruguay, tr. by Walter Owen), Pan American Union, Washington, D.C., 1956.

27

Una velada musical

P. *Pepe*   M. *su señora, Margarita*

P. Oye, Margarita, te traigo una buena noticia. La señora de Ayora ha tenido la gentileza de invitarnos a una velada literario-musical en su casa.

M. ¡Espléndido! Es muy amable de su parte. Pero, ¿no crees tú que será algo aburrido? Ya sabes, me cansan las tertulias formales: mucha etiqueta, muchos cumplidos, mucho chisme y mucha pérdida de tiempo.

P. No temas. Según me dicen, bien vale la pena. La Sra. de Ayora tiene fama de saber escoger muy bien sus amistades y de organizar veladas muy interesantes. Y

además nos dará la ocasión de conocer a la *gente bien,* como dicen, de esta ciudad.

M. Dime, Pepe, ¿sabes más o menos en qué va a consistir la velada?

P. Algo he oído, aunque, naturalmente, el programa se supone que sea una sorpresa. La parte literaria consistirá en la lectura de alguna de sus últimas poesías originales por el joven poeta Alonso Dorado. Dicen que es un excelente poeta y que recita maravillosamente. También es probable que la bellísima actriz Estrellita Alvarez nos recite un monólogo. ¡Qué bien declama! ¡Qué graciosa es!

M. No lo dudo viendo tu entusiasmo. Con todo, a mí me parece que me interesará más la parte musical. Pero te advierto que soy muy exigente.

P. Ya lo sé de sobras. También lo es la Sra. de Ayora. Nunca invita a nadie a tocar que no sea de primera categoría. Dicen que esta vez el plato fuerte será el concierto del Cuarteto Orfeo.

M. ¡Cómo! ¿Contrata un cuarteto profesional para una velada en su casa?

P. No, chica, no son profesionales. Son aficionados. Son cuatro amigos, figuras de la sociedad local, a quienes apasiona la música. Hace varios años que tocan juntos. El violín primero es un reputado doctor, el segundo es un abogado, la viola la toca un comerciante y el violoncelista es un profesor de literatura en el Instituto de Segunda Enseñanza.[1]

M. ¡Qué interesante! Pero me da miedo. Los que tocan instrumentos de cuerda son siempre o muy buenos o muy malos. Me temo que no[2] sea esto último. ¡Es tan difícil alcanzar la perfección requerida!

P. No te apures. Me han asegurado que tocan con la perfección de profesionales y con el fuego y entusiasmo de los aficionados. Parece que el Dr. Galíndez, el primer violín, es algo excepcional.

M. Empiezo a convencerme de que vamos a pasar una velada muy agradable.

P. De ello estoy seguro. La Sra. de Ayora, como te dije, sabe hacerlas muy bien. Y además tiene fama de preparar unos refrescos deliciosísimos. Su pastelería no tiene rival. Y sus hijas, que la ayudan a hacer los honores de la casa, son encantadoras. ¿No las conoces? Maruja, la de los ojos azules, Herminia, la vivaracha . . .

M. Sí, recuerdo haberlas visto[3] aunque nunca he sido presentada. Me gustará conocerlas. (*Después de una pausa.*) Supongo que has aceptado la invitación.

P. No faltaba más.[4]

---

[1] **Instituto de Segunda Enseñanza** is the term used in Spain, which corresponds to our "secondary school." In Mexico, **escuela secundaria** is used.

[2] **que no** *lest* (Spanish has a choice between **que** *that* and the negative **que no** *lest,* after verbs of fearing: *I fear lest he may come = I think fearingly, "Let him not come."*)

[3] **haberlas visto** *having seen them*

[4] **No faltaba más** *Of course*

● CUESTIONARIO

1. ¿A dónde han sido invitados Pepe y Margarita?
2. ¿Por qué no le gustan las tertulias formales a Margarita?
3. ¿Qué es una velada musical?
4. ¿Cuáles son las atracciones principales de la velada a que asistirán Pepe y su señora?
5. ¿En qué consiste un cuarteto musical?
6. ¿Quiénes componen el cuarteto Orfeo?
7. ¿Qué diferencia hay entre un cuarteto profesional y uno de aficionados?
8. ¿Por qué son famosas las tertulias de la señora de Ayora?

La música hispánica

La música hispánica merece ser mejor conocida. Sólo en los últimos años, gracias a la maravilla de los discos de larga duración y al perfeccionamiento de los aparatos de reproducción, el tesoro musical de España empieza a cruzar las fronteras. Desde las deliciosas *Cantigas* del rey Alfonso el Sabio (siglo XIII) hasta la música cortesana y religiosa del Renacimiento, España contribuye a la riqueza musical de Europa obras exquisitas. La guitarra se perfecciona en manos de los españoles para convertirse en un instrumento de concierto a la par que el acompañamiento ideal para la música popular. Los *romances*[1] han conservado

---

[1] **romances** *ballads*

desde el siglo catorce la poesía, la música y el encanto de la época medieval y se han extendido por todo el continente americano. Desde el siglo diecisiete la popularísima *zarzuela*[2] ha dado pie a no pocas obras inmortales que han sido por generaciones, y son todavía, el deleite del público amante de la música en todos los países hispanos.

Naturalmente todo el mundo conoce, o por lo menos ha oído hablar de la música flamenca. Pero lo que pocos conocen es su gran variedad. Hay modalidades que corresponden, no ya a las diferentes comarcas de Andalucía, sino hasta a las ciudades: malagueñas, sevillanas, cordobesas; o que reflejan distintas emociones, según las circunstancias: seguirías,[3] soleares,[4] peteneras,[5] y hasta fiestas religiosas, como las emocionantes saetas[6] de Semana Santa. Aun se puede decir que es menos conocida, y no porque no lo merezca,[7] la música folklórica tan rica y tan variada de las otras regiones de España: Galicia, Asturias, Países Vascos, Cataluña y Levante, Castilla y Extremadura. Pocos países pueden jactarse de música tan abundante y variada, en proporción con su extensión geográfica, como España.

En España todo el mundo canta y la música es una parte integrante de la cultura del pueblo en todas las ocasiones. Aquí hay una razón por la cual parece que España no tiene muchos grandes compositores cuyas composiciones son conocidas por todos los amantes de la música. Y además, la música española es demasiado española, porque está tan arraigada en el alma popular, para tener, como tal, una atracción universal. Con todo, desde el Scarlatti, pasando por Bizet, Berlioz, Ravel,[8] y otros,

la música española ha sido una fuente de inspiración para muchos compositores del resto de Europa. En las últimas generaciones se notan señales de cambio. Hay obras de los compositores españoles que, inspirados en motivos o melodías nacionales, han sido traducidas a un idioma musical contemporáneo, y ya han desbordado las fronteras. Todo el mundo conoce a músicos como Albéniz, Granados, Turina y de Falla.[9]

En música como en otras artes y en literatura, el genio creador español no se ha agotado. Después de cada período de producción febril sucede una época de descanso y pausa en que el genio hispano, como si cobrara nuevas energías, vuelve a resucitar de sus cenizas como ave fénix inmortal.

La música latinoamericana es mejor conocida, tal vez, por las cualidades populares. Pero para conocer bien esta música es necesario estudiar sus cuatro fases:

1. La cultura precolombina, es decir, anterior a 1492, se expresó musicalmente en ritmos marcados con los pies e instrumentos primitivos, tales como maracas, o calabazas de china, cajas y tambores, que hacían un gran ruido. Sabemos que los indios tenían una escala musical pentatónica, es decir de cinco tonos. La triste y monótona quena y el rondador o antara[10] de los pastores incaicos fueron instrumentos complejos.

2. La cultura colonial entre 1492 y 1750 se caracteriza por fiestas populares y música religiosa. En esos años los españoles quisieron, sin gran éxito, suprimir la antigua música india con la introducción de la música europea y la música de los negros importados con sus muchos

---

[2] **zarzuela,** a short musico-dramatic piece (with occasional dancing), written in popular language and rhythms, so called from the hunting lodge, *La Zarzuela,* near the Royal Palace in Madrid where the King had his entertainment. Among the most popular **zarzuelas** are "La verbena de la paloma" and "La revoltosa."

[3] **seguirías,** gypsy **seguidillas** (a quick, provocative dance with hip-swaying) accompanied usually by a four-line song.

[4] **soleares,** another favorite dance of the Spanish gypsies, with a rabesques and fantastic movements.

[5] **peteneras,** a flamenco dance brought from Spain to the New World and modified by Negro and *Criollo* influences. The dance is accompanied by songs.

[6] **saetas,** *arrows,* is a type of Spanish religious song, which is a regular feature of the Holy Week ceremonies, so called because of the sudden outbursts of religious song, often addressed to the Virgin Mary.

[7] **no porque no lo merezca** *not because it does not deserve it*

[8] Domenico Scarlatti, a seventeenth-century Italian, went to the Iberian Peninsula at the age of forty-four and remained there until his death, composing operas and sonatas. The Frenchman Georges Bizet is the composer of the opera *Carmen.* Hector Berlioz (1803–1869) composed many musical pieces with a Spanish flavor. Maurice Ravel, French composer, was influenced greatly by Spanish music and composed *habaneras* and rhapsodies.

[9] Both Albéniz (1860–1909) and Granados (1867–1916) were exponents of nationalism in music. De Falla (1867–1946) is perhaps the best known of all Spanish composers.

[10] **Quena, rondador,** and **antara** are Andean musical instruments.

ritmos. Resultó, pues, una música criolla, pero en los países de gran población india siempre ha subsistido la nota indígena.

3. La época moderna entre 1750 y 1900 se caracteriza por la formación de culturas nacionales. Es esa época fueron escritos también los himnos de varios países, pues el siglo diecinueve comunicó a toda América un espíritu de libertad y organización que se expresa en la música, con los himnos y marchas patrióticos.

4. La época contemporánea se caracteriza por la creación de orquestas sinfónicas, por la representación de óperas, por la fundación de conservatorios de música, por el renacimiento de la música indígena, por la llegada de músicos y artistas ilustres de varios países de Europa, Norte América y los otros países latinoamericanos. Hay festividades, concursos, coros, música de cámara, etc. Hay casas editoras en donde solamente se publica música, y finalmente hay, como aquí en los Estados Unidos, gran número de fábricas en donde se hacen discos, transcripciones, etc. Hay industrias cinematográficas musicales, y andando el tiempo sin duda habrá televisión en los países más remotos.

La historia de la música y del baile de América es muy interesante. La primera escuela de música en América fue fundada en México en 1524 por Pedro de Gante.[11] Este fraile enseñó a los indios y a los criollos a cantar y a tocar varios instrumentos. Los conquistadores habían traído consigo[12] toda clase de música, instrumentos y libros. El primer órgano importado en América fue introducido en Venezuela en 1711 y el primer piano en 1795. En la escuela de Gante se compusieron trescientas sesenta y cinco canciones, una para cada día del año. Además, en 1526 se organizó en México la primera academia de baile del Nuevo Mundo. El "Profesor del Baile", señor Juan Ortiz, enseñó a los indios la música y los bailes europeos. En México también introdujeron la ópera. La primera que se representó era *Parténope* de Manuel Zumaya (1711). En 1869

Melesio Morales escribió una ópera graciosa para conmemorar el primer ferrocarril. En la música se podía oir *ronronear* las ruedas de los ferrocarriles y el silbido de la locomotora.

La cuna de la civilización del Nuevo Mundo fue Santo Domingo en el Mar Caribe. Cristóbal Colón vio las danzas y oyó los cantos de los indios acompañados de tambores. Pero Cuba es la isla que ha comunicado su música típica a todas las partes del mundo. Su música se caracteriza por un estilo a la vez español y africano. Su primera aportación fue *La Habanera*[13] que Bizet dio a conocer al mundo entero con su ópera *Carmen*.

En Panamá, Paraguay, Nicaragua, Perú, Guatemala y Bolivia casi todos los rasgos musicales son indios. En Venezuela y Colombia la música es española, india y negra. Las melodías combinan la melancolía india con el temperamento ardiente africano y el donaire español. En Costa Rica, Argentina y Uruguay hay poca influencia negra e india, pero con la excepción de Costa Rica hay mucha música gauchesca. El payador gauchesco se parece al cantor de corridos[14] de México y al cowboy de los Estados Unidos.

Todo el mundo conoce la música de Brasil. Es una combinación de elementos europeos, especialmente portugueses, y africanos e indios. La musicología es una ciencia muy bien desarrollada en Brasil y estudiada en casi todas las escuelas. En Chile, más que en ningún otro país americano, se ha desarrollado el "folklore" español, pero la música más popular de Chile es la *Zamacueca,* o la cueca, una adaptación de una fiesta morisca. Con los zapateos la *cueca* simboliza el cacareo de la gallina. En la cueca chilena, como en el tango argentino, en el jarabe mexicano y el joropo venezolano, viven todos los sentimientos humanos: tristeza, alegría, dolor, gozo, indiferencia, buen humor, burla, sarcasmo, desesperación, etc. Si uno no conoce la música latinoamericana, no conoce la expresión musical de la vida y el espíritu de esas personas. En estos bailes se halla el auténtico

---

[11] Pedro de Gante, a native of Flanders, was a Franciscan friar who came to Mexico in 1523 and established his school in Texcoco.

[12] **consigo** *with them*(selves), reflexive, analogous to **conmigo** and **contigo** (see Unit 10 §54). Colloquially, **con ellos** (**con él,** etc.) is crowding out **consigo.**

[13] *La Habanera* type of music was composed by Sebastián Yradier, who was born in Spain in 1809. He lived for some time in Cuba and his famous song "La Paloma" is best known in Latin America.

[14] The **corrido** is a popular epic-lyric-narrative verse, or song, similar to the **romance, payada,** and ballad.

folklore. Todos los bailes dicen algo fundamental. Todas las hazañas se recuerdan en cantos. Todos los casamientos del pueblo se celebran con fiestas.

De los contemporáneos nos será interesante
observar a algunos: a Juan Orrego Salas, chileno; a Blas Galindo, mexicano; a José Ardévol,
español; a Juan José Castro, argentino; a Jesús

María Sanromá, puertorriqueño; a Aurelio de
la Vega, cubano; a Heitor Villa-Lobos, brasileño; a Rodolfo Halffter, español-mexicano; a
Carlos Chávez, mexicano; y a Claudio Arrau,
chileno.

¿Quién sabe? Tal vez la música va a reu-
nirnos a todos—los de Norte y Sud América.

● CUESTIONARIO

1. ¿De qué manera se ha conservado la música
   de la época medieval española?
2. ¿Cómo se ha difundido la música hispánica
   en la época contemporánea?
3. ¿Cuál fue el origen de la zarzuela?
4. ¿Por qué razón no tiene una atracción universal la música española?
5. ¿Para qué compositores europeos ha sido la
   música española una fuente de inspiración?
6. Mencione las cuatro fases de la música latinoamericana.
7. Mencione usted a los principales compositores españoles.
8. ¿Qué es una orquesta sinfónica?
9. ¿Cuál fue la primera escuela de música en
   América?

10. ¿Qué país introdujo la ópera en América?
11. ¿Qué características tenía la ópera de
    Melesio Morales?
12. ¿Qué estilos se combinan en la música
    cubana?
13. ¿Qué características tiene la música de
    Panamá, Paraguay, Nicaragua, Perú,
    Guatemala y Bolivia?
14. ¿Cuáles son los elementos raciales de la
    música de Venezuela y Colombia?
15. ¿En qué países hay mucha música gau-
    chesca?
16. ¿Qué simboliza la cueca chilena?
17. Mencione a algunos de los compositores
    latinoamericanos contemporáneos.

● SUGGESTED READINGS

Chase, Gilbert, *The Music of Spain,* Norton, New York,
    1941.
Chávez, Carlos, *Toward a New Music* (tr. by Herbert
    Weinstock), Norton, New York, 1937.

Slonimsky, Nicolas, *Music of Latin America,* Crowell,
    New York, 1945.
Stevenson, Robert, *Music in Mexico,* Crowell, New
    York, 1952.

28

El arte hispánico

El arte es una de las mayores contribuciones de España a la cultura del mundo. Desde los tiempos prehistóricos, unos miles de años antes de la era cristiana, en las cuevas de Altamira, provincia de Santander, unos formidables artistas han dejado en las rocas ejemplos de su genio creador. Y así a través de los siglos, representando muy distintas culturas: primitiva, ibérica, romana, musulmana, cristiana, renacentista y moderna, el arte de España ha producido obras eternas y ha influido en el resto del mundo civilizado.

Al hojear una historia general del arte ciertas características peculiares y constantes del arte español resaltan en forma poderosa. En él encontramos el eterno dualismo hispano; el idealismo y el realismo, lo espiritual y emotivo al lado de lo concreto y práctico, como puede verse en las mejores obras del Greco[1] y de Goya,[2] de Velázquez[3] y de Picasso.[4]

En el arte español encontramos también una fuerza de expresión que sabe jugar hábilmente con los contrastes de luz y sombra, de dibujo detallado y minucioso junto a las simplificaciones atrevidas. ¿Quién no recuerda los monjes de Zurbarán[5] y los atrevimientos de Dalí[6] y Picasso?

El arte español, lo mismo que el pensa-

[1] El Greco is the Spanish name of Doménico Theotocópuli (1541–1614), of Greek descent, who was one of Spain's greatest painters.

[2] Francisco de Goya y Lucientes (1746–1828) was an extraordinary Spanish painter of the late eighteenth and early nineteenth centuries. He painted pictures in fresco and in oil, specializing in incidents in life and portraits. He is also famous for his caricatures.

[3] Diego Rodríguez Velázquez (1599–1660) was the painter of the household of Philip IV. He was Grand Marshal (*Aposentador Mayor*) of the Palace of Philip (1652). He is known as one of the greatest realists.

[4] Pablo Picasso, born in Malaga in 1881, leader of the modern school of Paris, is considered by many to be the greatest painter in the twentieth century.

[5] Francisco de Zurbarán (1598–1664) was a painter in the court of Philip IV, called "painter to the king and the king of painters."

[6] Salvador Dalí, born in 1904, is a painter of considerable imagination and is famous for his surrealistic canvases.

miento filosófico, y la literatura, no puede clasificarse en escuelas. El español es un individualista incorregible y, por lo mismo, indisciplinado, que no quiere someterse a normas. Cuando el genio existe y las condiciones son favorables, el pintor español se asimila cualquier influencia extraña con la que entra en contacto e imprime muy pronto en su obra un sello de originalidad inconfundible. Por ser siempre tan hispano el arte peninsular no encaja fácilmente en las categorías que tienen validez para el resto del arte europeo. La Dama de Elche,[7] maravillosa escultura ibérica, las grandes catedrales desde las antiguas hasta la contemporánea de la Sagrada Familia de Gaudí,[8] igual que los cuadros de pintores como Ribera,[9] Valdés Leal,[10] Murillo,[11] Goya, Zuloaga[12] y Sorolla[13] tienen un sello español e individual inconfundible.

Es verdad que el arte español refleja también otras corrientes, especialmente mediterráneas o latinas. Pero también es cierto que nunca existe una perfecta sincronización. El español se deja influir o imita no sólo cuando es de modo, sino cuando le apetece, cuando necesita renovarse. A veces genialmente se anticipa, como en las pinturas murales románicas de las viejas *iglesiucas pirenaicas*[14] en los siglos XII y XIII o en las atrevidas innovaciones del Greco, de Goya y de Picasso. Otras siguen a remolque, pero siempre con acento propio.

Raramente es frío y académico el arte español. Cuando el artista siente, de veras siente intensamente y se expresa con emoción, con pasión y entusiasmo. En los siglos en que el sentimiento religioso ha sido intenso, casi todo el arte español ha sido religioso. Sus creencias, sus esperanzas y sus temores se reflejan con patetismo en las obras de los grandes pintores que llenan las iglesias de España—para donde estaban destinados casi todos los cuadros —y ahora los museos de España y del extranjero, donde lucen muchas veces como desplazados y fuera del ambiente apropiado. En una época como la presente, en que los motivos religiosos son menos intensos y sinceros, el arte de los tallistas e imagineros medievales es sumamente interesante. Poblaron de espléndidas esculturas las catedrales hasta incluso los lugares más recónditos e inverosímiles, los retablos y los cuadros de Bermejo,[15] Ribera, Murillo, Zurbarán, Valdés Leal y Coello,[16] como las patéticas de Cano[17] y Berruguete[18] y los Pasos de la Pasión del Salzillo.[19] Atestiguan una época en que la fe era viva y la emoción sincera. En vano el arte contemporáneo ha tratado de renovar la imaginería religiosa. Los cuadros o murales religiosos de Sert[20] y Dalí,

---

[7] A famous piece of Iberian sculpture, showing some Greek influence, discovered in ancient times near the town of Elche, in Alicante, Spain.

[8] Antonio Gaudí (1852–1925), who designed the unusual church in Barcelona, was one of the best-known architects in Europe.

[9] José Ribera (1588–1652), of humble origin, was trained in Valencia probably by Ribalta. A realist, he became one of the world's most avid followers of Caravaggio. He exported many paintings to the Spanish courts, both at Naples and Madrid.

[10] Juan Valdés Leal (1622–1690) was a painter, sculptor, and architect, one of the founders of the Seville Academy.

[11] Bartolomé Esteban Murillo (1617–1682), regarded as one of the world's greatest painters, is famous for his realistic paintings of popular types and for his many pictures of the Immaculate Conception.

[12] Ignacio Zuloaga y Zabaleta (1870–1945) was of Basque origin, trained in the family's ceramic factory and by his own study in museums. He studied and painted in Italy. Some of his works are now in the Vatican. His works show Italian and Flemish influence.

[13] Joaquín Sorolla (1863–1923) was a painter of humble origin. He was admitted as a prodigy to the Academy at fifteen. His pictures are bright but solid and he specialized in beach scenes. His pictures are very widely exhibited today (some of his best are in the Hispanic Society of America in New York City).

[14] These were poor, small churches in Catalonia and the Pyrenees Mountains.

[15] Bartolomé Bermejo, a fifteenth-century Spanish painter of Córdoba. Little is known about his life. His works suggest travels to Italy and the Flemish country. He introduced the oil technique into Aragon, Spain.

[16] Claudio Coello (1630–1693) is well known for his religious works. His principal work is the altarpiece in the sacristy of San Lorenzo, in the Escorial, representing the Adoration of the Miraculous Host. It took seven years to complete.

[17] Alonso Cano (1601–1667) is a universal man well known for his arrogance. He was more influential as a sculptor than as a painter. He was born in Granada and trained by a sculptor father. He was introduced into the court by Velázquez. He was then hired to restore the royal collection of paintings of Titian and Rubens, which consequently influenced his own painting a great deal.

[18] Alonso Berruguete (1486?–1561) was the first artist who introduced pure Italian style of the sixteenth century into Spain. He was patronized by Emperor Charles V and Philip II. He was a painter, sculptor, and architect.

[19] Francisco Salzillo (1707–1781) was a sculptor who studied in the Colegio de la Anunciata. His works are beautiful, expressive, tragic statues of religious figures.

[20] José María Sert (1876–1945) is well known for his mural paintings. Some of his works may be seen in Rockefeller Center, New York City.

cerebrales, retóricos y grandiosos, nos dejan fríos porque les falta la genuina inspiración y la emoción intensa de otras épocas de mayor fe.

El arte hispánico, que en los siglos de la Edad Media había logrado una fusión afortunada de lo oriental y lo occidental, desde la arquitectura mozárabe y las delicadezas mudéjares hasta la sofisticación y las filigranas del plateresco, cruza el océano con los conquistadores. Muy pronto, en Lima lo mismo que en México, en Colombia como en el sudoeste norte-americano y en California, produce obras que, aunque reflejan los modelos y el espíritu que las han inspirado, muy pronto logran personalidad propia. El arte hispano con la misma facilidad y soltura con que absorbe y asimila los elementos nórdicos, mediterráneos y orientales en los siglos medios, en los tres siglos de dominio colonial en México como en Perú, sabe asimilar y absorber armoniosamente las influencias precolombinas: mayas, aztecas e incas.

● CUESTIONARIO

1. ¿Qué importancia tienen las cuevas de Altamira en el arte español?
2. ¿Qué culturas han influido en el arte español?
3. Mencione algunas características del arte español.
4. ¿Qué características tiene la pintura de Salvador Dalí y Pablo Picasso?
5. ¿Por qué no se puede clasificar el arte español en escuelas?
6. Mencione algunos pintores representativos del arte español.
7. ¿Cuál fue el arte de los tallistas e imagineros medievales?
8. ¿Qué cambios se producen en el arte español importado en Hispanoamérica?
9. ¿Cuáles son las influencias precolombinas en el arte hispánico?

● SUGGESTED READINGS

Born, Esther, *The New Architecture in Mexico,* Morrow, New York, 1937.
Crosby, Sumner McK., ed., *Gardner's Art through the Ages,* 4th ed., Harcourt, Brace, New York, 1959.
Goya, *Drawings from the Prado* (Introduction by André Malraux; tr. by Edward Sackville-West), Horizon, London, 1947.

Post, Chandler R., *A History of Spanish Painting,* Harvard University Press, Cambridge, 1930.
Sanford, Trent E., *The Story of Architecture in Mexico,* Norton, New York, 1947.
Sculpture of the Western Hemisphere, International Business Machines Corporation, New York, 1942.

Las artes populares en México[1]

México es un país donde el arte popular, ejecutado con una gran lealtad de espíritu por el pueblo, asoma por todas partes. Manos preparadas para transformar la materia, educadas en una espontánea mística del volumen, saben dar a la piedra, a la madera, al vidrio, al cuero, y a los metales preciosos el signo de su carácter y personalidad, devolviéndole a la materia lo que de ella recibió el espíritu. El labriego, concluida su faena en el campo, con un puñado de barro entre los dedos, modela una vasija cuya forma algo tiene que ver con su propio equilibrio vital. Es que el diálogo entre el hombre y la tierra no se suspende al dejar el arado junto al surco. Continúa transformándose, penetrando su alma con el instinto de la realización plástica. Lo mismo le ocurre al minero y al obrero de cualquier condición; terminada su dura labor, labra y cincela en su casa, para su mujer y sus hijos, preciosas figurillas con los más diversos materiales.

Todo este trabajo de noble artesanía lo

---

[1] From Félix Coluccio, *Folklore de las Américas,* Librería Editorial "El Ateneo", Buenos Aires, 1948.

realizan los mexicanos a toda hora y en todas partes, gozosamente, naturalmente, como una parte esencial del ritmo que dirige la vida nacional. Cantando en la guitarra, tejiendo en el telar, decorando y dibujando los símbolos locales, soplando el vidrio, el mexicano es siempre un artista, el mismo que canta en la guitarra para dar satisfacción a su ser íntimo.

En todas partes encanta e impresiona la nota artística que el pueblo pone en la vida diaria: con el aserrín con que se limpian las manchas del piso, en los restaurantes los mozos de servicio, al esparcirlo, aprovechan para hacer extrañas flores en el suelo, que cambian de forma a medida que cumplen su trabajo, casi siempre cantando. Los muchachos que limpian los cristales y los espejos de las grandes tiendas, con la espuma del jabón van trazando marcos con bellos elementos decorativos; corazones, flores, frutas y pájaros. El mozo del café, mientras llega la clientela, con unas pequeñas tijeras va recortando en las servilletas, artísticas decoraciones. Los más modestos parroquianos de las cocinerías populares, de sobremesa, modelan también con la miga de pan, pequeños monitos que resultan deliciosas figurillas.

Así es México. Y no es exagerado afirmar que allí la creación artística del pueblo está presente en todos los aspectos de la actividad nacional como un impulso funcional de dignificación humana. Recordemos que antes de la conquista[2] el indio había levantado ya, en sus templos, verdaderos monumentos de afirmación cosmogónica, manifestaciones de un alma que integra las líneas del paisaje y quiere dejar una huella permanente de su tránsito histórico. Pensemos que es el mismo indio que hoy talla,

teje y pule la materia de acuerdo con las técnicas aprendidas de los españoles.

Frente a los cincelados escudos de los conquistadores, los artífices sintieron la presencia de una provechosa lección y de este primer encuentro surgirán los albores de la artesanía mexicana en el hierro, el cobre y el bronce. Los españoles también lo quieren. La alfarería, los tejidos, la industria típica de guitarras y violines, el complicado arte de los esmaltes de Uruapán,[3] la talla policromada y la platería dan muestra de las facultades del pueblo mexicano. Lo español y lo autóctono en un flujo y reflujo constante se mezclan y enriquecen la producción de arte popular.

El ángel de hojalata, que elabora el campesino, representa una imagen del credo católico español. El cántaro de greda que modela el alfarero algo tiene de la sobriedad castellana. Las espuelas de plata que forja el artesano, siguiendo su instinto emocional, está ligado a la integridad del caballo moro que trajo Hernán Cortés.

Las artes populares en México realizan una función eminentemente social. Disciplinado al contacto de la materia, el pueblo adorna su vida, su casa y su muerte. México sabe que en su arte popular está lo más puro de su esencia, el aliento histórico de su anhelo de equilibrio y armonía; su inocente júbilo de afirmación terrenal, pero también de su superación humana. Sabe, además, perfectamente bien que el arte es lo único capaz de crear la unidad nacional; un arte propio original, vigoroso, espulgado de extrañas modalidades que impidan la plena expresión de la raza.

● CUESTIONARIO

1. Mencione algunos ejemplos que demuestren la nota artística que el pueblo mexicano pone en la vida diaria.
2. ¿Qué sabe usted acerca del arte indígena en México antes de la conquista?
3. ¿Cómo se integró el arte indígena con el arte hispánico importado por los españoles?
4. ¿Cuál es la función social que realizan las artes populares en México?

---

[2] By the Spanish in the sixteenth century.
[3] A district in the state of Michoacán.

Arguedas, José María, *The Singing Mountaineers* (Songs and Tales of the Quechua People), University of Texas Press, Austin, 1957.

Boggs, R. S., and N. B. Adams, eds., *Spanish Folktales,* Crofts, New York, 1932. [This edited text contains nineteen well-known folk stories of universal appeal, written in easy Spanish, and scholarly notes on the selections.]

Born, Esther, *The New Architecture in Mexico,* Morrow, New York, 1937.

Clark, Sydney, *All the Best in Mexico,* Dodd, Mead, New York, 1956.

Cole, M. R., "Los pastores," *Memoirs of American Folklore Society,* Vol. IX, 1907. [A Christmas Play]

De Onís, Harriet, ed. and tr., *The Golden Land, an Anthology of Latin-American Folklore in Literature,* Knopf, New York, 1948. [Part I: The Discoverers of the New Land; Part II: The Sons of the New Land; Part III: The Creators of the Nations; Part IV: Rediscovering the American Tradition; Part V: Brazil. The book gives a panoramic view of the culture and beliefs of Spanish America and Brazil in fifty-four selections from forty-four writers.]

Deutsch, Leonard, *A Treasury of the World's Finest Folk Songs,* Howell, Soskin, New York, 1942. [Spanish, Catalan, and Basque songs, translated into English, are on pages 165–77.]

de Varona, Esteban, *A Handbook of Mexican Treasures,* Unión Gráfica, S.A., Mexico, D. F., 1958.

Haight, Anne Lyon, and Monroe Wheeler, *Portrait of Latin America As Seen by Her Print Makers* (Introduction by Jean Charlot), Hastings House, New York, 1946.

Kusch, Eugene, *Mexico in Pictures,* Architectural Book, New York, 1958.

Lado, Robert, *Linguistics across Cultures,* The University of Michigan Press, Ann Arbor, 1957: Ch. 6, "How to Compare Two Cultures."

Niggli, Josephina, *Mexican Folk Plays,* University of North Carolina Press, Chapel Hill, 1938. [A collection of five one-act plays in English.]

Parkes, Henry Bamford, *A History of Mexico,* Houghton Mifflin, Boston, 1950.

Romanell, Patrick, *Making of the Mexican Mind,* University of Nebraska Press, Lincoln, 1952.

Toor, Frances, *A Treasury of Mexican Folkways,* Crown, New York, 1947. [Customs, myths, folklore, traditions, beliefs, fiestas, dances, and songs of the Mexican people.]

Zelayeta, Elena, *Elena's Secrets of Mexican Cooking,* Prentice-Hall, New York, 1958.

29

Emigrantes

En el año 1519 cierto emigrante al Nuevo Mundo, llamado Don Fernando Cortés, escribió unas cartas al Rey de España.[1] Describía la ciudad que hoy llamamos México:

"Esta gran ciudad de Temixtitán[2] está fundada en una laguna salada y desde la Tierra-Firme hasta el cuerpo de la dicha ciudad, por cualquiera parte que quieran entrar en ella, hay dos lagunas. Tiene cuatro entradas, todas de calzada hecha a mano. Es tan grande la ciudad como Sevilla y Córdoba. Son las calles de ella, digo las principales, muy anchas y muy derechas, y algunas de éstas y todas las demás son la mitad de tierra, y por la otra mitad es agua, por la cual andan en sus canoas, y todas las calles de trecho a trecho están abiertas por donde atraviesa el agua de las unas a las otras. Y en todas estas aberturas hay sus puentes de muy anchas y muy grandes vigas juntas y recias y bien labradas; y tales, que por muchas de ellas pueden pasar diez de caballo a la par.

"Tiene esta ciudad muchas plazas, donde hay continuos mercados. Tiene otra plaza tan grande como dos veces la ciudad de Salamanca, toda cercada de portales alrededor, donde hay cotidianamente arriba de sesenta mil personas comprando y vendiendo; donde

[1] He addressed the King as "muy alto y poderoso, y muy católico Príncipe, invictísimo Emperador y señor nuestro."
[2] One of the old names of the valley of Mexico and Mexico City.

hay todos los géneros de mercadurías que en todas las tierras se hallan, así de mantenimientos como de vituallas, joyas de oro y plata, de estaño, de conchas, de caracoles y de plumas. Se vende piedra labrada y por labrar, adobes, ladrillos. Hay calle de casas donde venden todos los linajes de aves que hay en la tierra, así como gallinas, águilas, falcones y gavilanes. Venden conejos, venados y perros pequeños, que crían para comer. Hay calles de herbolarios, donde hay todas las raíces y yerbas medicinales que en la tierra se hallan. Hay casas como de boticarios donde se venden las medicinas hechas. Hay casas como de barberos, donde lavan y rapan las cabezas. Hay casas donde dan de comer y beber por precio. Hay hombres como los que llaman en Castilla ganapanes, para traer cargas. Hay todas las maneras de verduras que se hallan, especialmente cebollas, ajos, berros y tagarninas. Hay frutas de muchas maneras, en que hay cerezas y ciruelas que son semejantes a las de España. Venden miel de abejas y cera y miel de cañas de maíz, que son tan dulces como las de azúcar, y miel de una planta que llaman maguey, que es muy mejor que arrope; y de estas plantas hacen azúcar y vino. Hay a vender muchas maneras de hilado de algodón de todos colores en sus madejicas, que parece propiamente alcaicería de Granada en las sedas, aunque esto otro es en mucha cantidad. Venden mucha loza, jarros, ollas, ladrillos y otras infinitas maneras de vasijas, todas de singular barro, vidriadas y pintadas. Venden maíz en grano y en pan. Venden pasteles de aves y empanadas de pescado. Cada género de mercaduría se vende en su calle, sin que entremetan otra mercaduría ninguna, y en esto tienen mucha orden. Todo lo venden por cuenta y medida, excepto que hasta ahora no se ha visto vender cosa alguna por peso. Hay en esta gran plaza una muy buena casa como de audiencia, donde están siempre sentados diez o doce personas, que son jueces y libran todos los casos y cosas que en el dicho mercado acaecen, y mandan castigar los delincuentes . . .

"Por lo que yo he visto y comprendido acerca de la similitud que toda esta tierra tiene a España, así en la fertilidad como en la grandeza y fríos que en ella hace, me pareció que el más conveniente nombre para esta dicha tierra era llamarse la Nueva España del mar Océano; y así en nombre de vuestra majestad se le puso aquel nombre. Humildemente suplico a vuestra alteza lo tenga por bien y mande que se nombre así."

Otro emigrante—Bernardo de Balbuena[3]—describe la ciudad de esta manera: ". . . vi una soberbia y populosa ciudad; no sin mucha admiración dije en mi pensamiento: ésta sin duda es aquella grandeza mexicana, de que tantos milagros cuenta el mundo."

Bañada de un templado fresco viento,
donde nadie creyó que hubiese mundo
goza florido y regalado asiento.

Es ciudad de notable policía
y donde se habla el español lenguaje
más puro y con mayor cortesanía,

vestido de un bellísimo ropaje
que le da propiedad, gracia, agudeza,
en casto, limpio, liso y grave traje.[4]

Otro emigrante se llamaba Pedro de Valdivia. Después de pasar cinco años en el Nuevo Mundo fue a Chile y escribió unas cartas al Emperador, Carlos V de España. Pedro de Valdivia había nacido en Badajoz, España, a fines del siglo XV.

En 1541 Valdivia fundó la ciudad de Santiago de Chile; en 1550, Concepción; en 1551, Valdivia. Murió en 1553. Se dice que Valdivia (y otros cronistas de Indias también) sufrieron tal transformación a su contacto con el Nuevo Mundo que no quedaron de su hispanidad más que el idioma y la ambición.

"Al 11 de febrero de dicho año (1546) partí y caminé treinta leguas, que era la tierra que nos servía y habíamos corrido pasadas 10 leguas adelante, topamos mucha población, y a las diez y seis, gente de guerra que nos salían a defender los caminos y pelear. Nosotros corríamos la tierra, y los indios que tomaba los enviaba por mensajeros a los caciques comarcanos requeriéndolos con la paz: y un día por la mañana salieron hasta trescientos indios a

---

[3] Born in 1568 (died 1627) in La Mancha, Spain. He wrote the *Grandeza mexicana*, a long epic descriptive poem to express his great admiration for the New World. He is considered "the first American poet."

[4] Quoted from the *Grandeza mexicana*.

pelear con nosotros, diciendo que ya les habían dicho lo que queríamos, y que éramos pocos y nos querían matar: dimos en ellos y matamos hasta 50 y los demás huyeron.

"Aquella misma noche al cuarto de la prima, dieron sobre nosotros siete u ocho mil indios, y peleamos con ellos más de dos horas, y se nos defendían bárbaramente cerrados en un escuadrón como tudescos; al fin dieron lado y matamos muchos de ellos y al capitán que los guiaba. Nos mataron dos caballos, e hirieron cinco o seis y otros tantos cristianos. Huidos los indios, entendimos lo que quedaba de la noche

en curar a nuestros caballos y a nosotros, y otro día anduve cuatro leguas y di en un río muy grande donde entra en la mar que se llama Biubiu,[5] que tiene media legua de ancho; y visto buen sitio donde podía poblar, y la gran cantidad de los indios que había, y que no me podía sustentar entre ellos con tan poca gente. Supe además que toda la tierra de esta parte y de aquélla del río venía sobre mí, y a sucederme algún revés, dejaba en aventura de perderse todo lo de atrás,[6] di la vuelta a Santiago dentro de cuarenta días que salí de él con muy gran regocijo de los que vinieron conmigo".

[5] El Río Bío-Bío (see page 188)
[6] y . . . atrás *and to avoid the risk of losing everything already gained*

● CUESTIONARIO

1. Describa la ciudad de México en tiempos de Don Fernando Cortés.
2. Describa los mercados de la gran ciudad de Temixtitán.
3. ¿Quiénes administraban justicia en esos mercados?
4. ¿Qué nombre propuso Cortés al rey para llamar la ciudad de Temixtitán? ¿Por qué?
5. ¿Cómo describió Balbuena la ciudad de México?
6. ¿Qué es un emigrante?
7. ¿Quién reinaba en España en tiempos de la conquista del Nuevo Mundo?
8. ¿Cuáles son las ciudades chilenas que fundó Pedro de Valdivia?
9. ¿Por qué son importantes las cartas que escribían los conquistadores al rey?
10. ¿Qué dificultades encontró Pedro de Valdivia en la conquista de Chile?

● SUGGESTED READINGS

Alegría, Fernando, *Lautaro* (tr. by Delia Goetz), Farrar and Rinehart, New York, 1944.

MacLeish, Archibald, *Conquistador,* Houghton Mifflin, Boston, 1934 (sixth impression).

La llegada de un emigrante del siglo XX

El navío se detiene en el puerto de Nueva York. La primera impresión del viajero es abrumadora, aplastante. Conocía varios países en el viejo mundo, y nunca se sintió extraño ni desconcertado como ahora. Entre la niebla aparecieron grandes y pequeñas embarcaciones, veleros y remolcadores; la Estatua de la Libertad iluminando al mundo. Los altos rascacielos, con sus innumerables ventanas, parecían ojos inquisidores. En el muelle, notó un movimiento ruidoso de cargadores y de máquinas ensordecedoras al funcionar. Una multitud se

congregaba en espera de los recién llegados, y al irlos descubriendo gritaba y gesticulaba. Las complicaciones de la revisión de equipajes y otras formalidades del desembarco son demasiado para él; por todas partes hay gritos y conversaciones en una lengua que apenas entiende. Sí, éste es otro mundo en el que se siente perdido y desorientado.

Por fortuna para el viajero, un amigo suyo, que ahora vive en Nueva York, sale a recibirle y le sirve de ayuda para salvar sus dificultades. Y en su automóvil le lleva a la casa en que vive, donde le ofrece hospitalidad por unos días. Al ir cruzando por las calles, otra impresión extraña: es un domingo en la mañana, y a estas horas la ciudad parece casi desierta; los altos edificios, vacíos. ¿Dónde estará la gente? Otros días le asustará el movimiento y el ruido de estas calles y avenidas, ahora en completo abandono.

Y ya duda si podrá acostumbrarse a esta nueva vida. Entran en un restorán. La limpieza, el buen gusto y la variedad de platos suculentos que se le ofrecen, le dejan buena impresión. Después de una comida excelente, sus nervios agotados se equilibran poco a poco.

Llevándolo siempre en su automóvil, su amigo le va mostrando ahora parte de la ciudad, algunos parques y las orillas del río. Y la grandiosidad que antes le abrumaba, se le figura ahora admirable.

—Descansa unos días, y cuando quieras, empezarás a trabajar en la misma fábrica que yo; mientras aprendes el oficio te pagarán el salario completo que recibirás después.

Otra novedad sorprendente. En el viejo mundo había tenido que esperar y luchar tanto para poder malvivir; y aquí, acabado de llegar,[1] y sin esfuerzo por su parte, se encontraba con un trabajo bien pagado.

—Uno de estos días iremos al banco y abriremos una cuenta corriente para ti.

El nunca había tenido dinero en ningún banco; y lo de tener una cuenta corriente a su nombre era otra novedad que le sorprendía y le halagaba. Empezaba a sentirse como una persona muy diferente de la que había sido hasta entonces.

Unas semanas después, su amigo dijo al viajero:

—Veo que la nueva vida ya no te extraña, y te vas acostumbrando a ella sin dificultad.

—A lo bueno se acostumbra uno fácilmente.

---

[1] **acabado de llegar** *barely arrived*

● CUESTIONARIO

1. ¿Por qué razones vienen muchos emigrantes al Nuevo Mundo?
2. ¿Qué dificultades tiene la mayoría de los emigrantes recién llegados a un país?
3. ¿Por qué no hay mucha actividad en las ciudades los domingos por la mañana?
4. ¿De qué países ha venido la mayoría de los emigrantes del siglo XX?
5. ¿Qué ciudades norteamericanas tienen un mayor porcentaje de emigrantes?
6. ¿Qué trabajo hacen generalmente los emigrantes?
7. ¿Por qué se siente el emigrante como una persona diferente en los Estados Unidos?
8. ¿Cuáles son algunas de las comodidades que atraen a los emigrantes?

30

Charlas sobre el folklore

Algunas veces la charla se parece a una tertulia cuando varios contertulios forman, en cualquier café-nevería cerca del barrio estudiantil de una universidad, un grupo todos interesados en las costumbres de otros países. Las escenas que se exhiben aquí son típicas:

—Vamos a examinar hoy algunos aspectos del saber del pueblo, es decir el folklore. Casi todos conocen ciertas narraciones y se deleitan en repetirlas, exagerándolas sin medida. En los Estados Unidos, por ejemplo, el cuento de "Johnny Appleseed" es muy popular.

—Dígalo, ¿quién era Johnny Appleseed?

—Un vendedor ambulante que viajaba por toda la tierra hasta San Francisco plantando semillas de manzanas en lugares remotos. Le consideraban un santo místico o faná-tico porque crecían los manzanos por todas partes. Al llegar a una pobre casita siempre decía: "Me llamo Johnny Appleseed. He vivido aquí muchos siglos. En efecto, vine aquí cuando apenas fue explorado este continente. Me gustan los indios, me gusta la gente blanca, me gustan los animales y nunca he lastimado a ninguno de ellos. He plantado semillas y he puesto manzanos para los colonos y los he cuidado. He hablado a la gente de Dios y he tratado de ser buen americano en esta tierra. Quizás lo haya sido. Quizás yo no esté muerto todavía . . ."

—Sócrates dijo, ¿verdad?, que no hay mal para el hombre de bien ni en esta vida ni en la muerte.

—Verdad.

—Hagamos un breve examen. Yo no busco discusiones, pero no las rehuyo—voy a ser franco: El viajero que atraviesa rápidamente un país lo juzga, por lo común, sólo por las costumbres aparatosas o pintorescas. Por ejemplo, al tratarse de España se habla de las corridas de toros, del canto y el baile flamenco, las procesiones de Semana Santa, sin realmente entenderlos. Se juzga a México por el "indio pintoresco" y los mercados. Se juzga a Cuba por la samba o los casinos.

—Y muchos juzgan a todos los hispanos como aficionados a la siesta sin tomar en cuenta que en muchos países hace calor durante la tarde y es preferible descansar desde la una hasta las tres, y trabajar desde las tres hasta las siete u ocho, ¿verdad?

—Pues volvamos a la cuestión de folklore. Para conocer bien a cualquier pueblo es necesario oirle en sus cantares, mirarle en el ejercicio de sus diversas actividades. Todo lo relativo a tradiciones y costumbres es una verdadera enciclopedia, que se llama folklore. Las muchas sociedades de folklore del mundo fueron establecidas para investigar extensivamente el fenómeno etnográfico, histórico, político y sociológico de costumbres populares, de la vida familiar y social (que incluye alimentación, viviendas, indumentaria y diversiones).

—Otros aspectos de los estudios son: ferias, fiestas populares (que varían según los países o las regiones de un país), artes, bailes y danzas, juegos, deportes y pasatiempo, creencias y supersticiones, costumbres regionales y religiosas, poesía popular, refranes, adagios y proverbios, cuentos y leyendas.

—El canto popular español es el fruto de una improvisación que expresa el sentimiento del *pueblo*. Lo escucha y lo repite improvisándolo. Los cantos populares se consideran como importantes elementos en el estudio del folklore de cualquier país. Los cantos de España, tan bien como los de los otros países de habla española, tienen valor artístico. Estas manifestaciones de la actividad popular son universales en el espacio y en el tiempo.

—Muchos cantos revelan sabiduría sencilla:

El secreto de tu pecho
no lo digas a tu amigo;
que si la amistad le falta,
será contra ti un testigo.

Yo me enamoré de noche
y la luna me engañó;
otra vez que me enamore,
será de día y con sol.

Se lamentaba un sabio
de su miseria,
y al campo ha salido
a comer yerbas.
Volvió la cara
y vio que otro comía
las que él dejaba.

Es amor una senda
tan sin camino,
que el que va más derecho
va más perdido.

—Las vicisitudes del estudiante se describen en muchos cantos:

Esta capa que me tapa,
tan pobre y tan vieja está,
que sólo porque se va
se reconoce que es capa.

El amor del estudiante
es un amor muy profundo;
es como la leña verde;
poca lumbre y mucho humo.

Si el comer poco es salud,
como dice el refrán,
los pobrecitos alumnos,
¡cuántos años vivirán!

A todos les da claveles
la morena de la plaza;
a todos les da claveles,
y a mí me da calabaza.

Quiero que me des el sí;
quiero que me des el no;
quiero que me desengañes:
si vas a ser mía o no.

—Los españoles son, por su naturaleza, jocosos y alegres:

No sé cómo no estoy loco
con esta pena que tengo;
que me ha puesto tu querer
tonto, sordo, mudo y ciego.

Estaba un mudo cantando
y un sordo le estaba oyendo,
y un ciego estaba mirando,
y pasó un cojo corriendo.

Ayer me dijiste que hoy,
y hoy me dices que mañana,
y mañana me dirás:
—Ya se me quitó la gana.

Tú me dices que estoy loco;
yo te confieso que sí;
que si loco no estuviera,
¿cómo te quisiera a ti?

El amor de las mujeres,
es como el de las gallinas:
cuando falta el gallo grande
cualquier pollo las domina.

Cuando un pobre se emborracha
de un rico en la compañía
la del pobre es borrachera,
la del rico es alegría.

Cinco sentidos tenemos;
todos los necesitamos;
todos cinco los perdemos
cuando nos enamoramos.

Las estrellas del cielo
son ciento doce;
con las dos de tu cara
ciento catorce.

—Algunos cantos de Argentina, por ejemplo, toman la forma de un pericón:[1]

    EL—Querer una no es ninguna;
       querer dos es vanidad;
       el querer a tres o cuatro
       es gracia y habilidad.
  ELLA—Mocito de veinte novias
       y conmigo veintiuna,
       si todas son como yo,
       Se ha de quedar sin ninguna.

—Otros cantan la filosofía del gaucho:[2]

Respetar tan sólo a Dios;
y de Dios abajo a ninguno.

Mi gloria es vivir tan libre
como el pájaro del cielo;
no hago nido en este suelo,
donde hay tanto que sufrir;
y nadie me ha de seguir
cuando yo remonto el vuelo.

Cantando me he de morir,
cantando me han de enterrar,
y cantando he de llegar
al pie del Eterno Padre . . .

—La fábula siempre tenía moraleja:[3]

Los dos conejos

Por entre unas matas,
seguido de perros,
no diré corría,
volaba un conejo.

De su madriguera
salió un compañero,
y le dijo: "Tente,
amigo, ¿qué es esto?"—
"¿Qué ha de ser? responde:
sin aliento llego . . .
Dos pícaros galgos
me vienen siguiendo".—
"Sí (replica el otro)
por allí los veo,
pero no son galgos".—
"¿Pues qué son?—Podencos".—
"Qué? ¿Podencos dices?—
"Sí como mi abuelo.
Galgos, y muy galgos;
bien visto lo tengo".—
"Son podencos: vaya,
que no entiendes de eso".—
"Son galgos te digo".—
"Digo que podencos . . ."
En esta disputa,
llegando los perros,
pillan descuidados
a mis dos conejos.
Los que por cuestiones
de poco momento
dejan lo que importa,
llévense este ejemplo.

—Otros versos son jocosos y a la vez satí-
ricos:

No me mires, que miran
que nos miramos:
miremos la manera
de no mirarnos.
No nos miremos,
y cuando no nos miren
nos miraremos.

---

[1] **pericón,** a lively dance in which the performers wave a handkerchief to express emotions.
[2] José Hernández, author of the epic poem *Martín Fierro,* was an Argentinian. This poem is considered a New World masterpiece. (See pages 428–431.)
[3] Tomás de Iriarte (1750–1791) was one of Spain's best fabulists.

El que quiera ser dichoso
dos cosas ha de tener:
la conciencia muy tranquila
y el amor de una mujer.

Es el amor, señores,
como el cigarro:
nadie lo deja y todos
quieren dejarlo.
Y el que lo deja
es para volver luego
con mayor fuerza.

—Los refranes y proverbios revelan muy claramente el espíritu y el buen humor de un pueblo. Los refranes españoles son numerosos y muchos son humorísticos:

El maestro Ciruela
no sabía leer
y ponía escuela.

Quien tiene dineros, tiene compañeros.

Al cabo de cien años todos seremos calvos.

Quien dice de mí, mírese a sí.

A lo que Dios cría,
No hay que buscarle la mejoría.

En boca cerrada no entran moscas.

Más vale ser pobre y feliz que rico y triste.

El consejo de la mujer es poco,
Pero el que no lo toma es loco.

El que pega paga.

Cuando yo tenía dinero, me llamaban don Tomás
y ahora que no lo tengo, me llaman Tomás no más.

—Otros son de carácter doctrinal y universal:

Más vale maña que fuerza.

No es oro todo lo que reluce.

Quien madruga, Dios le ayuda.

A palabras locas, orejas sordas.

Si el vino te tiene loco, déjalo poquito a poco.

Quien mal anda, mal acaba.

—Los proverbios, por lo común, tienen un sentido figurado y también universal:

A Dios lo que es de Dios
y al César lo que es de César.

Allégate a los buenos y serás uno de ellos.

Aunque se viste la mona de seda, mona se queda.

Ayúdate y Dios te ayudará.

● CUESTIONARIO

1. ¿Qué se entiende por *folklore?*
2. ¿Cuáles son los juicios falsos con que generalmente se juzga a España, México y Cuba?
3. ¿Dónde hay que recurrir para conocer bien a un pueblo?
4. ¿Para qué fueron establecidas las sociedades de folklore del mundo?
5. ¿Qué reflejan los cantos populares españoles?
6. ¿Cuáles son las vicisitudes del estudiante que se describen en los versos correspondientes?
7. Mencione otros dos ejemplos de cantos populares que describan el carácter jocoso y alegre de los españoles.
8. ¿Qué es una fábula?
9. ¿Qué cantan los argentinos mientras bailan el pericón?
10. Diga algunos proverbios españoles.

El folklore español [1]

(El saber popular)

Folklore es la ciencia no escrita del pueblo. Es un espejo en que un pueblo puede reconocerse a sí mismo y verse retratado en su vida más íntima. Consta de tradiciones, cuentos, leyendas, supersticiones, recuerdos y fiestas populares, costumbres, refranes y proverbios, creencias, etnografía tradicional, trajes, juegos infantiles, etc.

En recientes años se ha empezado a estudiar científica y literariamente este ramo de las ciencias sociales. La palabra *folklore* es un término impreciso y vago. Puesto que no hay un término preciso ni concepto universalmente reconocido, las varias sociedades han adoptado la palabra *folklore*. En general, es la teoría que estudia la sabiduría del pueblo, que estudia y compara el qué y el cómo de lo que el pueblo hace, piensa y siente. Uno de los más necesarios objetos de las sociedades es la colección, arreglo y estudio de los hechos para generalizarlos y filosofarlos.

Casi todas las naciones del mundo sienten gran orgullo en las manifestaciones auténticas de su antigua cultura. Hace unos ochenta años fue creada en España una "Sociedad para la Recopilación y Estudio del Saber y de las Tradiciones Populares". Las bases eran:

Esta Sociedad tiene por objeto recoger, acopiar y publicar todos los conocimientos de nuestro pueblo en los diversos ramos de la ciencia (medicina, higiene, botánica, política, moral, agricultura, etc.); los proverbios, cantares, adivinanzas, cuentos, leyendas, fábulas, tradiciones y demás formas poéticas y literarias; los usos, costumbres, ceremonias, espectáculos y fiestas familiares, locales y nacionales; los ritos, creencias, supersticiones, mitos y juegos infantiles en que se conservan más principalmente los vestigios de las civilizaciones pasadas; las locuciones, giros, traba-lenguas, frases hechas, motes y apodos, modismos, provincialismos y voces infantiles; los nombres de sitios, pueblos y lugares, de piedras, animales y plantas; y, en suma, todos los elementos constitutivos del genio, del saber y del idioma patrios, contenidos en la tradición oral y en los monumentos escritos, como materiales indispensables para el conocimiento y reconstrucción científica de la historia y de la cultura españolas.

Esta Sociedad constará de tantos centros cuantas son las regiones que constituyen la nacionalidad española . . .

En la recolección de materiales, todos y cada uno de los centros del folklore que se constituyan, tendrán como principal objetivo la fidelidad en la transcripción y la mayor escrupulosidad en declarar la procedencia de las tradiciones o datos, etc., que recojan, utilizando, cuando el estado de sus recursos lo consiente, la escritura musical, dibujo, taquigrafía, fotografía y demás medios adecuados para obtener la fidelidad en la reproducción.

● CUESTIONARIO

1. ¿De qué consta el folklore de un pueblo?
2. ¿Por qué se ha adoptado la palabra folklore para designar a esta ciencia no escrita del pueblo?
3. ¿A qué ciencias pertenece el folklore?
4. ¿Cuál es el objeto de las sociedades que estudian el folklore?
5. ¿Cuál es la institución creada en España con el objeto de estudiar las manifestaciones auténticas de su cultura?
6. ¿Cuándo se empezó a estudiar el folklore en forma científica y literaria?
7. ¿Cómo está organizado el estudio del folklore en España?
8. ¿Qué importancia tiene el estudio del folklore?

● SUGGESTED READINGS

See those listed for Unit 28.

---

[1] Selections from *Biblioteca de las tradiciones populares españolas,* Tomo I, Madrid, 1884.

Appendix: Verbs

Regular Verbs

Simple Tenses

INFINITIVE	**hablar** *to speak*	**comer** *to eat*	**vivir** *to live*
–ndo FORM	hablando	comiendo	viviendo
–do FORM	hablado	comido	vivido
INDICATIVE *Present*	hablo hablas habla hablamos habláis[1] hablan	como comes come comemos coméis[1] comen	vivo vives vive vivimos vivís[1] viven
Imperfect	hablaba hablabas hablaba hablábamos hablabais[1] hablaban	comía comías comía comíamos comíais[1] comían	vivía vivías vivía vivíamos vivíais[1] vivían
Preterit	hablé hablaste habló hablamos hablasteis[1] hablaron	comí comiste comió comimos comisteis[1] comieron	viví viviste vivió vivimos vivisteis[1] vivieron
Future	hablaré hablarás hablará hablaremos hablaréis[1] hablarán	comeré comerás comerá comeremos comeréis[1] comerán	viviré vivirás vivirá viviremos viviréis[1] vivirán
Conditional	hablaría hablarías hablaría hablaríamos hablaríais[1] hablarían	comería comerías comería comeríamos comeríais[1] comerían	viviría vivirías viviría viviríamos viviríais[1] vivirían
Direct Command (**tú** and **vosotros** forms)	habla hablad[1]	come comed[1]	vive vivid[1]

[1] The **vosotros** form of the verb is included for completeness; see footnote Unit 2 §1.

SUBJUNCTIVE

Present	hable	coma	viva
	hables	comas	vivas
	hable	coma	viva
	hablemos	comamos	vivamos
	habléis	comáis	viváis
	hablen	coman	vivan
Imperfect (–**ra**)[2]	hablara	comiera	viviera
	hablaras	comieras	vivieras
	hablara	comiera	viviera
	habláramos	comiéramos	viviéramos
	hablarais	comierais	vivierais
	hablaran	comieran	vivieran
Imperfect (–**se**)[3]	hablase	comiese	viviese
	hablases	comieses	vivieses
	hablase	comiese	viviese
	hablásemos	comiésemos	viviésemos
	hablaseis	comieseis	vivieseis
	hablasen	comiesen	viviesen

Perfect Forms

INDICATIVE

Present Perfect	he / has / ha / hemos / habéis / han	hablado	comido	vivido
Past Perfect	había / habías / había / habíamos / habíais / habían	hablado	comido	vivido
Future Perfect	habré / habrás / habrá / habremos / habréis / habrán	hablado	comido	vivido
Conditional Perfect	habría / habrías / habría / habríamos / habríais / habrían	hablado	comido	vivido

[2] This is the imperfect subjunctive form most generally used, and is the one used exclusively in the dialogs.
[3] This is another imperfect subjunctive form, and is found in the readings. See Discussion Unit 19 §105.

SUBJUNCTIVE *Present Perfect*	haya hayas haya hayamos hayáis hayan	hablado	comido	vivido
Past Perfect (–**ra**)[4]	hubiera hubieras hubiera hubiéramos hubierais hubieran	hablado	comido	vivido
Past Perfect (–**se**)[5]	hubiese hubieses hubiese hubiésemos hubieseis hubiesen	hablado	comido	vivido

Stem-Changing Verbs[6]

INFINITIVE	**sentar**[7] *to seat*	**contar**[8] *to tell, count*	**perder**[9] *to lose*
–**ndo** FORM	sentando	contando	perdiendo
PRESENT INDICATIVE	**siento** **sientas** **sienta** sentamos sentáis **sientan**	**cuento** **cuentas** **cuenta** contamos contáis **cuentan**	**pierdo** **pierdes** **pierde** perdemos perdéis **pierden**
PRESENT SUBJUNCTIVE	**siente** **sientes** **siente** sentemos sentéis **sienten**	**cuente** **cuentes** **cuente** contemos contéis **cuenten**	**pierda** **pierdas** **pierda** perdamos perdáis **pierdan**
PRETERIT	senté sentaste sentó sentamos sentasteis sentaron	conté contaste contó contamos contasteis contaron	perdí perdiste perdió perdimos perdisteis perdieron

[4] This is the past perfect subjunctive form most commonly used.

[5] This is another past perfect subjunctive form, less commonly used than the one ending in –**ra**. Note that the two past perfect subjunctive forms parallel the two imperfect subjunctive forms.

[6] See Unit 4 § 16 and Discussion of Unit 16 §95. For **sentir, morir,** and **pedir,** see in addition Unit 9 §45. All the stem-changing verbs in the book are in this and following footnotes, and in the model verbs.

[7] Like **sentar** are **cerrar, comenzar, despertar, empezar,** and **pensar.**

[8] Like **contar** are **acordar, acostar, almorzar, apostar, colgar, costar, encontrar, jugar, mostrar, probar, recordar, rogar** and **volar.**

[9] Like **perder** are **defender, detener,** and **entender.**

INFINITIVE	soler[10] *to be accustomed to*	sentir[11] *to regret*	morir[12] *to die*	pedir[13] *to ask for, request*
–ndo FORM	soliendo	**sintiendo**	**muriendo**	**pidiendo**
PRESENT INDICATIVE	**suelo** **sueles** **suele** solemos soléis **suelen**	**siento** **sientes** **siente** sentimos sentís **sienten**	**muero** **mueres** **muere** morimos morís **mueren**	**pido** **pides** **pide** pedimos pedís **piden**
PRESENT SUBJUNCTIVE	**suela** **suelas** **suela** solamos soláis **suelan**	**sienta** **sientas** **sienta** **sintamos** **sintáis** **sientan**	**muera** **mueras** **muera** **muramos** **muráis** **mueran**	**pida** **pidas** **pida** **pidamos** **pidáis** **pidan**
PRETERIT	solí soliste solió solimos solisteis solieron	sentí sentiste **sintió** sentimos sentisteis **sintieron**	morí moriste **murió** morimos moristeis **murieron**	pedí pediste **pidió** pedimos pedisteis **pidieron**

Irregular Forms of Verbs

In the verbs which follow, only the tenses having one or more irregular forms are listed. Irregular forms are printed in bold-faced type, regular forms in lightface.

Present subjunctive forms like **caiga, diga, haga, influya, oiga, ponga, salga, tenga, traiga, valga, venga,** and **vea** are not listed because their formation is in accordance with the rules given. Likewise, imperfect subjunctive forms, such as **cayera, diera, dijera, estuviera, hubiera, hiciera, influyera, fuera, pudiera, pusiera, quisiera, supiera, produjera, tuviera, trajera,** and **viniera** are not given because their formation is in accordance with the rules given.

Verb forms which show only a spelling change, e.g., **cayendo, caído,** are given in footnotes, so as to separate changes in *spelling* from changes in *sound.*

References given in parentheses after the name of a verb form are to the sections in the grammatical discussions where the forms in question are explained.

---

andar *to walk, go*
Preterit (Unit 9 §44)   **anduve, anduviste, anduvo, anduvimos, anduvisteis, auduvieron**

---

caer[14] *to fall*
Present Indicative (Unit 5 §21) **caigo,** caes, cae, caemos, caéis, caen

---

conocer *to know (be acquainted with)*
Present Indicative (Unit 5 §21) **conozco,** conoces, conoce, conocemos, conocéis, conocen

---

[10] Like **soler** are **disolver, doler, envolver, llover,** and **volver.**
[11] Like **sentir** are **mentir, preferir,** and **sugerir.**
[12] Like **morir** is **dormir.**
[13] Like **pedir** are **conseguir, despedir, elegir, perseguir, reir, repetir,** and **seguir.**
[14] Forms which show only a *spelling* change are: –ndo form (**cayendo**); –do form (**caído**); preterit forms (**caíste, cayó, caímos, caísteis, cayeron**). See Table in Unit 8 §40.

dar *to give*

Present Indicative (Unit 5 §21)	**doy,** das, da, damos, dais, dan
Present Subjunctive (Unit 16 §95)	**dé, des, dé, demos, deis, den**
Preterit (Unit 6 §26)	**di, diste, dio, dimos, disteis, dieron**

---

decir *to say, tell*

–ndo form (Unit 8 §40)	**diciendo**
–do form (Unit 16 §92)	**dicho**
Present Indicative (Unit 5 §21)	**digo, dices, dice,** decimos, decís, **dicen**
Preterit (Unit 9 §44)	**dije, dijiste, dijo, dijimos, dijisteis, dijeron**
Future (Unit 20 §110)	**diré, dirás, dirá, diremos, diréis, dirán**
Conditional (Unit 20 §111)	**diría, dirías, diría, diríamos, diríais, dirían**
Direct Command (**tú** form) (Unit 5 §23)	**di**

---

estar *to be*

Present Indicative (Unit 3 §13)	**estoy, estás, está,** estamos, estáis, **están**
Present Subjunctive (Unit 16 §95)	**esté, estés, esté,** estemos, estéis, **estén**
Preterit (Unit 9 §44)	**estuve, estuviste, estuvo, estuvimos, estuvisteis, estuvieron**

---

haber *to have*

Present Indicative (Unit 16 §94)	**he, has, ha, hemos,** habéis, **han**
Present Subjunctive (Unit 16 §95)	**haya, hayas, haya, hayamos, hayáis, hayan**
Preterit (Unit 9 §44)	**hube, hubiste, hubo, hubimos, hubisteis, hubieron**
Future (Unit 20 §110)	**habré, habrás, habrá, habremos, habréis, habrán**
Conditional (Unit 20 §111)	**habría, habrías, habría, habríamos, habríais, habrían**

---

hacer *to do, make*

–do form (Unit 16 §92)	**hecho**
Present Indicative (Unit 5 §21)	**hago,** haces, hace, hacemos, hacéis, hacen
Preterit (Unit 9 §44)	**hice, hiciste, hizo, hicimos, hicisteis, hicieron**
Future (Unit 20 §110)	**haré, harás, hará, haremos, haréis, harán**
Conditional (Unit 20 §111)	**haría, harías, haría, haríamos, haríais, harían**
Direct Command (**tú** form) (Unit 5 §23)	**haz**

---

incluir[15] *to include*

Present Indicative (Unit 5 §21)	**incluyo, incluyes, incluye,** incluimos, incluís, **incluyen**

---

ir[16] *to go*

Present Indicative (Unit 5 §21)	**voy, vas, va, vamos, vais, van**
Present Subjunctive (Unit 16 §95)	**vaya, vayas, vaya, vayamos, vayáis, vayan**
Imperfect Indicative (Unit 10 §51)	**iba, ibas, iba, íbamos, ibais, iban**
Preterit (Unit 9 §44)	**fui, fuiste, fue, fuimos, fuisteis, fueron**
Direct Command (**tú** form) (Unit 5 §23)	**ve**

---

[15] Forms which show only a *spelling* change are: **–ndo** form (**incluyendo**); preterit forms (**incluyó, incluyeron**). Cf. **cayendo, cayó, cayeron** (from **caer**) and **oyendo, oyó, oyeron** (from **oir**). The following is a list of all the verbs with infinitive in **–uir** which have appeared in this book, and which are inflected like **incluir: atribuir, constituir, construir, contribuir, distribuir, fluir, huir, influir, rehuir,** and **sustituir.**

[16] The **–ndo** form (**yendo**) shows only a *spelling* change.

oir[17] *to hear*

Present Indicative (Unit 5 §21)　　　　**oigo, oyes, oye,** oímos, oís, **oyen**

---

poder *to be able*

−**ndo** *form* (Unit 8 §40)　　　　**pudiendo**
Present Indicative[18]　　　　**puedo, puedes, puede,** podemos, podéis, **pueden**
Preterit (Unit 9 §44)　　　　**pude, pudiste, pudo, pudimos, pudisteis, pudieron**
Future (Unit 20 §110)　　　　**podré, podrás, podrá, podremos, podréis, podrán**
Conditional (Unit 20 §111)　　　　**podría, podrías, podría, podríamos, podríais, podrían**

---

poner *to put, place*

−**do** *form* (Unit 16 §92)　　　　**puesto**
Present Indicative (Unit 5 §21)　　　　**pongo,** pones, pone, ponemos, ponéis, ponen
Preterit (Unit 9 §44)　　　　**puse, pusiste, puso, pusimos, pusisteis, pusieron**
Future (Unit 20 §110)　　　　**pondré, pondrás, pondrá, pondremos, pondréis, pondrán**
Conditional (Unit 20 §111)　　　　**pondría, pondrías, pondría, pondríamos, pondríais, pondrían**
Direct Command (**tú** form) (Unit 5 §23)　　　　**pon**

---

producir *to produce*

Present Indicative (Unit 5 §21)　　　　**produzco,** produces, produce, producimos, producís, producen
Preterit (Unit 9 §44)　　　　**produje, produjiste, produjo, produjimos, produjisteis, produjeron**

---

querer *to wish, want*

Present Indicative[19]　　　　**quiero, quieres, quiere,** queremos, queréis, **quieren**
Preterit (Unit 9 §44)　　　　**quise, quisiste, quiso, quisimos, quisisteis, quisieron**
Future (Unit 20 §110)　　　　**querré, querrás, querrá, querremos, querréis, querrán**
Conditional (Unit 20 §111)　　　　**querría, querrías, querría, querríamos, querríais, querrían**

---

saber *to know*

Present Indicative (Unit 5 §21)　　　　**sé,** sabes, sabe, sabemos, sabéis, saben
Present Subjunctive (Unit 16 §95)　　　　**sepa, sepas, sepa, sepamos, sepáis, sepan**
Preterit (Unit 9 §44)　　　　**supe, supiste, supo, supimos, supisteis, supieron**
Future (Unit 20 §110)　　　　**sabré, sabrás, sabrá, sabremos, sabréis, sabrán**
Conditional (Unit 20 §111)　　　　**sabría, sabrías, sabría, sabríamos, sabríais, sabrían**

---

salir *to leave, go out*

Present Indicative (Unit 5 §21)　　　　**salgo,** sales, sale, salimos, salís, salen
Future (Unit 20 §110)　　　　**saldré, saldrás, saldrá, saldremos, saldréis, saldrán**
Conditional (Unit 20 §111)　　　　**saldría, saldrías, saldría, saldríamos, saldríais, saldrían**
Direct Command (**tú** form) (Unit 5 §23)　　　　**sal**

---

[17] Forms which show only a *spelling* change are: −**ndo** for (**oyendo**); −**do** form (**oído**); present indicative form (**oímos**); preterit forms (**oíste, oyó, oímos, oísteis, oyeron**).

[18] The present of this verb is of the stem-changing type. See Unit 4 §16.

[19] The present of this verb is of the stem-changing type. See Unit 4 §16.

ser *to be*

Present Indicative (Unit 2 §2)	**soy, eres, es, somos, sois, son**
Present Subjunctive (Unit 16 §95)	**sea, seas, sea, seamos, seáis, sean**
Imperfect Indicative (Unit 10 §51)	**era, eras, era, éramos, erais, eran**
Preterit (Unit 9 §44)	**fui, fuiste, fue, fuimos, fuisteis, fueron**
Direct Command (**tú** form) (Unit 5 §23)	**sé**

tener *to have*

Present Indicative[20]	**tengo, tienes, tiene,** tenemos, tenéis, **tienen**
Preterit (Unit 9 §44)	**tuve, tuviste, tuvo, tuvimos, tuvisteis, tuvieron**
Future (Unit 20 §110)	**tendré, tendrás, tendrá, tendremos, tendréis, tendrán**
Conditional (Unit 20 §111)	**tendría, tendrías, tendría, tendríamos, tendríais, tendrían**
Direct Command (**tú** form) (Unit 5 §23)	**ten**

traer[21] *to bring*

Present Indicative (Unit 5 §21)	**traigo,** traes, trae, traemos, traéis, traen
Preterit (Unit 9 §44)	**traje, trajiste, trajo, trajimos, trajisteis, trajeron**

valer *to be worth*

Present Indicative (Unit 5 §21)	**valgo,** vales, vale, valemos, valéis, valen
Future (Unit 20 §110)	**valdré, valdrás, valdrá, valdremos, valdréis, valdrán**
Conditional (Unit 20 §111)	**valdría, valdrías, valdría, valdríamos, valdríais, valdrían**

venir *to come*

–ndo form (Unit 8 §40)	**viniendo**
Present Indicative[22]	**vengo, vienes, viene,** venimos, venís, **vienen**
Preterit (Unit 9 §44)	**vine, viniste, vino, vinimos, vinisteis, vinieron**
Future (Unit 20 §110)	**vendré, vendrás, vendrá, vendremos, vendréis, vendrán**
Conditional (Unit 20 §111)	**vendría, vendrías, vendría, vendríamos, vendríais, vendrían**
Direct Command (**tú** form) (Unit 5 §23)	**ven**

ver[23] *to see*

–do form (Unit 16 §92)	**visto**
Present Indicative (Unit 5 §21)	**veo, ves, ve, vemos, veis, ven**
Imperfect Indicative (Unit 10 §51)	**veía, veías, veía, veíamos, veíais, veían**

---

[20] Except for **tengo,** the present of **tener** is of the stem-changing type. See Unit 4 §16.
[21] Forms which show only a *spelling* change are: *–ndo* form (**trayendo**) and *–do* form (**traído**).
[22] Except for **vengo,** the present of **venir** is of the stem-changing type. See Unit 4 §16.
[23] Forms which show only a *spelling* change are: preterit forms (**vi, vio**).

Spanish-English Vocabulary

The vocabulary includes all words except the following: (1) words appearing only in the pronunciation and writing exercises; (2) adverbs ending in –mente when the adjective form is listed; (3) regular –do forms used as adjectives when the appropriate meaning is listed under the infinitive; (4) most proper names.

The words printed in extra large boldface comprise the "Active Vocabulary," that is, the words used in the Dialogs, grammar, and drills. Their definitions are followed by the number of the unit where they first appear.

The asterisk (*) indicates that the word is treated in the Grammar (see Index). A clue to the kind of irregularity of certain verbs (including the spelling alterations c ⟷ z, c ⟷ qu, g → j, gu → gü, and i → y) is given in parentheses after the entry.

ABBREVIATIONS

abr	abbreviation	dim	diminutive	pl	plural
adj	adjective	f	feminine noun	prep	preposition
adv	adverb	fig	figurative	sing	singular
aug	augmentative	inf	infinitive	v	verb
conj	conjunction	m	masculine noun		

a

*a   to, at, from, by, on [1]

abajo   down, under, downstairs [5]; **por —** below; **para—** downward; **hacia —** (turned) down; **de arriba para —** up and down; **venirse —** to come down

abandonar   to abandon, give up

abandono m   abandonment

abarcar (**qu**)   to comprise

abarrotes m pl   groceries

abeja f   bee

abertura f   opening

abierto,-a (see **abrir**)   open, opened [1]

abogado m   lawyer [8]

abono m   fertilizer

abreviatura f   abbreviation

abrigo m   overcoat, shelter; — **de pieles**   fur coat [15]

abril m   April [9]

abrir   to open [1]; —**se mucho** to be opened (wide); —**se paso** to make one's way

abrumador,-ra   overwhelming

abrumar   to overwhelm, oppress

absolutamente   absolutely

absorber   to absorb

absorción f   absorption

abuela f   grandmother [2]

abuelita f dim   granny

abuelo m   grandfather [2]; pl grandparents

abundancia f   abundance

abundante   abundant

abundar   to be numerous

aburrido,-a   boring [3]

acá   here [5]; **hacia —**   this way [23]

acabar   to finish, complete, end [3]; *— **de** + inf   to have just . . . , finish . . . ing [3]

academia f   academy

académico,-a   academic

acaecer (like **parecer**)   to happen

acción f   action [24]

aceite m   olive oil

aceituna f   olive

acento m   accent

aceptación f   acceptance

aceptar   to accept [9]

acerca de   about

acercarse (**qu**) (**a**)   to approach

acero m   steel

acervo m   heap, totality, storehouse

aclarar   to clear up

acompañamiento m   accompaniment

acompañar   to accompany, join [18]; — **en pena**   to extend sympathy [21]

aconsejar   to advise [21]

acontecer (like **parecer**)   to happen

acontecimiento m   event [13]

acopiar   to collect

acordarse (**ue**) (**de**)   to remember [12]

acortar   to cut (down), shorten [9]

acostar (**ue**)   to put to bed; —**se**   to go to bed [12]; *estar **acostado**   to be in bed [22]

acostumbrarse (**a**)   to become accustomed (to)

actitud f   attitude

actividad f   activity

activo,-a   active

acto m   act

actor m   actor

actriz f   actress

actuación f   action, activity, performance [24]

actual   present, real

acudir (**a**)   to go (to), consult, turn (to)

acuerdo m   accord [15]; **de —**   agreed, in agreement, accord-

ingly [15]; de — con according to, by means of; ponerse
de— to agree [17]
acurrucados,-as huddled together
adagio m adage
adaptación f adapting
adaptado,-a adapted
adarga f shield
adecuado,-a adequate
adelante forward; come in [12]
adelanto m advancement
ademán m gesture, movement
además adv besides [4]; *— de
prep besides
adentro within, inside [13]
adhesión f adhesion, adherence
adición f addition
adicional additional
adiestramiento m skill
adiós good-bye [1]
adiosito dim good-bye now
adivinanza f riddle
adjetivo m adjective [24]
administración f administration
administrador m administrator, manager [10]
administrar to administer
admirable admirable [13]
admiración f admiration, wonder
admirar to admire
admitir to admit
adobe m adobe (baked clay)
adolescente adolescent
adonde where [1]
* ¿Adónde? Where? [1]
adoptar to adopt
adornar to adorn
adquirir (ie) to acquire
advertir (ie,i) to warn
aeropuerto m airport
afectividad f affection, affectivity
afecto m feeling, affection
afición f (a) liking, fondness (for)
aficionado m (sports) fan
afirmación f affirmation
afirmar to affirm
aflojar to loosen; — los lazos to
break the ties
afortunado,-a fortunate
africano,-a African
afuera outside [5]; hacia — out
agente m agent
ágil agile
agitador m agitator
agitar to be active, agitate [10];
—se to be moved rapidly,
shake; el — moving
agosto m August [9]
agotar to exhaust; —se to be
worn out
agradable pleasant
agradecer (like parecer) to
appreciate, thank (for) [17]
agradecimiento m grati-
tude [24]
agresión f aggression

agrícola adj agricultural
agricultor m farmer [10]
agricultura f agriculture [24]
agua (el) f water; — potable
drinking water [10]
aguacate m avocado
aguardiente m brandy
agudeza f sharpness
águila (el) f eagle
ah ah, oh [3]
ahí there [3]; por — over there
ahijado m godchild
ahora now [1] por — for
now [15]; *— que since [18]
ahorrar to save
airado,-a angry
aire m air [10]
aislado,-a isolated
ají m chili
ajo m garlic
ajustarse to adjust (oneself), fit in
* al = a + el; — + inf upon + -ing
ala (el) f wing, brim
Alá Allah
álamo m poplar tree [10]
alarde m display; hacer — (de)
to show off, display
albor m beginning
alcaicería f raw-silk exchange
alcalde m mayor
alcanzar (c) to attain, reach [5],
manage
alcohol m alcohol
alcohólico,-a alcoholic
alegato m allegation
alegrar to cheer; —se (de) to
be glad (of) [15]
alegre gay
alegría f joy
alejarse to go off in the distance
alemán,-ana adj German; m
German
Alemania f Germany
alentar (ie) to breathe, encourage
alfarería f pottery
alfarero m potter
alfombra f carpet
álgebra (el) f algebra [9]
* algo something, anything [4];
adv somewhat [7]
algodón m cotton
alguacil m constable
* alguien someone [4]
* alguno (algún),-a some,
any [3]
alias otherwise, alias [22]
aliento m breath
alimentación f food
alimento m food, nourishment
alma (el) f spirit, soul, heart [21]
almendra f almond
almohada f pillow
almorzar (ue,c) to eat
lunch [14]
almuerzo m lunch [19]
aló hello [3]

alpinista m Alps mountain
climber
alquiler m rent [15]
alrededor adv around; a nuestro
—around us; — de prep around
Altamira home of the famous art
caves in the province of Santander, Spain
alteración f alteration, change
alterar to alter, change
alteza f highness
altiplanicie f high plain
alto,-a tall, high [8]; pasar
por — to pass over
altura f height
alumna f student [2]
alumno m student [1]
alzarse (c) to be raised, rise
allá there [3]; más — del beyond; por — over there
allegarse (gu) to go in the company (of)
* allí there [10]
amabilidad f kindness [24]
amable adj kind [2]
amado,-a beloved
amante m lover
amar to love
amargo,-a bitter; un — a strong
maté (served without sugar) [21]
amarillo,-a yellow [17]
ambición f ambition
ambicioso,-a ambitious
ambiente m setting, atmosphere,
environment
ámbito m environment
ambos,-as pl both [24]
ambulante walking, traveling
amenazar (c) to threaten
América f America; la — del
Norte North America; la —
del Sur South America; la —
española Spanish America; la
— hispánica Hispanic America; la — latina Latin America;
las —s the Americas
americanismo m Americanism
americano,-a American [2]
amiga f (girl) friend [2]
amigaso m old friend (gaucho
dialect)
amigo m friend [2]
amistad f friendship; hacerse
—es, trabar —es to make
friends
amistoso,-a friendly
amor m love
amoral amoral
amparar to help
amplio,-a large (spacious)
amueblado,-a furnished
anales m pl annals
analfabetismo m illiteracy [24]
analizar (c) to analyze
anaranjado,-a orange
(colored) [17]

anciano,-a old; *m* old man; **los —s** the old folks

ancho,-a wide; **de —** wide; **por lo —** widthwise

anchura *f* width; **de —** wide

Andalucía *f* Andalusia (province of southern Spain)

andaluz,-za *adj* Andalusian; *m* Andalusian

*   **andar** to go, walk [9]; **anda como siempre** he is as usual; **anda con ojo** be careful; **andando el tiempo** as time goes on

andinismo *m* mountain climbing (in the Andes)

andinista *m* Andes mountain climber

anegarse (gu) to be swamped

ángel *m* angel

angelito *m dim* little angel

anglicismo *m* Anglicism

angloargentino,-a Anglo-Argentinian

angloespañol,-la Anglo-Spanish

anglosajón,-ona Anglo-Saxon

angustia *f* anguish

anhelo *m* desire, zeal

animación *f* animation

animal *m* animal

animar to encourage; **—se** to cheer up, "get going"

ánimo *m* desire, mind

aniversario *m* anniversary [13]

anoche last night [18]

ansí = así (old and dialectal form)

ansioso,-a (a *or* **de)** anxious (for)

antara *f* ancient Peruvian musical instrument

antártico,-a Antarctic

ante in the presence of, before, to, (accredited) to [24] **— todo** especially

anteanoche night before last [10]

anteayer day before yesterday [19]

antebrazo *m* forearm

anteojos *m pl* (eye)glasses

anterior a before, prior to

antes *adv* before [10]; *—* **de** *prep* before, rather than [24]; *—* **(de) que** *conj* before [18]

antesala *f* waiting room

anticipación: con — in advance

anticiparse to anticipate, go ahead

anticuado,-a antiquated [8]

antiguo,-a ancient, old, former [24]

antihéroe *m* anti-hero

antimonio *m* antimony

antipático,-a disagreeable [19]

antípodo,-a antipodal

anualmente annually

anuncio *m* announcement, ad

añadir to add

año *m* year [4]: **al —** yearly, per year [9]

apagar (gu) to turn off [5]

aparato *m* machine

aparatoso,-a superficial, showy

aparecer (*like* **parecer**) to appear

aparente apparent

apariencia *f* appearance

apartar to part off, attract

aparte apart, separate

apasionado,-a passionate

apasionar to inspire a great liking (in)

apego *m* fondness [21]

apellido *m* surname

apenas scarcely, just [14]

apertura *f* opening

apetecer (*like* **parecer**) to appeal

apetecible cherished

aplastado,-a flat [22]

aplastante crushing

aplaudir to applaud

aplauso *m* applause [24]

aplicado,-a applicable; industrious

apoderarse (de) to take possession (of)

apodo *m* nickname

aportación *f* contribution

apostar (ue) to bet [7]; **te apuesto (que no)** I'll bet (not) [7]

apostólico,-a apostolic

apoyo *m* support

apreciar to appreciate

aprender (a) to learn (to) [7]

apresurar to hurry

aprobación *f* approval

aprobado,-a approved, "A" (in a course); **ser —s** to pass courses

aprobar (ue) to approve

apropiarse to appropriate, take to oneself

aprovechar to profit by, make use of; **— para** to be able to [23]

apurarse to worry

apuro *m* worry, hardship

aquel, aquella that; **aquellos, -as** those [11]

aquello that (idea)

*   **aquí** here [2]; **por —** this way [22]

árabe Arabic; *m* Arabic (language), Arab

arado *m* plough

aragonés,esa Aragonese (of the province of Aragon, Spain)

araucano *m* Araucanian (Indian of southern South America)

árbitro *m* umpire

árbol *m* tree [10]

arcaico,-a archaic

arco *m* arch

ardiente warm, hot

área (el) *f* area

arena *f* sand

arenero *m* bullring sweeper

argentino,-a Argentinian [14]

aristocracia *f* aristocracy

aritmética *f* arithmetic

armado,-a (de) armed (with)

armas *f pl* arms, weapons

armonía *f* harmony

armónico,-a harmonious

armoniosamente harmoniously

armonizado,-a in harmony

arquitectura *m* architecture

arraigar (gu) to become rooted, be popular

arraigo *m* roots

arrastrar to drag (off)

¡Arre! Get up!

arreglar to arrange, fix [6]

arreglo *m* arrangement

arremeter to charge

arriba up, upstairs, on top [5]; **hacia —** upward, up; **por —** above; **de — para abajo** up and down; **— de** upwards of, about

arrojado,-a rash, fearless

arrope *m* grape juice boiled to a syrup

arroyo *m* stream

arroz *m* rice [5]

arruinarse to be ruined, be bankrupt

arte *m f* art [7]

artesanía *f* artisanship

artesano *m* artisan

Artico *m* Arctic

articulado,-a articulate

artículo *m* article

artífice *m* artisan

artificial artificial [22]; **fuegos —es** fireworks [23]

artificio *m* artifice, craft [24]

artillero *m* artilleryman [23]

artista *m f* artist

artístico,-a artistic, art

asa (el) *f* handle

asado,-a roasted, cooked; *m* roast; **— a la parrilla** grilled meat; **— a tira** stripped beef; **— de costado** flank beef

ascensorista *f* elevator operator

asegurar to assure, secure, make certain

aserrín *m* sawdust

asesino *m* assassin, murderer [13]

así so, thus, like that [10]; **— como** just as; **— que** thus; **— es que** this is the way that

asiento *m* seat, place

asignar to assign

asignatura *f* course

asilo *m* asylum, home

asimilar to assimilate

asistir (a) to attend, perform

asociado: *see* **estado**

asociarse (a) to become a part (of)

asomar to appear; **—se** to look out of (from), go out [23]

asombrarse to be surprised

aspecto *m* aspect

aspiración *f* aspiration

aspirante aspirant

aspirar to aspire

aspirina *f* aspirin [12]

astronómico,-a astronomical [8]

Asturias Asturias (province of northern Spain)

asunto *m* affair, matter [15]

asustar to frighten

atacar (qu) to attack [13]

ataque *m* attack [10]

atardecer (*like* **parecer**) to grow dark

atención *f* attention

atender (ie) to care for

atento,-a attentive; **su atenta** your kind letter [18]; **— y seguro servidor** Sincerely yours [18]

atesorar to treasure, hoard up

atestiguar (gü) to bear witness, represent

Atlántico *m* Atlantic (Ocean)

atleta *m* athlete

atormentar to tease

atracción *f* attraction

atraer (*like* **traer**) to attract

atrás back, in (the) back [7]; **todo lo de —** all the gains

atravesar (ie) to cross

atrevido,-a bold

atrevimiento *m* boldness

atribuir (*like* **incluir**) to attribute

audacia *f* boldness, daring

audiencia *f* public hearing

augusto,-a august

aumentar to increase

aun, aún even, still

* **aunque** although, even though [18]

áureo,-a golden

auspicios *m pl* auspices

auténtico,-a authentic

auto, automóvil *m* car [8]

autobús *m* bus [19]

autóctono,-a native

autómata *m* automat

automático,-a automatic

autor *m* author

autoridad *f* authority

auxilio *m* aid

avance *m* advancement

avanzado,-a advanced, aggressive; **avanzada** modern young woman

avaricia *f* avarice, greed

ave (el) *f* bird

avellana *f* chestnut

avenida *f* avenue [4]

avenirse (*like* **venir**) **(a)** to compromise (with)

aventura *f* adventure, risk

aventurero *m* adventurer

avestruz *m* ostrich

aviador *m* aviator

avión *m* airplane

avisar to inform, advise, tell [23]

aviso *m* warning

avocado *m* = **aguacate** avocado

¡Ay! Oh! [3]

ayer yesterday [9]; **— por la mañana** yesterday morning

ayuda *f* aid

ayudante *m* assistant

ayudar to help, assist

azafrán *m* saffron

azteca *adj and m f* Aztec

azúcar *m* sugar [4]; **terrón de —** cube of sugar; **caña de —** sugar cane

azul blue [10]

azulejo *m* tile

b

bachillerato *m* bachelor's degree [9]

Badajoz Badajoz (city and province of southern Spain)

¡Bah! Bah! [8]

bahía *f* bay

bailar to dance [23]

bailarín,-ina dancing; *m f* dancer [23]

baile *m* dance [23]

bajar to lower

bajo,-a short [22], low; *adv and prep* under

balance *m* balancing

balbuceos *m pl* stammerings, lispings

balcón *m* balcony [23]

baldío,-a uncultivated, public (lands)

balón *m* ball

baloncesto *m* basketball

banana *f* banana

banco *m* bank [10]

banda *f* band

bandeja *f* tray

bandera *f* flag, banner

banderilla *f* dart

banderillero *m* dart thruster (in a bullfight)

banquero *m* banker

bañar to bathe [12]; **—se (de)** to be bathed (by,) take a bath

baño *m* restroom

barba *f* beard, chin

barbacoa *f* barbecue

barbaridad *f* barbarity; **¡Qué —!** What nonsense! [11]; How terrible!

bárbaro,-a barbarous

barbería *f* barbershop [7]

barbero *m* barber [7]

barón *m* baron

barrer to sweep [5]

barrio *m* neighborhood [15]

barro *m* mud, clay [10]

basado,-a based

base *f* base; **a — de** on the basis of

básico,-a basic

básquetbol *m* basketball [7]

bastante enough, a lot (of), very, a great deal, fairly [9]

bastar to suffice

batata *f* sweet potato

batería *f* battery [8]

baúl *m* trunk

bautismo *m* baptism

beber to drink [20]

bebida *f* drink

béisbol *m* baseball

belleza *f* beauty; **salón de —** beauty shop

bellísimo,-a very (most) beautiful

bello,-a beautiful

bendición *f* benediction, blessing

bendito,-a blessed, confounded [6]

beneficio *m* benefit; **a — de** for the benefit of [15]

berro *m* watercress (plant)

biblioteca *f* library

bibliotecario,-a *m f* librarian

bicicleta *f* bicycle

bien *adv* well, very, good [1]; **más —** rather [22]; **está —** all right [1]; *m* good

biftec *m* beefsteak; **— de lomo** beef loin; *also* **bife**

bilingüe bilingual

billete *m* bill (money), ticket [17]

billón billion (British), trillion (U.S.A.) [2]

biología *f* biology [9]

¡bis! encore!

blanco,-a white [17]; **ropa blanca** underwear

blando,-a bland, gentle, smooth

blasfemia *f* blasphemy

boca *f* mouth [14]

bocacalle *f* intersection (of streets) [23]

bocina *f* horn [8]

boda *f* wedding [15]

boleadora *f* lariat (with balls at ends)

boliviano,-a Bolivian; *m* monetary unit of Bolivia [14]

bolsillo *m* pocket [20]

bombachas *f pl* full, long bloomers

bondad *f* kindness, goodness [12]; **tenga (ten) la — (de)** please [12]

bonito,-a pretty [2]

bordar to embroider
borde *m* edge
bordear to go around, circle
borrachera *f* drunkenness
bosques *m pl* woods
bota *f* boot
botánica *f* botany
boticario *m* apothecary
botín *m* booty
boxeo *m* boxing [7]
brasileño,-a Brazilian
bravo,-a brave; ¡—! Bravo!
bravura *f* fierceness, bravery
brazo *m* arm; a — partido hand-to-hand
breve brief; en — in short
brevedad *f* brevity, speed
brevísimamente very briefly
brillante brilliant [24]
brillantina *f* brilliantine [7]
brillar to shine
brindar to toast
brioso,-a spirited
bronce *m* bronze
brusco,-a brusque, quick
brutal brutal [24]
bruto,-a crude [6]; *m* brute, rude
* bueno (buen),-a good, well [1]; Buenas noches Good evening; Buenas tardes Good afternoon [2]; Buenos días Good morning; lo — the good part [7]; Muy buenos días Good morning to you; visto — O. K. [14]
buey *m* ox
burla *f* jesting
burlador *m* mocker
burlarse (de) to make fun (of)
burrito *m dim* little donkey
burro *m* donkey
bus *m* bus [14]
busca: en — de looking for
buscar (qu) to get, look for, look up, meet [14]

c

¡Ca! Oh, no!
cabal exact, complete
cabalgadura *f* mount
cabalgatas *f pl* horseback riding
caballeresco,-a chivalrous
caballería *f* chivalry
caballero *m* gentleman, knight
caballo *m* horse [10]; a (de) — on horseback
cabaña *f* cabin
cabecera *f* head (of a table or bed)
cabello *m* hair
cabeza *f* head [12]; dolor de — headache
cabo *m* cape; al — de at the end of; al fin y al — in short

cacao *m* cocoa, chocolate (tree)
cacareo *m* cackling
cacique *m* chief
* cada each, every [5]
cadáver *m* corpse; el — fue velado the wake was held
cadete *m* cadet [23]
* caer to fall [4]; — bien to suit; —se to fall down [12]; dejarse — to drop, fall
café *m* coffee, café, restaurant [4]; —nevería ice-cream parlor; taza para — coffee cup
cafecito *m dim* cup of coffee
caída *f* fall
caja *f* box, musical box
cajeta *f* box of jelly
calabaza *f* gourd; *slang* "the air"
calcetín *m* sock [11]; calcetines socks
calculado,-a calculated
cálculo: *see* regla
calendario *m* calendar
cálido,-a warm; crafty
caliente hot [4]
calificar (qu) to grade (students)
calmar to calm; —se to calm down [6]
calor *m* heat; hace — it is hot, warm
calvo,-a bald
calzada: de — *f* footpath, causeway
calzoncillos *m pl* shorts [11]
calzones *m pl* breeches [11]
callar(se) to be quiet, hush ¡Calle!, ¡Cállate! Be still! [22]
calle *f* street [4]
cama *f* bed [11]; ropa de — bed linen [11]
cámara *f* chamber
* cambiar (de) to change, exchange [8]; — de tema to change the subject [17]
cambio *m* change, exchange [14]; en — on the other hand
caminar to travel, walk
caminata *f* walk, hike
camino *m* way, road
camisa *f* shirt [11]
camiseta *f* undershirt [11]
campanilla *f* bell
campaña *f* campaign
campechano,-a frank, cheerful
campeonata *m* championship
campesino *m* farmer, peasant [10]
campo *m* field, country, room, land [10]
camposanto *m* cemetery
can *m* dog
canal *m* canal
canasta *f* basket, canasta (card game)
canción *f* song

cancha *f* field or ground (for sports)
candela *f* candle
candor *m* candor
canoa *f* canoe
cansar to tire
Cantábrico *m* Cantabrian sea (north of Spain)
cantar to sing; — por to sing the praises of; *m* song
cántaro *m* pitcher
cantidad *f* quantity, amount, number [8]
cantiga *f* lyric
canto *m* song
cantor *m* singer
caña *f* cane; — de azúcar sugar cane
capa *f* cloak, cape
capacidad *f* capacity, ability
capaz capable
capilla *f* chapel [15]
capital *f* capital (city)
capitán *m* captain
capitaneado,-a headed, led
capítulo *m* chapter
capote *m* cloak
cara *f* face [6]
caracol *m* snail
carácter *m* (*pl* caracteres) character
característica *f* characteristic
caracterizar (c) to characterize
¡Caramba! Gosh!, My heavens! [5]
carbón *m* coal
carburador *m* carburetor [8]
cárcel *f* prison [13]
cardal *m* grove of thistles
carecer (*like* parecer) (de) to lack
carencia *f* scarcity [24]
carga *f* package
cargador *m* baggage carrier, porter
cargante annoying, boring [14]
cargar (gu) to charge
cargo *m* charge, responsibility
cariño *m* affection
carne *f* meat [5]
carnicería *f* butchershop
caro,-a expensive [7]; costar muy— to be very expensive [7]
carpintero *m* carpenter
carrera *f* career, race; — de maratón marathon race [7]
carrito *m dim* cart
carro *m* car [8]
carta *f* letter [15], charter
cartel *m* sign
cartera *f* purse, billfold, wallet, [9]
* casa *f* house [2]; a — home; en — at home [3]; — editora publishing house
casado,-a married [4]

casamiento *m* marriage

casar to marry (marry off) [4]; **estar sin** — to be unmarried; **—se** to get married [15]

casi almost [5]

casino *m* casino, club

casita *f dim* little house [4]

caso *m* case, affair [8]; **en todo** — anyway [8]; **no hacer al** — to have nothing to do with it, be beside the point

¡Cáspita! Gosh!

casta *f* line, lineage

castellano,-a *adj and m f* Castilian, [9]; *m* Castilian, Spanish (language) [9]

castigar (**gu**) to punish [12]

Castilla *f* Castile (province in central Spain)

castillo *m* castle

casto,-a pure

casual casual, accidental [24]

casualidad *f* casualty, chance [20]

Cataluña *f* Catalonia (province in northeast Spain)

Cataplum Kerplunk! [22]

catecismo *m* catechism

cátedra *f* professorship; **perder la** — to lose one's position

catedral *f* cathedral

catedrático *m* professor

categoría *f* category, class, rank

católico,-a Catholic

catorce fourteen [2]

causa *f* cause

causar to cause

caza *f* hunt

cazador *m* hunter

cazar (**c**) to hunt

cebolla *m* onion [10]

cejas *f pl* eyebrows

celebrar to celebrate, observe, hold (a meeting) [4]

celeridad *f* haste

celta *adj* Celtic

céltico,-a Celtic

célula fotoeléctrica electric eye

cementerio *m* cemetery [13]

cenizas *f pl* ashes

censura censorship

centavo *m* cent [5]

centenario *m* centenary

centímetro *m* centimeter

central central [4]

centro *m* center [14]; (**al**) — downtown

Centroamérica *f* Central America

cera *f* wax

cerca *adv* near [4]; *— de prep* near [4]; **de** — close at hand

cercado,-a (**de**) enclosed (in)

cerdo *m* pig [10]

cereal *m* cereal

cerebral cerebral

ceremonia *f* ceremony

ceremonioso,-a ceremonious

cereza *f* cherry

cerrar (**ie**) to close [1]; **—se** to close

certificado *m* certificate, credential [22]

César Caesar

cesar (**de**) to cease (to)

cicatriz *f* scar [22]

ciclismo *m* bicycle riding

ciego,-a blind

cielo *m* sky, heaven; **¡Ah —s!** My Heavens!

ciénagas *f pl* marshes

ciencia *f* learning, science, field of study

científico,-a scientific

* **ciento** (**cien**) a (one) hundred [5]; **por** — percent

cierto,-a certain; *adv* certainly

cigarro *m* cigar

cincelar to carve

cinco five [2]

cincuenta fifty [3]

cine *m* movie, movies [16]

cinematográfico,-a *adj* movie

cínico,-a cynic

circuito *m* circuit

círculo *m* circle

circunstancia *f* circumstance

ciruela *f* plum

cita *f* date, appointment

citar to cite

ciudad *f* city [10]

ciudadano,-a *adj and m f* citizen [24]

cívico,-a civic

civil civil

civilización *f* civilization

civilizado,-a civilized

clarín *m* bugle

claro,-a light, clear [12]; **¡—!** Of course! [3]; **—** **que** (**sí**) Of course [4] **¡—** **que no!** Of course not!

* **clase** *f* class [1], kind, kinds; **faltar a** — to miss class; **programas de** — courses; **sala de** — classroom

clásico,-a classic; *m* classic

clasificar (**qu**) to classify

clavar to pierce

clavel *m* carnation

clientela *f* clientele, customers

clima *m* climate

club *m* club [10]

cobarde *m* coward [13]

cobrar to collect

cobre *m* copper

cocina *f* kitchen, cooking [2]

cocinera *f* cook [22]

cocinería *f* kitchen, shop

cocinero *m* cook

coche *m* car [8]

coche-comedor *m* diner

cochino,-a filthy [19]; *m* pig

codo *m* elbow [15]; (**hablar**) **por los —s** to chatter [15]

coger (**j**) to take, assume

cojo,-a lame

colaboración *f* collaboration

colección *f* collecting

colectivo,-a collective; *m* bus [14]; *f* collective

colegio *m* school [9]

* **colgar** (**ue,gu**) to hang (up) [22]

colmado,-a abundant

colocar (**qu**) to place

colombiano,-a Colombian

colón *m* monetary unit (of Costa Rica and El Salvador) [14]; **Colón** Columbus

colonia *f* colony, section (of a city)

colonización *f* colonizing

colonizado,-a colonized

colono *m* colonizer

color *m* color [4]; **de —es** colored

columna *f* column

comarca *f* region bounded

comarcano,-a regional

combate *m* combat

combatir to fight

combinación *f* combination

combinar to combine

comedia *f* comedy

comedor *m* diner, dining room [3]

comentar to comment (on), gossip

comenzar (**ie, c**) to begin [23]

comer to eat [4]

comercial commercial

comerciante *m* merchant

comercio *m* commerce

comestibles *m pl* groceries; **tienda de** — grocery store

cómico,-a comical

comida *f* dinner, meal [4]; **hacer una** — to have a dinner (party); **hora de la** — dinner time; **de** — for dinner [5]

comienzos *m pl* beginnings; **a — de** at the beginning of

comisión *f* agency, commission, committee

comitiva *f* participants

* **como** like, as, how, about [4]; **no hay** — there's nothing like [9]

* **¿Cómo? ¡Cómo!** What? [1] How?, What (a)!; **— no** Of course [2]

comodidad *f* comfort, convenience [10]

cómodo,-a comfortable [24]

compañero,-a *m f* companion, colleague; **— de clase** (**escuela**) classmate [2]

compañía *f* company [15]

comparación *f* comparison
comparar to compare [14]
compartir to share [14]
compás: al — de to the time of
compasión *f* compassion
competencia *f* competition, competence [7]
competitivo,-a competitive
complaciente obedient, obediently
complejo,-a complex
complemento *m* complement, object
completar to complete
completo,-a complete
complicación *f* complication
complicado,-a complicated [8]
* **componer** (*like* **poner**) to compose [5]
comportarse to behave
composición *f* composition
compositor *m* composer
compra *f* purchase; (**ir**) **de —s** (to go) shopping; **hacer —s** to shop
* **comprar** to buy [11]
* **comprender** to understand [10]; comprise
comprensible understandable
comprensión *f* comprehension [24]
compresión *f* compression
comprometido,-a promised, dedicated, engaged
compromiso *m* engagement [18]
compuesto,-a (*see* **componer**) composed; *m* compound [24]
comulgar (**gu**) to go to communion [15]
común, comunes common [24]; **por lo —** usually
comunicación *f* communication
comunicar (**qu**) to communicate
comunión *f* communion [15]
* **con** with, by [2]; **— tal (de) que** provided [18]
conceder to allow, grant [6]; **—se** to be bestowed
concepto *m* concept
concesión *f* concession
conciencia *f* conscience
concierto *m* concert
concluido,-a finished
concordia *f* concord, agreement
concreto,-a concrete
concurso *m* concourse, contest
concha *f* shell
condecoración *f* decoration, badge, medal [24]
condenado "F" (in a course)
condenar to condemn
condición *f* condition, position [24]
conducir (*like* **producir**) to lead
conducta *f* conduct [22]
conducto *m* conductor, mediator
conectado,-a connected

conejo *m* rabbit
conferencia *f* conference, lecture
confesar (**ie**) to confess
confianza *f* confidence, trust; **tertulia de —** gathering of close friends
confiar (**í**) to trust
confirmación *f* confirmation
confitura *f* confection, preserves
conflicto *m* conflict [24]
conformarse to conform
confortado,-a comforted
congregarse (**gu**) to congregate
congreso *m* congress
conjugación *f* conjugation
conjunto *m* combination, whole; **en —** in all; **como —** as a whole
conmemorar to commemorate
* **conmigo** with me [4]
* **conocer** (**zc**) to know, be acquainted with, meet [3]; **dar a —** to make known; **—se de** to be known to
conocidísimo,-a very well known
conocimiento *m* knowledge, understanding [24]
conque then, well
conquista *f* conquest
conquistador *m* conqueror
conquistar to conquer
consciente conscious
consecuencia *f* consequence
conseguir (*like* **seguir**) to get [6], manage, accomplish
* **consejo** *m* advice; council [9]; *pl* advice [17]
consentir (*like* **sentir**) to consent, permit
conservador,-ra conservative
conservar to keep, preserve
conservatorio *m* conservatory
considerable considerable
consideración *f* consideration
considerar to consider [7]
consigo with them, with her, with him, with you, with it
consistencia *f* consistency
consistente consistent
consistir to consist
constante constant
constar (**de**) to have, consist (of); **hacer —** to inform, reveal
constitución *f* constitution
constitucional constitutional
constituir (*like* **incluir**) to constitute
constitutivo,-a constituent
construcción *f* construction
constructor *m* builder
construir (*like* **incluir**) to construct, build
consubstancial consubstantial
cónsul *m* consul [2]
consulta *f* consultation
consultar to consult [19]

consumo *m* consumption
contacto *m* contact
contar (**ue**) to tell, count, relate [10]; **¿Qué me cuenta (de)...?** How about...? What's the news?; **— con** to enjoy; **¿Qué cuenta?** What does she say? [15]
contemplar to contemplate [21]
contemporáneo,-a contemporary
contener (*like* **tener**) to contain
contenido *m* content, basic idea
contento,-a (**de**) happy (to); *m* **de —** with joy
contertuliano *m* guest (at a *tertulia*)
contestación *f* answer
contestar to answer [2]
contienda *f* struggle, contest
* **contigo** with you [6]
continental continental
continente *m* continent
continuación: a — at once
continuar (**ú**) to continue
continuo,-a continuous
* **contra** against [6]; **en — de** against [6]
contradanza *f* quadrille, cotillion, contredanse [23]
contradictorio,-a contradictory
contrario,-a opposite [24]; **(todo) lo —** (exactly) the opsite; *m* opponent
contraste *m* contrast
contratar to hire, offer a contract (to)
contribución *f* contribution
contribuir (*like* **incluir**) to contribute
convencer (**z**) to convince [17]
conveniente proper
convenir (*like* **venir**) to suit, be proper [21]
conversación *f* conversation [3]
conversar to converse
convertir (**ie,i**) to convert
convicción *f* conviction
cooperación *f* cooperation [24]
cooperar to cooperate [24]
cooperativo,-a cooperative
coordinar to coordinate [24]
coqueta *f* flirt
corazón *m* heart [10]
corbata *f* necktie [12]
corbina *f* (*also* **corvina**) a large white fish, similar to weakfish
corcho *m* cork
cordillera *f* mountain range
Córdoba Cordova (city in southern Spain)
cordobés,-esa Cordovan
Corinto Corinth
coro *m* chorus
corona *f* crown, funeral wreath [21]
coronado,-a (**de**) crowned (with)

coronilla *f dim* crown, top

correcto,-a correct

correo *m* mail [15]

correr to run, chase, travel [13]

correspondencia *f* correspondence department (in an office)

corresponder to correspond, belong

correspondiente corresponding

corresponsal *m* correspondent

correveidile *m* gossiper

corrida *f* course; **— de toros** bullfight [7]

corrido *m* Mexican ballad

corriente current, day-by-day; **lo más —** the usual thing; *f* current; **— de aire** draught

corrupción *f* corruption

cortabolsas *m* thief [24]

cortar to cut (off) [7]

cortedad *f* scantiness [24]

cortesanía *f* courtliness, politeness

cortesano,-a court, courtly

cortinao *m* curtain (gaucho dialect)

corto,-a short, narrow [7]

cosa *f* thing [4] **— de** a matter of; **una —** something [5]; **la de—s** how many things! [24]

cosecha *f* harvest [10]

cosmogónico,-a cosmogonic

cosmopolita cosmopolitan

costa *f* coast

costado: see asado

costar (**ue**) to cost [7] **— muy caro** to be very expensive [7]; **— tanto** to be so hard [17]

costarricense Costa Rican

costumbre *f* custom, way [9]; **como de —** as usual [9]

cotidianamente daily

cotizarse (**c**) to be quoted (on the market)

creación *f* creation

creador,-ra creative

crear to create, raise

crecer (*like* **parecer**) to grow [16]; *m* **el —** growing up [16]

credo *m* creed, belief

creencia *f* belief [24]

* **creer** (**y**) to believe [4]; **Ya lo creo** Yes, indeed [10]

crema *f* cream

cría *f* raising

criado,-a *m f* servant, maid [5]

crianza *f* breeding, raising [10]

criar (**í**) to raise, create

criollo,-a creole (born in the New World of Old World ancestry)

cristal *m* glass, window glass; *fig* drop of water

cristiano,-a *adj and m f* Christian

Cristo *m* Christ

crítica *f* criticism

criticar (**qu**) to criticize

crónica *f* newspaper column, account

cronista *m* chronicler, newspaper writer

cronología *f* chronology

crueldad *f* cruelty

cruzar (**c**) (**de**) to cross, be crossed (by)

cuadra *f* block [4]

cuadrado,-a square

cuadrilla *f* company, band, escort

cuadro *m* picture, design, chart; **— mural** mural

cual: el —, la —, los cuales, las cuales which [7]; **por lo —** therefore

* **¿Cuál?** Which? What? [3]

cualidad *f* quality

* **cualquier(a)** any, some, anyone [8]

* **cuando** when [1]

* **¿Cuándo?** When? [1]

cuanto,-a all (the) [12]; **unos cuantos** a few [8]; **— más ... mayor** the more ... the greater; **tantos ... cuantos** as many ... as; **en — a** as for, as regards [18]

* **¿Cuánto,-a?** How much? [3]

cuarenta forty [8]

Cuaresma *f* Lent [15]

cuarteto *m* quartet

cuarto,-a fourth [10]; *m* room [2], a fourth [2]

cuatro four [2]

cuatrocientos,-as four hundred [8]

cubano,-a Cuban

cubierto,-a (*see* **cubrir**) (**de**) covered (with) [16]

cubrir to cover [16]

cucharadita *f dim* teaspoonful

cucharita *f* teaspoon

cuchillo *m* knife

cueca *f* folk dance of Chile

cuello *m* neck

cuenta *f* account, count, bill [9]; **por su —** on one's (their, his, her, your) own; **tomar en —** to take into account; **darse — (de)** to realize [19]; **— corriente** checking account

cuento *m* story

cuerda: instrumentos de — string instruments

cuero *m* hide, leather [10]

cuerpo *m* body, group, corps [12]

cuestión *f* question [9]

cuestionario *m* set of questions

cueva *f* cave

cuidado *m* care [4]; **con (mucho) —** (very) carefully [10]; **¡—!** Be careful [4]!; **no tengas (tenga) —** don't worry

[5]; **tenga — (de)** be careful (to) [5]

cuidar to care for, tend

culminante culminating, climactic

culpa *f* blame, fault [6]; **tener la —** to be to blame [19]; **todo por — de él** it was all his fault [6]

cultivar to cultivate, grow

cultivo *m* cultivation, crops

cultura *f* culture

cultural cultural

cumpleaños *m* birthday [4]

cumplido *m* compliment

cumplimiento *m* accomplishment, compliment [24]

cumplir to accomplish, attain, carry out, do one's duty [15]

cuna *f* cradle

cuñado *m* brother-in-law [6]

cuñao = cuñado

curar to treat, cure

curiosidad *f* (**por**) curiosity (to)

curioso,-a curious

curso *m* course; **perder el —** to fail in a course.

cuyo,-a whose

ch

chaleco *m* vest [23]

chaparajos *m pl* chaps

chaperón,-ona *m f* chaperon [16]

chaqueta *f* jacket

charla *f* informal talk

chato,-a flat, flat-nosed [22]

cheque *m* check [14]

chicle *m* chewing gum

chico,-a small [6]; *m* boy; *f* girl [3]; **¡Chica!** My dear!

chicha *f* chicha (fermented liquor made of corn or fruit)

chile *m* chili, pepper

chileno,-a Chilean

china *f* china, porcelain

chiquero *m* stall

chiripá *m* raincoat (worn by the gaucho)

chirle insipid

chisme *m* gossip

chiste *m* joke

chistoso,-a funny

¡Chito! Sssh!

chivato *m* kid

choclo *m* roasting ear; **pastel de —** escalloped corn

choque *m* clash, collision

chuparse to lick

churrasco *m* barbecued meat [14]

d

dádiva *f* gift, honorarium

danza *f* dance

danzón *m* Cuban dance [23]

daño *m* harm; **hacer —** to hurt, harm

* **dar** to give, make [5]; **— de beber** to serve drinks; **— de comer** to feed; **— en** to come upon, attack; **— exámenes** to take exams; **—la vuelta** to turn around, return; **— saltos** to leap up and down; **—se cuenta (de)** to realize

dato *m* information, datum

* **de** of, from, to, as, concerning, by, with [1]

* **debajo de** under, below [12]

* **deber** to owe, ought, must [2]; **—se** to be due; *m* duty

débil weak

decidir(se) (a) to decide [17]

décimo,-a tenth [9]; *m* lottery ticket [20]

* **decir** to say, tell [1]; **es —** that is; **querer —** to mean; **digo** I mean; **se le dice** it is said

decisión *f* decision

decisivamente decisively

declamar to act, declare

declarar to declare

decoración *f* decoration

decorar to decorate

decorativo,-a decorative

dedicar (qu) to dedicate, use [17]

dedo *m* finger

defecto *m* defect

defectuoso,-a defective

defender (ie) to defend [13]

defensa *f* defense

defensivo,-a defensive

defraudar to defraud, cheat

* **dejar** to let, permit [3]; leave [5], put down; **— de** to stop, fail to; **—se caer** to drop, fall

* **del = de + el** [6]

delante de in front of

delegado *m* delegate

deleitarse to take delight

deleite *m* delight

delgado,-a slender [22]

delicadeza *f* delicacy

delicado,-a delicate, slender; **lo —** what is delicate

deliciosísimo,-a most delicious

delicioso,-a delicious, delightful

delincuente delinquent, offender

demás: los —, las — the others, the rest (of the) [9]

demasiado too much, too [9]

democracia *f* democracy

demócrata democratic

democrático,-a democratic

demostración *f* demonstration

demostrar (ue) to display, show

denominado,-a designated (as)

denso,-a dense, dark

dentista *m* dentist [15]

dentro *adv* within [3]; *— **de** *prep* within, inside of [3]

departamento *m* department

depender (de) to depend (on) [8]

dependienta *f* clerk [11]

dependiente *adj* dependent; *m* clerk [11]

deporte *m* sport [7]

deportista *adj* sports

derecho,-a right [4], straight; *m* right; **a (hacia) la derecha** to the right [4]; *adv* straight ahead

derivación *f* derivation

derivar to derive

derramar to shed, lose

desafortunadamente unfortunately

desagradable unpleasant

desaliñarse to disarrange

desarreglar to disarrange [24]

desarrollar to develop, engage in

desarrollo *m* development

desatento,-a inattentive [24]

desbastar to relieve, elevate

desbordar to cross

descansar to rest

descanso *m* rest

descender (ie) to descend

descendiente *m f* descendant

descomponer (ue) (*like* **poner)** to put out of order [24]

descompuesto,-a out of order [3]

desconcertado,-a confused

desconocido,-a unknown; **lo —** what is unknown

describir to describe

descripción *f* description [22]

descubierto,-a (*see* **descubrir)** discovered

descubridor *m* discoverer

descubrimiento *m* discovery

descubrir to discover, reveal

descuidado,-a reckless

desde from, since [11]; *— **que** since [18]

desear to want

desembarco *m* disembarking

desemejante dissimilar

desempeñar to perform

desengañar to undeceive

desengaño *m* disillusionment

deseo *m* desire

desesperación *f* desperation

desfilar to march in line

desfile *m* marching, parade [23]

desflecar (qu) to sprinkle, remove (flakes)

desgraciado,-a unfortunate [7]

* **deshacer** to undo [5]

desierto,-a deserted; *m* desert

designar to designate

deslumbrarse to be baffled, be dazzled

desnudez *f* nakedness

desorden *m* disorder, confusion [21]

desorientación *f* disorientation

desorientado,-a disoriented

despacho *m* office

despedida *f* farewell, leave-taking [24]

despedir (*like* **pedir)** to fire, send off [22]; **—se** to leave, take leave

despertar (ie) to awaken [22]; **—se** to wake up

despierto,-a awake

desplazado,-a displaced

despojos *m pl* spoils

despreciarse (de) to be ashamed (of)

desprecio *m* scorn

desprenderse (de) to give up one's responsibility (for)

después *adv* afterward, later, then [2]; *— **de** *prep* after [24]

destacarse (qu) to excel, be outstanding [17]

destinado,-a destined, made

destino *m* destiny

destreza *f* skill

desvelo *m* staying up late at night

desventaja *f* disadvantage [19]

detallado,-a detailed

detalle *m* detail

* **detener(se) (***like* **tener)** to stop [9]

determinar to determine, define

detrás *adv* behind, after [23]; *— **de** *prep* behind, back of

devoción *f* devotion

devolver (*like* **volver)** to return, give back

devoto,-a devout

D.F. = Distrito Federal Federal District

día *m* day [1]; **al — siguiente** on the following day; **Buenos —s** Good morning [1]; **de — ** in the daytime [22]; **del —** today's; **hoy —** nowadays [16]; **ocho —s** a week; **otro —** the next day [10]; **todos los —s** every day [10]

diablo *m* devil; **¡qué —s** the deuce!

diálogo *m* dialog

diámetro *m* diameter

diario,-a daily

dibujar to draw

dibujo *m* drawing

diccionario *m* dictionary

diciembre December [9]

dictador *m* dictator

dictar to dictate [18]

dicha *f* good fortune; **¡Qué —!** What luck!

dicho,-a (*see* **decir)** said, above-mentioned [16]; **he** — I have spoken [24]

dichoso,-a happy, lucky [23]

diecinueve (**diez y nueve**) nineteen, nineteenth [8]

dieciocho (**diez y ocho**) eighteen, eighteenth [8]

dieciséis (**diez y seis**) sixteen, sixteenth [8]

diecisiete (**diez y siete**) seventeen, seventeenth [3]

diez ten [2]; **un** — a dime [9]

diferencia *f* difference

diferente different [7]

***difícil** (**de**) difficult (to) [17]

dificultad *f* difficulty

difundir to diffuse, spread

dignidad *f* dignity, high position

dignificación *f* dignifying

digno,-a worthy

diminutivo *m* diminutive

dinamarqués,-esa; *m f* Dane

dinamismo *m* dynamism

dinastía *f* dynasty

dinero *m* money [7]

***Dios** God [2]; **Por** — For Heaven's sake [5]; — **mío** my Heavens [2]

diploma *m* diploma

dirección *f* direction, steering mechanism, address [4]

directo,-a direct, directly [19]

director *m* director [14]

dirigente leading, as a leader

dirigir (**j**) to direct, intend; —**se** to approach, speak (to), direct onself

disciplinado,-a disciplined

disco *m* disc, record [3]

discreto,-a discreet

disculparse (**de**) to make excuses (for)

discurso *m* speech, discussion [13]

discusión *f* discussion [24]

discutir to discuss, argue [8]

disfrutar (**de**) to enjoy

disfrute *m* enjoyment

disgustar to be furious, displeased

disgusto *m* displeasure

disimulado,-a feigned; **hacer** (**se**) **el disimulado** to pretend not to notice [23]

disolución *f* dissolving [24]

disolver (**ue**) to dissolve, disperse [13]

disparar to shoot [13]

disponer (*like* **poner**) (**de**) to command, have at its disposal; —**se a** to get ready to

disposición *f* disposition, state

disputa *f* dispute

distancia *f* distance

distar to be at a distance from

distinguir (**g**) to distinguish

distintivo,-a distinctive; *m* distinctive mark

distinto,-a (**de**) distinct, different (from)

distraer (*like* **traer**) to distract

distribuir (*like* **incluir**) to distribute, pass out

distrito *m* district

disuelto,-a (*see* **disolver**) dissolved [16]

diversificarse (**qu**) to become different, diversify

diversión *f* diversion

diverso,-a diverse, different

divertirse (**ie, i**) to have a good time

dividir to divide

divino,-a divine

división *f* division

doblar to turn, fold, bend, double [4]

doble double; *see* **paso**

doce twelve [8]

docena *f* dozen [5]

***doctor** *m* doctor [12]

doctorado *m* doctorate (degree)

doctrinal doctrinal; *m* catechism

documento *m* document, papers (identification) [6]

dogma *m* dogma

dólar *m* dollar [8]

doler (**ue**) to hurt, pain [12]

dolor *m* pain, sadness, grief; — **de cabeza** headache

domicilio *m* home

dominación *f* domination

dominante dominating, powerful

dominar to dominate, rule

domingo *m* Sunday [4]

dominical *adj* Sunday [24]

dominicano,-a Dominican

dominio *m* domination, control

don,-ña *m f* (title used before a given name to show respect) [4], [2]

donaire *m* grace

***donde** where [7]

*¿**Dónde?** Where? [2]

***dormir** (**ue, u**) to sleep [9]

dos two [2]

doscientos,-as two hundred [8]

Dr. = **doctor** [3]

dualismo *m* dualism

duda *f* doubt; **sin** — doubtless

dudar (**en**) to doubt, hesitate (to) [20]

duelo *m* grief, mourning [21]; **de** — in mourning [21]

dueño,-a *m f* owner; **dueña** (**de casa**) housewife [5]

dulce sweet; *m pl* sweets, candy

dúo: a — together

duración *f* duration; **a larga** — long-playing (record)

durante during

durar to last

duro,-a hard

e

***e** and [6]

E.U. = **Estados Unidos** (*also* **EE.UU.**)

¡**Ea!** Come on!

economía *f* economics

económico,-a economic [24]

ecuador *m* equator

ecuatorial equatorial

ecuatoriano,-a Ecuadorian

ecuestre equestrian

echar to throw, pour, give; —**de menos** to miss [15]; — **mirada** to glance [23]

edad *f* age [4]; **Edad Media** Middle Ages; ¿**Qué** — **tiene?** How old is she? [4]

edificio *m* building

editora: casa — *f* publishing house

educación *f* education [9]

educado,-a educated

EE.UU. = **Estados Unidos** *m pl* United States [2]

efecto *m* effect; **en** — sure enough; that's right, so it is

eficaz efficient

*¿**eh?** eh? huh? [3]

ejecutado,-a executed, performed

ejemplo *m* example [17]; **por** — for example [17]

ejercer (**z**) to exercise, act, exert

ejercicio *m* exercise

ejercitar to exercise, practice, train

ejército *m* army

***el** the [1]

***él** he, him [2]; **de** — his; — **no** not he

elaborar to work, fashion

elección *f* election [13]

electoral electoral

electricidad *f* electricity [15]

eléctrico,-a electric

elegancia *f* elegance, grace

elegantemente elegantly

elegir (**i, j**) to elect, choose [24]

elemento *m* element

elevar to elevate, be high, raise [24]

eliminar to eliminate [24]

elote *m* roasting ear

***ella** she, her; **de** — hers [2]

***ellas** they, them [2]

elle the letter **ll** [14]

***ello** it: **todo** — all of it

***ellos** *m* they, them [2]

emanciparse to emancipate, free

embajador *m* ambassador [24]

embarcación *f* vessel

embargo: sin — nevertheless, but [3]

emborracharse to get drunk

embromar to tease

emigrante *m* emigrant

eminente eminent
emoción *f* emotion
emocional emotional
emocionante exciting, emotional
emotivo,-a emotional
empanada *f* sandwich
empaparse to get soaked [23]
empatado,-a tied (in a score)
emperador *m* emperor
empezar (**ie, c**) to begin [22]
empleada *f* clerk, employee
empleado *m* clerk [10]
emplear to use
empleo *m* employment, job, use [6]
empresa *f* undertaking
* **en** in, into, on, at [2]; — **contra de** against [6]; — **cuanto (a)** as for; — **pro de** in favor of [24]; — **vez de** instead of [4]
enamorarse (**de**) to fall in love (with)
encajar to fit
encantado,-a (**de**) delighted (to) [4]
encantador,-ra charming
encantar to be enchanting
encanto *m* charm
encargar (**gu**) to charge, order [21]
encerrado,-a locked up
enciclopedia *f* encyclopedia
encima: por — de above, over
encogerse de hombros to shrug one's shoulders
encontrado,-a opposing, at odds with
encontrar (**ue**) to find, encounter [10]; — **se** to meet, find oneself, be [10]
encuentro *m* encounter; salir al — to go out to meet
enemigo *m* enemy
energía *f* energy
enero *m* January [9]
énfasis *m* emphasis
enfermarse to get sick
enfermedad *f* sickness, illness [21]
enfermera *f* nurse [12]
enfermo,-a sick [4]
enfrentarse (**con**) to meet
engañar to deceive
enlazado,-a joined, intertwined
enojadísimo,-a very angry [19]
enojar to anger [12] —**se** to get angry [12]
enorgullecerse (*like* **parecer**) (**de**) to be proud (of)
enorme enormous
enredado,-a complicated (14)
enriquecer (*like* **parecer**) to enrich
ensalada *f* salad [5]
ensanchar to widen

ensanche *m* widening
ensayarse to rehearse, train
enseñanza *f* teaching; **segunda** — secondary (school)
enseñar to teach, show [5]
ensordecedor,-ra deafening
ensuciar to dirty [5]; —**se** to get dirty
ensueño *m* dream, dreams
entender (**ie**) to understand [4], intend — (**en**) to spend (time) in; —**se** to be understood; —**se** (**con**) to get along with
entendimiento *m* understanding [24]
entero,-a entire, complete; **el** — *m* lottery ticket [20]
enterrar (**ie**) to bury
entidad *f* entity
entierro *m* burial, funeral [21]
entonación *f* intonation
entonces then [2]
entrada *f* entrance, doorway [3]
* **entrar** (**a**) (**en**) to enter, come in [1]
* **entre** between, among [19]; **por** — from
entregar (**gu**) to hand over
entremés *m* entrée (food)
entremeter to interfere, mix
entretenimiento *m* entertainment
entrevista *f* interview
entusiasmar to make enthusiastic [10]; —**se** to become enthusiastic [10]
entusiasmo *m* enthusiasm
entusiasta *m f* enthusiast, fan
enviar (**í**) to send [18]
envolver (**ue**) to wrap [11]
envuelto,-a (*see* **envolver**) (**de**) wrapped (in) [16]
épico,-a epic
época *f* epoch, time
equilibrarse to be balanced
equilibrio *m* balance, mind
equipajes *m pl* baggage
equiparse (**de**) to be equipped (with)
equipo *m* team, equipment [7]
equitación *f* equitation, horseback riding
equivalente similar
equivocado,-a mistaken [3]
era *f* era
erudito *m* erudite
errante errant
errar (**ye**) to err
escala *f* scale
escalar to climb
escalera *f* stairs; — **mecánica** escalator
escandalizado,-a scandalized
escándalo *m* scandal, racket [5]
escandaloso,-a scandalous

escapar(se) to escape, run away [18]
escasez *f* scarcity, want
escaso,-a scarce [7]; — **de dinero** short of money [7]
escena *f* scene
escenario *m* scene, setting
escoger (**j**) to draw, select, choose [13]
escolta *m* escort; *f* convoy [6]
* **escribir** to write [4]
escrito,-a (*see* **escribir**) written [16]; *m pl* writings
escritor *m* writer
escritura *f* writing
escrúpulo *m* scruple
escrupulosidad *f* scrupulousness
escuadrón *m* squadron
escuchar to listen (to)
escudo *m* shield
escuela *f* school [2]; — **superior** high school
esculpir to engrave, sculpture
escultura *f* sculpture
* **ese, esa** that; **esos,-as** those [3]
ése, ésa that, that one; **ésos,-as** those [11]
esencia *f* essence, being
esencial essential
esfuerzo *m* effort, struggle [24]
esmalte *m* enamel
eso that [3]; **por** — therefore, for that reason, that's why [3]
espaciado,-a spaced, located
espacio *m* space, period; **de** — carefully
espada *f* sword
espaldas *f pl* back
espantar to frighten (away), brush (off)
España Spain [7]
* **español,-la** Spanish; *m* Spanish (language) [1], Spaniard [15]
españolidad *f* Spanishness
españolizado,-a Hispanized
esparcir (**z**) to spread
especial special, especially
especialista *m f* specialist
especializarse (**c**) to specialize, major
especie *f* kind
específico,-a special, specific
espectacular spectacular
espectáculo *m* spectacle, pageant
espectador *m* spectator
espejo *m* mirror
espera: en — de waiting for
esperanza *f* hope [19]
esperar to wait (for) [2], expect, hope
espíritu *m* spirit
espiritual spiritual
espléndido,-a splendid
espontánea *f* spontaneity

espontáneo,-a spontaneous

esposa f wife

esposo m husband [24]: pl husband and wife [24]

espuela f spur

espulgado,-a closely examined

espuma f foam, suds

esquiador,-ra m f skier

esquiar to ski

esquina f corner [4]

esquivar to move gracefully, shift, dodge

establecerse (like **parecer**) to be established

establecimiento m establishment

estación f season; station

estado m state [2], office; — **libre asociado** commonwealth; *(los) **Estados Unidos** (the) United States [2]

estancia f room, ranch, quarters

estanciero m rancher (owner of an *estancia*)

estante m bookshelf

estaño m tin

* **estar** to be [1]

estatua f statue

estatura f height

este, esta this [4]; *esta noche** tonight [5]; **estos,-as** these

este m east

éste, ésta this, the latter [7]; **éstos,-as** these, the latter

estético,-a aesthetic; **estética** f aesthetics, style

estilizado,-a proper (according to style)

estilo m style [10]; **por el** — of that kind [10]

estimación f esteem; **dar** — (a) to honor (a check)

estimar to esteem, regard highly

estirpe f stock, lineage

esto this [6]; **en** — at this moment

estocada f sword thrust

estómago m stomach

estoque m sword

estratificado,-a stratified

estrechar la mano to shake hands

estrecho,-a narrow; m strait

estrella f star

estribillo m refrain (of a song)

estudiante m f student [13]

estudiantil adj student, of students [9]

estudiar to study [2]

estudio m study [17]

estupendo,-a stupendous

estúpido,-a stupid

etapa f stage, level

eterno,-a eternal

etimología f etymology

etiqueta f (table) etiquette, formality

étnico,-a ethnic

etnografía f ethnography

etnográfico,-a ethnographic

Europa f Europe [20]

europeo,-a European

evento m event

evitar to avoid

evolución f evolution

exacto,-a exact [4]; adv exactly

exageración f exaggeration

exagerar to exaggerate [8]

exaltar to exalt

examen m examination [9]; **dar (sufrir) exámenes** to take exams

examinar to examine

excelencia f excellence; **por** — outstanding

excelente excellent

excepcional exceptional

* **excepto** except [4]

exclusivo,-a exclusive

excursión f trip, excursion; — **a pie** hike

excursionista m f hiker

excusable excusable

exhibir to show, show off

exigente strict [19], discriminatory; **menos** — easiest

exigir (j) to require, take, demand [6]

existencia f existence [24]

existir to exist [13]: **dejar de** — to die

éxito m success [24]

éxodo m exodus, loss

expensas: a — **de** at the expense of

experiencia f experience

experimento m experiment

explicación f explanation

explicar (qu) to explain [5]

explorador m explorer

explorar to explore

explosivo m explosive

explotar to exploit

exportación f export

expresar to express

expresión f expression

expresivo,-a expressive

exquisito,-a exquisite

extender (ie) to extend

extensión f extension

extensivamente extensively

exterior foreign

externo,-a external

extinguir (g) to extinguish

extra extra [13]

extraacadémico,-a extracurricular

extracto m extract

extranjero,-a foreign [4]; m foreigner; **del** — from abroad; **en el** — abroad [4]

extrañar to seem strange

extraño,-a strange, foreign

extraordinario,-a extraordinary

extravagante extravagant

Extremadura f Extremadura (province of Spain)

extremar to lavish

extremista m f extremist

extremo,-a extreme; m extreme, end

f

fábrica f factory

fábula f fable

faceta f facet

* **fácil** (**de**) easy (to) [4]

facilidad f ease; **con** — easily

facilitar to make easy

facón m knife (word used by gauchos)

factor m factor

facultad f faculty, skill; division of a university

faena f act, task

falcón m falcon

falda f skirt

falsificar (qu) to falsify, forge [22]

falso,-a false

falta f lack [11]; **hacerle** — to need [19]; **Les hace falta** They need [19]; **sin** — without fail [11]

faltar to miss, be lacking [4]; need, be missing, fail; — **a la clase** to miss class; **faltan veinticinco para las nueve** it is twenty-five minutes to nine [19]; **no faltaba más** don't think of it [21]

fallar to fail [8]

fallecer (like **parecer**) to die

fama f reputation, fame

familia f family [2]

familiar adj familiar, family

familiaridad f familiarity

famoso,-a famous [22]

fanático,-a fanatical

fanfarrón m braggart

fantasía f fantasy

fantástico,-a fantastic [7]

farmacia f drugstore

fascinación f fascination

fase f phase

fatal fatal [24]

fatalismo m fatalism

favor m favor [1]; **¿Nos hará el** — (**de**) Will you please . . . ? **por** — please [1]; **si me hace el** — please [3]

favorable favorable

favorito,-a favorite

fe f faith

febrero m February [9]

febril feverish

fecundar to fertilize, enrich

fecha f date [4]

federación f federation

felicidad *f* happiness
felicitar to congratulate [4]
feliz happy
femenino,-a feminine
fénix *m* phoenix
fenomenal phenomenal [7]
fenómeno *m* phenomenon
feo,-a ugly; **una fea** an ugly woman
feria *f* fair [10]
feriado,-a: día — holiday [4]
feroz fierce, ferocious [14]
ferrocarriles *m pl* railroads
fertilidad *f* fertility
festividad *f* festival
feudal feudal
fiambrería *f* delicatessen shop
fiambres *m pl* cold cuts (of meat)
fidelidad *f* fidelity
fiebre *f* fever [12]
fiel loyal
fiereza *f* fierceness
fiero,-a wild, huge; *m* beast
fiesta *f* party, feast [23]
figura *f* figure, line
figurado,-a figurative
figurar(se) to figure, imagine [21]; **se le figura** he imagines
figurilla *f dim* little figure
fijar to fix [23]; **—se** to imagine, look [23]
fila *f* file
filiación *f* filiation, relationship
filigrana *f* filigree
filología *f* philology
filólogo *m* philologist
filosofar to study the philosophy (of), philosophize
filosofía *f* philosophy [9]
filosófico,-a philosophical
filósofo *m* philosopher [9]
fin *m* end [15]; **a —es de** at the end of; **al — y al cabo** after all; **en —** in short [21]; **por (al) —** finally [15]
finado *m* (the) deceased
final *m* end
finalmente finally
finanzas *f pl* finances
finca *f* farm, ranch [10]
fingir (**j**) to feign, pretend
fino,-a fine [10]
firma *f* company [18], signature
firmado,-a signed
firme firm, solid
física *f* physics [9]
físico,-a physical
flacón,-ona very thin
flamenco,-a Flemish
flan *m* flan (custard)
fleco *m* fringe, flounce
flecha *f* arrow [6]
flor *f* flower [13]
floral floral
floreo *m* show, glamor
florido,-a flowery

fluir (*like* **incluir**) to flow
flujo *m* flow
fogata *f* bonfire
fogón *m* fire
fomentar to encourage, sponsor
forjar to forge
forma *f* form [24]
formación *f* formation
formal formal
formalidad *f* formality
formar to form, make (up) [23]; **—se** to grow
formidable formidable
foro *m* bar, forum
fortalecer (*like* **parecer**) to strengthen
fortuna *f* good fortune; **por —** fortunately
forzado,-a forced
foto *f* picture
fotoeléctrica: *see* **célula**
fotografía *f* photography
fotógrafo *m* photographer
fracasar to fail
fractura *f* fracture
fragmento *m* fragment
fraile *m* friar
francés,-esa French; *m* Frenchman, French (language)
Francia France
franco,-a frank
frasco *m* vial, cup
frase *f* phrase, sentence
frecuencia: con (mucha) — (very) frequently
frecuente frequent
frenar to curb
freno *m* brake [8]
frente *f* face, forehead; **— a** facing, in the presence of, in front of
fresco,-a fresh
frijol *m* bean [5]
frío,-a cold; *m* coldness; **hace —** it is cold
frito,-a fried
frontera *f* border, frontier
fructífero,-a fruitful, profitable
fruta *f* fruit [5]
fruto *m* fruit (i.e., product); *fig* result
fuego *m* fire [23]; **—s artificiales** fireworks [23]
fuente *f* fountain, source
fuera *adv* outside (of) [24]; ***— de** *prep* outside, besides [24]
fuerte strong, loud [5]; **el plato —** the main course
fuerza *f* strength, force; **con todas sus —s** with all their might
Fulano de Tal So-and-So
función *f* (**de**) function (as), duty
funcional functional
funcionar to function, work

funcionario *m* official [8]
funda *f* pillowcase [11]
fundación *f* founding
fundamental fundamental, basic
fundamento *m* foundation, base
fundar to found
fundo *m* ranch
fúnebre *adj* funeral
furia *f* fury
furioso,-a furious [6]
fusión *f* fusion
fútbol *m* football [7]
futuro,-a future; **lo —** the future; *m* future

g

gabardina *f* gabardine
gala: hacer — to be proud
galgo *m* greyhound
Galicia Galicia (province in northwest Spain)
gallina *f* hen
gallo *m* cock
gama *f* gamut
gana *f* (**de**) desire (to) [3]; **tener —s (de)** to want to [7]
ganado *m* livestock [10]; **— vacuno** cattle
ganancia *f* gain, profit [10]
ganapán *m* (*disparaging*) errand boy (often one who carries bundles for a fee)
ganar to gain, earn, win [7]; beat [5]
ganso *m* goose
garganta *f* throat [12]
gastador,-ra *adj and mf* spendthrift
gastar to spend
gasto *m* expense
gato *m* cat [5]; **no se deje dar gato por liebre** don't let them cheat you [5]
gauchesco,-a pertaining to the gaucho
gaucho *m* gaucho (social or cultural type who inhabited the pampas of Argentina and Uruguay; in some respects suggests "cowboy")
gavilán *m* sparrow hawk
gemido *m* moan
generación *f* generation
general general [9]; **por lo —** usually
generalizar (**c**) to generalize
género *m* kind
generoso,-a generous
genial *adj* of genius
genialmente with genius
genio *m* genius
*gente *f* people [5]; **la — bien** the cultured people
gentileza *f* (**de**) kindness (to)
genuino,-a genuine
geografía *f* geography [9]

geográfico,-a geographical, geo-
graphically
geometría f geometry [9]
gerente m manager, boss [19]
germánico,-a Germanic
germano,-a German
gesticular to gesticulate; —se to
be shown by gestures
gesto m gesture [13]
gigantesco,-a gigantic
giro m turn (of phrase), characteristic way of expression
gitano m gypsy
glaciares m pl glaciers
gloria f glory
gobernador m governor
gobernante m governor
gobernar (ie) to govern
gobierno m government [8]
gol m goal
golpe m strike, hit
golpecito m dim tap
goma f rubber; zapatos de —
overshoes
gordo,-a fat; premio — first
prize [20]
gorro m cap
gozar (c) (de) to enjoy
gozo m joy
gozosamente joyously
gracia f grace; —s thank you,
thanks [1]
gracioso,-a gracious; funny
graderías f pl steps
grado m degree
graduación f graduation
graduado,-a graduate; m graduate
graduarse to be graduated
gral. = abr of general [24]
gramática f grammar
Granada Granada (province in
southern Spain)
* grande (gran) large, great,
big [6]
grandeza f greatness, grandeur
grandiosidad f grandeur
grandioso,-a grandiose
grandísimo,-a very great, greatest
grano m grain
grave grave, serious [13]
gravedad f seriousness
greda f clay, chalk
griego,-a adj and m f Greek
gripe m grippe, flu [12]
gris gray [17]
gritar to shout
grito m shout
grotesco,-a grotesque
grupo m group [7]
guantes m pl gloves
guapo,-a handsome [23]
guaraní m monetary unit of
Paraguay [14]
guarda: a la — on guard
guardar to keep, protect

guardia m guard; f guard
(corps) [6]
guascaso m big kick (gaucho
dialect)
guatemalteco,-a Guatemalan
¡Guay! Oh! Woe!
Guayanas f pl (the) Guianas
guerra f war
guerrillero,-a fighting
guía m guide; f guide book
guiar (í) to guide
guisado m stew
guitarra f guitar
* gustar to be pleasing, like [2];
me gusta I like it
gusto m pleasure [1]; taste;
a — de to the liking of; con
mucho — gladly [1]; el — es
mío it's my pleasure; mucho
— de conocerlo(la) I'm glad
to meet you; ¡Qué — de verte!
How nice to see you! [24]; tanto
— I'm glad to meet you

h

habanero,-a m f song and dance
of Havana
* haber to have, be [5]; —de to
be to, must; hay, hubo, había,
etc. there is (are), was (were),
etc.; hay que it is necessary [1]; ¿Qué hubo? Hi,
there [18]
hábil skillful
habilidad f skill
habitante m inhabitant
habitar to inhabit
hábito m habit
habla (el) f speech; de — española Spanish-speaking; los
de — inglesa English speakers
hablante m speaker
hablar to speak, talk [2]; modo
de— way of speaking; oir —
de to hear about
* hacer to do, make, perform [1];
hace como cuatro años for
about four years [4]; hace dos
años two years ago, for two
years [15]; me hará el favor
will you please; si me hace el
favor please [3]; — compras
to shop; — pregunta(s) to
ask (a) question(s) [9]; — una
comida to give a dinner [4];
— un papel to play a role;
—se to become, be made; —se
amistades to make friendships;
—se tarde to be getting late
* hacia to, toward [23]; — abajo
downward; — acá this way [23];
—afuera out; — arriba upward; —fines toward the end

hacienda f hacienda, estate [10]
halagar (gu) to flatter
hallar to find; —se to be, find
oneself, be found
hambre (el) f hunger [4];
tener — to be hungry [4]
harina f flour [5]
* hasta to, as far as, until, even [4];
— luegito bye-bye; *— que
conj until [18]
hay (see haber) there is (are) [5]
hazaña f deed, exploit
hazmerreir m laughing stock
hebreo,-a Hebrew
hecho,-a (see hacer) done,
made [13], already made; m fact
helado m ice cream [5]
hemisferio m hemisphere [24];
— del Oeste (Occidental)
Western Hemisphere
herbolario m herb growing
heredar to inherit
herido,-a wounded [13]; m
wounded man
herir (ie, i) to wound, hurt
hermana f sister [2]
hermanito m dim little brother
hermano m brother [2]; pl
brothers and sisters [2]
hermosísimo,-a very beautiful
hermoso,-a beautiful
héroe m hero
heroico,-a heroic
heroismo m heroism
herramienta f tool [8]
heterogeneidad f heterogeneity
hidalgo m nobleman
hielo m ice
hierro m iron
higiene m hygiene
hija f daughter [2]
hijo m son [2]; pl sons and
daughters [2]
hilado m thread
himno m hymn [23]
hincharse to swell (out)
hipódromo m hippodrome
hispánico,-a Hispanic
hispanidad f Hispanic characteristics
hispano,-a Hispanic; los —s
the Spanish peoples
Hispanoamérica f Hispanic
America
hispanoamericano,-a Hispanic
American
hispanoparlante m Spanish-
speaking person
historia f history, story [9]
histórico,-a historical
hmm hum [6]
hogar m home
hojalata f tin plate
hojear to leaf through, scan
hola, holá hello [3]
holandés,-esa Dutch

hombre *m* man [6] — **de bien** good man; — **del día** man of the hour [17]

hombrecillo *m dim* young man

hombro *m* shoulder

homenaje *m* homage

hondureño,-a Honduran

honesto,-a honorable, proper

honor *m* honor [24], fame, privilege

honra *f* honor, reverence

honrado,-a honored

honroso,-a honorable

* **hora** *f* hour, time [3]; **¿Qué — es?** What time is it? [3]; **tener —** to have an appointment [12]

horario *m* schedule [19]

horizontal horizontal

horizonte *m* horizon

horrible horrible [13]

horror *m* horror [10]

hospital *m* hospital

hospitalidad *f* hospitality

hostil hostile

hotel *m* hotel

hoy today [4]; — **día** nowadays [16]

hoyo *m* hole

huelga *f* strike [9]

huella *f* trace, track [22]

huevo *m* egg [5]

huir (*like* **incluir**) to flee

humanidad *f* humanity

humanista *m f* humanist

humano,-a human

humildad *f* humbleness, humility

humilde humble

humillación *f* humiliation

humillado,-a humiliated

humo *m* smoke

humor *m* humor

humorístico,-a humorous

hundirse to sink, fail

hurra hurrah

¡Huy! Ouch!

i

ibérico,-a Iberian

ibero,-a Iberian

idea *f* idea [3]

ideal *m* ideal

idealismo *m* idealism

idealista idealistic [17]; *m f* idealist

ideología *f* ideology

idioma *m* language

ídolo *m* idol

iglesia *f* church [15]

ignorancia *f* ignorance

ignorar to ignore, not to know

* **igual** equal, (the) same [6]; **sin — ** unequaled; — **que** as well as, the same as [9]

igualarse to be like

igualdad *f* equality [24]

igualmente the same (to you) [6]

iluminar to illuminate

ilusión *f* illusion

ilustrado,-a well-informed

ilustre illustrious

imagen *f* image, view

imaginación *f* imagination [24]

imaginar(se) to imagine [10]

imaginería *f* imagery

imaginero *m* painter of religious images

imán *m* magnet, charm

imitar to imitate

impasible indifferent

impedir (*like* **pedir**) to prevent (from)

imperatorio,-a of being an emperor

imperial imperial

imperio *m* empire

impermeable *m* raincoat

ímpetu *m* impetus, attack

impetuosidad *f* impetuousness

implícito,-a implicit

importación *f* import

importancia *f* importance [18]; **No tiene —** It doesn't matter [18]

importante important [8]

importantísimo,-a most important

importar to matter [8]; import

importunidad *f* importunity, annoyance

imposibilidad *f* impossibility [24]

* **imposible (de)** impossible (to) [11]

impreciso,-a imprecise

impresión *f* impression

impresionar to impress

imprimir to press, print

improvisación *f* improvisation

improvisar to improvise

impuesto *m* tax

impulso *m* impulse

inacción *f* inaction, inactivity [24]

inauguración *f* inauguration [8], opening

inca *adj and m f* Inca (Indian)

incaico,-a Inca

incierto,-a uncertain

incitar to incite

inclinarse to be bent, bow

* **incluir** (**y**) to include [5]

* **incluso** including [24]

incompleto,-a incomplete

incomprensible incomprehensible

inconfundible clear, unmistakable

inconscientemente unconsciously

inconsolable inconsolable

inconveniente: no tener— not to mind

incorregible incorrigible

indecible indescribable

independencia *f* independence [23]

independiente independent [13]

Indias *f pl* (the) New World

indicar (**qu**) to indicate, point, show [21], advise

índice *m* index finger

indiferencia *f* indifference

indiferente indifferent

indígena *adj and m f* indigenous, native

indigenismo *m* indigenousness

indio,-a Indian; *m f* Indian

indisciplinado,-a undisciplined

indiscutible undisputed

indispensable indispensable

individual individual

individualidad *f* individuality

individualista individualistic; *m f* individualist

individuo *m* individual

inducir (*like* **producir**) to induce

indumentaria *f* accessories, clothes

industria *f* industry

industriado,-a trained

inescapablemente inescapably

inevitable inevitable

inexcusable inexcusable

infame *m* scoundrel [13]

infamemente infamously

infantería *f* infantry [23]

infantil childlike, childish

infatigable tireless, untiring

infeliz unfortunate

inferior inferior

infestar to infest

infierno *m* inferno

infinito,-a infinite

influencia *f* influence

influir (*like* **incluir**) (**en**) to influence

información *f* information

informar to inform [18]

informe *m* information, item, report

ingeniería *f* engineering [17]

ingeniero *m* engineering

ingenioso,-a ingenious

Inglaterra *f* England

inglés,-esa English; *m* English (language), Englishman [2]

ingrediente *m* ingredient

ingresos *m pl* income

iniciar to initiate, begin

injusticia *f* injustice

inmediato,-a immediate [14]; **de —** immediately [18]

inmenso,-a immense, huge

inmigración *f* immigration

inmigrante *m* immigrant

inmortal immortal

inmortalizado,-a immortalized

inmóvil motionless

inmovilidad *f* immobility

innecesario,-a unnecessary [24]

innegable undeniable

innovación *f* innovation

innumerable innumerable

inocente innocent [13]

inquebrantable indestructible

inquietud *f* restlessness

inquisidor,-ra inquisitive

inscribirse to enroll

inscripción *f* inscription

insistencia *f* insistence [24]

insistente insistent

insistir (**en**) to insist [17]

insospechado,-a unsuspected

inspiración *f* inspiration

inspirar to inspire

instalar to install; **—se** to get settled [24]

instantáneo,-a instantaneous, sudden

instinto *m* instinct

institución *f* institution

instituto *m* institute, (high) school [9]

instrucción *f* instruction

instrumento *m* instrument

insuficiente insufficient

ínsula = isla *f* island

integrante integral

integrar to integrate, become a part of, comprise

integridad *f* integrity, composite

íntegro,-a whole

intelectualmente intellectually

inteligencia *f* intelligence

inteligente intelligent

intención *f* intention

intenso,-a intense

intento *m* attempt

interamericano,-a inter-American

intercambio *m* exchange

interdependencia *f* interdependence

interés *m* (**por**) interest (in)

interesante interesting

interesantísimo,-a very interesting

interesar to interest, be of interest

interior *adj* interior [11]; **ropa —** underwear [11]; *m* interior

interjección *f* interjection

intermitentemente intermittently

internacional international

interpretación *f* interpretation

interpretar to interpret

intérprete *m* interpreter

interrogativo,-a questioning

interrumpir to interrupt

interrupción *f* interruption

intimidad *f* intimacy

íntimo,-a intimate

intolerancia *f* intolerance

introducción *f* introduction

introducir (*like* **producir**) to introduce

inútil useless [9]

invadir to invade

inválido,-a ill, helpless

invasor *m* invader

inventar to invent

inventor *m* inventor

invernal *adj* winter [24]

inverosímil unusual

investido,-a (**de**) invested (with)

investigador,-ra *adj* investigating; *m f* investigator [24]

investigar (**gu**) to investigate [24]

invictísimo,-a most invincible

invierno *m* winter [10]

invitación *f* invitation [3]

invitado *m* guest [5]

*****invitar** to invite [1]

*****ir** to go [1]; **— de compras** to go shopping; **¡Qué va!** Nonsense! [8]; **vamos a...** let's...; **vaya, vaya** go on; **—se** to go out (away) [10]; **vámonos** let's be going [9]

ironía *f* irony

irrisorio,-a derisive

isla *f* island

istmo *m* isthmus

italiano,-a Italian

izquierdo,-a left [4]; **a la izquierda** to the left [4]

j

jabón *m* soap

jactarse to boast

jai-alai *m* jai-alai (a ball game from the Basque provinces of Spain) [7]

jalea *f* jelly

*****jamás** never, ever [13]

jarabe *m* folk dance of Mexico

jarcha *f* lyric refrain of Arabic origin

jardín *m* garden, yard [5]

jardinero *m* gardener [22]

jarrita *f dim* jar; **— para crema** cream pitcher

jarro *m* jug

jefe *m* boss, chief [6]

jerga *f* jargon

Jesucristo Jesus Christ

Jesús Jesus [2]

jinete *m* horseman

jocoso,-a jolly

jonrón *m* home run

joropo *m* folk dance of Venezuela [3]

*****joven** young [14]; *m* young man; *f* young lady

joya *f* jewel

júbilo *m* joy

juego *m* game [7]

jueves *m* Thursday [4]

juez *m* judge

jugador *m* player

jugar (**ue,gu**) to play [5]; **—se con** to fool with

jugoso,-a juicy [14]

juguete *m* plaything, toy [5]

juicios *m pl* judgments

julio *m* July [9]

junio *m* June [9]

junta *f* club, body (of scholars)

juntar to join, put close together

juntito,-a *dim* close together

junto,-a united; *pl* together [6]; *****— a** near, together with [24]; **— con** together with; **en —** together

Júpiter Jupiter

jurídico,-a juridical

jurisconsulto *m* jurist

justa *f* joust

justicia *f* justice

justo,-a exact, exactly

juventud *f* youth

juzgar (**gu**) to judge

k

kilo *m* kilogram (about 2.2 pounds) [5]

kilómetro *m* kilometer (about 0.62 mile) [10]

l

*****la** the [1], her, you, it [4]

labor *f* work

labrador *m* peasant

labrar to work, carve, make; **por —** to be carved

labriego *m* worker

lado *m* side [7]; **al — de** along with; **dar —** to give way; **del — de** with

ladrillo *m* brick

ladrón *m* thief [22]

lago *m* lake

lágrima *f* tear

laguna *f* lake

lamentarse to complain

lana *f* wool [10]

langosta *f* shrimp

lanza *f* lance

lanzar (**c**) to hurl; **—se (a)** to undertake

lápiz *m* pencil [9]

largo,-a long [7]; **a todo lo — de** all along; *m* length

largote *aug* very long

*****las** the [2], them, you [4]

*****lástima** *f* shame, pity [2]; **— que** it's too bad that [2]

lastimar to hurt

lata *f* tin can

lateral lateral [24]

látigo *m* whip
latín *m* Latin
latinista *m f* Latin scholar
latino,-a *adj* Latin; *m* Latin
Latinoamérica *f* Latin America [8]
latinoamericano,-a Latin American
latitud *f* latitude
lavamanos *m* lavatory [24]
lavaplatos *m* dishwasher [24]
lavar to wash [8]; —se to wash [8]
lazo *m* tie, bond, lasso
le him, you, to him, to her, to you, to it [3]
leal loyal [12]
lealtad *f* loyalty
lección *f* lesson
lector,-ra *m f* reader
lectura *f* reading
leche *f* milk [4]
lechera: *see* res
lechería *f* dairy [10]
lechuga *f* lettuce
leer (y) to read
legar (gu) to bequeath
legua *f* league (about 2.4 miles)
lejano,-a distant
lejos far, far away [4]
lengua *f* language, tongue [12]
lenguaje *m* language
lentejas *f pl* lentils [10]
leña *f* firewood
* **les** to them, to you [4]
lesión *f* lesion, injury
letanía *f* litany
letra *f* letter
levantar to raise, build; —se to get up, be raised [12]
levantaválvulas *m* valve lifter [24]
leve slight
léxico *m* lexicon
leyenda *f* legend
libertad *f* liberty; poner en — to free
libertador *m* liberator
libra *f* pound
librar to free, spare
libre free [13]: *see* estado
libro *m* book [1]
licenciado *m* lawyer; licentiate (in Europe, a university degree intermediate between bachelor's and doctor's) [24]; — en Derecho Bachelor of Laws (degree)
licenciatura *f* law degree
liceo *m* school (primary or secondary) [9]
líder *m* leader [13]
lidia *f* fight
lidiar to fight
liebre *m* hare [5]; *see* gato
lienzo *m* linen
liga *f* league, bond

ligar (gu) to join, link
ligereza *f* grace, skill
ligero,-a light (in weight)
limitar to limit, form (the) boundaries (of)
límite *m* boundary
limón *m* lemon
limonada *f* lemonade [12]
limosna *f* alm
limpiar to clean
límpido,-a limpid
limpieza *f* cleanliness
limpio,-a clean
linaje *m* species, family
linda *f* dear [24]
lindo,-a pretty, quaint [23]
línea *f* line
lingüístico,-a linguistic
lío *m* confusion, fight, mix-up [6]
liquidación *f* sale, clearance sale
liquidar to settle (an account)
lírico,-a lyric
liso,-a plain, smooth
lista *f* list, roster [1]; pasar — to call the roll [1]
literario,-a literary, in literature
literatura *f* literature
litro *m* liter [5]
* **lo** it, him, you [4]; the [5]; *—de the matter of [14]; *— que what [14]
local local
loco,-a crazy [5]; *m* fool [17]
locomotora *f* locomotive
locución *f* locution, expression, phrase
locura *f* madness
lógicamente logically
lograr to attain, achieve, succeed (in), manage (to)
loma *f* hill
lomo: *see* biftec
longitud *f* longitude
* **los** them [4]; you; the [1]
lotería *f* lottery [20]
loza *f* pottery, chinaware
lucir (*like* parecer) to be displayed, be spectacular, show off
luchar to struggle, fight
luego then, later [4]; hasta — so long, until later; — que as soon as
lueguito *dim:* hasta — bye-bye
lugar *m* place [5]; tener — to take place
lugarcito *m dim* little place
lumbre *f* light
luna *f* moon; a la luz de la — in the moonlight; — de miel honeymoon
lunes *m* Monday [4]
luto *m* mourning [21]; de — in mourning [21]
luz *f* light [10]; a la — de la luna in the moonlight; traje de luces bullfighter's costume

ll

llama *f* flame [17]
llamar to call [3]; knock (at the door) [2]; —se to be named, be called [2]
llamativo,-a gaudy
llanero *m* plainsman
llano *m* plain, plains
llanta *f* tire [8]
llanto *m* tears
llanura *f* plain
llave *f* key [22]
llegada *f* arrival
llegar (gu) (a) to arrive, reach, come, go [1] — a ser to become; no — a tanto not to go that far, not to be so bad as that
llenar to fill [21]
lleno,-a full
llevar to carry, take, wear, have, be [5]; — tras sí to produce, bring in its wake; — una vida to live, lead a life; —se to carry away, take [12], get [15]
llorar to weep [21]
llover (ue) to rain [23]
llovizna *f* shower, drizzle
lluvia *f* rain [10]

m

macarrónico,-a fractured, garbled
madejica *f dim* small skein
madera *f* wood
madre *f* mother [2]; — Patria Mother Country (i.e., Spain)
madriguera *f* burrow, hole
madrugada *f* early morning
madrugar (gu) to get up early
madurar to mature
maduro,-a mature, ripe
maestría *f* M.A. degree
maestro,-a master; obra maestra masterpiece; *m f* teacher
mágico,-a magic, magical
magnífico,-a magnificent, wonderful [8]
maguey *m* maguey (cactus plant)
maíz *m* corn [10]; — tierno tender corn (in milk stage)
majadero,-a foolish; *m* fool
majestad *f* majesty
majo *m* dude, dandy
* **mal** ill, bad, badly [3]; *m* evil
malagueño,-a of Málaga (a city in Spain); *f* name of a dance and music
maldad *f* illness, badness [24]
maldición *f* curse
maleta *f* suitcase
malicioso,-a malicious
* **malo (mal),-a** bad, sick, out of order [3] de — bad [17]
malvivir to live badly, dissipate

mamá *f* mother [2]
mamacita *f dim* mommy
mancha *f* spot
mandar to send, order [4]
manejo *m* managing, handling
manera *f* manner, kind [24]; **de ninguna** — by no means; **de una** — in a manner, **la** — **de** in a way that
manifestación *f* manifestation, demonstration [13]
manifestar (**ie**) to show
mano *f* hand [5]; **a** — by hand
manso,-a gentle
manteca *f* lard [5]
mantener (*like* **tener**) to support, keep
mantenimiento *m* maintenance, livelihood
mantequilla *f* butter [5]
manual *m* manual
manzana *f* apple
manzano *m* apple tree
maña *f* skill
* **mañana** *f* morning [1]; **ayer por la**— yesterday morning; **de la** — A.M. [18]; *adv* tomorrow [4]
mapa *m* map
máquina *f* machine [19]; **escribir a** — to type
maquinilla *f dim* little machine; clippers [7]
mar *m* sea [21]; *see* **puerto**
maracas *f pl* musical gourds
maratón *m* marathon [7]
maravilla *f* marvel
maravilloso,-a marvelous
marcar (**qu**) to mark, place
marco *m* mark, frame
marcha *f* march [23]; **en** — on the march
margen *m* margin
marido *m* husband
martes *m* Tuesday [4]
mártir *m* martyr [13]
martirizado,-a martyred, martyrized
marzo *m* March [9]
* **más** more, most [3]; — **de** (**que**) more than [13]; —**tarde** later; **lo** — **pronto posible** as soon as possible; **no** — just, only [18]; **no hay** — **remedio que** there's nothing to do but [9]; **¡Qué cosa** — **ridícula!** How ridiculous! [8]
masa *f* mass
mascota *f* mascot
matacán *m* dog poison
matacandelas *m* candle extinguisher
matador *m* matador (in a bullfight)
matafuego *m* fire extinguisher
matamoros *m* bully

matamoscas *m* fly swatter
matapolvos *m* drizzle, sprinkle
matar to kill [8]; —**se** to get killed [8]
matas *f pl* thickets
matasano *m* quack doctor
matasiete *m* bully
mate *m* maté (a kind of tea)
matemáticas *f pl* mathematics
materia *f* course, matter, material [9]
materialmente literally, materially
matiz *m* shade, hue
matrícula *f* enrollment
matricularse (**qu**) to enroll
matrimonio *m* matrimony; married couple
máximo,-a maximum, greatest
maya Maya, Mayan (Indian)
mayo *m* May [9]
mayonesa *f* mayonnaise
* **mayor** greater, greatest, older, oldest [14]; **la** — **parte de** most of; *m pl* **mayores** the elders
* **mayoría** *f* majority [19]
mazamorra *f* boiled corn
* **me** me, to me [3]
mecánico,-a: *see* **escalera**
mecanismo *m* mechanism, system
mecanógrafa *f* typist
medalla *f* medal [23]
mediano,-a medium
medianoche *f* midnight
mediante by means of
medias *f pl* hose
medicina *f* medicine [17]
medicinal medicinal
médico,-a medical; *m* doctor [8]
medida *f* size, measure; **a** — **que** while, as; **sin** — greatly
medieval medieval
medio,-a half (a) [3], middle, middle-class; **Edad Media** Middle Ages; *m* means, way; **en** — (**de**) in the midst (middle) (of); **por** — **de** by means of
mediodía *m* noon [23]
Mediterráneo,-a Mediterranean (Sea)
* **mejor** better, best [5]; **muy** — **que** much better than
mejora *f* improvement
mejoramiento *m* improvement [24]
mejorar to improve, better [24]
mejoría *f* improvement
melancolía *f* melancholy
melancólico,-a melancholic
melodía *f* melody
melón *m* melon
memoria *f* memory [9] **de** — by memory, by heart
mencionar to mention [8]
menear to stir
menguante *f* decline, end, waning

* **menor** younger, less, lesser, least, youngest [2]
menos less, except [7]; ***a** — **que** unless [17]; **al** — at least [22]; **echar de**— to miss [15]; **en (a)** — **de** in less than; **las nueve** — **cuarto** a quarter to nine [19]; **lo de** — the least important thing [10]; **lo** — **posible** as little as possible; **por (a) lo** — at least [7]
mensaje *m* message
mensajero *m* messenger
menta *f* mint (herb)
mental mental
mente *f* mind
mentir (**ie, i**) to lie [16]
mentira *f* lie
menú *m* menu
menudo: a — often [15]; **muy a** — very often
meñique *m* little finger
mercado *m* market [5]
mercaduría *f* merchandise
mercurio *m* mercury
merecer (*like* **parecer**) to merit, deserve [5]
merecimiento *m* merit, reward [24]
meridional south, southern
mérito *m* merit, praise
mero,-a mere
mes *m* month [4]; **al** — per month; **hace algunos meses** some months ago
mesa *f* table [23]
meseta *f* mesa, table land
mestizaje *m* race mixture
mestizo,-a part Spanish, part Indian; *m* mestizo
metal *m* metal
meter to put, place [6]; —**se** to get, put oneself [6]
método *m* method
metro *m* meter (39.37 inches) [6]
mexicano,-a *adj and m f* Mexican [4]
mezcla *f* mixture
mezclar to mix, mingle
* **mi** my [2]
* **mí** me [5]
micro *m* (small) bus [14]
miedo *m* fear; **dar** — to frighten; **tener** — to be afraid
miel *f* honey; **luna de** — honeymoon
miembro *m* member
* **mientras** while [10]; — **tanto** meanwhile
miércoles *m* Wednesday [4]
miga *f* crumb
mil (a) thousand [9]
milagro *m* miracle
militante militant
militar military [23]
millares *m pl* thousands

millón *m* million [8]

mimo *m* pampering

mina *f* mining; **de —s** mining

mineral *adj and m* mineral

minero *m* miner

ministerio *m* ministry [6]

ministro *m* minister

minoría *f* minority

minucioso,-a minute

minutito *m dim* minute [18]

minuto *m* minute [3]

mío,-a my, (of) mine [2]; **Dios —** My heavens! [2]

mira *f* design; leveling rod

mirada *f* look [23]

miradores *m pl* locks (in a canal to control water level)

mirar to look (at) (upon) [5]

misa *f* mass [15]

miseria *f* misery, poverty

misión *f* mission

mismo,-a same, self [7]; **— ... que** same ... as; **lo —** the same thing; the same to you; **(por) lo — que** (just) the same as; **por lo —** therefore; **yo —** I myself

misterio *m* mystery

misterioso,-a mysterious

misticismo *m* mysticism

místico,-a *adj and m* mystic

mitad *f* half

mito *m* myth

mocito *m dim* young man

moda: de — in fashion

modales *m pl* manners

modalidad *f* manner, model, variety

modelar to model, fashion

modelo *m f* model

moderado,-a moderate

moderno,-a modern [8]

modesto,-a modest, humble

modificación *f* change

modificar (qu) to modify

modismo *m* idiom

modo *m* way, manner; **de este —** in this way; **del mismo —** in the same way; **de todos —s** to make a long story short, anyway [17]

molestar(se) to bother

molestia *f* bother, trouble [4]

momentito *m dim* moment [16]

momento *m* moment, minute [15]; **de —** momentarily

mona *f* monkey

mondadientes *m* toothpick

moneda *f* money

monetario,-a monetary

monito *m dim* monkey

monja *f* nun

monje *m* monk

monólogo *m* monologue

monosabio *m* "wise monkey" (bullring attendant)

monótono,-a monotonous

monstruo *m* monster

montaña *f* mountain

montañoso,-a mountainous

montar to ride (a horse, bike, etc.)

monte *m* mountain

monumento *m* monument

morado,-a purple [17]; brown

moral *adj* moral; *m* moral, morals

moraleja *f* moral

moreno,-a dark brown [17]; **la morena** brunette [2]; **Sierra Morena** mountains in Spain

morir (ue, u) to die [9]

morisco,-a Moorish

moro,-a Moorish; *m* Moor

mortal mortal [24]

mosca *f* fly

mosquito *m dim* mosquito

mostrar (ue) to show [6]

mote *m* motto, slogan

motivación *f* motivation

motivo *m* motif, motive

mover (ue) to move; **—se** to move around

movimiento *m* movement

mozárabe Mozarabic

mozo *m* servant, waiter, boy

muchacha *f* girl [4]

muchacho *m* boy [4]; *pl* boys and girls

muchedumbre *f* crowd

muchísimo,-a much, very much [10]; **muchísimas gracias** thank you very much [12]

mucho,-a much, many [2]; *adv* a great deal, too long (much) [5]

mudarse to change

mudéjar *adj* Mudejar (e.g., Moorish architecture); *m* a Moslem living under Christian king (in Spain) but retaining own culture and religion

mudo,-a dumb

mueble *m* (piece of) furniture [18]; **—s** furniture [5]

muelle *m* dock

muerte *f* death [13]; **dar — (a)** to kill

muerto,-a (*see* **morir**) dead [13]; *m* dead person [13]

muestra *f* evidence, sign, token, sample

mujer *f* woman, wife [15]

mujercita *f dim* dear (wife) [19]

mula *f* mule

mulato *m* mulatto

muleta *f* muleta (used by bullfighters)

multa *f* fine [5]

múltiple multiple

multiplicar(se) (qu) to multiply

multitud *f* multitude

mundial *adj* world

mundo *m* world [12]; **del —** in the world; **todo el —** everybody [12]

mural mural

murmuración *f* muttering, gossip

murmurar to mutter, gossip

músculo *m* muscle

museo *m* museum

música *f* music

músico *m* musician

musicología *f* musicology

musulmán,-ana Moslem, Moorish; *m f* Moslem

mutilación *f* mutilation

mutuo,-a mutual

muy very, too [2]

n

na = **nada**

nacer (*like* **parecer**) to be born

nacimiento *m* birth

nación *f* nation [24]

nacional national [6]; *m* coin of Argentina [14]

nacionalidad *f* nationality

nada nothing, anything [5]; **de —** don't mention it [1]; *adv* at all [6]

nadar to swim

nadie nobody, anybody [5]

naipes *m pl* cards

naranja *f* orange [17]

naranjo *m* orange tree

nariz *f* nose [22]

narración *f* narration

natación *f* swimming [7]

natural native, natural

naturaleza *f* nature

naturalidad *f* naturalness

navegante *m* navigator

Navidad *f* Nativity, Christmas; **las —es** the Christmas season

navío *m* ship

necesario,-a necessary [10]

necesidad *f* need

necesitar to need [2]

necio,-a foolish, fool

neerlandés,-esa Dutch; *m f* Dutch person

negado,-a denied

negocio *m* (piece of) business [18]; **—s** business [8]

negro,-a black [4]; *m* Negro

neolatino,-a neo-Latin

neologismo *m* neologism

nervios *m pl* nerves

nervioso,-a nervous [22]

netezuelo *m dim* grandchild

nevar (ie) to snow

nevería: *see* **café**

ni nor, or [5]; **— ... —** neither ... nor, either ... or; **— papa** absolutely nothing [7]; **no ... —** not even

nicaragüense Nicaraguan

nido *m* nest
niebla *f* mist
nieto *m* grandson
nieve *f* snow
nilón *m* nylon
* **ninguno (ningún),-a** any, no, none [4]
niña *f* girl [10]
niño *m* boy [10]; *pl* children [10]
nítido,-a bright
nitrato *m* nitrate
nivel *m* level [21]
* **no** no, not [2]; — **más** only, no more, just [18]
nobleza *f* nobility
noción *f* notion
* **noche** *f* night [5]; **de** — at night, by night [11]; **esta** — tonight [5]; **por la** — in the evening [11]
nombrar to name
nombre *m* name [12]; noun
nórdico,-a Nordic
norma *f* norm
noroeste *m* northwest
norte *m and adj* north, northern [4]
Norteamérica *f* North America
norteamericano,-a North American [4]
* **nos** us, to us, ourselves [6]
* **nosotros,-as** we, us [2]
nota *f* note
notar to notice, note
notaría *f* profession of notary
notario *m* notary
* **noticia** *f* (piece of) news [6]; —**s** news [18]
novecientos,-as nine hundred [9]
novedad *f* novelty, something new [18]
novela *f* novel
noveno,-a ninth [9]
noventa ninety [8]
novia *f* sweetheart, girl friend [15]
noviembre *m* November [9]
novio *m* lover, boy friend [15]
nube *f* cloud [10]
nuca *f* neck, nape of the neck
nudillo *m dim* knuckle
* **nuestro,-a** our, ours [7]
nueve nine [2]
nuevecito,-a *dim* new, brand new [19]
nuevo,-a new [2]; **de** — again
nuez *f* nut
núm. *abr of* **número**
numérico,-a numerical
número *m* number [3]
numeroso,-a numerous
numismática *f* numismatics (study of coins)
* **nunca** never, ever [4]
nutritivo,-a nourishing

ñ

ñoquis (*or* **ñoque**) a kind of macaroni

o

* **o** or [4]; — ... — either ... or
obediencia *f* obedience
obediente obedient
objetivo *m* object, objective
objeto *m* object
obligación *f* obligation
obligar (**gu**) to oblige, force [13]
obra *f* work; — **maestra** masterpiece
obrero *m* worker
obsceno,-a obscene
observación *f* observation
observar to observe; **obsérvese** note
obstáculo *m* obstacle
obtener (*like* **tener**) to obtain, get
obvio,-a obvious
ocasión *f* occasion, opportunity
occidental western [24]
occidente *m* occident, west [24]
océano *m* ocean
octavo,-a eighth [9]
octubre *m* October [4]
ocupado,-a busy [5]
ocupar to occupy
ocurrir to occur
ochenta eighty [8]
ocho eight [2]; — **días** a week
ochocientos,-as eight hundred [8]
odiar to hate [17]
OEA = Organización de Estados Americanos Organization of American States (Pan-American Union) [24]
oeste *m* west; **Hemisferio del** — Western Hemisphere
ofensivo,-a offensive; *f* **ofensiva** offense
oficial official [22]; *m* officer [22]
oficina *f* office [15]
oficio *m* job, office, business [5]
ofrecer (*like* **parecer**) to offer, present [10]; **¿Qué se le ofrece?** What may I do for you? [11]
ofrecimiento *m* offering, offer [24]
ofrenda *f* offering
oídas: de — by ear, hearsay
oído *m* ear
* **oir** to hear [3]; **¡Oiga!** Hey!
* **!Ojalá!** Would that ..., I hope ... [17]
ojo *m* eye [15]; **anda con** — be careful
olímpico,-a Olympic [7]
olvidar(se) to forget, be for-

gotten [12]; **se me olvidó** I forgot [22]
olla *f* stew, pot
ombú *m* a great tree on the pampas
once eleven [8]; **la clase de las** — the eleven o'clock class; **para las** — by (for) eleven o'clock [12]
onceavo,-a eleventh [9]
ópera *f* opera
operación *f* operation [24]
operante *m and adj* operator, operating, guiding [24]
opinión *f* opinion
oponer (*like* **poner**) to oppose; —**se** (**a**) to resist, be opposed (to) [17]
oportuno,-a opportune, timely [24]
oportunidad *f* opportunity [7]
oposición *f* opposition [13]
opresión *f* oppression
opuesto,-a (*see* **oponer**) opposite
oración *f* prayer
oral oral
orbe *m* orb, world
orden *m* order (series); *f* order (command); **a tus órdenes** certainly [6]
ordinario,-a ordinary
oreja *f* ear, outer ear
Orfeo Orpheus
organismo *m* organization, organ
organización *f* organization [24]
organizar (**c**) to organize [7]
órgano *m* organ
orgullo *m* pride
orgulloso,-a proud
oriental east, eastern
origen *m* origin
original *adj and m* original
originalidad *f* originality
originar to bring (into being); —**se** to have (its) origin
originario,-a native, of ... origin
orilla *f* shore, bank
oro *m* gold [23]
orquesta *f* orchestra
os *pl* you, to you [2]
oscuro,-a obscure, dark [19]
otoño *m* autumn [4]
* **otro,-a** other, another [5]; — **día** the next day; **las unas de las otras** some from (the) others, each other
oveja *f* sheep [10]
ovejuno,-a pertaining to sheep

p

paciencia *f* patience
pacífico,-a peaceful; *m* **el Pacífico** the Pacific Ocean
padecer (*like* **parecer**) to suffer

* **padre** *m* father [2]; *pl* parents
padrino *m* godfather [4]
paella *f* a Spanish rice dish [5]
pagar (**gu**) to pay (for) [6]
página *f* page
país *m* country [7]
paisaje *m* landscape
paisano *m* countryman
paja *f* straw [10]
pájaro *m* bird
palabra *f* word [1]
palacio *m* palace [23]
paladar *m* palate, mouth
palco *m* box (seat in a theater)
palenque *m* parade ground
pálido,-a pale [21]
palma *f* palm
palo *m* stick, pole [13]; **a —s** with clubs [13]
palpitante palpitating
pampa *f* pampa (extensive treeless plains of Argentina and Uruguay)
pan *m* bread [5]
panadería *f* bakery
panamericano,-a Pan-American [7]
pantalones *m pl* pants
panteón *m* cemetery
paño *m* cloth
pañuelo *m* handkerchief
papa *f* potato [7]; **ni —** absolutely nothing [7]
papá *m* father [2]
papel *m* paper, role [6]; **hacer un —** to play a role [24]
papeleta *f dim* slip of paper
paquete *m* package [11]
par *m* pair, couple [11]; **al — que** while; **a la —** abreast; **a la — que** as well as; **la —** peer, equal; **sin —** unequaled
* **para** to, for, in order to, toward, to the end that, by [3]; **— que** in order that [18]
parabrisas *m* windshield
paracaídas *m* parachute [24]
paracaidista *m* parachutist [23]
parachoques *m* bumper
* **parado,-a** standing, stationed [20]
paradoja *f* paradox
paradójico,-a paradoxical
paraguas *m sing and pl* umbrella, umbrellas [23]
paraguayo,-a Paraguayan [14]
paralelo *m* parallel
páramos *m pl* high, cold regions
parar to stop [6]
pararrayos *m* lightning rod
parasol *m* sunshade [24]
* **parecer** *m* opinion; **a mi —** in my opinion; *v* (**zc**) to seem, appear (to be) [5]; **¿No le parece?** Don't you think so? [10]; **¿Qué le parece?**

What do you think of . . .? [5]; **—se** (**a**) to resemble, be alike
parecido,-a (**a**) similar (to)
pared *f* wall [2]
pareja *f* couple, pair [5]
parejero *m* couple
parejo,-a equal
pariente *m* relative [4]
parodia *f* parody
párpados *m pl* eyelids
parque *m* park [4]
parrilla *f* grill; **asado a la —** grilled
parroquiano *m* customer
* **parte** *f* part [3]; **a** (**por**) **todas —s** everywhere [16]; **de** (**por**) **—** by, on the part of [3]; **en mucha —** in great part; **gran — de** most of; **la mayor —** most
partición *f* partition, dividing [24]
participar to participate [7]; make known, share; **— de** to partake of, share
particular particular, personal, private
partido,-a parted; **a brazo —** hand-to-hand; *m* party [13], faction, game, platform
partir to leave [24]; divide, split, break [21]; **a — de** starting from
pasado,-a *adj and m* past [4]
pasajero *m* passenger
* **pasar** (**a**) to pass, enter [1]; go; happen; spend; endure; **— lista** to call the roll [1]; **—lo mal** to have a hard time [10]; **— de** to be more than; **— por** to pass (by) for, come for [3]; **— por alto** to pass over, skip; **—se** to pass away
pasatiempo *m* pastime [24]
Pascua *f* Easter (or any of the other Church holidays—Christmas, Twelfth-Night, Pentecost)
pase *m* pass
pasear(**se**) to pass, walk, take a walk [21]
paseíllo *m dim* parade
pasión *f* passion
pasivo,-a passive
paso *m* passage, station, step; **abrirse —** to make one's way; **— doble** two-step (dance)
pasta *f* paste [19]
pastel *m* pastry, pie; **— de choclo** escalloped corn, corn pudding
pastelería *f* pastry, pastry shop
pastilla *f dim* pill [12]
pasto *m* pastureland
pastor *m* shepherd
pata *f* foot [14]; **meter la —** to put one's foot in one's mouth, blunder [14]

patata *f* potato
patéticas *f pl* pathetics (sorrowful paintings)
patetismo *m* pathos
patio *m* patio [2]
pato *m* duck
patria *f* fatherland [17]
patriarcal patriarchal
patrio,-a of the country
patriota *m* patriot
patriótico,-a patriotic
patrón *m* owner of an estate
pausa *f* pause
pavo *m* turkey
payador *m* gaucho ballad singer
paz *f* peace [5]
pecador,-ra *m f* sinner
pecho *m* chest, heart
pedido *m* request, order [18]
* **pedir** (**i**) to order, request, ask (for) [4], borrow
pegar (**gu**) to strike; **—se** to stick
peinar to comb [7]; **—se** to comb one's hair [7]
peine *m* comb [7]
pelear(**se**) to fight, quarrel [6]
película *f* film
peligro *m* danger [24]
peligroso,-a dangerous
pelo *m* hair [7]
pelota *f* ball
pelotari *m* ballplayer
pena *f* pain, grief [7]; **acompañar en —** to extend sympathy [21]; **valer la —** to be worthwhile [7]
penal *m* penalty
penetrar to penetrate
península *f* peninsula
peninsular peninsular
pensador *m* thinker
pensamiento *m* thought
* **pensar** (**ie**) to think, intend [4]; **— en** think about [8]
pensativo,-a pensive
pentatónico,-a pentatonic (five-tone scale)
peón *m* peon, footman
* **peor** worse, worst [14]; **si pasa lo—** if worse comes to worse
pequeñez *f* smallness
pequeño,-a small
* **perder** (**ie**) to miss, lose [5]; **— al curso** to fail in a course; **—se** to lose, get lost [12]
perdición *f* perdition [24]
pérdida *f* loss
perdón *m* pardon, pardon me [3]
perdonar to pardon [18]
perdurable enduring
perezoso,-a lazy [22]
perfección *f* perfection
perfeccionamiento *m* perfecting
perfeccionarse to be perfected

perfecto,-a perfect [2]

perfilarse to be outlined

pericón *m* lively dance and song of Argentina

periódico *m* newspaper [13]

periodismo *m* journalism

periodista *m* newspaperman

período *m* period

perito,-a skillful, expert

permanecer (*like* **parecer**) to remain

permanente *adj* permanent; *m* permanent wave

permiso *m* permission, permit [2]; **con** — excuse me [2]

permitir to permit

pero but [3]

perpetuo,-a perpetual, year-'round

perrito *m dim* little dog

perro *m* dog

perseguir (*like* **seguir**) to persecute

persistente persistent

persona *f* person [14]; **por** — per person

personal personal [14]

personalidad *f* personality

personalizar (**c**) to make personal

perspectiva *f* perspective

pertenecer (*like* **parecer**) to belong [5]

peruano,-a Peruvian

pésame *m* condolence [21]

pesar *m* regret; *a* — **de** in spite of [17]; *v* to weigh [22]; grieve

pesca: de — fishing

pescado *m* fish (caught)

pescador,-ra *adj* fishing; *m f* fisherman

peseta *f* peseta (monetary unit of Spain) [5]

peso *m* peso (monetary unit of several Hispanic countries) [5]; grief; weight

petenera *f* Andalusian dance

petición *f* petition

petróleo *m* petroleum, oil [8]

pez *f* fish (in the water)

piadoso,-a pious

pica *f* pike, lance

picador *m* picador (bullfighter on horseback who thrusts the lance at the bull)

picante hot

picar (**qu**) to sting, bite

pícaro,-a roguish; *m* rogue

pico *m* peak

pie *m* foot [5]; **dar** — **a** to be the basis for; **excursión a** — hike; **ponerse de** — to stand up

piedad *f* pity

piedra *f* stone

piel *f* hide [8]; **abrigo de pieles** fur coat [15]

pierna *f* leg

pieza *f* piece, item

pillar to pillage, grasp, catch, nab

pintar to paint

pintor *m* painter

pintoresco,-a picturesque

pintura *f* painting, picture [5]; **ni en** — by no means [10]

piña *f* pineapple

pionero *m* pioneer

pique de puntos drawing of points

Pirineos *m pl* Pyrenees mountains

piso *m* floor

pistola *f* pistol [22]

pizarra *f* blackboard [9]

placer *m* pleasure

plan *m* plan [24]

planchador *m* presser, ironer

planeta *m* planet

planta *f* plant [8]

plantar to plant

plástico,-a plastic

plata *f* silver; money [5]

plátano *m* banana

plateresco,-a plateresque; ornate

platería *f* silverwork

platillo *m dim* saucer

plato *m* dish, plate, course (of a meal [5]; **el** — **fuerte** the main course

Platón Plato [9]

playa *f* beach [21]

plaza *f* square, marketplace [9]; — **de toros** bullring

pleito *m* lawsuit; dispute [17]

plenitud *f* fullness, richness

pleno,-a full

plomo *m* lead

pluma *f* feather, pen

población *f* population

poblar (**de**) (**con**) to fill (with), settle, people

pobre poor [5]; — **de mí** (**ti**) poor me (you); *m f* poor person [5]

pobrecito,-a *dim* poor

* **poco,-a** little, few; **un** — (**de**) a little [7]; **unos pocos** a few; *adv* little [7]; — **a** — little by little

podenco *m* hound

* **poder** *m* power; *v to be able, may, can [13]

poderoso,-a powerful

poema *m* poem

poesía *f* poetry, short poem

poeta *m* poet

poético,-a poetic

poetisa *f* poetess

poetizado,-a made into poetry, versified

policía *m* policeman [6]; *f* police [6], police station; politeness

policromado,-a polychrome

político,-a political; **hijo** — son-in-law; *m* politician; *f* politics [13], policy [17]

polo *m* pole

polvo *m* dust [10]

pollo *m* chicken [5]; dude

poncho *m* poncho (blanket)

ponderativo,-a ponderative, exaggerating

* **poner** to place, put, make [5]; —**se** to put on, get [12]; — **se a** to begin, get, make [12]; —**se de acuerdo** to agree [17]; —**se de pie** to stand up

pontificio,-a pontifical

popular popular

popularidad *f* popularity

popularísimo,-a very popular

populoso,-a heavily populated

poquito *dim* a very little [4]; — **a poco** little by little; **un** — a little bit

* **por** per, by, for, through, across, during, in behalf of, on account of [1]; **¿**— **que?** why? [2]

porcentaje *m* percentage

porción *f* portion

* **porque** because [4]

porqué *m* reason

portal *m* portal, entry

portátil portable [3]

porte *m* conduct, carriage

portugués,-esa *adj and m f* Portuguese; *m* Portuguese (language)

porvenir *m* future

poseer (**y**) to have, possess

posesión *f* possession

posibilidad *f* possibility [24]

* **posible** (**de**) possible (to) [5]

posición *f* position

postal postal [14]; **tarjeta** — postcard [14]

postre *m* dessert [5]; *pl* dessert; **de** — for dessert [5]

postura *f* posture

potable drinkable, drinking [10]

potestad *f* power

práctica *f* practice

practicar (**qu**) to practice, play, engage in [7]; —**se** to be performed, be played [15]

práctico,-a practical

pradera *f* prairie

preceder (**de**) to precede, be preceded (by)

precepto *m* precept

preciarse to be proud

precio *m* price; **por** — for a charge

precioso,-a precious

precisión *f* precision

preciso,-a precise, exact; necessary

precolombino,-a pre-Columbian

predilección *f* choice, favor

predominantemente predominantly

predominar to predominate

preferencia *f* preference [24]

preferible preferable

preferir (**ie, i**) to prefer [5]

pregunta *f* question [9]; **hacer** **—s** to ask questions [9]

preguntar to ask [11]; **— por** to ask for (about)

prehistórico,-a pre-historic

preludio *m* prelude

prematuramente prematurely

premiado,-a winner [20]; *m* awardee

premiar to reward [20]

premio *m* prize, reward [9]; **— gordo** first prize [20]

prender to seize, apprehend, take

prensa *f* press

preocupar to concern, divert; **—se** (**de**) to be concerned (about) (with), worry [5]

preparación *f* preparation [24]

preparar to prepare, be ready, make ready

preparativos *m pl* preparations

presencia *f* presence

presenciar to watch, be present (for) (at), witness

presentación *f* (good) appearance

presentar to present, introduce [24]; **—se** to appear, come

presente present [1]; **del —** of this month [18]

presidencia *f* presidency [24]

presidencial presidential [23]

presidente *m* president [13]

presidir to preside

préstamo *m* loan

prestar to lend, give [7]

prestigio *m* prestige [17]

pretender to try

pretensión *f* pretension

pretérito *m* preterit (tense)

pretexto *m* pretext, excuse [13]

prevaleciente prevalent

prevención *f* prevention

prevenir (*like* **venir**) to prevent

priéndalé = préndalo take it, drain it

prima *f* cousin [2]; early morning; **al cuarto de la —** at the fourth hour of the morning

primario,-a primary

primavera *f* spring [4]

*****primero** (**primer**),**-a** first [4]; **el — en** the first to [23]; **a—s de** at the first of; *adv* first

primitivo,-a primitive

primo *m* cousin

principal principal, main [8]

príncipe *m* prince

principiar to begin

principio *m* principle, beginning [22]; **al —** at first [10]; **a —s** at the beginning

prisa: con — hastily

privilegiado,-a privileged

privilegio *m* privilege [24]

*****pro: en — de** in behalf of [24]

probabilidad *f* probability [24]

probable probable [7]

probar (**ue**) to try [19]; taste; **—se** to try on

problema *m* problem [5]

procedencia *f* source

proceder to proceed

procesión *f* procession

procurar to try

producción *f* production

*****producir** (**zc**) to produce [9]

producto *m* product

profesión *f* profession [7]

profesional professional [8]

profesor *m* professor [1]

profesora *f* professor

profundidad *f* depth

profundo,-a profound, deep

programa *m* program; **— de clase** course

progresar to progress, get ahead [8]

progreso *m* progress [24]

prohibido,-a prohibited

prolongarse (**gu**) to be prolonged

promesa *f* promise

prometer to promise [10]

promover (**ue**) to promote

pronto fast, soon [5]; **lo más — posible** as soon as you can [5]; **tan — como** as soon as [18]

pronunciación *f* pronunciation [14]

pronunciar to pronounce

propiamente similar (to), characteristic

propiedad *f* propriety, ownership

propio,-a own, one's (their) own, itself, very

proponer (*like* **poner**) to propose

proporción *f* proportion

proporcionar to give, afford

propósito *m* purpose; **a —** by the way [4]

prosa *f* prose

protección *f* protection

protegido,-a protected, secure

protesta *f* protest

protestar to protest

provecho *m* profit, good

provechoso,-a profitable

proverbio *m* proverb

providencia *f* providence

provincia *f* province

provincialismo *m* provincialism

provocado,-a provoked

próximo,-a next; *adv* next [7]

proyectar to project, cast

prudencia *f* prudence

prueba *f* evidence, proof

psicología *f* psychology [9]

pst (exclamation used to attract attention) [9]

publicar (**qu**) to publish

público,-a *adj* public; *m* audience

puchero *m* stew

*****pueblo** *m* people; town [17]

puente *m* bridge

puerco *m* pig

puerta *f* door [1]

puerto *m* port; **— de mar** seaport

puertorriqueño,-a *adj and m f* Puerto Rican

*****pues** well, then [4]; *conj* since

puesto,-a (*see* **poner**) put, made; *m* job, position, stall [10]; ***—que** since [18]; **llevar —** to have on [23]

¡Puf! Pooh!

pulgar *m* thumb

pulir to polish

pulpería *f* general store

punta *f* point, end, tip

puntapié *m* kick

punto *m* point; **dos —s** colon [18]; **en —** sharp, on the dot

puntual punctual

puntualidad *f* promptness; **con —** punctually

puñado *m* handful

puñal *m* dagger

puño *m* fist

puro,-a pure [10]

q

*****que** that, who, which [1]; for; than [7]; **lo —** what [9]

*****¡qué! ¿qué?** what (a), how!, what? [2]; **¿— tal?** how are you? [3]; **¿Por —?** Why [3]

quebrantado,-a broken

*****quedar** to be left, remain, be [5]; **—(se) (en)** to remain, agree [9]; **—se** to stay [10]

quedirán *m* public opinion

quehacer *m* chore

quemar to burn

quena *f* primitive musical instrument

*****querer** to wish, want, love [4]; **— decir** to mean; **tu —** loving you; **¿Quieres?** Will you? [5]

querido,-a dear

quetzal *m* monetary unit of Guatemala [14]

¡Quiá! Nonsense!

*****quien** who, whom, he (him) who, which [15]

*¿quién? who?, whom [1]; **¿de —?** whose [3]; **¿con —?** with (to) whom? [3]

quijotescamente quixotically

química *f* chemistry [9]

químico,-a chemical

quince fifteen [4]

quinientos,-as five hundred [8]

quinto,-a fifth [9]

quitapinturas *m* paint remover [24]

*quitar to take away [6]; **—se** to take off, brush off [12]

quite *m* maneuver, hindrance

quizá, quizás perhaps [20]

r

rabiar to rave [16]

racial racial

radical radical [17]

radio *m* radio [5]; **poner el —** to turn on the radio [5]

raíz *f* root

ramo *m* branch, line of goods

rana *f* frog

ranchero *m* rancher

rancho *m* ranch

rapar to shave, cut (hair)

rápido,-a rapid, rapidly

raro,-a rare, strange [23]

rascacielos *m* skyscraper

rasgo *m* trait, flourish (in handwriting)

rato *m* short time, while [4]

ratón *m* mouse [22]

ravioles *m* ravioli

rayo *m* ray

raza *f* race

razón *f* reason, reasoning [7]; **con —** rightly, no wonder; **tener —** to be right

razonable reasonable

razonarse to be rationalized

reacción *f* reaction

reaccionar to react

real real, royal [24]

realidad *f* reality [7]

realismo *m* realism

realista realistic

realización *f* achievement

realizar (c) to accomplish, realize, show

reata *f* rope

rebaño *m* flock

recado *m* message, note [3]

recepción *f* reception [24]

receta *f* prescription [12], recipe

recetar to prescribe

recibimiento *m* reception, receiving [24]

recibir to receive, meet, get [6]

recibo *m* reception, receiving, receipt [11]

reciente (recién) recent; **recién llegado** newcomer

recio,-a strong

recitar to recite, read

recobrarse (de) to recover (from)

recoger (j) to collect, catch

recolección *f* assembling, collecting

recomendación *f* recommendation [24]

recomendar (ie) to recommend, suggest

recóndito,-a hidden

reconocerse (*like* conocer) to be recognized, recognize oneself

reconstrucción *f* reconstruction

recopilación *f* collecting and classifying

*recordar(se) (ue) to remember, recall, remind [4]

recortar to cut

recrear to recreate

recuerdo *m* memory; **—s** regards

recurrir to go, resort, have recourse

recurso *m* recourse, resource, income

rechazar(se) (c) to reject, be rejected

red *f* net, series

redondear to round off, make unique

reducción *f* reduction

*reducir (*like* producir) to reduce [9]

reemplazar (c) to replace, refill

referencia *f* reference [22]

referirse (ie,i) to refer, mention

refinado,-a refined, proper

refinería *f* refinery [8]

reflejar to reflect

reflejo reflection

reflujo *m* reflux, ebb

reformador,-ra reforming, liberal

refrán *m* refrain, saying

refrescar (qu) to refresh

refrescos *m pl* refreshments

regalado,-a pleasant

regalar to give [20]

regalo *m* gift [15]

regata *f* regatta

regatear to bargain [5]

regeneración *f* regeneration

régimen *m* (*pl* **regímenes**) regime, regimen

región *f* region

regional regional

regionalista regionalistic

regla *f* rule; **— de cálculo** slide rule

regocijo *m* rejoicing

regresar to return, come back [3]

regular regular, fair, usual [12]

rehuir (*like* incluir) to reject, shun

reinar to reign

reino *m* kingdom, monarchy

reir(se) (í) to laugh

relación *f* relation, story

relacionado,-a related

relatado,-a related, told

relatividad *f* relativity [24]

relativo,-a relative [14]; **todo lo — (a)** everything pertaining to; *m* relative

religión *f* religion [9]

religioso,-a religious

reló = reloj *m* clock, watch

relucir (*like* parecer) to shine

remedar to mock

remedio *m* remedy; **no hay más — que** there's nothing to do except [9]

remiendo *m* patch

reminiscencia *f* reminiscence

remolcador *m* tugboat

remolque: a — close behind; in his wake

remontar to go up; **— el vuelo** to take off

remoto,-a remote, extreme

remuneración (de) *f* remuneration (for)

renacentista *adj* Renaissance

renacimiento *m* Renaissance

rendir (i) to render, pay

renovar (ue) to change, renew; **—se** to improve

renunciar to renounce, resign [19]

repechar to go uphill

repente: de — suddenly

repetir (i) to repeat [2]

replicar (qu) to reply, retort

reporte *m* report [24]

repórter *m* reporter [24]

representación *f* production, presentation

representante *m* representative

representar to represent, show

representativo,-a representative

reprimenda *f* reprimand

reprobado: salir — to fail (a course)

reproducción *f* reproduction

república *f* republic [24]

republicano,-a republican

repuesto *m* stock, goods, spare part [18]

reputado,-a well-known

requerir (*like* querer) to demand, require, be necessary

requisito *m* requisite, prerequisite

res *f* cattle; **reses lecheras** milk cows

resaltar to stand out

reserva *f* reserve

resfriado *m* cold [12]: **estar —** to have a cold [12]

residencia *f* residence

resignarse to be resigned

resistir to resist, fight off

resolver (ue) to resolve

respectar to concern; **por lo que respecta a** as for

respectivamente respectively

respecto (a) with respect to [18]; compared to; — (de) pertaining (to)

respetabilidad *f* respectability

respetable respectable [8]

respetar to respect [13]

respeto *m* respect

responder to answer

responsabilidad *f* responsibility

responsable responsible

restaurán, restaurante *m* restaurant (*see* **restorán**)

restaurar to restore

restitución *f* restitution

resto *m* rest

restorán *m* restaurant [4]

restricción *f* restriction

resucitar to rise, revive

resuelto,-a (*see* **resolver**) resolute, resolved, determined

resultado *m* result, outcome

resultar to result, be, come out, work out [19]

resumen: en — in short

resumir to sum up

retablo *m* altarpiece, series of historical pictures

retirar to retire, take away

retórico,-a rhetorical

retratado,-a photographed

reunión *f* meeting [9]

reunir to unite; **—se** to meet

revelar to reveal, develop (pictures), show [14]

reverencia *f* reverence

reverente reverent

revés *m* reversal, mishap

revisión *f* inspection

revista *f* review, magazine [15]

revolución *f* revolution

revólver *m* revolver

* **rey** *m* king; *pl* king and queen [23]

rezar (c) to pray [15]

rico,-a rich; delicious; *m* rich man; **los ricos** the rich (people)

ridículo,-a ridiculous [8]

riesgo *m* risk; **con — de** at the risk of

rifa *f* raffle [15]

rifar to raffle [15]

rincón *m* corner

rinconcito *m dim* corner

riña *f* fight

río *m* river

rioplatense of the River Plate basin

riqueza *f* wealth; *pl* wealth, riches

risa *f* laughter

ristre *m* rest (for a lance)

ritmo *m* rhythm

rito *m* rite

rival *m* rival, equal

robar to steal, rob

robo *m* robbery [22]

robustecer (*like* **parecer**) to strengthen

roca *f* rock

Rocosas *f pl* Rockies

rodear (de) to surround (with)

rodillas: de — kneeling

rogar (ue,gu) to ask, pray [17]

rojizo,-a reddish [24]

rojo,-a red [17]

romance *m* ballad

romancero *m* collection of ballads

románico,-a Romance

romano,-a Roman

romántico,-a romantic

rompecabezas *m* puzzle [24]

romper to break [5]

rompimiento *m* breaking, destruction [24]

roncar (qu) to snore [16]

ronda *f* round, patrol [22]

rondador *m* Ecuadorian musical instrument

ronronear to rumble

ropa *f* clothes [5]; — **blanca** (**interior**) underwear [11]; **— de cama** bed linen [11]

ropaje *m* clothing

rosbif *m* roast beef [5]

rostro *m* face

rotación *f* rotation; **contar en —** to count off [8]

roto,-a (*see* **romper**) broken [16]

rozar (c) to graze, clear

rubio,-a blond [2]

rúbrica *f* flourish (used with a signature as a distinguishing mark)

rudeza *f* crudeness

rueda *f* wheel

ruido *m* noise [3]

ruidoso,-a noisy

ruina *f* ruin, ruins [17]

rumano,-a Rumanian

rumor *m* rumor

rural rural

ruso,-a Russian

rústico,-a rustic

s

S.A. = Sociedad Anónima Corporation

sábado *m* Saturday [9]

sabana *f* savannah

sábana *f* sheet [11]

saber *m* knowledge; *v to know (how), find out, can [2]

sabiduría *f* wisdom

sabio,-a wise; *m* wise man

sable *m* sabre

sacar (qu) to get, take out, pull out [20]; — **una foto** to take a picture

sacerdote *m* priest

sacrificar (qu) to sacrifice

sacrilegio *m* sacrilege

sacudimiento *m* shaking, waving [24]

sacudir to shake, wave; dust [5]

sagrado,-a sacred [13]

sal *f* salt

sala *f* room, living room [2]; **de clase** classroom; **— de matrícula** enrollment room

salado,-a salty, salt

Salamanca Salamanca (city in western Spain)

salario *m* salary, wages

* **salir** (de) to leave, come (go) out (of) [3]

salmonado,-a salmon

salón *m* shop; **— de belleza** beauty shop; **— de té** tearoom

salpicar (qu) to sprinkle

salsa *f* sauce

saltar to jump

salto *m* jump; **dar —s** to leap up and down; **de un —** with a start

salud *f* health

saludar to greet, recognize

saludo *m* greeting [6]

salvador,-ra saving, of salvation

salvadoreño,-a Salvadorian

salvaje *m* savage, wild

salvar to save, spare

salvavidas *m* life saver [23]

salvo except

salvoconducto *m* safe-conduct, pass

samba *f* Cuban dance

sangre *f* blood

sanitario,-a sanitary [24]

sano,-a in good health

Santander Santander (province in northern Spain)

* **santo** (**san**),-a holy, saint [4]; *m f* saint; **el día del —** Saint's Day [4]

santuario *m* sanctuary

saquear to sack, destroy

sarcasmo *m* sarcasm

sargento *m* sergeant [22]

satírico,-a satirical

satisfacción *f* satisfaction

satisfecho,-a satisfied

saturar (de) to saturate (with)

* **se** (one's) self; one; to him, to her, to you, to them [5]

sección *f* section, department
secretaria *f* secretary [15]
secretaría *f* secretariat [24]
secretario *m* secretary [24]
secreto *m* secret
sector *m* sector, cross section, section
secundario,-a secondary [9]
seda *f* silk
sede *f* seat, location
seductor *m* seducer
seguido,-a (de) followed (by); **en seguida** immediately.
* **seguir (i, g)** to continue, follow, keep on, go on [4]; **— cursos** to take courses; **usted sigue** you're next [7]
seguiría *f* gypsy dance
* **según** according to (what) [18]
segundo,-a second [9]
seguridad *f* security, assurance [22]
seguro,-a sure [18]; **lo —** what is certain
seis six [2]
seiscientos,-as six hundred [8]
selva *f* forest
sello *m* stamp, characteristic
semana *f* week [4]; **la otra —** next week [18]; **la — pasada** last week
semejante similar
semestre *m* semester
semicírculo *m* semicircle [23],
semilla *f* seed
semisalvaje half-savage
sencillo,-a simple [8]
senda *f* path
seno *m* bosom
* **sentado,-a** seated [22]
sentarse (ie) to sit (down) [1]
sentido,-a heartfelt [21]; *m* sense, feeling, meaning [21]
sentimental sentimental
sentimiento *m* sentiment, feeling
sentir *m* feeling; **el común —** the common feeling; *v* (**ie, i**) to feel [12]; regret [11]; (**lo**) **siento** I am sorry [11]; **—se** to feel, be felt [12]
señal *f* sign, indication
señalar to point (to), indicate, show the way (to)
* **señor** *m* Mr., sir, man, lord [3]; **—es** Mr. and Mrs., ladies and gentlemen; **Muy —es míos** Gentlemen [18]
* **señora** *f* Mrs., lady, wife [2]
señoría *f* lordship
señorial lordly [24]
señorita *f* Miss, lady [1]
separación *f* separation
separar to separate; **—se (de)** to leave
séptimo,-a seventh [9]

ser *m* being; **v* to be [2]
serenidad *f* serenity, calmness
serie *f* series
seriedad *f* seriousness [24]
serio,-a serious [6]; **en—** seriously
serpentina *f* serpentine, streamer [23]
servicio *m* service
servidor,-ra *m f* at your service, here [18]; **su seguro —* sincerely yours [18]
servilleta *f* napkin
servir (i) (de) to serve (as), help [16]; **¿En qué puedo —la?** May I help you?, What can I do for you?; **sírvase** help yourself
sesenta sixty [8]
sesgado,-a slanting
sesión *f* session
setecientos,-as seven hundred [8]
setenta seventy [8]
setiembre *m* September [4]
Sevilla Seville (city in southern Spain)
sevillano,-a from Seville
sexto,-a sixth [9]
shh shh [22]
* **si** if, whether [3]
sí yes [1]; oneself, themselves
siempre always [5]
sierra *f* mountain range; **Sierra Nevada** mountain range in Spain
* **siesta** *f* siesta, nap [19]
siete seven [2]
siglo *m* century
significación *f* meaning
significado *m* meaning
significar (qu) to mean [24]
signo *m* sign, stamp
siguiente following; **al día —** on the following day
silbido *m* whistling, whistle
silencio *m* silence
silueta *f* silhouette
siluetado,-a silhouetted
silla *f* chair
simbolizar (c) to symbolize
símbolo *m* symbol
simétrico,-a symmetrical
simiente *f* seed
similar similar
similitud *f* similarity
simpatía *f* sympathy, understanding
simpático,-a nice, fine, charming [19]
simple simple
simplicidad *f* simplicity
simplificación *f* simplification
simulado,-a pretended
* **sin** without [10]; **— embargo**

nevertheless [3]; **— que** *conj* without [18]
sincero,-a sincere [17]
sincronización *f* synchronism, synchronization
sinfonía *f* symphony
sinfónico,-a symphonic
sino but [6]; **no sólo . . .—** not only . . . but also [6]; **— que** *conj* but [18]
sintaxis *f* syntax
síntesis *f* synthesis
siquiera: ni — not even
sistema *m* system, range [6]
sitio *m* place
situación *f* situation [13]
situado,-a situated
soberanía *f* sovereignty
soberbio,-a haughty, high
sobras: de — too well
* **sobre** over, on, about [9]; **— todo** especially [21]
sobremesa: de — after dinner
sobrenatural supernatural
sobresalir (*like* **salir**) to be conspicuous
sobretodo *m* overcoat [21]
sobriedad *f* sobriety
sobrina *f* niece [4]
sobrino *m* nephew
social social [18]
sociedad *f* society; **— anónima** corporation
socio-económico,-a socioeconomic
sociológico,-a sociological
Sócrates Socrates [9]
sofá *m* sofa
sofisticación *f* sophistication
sol *m* sun; monetary unit of Peru [14]
solamente only [23]
solear *m* gypsy dance
solemne solemn
soler (ue) to be accustomed (to)
solicitar to solicit; **se solicita** wanted
sólidamente solidly
solidaridad *f* solidarity
solo,-a single, mere, only, alone [5]; **café —** black coffee
sólo (solamente) *adv* only [6]; **no —. . . sino también** not only . . . but also [6]
soltero,-a unmarried
solterón *m* old bachelor
soltura *f* freedom, agility
solución *f* solution
solucionar to solve, resolve [24]
sollozo *m* sobbing, sob
sombra *f* shadow
sombrero *m* hat [23]
sombrerote *m aug* big hat [23]
someter to subdue; **—se (a)** to submit (to)
sonar (ue) to sound, ring, play

sonido *m* sound
sopa *f* soup
soplar to blow
sordo,-a deaf
sordomudo *m* deaf mute
sorprendente surprising
sorprender to surprise
sorpresa *f* surprise
sospecha *f* suspicion
sospechoso,-a suspicious [22]
sostenido,-a held
Sr. = señor
Sra. = señora
* su his, her, your, their, its [4]
suave gentle, soft
suavidad *f* gentleness
subantártico,-a subantarctic
subártico,-a subarctic
subir to go up, rise
súbito,-a sudden
subjeto *m* (*also* sujeto) subject
sublimación *f* sublimation
subrayar to emphasize, underscore
subsistir to subsist
subteniente *m* second lieutenant [23]
subterráneo *m* subway
subtropical subtropical
suceder to happen, follow [6]
sucesivo,-a successive, following
suceso *m* event
sucio,-a dirty [5]
sucre *m* monetary unit of Ecuador [14]
suculento,-a nourishing
Sud South
Sudamérica *f* South America
sudamericano,-a South American
sudoeste *m* southwest
sueldo *m* salary [10]
suelo *m* ground, floor
suelto,-a loose, relaxed
sueño *m* dream
suerte *f* luck [8], play; ¡Que buena — la suya! How lucky you were!; ¡Qué — de hombre! What a lucky man! [15]; tocar en — to fall to one's lot
suficiente sufficient; lo — enough, what is sufficient
sufijo *m* suffix
sufrimiento *m* suffering
sufrir to suffer, undergo; — exámenes to take exams
sugerencia *f* suggestion [24]
sugerir(ie,i) to suggest [14]
suicida suicidal
Suiza Switzerland
sujeto *m* subject
suma *f* sum; en — in short
sumamente exceedingly
sumisión *f* submission
sumo,-a highest

superación *f* excelling
superficie *f* surface
superior higher; escuela — high school
supermercado *m* supermarket
superstición *f* superstition
suplicar (qu) to supplicate, beg [21]
suponer (*like* poner) to suppose [8]
suposición *f* supposition [24]
suprimir to suppress
supuesto,-a (*see* suponer) supposed [16]
sur *m* south; al — de south of
surco *m* furrow
surgir (j) to emerge
suroeste *m* southwest
surtido,-a supplied, stocked
¡Sus! Hey!
suspenderse to stop
suspiro *m* sigh
sustancia *f* substance
sustancioso,-a substantial
sustantivo *m* noun [24]
sustentar to sustain, nourish
sustituir (*like* incluir) to substitute (for), replace
susto *m* fright
sutileza *f* subtlety
* suyo,-a (of) his, hers, theirs, its, yours [11]

t

tabaco *m* tobacco
tacita *f* *dim* small cup, demitasse
taco *m* taco
tagarnina *f* a kind of thistle
tal such, such a [3]; con — que provided [18]; ¿Qué—? How are you? [3], How about it? [10]; — (tales) como such as; *— vez perhaps [3]
talento *m* talent
talla *f* size
tallar to form, carve
tallarines *m pl* a kind of spaghetti
tallista *m* carver, engraver
tamal *m* tamale
* también also [2]
tambor *m* tambour, drum
* tampoco neither, either [4]; yo — neither do I
* tan so, as [4]; — ... como as ... as; — pronto (como) as soon as [18]; — ... que so ... that
tango *m* tango (dance) [23]
* tanto,-a *adj* so (as) much, so (as) many [2]; mientras — meanwhile; otros —s as many; por lo — *adv* therefore; tantas ... cuantas as many ...

as [14]; — ... como *adv* both ... and, as much as [14]
tapar to cover
taquigrafía *f* typing
tardar (en) to delay, be late [5]
tarde late [5]; se hace—it is getting late; * *f* afternoon, evening [2]; Buenas tardes Good afternoon [2]
tarea *f* task, job [24]
tarjeta *f* card [14]; — postal post card [14]
¡Tate! Well!
taza *f* cup [4]; — para café coffee cup
* te you, to you, yourself [2]
té *m* tea; tomar — to have tea
teán *m* team
teatral theatrical
teatro *m* theater [6]
técnica *f* technique [24]
técnico,-a technical *m* technician [8]
techo *m* roof [10]
tejer to weave
tejido *m* weaving
telar *m* loom
teléfono *m* telephone [3]; por — on the telephone
televisión *f* television
tema *m* theme, subject [7]; cambiar de — to change the subject [17]
temer to fear
temor *m* fear
temperamento *m* temperament
temperatura *f* temperature
templado,-a temperate
templo *m* temple
temporada *f* season
temprano early [15]
tendencia *f* tendency
tender (ie) (a) to tend (toward)
tenedor *m* fork
* tener to have, hold, possess [2]; — cuidado to be careful [5]; — de todo to have (some) of everything [20]; — ganas de to want to [15]; — hambre to be hungry [4]; — la bondad de to be so kind as to [12]; *— que to have to [3]; — razón to be right [9]; (no) — cuidado (not) to worry [5]; —se to stop
teniente *m* lieutenant [22]
tentado,-a tempted
teología *f* theology
teológico,-a theological
teoría *f* theory, method
* tercero (tercer),-a third [9]
terminar to finish [13]; —se to come to an end
término *m* term
terminología *f* terminology

termómetro *m* thermometer [12]

terrenal earthly

territorial territorial

territorio *m* territory

terrón *m*: — de azúcar cube of sugar

tertulia *f* party, social gathering; — de confianza gathering of close friends

tesoro *m* treasure

testamento *m* will

testigo *m* witness

testimoniar to testify

textiles *m pl* textiles

* ti you [3]

tía *f* aunt [2]

tiempo *m* time, weather [5]; en mis —s in my day [16]

tienda *f* shop, store; — de comestibles grocery store; de — en — from store to store

tierno,-a gentle, tender

tierra *f* land

tijeras *f pl* scissors [7]

timbal *m* timbal, kettledrum

timbre *m* stamp

tinte *m* tint, color

tintorería *f* cleaning shop [11]

tío *m* uncle [2]

típico,-a typical [5]

tipo *m* type, guy, fellow [20]

tira: *see* asado

tirador *m* marksman, handle, knob

tiranía *f* tyranny

tirano *m* tyrant [13]

tirar to pull [7]

tiro *m* shot [13]; a —s with shots [13]

titiritera *f* puppet-player

titulares *m pl* headlines [13]

titularse to be entitled, be named [13]

título *m* title, headline

tiza *f* chalk [1]

toalla *f* towel [2]

tocadiscos *m* record player [3]

tocar (qu) to play (a musical instrument) [23], touch [16]; — en suerte to fall to one's lot

todavía still, yet [4]

* todo,-a all, every [3]; ante — especially; del — completely; en — caso anyway; hay de — there is (some) of everything; sobre — especially [21]; — el mundo everybody [12]; —s everybody [6]; todas partes everywhere [16]; de todos modos by all means [17]

tolerar to tolerate

tomar to take, drink, eat [5]; ¡Toma! Here!

tomate *m* tomato

tono *m* tone, note

* tontería *f* (piece of) foolishness [6]; —s trifles, nonsense [18]

tonto,-a foolish; *m* fool

topar to come upon

toque *m* play, note (struck on a musical instrument)

toreo *m* bullfighting [7]

torero *m* bullfighter

torno: en — a around

toro *m* bull [7]

tortilla *f dim* tortilla

tortita *f dim* tart, cookie

total *m* total, whole [2]; en — in all [2]

trabajar to work [1]

trabajo *m* work, job [8]

trabalenguas *m* tongue-twister

trabar to unite; — nuevas amistades to make new friends

tradición *f* tradition

tradicional traditional

traducción *f* translation

traducir (*like* producir) to translate

traductor *m* translator

* traer to bring, carry [3], have

tráfico *m* traffic [6]

tragedia *f* tragedy

traicionero,-a treacherous [21]

traje *m* suit, clothes [11]; — de luces bullfighter's costume

tranquilo,-a tranquil, quiet [18]

transcripción *f* transcription

transcurso *m* passing (of time)

transformación *f* transformation

transformar to transform

tránsito *m* traffic [6], existence

transportado,-a transported

tranvía *m* streetcar [10]

tras after, with

trasladar(se) to move

tratar to treat, discuss, have dealings [17]; — de to try to [17], have dealings (with); —se (de) to be a question of; de que se trata in question

través: a — de across

trazar (c) to trace, draw

trece thirteen [2]

trecho *m* way, space; de — a — at intervals

treinta thirty [8]

tremendo,-a tremendous [6]

tren *m* train; entre — y — between trains

trenzar (c) to prance; braid (one's hair)

tres three [2]

triangular triangular

triángulo *m* triangle

tribu *f* tribe

trigo *m* wheat [10]

trinchado *m* carving

triste sad [6]

tristeza *f* sadness

triunfar to triumph

triunfo *m* triumph

tronco *m* trunk

tropical tropical

trucha *f* trout; — salmonada salmon

* tu your [2]

* tú you [2]

tudesco,-a German

tumba *f* tomb [13]

tungsteno *m* tungsten

turbar to disturb

turista *m f* tourist [14]

turnarse to take turns

* tuyo,-a yours, of yours [8]

u

* u or [6]

Ud. = *abr of* usted

¡Uf! Oh!

úlcera *f* ulcer [10]

último,-a last, final [4]; por — finally

unánime unanimous [24]

undécimo,-a eleventh [9]

* único,-a only, unique [9]

unidad *f* unit, unity

uniforme uniform, alike; *m* uniform [23]

uniformidad *f* uniformity

unión *f* union [10]; la Unión Panamericana the Pan-American Union [24]

unir to unite; —se (a) to join

universal universal; name of a newspaper in Mexico

universidad *f* university [13]

* universitario,-a *adj* university [13]

* uno(un),-a a, an, one [2]; la una one o'clock [11]; *pl* some

uña *f* fingernail

urgente urgent

urgir (j) to be urgent, be needed

urna *f* urn

uruguayo,-a Uruguayan

usar to use [3]

uso *m* use, custom

usté = usted

* usted you [1]

útil useful [24]

utilizar (c) to utilize

uva *f* grape

v

vaca *f* cow [10]

vacación *f* vacation; vacaciones vacation [7]

vacilar to vacillate, hesitate

vacío,-a empty; *m* vacuum

vacuno: *see* ganado

vago,-a vague
vagón m wagon, car
vaivén m seesaw, confusion
vajilla f dishes, table
service [22]
valentón m braggart
valer to be worth [7]; — **la pena** to be worthwhile [7]
valeroso,-a brave
validez f validity
valiente valiant, brave
valor m worth, value, bravery
vanidad f vanity
vano: en — in vain
vaquero m cowboy
variado,-a varied
variar (í) to vary
variedad f variety
varios,-as several [13]
varón m man, male
vasco,-a Basque (from the northern provinces of Spain)
vascongado m Basque
vasija f vessel, receptacle
vasto,-a vast
vecindad f nearness, neighborhood
vecino,-a neighboring; m neighbor
vehemente vehement
veinte twenty [3], **veintiuno** twenty-one [8]
vejez f old age
velada f evening party (usually with music and literary discussion); wake (before a funeral)
velar to watch, stay awake (for the wake) [21]; **el cadáver fue velado** the wake was held
velero m sailboat
velocidad f speed
velorio m wake [21]
venado m deer
vencer (z) to conquer, overcome
vendedor m paper boy; seller [13]
vender to sell [5]; **a —** for sale
veneno m poison
venerar to venerate
venezolano,-a Venezuelan [3]
* **venir** to come [3]; **¿A qué viene?** How come?
venta f sale
ventaja f advantage [8]
ventajosamente advantageously
ventana f window [2]
* **ver** to see [4]; **a —** let's see [11]; **tener que — con** to have something to do with [16]; **por lo visto** apparently [10]
verano m summer [10]
veras: de — truly, really [15]
verbo m verb [24]
verdad f truth [3]; *¿—? isn't

it?, aren't they?, etc. [3]; **es —** that's right
verdadero,-a true, real [7]
verde green [4]
verdoso,-a greenish
verduras f pl green vegetables [5]
vergüenza f shame
verso m verse
vertebral vertebral
vestido,-a (de) dressed (in) [21]; m dress [11]; pl clothes [17]
vestigio m vestige
vestir (i) to dress; **—se (de)** to dress (in) [21]
* **vez** f time [3]; **a la —** at the same time, at a time; **alguna —** ever, sometime [8]; *en — de instead of [4]; **otra —** again; **tal —** perhaps [3]; **una —** once; **a veces** at times; **muchas veces** often; **unas (algunas) veces** sometimes
vía f way; **por — de** by way of
viajar to travel
viaje m journey, trip [7]; **hacer un —** to take a trip [20]
viajero m traveler
víbora f viper
vicisitud f vicissitude
víctima f victim
vida f life [10]
vido = vio
vidriado,-a glasswork
vidrio m glass
* **viejo,-a** old [14]; m f old person; old boy [14]; **viejos** old folks
viento m wind [10]; **hace —** it is windy
viernes m Friday [4]
viga f beam
vigilado,-a watched
vigoroso,-a vigorous
villancico m song, carol
vinculado,-a linked
vínculo m bond
vino m wine
violento,-a violent
violín m violin, violinist
violoncelista m cellist
virgen f virgin
virrey m viceroy
virtud f virtue
virtuoso,-a virtuous
visigodo m Visigoth
visión f vision
visita f visit [12]
visitante m visitor
visitar to visit
vista f view; **hasta la —** I'll see you later
visto: por lo — apparently [10]; **— bueno** O.K. [14]

vistoso,-a colorful
vital vital, living
vitaminas f pl vitamins
vituallas f pl victuals, provisions
viuda f widow [21]
vivaracho,-a lively
vivienda f dwelling, lodging; **—s** housing [24]
vivir to live [4]
vivo,-a alive, lively, real, bright
vocablo m word
vocabulario m vocabulary
volar (ue) to fly [17]
volumen m volume
voluntad f will
* **volver (ue)** to return, turn [5]; **— a + inf** to . . . again [15]; **— loco** to drive (one) crazy [5]; **—se loco** to go crazy; **—se** to become
vosotros,-as you (pl)
votación f vote, voting [24]
votar to vote [24]
voz f voice, word [24]; **a media —** in a low voice; **de — grave** in a serious voice; **voces** shouts [24]
vuelo m flight
vuelta f change; **dar la —** to turn around, return
vuelto,-a (see volver) returned, turned; m change
vuestro,-a your
vulgar vulgar, of the common people

y

* **y** and [2]
ya already, now, presently [4]; **— lo creo!** Yes, indeed! [10]; **— . . . —** whether . . . or; **¡—!** Ready!; *—**que** since [4]
yámbico,-a iambic
yate m yacht
yelmo m helmet
yerba f herb
* **yo** I, me [2]
yuxtaposición f juxtaposition

z

zamacueca = cueca f folk dance of Chile
zapateado m foot-tapping dance [23]
zapateo m foot beat
zapatería f shoe store
zapato m shoe [5]; **—s de goma** overshoes, galoshes
zarzuela f musicodramatic composition
zeta f the letter z
zona f zone

Index

Spanish words are in boldface, and English translations in italics. The boldface numbers are those of the grammar sections which are numbered consecutively throughout the book. The lightface numbers are page numbers. The entries are in English alphabetical order.

ABBREVIATIONS

adj	adjective	imperf	imperfect	pret	preterit
adv	adverb, adverbial	indef	indefinite	pron	pronoun
art	article	indic	indicative	ref	refer(ring), reference(s)
cn	cultural note	inf	infinitive	refl	reflexive
cond	conditional	interrog	interrogative	sing	singular
const	construction	masc	masculine	subj	subject
def	definite	obj	object	subjunc	subjunctive
fem	feminine	perf	perfect	vb	verb
ff	and following	pl	plural	vs	versus
fn	footnote	prep	preposition	w/p	with-preposition
fut	future	pres	present	w/v	with-verb

a, + **el** → **al, 29**:98; vs **en** for *at,* **123**:358; **ir a jugar al jardín, 33**:107; vs **para,** with vbs of motion, **33**:107, **129**:383; preps, to make compound, **136**:406; sign of personal obj, **25**:86, **73**:213; before w/p prons, **55**:161; w/p prons after, **137**:408

-a, fem marker, **4**:32

[a], 6, 27, 137; fusion, 152

a menos que, subjunc, after, **102**:299

a pesar de, compound prep, **136**:406

about, meaning of **de, 126**:372

acá, vs **aquí,** cn, 76

acabar de, + inf, **39**:123

accent mark, indicator of stress, 4; on advs with **-mente** suffix, **96**:274; on demonstratives, **59**:177 fn; on **habláramos, dijéramos,** etc., **105**:313 fn; on vbs with attached prons, **24**:84 fn; on vbs with stem ending in vowel, **26**:93 fn, **92**:265 fn

acceptance-rejection, criterion for subjunc, **97**:282, **105**:313, **117**:349

acostado, posture, **127**:375

across, meaning of **por, 125**:369

action-going-on, criterion for subjectless use of refl, **37**:113

activity, criterion for derivation, **134**:402

address, forms of, **1**:27

además de, compound prep, **136**:406

adjective clauses, indic and subjunc in, **103**:304, **105**:313; nominalization, **59**:177; vs noun clauses that modify nouns, **132**:389; pres perf subjunc in, with past meaning, **106**:319

adjectives, vs adv, with **tener** and **dar, 90**:254; advs from, **96**:274; agreement with noun, **6**:35; demonstratives, **27**:96; derivation, from nouns, **134**:402; descriptive, **64**:192; **-do** form as, **92**:265; gender of, **6**:35; limiting, **46**:141; nominalization, **59**:177,

77:226; nouns derived from, **134**:402; of order, + inf, **132**:389; position of, **64**:192, with **qué, 88**:252; possessive, **19**:69, used less than in English, **31**:100; shortened, **50**:145; sing and pl of, **6**:35

administrador, cn, 152

adónde, interrog word, **8**:44

adverb, vs adj, with **tener** and **dar, 90**:254; adj clauses used adverbially, **103**:304; **lo más, lo menos** with, **80**:233; *-ly,* equivalents of, **96**:274; modifying descriptive adjs, **64**:192; **-ndo** form, adverbial use of, **40**:125; preps, to make compound, **136**:406

adverb clauses, indic and subjunc in, **102**:299, **105**:313

adverbial conjunctions, to begin adv clauses, **102**:299

affix, derivation with, **134**:402; **-ito, -ico, -illo, 108**:322; **-mente, 96**:274; prefixes in vbs (**tener- detener,** etc.), **44**:137

affricate, 4, 18

after, meaning of **por, 125**:369

age, **mayor, menor, viejo,** and **joven** ref to, **78**:228

agency, criterion for **por, 121**:355, **125**:369

ago, **hacer, 91**:257

agreement, see Gender, Number, Person

ahí, vs **allí** and **allá,** cn, 42

ahora que, indic after, **102**:299

aim, criterion for **para, 129**:383, **130**:385

al, from **a** + **el, 29**:98, 153; + inf, **35**:111

-al, derivation with, **134**:402

algo, affirmative word, **70**:210; in affirmative questions, **74**:214; **de** after, **126**:372; *something* vs *somewhat,* **84**:245

alguien, affirmative word, **70**:210; in affirmative questions, **74**:214; vs **alguno, 73**:213; personal **a** with, **73**:213

alguno, -a, -os, -as, affirmative word, **70**:210; in affirmative questions, **74**:214; vs **alguien, 73**:213; **algún, 50**:145; **algunos** vs **unos, 83**:235; nominalization, **84**:245; personal **a** with, **73**:213; position, **46**:141

all, **todo** for, vs *every*, **75**:215

allá, allí, vs **ahí,** cn, 42

aló, telephone greeting, cn, 42

along, meaning of **por**, **125**:369

alveolar, 3

amounts, no repeating pron required with when obj, **56**:162

-ancia, derivation with, **134**:402

andar, pret, **44**:137

ante-, derivation with, **134**:402

antes de, compound prep, **136**:406

antes (de) que, compared to **antes de**, **102**:299; subjunc after, **102**:299, **105**:313

anti-, derivation with, **134**:402

anticlimax, see Word order

any, **cualquier(a)**, **50**:145; **ninguno**, **70**:210

apocopation, see Shortening

aquel, aquella, -os, -as, vs **ese,** cn, 170

aquí, vs **acá,** cn, 76

-ar verbs, pres, **3**:29; see Verb conjugation

Argentina, def art with, **76**:217

around, meaning of **por**, **125**:369

arroz, cn, 76

article, definite, **a + el → al**, **29**:98; classifying nouns, with, **30**:99; days and places, with, **76**:217; **de** phrases to modify particularized nouns, in, **131**:387; "definite wholes," for, **75**:215, cn, 264, **101**:291; **el** with fem nouns, **120** 354; forms and agreement, **4**:32; **la una, las dos,** etc., **62**:183; **lo** with compared advs, **80**:233; nominalization with **el, la, los, las,** **59**:177, with **lo,** **77**:226, **92**:265; position, **46**:141; things possessed, with, **31**:100

article, indefinite, **de** phrases to modify particularized nouns, in, **131**:387; forms and use, **4**:32; individualization, for, **83**:235; position, **46**:141; **un** with fem nouns, **120**:354; **unos,** **83**:235

as, meaning of **de**, **126**:372

as if, imperf subjunc with, **107**:320

aspiration, 171; see Unaspirated

assimilation, [n], 15, 18, 20, 120, 121; [s], 10, 171, 208

at, **en** and **a** for, **123**:358; meaning of **por**, **125**:369

atento y seguro servidor, cn, 298

aunque, indic and subjunc after, **102**:299

auxiliary, see Verbs

[b], 15, 19; vs [b̶], 43; vs [p], 106; sequence [mb], 15; pause before, 19; spelled **v,** 15, 121, 265

[b̶], 11; vs [b], 43; spelled **v,** 19, 121, 265

back vowel, 3

background, criterion for imperf, **52**:155

be, **estar** vs **ser**, **14**:55; idioms with **tener** and **dar**, **90**:254

because of, meaning of **por**, **125**:369

becoming, criterion for **estar**, **14**:55

belongingness, criterion for **de**, **126**:372; for **ser**, **14**:55

benefit, criterion for indirect obj, **58**:175, **67**:198

bilabial, 3

-ble, derivation with, **134**:402

boliviano, monetary unit, cn, 224

Brasil, def art with, **76**:217

bueno, -a, -os, -as, buen, **50**:145; usually precedes noun, **64**:192

busses, Spanish equivalents, cn, 224

by, **de** and **por** for, after a **-do** form, **121**:355, **126**:372

c, sequences **ce, ci,** 16, 191, 208; see [k] and [s]

[č], 18

cada, cada uno, -a, **84**:245

caer, caerse, **67**:198; **-ndo** form, **40**:125; pres, **21**:77; **tú** commands, **23**:82; **usted, -es** commands, **22**:79

calendar periods, days, months, years, **48**:144

cambiar, de after, **126**:372

can, criterion for pres, **17**:65

Canadá, def art with, **76**:217

capacity, criterion for **de**, **126**:372

cardinal numerals, see Numerals

casa, omission of def art with, **76**:217

castellano, cn, 136

Castilian pronunciation, 208, 281

cause, criterion for **por**, **125**:369, **130**:385

cerca de, compound prep, **136**:406

certificado de buena conducta, cn, 366

ch, see [č]

Chalo, cn, 136

change, criterion for **estar**, **14**:55, **41**:126

change of feelings, calls for refl const, **66**:196

ciento, -os, -as, **43**:130

-ción, derivation with, **134**:402

clase, omission of def art with, **76**:217

classification, criterion for position of adj, **64**:192; for **qué** vs **cuál**, **138**:410

classifying nouns, art with, **30**:99

clauses, definition, **97**:282; vs phrases, **102**:299; see Noun clauses, Adjective clauses, Adverb clauses

climax, see Word order

co-, derivation with, **134**:402

colectivo, *bus*, cn, 224

colegio, cn, 136

colgado, posture, **127**:375

collective nouns, sing and pl vbs with, **109**:323

colón, monetary unit, cn, 224

colors, **100**:290

commands, direct, with **tú**, **23**:82, with **usted, -es,** **22**:79; indirect, **98**:287; negative, **23**:82; pres subjunc, compared to, **95**:270; w/v prons in, **24**:84

communication, vbs of, for suasion, **118**:351; indirect obj with, **118**:351

como, vs **de** *as*, **126**:372; indic after, **102**:299; preceded by **tan, tanto,** **81**:233; subj prons after, **137**:408

como si, **107**:320

cómo, interrog word, **8**:44

comparison, of equality, **81**:233; of identity, **82**:234; of inequality, **79**:230; comparative words, **78**:228; **lo** with compared advs, **80**:233; criterion for **estar**, **14**:55, **41**:126; for **para**, **129**:383

complements, vbs not requiring, **128**:376; vbs often requiring, cn, 264

complimentary close, cn, 298

componer, pres, **21**:77

compounds, formation, **135**:405; preps, **136**:406; stress, 4, 5

comprar, indirect obj with, **58**:175

comprender, pret vs imperf, **52**:155

con, conmigo, contigo, **54**:160; expressing means to action, **122**:357; omission of indef art after, **83**:235; phrases equivalent to *-ly*, **96**:274; w/p prons after **137**:408

con tal (de) que, subjunc after, **102**:299, **105**:313

concerning, meaning of **de, 126**:372

conditional, **111**:332; fut and imperf, relation to, **111**:332; probability, to show, **124**:367; not usual after **si** *if,* **115**:338; softened requests and criticisms, in, **116**:342; see Verb conjugation

conditional sentences, see *If* clauses

conducta, certificado de buena, cn, 366

conjunctions, **e** for **y, 28**:97; to begin adv clauses, **102**:299; **u** for **o, 28**:97

conjunctive pronouns, see Pronouns, ref to w/v

conmigo, 54:160

conocer, pres, **21**:77; vs **saber, 32**:100; **tú** commands, **23**:82; **usted, -es** commands, **22**:79

consejo, countable noun, **104**:307

consonants, 3 ff

contact, criterion for **por, 130**:385

contigo, 54:160

contra, w/p prons after, **137**:408

contra de, en, compound prep, **136**:406

contraction, **a + el → al, 29**:98; **de + el → del, 29**:98 fn; **veinte y uno → veintiuno,** etc., **43**:130

contradanza, cn, 383

contradictions, position of **no** in, **72**:212

contrary-to-fact *if* clauses, **115**:338

contrast, criterion for position of adj, **64**:192

correspondence, criterion for **por, 125**:369

corrida de toros, cn, 106

could, equivalents of, **116**:342, **124**:367

countables, mass nouns and, **104**:307

counting forms, see Numerals

creer, creí, etc., with accent mark and **creyó,** etc., with **y, 26**:93 fn; **-ndo** form, **40**:125

criticisms, softened requests and, **116**:342

cuál, -es, interrog word, **8**:44; nominalization with, **59**:177; vs **qué** for *what,* **138**:410

cualquier(a), cualesquier(a), 50:145; vs **ninguno, 70**:210

cuando, indic and subjunc after, **102**:299

cuándo, interrog word, **8**:44

cuánto, -a, -os, -as, interrog word, **8**:44

cuanto, en, indic and subjunc after, **102**:299

cuanto a, en, compound prep, **136**:406

cutoff point, criterion for pret, **52**:155, **53**:159

[d], 16, 19; vs [d̶], 43; vs [t], 106; sequence [nd] 16

[d̶], 14, 61; vs [d], 43

-dad, derivation with, **134**:402

dar, idioms with, **90**:254; pres, **21**:71; pret, **26**:93; **tú** commands, **23**:82; **usted, -es** commands, **22**:79

dates, **48**:144

days of week, **48**:144; def art with, **76**:217; pl of, **49**:145

de, in dates, **48**:144; inf, with, after **fácil,** etc., **132**:389; meanings, **126**:372; **millón, millones,** after, **43**:130; phrases with, **126**:372; as equivalents of nouns, etc., modifying nouns in English, **131**:387, **132**:389; nominalization, **59**:177, **77**:226; vs **por** for *by* after a **-do** form, **121**:355; in telling time, **62**:183, **126**:372; possession, for, **20**:71; preps, to make compound, **136**:406; *than,* **79**:230; *with* and *in,* **122**:357; w/p prons after, **137**:408

de quién, 139:411

debajo de, compound prep, **136**:406

deber, imperf sunjunc of, in softened requests and criticisms, **116**:342; inf obj, with, **33**:107; *must, ought,* **114**:337

décimo, lottery ticket, cn, 329

decir, he dicho, cn, 401; **-ndo** form, **40**:125; pres, **21**:77; pret, **44**:137; **tú** commands, **23**:82; **usted, -es** commands, **22**:79; see Communication

definition, criterion for **cuál** and **qué, 138**:410

degrees, see Comparison

dejar, direct obj with, **118**:351; vs indirect commands, **98**:287; inf obj, with, **33**:107; vb of suasion followed by inf, **118**:351

del, from **de + el, 29**:98 fn, 153

demonstratives, **27**:96; accent mark with, **59**:177 fn; **de** phrases to modify particularized nouns, in, **131**:387; nominalization, **59**:177; position, **46**:141

dental, 3

dentro de, compound prep, **136**:406

derivation, **134**:402

des-, derivation with, **134**:402

descriptive adjectives, **64**:192; see Adjectives

desde que, compared to **desde, 102**:299; indic after, **102**:299

deshacer, pres, **21**:77

después de, compound prep, **136**:406

detener, pret, **44**:137

determinateness, criterion for indic in adj clauses, **103**:304, **105**:313

determinative adjectives, **46**:141; see Adjectives

detrás de, compound prep, **136**:406

día, de día vs **por el día, 126**:372; saints' days, cn, 61

differentiating, criterion for position of adjs, **64**:192

difícil, takes **de** before inf, **132**:389

dimensions, criterion for **en** *at,* **123**:358

diminutives, **-ito, -ico, -illo, 108**:322

Dios, exclamation, cn, 26

direct objects, see Objects

direction, criterion for **para, 129**:383

disjunctive pronouns, see Pronouns, ref to w/p

disservice, criterion for indirect obj, **67**:198

distance, criterion for **ahí, allí, allá,** cn, 42; for **ese** vs **aquel,** cn, 170

distributive, see "One each"

do, did, no parallel in Spanish questions, **9**:46

-do form, as adj, **92**:265; **de** and **por** for *by* after, **121**:355; postures, for, **127**:375

doctor, cn, 401

documento, cn, 91

don, no art with this title, **30**:99; to show respect, cn, 61

doña, no art with this title, **30**:99; vs **señora,** cn, 26

donde, introducing adj clauses, **103**:304

dónde, interrog word, **8**:44

dormir, pret and **-ndo** form, **45**:140

down, meaning of **por, 125**:369

-ducir verbs, pres, **21**:77; pret, **44**:137

duration, criterion for **por, 125**:369

duty, criterion for **por, 125**:369

e, for **y** *and,* **28**:97

[e], 7, 27, 76; fusion, 152

each-other construction, **85**:248

-ecer verbs, pres, **21**:77

¿ eh?, tag in questions, **12**:52

el, see Article, definite

él, subj pron, **1**:27; w/p pron, **54**:160, **55**:161

ella, subj pron, 1:27; w/p pron, 54:160, 55:161
ellos, -as, subj pron, 1:27; w/p pron, 54:160, 55:161
emotion, criterion for subjunc, 97:282; for intonation, 11:48
emphasis, shown by **de** const in possessives, 20:71; by **mismo,** 65:195; by pitch, 11:48; by position of word, 9:46, 37:113, 87:251; by subj prons, 2:28; by w/p prons, 55:161
en, vs **a** for *at*, 123:358; inf after **único** and adjs of order, with, 132:389; means to action, expressing, 122:357; w/p prons after, 137:408
en contra de, compound prep, 136:406
en cuanto, indic and subjunc after, 102:299
en cuanto a, compound prep, 136:406
en pro de, compound prep, 136:406
en vez de, compound prep, 136:406
enhancing, criterion for position of descriptive adjs, 64:192
entero, lottery ticket, cn, 329
entrar, takes **a** before inf, 33:107
entre, subj prons after, 137:408
equality, see Comparison
equivalence, lack of, in translation, cn, 42
-er verbs, pres, 15:62; see Verb conjugation
escribir, see Communication
ese, -a, -os, -as, -o, vs **aquel,** cn, 170; see Demonstratives
español, equivalent to English noun and adj, 131:387; language, cn, 136
esposa, vs **mujer** and **señora,** cn, 61
esta noche, *this evening, tonight,* 27:96
Estados Unidos, def art with, 76:217
estar, complements, without, 128:376; **-do** form, with, 93:267; fut and cond of, for probability, 114:337, 124:367; pres, 13:54; pret, 44:137; progressive, to form, 41:126, 53:159, 112:334; vs **ser,** 14:55, 41:126, 93:267, cn, 299; **tú** commands, 23:82; **usted, -es** commands, 22:79
este, -a, -os, -as, -o, see Demonstratives
evening, **tarde** vs **noche,** 62:183
every, **todo** for, vs *all,* 75:215
excepto, subj prons after, 137:408
exchange, criterion for **por,** 125:369, 130:385
exclamations, adjs with **qué** in, 88:252; indic or subjunc in, 117:349
excuse me, **perdón** vs **con permiso,** cn, 42
existence, omission of indef art to stress mere, 83:235

[f], 16
fácil, takes **de** before inf, 132:389
factuality, criterion for indic in adv clauses, 102:299
falling terminal juncture, see Juncture
feminine, see Gender
for, criterion for **hacer** in expressions of time, 91:257; meaning of **de,** 126:372; of indirect obj, 18:66, 58:175; of **para,** 58:175, 129:383; of **por,** 58:175, 125:369
for me to, meaning of **para,** 129:383
fraction of the whole, criterion for pl with collective noun, 109:323
frequency, see Pitch
fricative, 4, 8, 9, 11, 14, 16, 17, 20; **y** in **trayendo,** etc., 40:125 fn; see [b̵], [d̵], [g̵]
from, meaning of **de,** 58:175; of indirect obj, 58:175
front vowel, 3
fuera de, compound prep, 136:406

fusion, 12, 152; see Linking
fútbol, cn, 106
future, 110:329; fut meaning determines subjunc in adv clauses, 102:299; fut tense and **ir a,** 34:109, 110:329; fut tense not usual after **si** *if,* 115:338; pres indic with fut meaning, 17:65, 41:126, 112:334; pres subjunc with fut meaning, 95:270; probability, to show, 114:337; vs willingness, 115:338; see Verb conjugation

g, sequences **ge, gi,** 21, 225; [g] [g̵], [x]
[g], 18; vs [g̵], 43, 153; vs [k], 106; sequence [gw], 171; spelling, 153
[g̵], 8; vs [g], 43, 153; sequence [g̵s], 208, [g̵w], 171; spelling, 153
gain, criterion for indirect obj, 58:175
gender, **el** and **un** with fem nouns, 120:354; fem nouns made masc, cn, 91; neuter demonstratives, 27:96; of adjs, 6:35; one adj modifying nouns of different genders, 64:192; nouns, 4:32; nouns and prons ref to both sexes, 1:27, 85:248, 133:392; numerals, 7:38, 43:130, 47:143; possessive adjs, 19:69; w/v prons, 18:66
gente, sing vb with, 109:323
geographical names, def art with, 76:217
get, criterion for refl and **ponerse,** 66:196
glide, 76
goal, criterion for **para,** 129:383, 130:385
going on, criterion for progressive, 41:126
gordo, premio gordo, cn, 329
grande, gran, 50:145
gu, spelling of /g/, 153; of /gw/, 171
guaraní, monetary unit, cn, 225
gustar, indirect obj with, 56:162; w/v pron with, 56:162

h, 19, 245
[h], vs [s, x], 171
haber, complements, without, 128:376; fut and cond of, for probability, 114:337, 124:367; **haber de todo,** 126:372; **haber que** + inf, 39:123; imperf subjunc of, in softened requests and criticisms, 116:342; indef art after, omission of, 83:235; perf consts, to form, 94:268, 95:270, 113:335, 116:342; position of w/v prons with **hay que,** 42:128; pres, 94:268; pret, 44:137; progressive consts, in, 112:334; vs **tener,** 94:268; *there to be,* 36:112, 95:270, 113:335
habitual, criterion for pres tense, 41:126
hacer, direct obj with, 118:351; pres, 21:77; time, in expressions of, 91:257; **tú** commands, 23:82; **usted, -es** commands, 22:79; vb of suasion followed by inf, 118:351
hacia, w/p prons after, 137:408
happening, criterion for **-ndo** form, 40:125
happening-and-then-over-with, criterion for pret, 52:155
hard palate, 2
hasta, w/p prons after, 137:408
hasta que, compared to **hasta,** 102:299; indic and subjunc after, 102:299
he dicho, cn, 401
high pitch, 5
high vowel, 3
hora, in telling time, 62:183

hortatory, see *Let's*
hours, **62**:183

i, see [i], [y]
[i], 15, 27, 76
-ico, -a, -os, -as, 108:322
identification, criterion for **de, 126**:372; for omission of indef art, **83**:235
identity, see Comparison
if clauses, **115**:338; *whether*, **115**:338; see *As if*
igual, -es, comparative word, **82**:234; vs **mismo, 82**:234
-illo, -a, -os, -as, 108:322
im-, derivation with, **134**:402
imperative, see Commands
imperfect, **51**:153; vs imperf progressive, **53**:159; vs pret, **52**:155, **53**:159; probability corresponding to, shown by cond, **124**:367; telling time, in, **62**:183; see Subjunctive, Verb conjugation
imperfect progressive, see Progressive
imposible, takes **de** before inf, **132**:389
in, **de** as equivalent of, **122**:357, **126**:372
in-, derivation with, **134**:402
in order to, meaning of **para, 129**:383
incluir, -ndo form, **40**:125; pres, **21**:77; **incluyó,** etc., with **y, 26**:93 fn
incluso, subj prons after, **137**:408
inconclusiveness, intonation to show, **11**:48
indefinites, affirmative questions, in, **74**:214; indef use of refl, **37**:113; no repeating pron required with when obj, **56**:162; nominalization, **84**:245; omission of art for indefiniteness, **75**:215; of indef complement, **128**:376; personal **a** with, **73**:213; **-quiera** compounds, **135**:405
indicative, in adj clauses, **103**:304; adv clauses, **102**:299; exclamations, after expressions of welcoming-spurning, **117**:349; *if* clauses, **115**:338; noun clauses, **97**:282, **132**:389; with **tal vez, 95**:270; see Verb conjugation
indirect commands, **98**:287
indirect object, see Objects
individualization, criterion for indef art, **83**:235
inequality, see Comparison
inertness, criterion for derivation, **134**:402
infinitive, after another vb, **33**:107; **al** +, **35**:111; def art with, cn, 264; vs clause, **97**:282, **105**:313, **118**:351, **119**:353; fut, stem of, **110**:329; vs *-ing* form, **97**:282, **132**:389; modifier, as, **132**:389; vs **-ndo** form, **119**:353; noun, functions as, **33**:107, **38**:121; passive, cn, 76; preps before, **33**:107, **35**:111, **38**:121, **129**:383; **tener que,** etc., after, **39**:123; w/v prons in consts with, position of, **42**:128
influence, criterion of subjunc, **97**:282, **105**:313, **118**:351, **132**:389
information, criterion for question intonation, 5; for indic, **97**:282, **132**:389
informativeness, criterion for position of adj and noun, **64**:192
-ing form, vs clause, **105**:313; corresponds to Spanish inf, etc., **38**:121; vs inf, **97**:282, **132**:389; see **-ndo** form
initial position, criterion for stop consonant, 19
intelligibility, criterion for omission of complement, **128**:376
interest, criterion for indirect obj, **58**:175

interrogative words, **8**:44; intonation of questions beginning with, 5; no repeating pron required with when obj, **56**:162; position, **9**:46, **87**:251; see Questions
intonation, **11**:48; see Pitch
intransitive verbs, + refl prons, **67**:198; where English intransitive same as transitive, Spanish has refl, **37**:113
invitar, takes **a** before inf, **33**:107
ir, ir a, as fut and *let's,* **34**:109, + inf, **33**:107, **34**:109, position of w/v prons in consts with, **42**:128; **irse, 67**:198; pres, **21**:77; pret, **44**:137; **tú** commands, **23**:82; **usted, -es** commands, **22**:79; **vámonos, 99**:289; **vamos a** *let's* vs pres subjunc, **99**:289
-ir verbs, pres, **15**:62; pret of stem-changing, **45**:140; see Verb conjugation
irregular verbs, see Verb conjugation
it, as material subj and stopgap subj, **132**:389; not normally expressed as subj, **2**:28
-ito, -a, -os, -as, 108:322

j, see [x]
jamás, negative word, **70**:210
joven, más joven vs **menor** *younger*, **78**:228
juncture, 8, 9, 11, 20
junto a, compound prep, **136**:406

[k], 12, 16; vs [g], 106; sequence [ks], 208, [ŋk], 121; spelling, 137
kilo, kilómetro, metric system, cn, 76

[l], 6, 76; sequences [rl], [ʀl], 20, [lʀ], 62
la, las, indef **la,** cn, 152; see Article, definite; Objects, ref to direct; Pronouns, ref to w/v
lástima, indic or subjunc after, **117**:349
lateral, 4, 6, 281
le, les, see Objects, ref to indirect; Pronouns, ref to w/v
let's, pres subjunc for, vs **vamos a, 99**:289; **vamos a, 34**:109
level terminal juncture, see Juncture
levels of pitch, 5, 7; signal of juncture, 5
like-dislike, criterion for subjunc, **97**:282, **105**:313, **117**:349
limiting adjectives, **46**:141
linking, 10, 12; of [y], 20; see Fusion
lips, 2
ll, [y], 8; cn, 225; 281
lo, complement with **creer, saber,** etc., cn, 264; with **todo,** cn, 280; see Article, definite; Objects, ref to direct; Pronouns, ref to w/v
lo de, *business, concern, part,* etc., *of,* **77**:226
lo que, *what,* **77**:226
location, criterion for **por, 125**:369; when unexpressed after **estar, 128**:376
los, see Article, definite; Objects, ref to direct; Pronouns, ref to w/v
loss, criterion for indirect obj, **58**:175
loudness, see Stress
low pitch, 5
low vowel, 3
-ly, equivalents of, **96**:274

[m], 10, 98, 99; sequences [mb, mp, mm], 15, 121; spelled **n,** 15, 121

make, **dar, 90**:254; **poner, 66**:196

malo, -a, -os, -as, mal, 50:145; usually precedes noun, **64**:192

manner of articulation, 3

mañana, in telling time, **62**:183

María, cn, 42

más, comparative word, **78**:228; in exclamations, **88**:252; position, **46**:141

masculine, see Gender

mass nouns, and countables, **104**:307

mayor, comparative word, **78**:228; vs **más viejo** *older,* **78**:228

mayoría, pl vb with, **109**:323

me, see Pronouns, ref to w/v; see Reflexive

means to action, criterion for **con** or **en, 122**:357

mejor, comparative word, **78**:228

Memo, cn, 329

menor, comparative word, **78**:228; vs **más joven** *younger,* **78**:228; vs **menos** *least,* **78**:228

menos, comparative word, **78**:228; vs **menor** *least,* **78**:228; position, **46**:141; telling time, in, **62**:183

menos que, a, subjunc after, **102**:299

-mente, *-ly,* **96**:274; stress, 5, **96**:274

metric system, cn, 76

metro, metric system, cn, 76

mi, mis, 19:69, **60**:180; see Possessives

mí, 54:160, **55**:161; repetition of prep with, **137**:408; see Pronouns, ref to w/p

micro, *bus,* cn, 224

mid vowel, 3

middle pitch, 5

-miento, derivation with, **134**:402

mientras, indic and subjunc after, **102**:299

millón, millones, 43:130; **de** after, **43**:130

minutes, **62**:183

mío, -a, -os, -as, 60:180, **61**:182; see Possessives

mirar, see Perceived actions

mismo, -a, -os, -as, comparative word, **82**:234; emphasis, for, **65**:195; vs **igual, 82**:234; position, **46**:141

monetary units, cn, 224

months, **48**:144

morir, morirse, 67:198

motion, criterion for **a** *at,* **123**:358; vbs of, take **a** before inf, **33**:107, **129**:383

motive, criterion for **por, 125**:369

mouth, 2

mucho, -a, -os, -as, nominalization, **84**:245; position, **46**:141

mueble, countable noun, **104**:307

mujer, vs **esposa** and **señora,** cn, 61

must, see **Deber**

n, see [m], [n], [ŋ]

[n], 9; assimilation in [nd], 16, 121; in [nm], 18, 121; in [nt], 15, 121; sequence [nʀ], 62

[ŋ], sequence [ŋx], 21; sequences [ŋk, ŋg, ŋw, ŋx], 121

[ñ], 13

nacional, monetary unit, cn, 224

nada, de after, **126**:372; negative word, **70**:210

nadie, negative word, **70**:210; vs **ninguno, 73**:213; personal **a** with, **73**:213

nasal, nasality, nose, 3, 9, 13; see [m], [n], [ŋ], [ñ]

-ncia, derivation with, **134**:402

-ndo form, vs inf and clause with vbs of perception, **119**:353; progressive, to form, **41**:126, **112**:334; uses of, **40**:125, **41**:126; w/v prons in consts with, position of, **42**:128; see Verb conjugation

negation, commands, negative, **23**:82; *let's not,* **99**:289; negative words other than **no, 69**:209, **70**:210, **71**:211; position of **no, 10**:48, **72**:212; of other negative words, **69**:209; of w/v prons in negative commands, **24**:84; of w/v prons with pres subjunc for *let's not,* **99**:289; prefixes denoting, **134**:402; tags, negative questions with, **12**:52

negocio, countable noun, **104**:307, **131**:387 fn

neuter, see Article, definite, ref to **lo**; Gender

neutral *if* clauses, **115**:338

ni, negative word, **70**:210

ninguno, -a, -os, -as, vs **cualquier(a), 70**:210; vs **nadie, 73**:213; negative word, **70**:210; **ningún, 50**:145; personal **a** with, **73**:213

no, position, **10**:48, **24**:84, **72**:212

¿ **no** ?, tag in questions, **12**:52

noche, de noche and **por la noche** *at night,* **62**:183, **126**:372; **esta noche** *this evening, tonight,* **27**:96; vs **tarde, 62**:183; telling time, in, **62**:183

nominalization, of adj clauses, **103**:304; **-do** form, **92**:265; indefinites, **84**:245; possessives, **61**:182; with def art, demonstratives, and **cuál, 59**:177; **lo, 77**:225

nos, loss of final **s** in vb before, **99**:289; see Pronouns, ref to w/v; see Reflexive

nosotros, -as, de nosotros for **nuestro, 60**:180; in addition to noun, **101**:291; subj pron, **1**:27; w/p pron, **54**:160, **55**:161

noticia, countable noun, **104**:307

nouns, adjs derived from, **134**:402; adjs, from, see Nominalization; art with classifying, **30**:99; collective, sing and pl vbs with, **109**:323; compound, **135**:405; derivation, from adjs and vbs, **134**:402; first and second person with, **101**:291; inf as, **33**:107; mass and countable, **104**:307; nouns modifying nouns in English, equivalents of, **131**:387; sing and pl of, **5**:33; subj of vb, as, **2**:28; see Objects

noun clauses, indic and subjunc in, **97**:282, **105**:313, **117**:349; vs inf and *-ing* form, **97**:282; vs inf and **-ndo** form with vbs of perception, **119**:353; modifying nouns, **132**:389; pres perf subjunc in, with past meaning, **106**:319

nuestro, -a, -os, -as, 19:69, **60**:180, **61**:182; see Possessives

number, pl adj modifying two or more nouns, **64**:192; pl, anticipation of, **63**:185; pl commands, **22**:79, **23**:82; pl **cualesquier(a), 50**:145; pl **ningunos** infrequent, **70**:210 fn; pl of nouns ending in [s], **49**:145; pl vb with sing nouns joined by **o** or **ni, 70**:210 fn; sing for "one each," **89**:254, **131**:387 fn; sing and pl of adjs, **6**:35; with collective nouns, **109**:323; in **de** phrases modifying nouns, **131**:387; of mass nouns and countables, **104**:307; of nouns, **5**:33, **49**:145; of numerals, **47**:143; of possessive adjs, **19**:69; in telling time, **62**:183; of w/v prons, **18**:66

numerals, cardinal, to *ten,* **7**:38; above *ten,* **43**:130; vs ordinal, **47**:143; dates, in, **48**:144; ordinal, **47**:143; position, **46**:141, **47**:143; shortening, **50**:145; telling time, in, **62**:183; see Order, adjectives of

nunca, negative word, **70**:210

o, affirmative word, **70**:210; **u** for, **28**:97

-o, masc marker, **4**:32

[o], 9, 27, 76, 137

objects, **a quien, 86**:249; direct, with vbs of perception, **119**:353; direct and indirect, meaning, **18**:66, in refl consts, **65**:195, **66**:196, **67**:198, with vbs of suasion, **118**:351; indirect, **gustar, parecer,** etc., with, **56**:162, meaning, **58**:175, service-disservice criterion for, **67**:198; infs as, **33**:107; nouns as, **a** with, **25**:86, **73**:213, art with, **75**:215, repeated by pron objs, **56**:162; prons, **a** with, **55**:161, forms of direct and indirect, **18**:66; subj = obj in English, criterion for refl, **37**:113; see Pronouns, ref to w/p and w/v

obligation, **tener que, haber que,** etc., **39**:123; see **Deber**

occupational names, **estudiar para (ser) médico,** etc., **129**:383

of, meaning of **de, 126**:372; of indirect obj, **58**:175; *of mine, of his,* etc., **60**:180

oir, -ndo form, **40**:125; pres, **21**:77; pret, **26**:93 fn; **tú** commands, **23**:82; **usted, -es** commands, **22**:79; see Perceived actions

ojalá, cn, 281; imperf subjunc after, **107**:320

on, + *-ing,* criterion for **al** + inf, **35**:111; meaning of indirect obj, **58**:175, **67**:198; of **para, 129**:383; of **por, 125**:369

one, criterion for nominalization, **59**:177

"one each," sing for, **89**:254

operational, criterion for **por** *by,* **121**:355

optative, see Wish

-or, derivation with, **134**:402; masc marker, **4**:32

order, adjectives of, **primero en salir,** etc., **132**:389

order of words, see Word order

ordinal numerals, see Numerals

organs of speech, 2

orthographic changes, see Spelling changes

-ote, 134:402

otro, -a, -os, -as, nominalization, **84**:245; position, **46**:141; **uno a otro,** see *Each-other* construction

ought, see **Deber**

outcome, criterion for pret, **52**:155

[p], 6; vs [b], 106

padre, padres *father and mother,* **133**:392

padrino, cn, 61

palate, palatal, 2, 3, 281

para, vs a, with vbs of motion, **129**:383; *in order to, for . . . -ing,* **38**:121; meanings, **129**:383; vs **por, 130**:385; vs **que, 39**:123; w/p prons after, **137**:408

para que, compared to **para, 102**:299; subjunc after, **102**:299

parado, posture, **127**:375

parecer, indirect obj with, **56**:162; pres, **21**:77; **usted, -es** commands, **22**:79; w/v pron with, **56**:162

parte, pl vb with, **109**:323

participation of actor, criterion for adding refl pron, **67**:198

participle, past, see **-do** form

participle, present, see *-ing* form and **-ndo** form

particularity, criterion for art, **131**:387

partitive, criterion for **de, 126**:372

pasar, takes **a** before inf, **33**:107

passive, infinitive, cn, 76, cn, 225; refl with nonpersonal subjs, **37**:113; **ser** and **estar** + **-do** form, **93**:267

past, compared with pres, in indic and subjunc, **102**:299; past form with pres meaning, **115**:338; see Imperfect, Preterit

past participle, see **-do** form

past perfect, see Perfect

past progressive, see Progressive

pause, 4, 7; criterion for following a stop consonant, 15

pedir, pres, **16**:63; pret and **-ndo** form, **45**:140; **tú** commands, **23**:82; **usted, -es** commands **22**:79

pending, criterion for subjunc in adv clauses, **102**:299

penetration, criterion for **por, 130**:385

pensar, pres, **16**:63; **tú** commands, **23**:82; **usted, -es** commands, **22**:79

peor, comparative word, **78**:228

Pepe, cn, 42

per, meaning of **por, 125**:369

perceived actions, inf, clause, and **-ndo** form with, **119**:353

perception, vbs of, inf, clause, and **-ndo** form with, **119**:353

perder, tú commands, **23**:82; **usted, -es** commands, **22**:79

perdón, vs **con permiso,** cn, 42

perfect, fut and cond perf after **si** *whether,* **115**:338; fut perf to show probability, **124**:367; past perf subjunc in softened requests and criticisms, **116**:342; pres perf indic, **94**:268; pres perf subjunc, **95**:270, after vb in pres, **106**:319, with past meaning, **106**:319; additional forms, **113**:335; see Verb conjugation

period, see Punctuation

permiso, con, vs **perdón,** cn, 42

person, anticipation, **63**:185; commands, etc., **22**:79, **23**:82, **98**:287, **99**:289; *each-other* const, **85**:248; nouns and **todos, 101**:291; possessives, **19**:69, **61**:182; subj prons, **1**:27; **tú** vs **usted, 1**:27, **22**:79, **23**:82; w/p prons, **54**:160; w/v prons, **18**:66, **65**:195

pésame, cn, 349

pesar de, a, compound prep, **136**:406

phrases, vs clauses, **102**:299

pitch, 4, 5; determined by stress, 9; element of stress, 7; intonation, **11**:48; see Levels of pitch

places of articulation, 3

places, def art with names of, **76**:217

planning, criterion for simple pres and imperf, **41**:126, **53**:159, **112**:334

plural, see Number

poca, -a, -os, -as, de after, **126**:372; nominalization, **84**:245

poder, forms of, = *could,* **116**:342; imperf subjunc of, for softened requests and criticisms, **116**:342; inf obj, with, **33**:107; **-ndo** form, **40**:125; pres, **16**:63; pret, **44**:137; pret vs imperf, **52**:155, **53**:158 f n

point, criterion for **a** *at,* **123**:358

policía, vs **policías,** cn, 91, **109**:323; sing vb with, **109**:323

poner, pres, **21**:77; **poner, ponerse** *to make, to get,* **66**:196; pret, **44**:137; **tú** commands, **23**:82; **usted, -es** commands, **22**:79

por, vs de, after a **-do** form, **121**:355; in telling time, **62**:183, **126**:372; meanings, **125**:369; phrases with, **125**:369; w/p prons after, **137**:408

por qué, interrog word, **8**:44

porque, indic after, **102**:299

posible, takes **de** before inf, **132**:389

position, meaning of preps, **130**:385
position of words, see Word order
possessives, **de** phrases, **20**:71, **60**:180, **126**:372; modifying particularized nouns, **131**:387; indirect obj, **67**:198; nominalization, **61**:182, **77**:226; possessive adjs, long forms not preceding nouns, **60**:180, position, **46**:141, short forms preceding nouns, **19**:69, used less than in English, **31**:100; things possessed, def art with, **31**:100, sing for "one each" of, **89**:254
postures, **-do** form for, **127**:375
pre-, derivation with, **134**:402
prefix, see Affix
prepositions, adv conjunctions, compared to, **102**:299; compound, **136**:406; inf and clause, before, **33**:107, **38**:121, **97**:282; position in *each-other* const, **85**:248, with **de quién**, **139**:411; prep phrases, of location to modify nouns, **86**:249, with **de**, nominalization of, **77**:226, with names of places (**a casa**, etc.), **76**:217; repetition with **mí** and **ti**, **137**:408; space and time, to show position in, **130**:385; subj prons with, **137**:408; see *A, Across, After, Along, Around, At, Because of, By,* **Como, Con,** *Concerning,* **Contra, De,** *Down,* **En, Entre, Excepto,** *For, From,* **Hacia, Hasta,** *In, In order to,* **Incluso,** *Of, On,* **Para,** *Per,* **Por, Según, Sin, Sobre,** *Than, Through, To, Toward, With*
present, fut meaning, **17**:65, **106**:319, **112**:334; vs pres progressive, **41**:126; pres subjunc after vb in pres, **106**:319; see Verb conjugation
present participle, see *-ing* form
present perfect, see Perfect
preterit, vs imperf, **52**:155, **53**:159; probability corresponding to, shown by fut perf, **124**:367; see Verb conjugation
preterit progressive, see Progressive
primero, -a, -os, -as, primer, **47**:143, **50**:155
probability, shown by fut and **deber**, **114**:337; by fut perf and cond, **124**:367
producir, pres, **21**:77; pret, **44**:137
progressive, fut and cond after **si** *whether*, **115**:338; fut, vs simple pres, **112**:334; imperf, **53**:159; past, in English, as criterion for simple imperf, **52**:155; pres, **41**:126; pret, **53**:159; additional forms, **112**:334; prons, position of w/v, **42**:128
pronouns, relative, see Relative words; subj, **1**:27, **2**:28, in addition to noun, **101**:291, with relator words, **137**:408; w/p, **137**:408, added for emphasis, **55**:161, possessives, forms in, **20**:71, to replace w/v in absence of vb, **55**:161; w/v, **18**:66, noun objs, to repeat, **56**:162, position in commands, **24**:84, **98**:287, with pres subjunc for *let's,* **99**:289, in vb consts, **42**:128, refl, **65**:195, **66**:196, two together, **57**:171, **67**:198; see **Lo;** Objects
proper name, high pitch for, 20
proxy, criterion for **por,** **125**:369, **130**:385
pueblo, sing vb with, **109**:323
pues, indic after, **102**:299
puesto que, indic after, **102**:299
punctuation, period in numerals, **43**:130 fn; see Accent mark
purpose, criterion for **para** and **por,** **38**:121, **129**:383, **130**:385

qu, see [k]
quantitative, omission, **128**:376

que, adv conjunctions formed with, **102**:299, **136**:406; *as,* **82**:234; indirect commands, with, **98**:287; nominalization of clauses with, **59**:177; **ojalá, ojalá que,** **107**:320; **tener que,** etc., **39**:123; *than,* **79**:230; *that, which, who, whom,* **86**:249, **103**:304
qué, adjs with, position of, **88**:252; **de** after, **126**:372; interrog word, **8**:44; vs **cuál** for *what,* **138**:410
quedar, quedarse, **67**:198
querer, imperf subjunc for softened requests and criticisms, **116**:342; pres, **16**:63; pret, **44**:137
questions, indefinites in affirmative questions, **74**:214; interrog words, **8**:44; intonation, 5, **11**:48; tag questions, **12**:52; word order in, **9**:46
quetzal, monetary unit, cn, 224
quien, *who, whom,* **86**:249
quién, -es, interrog word, **8**:44; **de quién, -es** *whose,* **139**:411
-quiera, **135**:405
quitar, indirect obj with, **58**:175

[r], 15, 17, 61; sequence [rl], 20
[ʀ], 7, 18, 61; sequence [ʀl], 20, [lʀ, nʀ, zʀ], 62
re-, derivation with, **134**:402
reality, criterion for indic in adv clauses, **102**:299
recipient, criterion for **para,** **129**:383, **130**:385
reciprocal, see *Each-other* construction
recordar, pres, **16**:63; **tú** commands, **23**:82; **usted, -es** commands, **22**:79
reducir, pret, **44**:137
redundant pronouns, w/p added for emphasis, **55**:161; w/v in addition to noun objs, **56**:162
reflexive constructions, direct objs, with, **66**:196; indirect objs, with, **67**:198; nonpersonal subjs, with, **37**:113; vs **ser** + **-do** form, **93**:267; unplanned occurrences, for, **68**:201; see *Each-other* construction
reflexive pronouns, w/v, **65**:195; see Pronouns
regatear, cn, 76
relational, criterion for **de** *by, with,* **121**:355, **122**:357
relative words, equivalents of *that, which, who, whom,* **86**:249; added with **de quién,** **139**:411
relator words, **tener que,** etc., **39**:123; subj prons after, **137**:408; see Conjunctions, Prepositions, Relative pronouns
remoteness, criterion for **ahí, allí, allá,** cn, 42; for **ese** vs **aquel,** cn, 170
requests, softened, and criticisms, **116**:342
reservations, position of **no** in, **72**:212
resonance, 2
rey, reyes *king and queen,* **133**:392
ronda, cn, 366
round lips, 3

[s], 9, 16, 17, 137; voicing, 10; vs [h, z], 171; sequences [gs, ks], 208; spelling, 191, 208
saber, pres, **21**:77; pret, **44**:137, vs imperf, **52**:155; vs **conocer,** **32**:100; **tú** commands, **23**:82; **usted, -es** commands, **22**:79
salir, pres, **21**:77; **tú** commands, **23**:82; **usted, -es** commands, **22**:79
san, santo, -a, no art with, **30**:99
se, for **le, les,** **57**:171; refl, **65**:195; see Pronouns, ref to w/v; see Reflexive
seguir, progressive, to form, **41**:126; **tú** commands, **23**:82
según, indic and subjunc after, **102**:299, **105**:313; prep and conjunction, as, **102**:299; subj prons after, **137**:408

selection, criterion for **cuál** vs **qué**, **138**:410

semi-, derivation with, **134**:402

semiconsonant, 6, 20

semivowel, 76

señor, *master*, cn, 170; **señores** *Mr. and Mrs.*, **133**:392

señora, vs **doña**, cn, 26; vs **esposa** and **mujer**, cn, 61; *mistress*, cn, 170

sentado, posture, **127**:375

separation, criterion for **para**, **130**:385

sequence of tenses, **105**:313, **106**:319

ser, agreement with predicate noun, **63**:185; **de quién**, with, **139**:411; **-do** form, with, **93**:267, cn, 299; vs **estar**, **14**:55, **93**:267, cn, 299; **estudiar para (ser) médico**, **129**:383; fut and cond of, for probability, **114**:337, **124**:367; **mío**, etc., after, **60**:180; pres, **2**:28; pret, **44**:137; telling time, in, **62**:183; **tú** commands, **23**:82; **usted, -es** commands, **22**:79

series, pret vs imperf in series action, **52**:155

service, criterion for indirect obj, **67**:198

sex, see Gender

shortening, **algún, buen, cien, cualquier, gran, mal, ningún, veintiún**, etc., **50**:145; **primer, tercer**, **47**:143, **50**:145; **un**, **7**:38, **43**:130, **50**:145

should, see **Deber**

si, clauses with, see *If* clauses; *whether*, **115**:338

siesta, cn, 312

simultaneity, criterion for **al** + inf, **35**:111

sin, implied negative, **71**:211; omission of indef art after, **83**:235; w/p prons after, **137**:408

sin que, compared to **sin**, **102**:299; subjunc after, **102**:299, **105**:313

singular, see Number

so that I can, meaning of **para**, **129**:383

sobre, w/p prons after, **137**:408

soft palate, 2

softened requests and criticisms, cond indic and imperf subjunc for, **116**:342

sol, monetary unit, cn, 224

sounds, 2 ff

space, preps show position in, **130**:385

speech organs, 2

spelling, relation to sound, 4

spelling changes, **c** vs **z**, **23**:82 fn; **g** vs **gu**, **16**:63 fn; **i** vs **y**, **26**:93 fn, **40**:125 fn

sports, cn, 106

spread lips, 3

state, change of, calls for reflexive and **ponerse**, **66**:196

stem-changing verbs, pres, **16**:63; pres subjunc, **95**:270; pret of **-ir**, **45**:140; **tú** commands, **23**:82; **usted, -es** commands, **22**:79

stop consonants, 3, 6 ff, 17, 18; see [k], [p], [t]

stopped action, criterion for pret, **52**:155

stress, 4 ff; in cognates, 92, 93; and intonation, **11**:48; **-mente**, on, 5, **96**:274; possessive adjs, on, **60**:180; *-self* words in English, on, **65**:195; strong, 4, 5, 6, 7 ff; determines pitch level, 9; weak, 4, 5, 6 ff; w/v prons weak-stressed, **55**:161; word order, and, **9**:46, **37**:113, **87**:251; see Emphasis

strong stress, see Stress

su, sus, **19**:69, **60**:180; see Possessives

suasion, criterion for subjunc, **97**:282, **105**:313, **118**:351; inf after vbs of, **118**:351

sub-, derivation with, **134**:402

subjects, def art with subj nouns, **75**:215; emphasis, subj prons for, **1**:27, **98**:287; = obj in English, criterion for refl, **37**:113; omission in questions,

9:46; position, **9**:46, **87**:251; refl, subjectless use of, **37**:113; **se** unambiguous, to make, **65**:195; see Nouns, Pronouns

subjunctive, adj clauses, in, **103**:304; adv clauses, in, **102**:299; exclamations after expressions of welcoming-spurning, in, **117**:349; imperf, for *as if*, **107**:320, in *if* clauses, **115**:338, in wishes, **107**:320; imperf and past perf in softened requests and criticisms, **116**:342; indirect commands, in, **98**:287; vs inf, after vbs of suasion, **118**:351; noun clauses, in, **97**:282, **132**:389; pres, for *let's*, **99**:289, not usual after **si** *if*, **115**:338; **tal vez**, with, **95**:270; see Commands, Verb conjugation

substitution, criterion for **de**, **126**:372; for **por**, **125**:369

successive events, criterion for pret, **52**:155

sucre, monetary unit, cn, 224

suffix, see Affix

superlative, see Comparison

suyo, -a, -os, -as, **60**:180, **61**:182; see Possessives

syllable, 4, 5; division, 9

[t], 7; vs [d], 106; sequence [nt], 15, 121

tag, **¿eh?, ¿no?, ¿verdad?**, **12**:52; statement tags, **11**:48

tal vez, indic or subjunc with, **95**:270

también, affirmative word, **70**:210

tampoco, negative word, **70**:210

tan, followed by **como**, **81**:233; in exclamations, **88**:252

tan pronto (como), indic and subjunc after, **102**:299

tanto, -a, -os, -as, followed by **como**, **81**:233

tap, 4, 7, 15

tarde, vs **noche**, **62**:183; telling time, in, **62**:183

te, see Pronouns, ref to refl and w/v

teeth, 2

telephone greetings, cn, 42

tener, complements, without, **128**:376; fut and cond of, for probability, **114**:337, **124**:367; vs **haber**, **94**:268; idioms with, **90**:254; indef art, omission, **83**:235; personal **a** unnecessary, **25**:86; pres, **16**:63; pret, **44**:137; **tener de todo**, **126**:372; **tener que** + inf, **39**:123; **tú** commands, **23**:82; **usted, -es** commands, **22**:79

tense, **2**:28 fn

tenses, forms, see Verb conjugation; form-meaning correspondence in *if* clauses, **115**:338; inf and *-ing* in English do not show, **105**:313; meanings, see Conditional, Future, Imperfect, Perfect, Present, Preterit, Progressive; sequence, **105**:313, **106**:319

tercero, -a, -os, -as, tercer, **47**:143, **50**:145

terminal juncture, see Juncture

than, **de**, **79**:230, **126**:372

that, equivalent of, **86**:249; **ese** vs **aquel**, cn, 170; vs *which* as criterion for noun clauses, **132**:389

there, **ahí, allí, allá**, cn, 42

those, criterion for nominalization, **59**:177

throat, 2

through, meaning of **por**, **125**:369

ti, **54**:160, **55**:161; repetition of prep with, **137**:408; see Pronouns, ref to w/p

time, days, months, years, **48**:144; **hacer** in expressions of, **91**:257; hours, minutes, **62**:183; preps, criterion for, **130**:385

time deadline, criterion for **para**, **129**:383

titles, art with, **30**:99

to, **a**, **58**:175; **de**, **126**:372; indirect obj, meaning of, **18**:66, **58**:175; inf in English, sign of, **38**:121; **para**, **129**:383; **por**, **125**:369

to be a, meaning of **para**, **129**:383

todo, -a, -os, -as, art with in senses *all* and *every*, **75**:215; **de todo** partitive, **126**:372; first and second person with **todos, 101**:291; **lo** with, cn, 280

tongue, 2

tontería, countable noun, **104**:307

totality, see **Todo**

toward, meaning of **para**, **129**:383, **130**:385

traer, -ndo form, **40**:125; pres, **21**:77; pret, **44**:137; **tú** commands, **23**:82; **usted, -es** commands, **22**:79

translation, lack of equivalence in, cn, 42

trill, see Vibrant

tu, tus, 19:69, **60**:180; see Possessives

tú, direct commands, **23**:82; subj pron, **1**:27

tuyo, -a, -os, -as, 60:180, **61**:182; see Possessives

u, see [u] and [w]

u, for **o** *or*, **28**:97

[u], 10, 27, 76

-uir verbs, see **Incluir**

un, una, see Article, indef

unaspirated, [k], 12; [p], 6; [t], 7

unfinished business, criterion for imperf, **52**:155

único, takes **en** before inf, **132**:389

universitario, -a, -os, -as, like English noun to modify noun, **131**:387

unlikely *if* clauses, **115**:338

uno, -a, -os, -as, vs **algunos, 83**:235; art and numeral, **7**:38, **43**:130; nominalization, **84**:245; position, **46**:141; **uno a otro,** etc., see *Each-other* construction; **uno** vs **un, 7**:38, **43**:130, **50**:145; **unos** the pl of **un, 83**:235

unplanned occurrences, criterion for refl, **68**:201

unreality, imperf subjunc for, **107**:320, **115**:338

unstopped action, criterion for imperf, **51**:153, **52**:155

used to, criterion for imperf, **52**:155

usted, -es, subj pron, **1**:27; in addition to noun, **101**:291; direct commands, **22**:79; w/p pron, **54**:160, **55**:161

v, see [b] and [ƀ]

value judgments, criterion for position of descriptive adjs, **64**:192

vámonos, 99:289

vamos a, see **Ir**

velorio, cn, 349

velum, velar, 2, 3

venir, inf after takes **a, 33**:107; **-ndo** form, **40**:125; pres, **16**:63; pret, **44**:137; **tú** commands, **23**:82; **usted, -es** commands, **22**:79

ver, pres, **21**:77; **tú** commands, **23**:82; **usted, -es** commands, **22**:79; see Perceived actions

verb conjugation, cond, **111**:332; cond perf, **113**:335; direct commands, **22**:79, **23**:82; **-do** form, **92**:265; fut, **110**:329; fut perf, **113**:335; imperf, **51**:153, subjunc, **105**:313; **-ndo** form, **40**:125, **45**:140; past perf, **113**:335; pres of **-ar** vbs, **3**:29, of **-er, -ir** vbs, **15**:62, of **estar, 13**:54, of irregular vbs, **21**:77, of **ser, 2**:28, of stem-changing vbs, **16**:63; pres and pres perf subjunc, **95**:270; pres perf, **94**:268; pret of **-ir** stem-changing vbs, **45**:140, of irregular vbs, **44**:137, of regular vbs and **dar, 26**:93; progressive forms, **41**:126, **112**:334; see Infinitive

verbs, of motion, **33**:107, **129**:383; of perception, **119**:353; of suasion, **118**:351; auxiliary to inf, **33**:107, **39**:123, to **-ndo** form, see Progressive; nouns from, **134**:402, **135**:405; position, **9**:46, **87**:251

¿ **verdad**?, tag in questions, **12**:52

vez de, en, compound prep, **136**:406

vibrant, 4, 7

viejo, más viejo vs **mayor** *older*, **78**:228

vocal folds, 2

voiceless consonants, 3, 6 ff, 10

voicing, voiced, 3, 6 ff, 10, 171

volver, tú commands, **23**:82; **usted, -es** commands, **22**:79

vosotros, -as, 1:27 fn

vowels, 3, 6 ff; articulation of, 3; shortness of, 6, 10; see [a], [e], [i], [o], [u]

[w], 6; sequence [gw], 171, [ŋw], 121

weak stress, see Stress

week, days of, **48**:144, **49**:145

welcoming-spurning, criterion for subjunc, **97**:282, **105**:313, **117**:349

what, **cuál** and **qué** for, **138**:410

whether, see **Si**

which, equivalent of, **86**:249; vs *that* as criterion for adj clauses, **132**:389

who, equivalent of, **86**:249

whom, equivalent of, **86**:249

whose, **de quién, 139**:411

wife, **esposa, mujer, señora,** cn, 61

willingness, vs fut, **115**:338

wish, **ojalá** + imperf subjunc, **107**:320

with, **de, 122**:357, **126**:372

with-preposition pronouns, see Pronouns

with-respect-to, criterion for indirect obj, **58**:175

with-verb pronouns, see Pronouns

word order, adjs, descriptive, **64**:192, limiting, **46**:141, possessive, **19**:69, **60**:180, **qué,** with, **88**:252; climactic and anticlimactic, **87**:251; **cualquier(a), 50**:145; **de quién,** with, **139**:411; **hacer** in expressions of time, **91**:257; intonation and, **11**:48; **más, muchos, otros, todos,** and ordinal numerals, **46**:141; negative words, **69**:209, **70**:210, **71**:211, **72**:212; noun obj before vb repeated by pron, **56**:162; perf not divided, **94**:268; prep in *each-other* const, **85**:248; questions, **9**:46; refl consts, **37**:113; **tener que,** etc., **39**:123; w/v prons, **18**:66, commands, **24**:84, **98**:287, pres subjunc for *let's*, **99**:289, two together, **57**:171, **67**:198, vb consts, **42**:128; see Emphasis

would, equivalents of, **111**:332; imperf, criterion for, **52**:155

x, 208

[x], 20, 21; vs [h], 171; sequence [ŋx], 21, 121; spelling, 225

y, e for, **28**:97; numerals, in, **43**:130; telling time, in, **62**:183

[y], 8, 11; cn, 225; linking, 20; spelling, 281

ya que, indic after, **102**:299

years, **48**:144

yo, subj pron, **1**:27

z, see [s]

[z], 10; vs [s], 171, 208; sequence [zʀ], 62

zapateado, cn, 383